MICROPROCESSOR TECHNOLOGY AND MICROCOMPUTERS

MICROPROCESSOR TECHNOLOGY AND MICROCOMPUTERS

Edward J. Pasahow

McGRAW-HILL BOOK COMPANY

NEW YORK   ATLANTA   DALLAS   ST. LOUIS   SAN FRANCISCO   AUCKLAND
BOGOTÁ   GUATEMALA   HAMBURG   LISBON   LONDON   MADRID   MEXICO
MILAN   MONTREAL   NEW DELHI   PANAMA   PARIS   SAN JUAN   SÃO PAULO
SINGAPORE   SYDNEY   TOKYO   TORONTO

Sponsoring Editor: Gordon Rockmaker
Editing Supervisor: Suzette André
Design and Art Supervisor/Cover and Interior Design: Meri Shardin
Production Supervisors: Priscilla Taguer and Kathleen Donnelly

Technical Studio: Hadel Studio
Cover Photographer: Joel A. Levirne, Graphic Images, Ltd.

*Use of PCturbo 286e™ for cover photo courtesy of
Orchid Technology, Inc., Fremont, California*

Library of Congress Cataloging-in-Publication Data

Pasahow, Edward.
  Microprocessor technology and microcomputers.

  Includes index.
  1. Microprocessors. 2. Microcomputers. I. Title.
QA76.5.P324   1988   004.16   86-31275
ISBN 0-07-048729-4

1 2 3 4 5 6 7 8 9 0 SEMBKP 8 9 4 3 2 1 0 9 8 7

ISBN 0-07-048729-4

For Rosemarie

CONTENTS

PREFACE   xi

CHAPTER 1   **An Introduction to Microprocessors and
             Microcomputers**   1
             Microprocessors and Microcomputers 2 • Micro-
             computer Characteristics 2 • Microprocessor Regis-
             ters 4 • Arithmetic and Logic Section 6 • Control
             Section 6 • Memory 7 • Bit-Sliced Microproces-
             sor Architecture 13 • Input/Output 15 • Micro-
             processor Products 17 • Chapter Summary 22 •
             Key Terms and Concepts 23

CHAPTER 2   **Number Systems and Codes**   24
             Positional Number Systems 25 • Conversion Between
             Bases 26 • Arithmetic in Other Bases 30 • Com-
             plement Systems 33 • Double-Precision Arithme-
             tic 35 • Codes 36 • Chapter Summary 41 • Key
             Terms and Concepts 41 • Problems 42

CHAPTER 3   **Programming**   43
             The Programming Process 44 • Flowchart Prepara-
             tion 46 • Debugging Techniques 48 • Chapter
             Summary 51 • Key Terms and Concepts 51 •
             Problems 51

CHAPTER 4   **8085 Microprocessor Architecture**   54
             The 8085 Microprocessor Integrated Circuit 55 •
             Clock and Control Signals 57 • Demultiplexing and
             Buffering the System Buses 62 • Memory 64 • Bi-
             directional Bus Drivers 68 • Introduction to 8085 Pro-
             gramming 69 • Chapter Summary 71 • Key Terms
             and Concepts 72 • Problems 72

CHAPTER 5   **6800 Microprocessor Architecture**   74
             The 6800 Microprocessor Integrated Circuit 75 •
             Clock and Control Signals 77 • Timing Con-

trol 79 • Demultiplexing and Buffering the System Buses 79 • Memory 81 • Bidirectional Bus Drivers 85 • Introduction to 6800 Programming 85 • Chapter Summary 88 • Key Terms and Concepts 89 • Problems 89

CHAPTER 6 **An Introduction to the Instruction Repertoire**   91
8085 Memory, Register, and I/O Device Notation 92 • 8085 Addressing Modes 94 • Encoding and Decoding 8085 Instructions 95 • Introduction to 8085 Instructions 96 • 8085 Programming Efficiency 102 • 6800 Memory, Register, and I/O Device Notation 104 • 6800 Addressing Modes 106 • Encoding and Decoding 6800 Instructions 107 • Introduction to 6800 Instructions 108 • 6800 Programming Efficiency 114 • Chapter Summary 116 • Key Terms and Concepts 117 • Problems 117

CHAPTER 7 **Arithmetic and Logic**   120
The Status Register in Detail 121 • 8085 Carry Bit Modification 123 • 6800 Carry Bit Modification 123 • 6800 Overflow Bit Modification 124 • 8085 Register Instructions 125 • 6800 Register and Memory Instructions 127 • Addition 132 • Subtraction 136 • Boolean Operations 140 • Introduction to BCD Arithmetic 146 • Compare Instructions 148 • Chapter Summary 151 • Key Terms and Concepts 151 • Problems 152

CHAPTER 8 **Jumps**   155
Unconditional and Conditional Jumps 156 • 8085 Conditional Jump Instructions 157 • 6800 Conditional Jump and Branch Instructions 160 • Multibyte Addition 164 • Multibyte Subtraction 166 • Multibyte BCD Addition 169 • Multibyte BCD Subtraction 169 • Chapter Summary 173 • Key Terms and Concepts 174 • Problems 174

CHAPTER 9 **Shifting**   175
Shifting Concepts 176 • 8085 Rotate Accumulator Instructions 177 • 6800 Rotate Accumulator and Memory Instructions 178 • Software Multiplication 181 • Software Division 183 • Chapter Summary 184 • Key Terms and Concepts 186 • Problems 186

CHAPTER 10 **Loops and Indexing**   187
Loop Functions 188 • Counting Loops 189 • Noncounting Loops 195 • Timing Loops 195 • Address Modification Loops 197 • Nested Loops 197 • Chapter Summary 200 • Key Terms and Concepts 200 • Problems 201

CHAPTER 11 **Subroutines**   203
Subroutines in General 204 • 8085 Conditional Subroutine Calls 208 • 8085 Conditional Return

Instructions 211 • Advanced Subroutine Concepts 214 • Other 8085 Stack Instructions 223 • Other 6800 Stack Instructions 226 • Chapter Summary 226 • Key Terms and Concepts 228 • Problems 228

CHAPTER 12 **An Introduction to Interfacing and Peripheral Equipment**   229
Interfaces 230 • Design Examples 231 • Printers 232 • Keyboards 234 • CRT Terminals 235 • Modems 237 • Floppy-Disk Drives 237 • Magnetic Tape Recorders 240 • Local-Area Networks 240 • Chapter Summary 242 • Key Terms and Concepts 243 • Problems 244

CHAPTER 13 **Parallel Input/Output**   245
I/O Concepts 246 • 8085 Accumulator I/O 246 • I/O Devices 247 • Memory-Mapped I/O 251 • Interrupts 253 • Priority Interrupt Control Unit 260 • Direct Memory Access 266 • The 8257 DMA Controller 268 • Chapter Summary 274 • Key Terms and Concepts 275 • Problems 275

CHAPTER 14 **Serial Input/Output**   277
Serial Data Exchange 278 • Synchronous Serial Protocol 281 • Asynchronous Serial Protocol 281 • Modem Control Signals 282 • The Synchronous Receiver-Transmitter 283 • The 8251 Universal Synchronous-Asynchronous Receiver-Transmitter 284 • Chapter Summary 288 • Key Terms and Concepts 289 • Problems 289

CHAPTER 15 **Teletype Current Loops**   291
Teletype Characteristics 292 • Current Loops 293 • System Operation 295 • Software Interfacing to Teletypes 296 • Chapter Summary 298 • Key Terms and Concepts 299 • Problems 299

CHAPTER 16 **EIA Standard RS-232C Interface**   300
RS-232C Capabilities 301 • Signal Description 301 • Electrical Characteristics 304 • Mechanical Characteristics 306 • Converting RS-232 Levels 306 • Chapter Summary 307 • Key Terms and Concepts 308 • Problems 308

CHAPTER 17 **IEEE-488 General-Purpose Interface Bus**   309
IEEE-488 Bus Overview 310 • Bus Structure 310 • Functional Repertoire 311 • Electrical Characteristics 312 • Mechanical Characteristics 313 • Bus Operations 313 • Software Interfaces 318 • A Typical GPIB Instrument 318 • A Practical Note 319 • Chapter Summary 319 • Key Terms and Concepts 320 • Problems 320

CHAPTER 18   **Microcomputer Buses**   321
Multiplexed Buses 322   •   The S-100 Bus 324   •
The Multibus 329   •   Chapter Summary 333   •
Key Terms and Concepts 334 • Problems 334

CHAPTER 19   **Analog Interfaces**   335
The Simple Analog Interface 336 • Digital-to-Analog
Converters 336 • Analog-to-Digital Converters 343 •
Characteristics of Converters 345   •   Sample-and-
Hold Circuits 347   •   Voltage-to-Frequency Con-
verters 348 • Chapter Summary 349 • Key Terms
and Concepts 350   •   Problems 350

CHAPTER 20   **Support Devices and Troubleshooting**   352
Data Encryption Unit 353   •   Floppy-Disk Controller 356 • CRT Controller 359 • An Approach
to Microcomputer Troubleshooting 360   •   Pulsers
361 • Logic Probes 362 • Logic Analyzers 363 •
In-Circuit Emulators 365   •   Software Diagnostics
365 • Chapter Summary 368 • Key Terms and Concepts 368   •   Problems 369

CHAPTER 21   **An Introduction to 16- and 32-Bit Microprocessors** 370
The 80186 Microprocessor 371 • The 80286 Microprocessor 376 • The 68020 Microprocessor 378 •
Chapter Summary 380   •   Key Terms and Concepts 381 • Problems 381

APPENDIX   382
The 8080A Microprocessor 383   •   The 8224 Clock
Generator 387 • The 8228 System Controller and Bus
Driver 388 • The Z80 Microprocessor 389 • Ex-
planatory Note on the Decimal Adjust Accumulator In-
struction 392

INDEX   395

PREFACE

This book is intended for students of electronics technology who require in-depth, practical knowledge of microprocessors and microcomputers. Technicians and computer specialists will also find this material directly applicable in working with microcomputers. Coverage emphasizes the hardware aspects of these small systems, but enough discussion on software topics is supplied to demonstrate the interactions between the two.

In selecting the microcomputer on which to base such a book as this, I had essentially three choices: use a generic microprocessor, range through a large number of different processors trying to communicate the "flavor" of each, or analyze a particular processor in detail. Regardless of the approach, the shortcomings of each are readily apparent. The generic processor does not support lab experiments, nor does it prepare students for real-world situations. Skipping from one processor to another is guaranteed to hopelessly confuse the reader and also makes experimentation difficult. In selecting a few processors, the risk is that they may not be the ones the student will meet on the job.

Given this type of choice, one can only take a deep breath and plunge ahead. The 8085 and 6800 family of processors were chosen for this book. The reasons for this choice are based on my belief that it results in the most favorable outcome. First, if a widely used processor is adopted, the broadest range of students will find the book useful. Second, symbology and terminology that are commonly accepted by industry can be employed. And finally, the student acquires knowledge that can be readily utilized.

Signal flow diagrams can be powerful teaching tools in this approach; they are used in this book to tie together what the processor is currently doing with the signals present on the system buses. State-of-the-art devices are used as examples throughout, together with such important software techniques as top-down design, reentrant code, and recursive subroutines.

Mathematics is limited to basic algebra, and an understanding of basic integrated circuits is assumed. Beginning chapters provide an overview of microprocessors, followed by a study of number system concepts. Many students will have had earlier courses on this subject, so the chapter can serve as a review. (On the other hand, it is a complete development to serve the student who has never been introduced to number systems other than decimal.)

An outline of programming sets the stage for the assembler and machine code listings used in the examples. The 8085 and 6800 supply the basis for an architectural description which leads into detailed consideration of the instruction repertoire, explanations of how the instructions are used, means of input and output, and interfacing to external devices. With this preparation, the student should be comfortable analyzing microcomputer components and circuitry as well as writing diagnostic software routines.

Certain sections in this book are chip specific. In order to focus on these particular discussions I have used the symbol **80** to denote information relating to the Intel 8085 and the symbol 68 when referring to the Motorola 6800 series.

The electrical and mechanical characteristics of almost any interface likely to be encountered are then described. The chapter on teletype current loops includes conversion to or from TTL logic and use of opto-isolators. The frequently used communications standards RS-232C and IEEE-488 are discussed in detail, together with implementation techniques. Computer buses, such as the hobbyist S-100 and the Multibus, receive a full treatment which extends to troubleshooting problems in bused equipment.

An especially important area covered is analog interfacing. Here analog circuits, with working applications of such devices as multiplying DACs and V/F converters, D/A and A/D converters, and sample-and-hold devices, receive a complete analysis.

A work of this kind requires the efforts and cooperation of many people. The ideas and suggestions of colleagues and students, both past and present, have contributed much to this text. The same can be said for the manufacturers who generously supplied photographs and technical data. To each I extend a grateful acknowledgment and thanks.

Edward J. Pasahow

AN INTRODUCTION TO MICROPROCESSORS AND MICROCOMPUTERS

A remarkable change has occurred in the electronics industry during the last two decades. Previously, the number of computers in the world had been counted in the thousands, but with the invention of the microcomputer that quantity has reached the millions, and the number continues to grow. Technicians who design, build, or maintain electronics equipment will be seeing microprocessors in their work with increasing frequency. An understanding of microcomputer components, circuitry, and signal flow will become as fundamental to a technician's job as is a knowledge of Ohm's law and resistor theory. An understanding of microcomputers requires some familiarity with programming features, as well as with the hardware, to aid you in assessing problems and localizing faults.

CHAPTER OBJECTIVES

Upon completion of this chapter, you should be able to:

1. Define the terms "microcomputer" and "microprocessor."
2. List the components of a typical microprocessor.
3. Name the data and instruction registers usually found within a microprocessor.
4. Explain the operations performed in the arithmetic and logic section.
5. Distinguish between the various flags used in the status register.
6. Describe how a microprogram controls the sequence of events to be executed.
7. Describe the timing and the sequencing of instruction execution.
8. Draw a block diagram of a microprocessor.
9. Describe memory usage in a microcomputer.
10. Discuss bit-sliced microprocessor architecture.
11. Distinguish between programmed input/output, interrupt servicing, and direct memory access.
12. Describe the most commonly used microprocessor products now available from manufacturers.

MICROPROCESSORS AND MICROCOMPUTERS

A *digital computer* is an electronic device that can receive, store, manipulate, and send data. The data is manipulated as specified by a series of instructions, called a *program*, which is also stored in the computer. A digital computer consists of control, arithmetic and logic, memory, input, and output sections.

There is a special class of digital computers called *microcomputers,* which are based on microprocessor integrated circuits (ICs). To perform its functions, the microcomputer requires input/output logic, read-only memory, power supplies, an oscillator, and possibly random-access memory, in addition to the microprocessor. Figure 1-1 shows an example of a microcomputer based on a microprocessor.

The *microprocessor unit (MPU)* is made up of one or more programmable integrated circuits containing control, arithmetic, and logic sections as well as a portion of the input/output logic and sometimes memory. Providing some or all of the arithmetic and control sections of a computer, microprocessors come in a variety of word sizes ranging from 4 to 32 bits.

In this chapter we will use a typical 8-bit microprocessor to study the capability and operation of these devices and then take a look at some examples of microprocessors. The concepts in this chapter provide an overview of the remainder of the book, so many of the examples are of a general nature. Details in later chapters will explain how or why the operations are actually carried out.

Fig. 1-1 The IBM AT personal computer. *(Courtesy of International Business Machines Corporation)*

MICROCOMPUTER CHARACTERISTICS

Many common microcomputers work with binary numbers 8 bits long. This grouping of data into 8-bit units is an example of the *word size* of the computer. The 8-bit data unit is also often called a *byte,* so referring to a 1-byte computer is the same as saying that the computer has an 8-bit word size. Because the microprocessor and the memory in the microcomputer must work with the same data, they often have the same word size.

Typically, most microprocessors consist of a 40-pin dual in-line package (DIP). One or more pins are dedicated to power supply inputs. (For instance, the 8085 uses 1 pin for the power supply voltages.) One pin is used for ground and another two for the clock input. Frequently, 16 pins are needed for the memory address output. Data input/output (I/O) uses another 8 pins. One or more pins are needed to determine whether the memory reference is to be reading or writing. The remaining pins are associated with other control signals used for input, output, and timing. Newer packaging techniques for microprocessors are also appearing, such as the surface mount packs.

The interconnection of various components of a microcomputer is shown in Fig. 1-2. The MPU acts as the controller for the system. Either *read-only memory (ROM)* or *random-access memory (RAM),* or both, may be used as storage. Many types of input/output transfers can be implemented. The simplest is an I/O interface to the peripheral device. [Some peripheral equipment that you may be familiar with includes magnetic tape cassettes, printers, cathode-ray tube (CRT) terminals, and floppy disks.] When faster data transfer is necessary, interrupt logic or direct memory access may be used.

The key to a flexible microcomputer architecture is the use of *bidirectional buses* between the microprocessor and the other components. Most of the buses are *three-state buses;* that is, a device can set its output signals to high, low, or high-impedance states. In the latter case the device is essentially disconnected from the bus. Three different microcomputer buses are required, although some designs may *multiplex* two types of information over a signal set of bus lines (i.e., use the same line to carry more than one type of information at different times).

The *data bus* is an 8-bit bidirectional three-state bus. All data moving between the microprocessor and the other components travels along this path. Examples of data bus usage include reading data from memory to the microprocessor, storing results calculated by the microprocessor back into memory, fetching instructions

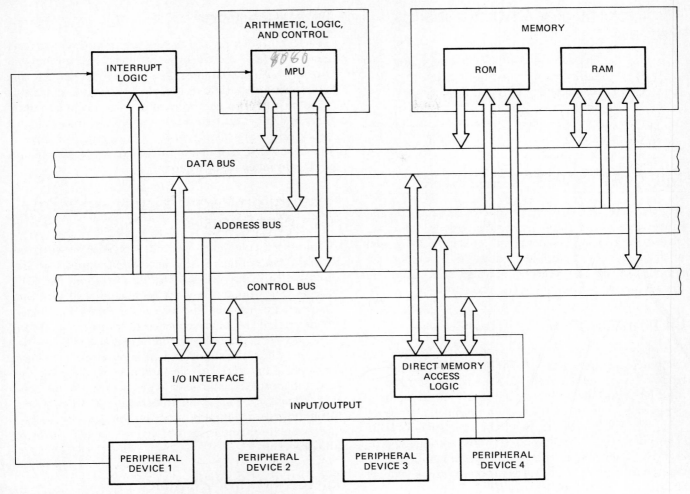

Fig. 1-2 Architecture of a typical microcomputer.

from memory for the microprocessor to execute, and transferring data from the MPU to or from peripheral devices.

The number of parallel bits in the *address bus* determines the maximum memory capacity that a microprocessor can use. Frequently, the address bus is 16 bits wide; this bus is three-state. The address bus specifies the source or destination address for data. With 16 bits, there are 65,536 possible addresses ($2^{16} = 65,536$). The address can indicate either memory or an I/O device.

Each operation to be performed is under the direction of the *control bus*. The number of control lines varies

a great deal from microprocessor to microprocessor, but generally there are 10 to 12 lines. These lines carry discrete signals (that is, a particular condition is true or false depending on the voltage level), so they are usually not three-state. The sequence and nature of the operation are specified by setting the correct control line; for example, "read data from RAM to the microprocessor" may be one control line, and "send data to the peripheral device from the MPU" could be another. Table 1-1 lists the data the address bus widths for some of the microprocessors that we will discuss later in this chapter.

Table 1-1 Typical Microprocessor Buses

	Microprocessors				
	8085	6800	8086	Z8000	68000
Data bus width (bits)	8	8	16	16	16
Address bus width (bits)	16*	16	20	16	24

*Multiplexed bus.
Note: The 8080A and Z80 have the same-size buses as the 8085.

Microcomputer Characteristics Review

1. Define the characteristics of a digital computer.
2. List the components of a microcomputer.
3. Describe the functions of a microprocessor.
4. How many bits are in 1 byte?
5. Discuss the purpose of the data, address, and control buses.

MICROPROCESSOR REGISTERS

Registers are used within the microprocessor to hold instructions and data for short time periods. While the instruction is being executed or when data is being used in arithmetic or logical operations, it is temporarily stored in a register. Registers are also used as buffers for data moving from one section to another.

Bit Numbering

The bits of the registers and memory cells in a microcomputer are numbered, so any particular bit can be readily designated. As Fig. 1-3*a* shows, the *most significant bit (MSB)* in an 8-bit register is bit 7, and the *least significant bit (LSB)* is bit 0. In a 16-bit register (Fig. 1-3*b*), the MSB is bit 15, while bit 0 is still the LSB. (This numbering scheme is not standard throughout the industry. Some manufacturers reverse the numbering so that the MSB is bit 0. The microprocessor user's manual always specifies the method used.)

Accumulator

The primary register in arithmetic and boolean operations is the *accumulator,* often called the *A register.* The results of operations performed by the *arithmetic-logic unit (ALU)* are placed in the 1-byte accumulator; that is, "accumulated answers" are to be found in the A register. Some microprocessors have more than one accumulator, so each one must be given a distinguishing designation, such as A1, A2, A3, and so on. Data moving between memory and the arithmetic sections may be held in the accumulator. Also, the accumulator may contain information being transmitted to or received from a peripheral device.

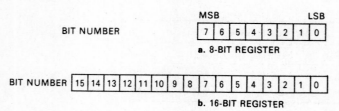

Fig. 1-3 Bit numbering.

Index Register

The 16-bit index register is very useful in serving as an incrementing or decrementing counter. The count might possibly tell the computer how many times to perform a particular operation, or it could be a memory address. In some microprocessors the functions of the accumulator and the index register are combined into a single entity called a *general register.* Thus, general registers can be used in arithmetic and logical instructions as well as in indexing operations.

Instruction Register and Program Counter Register

While the accumulator and index register are used to contain data, other registers in the microprocessor are used with the instructions. During execution, each instruction is held in the 8-bit instruction register. The control unit interprets the instruction register contents to determine the next sequence of control signals to generate. The program counter register contains the memory address of the next instruction. Because it must be capable of addressing all the memory, the program counter must have the same word size as the address bus, usually 16 bits. Once the starting address of the program is loaded into the program counter, its contents are normally incremented one by one to step through the program.

Stack Pointer Register

A stack can be implemented in two different ways in a microcomputer. In one method a file of 8-bit registers can be used by the microprocessor for additional storage. In the other method the stack may be in memory. A block of contiguous memory cells is used in the same way as the register file. The length of the stack is equal to the number of registers in the file or the number of memory locations set aside for stack use.

The stack can be compared to the spring-loaded plate servers found in many cafeterias—when the top plate is removed, the next one pops up. Clean plates placed on top cause the bottom plates to be pushed down.

From that analogy you should be able to understand that only information at the top of the stack is available for access. If you want to obtain this top data, the stack is *popped* and the information in the top cell or register is read. Placing information on the stack is called a *push.* In essence, all the stack contents are forced down one position to receive the new data word. Because the newest information is always available on top, this stack structure is called *first-in last-out (FILO).*

The *stack pointer* always keeps track of the top of the stack. Figure 1-4 shows how the pointer changes in pushing or popping operations. When the stack is

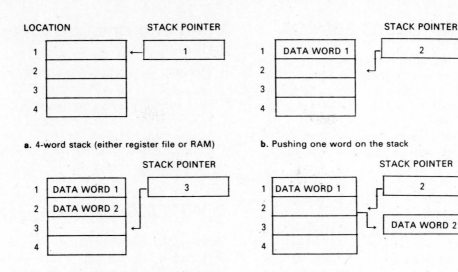

a. 4-word stack (either register file or RAM)

b. Pushing one word on the stack

c. Pushing second word on the stack

d. Popping the stack

Fig. 1-4 Stack operations.

empty, the pointer content indicates the first location (Fig. 1-4a). When data is pushed on the stack, the pointer increments to the next location (Fig. 1-4b and c). When the data is removed from the top of the stack, the stack pointer decrements and the data is made available (Fig. 1-4d).

Two errors can occur if the stack is not used correctly. If more items are pushed on to the stack than it can hold, a *stack overflow* error has been committed. Popping an empty stack will result in *stack underflow*. Stack operations are controlled by the program, so the programmer of a microprocessor must use care to prevent stack overflow or stack underflow, as both conditions will produce wrong answers.

Status Register

Many microprocessors provide single-bit indicators called *flags*, which show the results of the last arithmetic or logical function performed. Common status (or condition) flags are carry, zero, sign, and parity indicators. The status flags are conveniently grouped into a status register. The program can test each flag to determine whether it is set or cleared.

The carry flag is set or reset after such operations as addition or subtraction. If an addition produces a carry from the high-order bit position (the most significant bit), the carry flag will be set; alternatively, if no carry results, the bit is reset. The sign flag simply contains a 0 if the number is positive and a 1 if the number is negative. The zero flag is set if the result of the last instruction executed is equal to 0; otherwise, the zero flag is reset.

The parity flag is often used to check the correctness of an input or an output. Before discussing this flag, we must discuss the concept of *parity*. Simply stated, the number of set bits in a byte is an indication of the parity. If there is an odd number of bits set in the word, the parity is odd; if not, the parity is even. Consider a few examples, as shown in Table 1-2.

In the microprocessor, the number of 1s in the byte is determined, and the parity flag is set to 1 for even parity and to 0 for odd parity.

Microprocessor Registers Review

1. List the purpose of each register in a microprocessor.
2. Explain why the program counter is incremented.
3. Describe "pushing" and "popping" a stack.
4. Define the terms "FILO," "overflow," and "underflow" in reference to the stack and the stack pointer.
5. What is the parity of $0100\ 0001_2$? What value would the parity status flag have to indicate this parity?

Table 1-2 Parity Bits

Byte	Number of Bits Set to 1	Parity
$0000\ 0001_2$	1	Odd
$0000\ 0010$	1	Odd
$0000\ 0000_2$	0	Even
$0000\ 0011_2$	2	Even
$1001\ 1111_2$	6	Even
$0111\ 1111_2$	7	Odd

ARITHMETIC AND LOGIC SECTION

The manipulation of data is carried out in the arithmetic and logic section of the microprocessor. This section consists of the ALU and its arithmetic registers. Working on one or two 8-bit words in parallel, the ALU performs addition, subtraction, logical operations, and complementing. Most microprocessors cannot multiply or divide without the help of external circuitry or the use of a computer program.

A typical arithmetic and logic section is shown in Fig. 1-5. The major sections are the ALU itself (which performs complementing, adding, and boolean functions), a shift register, and a buffer register. There are two data inputs, a control input, and a single output. There is also a path for recirculating data from the shifter to the ALU. All registers and data paths are 8 bits wide.

The inputs for the operation, such as boolean AND, are sent to the arithmetic and logic section prior to application of the control input. The control input commands the ALU to perform an ANDing of input A with input B. After the AND has been completed, the answer passes through the shifter (unchanged) and into the buffer register, where it is available on the output lines. Other operations of the ALU are computed in a similar manner. (We will study computer arithmetic in more detail in Chaps. 2 and 7.) The shifter allows the programmer to shift the data left or right (see Chap. 9 for a full discussion).

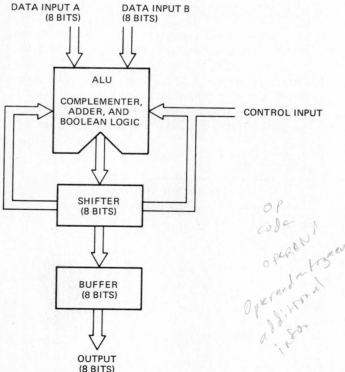

Fig. 1-5 Arithmetic-logic unit.

Arithmetic and Logic Section Review

1. List the components of the arithmetic and logic section.
2. Describe the purpose of the shifter.
3. How many inputs are required for an addition? For complementing?
4. Describe a possible use for the data path between the shifter and the ALU.

CONTROL SECTION

The control section maintains the correct timing and sequencing for the microcomputer. The crystal oscillator is the basis for timing, while sequencing is driven by the contents of the instruction register. Each instruction is actually a bit pattern that generates a series of enabling signals throughout the processor.

Each instruction requires one or more clock periods to complete execution. The timing pulses are generated by a crystal oscillator; together, this oscillator and the clock logic form the master clock. The clock period in modern microprocessors is 100 nanoseconds (ns) to 1 microsecond (μs). The clock logic may or may not be on the microprocessor chip. Figure 1-6 shows how a clock phase may be used for timing. The clock phases delineate the beginning or the end of each event within a single clock period.

Every *instruction cycle* consists of fetching and executing the instruction.

During the instruction-fetching portion of the cycle, the instruction is read from memory. Table 1-3 lists the steps necessary to obtain the instruction. First, the contents of the program counter are transferred to memory. The word in that memory location (the instruction) is sent to the data bus and then to the instruction register. Finally, the program counter is incremented to be ready to fetch the next instruction.

"Instruction execution" is another way of saying that the instruction is being decoded and the operation carried out. Instruction execution may require another memory reference to get the data, called the *operand*, to be processed, or, alternatively, memory may be referenced to write data back into some location.

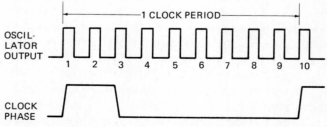

Fig. 1-6 Clock period and phases.

Table 1-3 Instruction Fetching

STEP 1. The contents of the program counter are sent to memory.

STEP 2. The contents of the memory cell are transferred to the data bus.

STEP 3. The data moves into the instruction register.

STEP 4. The program counter increments.

Microprogramming

The instruction-fetching sequence is an example of a *microprogram*. Each instruction in the computer instruction set, such as the one to complement the contents of the A register, requires a series of commands to move or operate on the data. The user need not be too concerned with the microprogram, as most microcomputers already have one developed for them. For special applications, a user can microprogram some models of MPUs, although this would be an unusual circumstance. Knowledge of the microprogram is quite useful in tracing a signal from within the processor, so an understanding of this concept will enhance your abilities to work with microcomputers.

Now consider the complement instruction. The microprogram steps necessary for the instruction's execution are illustrated in Fig. 1-7. All registers except for the program counter and A register were cleared prior to this sequence. The instruction fetch was also completed before execution of the microprogram began, as shown in Fig. 1-7a. A brief review of the instruction-fetching steps will explain the current contents of the registers: The program started at address 1000 0000 0000 0000$_2$; this is the original value in the program counter that is sent to the memory to obtain the instruction. The contents of cell 1000 0000 0000 0000$_2$ were transferred to the instruction register and the program counter incremented to 1000 0000 0000 0001$_2$.

The bits in the instruction are a coded message to control the start of the complementing microprogram. (The code 0010 1111$_2$ means to complement the A register.) First, the contents of the A register are gated onto the internal bus and then into the ALU, where complementing takes place. Note that input B is not necessary for this instruction (Figs. 1-7b and d). The data is passed through the shifter and buffer, is then placed on the bus, and is finally returned to its complemented form to the A register (Figs. 1-7e and f). The complement of 1101 0001$_2$ is 0010 1110$_2$, as shown in Fig. 1-7.

Five microprogram steps were necessary to execute the instruction. On completion of the instruction execution, the shifter and buffers registers still hold the result, but this data will be overwritten during the next operation. Because detailed knowledge of the signal and data flow within the processor is required, micropro-gramming a computer is a significant effort. Not every microprocessor can be microprogrammed by the user, but for those which can be, a microprogram development system is used.

Microprogram Development Systems

The microprogram must not be altered, so a ROM is used to store the control program. This memory is called a *control ROM (CROM)* to distinguish it from other ROMs used in the computer. Microprogramming consists of writing the microsequences for the control section. Development systems are available to make microprogramming easier.

Development systems usually consist of three parts: a microprogram controller, a storage device, and a display unit. The microprogram controller operates in the same manner as the control section of the microprocessor; that is, the microprogram controller *emulates* the control section. The microprogram being developed and tested is written and read into the storage device. The storage device is usually a read-write memory so that the program can be changed to correct errors; after the microprogram is completely debugged, it is copied into a ROM. The display unit permits the operator to read or write microcode in the storage unit, cause the controller to execute the microcode, and inspect the results of each *microinstruction* (which make up the microprogram).

After the microprogram is checked out, prototype control ROMs are produced. These ROMs are exercised in the actual MPU to ensure that the microprogram runs the same in the MPU as it did in the development system. On completion of this testing, the program is placed in production to generate as many CROMs as required.

Control Section Review

1. Describe the two parts of the instruction cycle.
2. List the events required to fetch the instruction.
3. Why must the program counter be incremented after fetching the instruction?
4. List the microprogram steps needed to complement the contents of the accumulator.
5. Describe the function of the internal bus in microprocessor operations.

MEMORY

Two types of memory are commonly used in microcomputers. Read-only memory is used to store programs and data that are not to be changed. (Do not confuse this use of ROM with the CROM; the CROM is read

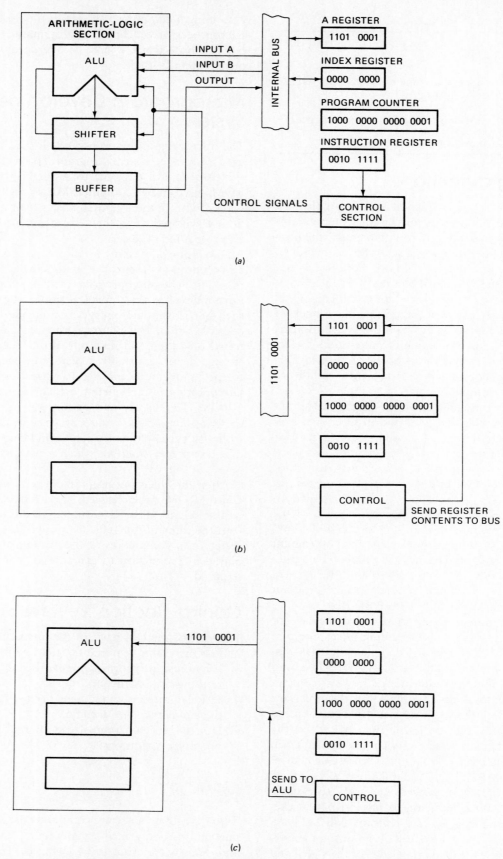

Fig. 1-7 Microprogram for complementing the contents of the accumulator.

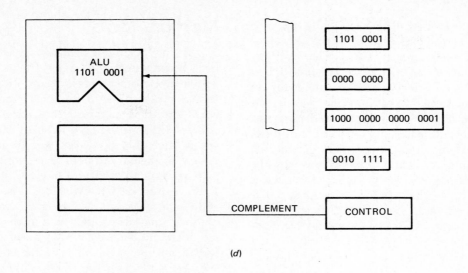

(d)

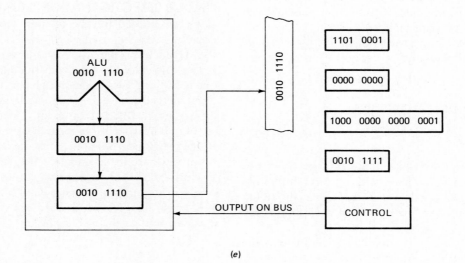

(e)

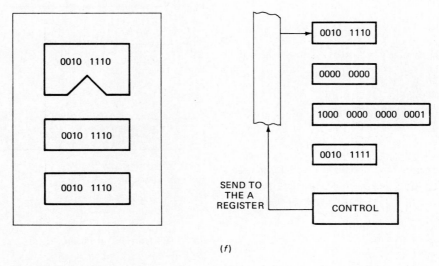

(f)

Fig. 1-7 (cont'd)

by the control section, while ROM is read by the MPU and contains the instructions needed for the microprocessor to perform its designated tasks.) [The read-only memory may be an electrically programmable ROM (EPROM). Where the distinction between these devices is unimportant, the term "ROM" will be used in this book.] Read-write memory stores data and programs that are frequently altered. Random-access memories are further divided into static or dynamic memories. *Static memories* must constantly receive power, while *dynamic memories* require only periodic refresh cycles (requiring less power). The memory area is often partitioned into a ROM area and a RAM area. For example, a memory with 65,536 locations may have addresses 0000_{10} through 4095_{10} assigned to ROM and the remainder to RAM. Usually, the two types of memory are packaged in separate DIPs.

The size of memory is often indicated by a symbolic notation. The 65,536 memory mentioned above could also be written as 64K, where K means that the number to the left should be multiplied by 1024 to obtain the actual number of locations in the memory ($64 \times 1024 = 65,536$). The 8-bit word size can also be indicated as in 8K $\times$ 8 (bits).

Addressing

Memory capacity is always a power of 2. For example, the 64K memory is equal to 2^{16} ($2^{16} = 65,536$). The reason for this relationship is that memory must be addressed by use of the address bus. A given number of address bus lines (say, n) allow us to address 2^n different locations in memory. Each address line corresponds to 1 bit of the binary address.

Every memory location is capable of holding 1 byte of data. To find the total number of bits in a memory, simply multiply the memory capacity by the word length. Two examples are provided to illustrate these relationships:

☐ **EXAMPLE 1** How many bits are there in an 8K $\times$ 8-bit memory?

$$8K = \quad 8192 \quad \text{words}$$
$$\underline{\times\ 8} \quad \text{bits per word}$$
$$65,536 \quad \text{total bits in memory}$$

☐ **EXAMPLE 2** A certain memory requires 10 address bits to specify the location of each word, and each word is 8 bits long. How many bits does the memory hold?

$$2^{10} = \quad 1024 \quad \text{words}$$
$$\underline{\times\ 8} \quad \text{bits per word}$$
$$8192 \quad \text{total bits in memory}$$

Memory Map

A plan for laying out memory, called a *memory map*, must be prepared when a new microcomputer is being designed. Consider a case where 8K $\times$ 8 RAMs and ROMs are being used for the memory. Because each RAM or ROM contains 8192 different locations, 13 address bits must be used to select the correct location within each chip ($2^{13} = 8192$). In addition, we must design the memory to hold several of each type of chip.

If we want 8K of ROM and 8K of RAM, a total of 1 ROM chip and 1 RAM chip will be needed. Then the addressing process must select the correct chip in addition to the address bits within the chip. As we will see later, the *chip-select (CS) input* to each RAM or ROM can be used to activate the correct memory IC. We also must designate whether the operation is to be read or write for the RAM chips.

LINEAR SELECTION ADDRESSING If only a few chips are needed for the memory, linear selection addressing may be used. For an 8192-word ROM or RAM, bits 0 through 12 can address the 8192 locations in the chip. Now assume that our microcomputer uses one ROM and two RAMs and has a 16-bit address bus. Then we can let bit 15 of the address select the ROM, bit 14 select RAM 1, and bit 13 select RAM 2. By setting bit 15 to a 1, we mean that the address is in the ROM (see Fig. 1-8a). The consequences of this address assignment are listed in Table 1-4. Because an MSB of 1 selects the ROM, addressing conflicts can occur with careless programming, as shown in the last case in Table 1-4. Here, bits 15, 14, and 13 are all set selecting all three memories; this programming is clearly wrong.

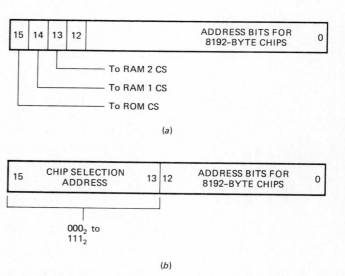

(a)

(b)

Fig. 1-8 Addressing methods: (*a*) linear selection addressing, (*b*) fully decoded addressing.

Table 1-4 Linear Selection Addressing Example

Address	Memory Selected
0000 0000 0000 0000$_2$ to 0001 1111 1111 1111$_2$	None (illegal addresses)

0010 0000 0000 0000$_2$
 	
to 0011 1111 1111 1111$_2$
    ↑
  bit 13
	RAM 2 (addresses above 0011 1111 1111 1111$_2$ are illegal)

0100 0000 0000 0000$_2$
 	
to 0101 1111 1111 1111$_2$
  ↑
  bit 14
	RAM 1 (addresses above 0101 1111 1111 1111$_2$ are illegal)

0110 0000 0000 0000$_2$ to 0111 1111 1111 1111$_2$ ↑↑ bit 14 bit 13	RAM 1 and RAM 2 (illegal)
1000 0000 0000 0000$_2$ to 1001 1111 1111 1111$_2$ ↑ bit 15	ROM (addresses above 1001 1111 1111 1111$_2$ are illegal)
1010 0000 0000 0000$_2$ to 1111 1111 1111 1111$_2$ ↑↑↑ bit 15 bit 14 bit 13	Combinations of ROM, RAM 1, and RAM 2 (illegal)

As Table 1-4 shows, a major shortcoming of linear selection is that some addresses are unusable, or "illegal." The total number of chips that can be addressed is limited, should you want to expand the memory. In this case the use of bits 13 through 15 limits the maximum number of memories to three. However, the scheme is simple, and no logic is required to decode the address of the memory chip selected; in fact, each is selected by a dedicated address bit. Small microcomputer memories are often designed to use linear selection addressing to minimize costs.

FULLY DECODED ADDRESSING If the capability for addressing a 64K memory is to be provided, fully decoded addressing must be used. Each RAM or ROM is given a unique address corresponding to the binary number in bits 13 through 15. If we let those addresses be

```
ROM      000X  XXXX  XXXX  XXXX
RAM 1    001X  XXXX  XXXX  XXXX
RAM 2    010X  XXXX  XXXX  XXXX
```

(where X may be 0 or 1), we get for each memory chip the address range shown at the top of page 12.

The remaining addresses available, but not used, will provide for an expansion to a total of 8 chips, each with 8K bytes (see Fig. 1-8b). Total memory size will be 64K [(8 × 8K) = 65,536]. Because consecutive addresses are used in this method, none is illegal; however, the cost of decoding the address is a disadvantage.

Decoding the address is simple in theory. Figure 1-9 shows a NAND gate used to decode the address for the ROM chip and then to select that chip. The CS input

Address Range

	Low				High			
ROM	0000	0000	0000	0000	0000	0000	1111	1111
RAM 1	0010	0001	0000	0000	0010	0000	1111	1111
RAM 2	0100	0010	0000	0000	0100	0000	1111	1111

These bits designate the memory chip   These bits address the 8192 bits within each chip

These bits designate the memory chip   These bits address the 8192 bits within each chip

to the ROM will be set only if bits 13 through 15 on the address bus are all 0.

A more practical device that can be used for address decoding is the 74138 3-to-8 decoder. Three address lines connected to the inputs will set only one of the output lines (S0 through S7), the one corresponding to that address. If only 8 memory chips are used, one 74138 IC with address bus bits 13 through 15 as inputs will fully decode the address (see Fig. 1-10). If more than eight memory chips are used, several 74138 ICs can be combined to select the proper memory chip.

ADDRESSING DYNAMIC RAM Dynamic RAM requires special addressing consideration. A typical 4K × 1 RAM will be used in the following discussion on addressing dynamic memories. In this case 12 address pins are required (2^{12} = 4096). Other pins are needed in this RAM as well; one is needed for power, one for ground, one for the input, one for the output, one for chip selection, and one for read-write selection. The total number of pins needed is far in excess of the 14 available on the IC. How can this be?

In fact, there are not 12 address pins needed, but only 6 (A0 through A5). The pins are used twice in a *split addressing cycle*. To understand split-cycle (multiplexed) addressing, first refer to Fig. 1-11, which presents a conceptual picture of the addressing arrangement. The memory is a matrix of 64 rows by 64 columns. At the intersection of each row and column is a memory address, so there are (64 × 64) = 4096

addresses. Now each address for the RAM is divided into two groups of bits, which are applied to the pins in two cycles. The 6-bit address for the row is first applied through an external multiplexer, and a row-address strobe ($\overline{RAS}$) is set, which latches the row address into bits A0 through A5. Then the second group of address bits designating the column is applied, and

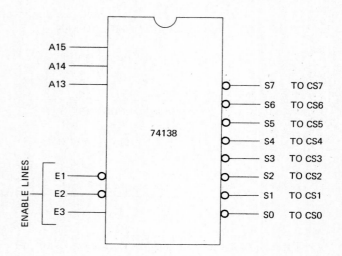

74138 FUNCTION TABLE			
INPUTS			OUTPUT HIGH
A15	A14	A13	S7
A15	A14	$\overline{A13}$	S6
A15	$\overline{A14}$	A13	S5
A15	$\overline{A14}$	$\overline{A13}$	S4
$\overline{A15}$	A14	A13	S3
$\overline{A15}$	A14	$\overline{A13}$	S2
$\overline{A15}$	$\overline{A14}$	A13	S1
$\overline{A15}$	$\overline{A14}$	$\overline{A13}$	S0

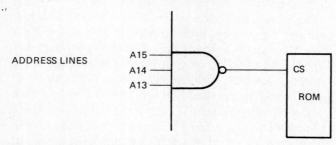

Fig. 1-9 Simple address decoding.

Fig. 1-10 Three-to-eight address decoder.

ROWS

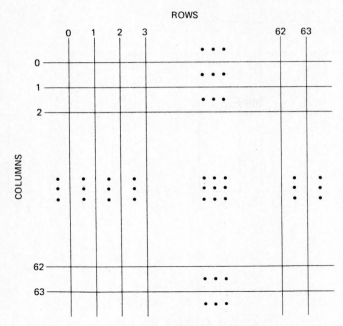

Fig. 1-11 Row and column addresses in dynamic RAM.

the column-address strobe ($\overline{CAS}$) latches the column address into bits A6 to A11. By using a multiplexed addressing scheme, 6 address pins are made to do the job of 12.

All the pins on the RAM are identified in Fig. 1-12. The bars over some of the signals ($\overline{RAS}$ and $\overline{CAS}$, for example) indicate that the signal is true when it is low.

This memory has a word length of only a single bit, but our microprocessor requires 8 bits. To achieve the desired word length, eight of the RAMS are used in parallel (Fig. 1-13). The address bits, $\overline{RAS}$, $\overline{CAS}$, and $\overline{WRITE}$, are paralleled to each RAM, while input data (D_{in}) and output data (D_{out}) are connected to individual data lines from the microprocessor.

Because this RAM is dynamic, it must be *refreshed*, that is, periodically rewritten; otherwise, the data stored in the memory will be lost. Reading or writing of the memory is prohibited during the refresh cycle. To refresh the memory, bits A0 to A5 are set to the row address to be refreshed. Because it is necessary only to refresh the rows, a total of 64 cycles will take care of the entire 4K RAM. After each cycle, the row address is simply incremented by one until all rows have been refreshed.

Memory Review

1. Distinguish between the uses of ROM and RAM in microcomputers.
2. List the two types of read-write memories.
3. How many words are there in a 16K memory?
4. Explain why memory capacity is always some power of 2.

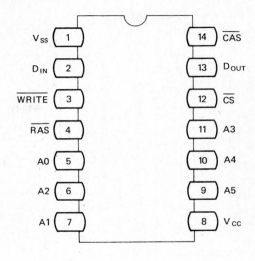

A0–A5	ADDRESS PINS
$\overline{CS}$	CHIP SELECT
$\overline{CAS}$	COLUMN ADDRESS STROBE
$\overline{RAS}$	ROW ADDRESS STROBE
D_{IN}	DATA IN
D_{OUT}	DATA OUT
$\overline{WRITE}$	WRITE/READ SELECT
V_{CC}	+5 V
V_{SS}	GROUND

Fig. 1-12 4K RAM pin assignments.

5. Discuss the advantages and disadvantages of linear selection and fully decoded addressing.
6. Describe how split-cycle addressing saves pins on a dynamic RAM integrated circuit.

BIT-SLICED MICROPROCESSOR ARCHITECTURE

There are some applications for which a general-purpose microprocessor is quite inefficient. In those cases, characterized by the need for a special-purpose MPU and by high volume for cost-effectiveness, *bit-sliced microprocessors* can be used with success. These microprocessors differ in two ways from those which we have discussed to this point. First, they are available in 4-bit segments, thus allowing the designer to construct a microcomputer with word lengths of 4 to 32 bits or more. Second, the microprograms for these machines must be written by the user, so the instruction set can be dedicated to the task.

This general nature of bit-sliced MPUs has a price, however, in that these MPUs are more difficult to use

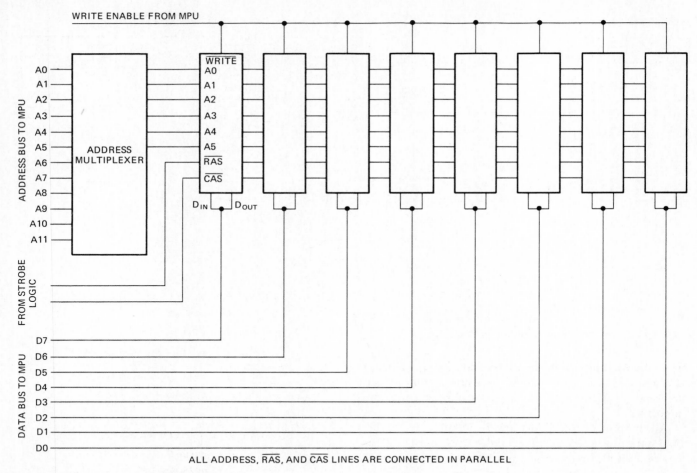

WRITE ENABLE FROM MPU

ADDRESS BUS TO MPU

A0
A1
A2
A3
A4
A5
A6
A7
A8
A9
A10
A11

ADDRESS MULTIPLEXER

WRITE
A0
A1
A2
A3
A4
A5
RAS
CAS

D IN   D OUT

FROM STROBE LOGIC

DATA BUS TO MPU

D7
D6
D5
D4
D3
D2
D1
D0

ALL ADDRESS, RAS, AND CAS LINES ARE CONNECTED IN PARALLEL

Fig. 1-13   8-bit dynamic RAM organization.

than are fixed-word-size devices. Designing the instruction set means that the control section must be uniquely tailored to each usage of the microprocessor. A great deal of effort and expense goes into producing the sequencing logic and microprogram of the control section.

A bit-sliced microprocessor provides all the registers, data paths, and ALU for the arithmetic section in segments that can be joined together. Earlier versions of these devices were available in 2- or 4-bit increments, but the 4-bit configuration is most common today. Figure 1-14 provides a conceptual view of how a 12-bit and a 32-bit microcomputer can be constructed from the bit-sliced *register arithmetic-logic units (RALUs)*. Note that the control sections for the two microcomputers are different. Trying to expand the 12-bit control section to 32 bits would be difficult. Starting with a new 32-bit design would be more feasible.

The *sequencer* decides on the order for executing the microinstructions. The sequencer can step through the program consecutively, or it can jump from one program location to another. Sometimes the same series of microinstructions is to be repeated several times, so the sequencer must be able to maintain a count and decide when to terminate the repetitive series. In Fig. 1-14c we

can see that the sequencer contains three components. The CROM was already covered in "Microprogram Development Systems" on page 7. The *sequencing logic* interprets the microinstructions, decides the order for stepping through the microprogram, and orders the control signal generator to send commands to the other sections of the microcomputer.

The RALU is similar to the arithmetic section discussed earlier, except for the fact that the RALU is sliced into 4-bit segments. Figure 1-15 illustrates this concept. Data is received from the input data bus and is temporarily stored in a register file that is equivalent to 16 general registers. From the file, data can be sent either to the ALU, where the arithmetic, boolean, and complement operations are performed, or to the shifter. A second shifter is in series with the data stream from the ALU, so a data word can be shifted in either of two shift registers. The buffer holds ALU results until they are placed back into the register file or on the output bus. All these components are 4 bits wide. The RALU can be joined together with another identical unit; in Fig. 1-16 an 8-bit RALU has been formed by paralleling two slices. The ALU and all the registers and data paths now provide 8-bit parallel word handling.

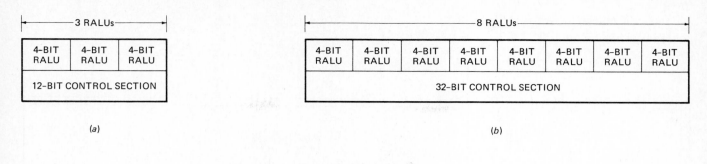

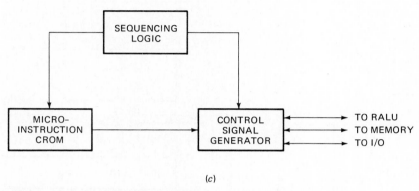

Fig. 1-14 Bit-sliced microprocessors: (*a*) 12-bit microprocessor, (*b*) 32-bit microprocessor, (*c*) sequencer.

The *control-signal generator* section must direct all the processing. Data must be routed along the paths at the correct time. The source registers for operands and the destination register for results must be designated. The input to the ALU and the operation to be performed on them must be controlled, and a destination for ALU results must be specified. Even when control is considered from this simplified point of view, the complexity of designing this section of a microprocessor is obvious. Because of the work involved in using bit-sliced microprocessors, these devices are not as widely used as those with fixed word sizes.

Bit-Sliced Architecture Review

1. How many RALUs would be needed in a 24-bit microcomputer? How many control sections?
2. Describe the function of the sequencer and list its components.
3. How does the bit-sliced RALU differ from one with a fixed word size?
4. Discuss the operations that the control-signal generator section must direct.

INPUT/OUTPUT

There are three methods for exchanging information between the microcomputer and its outside environment. *Programmed I/O* transfers data under control of the computer instructions, so the external logic is commanded by the program. In contrast to programmed I/O are *interrupts*; these force an input data exchange even though the processor was not expecting it. The most complex I/O logic is required for *direct memory access (DMA)*, which moves data to and from memory

Fig. 1-15 4-bit sliced RALU.

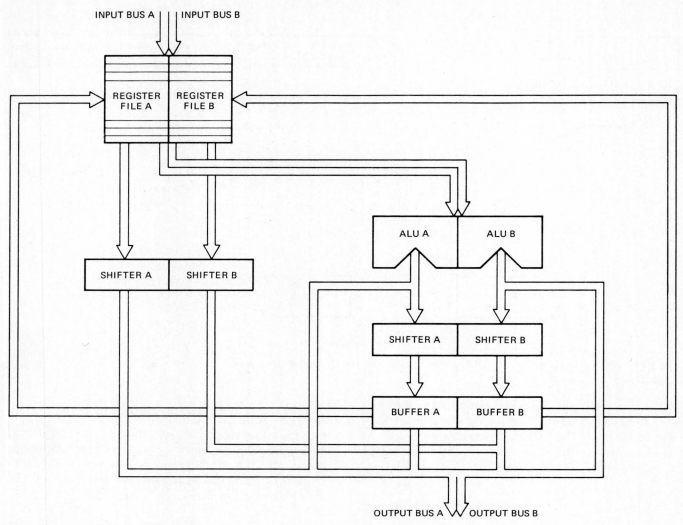

INPUT BUS A   INPUT BUS B

REGISTER FILE A   REGISTER FILE B

SHIFTER A   SHIFTER B

ALU A   ALU B

SHIFTER A   SHIFTER B

BUFFER A   BUFFER B

OUTPUT BUS A   OUTPUT BUS B

Fig. 1-16 Joined RALUs.

without involving the microprocessor in the data transfer.

The I/O concepts introduced in this section are more fully covered in Chaps. 12, 13, and 14.

Programmed I/O

Most commonly, microcomputer I/O uses serial data transfer. The serial data from the I/O is converted to parallel before the bits are placed on the system bus. Data from the processor must also be converted to serial. Most MPUs move data through some register in performing programmed I/O.

Interrupts

When a computer system is used in real-time operations, the processor must be notified of unscheduled events from the outside. Interrupt signals are used for this

function. An interrupt request signal is transmitted to the processor by an external system-bus control line. The microprocessor, under program control, can accept or reject the interrupt. If the interrupt is accepted, the processor sets the interrupt acknowledge signal and enters an interrupt-handling program. When the external device senses the acknowledge signal, the device transfers the input data to the I/O port.

Remember that the interrupt was unscheduled, so the microprocessor must suspend whatever action it had been doing prior to servicing the interrupt. Table 1-5 lists the microprogram steps for interrupt processing. First, the processor and arithmetic registers must be saved in memory. Then the program counter and other registers are loaded with the address of the interrupt-handling program. After that program has completed processing the interrupt, the registers are reloaded with their orginal contents so that the main program can resume operations at the same point where it left off.

Table 1-5 Interrupt Servicing Program

STEP 1. Store the contents of the A register, the program counter, and the status flags (in some microcomputers memory is used for storage; alternatively, the stack can be employed).

STEP 2. Load the program counter with the address of the interrupt-handling program.

STEP 3. Execute the interrupt-handling program.

STEP 4. Restore the contents of the A register, the program counter, and the status flags.

Direct Memory Access

Using a direct access to memory, an external device can read or write data and bypass the microprocessor entirely. The advantage of direct memory access (DMA) is that the processor is not involved in I/O operations. As we will see in Chap. 12, the disadvantages are the need for a sophisticated I/O device and the fact that instruction execution time may increase. The use of DMA is most commonly required when the processor would otherwise be overloaded in executing its program and managing I/O.

The scheme used to implement DMA is called *memory cycle stealing*. The external equipment sets a memory request signal high when it wants to access memory. The microprocessor logic responds with an acknowledge signal. The signal is an automatic response by the microprogram and does not require execution of an I/O instruction by the processor. (Until the acknowledge signal becomes high, the requesting device must wait.) While the I/O device is referencing memory, the processor can perform any operation except using memory; hence the term "cycle stealing." Some processors allow the device to continue to use memory for many cycles; others only allow a single memory reference before the processor regains control. Because only one user can reference memory at one time, the processor may have to wait for the peripheral equipment to finish. This delay in accessing memory could result in slowing down the speed of instruction execution.

Once the information transfer is complete, the I/O device drops the request, and the processor again can use memory. A device that employs DMA must have the same memory logic as the processor; that is, the device needs a counter to keep track of the number of words to read or write, a status register, an I/O clock, and memory addressing and memory control logic.

Input/Output Review

1. List the I/O methods used by microprocessors.
2. List the sequence of events that an interrupt triggers if it arrives while the microprocessor is executing another program.
3. List the signals required to access memory directly.

MICROPROCESSOR PRODUCTS

Having covered microprocessor concepts in general, we now examine some specific devices. Figure 1-17 is a

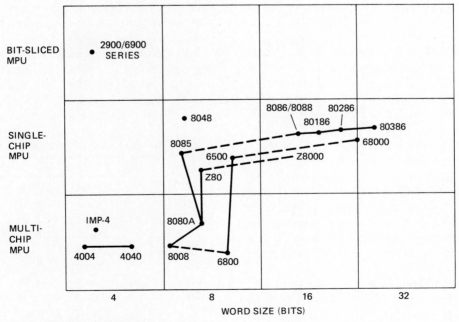

Note: Lines show family relationships

Fig. 1-17 A microprocessor family tree.

chart relating the characteristics of several microprocessors. It shows that microprocessors can be grouped by their word size, that is, 4, 8, or 16 bits. They can also be classed as multichip MPUs, single-chip MPUs, or bit-sliced MPUs. The chart provides the genealogy for MPUs that grew from earlier versions. From the fact that some microprocessor families have already produced three generations, we can see how much the industry has advanced in just a few years.

4-Bit Microprocessors

The earliest microprocessors had 4-bit word lengths instead of the more common 8 and 16 bits of the present microprocessors. This constraint was logical, for the designers wanted to limit the risk in developing the large-scale integration (LSI) technology necessary for the microprocessor. As they gained experience with the technology, the more cost-effective 8-bit device evolved.

The early 4-bit MPUs included the Intel 4004 and 4040 and the National Semiconductor IMP-4. Because these microprocessors were fabricated as multichip devices, they can no longer compete economically with the 8- and 16-bit MPUs.

8-Bit Microprocessors

The 8-bit microprocessor has become the industry standard today. The trend in this group of MPUs has been to decrease the number of chips and power supply voltages needed to construct a microcomputer. This trend has grown to the point that manufacturers now produce single-chip microprocessors that need just one compatible +5-V power supply with the transistor-transistor logic (TTL).

THE 8080A The 8080A is now being used in more different applications than is any other microprocessor. The 8080A is both a descendant of and an improvement on the 8008 MPU. Of special interest to designers is the extensive range of supporting ICs available for use with the 8080A.

The 8080A is the basis for a three-chip microprocessor. In addition to the 8080A, an 8224 System Clock Generator and the 8228 or 8238 System Controller ICs are necessary to provide all functions of a microprocessor. The 8224 is used to generate the timing signals for the 8080A MPU system from an external oscillator, and the 8228/8238 demultiplexes the data lines of the 8080A. The Appendix provides a detailed description of the 8080A architecture.

The 8080A requires three power supplies of +5 V, +12 V, and −5 V. Using a 50-ns clock, the 8080A instruction execution times range from 2 to 9 μs. All signals are TTL-compatible.

The other devices in the 8080A family are listed in Table 1-6. The 8224, 8228, and 8238 were described above. The 8251 provides either synchronous or asynchronous data communications in a single IC. The 8255 provides from one to three 8-bit I/O ports to the MPU. A multipurpose device, the 8212 I/O port can be used as an address buffer and decoder, a priority interrupt arbitrator, or an I/O peripheral interface. Direct memory access can be implemented by using the 8257 IC. Programmable delays or timed pulses can be created with the 8253.

Interrupt processing is facilitated by the 8259 or the 8214. The 8259 arbitrates priority among eight interrupts and initiates the software servicing routine. The 8214 allows several simultaneous interrupt requests to be received and serviced by the software. The 8205 is a 1-of-8 decoder that can be used for memory selection. Proper signals on the bidirectional bus rely on such devices as the 8216 or the 8226. Except for those devices made by Intel Corporation, all 8080A and support ICs are manufactured by unauthorized second sources. Differences are often found between the Intel and second-source parts. Table 1-7 lists the similar components made by Advanced Micro Devices (AMD), NEC, Texas Instruments (TI), and National Semiconductor (NS).

THE 8085 This MPU is Intel's next generation of the 8080A. A single chip replaces the three ICs needed in the earlier model. The 8085 package contains the ALU, the control unit, the accumulator and registers, and the clock logic. An external crystal or an RC network drives the clock logic. All bus interface logic is also provided by the 8085. Only a single +5-V power supply is needed by this N-channel silicon-gate device. Its instruction set includes all 8080A instructions plus two new ones.

In addition to being able to use many of the 8080A support devices, the 8085 also has some unique components (Table 1-8). The 8155 and 8156 were specifically designed for use with the 8085. They supply 256 bytes of static RAM, two or three (two 8-bit and one

Table 1-6 8080A Support Devices

Device	Purpose
8224	System clock generator
8228/8328	System controller
8251	Serial I/O communications interface
8255/8255A	Programmable parallel I/O interface
8212	I/O port
8253	Programmable timer
8259	Priority interrupt controller
8214	Priority interrupt device
8205	Address buffer decoder
8216/8226	Bidirectional bus drivers

Table 1-7 Second Sources for the 8080A Family

Device	Intel	AMD	NEC	TI	NS
8080A	8080A	9080A	8080A	TMS8080A	8080A
8205	8205	25LS138			
8212	8212	8212	8212	SM74S412	
8214	8214		8214		
8216/8226		8216/8226	8216		
8224	8224	8224	8224	SM74LS424	8224
8228/8238	8228/8238	8228/8238	8228/8238	SM74LS428	8228/8238
8251	8251	9551	8251		
8253	8253		8253		
8255	8255	9555	8255		8255
8259	8259				

16-bit) parallel I/O ports, and a programmable timer. The 8355 has 2048 bytes of ROM with two 8-bit I/O ports. The only difference between the 8755 and the 8355 is that the former has erasable programmable read-only memory (EPROM).

THE MC6800

While Intel was developing the 8080A, Motorola produced the MC6800 as its answer to an improved 8008. The MC6800 is probably the second most popular microprocessor family. There are considerable differences between the 8080A and MC6800, even though they may have a common ancestor. The MC6800 uses simpler timing signals and control signals than does the 8080A. The MC6800 does not multiplex the data bus, so no system controller (like the 8228) is required.

Only a single +5-V power supply is used. The MC6800 is fabricated by using N-channel silicon-gate depletion MOS. Of course, the MC6800 has a different instruction repertoire; there are fewer basic instruction types than those provided by the 8080A. An off-chip clock device is required. The MC6800 uses a 1-μs clock and can execute instructions in 2 to 12 μs. (A faster instruction cycle is possible with the MC6800A, which uses a 750-ns clock, and the MC6800B, which uses a 500-ns clock.)

A family of support devices, listed in Table 1-9, is also available for the MC6800. The MC6802 provides 128 bytes of RAM with the MPU, but some pins and signals differ from those of the MC6800. The two-phase clock signals are generated by the MC6870 series clock

chips, which contain both the crystal and the oscillator. General parallel I/O functions are supported by the MC6820, which provides two 8-bit I/O ports. For asynchronous serial data transfer and control, the MC6850 is used. The XC6852 performs synchronous serial I/O logic functions. The MC8507 priority interrupt controller has two part numbers because it is a bipolar component compatible with the NMOS MC6800 family.

THE 8048

The 8048 is a series of single-chip microprocessors. This family is at the low-capability end of microcomputers, designed for low-cost, high-volume applications. Only one +5-V power supply is used by any of the chips. All I/O is TTL-compatible. The user can select either a 2.5-μs or a 5-μs clock, and all these devices have a built-in timer. The members of the 8048 family are listed in Table 1-10.

Any of these processors can interface with the 8155, the 8355, or the 8755 chips developed for the 8085 MPU. In addition, an I/O expander, the 8243, is unique to this series. The 8243 expands I/O port 2 into four

Table 1-8 8085 Support Devices

Device	Purpose
8155 8156	Static RAM with I/O ports and timer
8355 8755	ROM with I/O ports

Table 1-9 MC6800 Support Devices

Device	Purpose
MC6802	MPU with RAM
MC6870A MC6871A MC6871B MC6875	Clock generator
MC6820	Peripheral interface adapter
MCS6850	Asynchronous communications interface adapter
XC6852	Synchronous serial data adapter
MC8507 (MC6828)	Priority interrupt controller

Table 1-10 8048 Family

Designator	ROM (bytes)	EPROM (bytes)	RAM (bytes)	Clock Period (µs)	I/O Ports (8-bit)
8035	0	0	64	2.5	3
8035–8	0	0	64	5	3
8048	1024	0	64	2.5	3
8748	0	1024	64	2.5	3
8748–8	0	1024	64	5	3

individually addressable 4-bit ports. N-channel MOS (NMOS) is used in these 24-pin DIPs.

THE Z80 All the 8085 instructions can be executed by the Z80; consequently, the programs given throughout this book will run on the Z80 without modification. In addition, the Z80 has features that allow it to perform more instructions than the 8085. Because the 8085 instruction set plus new instructions can be run on the Z80, we say that the 8085 instruction set is a *subset* of the Z80 repertoire. The Appendix provides an overview of the Z80 architecture. The NMOS microprocessor is based on the 8080A architecture, but it is not pin-for-pin compatible. The Z80 also has more registers and addressing modes than the 8080A has. Only one power supply is necessary, and clock logic is in the Z80. A novel feature of the MPU is automatic dynamic memory refresh. The original TRS-80 microcomputer had a Z80 chip for its processor.

All 8080A support devices except the 8259 priority interrupt control unit can be used with the Z80, although the 8155, the 8355, and the 8755 are not recommended. Other support ICs are listed in Table 1-11. The parallel I/O interface (PIO) is a functional equivalent to the 8255 of the 8080A support devices. It provides two 8-bit I/O ports. The clock timer circuit (CTC) is a programmable timer. It can serve as an internal timer or external event counter. There are four individual counters-timers within the circuit.

THE MCS6500 FAMILY Although this family of NMOS microprocessors does not use the same instruction set or system bus, it can be considered a derivation of the MC6800. In some cases the clock logic is on the chip. These MPUs use a $+5$-V power supply. Instruction execution times vary between 2 and 12 µs with a 1-µs clock.

Table 1-11 Z80 Support Devices

Device	Purpose
PIO	Parallel I/O interface
CTC	Clock timer circuit

Table 1-12 lists the capabilities of the processors in the family. While the data bus is always 8 bits, the address bus ranges from 12 to 16 bits in length. Packaging is either a 28- or a 40-pin DIP.

Two support devices are available (Table 1-13). The MCS6522 can be considered to be an improved MC6820 with general-purpose parallel I/O logic, two 8-bit I/O ports, a counter-timer, and serial I/O logic. The MCS6530 provides 1024 bytes of ROM, 64 bytes of RAM, an internal timer, and interrupt servicing logic.

THE 8086 The 8086 extends the 8080A family into the 16-bit word microprocessors. Much of the 8080A/ 8085 software can be run on the 8086 after being translated by a special program. In addition to these features, the 8086 provides 16-bit arithmetic (including multiplication and division), string operations, and bit manipulation. Extremely sophisticated programming techniques, such as reentrant routines, relocatable programs, and multiprocessing, have been designed into this processor. The extended set of addressing modes allows the microprocessor to address 1 megabyte (Mbyte) (10^6 bytes) of memory.

The 8086 is also considerably faster than its predecessors because it is fabricated from silicon gate HMOS. The reduced propagation delays allow a 5-megahertz (MHz) clock to be used. The instruction and memory efficiency allow the 8086 to run 12 times faster than the 8080A. The IC has 40 pins and uses a single power supply and two grounds.

The 8086 is supported by a large family of components. In addition to such devices as I/O ports and bus drivers like those we saw in other processors, this family also includes peripheral controllers: the 8251A programmable communications interface, the 8271 floppy-disk controller, the 8275 CRT controller, and the 8278 keyboard interface.

THE Z8000 This 16-bit microprocessor is also in the category of competing with minicomputers in terms of the instruction set and speed. It is 5 to 10 times faster than the Z80A, with a 4-MHz clock rate. The processor instructions include 32-bit operations (including multiplication) as well as 16-bit operations. It, too, performs

Table 1-12 MCS 6500 Family

MPU	Address Bus (bits)	Data Bus (bits)	Pins	On-Chip Clock
6502	16	8	40	Yes
6503	12	8	28	Yes
6504	13	8	28	Yes
6505	12	8	28	Yes
6506	12	8	28	Yes
6512	16	8	40	No
6513	12	8	28	No
6514	12	8	28	No
6515	12	8	28	No

string manipulations and can run in a multiprocessor environment.

The Z8000 comes in two versions. The 40-pin nonsegmented version can directly access 64K bytes of memory, while the 48-pin segmented version can address 8 Mbytes. The segmented version must be supported by the Z-MMU memory management unit for address translation and other memory overhead functions. The segmented version is upward-compatible with the nonsegmented Z8000.

Other chips in the family include the Z-MBU microprocessor buffer unit, the Z-FIFO first-in first-out buffer memory, the Z-CIO and the Z-SIO I/O circuits, and the Z-UPC universal peripheral controller.

THE MC68000 FAMILY A design goal of the MC68000, including the 68020, was to support high-level software languages efficiently by providing a suitable instruction set. This MPU, like the two previous ones, can run in a multiprocessor configuration.

Although the data bus is 16 bits wide, all registers within the MC68000 family are 32 bits. Memory addresses of up to 16 Mbytes can be reached by the 24-bit program counter. The processor is housed in a 64-pin DIP to provide a 16-bit data bus and a 23-bit address bus, together with control and power pins. The 24th bit of the address bus is a combination (by external gating) of the address strobe with two data lines.

A +5-V power supply and two grounds are required. A single-phase TTL-level clock with a frequency of up to 8 MHz provides timing. Many of the existing MC6800 family support chips can be used with this family.

Table 1-13 MCS 6500 Support Devices

Device	Purpose
MCS6522	Peripheral interface adapter
MCS6530	Multifunction support logic device

Other 16- and 32-Bit Microprocessors

Even higher scales of integration have led to the 16- and 32-bit families of microprocessors, such as the 80186, 80286, and 80386. Interestingly, all these processors can execute software written for the 8086 without modification; hence, they are said to be *upward-compatible* with the 8086. Chapter 21 provides an overview of these processors as well as of the 68000 family. In general, these processors provide built-in features for high performance, multitasking (execution of more than one program in the same time frame), and rapid communications.

The 16-bit 80186 provides two high-speed direct memory access channels, timers, and I/O control on the chip. Its performance is about twice that of the 8086. Much more memory can be addressed by this processor as well. It has a direct memory address capability of 1 Mbyte. With its numerical coprocessor, the 8087, it offers direct execution of trigonometric, exponential, and logarithmic instructions.

The 16-bit 80286 processor executes at a rate of 6 times that of the 8086. This processor is characterized by a large memory capacity of 16 Mbytes, and by means of *virtual memory* each task can reach 1 gigabyte (Gbyte) (2^{30}). Memory management and protection facilities are integrated into the microprocessor. With the high-performance 80287, high-performance numerical processing is supported.

The 80386 is a 32-bit machine. Even more performance is packaged into this chip. For example, its direct memory access is 4 Gbyte. Multiple on-chip features offer flexible memory management and protection. System performance can be increased by using the pipelined instruction execution, the address translation caches, the 16-MHz clock, and the 32-Mbyte/s bus bandwidth. All these features are explained in Chap. 21. As you might expect, the processor also works with a math coprocessor: either the 80287 or the 80387. Moving all these signals on and off the chip necessitates a 132-pin grid array package.

Bit-Sliced Microprocessors

THE 2900 SERIES The 2900 series microprocessor products (and the similar 6900 series) support a 4-bit sliced microprocessor architecture similar to that described earlier in this chapter. Bit-sliced microprocessors are expensive to develop, so they are only used when very high speeds are necessary. The processor is driven by a microprogram stored in ROM. Provided in the RALU 4-bit sections are the input and output buses, the ALU, complementer, shifter, register file, and buffer registers.

The 2909 microprogram sequencer creates the addresses for the proper microinstruction routines stored in ROM. Each microinstruction takes about 100 μs to execute. Operating directly on the ALU and buses, the microinstructions must specify the sources of data for each operation and the destination for the results of the operation. The microinstruction sequences will permit fetching instructions, moving data, performing arithmetic, carrying out boolean algebra operations, complementing, and shifting.

CHAPTER SUMMARY

1. Digital computers receive, store, manipulate, and send data. Operations are directed by the instructions of the program. The computer is composed of control, arithmetic and logic, memory, and I/O sections.

2. Microcomputers are digital computers based on microprocessors. The microprocessor forms the control, the arithmetic and logic, and part of the I/O sections of the computer. Additional I/O logic, memory, an oscillator, and power supplies are used with the microprocessor in the microcomputer.

3. The microprocessors have data, address, and control buses to transmit and receive signals. Most of the buses use three-state logic.

4. Bits in computer words are numbered to facilitate referencing a specific bit. In this book the LSB is bit 0. The MSB is bit 7 in 8-bit words and bit 15 in 16-bit words.

5. The accumulator, or A register, is the primary arithmetic and logic register. The accumulator may also temporarily store memory and I/O data.

6. The index register is most frequently used for counting the number of times an operation is to be repeated. Some microprocessors combine the function of the accumulator and index register into a general register.

7. The instruction currently being executed is held in the instruction register for interpretation. The program counter contains the address of the next instruction.

8. Data can be pushed on top of the stack, and the item on top can be retrieved by popping. The stack pointer maintains an indication of the top location in the stack. In using the stack, errors of overflow or underflow must be prevented.

9. The result of the last arithmetic or logical operation is indicated by the flags of the status register. Most microprocessors provide carry, zero, sign, and parity flags.

10. The arithmetic and logic section is composed of an ALU, a shift register, and a buffer register. Arithmetic, boolean algebra, and complement operations are capabilities of the ALU. The control input to this section specifies which function is selected.

11. Timing and sequencing are the responsibilities of the control section. Instruction cycles consist of fetching the instruction from memory and then executing the instruction. Fetching the instruction requires several steps.

12. The steps necessary to execute and fetch instructions are specified by the microprogram. Microprogram development systems are used to debug and verify and program before the CROM is fabricated.

13. Memory is often partitioned into ROM and RAM. Memory address bits specify an individual location. The memory map depicts the layout of the ROMs and RAMs in the memory. Both linear selection and fully decoded addressing have been used in microcomputer memories. Dynamic RAM uses split-cycle addressing to minimize pin count on the DIP.

14. Bit-sliced microprocessors allow designers to build computers with almost any word length and instruction set. Each such computer requires a unique control section.

15. Programmed I/O is the most commonly used data-exchange method for microcomputers. A peripheral device can signal its need for attention by sending the computer an interrupt. When large amounts of data must be transferred, DMA can be used.

KEY TERMS AND CONCEPTS

Digital computer

Program

Microcomputer

Microprocessor unit (MPU)

Word size

Byte

Read-only memory (ROM)

Random-access memory (RAM)

Bidirectional buses

Three-state buses

Most significant bit (MSB)

Least significant bit (LSB)

Accumulator (A register)

Arithmetic-logic unit (ALU)

Index register

General register

Instruction register

Program counter register

Stack and stack pointer

Pushing and popping

Status register and flags

Arithmetic and logic section

Control section

Instruction cycle

Operand

Microprogramming and microinstructions

Microprogram development systems

Control ROM (CROM)

Static and dynamic RAM

Memory map

Chip-select (CS) input

Linear selection addressing

Fully decoded addressing

Split-cycle addressing of dynamic RAM

Refreshing dynamic RAM

Bit-sliced microprocessors

Register arithmetic-logic unit (RALU)

Input/output (I/O) section

Programmed I/O

Interrupts

Direct memory access (DMA)

NUMBER SYSTEMS AND CODES

A microcomputer works exclusively with numbers. To reduce costs and simplify the implementation, the binary number system is used instead of the more familiar decimal system. You saw binary numbers used in Chap. 1 to illustrate how data and addresses are routed in the computer. A good grasp of binary number systems and computer arithmetic is essential to anyone involved with microcomputers. In addition, knowledge of the codes used for representing information and for error detection and correction is necessary to understand the processing of textual data and the accurate transmitting of information over noisy data channels.

CHAPTER OBJECTIVES

Upon completion of this chapter, you should be able to:

1. Discuss the concept of positional number systems.
2. Convert numbers in the binary, octal, or hexadecimal systems to their decimal equivalents and vice versa.
3. Add, subtract, multiply, and divide binary, octal, or hexadecimal numbers.
4. Perform arithmetic operations using complement systems.
5. Define the requirements for double-precision arithmetic.
6. Encode or decode data using common digital coding methods.
7. Describe the techniques used for error detection and correction in digital communications systems.

POSITIONAL NUMBER SYSTEMS

You are so well acquainted with the decimal number system that you hardly think about it in counting or performing arithmetic. In elementary arithmetic courses you were taught rules for counting and adding, but these rules have been used so many times that you can perform the operations even though the basic principles are not explicitly recalled. When you start to use another number system, you will be required to remember these basic concepts until your aptitude with other systems becomes as good as it is with the decimal system.

All the number systems that we are interested in use a *positional weighting* for each of the symbols, which are called *digits*. The quantity of digits in a number systems is equal to the *base* of that system. A positional number system can be represented in the form

$$(\cdots d_3 d_2 d_1 d_0 \cdot d_{-1} d_{-2} d_{-3} \cdots)_b \qquad (2\text{-}1)$$

where d_i is a digit and b is the base. Table 2-1 lists the base and digits for each of the number systems that we will be interested in. For the *binary* (or base 2) system, there are two digits—0 and 1. In *octal* there are eight, in *decimal* 10, and in *hexadecimal* (or *hex*) 16. The hexadecimal system uses the letters A through F as symbols for the digits equal to the decimal numbers 10 through 15. In each number system the largest digit is always one less than the base. The largest decimal digit is 9 ($10 - 1 = 9$), while the largest octal digit is 7 ($8 - 1 = 7$).

Radix is another term with the same meaning as base. The two words are used interchangeably. You already know that a period separates the fractional part of a number from the integer in the decimal system. We call it a *decimal point*. In general, that mark is called a *radix point*, and it is used in the other bases as well.

The position a digit occupies in a number represents its *weight* in a positional number system. By using the representation of Eq. (2-1), we can express the weighting as

$$d_3 d_2 d_1 d_0 \cdot d_{-1} d_{-2} d_{-3} = d_3 b^3 + d_2 b^2 + d_1 b^1$$
$$+ d_0 b^0 + d_{-1} b^{-1} + d_{-2} b^{-2} + d_{-3} b^{-3} \qquad (2\text{-}2)$$

Each digit's position represents the base raised to an appropriate power. In decimal, the first column to the left of the decimal point is weighted by 1 (10^0), the second column to the left by 10 (10^1), the third column to the left by 100 (10^2), and so on in positive powers of 10. To the right of the decimal point, the weighting is in negative powers of 10: that is, $\frac{1}{10}$ (10^{-1}), $\frac{1}{100}$ (10^{-2}), and so forth. We can portray this concept in the following manner:

	Decimal point				
			↓		
Decimal number	7	9	4.	8	0
Column weight	10^2	10^1	10^0	10^{-1}	10^{-2}

The same procedure is used in other bases. Again, the columns are weighted by increasing positive powers of the base to the left of the radix point and by increasing negative powers of the base to the right of the radix point. Examples in binary, octal, and hexadecimal follow:

	Radix point					
			↓			
Binary number	1	1	0.	0	0	1
Column weight	2^2	2^1	2^0	2^{-1}	2^{-2}	2^{-3}
Octal number	7	0	3.	4	2	
Column weight	8^2	8^1	8^0	8^{-1}	8^{-2}	
Hexadecimal number	F	2	B.	A	9	
Column weight	16^2	16^1	16^0	16^{-1}	16^{-2}	

To make the base of a number readily apparent, a subscript is appended to indicate the radix; otherwise, it might be impossible to distinguish between the values of numbers in different bases. For example, consider numbers composed of the same digits in several bases:

11.101_2	binary
11.101_8	octal
11.101_{16}	hexadecimal

Positional Number Systems Review

1. Define the terms "base," "radix," and "radix point."
2. List all the digits in the base 16 number system.
3. What would be the largest admissible digit in a base 4 number system?
4. What does the subscript 8 on a number imply?
5. In the number $70.8F_{16}$, what are the column weights for each digit?

Table 2-1 Number Systems

Number System	Base	Digits
Binary	2	0, 1
Octal	8	0, 1, 2, 3, 4, 5, 6, 7
Decimal	10	0, 1, 2, 3, 4, 5, 6, 7, 8, 9
Hexadecimal	16	0, 1, 2, 3, 4, 5, 6, 7, 8, 9, A, B, C, D, E, F

CONVERSION BETWEEN BASES

In our everyday business we use the decimal system, but when using digital computers the base 2 system will be of most importance to us. Converting between binary and decimal will become necessary in many cases to check answers, verify memory addresses, or decode data. Octal and hexadecimal numbers will also be encountered frequently because they are used to express binary numbers in a compact form.

Polynomial Expansion

The value of each digit in a number is determined by three factors: (1) the digit itself, (2) the number system base, and (3) the position of the digit in the number. The value of 159.8_{10} can be expanded by using these factors in a form similar to Eq. (2-2):

$$159.8_{10} = 1 \times 10^2 + 5 \times 10^1 + 9 \times 10^0 + 8 \times 10^{-1}$$

Writing a number in this way is called *polynomial expansion*. The same means of expansion can be used in any other base.

Polynomial expansion is the principle behind conversion from one number system to another. More efficient methods will be presented later in this chapter, but by understanding polynomial expansion you will gain insight into the conversion process. With the use of polynomial expansion, the number 111.01_2 can be converted to decimal by a series of multiplications and additions:

$$111.01_2 = 1 \times 2^2 + 1 \times 2^1 + 1 \times 2^0 + 0 \times 2^{-1}$$
$$+ 1 \times 2^{-2}$$
$$= 4 + 2 + 1 + 0 + 0.25$$
$$= 7.25_{10}$$

All the arithmetic operations needed to make the conversion are accomplished by using decimal numbers. Because the original base of the number was 2, the multiplications involved powers of 2.

By using the same approach but changing the multiplier to powers of the appropriate bases, octal and hexadecimal numbers can also be converted to decimal:

$$604.52_8 = 6 \times 8^2 + 0 \times 8^1 + 4 \times 8^0 + 5 \times 8^{-1}$$
$$+ 2 \times 8^{-2}$$
$$= 384 + 0 + 4 + 0.625 + 0.03125$$
$$= 388.65625_{10}$$
$$CFA.9_{16} = 12 \times 16^2 + 15 \times 16^1 + 10 \times 16^0$$
$$+ 9 \times 16^{-1}$$
$$= 3072 + 240 + 10 + 0.5625$$
$$= 3322.5625_{10}$$

With hexadecimal numbers, you must change digits larger than 9 (that is, A through F) to their decimal equivalents before expanding the number.

Polynomial Expansion Review

1. List the three factors that determine the value of each digit of a number.
2. What is the weight of the digit 4 in the number 746.21_{16}?
3. What must be done to digits larger than 9 before expanding a hexadecimal number?

Conversion by Grouping

Octal and hexadecimal numbers are used because it is easy to convert from binary to either of those larger bases. The larger bases are a convenient, short way of writing long binary numbers because fewer digits are involved; for example,

$$101\ 001\ 110\ 101\ 011\ 000\ 111_2 = 5,165,307_8$$

It took only seven octal digits to represent the same quantity as 21 binary digits, so it is easier to write the number in octal rather than in a long string of 1s and 0s. Simple mistakes, such as inserting or deleting a digit, can more easily be avoided by using the base 8 or 16 number systems.

A binary number can be converted to another base that is a power of 2 by properly grouping the bits to the right and the left of the radix point. In converting to octal, the binary number is arranged in groups of three digits:

$$1|100|111|011|010|101||111|011.|101|110_2$$
$$= 001\ 100\ 111\ 011\ 010\ 101\ 111\ 011.\ 101\ 110_2$$

It may be necessary to insert leading and trailing zeros to form groups of exactly three digits. Next, the digits in each group are converted to their octal equivalents (which are listed in Table 2-2). The result for the number above is

$$= 14,732,573.56_8$$

Converting to hexadecimal requires that the groups be 4 bits long; for example,

$$1,111,100,101,011.011,01_2$$
$$= 1\ |\ 1111\ |\ 0010\ |\ 1011.\ |\ 0110\ |\ 1_2$$

Grouping these and inserting leading and trailing zeros,

$$= 0001\ 1111\ 0010\ 1011.\ 0110\ 1000_2$$
$$= 1F2B.68_{16}$$

Obviously, the process can be reversed. It is possible to go from octal and hexadecimal numbers to binary by converting each digit in the higher base number to its direct binary equivalent:

$$65{,}231.4_8 = 110\ 101\ 010\ 011\ 001.\ 100_2$$

$$C01.A_{16} = 1100\ 0000\ 0001.\ 1010_2$$

It does not matter whether you use the octal or the hexadecimal system. Every binary number can be represented in either base. In this book we will concentrate on the hexadecimal system because it is easier to understand the manufacturer's literature for the microprocessor if we use that base. You should have knowledge of the octal system as well, because some equipment manufacturers use this system in their documentation.

Conversion by Grouping Review

1. Explain why the octal and hexadecimal number systems are often used in microcomputer documentation.
2. Describe the grouping process for converting from binary to octal and from hexadecimal to binary.
3. Discuss what you would do if the bits are not evenly divisible into groups of four digits when you are converting from binary to hexadecimal.

Conversion From Other Bases to Decimal

To convert to decimal from another base, an efficient method called "explosion" can be used. The explosion procedure consists of several steps, so it is more like a recipe than an equation. Mathematical descriptions of such processes are called *algorithms*. Algorithms are named after al-Khwārizmī, a ninth-century Arabian mathematician who wrote a textbook on decimal arithmetic. Strictly speaking, an algorithm consists of the precise rules for transforming specified inputs into specified outputs in a finite number of steps. In the following example, converting from an octal number to decimal is used to illustrate this concept. The conversion method is called the *explosion algorithm*.

INTEGER CONVERSION   If we want to convert the number 421.702_8 to decimal, we must first separate it into integer and fractional components. The reason for making the split is that the explosion algorithm uses one procedure for integers and another with fractions.

The first step in the algorithm is to write the old base (octal) as a decimal number, that is, 8_{10}. Next, the most significant digit (MSD) of the number to be converted is multiplied by the old base, and the product is added to the next digit to the right. The multiplication and addition are repeated as many times as there are digits. The final sum is the answer.

The conversion process is shown below. The octal digits are exploded across the page to allow room for the multiplication and addition.

Start with the most significant digit

$$
\begin{array}{ccc}
\downarrow & & \\
4 & 2 & 1 \\
\times\ 8 & \rightarrow +32 & \rightarrow +272 \\
\hline
32 & 34 & 273 \quad \leftarrow\text{Stop after adding} \\
 & \times\ 8 & \qquad\quad\text{the last digit} \\
 & \hline \\
 & 272 &
\end{array}
$$

$$421_8 = 273_{10}$$

Explosion also works with hexadecimal. To convert CBA_{16} to decimal, the old base used as a multiplier is 16_{10}.

$$
\begin{array}{ccc}
C = 12 & B = 11 & A = 10 \\
\times\ 16 & \rightarrow +192 & \rightarrow +3248 \\
\hline
192 & 203 & 3258 \\
 & \times\ 16 & \\
 & \hline \\
 & 3248 &
\end{array}
$$

$$CBA_{16} = 3258_{10}$$

Each hexadecimal digit larger than 9 must first be converted to its decimal value by using Table 2-2.

FRACTIONAL CONVERSION   Next we will convert the octal fraction to a decimal fraction. Recall that the number was 421.702_8. The process for fractional conversion uses division. First, the least significant digit

Table 2-2   Decimal, Binary, Octal, and Hexadecimal Equivalents

Decimal	Binary	Octal	Hexadecimal
0	0000	0	0
1	0001	1	1
2	0010	2	2
3	0011	3	3
4	0100	4	4
5	0101	5	5
6	0110	6	6
7	0111	7	7
8	1000	10	8
9	1001	11	9
10	1010	12	A
11	1011	13	B
12	1100	14	C
13	1101	15	D
14	1110	16	E
15	1111	17	F

(LSD) of the fraction is divided by the original base expressed in decimal (8_{10}). The quotient is added to the next digit to the left, and the process repeated as many times as there are digits. The final quotient is the answer. Converting 0.702_8 to decimal:

Start with the least significant fractional digit

$$\frac{2}{8} = 0.25$$

Stop with the most significant fractional digit →

$$\frac{0 + 0.25}{8} = 0.03125$$

$$\frac{7 + 0.03125}{8} = 0.879$$

$$0.702_8 = 0.879_{10}$$

The original octal number can now be converted to decimal by adding the integer, found previously, to the fraction above:

$$421.702_8 = 273_{10} + 0.879_{10}$$
$$= 273.879_{10}$$

Hexadecimal fractions can be converted by using the same algorithm, but the divisor must be 16_{10}. Converting $0.C16_{16}$ to decimal:

$$\frac{6}{16} = 0.375$$

$$\frac{1 + 0.375}{16} = 0.0859$$

Before the next stop, remember to convert C_{16} to 12_{10}:

$$\frac{12 + 0.0859}{16} = 0.755$$

$$0.C16_{16} = 0.755_{10}$$

The accuracy of the conversion depends on the number of places to the right of the decimal point in each quotient. Often the conversion is carried to one greater than the desired number of places of accuracy and is then rounded. For example, to get a conversion that is accurate to two places past the decimal point, carry all arithmetic to three places and then round to two places as a final step.

ROUNDING The rule for rounding a number in any base depends on whether the number is positive or negative. For positive numbers, add half the base (5 for decimal, 4 for octal, and 8 for hexadecimal) in the position to the right of the final length. Then *truncate*

the sum at that position. For example:

	Decimal	Octal	Hexadecimal
	Final length ↓	Final length ↓	Final length ↓
	0.972_{10}	0.0756_8	$0.AFF_{16}$
Add in third position	+ 5 ←Half the base	+ 4	+ 8
	$0.97\underline{|7}$	$0.10\underline{16}$	$0.B0\underline{|7}$
	Truncate		

The final results are:

$$0.97_{10} \qquad 0.10_8 \qquad 0.B0_{16}$$

In the octal and hexadecimal cases, a carry was propagated into the higher-order positions, thus causing the final result to be *rounded up*.

For negative numbers, half the base is subtracted from the position to the right of the final length and the difference is truncated. For example:

	Decimal	Octal	Hexadecimal
	Final length ↓	Final length ↓	Final length ↓
	-0.6512_{10}	-0.076_8	$-0.CF2_{16}$
Subtract in third position	− 5 ←Half the base	− 4	− 8
	$-0.65\underline{|62}$	$-0.10\underline{|2}$	$-0.CF\underline{|A}$

The final results are:

$$-0.65_{10} \qquad -0.10_8 \qquad -0.CF_{16}$$

In the octal example, a carry was propagated to the higher-order positions, thus causing the number to be rounded up.

Conversion-by-Explosion Summary

The explosion algorithm for converting any base to decimal is summarized as follows:

EXPLOSION ALGORITHM

STEP 1. Separate integers and fractions.

STEP 2. Integer conversion.
  a. Express the original base as a decimal number.
  b. Multiply the MSD by the original base.
  c. Add the product to the next digit to the right.

EXPLOSION ALGORITHM *(cont'd)*

    d. Multiply the sum by the original base. Repeat steps **c** and **d** as many times as there are digits. The final sum is the answer.

STEP 3. Fractional conversion.
    a. Express the original base as a decimal number.
    b. Divide the LSD by the original base.
    c. Add the quotient to the next digit to the left.
    d. Divide the sum by the original base. Repeat steps **c** and **d** as many times as there are digits remaining. The final quotient is the result.

Conversion From Decimal to Other Bases

The *digit-by-digit* conversion algorithm is used in converting from decimal to other bases. Here, too, mixed numbers must be separated into integer and fractional portions. Conversion of the integer is discussed first.

INTEGER CONVERSION   Integer conversion using the digit-by-digit algorithm requires that the number to be converted be divided by the new base expressed in decimal. The remainder is saved, and the residual quotient is again divided. The process is repeated until the quotient is zero. The MSD of the number is the last remainder generated. Find the octal equivalent of 75_{10} as follows:

$$\text{Divide by } 8_{10}: \qquad \overset{\text{Remainders}}{\underset{}{8\,\lceil\overline{75}}}$$

$$9$$
$$3 \leftarrow \text{LSD}$$
$$\text{Residual quotient}$$
$$8\,\lceil\overline{9} \quad 1$$
$$\underset{8\,\lceil\overline{1}}{\overset{0}{}} \quad 1 \leftarrow \text{Last remainder is MSD}$$

$$75_{10} = 113_8$$

Converting 109_{10} to hexadecimal, we have

$$\overset{\text{Remainders}}{}$$
$$16\,\lceil\overline{109} \quad 13 = D \leftarrow \text{LSD}$$
$$16\,\lceil\overline{6} \quad 6 \leftarrow \text{MSD}$$

$$109_{10} = 6D_{16}$$

FRACTIONAL CONVERSION   Fractional conversion by the digit-by-digit algorithm starts with the new base expressed as a decimal number. The fraction to be converted is multiplied by the new base, and the integer generated in the product is removed and saved. The process is repeated with the residual product until the desired number of significant digits has been generated. The first generated digit is the most significant.

Converting 0.896_{10} to octal (two places past the radix point), we have

Integers generated

$$
\begin{array}{ll}
 & 0.896 \\
 & \times\ \ 8 \\
\hline
\text{MSD } 7 & \leftarrow \boxed{7}.168 \\
 & 0.168 \\
 & \times\ \ 8 \\
\hline
1 & \leftarrow \boxed{1}.344 \\
 & 0.344 \\
 & \times\ \ 8 \\
\hline
\text{LSD } 2 & \leftarrow \boxed{2}.752
\end{array}
$$

Rounding to two places, the result is 0.71:

$$0.896_{10} = 0.71_8$$

Converting 0.32_{10} to hexadecimal, we proceed in the same manner. We use 16 as the multiplier in that case.

$$
\begin{array}{ll}
 & 0.32 \\
 & \times\ 16 \\
\hline
5 & \leftarrow \boxed{5}.12 \\
 & 0.12 \\
 & \times\ 16 \\
\hline
1 & \leftarrow \boxed{1}.92 \\
 & 0.92 \\
 & \times\ 16 \\
\hline
14 = E & \leftarrow \boxed{14}.72
\end{array}
$$

Rounding to two places gives 0.52, so

$$0.32_{10} = 0.52_{16}$$

Digit-by-Digit Conversion Summary

The digit-by-digit algorithm used to convert from decimal to any other base is summarized as follows:

DIGIT-BY-DIGIT ALGORITHM

STEP 1. Separate integers and fractions.

STEP 2. Integer conversion.
    a. Express the new base as a decimal number.
    b. Divide the number to be converted by the new base.
    c. Collect the remainders.

    d. Divide the remaining quotient by the new base. Repeat steps **c** and **d** until the quotient is 0. To find the equivalent number, collect the remainders in the reverse order in which they were generated.

STEP 3. Fractional conversion.
    a. Express the new base as a decimal number.
    b. Multiply the number to be converted by the new base.
    c. Collect the integer portion of the product and multiply the residue by the base. Repeat this step until the desired number of significant digits is obtained.

ARITHMETIC IN OTHER BASES

Checking of computer results can be accomplished most quickly by converting all numbers to decimal and using ordinary arithmetic. Because we are most experienced with decimal arithmetic, this manner of working will be the easiest to use. When it is necessary to perform arithmetic in other bases, possibly to follow step-by-step execution in the processor, we must use the arithmetic rules of the appropriate base.

Before looking at the rules in other bases, we will briefly review those for decimal. In addition, the *addend* is added by columns to the *augend* to calculate the *sum*. How do we know what the sum is? We use an addition table that we memorized long ago. Any column that adds up to more than 9 propagates a *carry* into the column to the left.

$$
\begin{array}{rl}
1 & \text{carry} \\
29 & \text{augend} \\
+37 & \text{addend} \\
\hline
66 & \text{sum}
\end{array}
$$

When we subtract, the *subtrahend* is subtracted in columns from the *minuend* using a subtraction table. The answer is called the *difference*. If a digit in the subtrahend is larger than that of the minuend in the same column, a *borrow* from the column to the left is required.

$$
\begin{array}{rl}
6 & \text{borrow} \\
\not{7}3 & \text{minuend} \\
-18 & \text{subtrahend} \\
\hline
55 & \text{difference}
\end{array}
$$

If the subtrahend is larger than the minuend, the order of subtraction is inverted. A minus sign is placed on the difference, showing that the inversion was necessary.

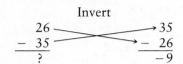

Invert

difference is a negative number

The rules for adding and subtracting in bases 2, 8, and 16 are the same, except that we use new addition or subtraction tables. These sums and differences are listed in Tables 2-3 and 2-4.

Table 2-3   Addition Tables

a   Binary

		Augend	
		0	1
Addend	0	0	1
	1	1	10

b   Octal

		Augend						
		0	1	2	3	4	5	6	7
Addend	0	0	1	2	3	4	5	6	7
	1	1	2	3	4	5	6	7	10
	2	2	3	4	5	6	7	10	11
	3	3	4	5	6	7	10	11	12
	4	4	5	6	7	10	11	12	13
	5	5	6	7	10	11	12	13	14
	6	6	7	10	11	12	13	14	15
	7	7	10	11	12	13	14	15	16

c   Hexadecimal

	0	1	2	3	4	5	6	7	8	9	A	B	C	D	E	F
0	0	1	2	3	4	5	6	7	8	9	A	B	C	D	E	F
1	1	2	3	4	5	6	7	8	9	A	B	C	D	E	F	10
2	2	3	4	5	6	7	8	9	A	B	C	D	E	F	10	11
3	3	4	5	6	7	8	9	A	B	C	D	E	F	10	11	12
4	4	5	6	7	8	9	A	B	C	D	E	F	10	11	12	13
5	5	6	7	8	9	A	B	C	D	E	F	10	11	12	13	14
6	6	7	8	9	A	B	C	D	E	F	10	11	12	13	14	15
7	7	8	9	A	B	C	D	E	F	10	11	12	13	14	15	16
8	8	9	A	B	C	D	E	F	10	11	12	13	14	15	16	17
9	9	A	B	C	D	E	F	10	11	12	13	14	15	16	17	18
A	A	B	C	D	E	F	10	11	12	13	14	15	16	17	18	19
B	B	C	D	E	F	10	11	12	13	14	15	16	17	18	19	1A
C	C	D	E	F	10	11	12	13	14	15	16	17	18	19	1A	1B
D	D	E	F	10	11	12	13	14	15	16	17	18	19	1A	1B	1C
E	E	F	10	11	12	13	14	15	16	17	18	19	1A	1B	1C	1D
F	F	10	11	12	13	14	15	16	17	18	19	1A	1B	1C	1D	1E

(Augend across the top; Addend down the left side)

Table 2-4 Subtraction Tables

a Binary

		Minuend	
		0	**1**
Subtrahend	0	0	1
	1	−1	0

b Octal

		Minuend							
		0	**1**	**2**	**3**	**4**	**5**	**6**	**7**
Subtrahend	**0**	0	1	2	3	4	5	6	7
	1	−1	0	1	2	3	4	5	6
	2	−2	−1	0	1	2	3	4	5
	3	−3	−2	−1	0	1	2	3	4
	4	−4	−3	−2	−1	0	1	2	3
	5	−5	−4	−3	−2	−1	0	1	2
	6	−6	−5	−4	−3	−2	−1	0	1
	7	−7	−6	−5	−4	−3	−2	−1	0

c Hexadecimal

		Minuend															
		0	**1**	**2**	**3**	**4**	**5**	**6**	**7**	**8**	**9**	**A**	**B**	**C**	**D**	**E**	**F**
	0	0	1	2	3	4	5	6	7	8	9	A	B	C	D	E	F
	1	−1	0	1	2	3	4	5	6	7	8	9	A	B	C	D	E
	2	−2	−1	0	1	2	3	4	5	6	7	8	9	A	B	C	D
	3	−3	−2	−1	0	1	2	3	4	5	6	7	8	9	A	B	C
	4	−4	−3	−2	−1	0	1	2	3	4	5	6	7	8	9	A	B
	5	−5	−4	−3	−2	−1	0	1	2	3	4	5	6	7	8	9	A
Subtrahend	**6**	−6	−5	−4	−3	−2	−1	0	1	2	3	4	5	6	7	8	9
	7	−7	−6	−5	−4	−3	−2	−1	0	1	2	3	4	5	6	7	8
	8	−8	−7	−6	−5	−4	−3	−2	−1	0	1	2	3	4	5	6	7
	9	−9	−8	−7	−6	−5	−4	−3	−2	−1	0	1	2	3	4	5	6
	A	−A	−9	−8	−7	−6	−5	−4	−3	−2	−1	0	1	2	3	4	5
	B	−B	−A	−9	−8	−7	−6	−5	−4	−3	−2	−1	0	1	2	3	4
	C	−C	−B	−A	−9	−8	−7	−6	−5	−4	−3	−2	−1	0	1	2	3
	D	−D	−C	−B	−A	−9	−8	−7	−6	−5	−4	−3	−2	−1	0	1	2
	E	−E	−D	−C	−B	−A	−9	−8	−7	−6	−5	−4	−3	−2	−1	0	1
	F	−F	−E	−D	−C	−B	−A	−9	−8	−7	−6	−5	−4	−3	−2	−1	0

Addition

We will use Table 2-3 to compute binary, octal, and hexadecimal sums. Remember that carrying is accomplished in these bases the same as in decimal, but the value carried into the next column is equal to the base.

$$\begin{array}{r} 11 \leftarrow \text{carries} \\ 01_2 \\ +\ 11_2 \\ \hline 100_2 \end{array}$$

$$\begin{array}{r} 11 \leftarrow \text{carries} \\ 2.7_8 \\ 7.3_8 \\ +\ 4.2_8 \\ \hline 16.4_8 \end{array}$$

$$\begin{array}{r} 1 \leftarrow \text{carry} \\ 2A_{16} \\ +\ B_{16} \\ \hline 35_{16} \end{array}$$

Starting with the rightmost column in the binary addition example, we have $(1 + 1) = 10_2$ (from Table 2-3a). So we put down 0 in the first column and carry 1. In the next column we have $(1 + 0 + 1) = 10_2$, so again we put down 0 and carry. Finally, the last column has only a 1 in it, so we put down 1.

The octal and hexadecimal additions also rely on the tables. In the rightmost column of the hexadecimal example, we have $(A + B) = 15_{16}$, so we write the 5 in that column and carry 1. We next have $(1 + 2) = 3$. That sum is put down in the second column.

Subtraction

As in addition, we start with the two numbers vertically aligned on the radix point. (After the numbers are properly aligned, the operations of addition or subtraction ignore the radix point.) Direct subtraction is performed column by column in any base. First, the minuend is found along the top row of the subtraction table, and then the row of the subtrahend is located. The difference will be found directly below the minuend, in the row of the subtrahend.

$$\begin{array}{r} 01 \leftarrow \text{borrows} \\ 1\cancel{0}0_2 \\ -\ 11_2 \\ \hline 001_2 \end{array}$$

If the digit in the minuend is smaller than that in the subtrahend, we must borrow from the next column to the left. Remember that in binary we are borrowing 2 from the next column. In octal the borrow is 8 and in hexadecimal, 16, of course. If the subtrahend is a larger number than the minuend, we simply invert the order of the subtraction and put a minus sign on the difference.

In this octal subtraction problem the subtrahend is larger than the minuend.

$$3 \leftarrow \text{borrows}$$

$$\begin{matrix} 27_8 & & 46 \\ -46_8 & & -27_8 \\ ? & & -17_8 \end{matrix}$$

A similar procedure is followed in hexadecimal subtraction.

$$1 \leftarrow \text{borrows}$$
$$\begin{matrix} 2.A_{16} \\ -1.F_{16} \\ \hline 0.B_{16} \end{matrix}$$

Multiplication

The multiplication tables in Table 2-5 provide the rules for this operation. Multiplication in other bases uses the same process as decimal. That is, each digit of the *multiplier* is multiplied by the *multiplicand,* and then the *partial products* are added. The position of the radix point in the *product* is found by adding the number of places in the multiplier and the multiplicand. An example of binary multiplication is

$$\begin{matrix} 111\ 001_2 & \text{multiplicand} \\ \times\ 101_2 & \text{multiplier} \end{matrix}$$

$$\left.\begin{matrix} 111\ 001 \\ 0\ 000\ 00 \\ 11\ 100\ 1 \end{matrix}\right\} \begin{matrix} \text{partial products (move over} \\ \text{one place for each} \\ \text{row)} \end{matrix}$$

$$100\ 011\ 101_2 \quad \text{product}$$

The octal multiplication below shows how the radix point position is found.

$$\left.\begin{matrix} 7.45_8 \\ \times\ 2.1_8 \end{matrix}\right\}$$

$$\begin{matrix} 745 \\ 1712 \\ \hline 20.065_8 \end{matrix} \quad \text{3 radix places}$$

Similarly, in hexadecimal:

$$\begin{matrix} B.E_{16} \\ \times\ 9_{16} \\ \hline 6A.E_{16} \end{matrix}$$

Division

Straight division in other bases is quite difficult. Instead, a multiplication table is constructed for the problem to prevent error. An octal example using such a table and illustrating the general rules of division is given below. The easiest way of developing the multiplication table is by repeated addition of the divisor. Instead of multi-

Table 2-5 Multiplication Tables

a Binary

Multiplier	Multiplicand 0	Multiplicand 1
0	0	0
1	0	1

b Octal

Multiplier	0	1	2	3	4	5	6	7
0	0	0	0	0	0	0	0	0
1	0	1	2	3	4	5	6	7
2	0	2	4	6	10	12	14	16
3	0	3	6	11	14	17	22	25
4	0	4	10	14	20	24	30	34
5	0	5	12	17	24	31	36	43
6	0	6	14	22	30	36	44	52
7	0	7	16	25	34	43	52	61

(Multiplicand across top; Multiplier down the side)

c Hexadecimal

Multiplier	0	1	2	3	4	5	6	7	8	9	A	B	C	D	E	F
0	0	0	0	0	0	0	0	0	0	0	0	0	0	0	0	0
1	0	1	2	3	4	5	6	7	8	9	A	B	C	D	E	F
2	0	2	4	6	8	A	C	E	10	12	14	16	18	1A	1C	1E
3	0	3	6	9	C	F	12	15	18	1B	1E	21	24	27	2A	2D
4	0	4	8	C	10	14	18	1C	20	24	28	2C	30	34	38	3C
5	0	5	A	F	14	19	1E	23	28	2D	32	37	3C	41	46	4B
6	0	6	C	12	18	1E	24	2A	30	36	3C	42	48	4E	54	5A
7	0	7	E	15	1C	23	2A	31	38	3F	46	4D	54	5B	62	69
8	0	8	10	18	20	28	30	38	40	48	50	58	60	68	70	78
9	0	9	12	1B	24	2D	36	3F	48	51	5A	63	6C	75	7E	87
A	0	A	14	1E	28	32	3C	46	50	5A	64	6E	78	82	8C	96
B	0	B	16	21	2C	37	42	4D	58	63	6E	79	84	8F	9A	A5
C	0	C	18	24	30	3C	48	54	60	6C	78	84	90	9C	A8	B4
D	0	D	1A	27	34	41	4E	5B	68	75	82	8F	9C	A9	B6	C3
E	0	E	1C	2A	38	46	54	62	70	7E	8C	9A	A8	B6	C4	D2
F	0	F	1E	2D	3C	4B	5A	69	78	87	96	A5	B4	C3	D2	E1

(Multiplicand across top; Multiplier down the side)

plying 26_8 by each digit from 0 to 10, simply add 26_8 to the product above for each row in the table. As a check, the last addition should be the original number (26_8) with a 0 to the right (260_8).

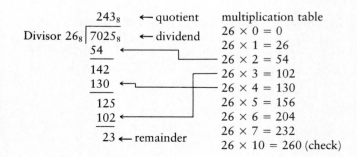

$$\begin{array}{r} 243_8 \leftarrow \text{quotient} \\ \text{Divisor } 26_8\,\overline{)\,7025_8} \leftarrow \text{dividend} \\ 54 \\ \hline 142 \\ 130 \\ \hline 125 \\ 102 \\ \hline 23 \leftarrow \text{remainder} \end{array}$$

multiplication table
$26 \times 0 = 0$
$26 \times 1 = 26$
$26 \times 2 = 54$
$26 \times 3 = 102$
$26 \times 4 = 130$
$26 \times 5 = 156$
$26 \times 6 = 204$
$26 \times 7 = 232$
$26 \times 10 = 260$ (check)

Binary division is so simple that a multiplication table is unnecessary. If the divisor is less than or equal to the dividend, the quotient is 1 in that position; otherwise, the quotient is 0. In the following problem the radix points in the divisor and dividend are both moved two places to the right to properly align the quotient. The general rule for the radix is to move it as many places as necessary to have it appear at the extreme right of the divisor.

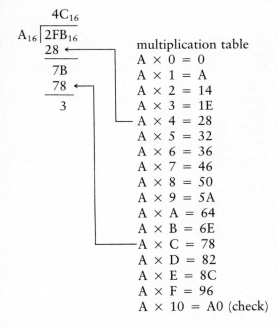

Hexadecimal division requires a multiplication table constructed in a manner similar to the one for octal division.

multiplication table
$A \times 0 = 0$
$A \times 1 = A$
$A \times 2 = 14$
$A \times 3 = 1E$
$A \times 4 = 28$
$A \times 5 = 32$
$A \times 6 = 36$
$A \times 7 = 46$
$A \times 8 = 50$
$A \times 9 = 5A$
$A \times A = 64$
$A \times B = 6E$
$A \times C = 78$
$A \times D = 82$
$A \times E = 8C$
$A \times F = 96$
$A \times 10 = A0$ (check)

Arithmetic Review

1. Describe how a table is used for the addition rules in any positional number system.
2. How is the radix point handled in binary subtraction?
3. Discuss the position of the radix point in the product of hexadecimal multiplication.
4. Describe the purpose of the multiplication table con-

structed for division of octal numbers. What simple check can be made to ensure that the multiplication table is correct before using it to carry out the division?

COMPLEMENT SYSTEMS

Digital circuits that perform arithmetic must be able to represent both positive and negative quantities. Because the circuits do not provide an easy method of indicating plus and minus signs, another indication is used in their place. The most significant bit of a binary number is used to show whether it is positive or negative. Recall that the quantity of bits in a number is the word length, so the sign bit is the leftmost bit in a word.

Figure 2-1 shows the range of hexadecimal numbers for an 8-bit word. A 0 in the most significant bit position indicates a positive number, and a sign bit of 1 is a negative value. In Fig. 2-1 the positive numbers run from 00_{16} ($0000\ 0000_2$) to $7F_{16}$ ($0111\ 1111_2$). Negative numbers range from 80_{16} ($1000\ 0000_2$) through FF_{16} ($1111\ 1111_2$). We can distinguish a positive number from a negative by just examining 1 bit. Arranging the numbers in a circle (as in Fig. 2-1) shows the cyclic nature of the numbers.

1's Complement

While not immediately obvious, there are two common ways of assigning the negative numbers to the quantities listed in Fig. 2-1. With either method, a complement system is used for negative numbers. One way that the negative numbers can be assigned is to convert each digit to its negative equivalent by binary subtraction in each column. Expressing the 8-bit number $-2A_{16}$ in

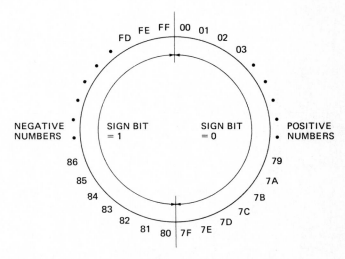

Fig. 2-1 A hexadecimal 8-bit complement system.

this way, we start with the positive number $2A_{16}$ = $0010\ 1010_2$. Subtracting each bit from 1:

$$
\begin{array}{cccccccc}
1 & 1 & 1 & 1 & 1 & 1 & 1 & 1 \\
-\,0 & -\,0 & -\,1 & -\,0 & -\,1 & -\,0 & -\,1 & -\,0 \\
\hline
1 & 1 & 0 & 1 & 0 & 1 & 0 & 1
\end{array}
$$

$$= 1101\ 0101_2 = D5_{16}$$

The word length must be specified prior to converting the number to its negative equivalent, so we know where the sign bit is to appear.

This convention is called the *1's complement*, or the *radix minus 1* complement. Its properties are shown in Table 2-6. Table 2-6 shows that all positive numbers are not changed in value but that negative numbers must be converted in the manner used above. The conversion can also be carried out in hexadecimal by subtracting each digit from F_{16}.

The 1's complement system has an unusual property. There are both positive and negative representations for zero. Both 00_{16} and FF_{16} equal the same quantity. Proof of their equivalence is straightforward. The conversion process is accomplished in hexadecimal this time. Converting FF_{16} to its positive equivalent, we subtract each digit from F_{16}.

$$
\begin{array}{cc}
F & F \\
-\,F & -\,F \\
\hline
0 & 0
\end{array}
$$

Thus the complement of FF_{16} is -00_{16}. (Of course, -0 is the same as $+0$.)

The negative zero in the 1's complement system

makes counting clumsy. On the other hand, there are equal quantities of positive and negative numbers in the 1's complement system; that is, we can make a one-to-one match of positives and negatives.

Positive	Negative
7F	80
7E	81
7D	82
.	.
.	.
.	.
02	FD
01	FE
00	FF

2's Complement

Even more widely used than the 1's complement system is the 2's complement. Using 8-bit words, the 2's complement is found by first determining the 1's complement and then adding 1 to the number that results. We showed in the last section that the 1's complement of $-2A_{16}$ is $D5_{16}$. The 2's complement is simply

$$D5_{16} + 1 = D6_{16}$$

Thus $D6_{16} = -2A_{16}$ in the 2's complement system. You may wonder why more than one complement system is necessary. Only one of these two ways of indicating negative numbers is used in any given microprocessor. Although the 2's complement is most popular, some manufacturers have built machines that use the 1's complement.

We emphasize the use of the 2's complement in this book. Using this conversion method, several other examples of finding the 2's complement are worked below.

☐ **EXAMPLE 1** What is the 2's complement of 35_{16}? First, obtain the 1's complement.

$$
\begin{array}{cc}
F & F \\
-\,3 & -\,5 \\
\hline
C & A \\
\end{array}
$$

Add 1:
$$
\begin{array}{cc}
C & A \\
+ & 1 \\
\hline
C & B
\end{array}
$$

$$CB_{16} = -35_{16}$$

☐ **EXAMPLE 2** Find the 2's complement of -00_{16}.

$$
\begin{array}{cc}
F & F \\
-\,0 & -\,0 \\
\hline
F & F \\
+ & 1
\end{array}
$$

Discard the MSD: ①0 \quad 0

$$-00_{16} = 00_{16}$$

Table 2-6 Hexadecimal 8-Bit 1's Complements

Number	Representation	
+7F	7F	
+7E	7E	
+7D	7D	
.	.	
.	.	Positive numbers
.	.	
+02	02	
+01	01	
+00	00	
−00	FF	
−01	FE	
−02	FD	
−03	FC	
.	.	
.	.	Negative numbers
.	.	
−7D	82	
−7E	81	
−7F	80	

There is only one representation for zero in this complement system.

☐ EXAMPLE 3

What is the 2's complement of $-FA_{16}$?

$$
\begin{array}{cc}
F & F \\
-\,F & -\,A \\
\hline
0 & 5 \\
+ & 1 \\
\hline
0 & 6
\end{array}
$$

$$-FA_{16} = 06_{16}$$

The sign bit was set, and the minus sign precedes the number. The two negative signs cancel, thus giving a positive result.

Table 2-7 shows that there are two major differences between the 1's and the 2's complements. First, there is only a single value for zero in the 2's complement. Thus the counting properties of the 2's complement are better. Second, the 2's complement has more negative numbers than positive. The value -80_{16} is included in Table 2-7, but there is no corresponding positive value of $+80_{16}$. The difference in the quantity of positive and negative numbers is mostly of interest to programmers and has little electronic significance.

Subtraction Using Complements

The main reason for using complements in microprocessors is that they make it possible to subtract by means of addition, thus allowing the same circuitry to be used in the processor for both operations.

Table 2-7 Hexadecimal 8-Bit 2's Complements

Number	Representation	
+7F	7F	
+7E	7E	
+7D	7D	
.	.	
.	.	Positive numbers
.	.	
+02	02	
+01	01	
+00	00	
−01	FF	
−02	FE	
−03	FD	
.	.	
.	.	Negative numbers
.	.	
−7E	82	
−7F	81	
−80	80	

SUBTRACTING BY 1'S COMPLEMENT

If we want to subtract by 1's complement, the minuend of the problem is not changed, but the subtrahend is converted to its 1's complement. We then add the two numbers. If the last column generates a carry, a 1 is "ended around" and added to find the final answer. Using an 8-bit word, subtract 14_{16} from 53_{16}.

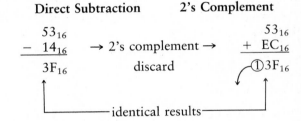

SUBTRACTING BY 2'S COMPLEMENT

Subtraction can also be carried out in the 2's complement system, as you might expect. The subtrahend is converted to its 2's complement and the numbers added. In this case any carry generated from the last column is just discarded.

Direct Subtraction

$$
\begin{array}{c}
53_{16} \\
-\ 14_{16} \\
\hline
3F_{16}
\end{array}
\quad \rightarrow \text{ 2's complement } \rightarrow \quad
\begin{array}{c}
53_{16} \\
+\ EC_{16} \\
\hline
①3F_{16}
\end{array}
$$

2's Complement

discard

identical results

Complement Systems Review

1. Distinguish between the 1's and the 2's complement systems. Why are both in use?
2. List some 8-bit octal numbers. Separate the list into positive and negative numbers and assign values to these numbers by using the 2's complement system.
3. Describe how subtraction can be performed by using addition with the 2's complement system.
4. What do you do if there is a carry out of the last column in the sum during 2's complement subtraction?

DOUBLE-PRECISION ARITHMETIC

A microprocessor word size limitation of 8 bits may seem to put some mathematical problems outside the reach of a small processor. Considering that the largest positive number is only $7F_{16}$ (127_{10}), how can the MPU be used in applications with numbers that extend beyond this range? Double-precision arithmetic is one way of overcoming this problem. As shown in Fig. 2-2, two 8-bit words can be joined to hold a larger number. A

Fig. 2-2 Double precision word format.

total of 15 bits for magnitude and the 16th bit for a sign will provide a range of numbers from $+32,767_{10}$ to $-32,768_{10}$ in the 2's complement. Even more capacity can be obtained by the use of triple-precision or longer multibyte word lengths, but microprocessors seldom need such precision.

The double-precision word consists of two half words called the *most* and *least significant halves* (MSH and LSH) or bytes. Addition and subtraction can easily be accomplished using complement arithmetic. The *double-precision addition algorithm* requires three steps:

1. Add the LSH of the augend to the LSH of the addend.
2. Add the carry from bit 7 of step 1 to the MSH of the augend.
3. Add the MSH of the augend and the MSH of the addend.

□ **EXAMPLE 1**   Add $07FA_{16}$ to $02AB_{16}$.

Add the LSH.

$$\begin{array}{r} AB \\ + \ FA \\ \hline ①A5 \end{array}$$

Carry out ← ①A5 ← LSH sum

Add the carry to the MSH of the augend.

$$\begin{array}{r} 02 \\ + \ 1 \\ \hline 03 \end{array}$$

Add the MSH of the augend and the addend.

$$\begin{array}{r} 03 \\ + \ 07 \\ \hline 0A \end{array} \leftarrow \text{MSH sum}$$

The double-precision sum is

$$0AA5_{16}$$

Check.

$$\begin{array}{r} 02AB_{16} \\ + \ 07FA_{16} \\ \hline 0AA5_{16} \end{array}$$

□ **EXAMPLE 2**   Subtract 0726_{16} from $0B3C_{16}$. Convert the subtrahend to the 2's complement.

$$-\ 0726_{16} = F8DA_{16}$$

Add the LSH.

$$\begin{array}{r} 3C_{16} \\ + \ DA_{16} \\ \hline 116_{16} \end{array}$$

Add the carry to the augend MSH.

$$\begin{array}{r} 0B_{16} \\ + \ 1_{16} \\ \hline 0C_{16} \end{array}$$

Add the MSH of the augend and the addend.

$$\begin{array}{r} 0C_{16} \\ + \ F8_{16} \\ \hline 104_{16} \end{array} \quad \text{discarding carry from last position} = 04_{16}$$

The double-precision sum is therefore

$$0416_{16}$$

As a check, we will carry out the subtraction in the normal manner:

$$\begin{array}{r} 0B3C_{16} \\ - \ 0726_{16} \\ \hline 0416_{16} \end{array}$$

Double-Precision Arithmetic Review

1. Describe the word format for double-precision arithmetic.
2. List the steps for double-precision addition. Why can the same algorithm be used for subtraction?
3. How is the carry from bit 7 of the LSH of the sum handled?
4. Why was the final carry from bit 15 in the answer to Example 2 discarded?

CODES

Much of the data processed by computers is nonnumeric. Text characters, shaft angles, and control signals are only a few types of information that can be manipulated by the processor. Because microprocessors are limited to storing only 1s and 0s, many codes have been developed to translate other forms of data into binary numbers.

Table 2-8 Binary-Coded Decimal

Decimal Digit	BCD Code
0	0000
1	0001
2	0010
3	0011
4	0100
5	0101
6	0110
7	0111
8	1000
9	1001

Binary-Coded Decimal

Binary-coded decimal (BCD) is commonly used by input/output (I/O) devices. The keyboards of many pocket calculators encode data into BCD. The encoded data represents the decimal digits in the range of 0 through 9 as 4-bit quantities. Table 2-8 lists the coded value for each digit.

While BCD is a good way of representing the decimal values, the coded versions of the numbers will not give the correct answer if used in normal arithmetic. This problem can easily be seen in the following example:

$$
\begin{array}{ll}
\textbf{Decimal} & \textbf{BCD} \\
19_{10} & 0001\ 1001 \\
+\ 1 & +\ \ \ \ \ 0001 \\
\hline
20_{10} = 1\ 0100_2 & 0001\ 1010
\end{array}
$$

But $\qquad 1\ 0100_2 \neq 0001\ 1010$

The problem arises because BCD cannot represent the true binary value of the sum. A correct solution results if the BCD is first converted to the true binary representation.

$$
\begin{array}{llll}
\textbf{Decimal} & \textbf{BCD} & & \textbf{Binary} \\
19_{10} = & 0001\ 1001 & = & 1\ 0011_2 \\
+\ 1_{10} = & +\ \ \ \ \ 0001 & = & +\ 0001_2 \\
\hline
20_{10} = & 1\ 0100_2 & = & 1\ 0100_2 \\
= & 1\ 0100_2
\end{array}
$$

Chapter 6 provides a detailed description of the use of BCD with microprocessors.

The American Standard Code for Information Interchange (ASCII)

The ASCII code is widely used by digital communications systems and computers. The code, shown in Table 2-9, is a 7-bit code. The characters, their coded values, and their meanings are listed in the table.

This code can be divided into subsets if the applica-tion does not require all 128 characters. There are 64 of the codes (20_{16} to $5F_{16}$) used for uppercase letters, numbers, common punctuation marks, and the blank space (SP). Another 32 codes (60_{16} to $7F_{16}$) specify lowercase letters and less commonly used punctuation marks; these codes are not frequently encountered. The final 32 codes (00_{16} to $1F_{16}$) specify machine commands such as line feed (LF), carriage return (CR), and ring the bell (BEL). They do not appear in a message or in print, but they control the communications equipment from both ends of the line.

In practice, an eighth bit is usually appended to the MSB position. This bit can be used for error detection or may be always 0. The 8 bits of the complete code may be sent either serially (1 bit at a time) or in parallel (all 8 bits at once).

The meanings of all the control codes may not be obvious from Table 2-9. A brief description of each should clarify their use. The "start of heading" char-acter is used to begin a character sequence that includes the address and routing information, called the *message heading*. The "start of text" character terminates the heading and signals the start of the message. The mes-sage ends with the "end of text" character. When an entire transmission is concluded, the "end of transmis-sion" character is sent.

An "enquiry" is used to request a response from a remote station, such as identification or status. "Acknowledge" is sent by the receiver as an affirmative response to the sender; "NAK" is used for a negative response.

Many of the characters control the message-handling equipment. The "bell" character sounds an alarm or buzzer. Backspace, line feed, horizontal and vertical tab-ulation, form feed, and carriage return position the print head on the page. "Delete" is used to erase an unwanted character.

When one or more characters outside the standard ASCII set are to be sent, they are preceded by the "shift out" control. "Shift in" is sent after those codes have been transmitted. "Data link escape" and "escape" pro-vide supplementary controls in data communications networks to change the meaning of a limited number of characters that follow. The DLE and ESC characters are usually terminated by the shift-in character.

Device controls are used to switch teleprocessing de-vices on or off. "Synchronous idle" is used to provide a synchronism signal when there are no other characters to be sent. The "end of transmission block" allows blocking of data for communications purposes. The "cancel" character indicates that erroneous data has been sent and should be disregarded. "End of medium" indicates the conclusion of useful data. "Substitute" is used in place of a character that has been found to be invalid. File, group, record, and unit separators can divide data into segments.

Table 2-9 ASCII Code

Character	Code (hex)	Meaning	Character	Code (hex)	Meaning
NUL	00	All-zero character	3	33	3
SOH	01	Start of heading	4	34	4
STX	02	Start of text	5	35	5
ETX	03	End of text	6	36	6
EOT	04	End of transmission	7	37	7
ENQ	05	Enquiry	8	38	8
ACK	06	Acknowledge	9	39	9
BEL	07	Bell	:	3A	Colon
BS	08	Backspace	;	3B	Semicolon
HT	09	Horizontal tabulation	<	3C	Less than
LF	0A	Line feed	=	3D	Equal to
VT	0B	Vertical tabulation	>	3E	Greater than
FF	0C	Form feed	?	3F	Question mark
CR	0D	Carriage return	@	40	Commercial "at"
SO	0E	Shift out	A	41	A
SI	0F	Shift in	B	42	B
DLE	10	Data link escape	C	43	C
DC1	11		D	44	D
DC2	12	Device controls	E	45	E
DC3	13		F	46	F
DC4	14		G	47	G
NAK	15	Negative acknowledge	H	48	H
SYN	16	Synchronous idle	I	49	I
ETB	17	End of transmission block	J	4A	J
CAN	18	Cancel	K	4B	K
EM	19	End of medium	L	4C	L
SUB	1A	Substitute	M	4D	M
ESC	1B	Escape	N	4E	N
FS	1C	File separator	O	4F	O
GS	1D	Group separator	P	50	P
RS	1E	Record separator	Q	51	Q
US	1F	Unit separator	R	52	R
SP	20	Space	S	53	S
!	21	Exclamation point	T	54	T
"	22	Quotation marks	U	55	U
#	23	Number (pound) sign	V	56	V
$	24	Dollar sign	W	57	W
%	25	Percent	X	58	X
&	26	Ampersand	Y	59	Y
'	27	Apostrophe	Z	5A	Z
(	28	Opening parenthesis	[	5B	Opening bracket
)	29	Closing parenthesis	\	5C	Reverse slant
*	2A	Asterisk	]	5D	Closing bracket
+	2B	Plus	∧	5E	Circumflex (caret)
,	2C	Comma		5F	Underline
-	2D	Hyphen	`	60	Accent grave
.	2E	Period	a	61	a
/	2F	Slant	b	62	b
0	30	0	c	63	c
1	31	1	d	64	d
2	32	2	e	65	e

Table 2-9 *(cont'd)*

Character	Code (hex)	Meaning	Character	Code (hex)	Meaning
f	66	f	s	73	s
g	67	g	t	74	t
h	68	h	u	75	u
i	69	i	v	76	v
j	6A	j	w	77	w
k	6B	k	x	78	x
l	6C	l	y	79	y
m	6D	m	z	7A	z
n	6E	n	{	7B	Opening brace
o	6F	o	|	7C	Vertical line
p	70	p	}	7D	Closing brace
q	71	q		7E	Overline
r	72	r	DEL	7F	Delete

Error Detection and Correction Codes

When data is transmitted from one place to another in a digital system, the receiver may question the validity of the data. Noise, crosstalk, or malfunction can introduce errors in the received bit stream. Through the use of error detection and correction (EDAC) codes, data can be checked for the possibility of error, and it can be modified to restore the original message if errors are found.

PARITY The concept of parity was introduced in Chap. 1. Here we examine how parity can indicate inaccuracies in the data. Commonly, an extra bit is appended to the ASCII code character to be used for a parity indicator. The *parity bit* is a form of redundancy that is part of the message. However, the redundancy has a price. By increasing the number of bits per character from 7 to 8, an overhead of 14 percent is incurred. The overhead of any error detection code is a measure of its *efficiency*.

Continuing the discussion, we pick the capital letter E as the ASCII character to be transmitted. Referring to Table 2-9, the code 45_{16} is found to represent an uppercase E. The parity bit will occupy the MSB position. We have a choice of using even or odd parity, so both possibilities are investigated. Writing the code in binary $0100\ 0101_2$ shows that the parity is odd. By setting the parity bit ($1100\ 0101_2$), the overall parity for the 8 bits becomes even. Making the parity bit 0 is equivalent to giving the word odd parity.

Starting with the even-parity situation, we look into the consequence of errors. Assume that the letter E is transmitted 4 times in a message: the first time, with no errors; the second time, bit 1 was read as a 1 because of noise on the line; the third time, bit 2 became a 0 and bit 4 became a 1; and the fourth time, bits 3, 4,

and 5 were set erroneously. The received characters are summarized as follows:

		Binary Data Received	Received Parity
	Bit number	7 6 5 4 3 2 1 0	
Case 1		1 1 0 0 0 1 0 1	Even
Case 2		1 1 0 0 0 1 1 1	Odd
Case 3		1 1 0 1 0 0 0 1	Even
Case 4		1 1 1 1 1 1 0 1	Odd

In case 1 the received character had even parity, as was expected. In case 2 the word was received as having odd parity, but we know it was transmitted with even parity. Receiving a character which has improper parity implies that some bit changed state; either a 1 was reset to 0 or a 0 was set to 1 by noise. Case 3 has two errors, but the parity does not show any irregularity. Why? The reason is that even parity can only detect an odd number of bits in error. An even number of incorrect bits gives a seemingly correct indication of even parity. Case 4, with 3 bits in error, again shows the wrong parity, but we see that there is no way to distinguish between 1-bit and 3-bit errors. In fact, any odd number of incorrect bits will produce odd parity. While this parity code can detect an odd number of bit errors, it cannot indicate how many errors occurred or which bits are actually wrong.

Had we started with odd parity at the transmitter, the situation would be just the reverse. An odd number of bits in error (1, 3, 5, . . .) would be received with even parity, but an even number (2, 4, 6, . . .) would be seemingly correct at the receiving station. Using more bits for parity strengthens the detection of multiple errors and can even indicate which bit or bits are wrong. An elaborate theory for EDAC coding has been developed and can be used to ensure reliable data communications.

CHECKSUMS Sometimes we are not concerned with the correctness of one word, but with an entire block of data composed of many words. An efficient code for verifying data blocks is the *checksum* (also called a *hash total*). Generation of the checksum requires that the transmitting station add all the data codes and append the sum as a final word in the message. The receiving station also sums the data and compares its answer with the last word. If the data sums agree, there is a high probability that the data is correct.

You may wonder why the receiving station cannot be sure whether the data was correct if the checksums agree. First, there may be compensating errors in the data; that is, one word may have increased by the same amount that another decreased. Second, the addition is performed in an adder of finite length. In most microprocessors that could be 8 bits. That means that all carries from the MSB position are discarded, and errors may occur that are hidden by this loss of information.

The data block shown below will be used to demonstrate the checksum procedure. Each word in the block is 8 bits long. Adding the first two words gives 60_{16}, but when that partial sum is added to FF_{16}, the result is $15F_{16}$. Because we are limited to 8 bits, the MSB of 1 is lost and the resulting sum is $5F_{16}$. Finally, adding $0E_{16}$ gives $6D_{16}$.

a. Generating the checksum:

Data block   checksum development

```
20 ┐
   │ + = 60
40 ┘       │
           │ + = ①5F   (discarding carry from
FF ────────┘   ↙    │   bit 7)
             + = 6D₁₆
0E ──────────────┘
```

b. Transmission block:

```
20 ┐
40 │
FF │  data
0E ┘
6D ← checksum
```

c. Correctly received data:

```
20 ┐
40 │
FF │ calculated checksum = 6D₁₆
0E ┘                           ↑
6D ←────── match ──────────────┘
```

d. Incorrectly received data:

```
         ┌→ 21 ┐
errors ──┤  C0 │
         └→ FF │  calculated checksum = EE₁₆
            0E ┘                            ↑
            6D ←─── no match ───────────────┘
```

The data is blocked for transmission with the checksum in an extra word (not part of the data). In this case the checksum has an efficiency of 25 percent (1 code word per 4 data words). If the data is received correctly, the checksum independently calculated by the receiver will match the last word in the block; however, bits that have changed will cause a different sum to be produced. No indication of which word has the error is provided, so the entire block must be retransmitted when a mistake is detected.

CYCLIC REDUNDANCY CHECK Another code that can be used to provide error detection capability on blocks of data is the cyclic redundancy check (CRC). The CRC uses fewer bits than do parity codes and has been implemented in both hardware and software. There are ICs on the market that will automatically calculate the CRC bit pattern that is appended to the data block as an extra word, much like the checksum. Computer programs have also been written that can generate the same bit pattern. Almost all floppy disks and digital tape cassettes use the cyclic redundancy check when recording data.

The CRC is a bit pattern for a polynomial of degree 7. The pattern of the data words can be expressed as

$$D(x) = D_7x^7 + D_6x^6 + D_5x^5 + D_4x^4$$
$$+ D_3x^3 + D_2x^2 + D_1x^1 + D_0x^0 \qquad (2\text{-}3)$$

where x is a *dummy variable*.

A *generator polynominal* is used as the divisor of $D(x)$:

$$\frac{D(x)}{G(x)} = Q(x) + R(x) \qquad (2\text{-}4)$$

where $G(x)$ is the generator polynominal, $Q(x)$ is the quotient, and $R(x)$ is the remainder. The purpose of the CRC, which is appended to the data, is to make the remainder in Eq. (2-4) become zero. By rewriting that equation, we can see how to accomplish this task.

$$D(x) - R(x) = Q(x)G(x) \qquad (2\text{-}5)$$

In other words, if the remainder is used for the CRC word, the generator polynomial will exactly divide the total data string.

The CRC transmitted in the last word in the block is thus the remainder of the generator division. When the receiving station divides by $G(x)$ and subtracts $R(x)$, it will find that there is a nonzero remainder if an error has occurred. If the remainder is zero, either the data has been correctly received or an undetectable error appears in the data stream.

Codes Review

1. List the reasons for the use of codes in digital communications.

2. When would the use of BCD instead of binary cause an incorrect result?
3. List the ASCII codes for the characters T, ?, $, and 7.
4. What are the meanings of the control characters DLE, SOH, ENQ, and LF?
5. Why does a single parity bit, used to check ASCII codes, for instance, seem correct when there are two received errors in the code?
6. Compare the efficiency of parity bits with checksums. Which would be more efficient for a 1000-word data block?
7. How do CRC bits make the bit pattern $D(x)$ exactly divisible by the generator polynomial?

CHAPTER SUMMARY

1. The place occupied by a digit in a positional number system signifies its weight in terms of the base raised to an appropriate power. Examples of positional number systems are binary, octal, decimal, and hexadecimal systems.
2. The quantity of symbols, or digits, in a positional number system is always equal to the base.
3. The radix point separates the integer and the fraction in a number. A subscript indicates its base.
4. Polynomial expansion allows us to convert between bases by considering the digits, the radix, and the weight of each digit.
5. Conversion from binary to another base that is a power of 2, such as octal or hexadecimal, is most easily accomplished by grouping.
6. The explosion algorithm is used to convert from other bases to decimal, and the digit-by-digit algorithm is used for conversion in the opposite direction.
7. Arithmetic in other bases employs addition and multiplication tables similar to those used in decimal. The rules of arithmetic in binary, octal, and hexadecimal are identical to those used in base 10 operations.
8. Complement systems make it possible to use the same circuitry for addition and subtraction. Both 1's and 2's complements are frequently encountered in microprocessor ALUs.
9. Because many microprocessors do 8-bit arithmetic, double precision is often necessary to prevent overflow.
10. Codes are employed to represent numbers and letters in binary form. Common codes include BCD and ASCII. Alternatively, coding may be used to provide error detection and correction of data transmitted over some digital communications network. Parity, checksums, and CRCs are examples of the latter types of codes.

KEY TERMS AND CONCEPTS

Positional number systems

Positional weighting

Digits

Base

Binary

Octal

Hexadecimal (hex)

Radix

Radix point

Polynomial expansion

Conversion by grouping

Explosion algorithm

Rounding

Truncation

Digit-by-digit algorithm

Arithmetic in other bases

Augend, addend, and sum

Carry

Minuend, subtrahend, and difference

Borrow

Multiplicand, multiplier, and product

Divisor, dividend, quotient, and remainder

1's complement

2's complement

Double-precision arithmetic

Codes

Binary-coded decimal (BCD)

American Standard Code for Information Interchange (ASCII)

Error detection and correction (EDAC) codes

Parity

Checksum

Cyclic redundancy check (CRC)

2-1 Convert the following numbers to decimal by use of polynomial expansion.

   a. 1276_8
   b. $011\ 110\ 010\ 000_2$
   c. $F7D_{16}$

2-2 Convert to decimal. All fractions should have accuracy to two places past the radix point.

   a. 47_8 **d.** 563.22_8
   b. $A9_{16}$ **e.** $A.F12_{16}$
   c. $1\ 000\ 111_2$

2-3 Convert the following numbers from decimal to octal. Compute all fractional values to two places past the radix point.

   a. 802_{10} **c.** 0.75_{10}
   b. 9999_{10} **d.** 196.017_{10}

2-4 Find the hexadecimal equivalents of the following decimal numbers, with two-place accuracy for all fractions.

   a. 999_{10} **c.** 295.156_{10}
   b. $42,769_{10}$ **d.** 13.86_{10}

2-5 Perform the indicated arithmetic operations using the binary number system.

   a. $\quad 110\ 011\ 011_2$ **c.** $\quad 110\ 011_2$
   $\quad + \quad 1\ 011\ 111_2$ $\times\ 1\ 101_2$

   b. $\quad 001\ 110\ 111_2$ **d.** $\underline{101\ 111\ 010_2}$
   $\quad - \ 010\ 000\ 000_2$ $1\ 110_2$

2-6 Perform the indicated octal arithmetic operations.

   a. $\quad 37_8$ **b.** $\quad 432_8$ **c.** $\quad 21.76_8$ **d.** $\underline{76,532_8}$
   $\quad + \ 26_8$ $- \ 264_8$ $\times \ 3.2_8$ 33_8

2-7 Perform the following arithmetic operations using the hexadecimal number system.

   a. $\quad B73_{16}$ **c.** $\quad 3.1F_{16}$
   $\quad + \ 2FD_{16}$ $\times \ 2.05_{16}$

   b. $\quad B64_{16}$ **d.** $\underline{715.C_{16}}$
   $\quad - \ DC1_{16}$ 2.17_{16}

2-8 Convert these binary numbers to their octal and hexadecimal equivalents by grouping.

   a. $101\ 111\ 011\ 010\ 001_2$
   b. $1\ 000\ 010.110\ 100_2$
   c. $110.001\ 000\ 1_2$
   d. $10\ 111.110\ 01_2$

2-9 Convert the octal and hexadecimal numbers below to their binary equivalents.

   a $67,014_8$ **c.** 216.425_8
   b. $F,C75_{16}$ **d.** $5B2.6175_{16}$

2-10 Find the parity of the following numbers.

   a. $1\ 110\ 111_2$ **c.** $12F_{16}$
   b. 37_8 **d.** 7776_8

2-11 Is the parity of these ASCII characters even or odd?

   a. A   **b.** f   **c.** ?   **d.** 2

2-12 What is the checksum for the data block below? (An 8-bit adder is to be used in computing the sum.)

   200_8
   177_8
   126_8
   515_8

2-13 Instead of using a single parity bit with an ASCII character, two are used in a 9-bit word. Bit 7 is set or cleared to make the parity of bits 1 through 7 even. Bit 8 is chosen to make the parity of bits 1 through 8 odd. What should the value of these bits be for the ASCII character %?

2-14 If the character transmitted in Prob. 2-13 were received with odd parity over bits 1 through 7 and even parity over bits 1 through 8, what could be concluded?

PROGRAMMING

A digital computer differs from every other electronic device in one important respect—the computer can do no useful work without its program. This combination of hardware and software forms the processing entity that is useful in solving a wide range of problems. The hardware-software interactions often result in situations in which it is difficult to decide if a failure was caused by the electronics or by the program. Everyone intending to work with computers must therefore have some knowledge of software. With programming skills, you will be able to develop simple software routines to help in assessing the causes of problems and in localizing faulty circuits. In addition to assisting in isolating problems, some elementary programming background will improve your ability to communicate with programmers.

CHAPTER OBJECTIVES

Upon completion of this chapter, you should be able to:

1. List the steps necessary to write a program.
2. Draw flowcharts using the proper American National Standards Institute (ANSI) symbols.
3. Describe the use of test cases, tracing, and simulation in debugging.
4. Debug programs by manually checking them before running them on the computer.

THE PROGRAMMING PROCESS

A *program* is a logical sequence of instructions and data which can be understood by a computer and which produces a specified result after execution. As such, the program might be considered to be an overall plan for the solution to a problem. Programs of any length are divided into several routines. A *routine* is a set of instructions within a larger program. This set of instructions is properly arranged to cause the computer to carry out frequently needed tasks. A further subdivision, the *subroutine,* is a short sequence of instructions designed to solve a specific part of the problem; subroutines usually have application to more than one routine.

For example, consider a simplified navigation problem on a coast-to-coast airline route. The program must be capable of calculating the course and speed changes necessary for travel between any two points on the earth. One of the routines in this program will be able to find the distance between those points. To measure this quantity, the distance routine may require a square root function to calculate the distance between given cartesian coordinates (as shown in Fig. 3-1):

$$d = \sqrt{(x_2 - x_1)^2 + (y_2 - y_1)^2} \qquad (3\text{-}1)$$

where
d = distance
x_1, x_2 = x coordinates of the two points
y_1, y_2 = y coordinates of the two points

The square root function can be written as a subroutine to be used not only by the distance routine, but perhaps by the speed routine as well. Figure 3-2 shows the relationship among the routines, the subroutines, and the data in a computer program.

The computer program written to solve a problem must completely specify what to do and how to do it

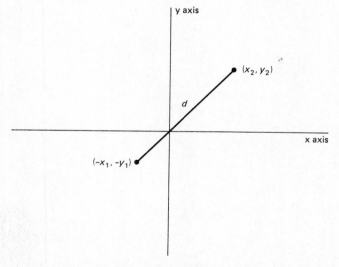

Fig. 3-1 Distance between two points in cartesian coordinates.

NAVIGATION PROGRAM

SQUARE ROOT SUBROUTINE

ARCTANGENT SUBROUTINE

SPEED ROUTINE

DISTANCE ROUTINE

COURSE ROUTINE

⋮

DATA SECTION

Fig. 3-2 Program structure.

and what data is involved. Should any of these questions be ignored or erroneously answered, the program will contain an error, or *bug*. To be sure that all necessary details have been covered, the programmer will generally follow a systematized series of steps. For small programs, the outcome of this process may simply be a mental discipline, but on large software projects each step will be formally documented. The process described in this section is the *top-down approach,* which is frequently used in structured programming.

Problem Statement

The first step required of the programmer or analyst is to write a clear, complete statement of the problem. Many times the person who will use the program is not exactly sure what the program is to do. For this reason, it is especially important for the programmer and user to mutually define the limits and capabilities of the program.

The problem statement for a computer must be much more comprehensive than instructions to another person would be. For instance, the system to be used in running the program must be described. In addition to designating the computer, the description must list the *peripheral equipment* (such as paper tape readers, printers, display terminals, and floppy disks) to be used.

A full summary of the data to be manipulated and the formats for input and output must be provided. Input parameters might include the source of the data, the format of the data (such as binary, BCD, or ASCII), the range of numbers to be handled, and the rate at which the information arrives. Important output parameters are the desired format, the accuracy requirements, the distribution of the output reports, and the *media* (magnetic disks, printer paper, CRT display) for the output. Furthermore, restrictions concerning compatibility with other programs, memory space available, and time available to run the program must be known.

Analysis

Once the problem has been fully defined, the programmer begins to analyze it. The analysis will survey the methods of solution available. For common problems, the programmer may already know the methods and be able to reference the proper manuals immediately; otherwise, an in-depth study of the programming literature and consultation with experts in the field may be necessary. Usually a wide variety of solutions will be found.

The ultimate result of the analysis phase is to select the one solution that best suits the problem. One of the considerations that enters into this decision is the amount of memory space needed to hold the program and data. Another consideration is the time available to develop the program; any sizable program involves a large amount of time to write and test, and thus a simple solution can produce significant savings here. A third consideration is how much computer time is allocated to executing the program; if the program is to be run frequently, it may be less costly to select a solution that minimizes the run time. As Fig. 3-3 shows, these three aspects of the program are not independent. Production

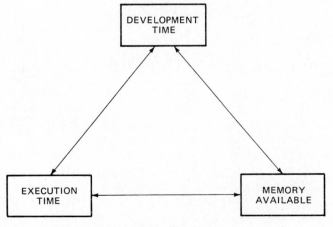

Fig. 3-3   Programming trade-offs.

of a program that runs very fast will require more time to be spent in refining the program; hence, the development time increases, and the written program may occupy more memory. Production time almost always increases when memory conservation is emphasized; as memory constraints become quite stringent, the development time can increase markedly.

When the solution is selected, the programmer reviews it to ensure that accuracy requirements, compatibility with other programs, and other restrictions in the problem statement are satisfied.

Problem Model

The formulas and the equations that will be used in the computer solution become a model of the actual situation. In selecting a mathematical representation, many variables are excluded from consideration. For example, if Newton's laws of motion are used as a model for automobile acceleration, such factors as temperature, humidity, type of rubber in the tires, and altitude cannot affect the computed solution, but they may be significant to automotive performance.

Not all programs require a model. Business programs may be of such a nature that only simple arithmetic is necessary. Complicated scientific programs, such as sending a rocket to the moon, almost always require a sophisticated model. The model is derived from the solution selected during analysis. The model will guide the programmer during the development of a step-by-step procedure for solution.

Before a model has been selected, it is not uncommon for the programmer to have uncovered some facets of the problem statement that are incomplete or incompatible. A complication may arise that changes the initial conclusion derived from the analysis. If so, the results of the earlier steps must be reconsidered and revised. This method of going back and forth among these steps in a repeated fashion shows the iterative nature of programming. The final program may be the outcome of many cycles of problem statement, analysis, and modeling.

Flowcharts

The next step of programming involves construction of a graphic representation of the logic to be used in the problem solution. The graphic technique most frequently used is the flowchart. The following section will describe the specifics of flowcharts in more detail. Here it is sufficient to note that a flowchart is constructed by using symbols and notations to further communications between programmers, analysts, and users. The flowcharts often form part of the permanent documentation of the program.

Coding

Many people who are not familiar with programming (and, unfortunately, too many inexperienced programmers) are surprised to find that coding is the fifth step of the effort. The actual instructions for the computer are prepared at this time. Using the flowcharts or other graphic aids as a guide, the programmer writes the instruction sequence. Usually a special coding sheet is used, so the instructions are in the proper format for computer data entry.

There is a large number of programming languages to choose from. One special language must be selected from the general category of machine codes, assemblers, or compilers. Most microcomputer manufacturers provide only a limited number of languages, so this choice may be dictated more by the languages that are available than by desirability. All these options mean that programmers are frequently required to learn new languages for microcomputers, languages that they have not previously used.

Debugging

Any type of program error may be called a bug. The error may have been caused by faulty logic, failure to follow the coding language rules, or simply a data entry mistake. Regardless of the cause, *debugging* is the method used in an attempt to eliminate all program problems.

Debugging begins with a manual check by the programmer, who reads through the *listing* of instructions and data. The first time through the listing, the programmer eliminates typographical errors, misspellings, and format errors. Next, the listing is compared to the flowchart; there should be a corresponding area of code for each flowchart symbol. Finally, the programmer *simulates* the computer processing by stepping through the program, instruction by instruction. All operations—such as data transfers, mathematical processes, and input/output—are checked.

In spite of a careful desk check, the program is rarely bug-free at completion of the manual checking. The program generation and execution processes will usually uncover additional errors. The testing of a large program to eliminate bugs can easily consume half the development effort. Normally, the programmer will be expected to test small programs. Test data is prepared to verify that the program can handle the full range of data values, including positive and negative numbers. It is important to realize that debugging cannot prove that all errors have been eliminated. Only those which have been detected can be corrected. Examples of debugging are provided later in this chapter, but you will probably gain more experience in this art as you write programs.

Documentation

The final and possibly most important step of the programming process is documentation. Documentation is not as interesting to most programmers as are coding and debugging, so it is too often slighted. The operator's description of how to use the program, as well as the permanent record of program structure necessary for future error correction or changes, are needed as much as is the object code itself. There is no standard method for documentation, but three levels of program description are commonly used: design documents, operator manuals, and descriptive documents.

Design documents are the result of the problem statement, the analysis, and the model. They are guides on how the program is expected to perform.

Operator manuals specify all procedures necessary for use of the program. Every control, switch, readout, and display affected by the program should be covered in sufficient detail for an untrained operator to learn how to use the system from the manual.

Descriptive documents are written after the fact to describe the software for those who must maintain it. Complete details, in programmer's terms, describe the code and data of each program. Flowcharts are frequently included in these documents. Programs of any size at all require several additional documents; typically, these include test plans and procedures, descriptions of the *interfaces* between the hardware and the software (how the two will communicate with each other), and reports on specific project areas.

Programming Process Review

1. List the steps of programming in their proper order.
2. List what should be included in the problem statement.
3. Describe what is accomplished during the program model step.
4. Define the term "bug."
5. How is debugging accomplished?
6. Why is documentation important?

FLOWCHART PREPARATION

Before coding a program, the programmer must analyze the problem and break it into well-defined segments. Graphic aids provide a visual representation of the problem that makes it easier to understand the component parts. By using graphic aids as a blueprint, the programmer is able to grasp the overall picture as well as the details of a particular element.

Flowcharts are diagrams consisting of symbols and statements that represent computer operations. Data transfers, arithmetic and logical functions, and the flow of program logic can all be depicted on a flowchart. The symbols indicate the type of operation to be performed, and the lines connecting the symbols show the sequencing that the computer is to carry out. American National Standards Institute symbols are used in this book, but other flowcharting standards exist.

Terminals

The terminal shown in Fig. 3-4a designates starting, stopping, delay, or interrupt points in the normal flow of a program. Every flowchart begins with a terminal. Every program has a single starting point, although the program may have as many delay, interrupt, or stop terminals as desired. The start terminal (see Fig. 3-4b) has an arrow leading out, thus indicating that the flow of logic begins from that point. The word "start" or the name of the program or routine is usually written in the symbol. The stop terminal (see Fig. 3-4c) depicts a stop, a delay, or an interrupt point, depending on what is written in the symbol.

Processes

A process is indicated by a rectangle, as shown in Fig. 3-4d. The *process* box means that some action is to be taken that will change the value of some data unit. In this example a counter is to be set to the value of 1. Only one input and one output are permitted by the process (denoted by a single arrow leading in and out of the symbol).

Flowlines

The arrows in Fig. 3-4e are called *flowlines*. They are used to show operational sequence and data flow directions. Arrowheads show the direction of movement. The lines are always drawn either vertically or horizontally and never cross one another. If arrows are not provided on the flowlines, the presumed flow direction is from top to bottom for vertical lines and from left to right for horizontal ones. Normally, no more than two 90° bends are allowed in a flowline (see Fig. 3-4e).

Connectors

There are two symbols used for connectors (see Fig. 3-4f). The circle is used to show continuation to or from another part of the flowchart on the same page. The pentagon shows connections from or to another page. Letters, numbers, or a combination of these are used to identify matching continuation points. Connector symbols can be used in pairs to replace long flowlines or to prevent flowlines from crossing.

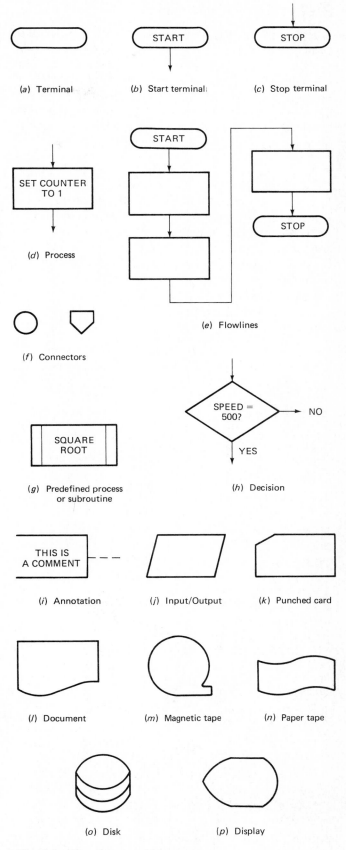

(a) Terminal (b) Start terminal (c) Stop terminal

(d) Process (e) Flowlines

(f) Connectors

(g) Predefined process or subroutine (h) Decision

(i) Annotation (j) Input/Output (k) Punched card

(l) Document (m) Magnetic tape (n) Paper tape

(o) Disk (p) Display

Fig. 3-4 Flowchart symbols.

Predefined Processes

A subroutine, or *predefined process,* is a named operation consisting of a series of program steps specified in another flowchart. Any widely used routine can be formed into a predefined process. The symbol for a subroutine is shown in Fig. 3-4*g*. The subroutine can be inserted into another program any time that function is to be used. When a subroutine is referenced, or *called,* the predefined operation will be executed.

Decisions

The decision diamond (see Fig. 3-4*h*) indicates that a choice must be made to decide which of two output paths will be taken. If the answer to the question in the diamond is "yes," then the flowline labeled "yes" indicates the next step; otherwise, the "no" direction is followed.

Other Symbols

When further explanation than will fit into one of the flowchart symbols is needed, additional descriptive comments can be placed in an annotation box (see Fig. 3-4*i*). The annotation should help clarify a difficult portion of the flowchart. The I/O symbol shows that data is entering or leaving the computer at that point. The I/O medium can also be indicated by using an appropriate symbol. Input/output media symbols are shown in Figs. 3-4*j* through 3-4*p*. Identification of the I/O data can be written in the symbol.

Example Flowchart

A flowchart presenting samples of the use of these symbols is shown in Fig. 3-5. This program reads a punched card containing an employee's time clock information and records it on the master payroll tape. If the pay exceeds $200, a check is prepared in addition to recording the data.

Flowcharts Review

1. List the primary uses for a terminal.
2. Describe the two types of connectors.
3. How many right angles are allowed in flowlines?
4. How many exits does a decision symbol have? A subroutine?
5. List the I/O media symbols available for flowcharting.

DEBUGGING TECHNIQUES

As surprising as it seems, the time a programmer spends in debugging and testing a program will be almost twice

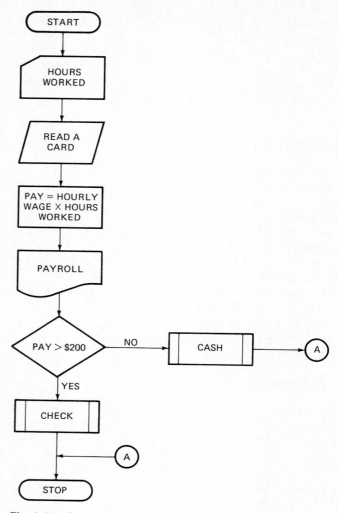

Fig. 3-5 Flowchart example.

as long as the time spent in initially coding the program. Because the computer interprets every instruction literally, nothing can be left to chance. Every possible situation must be visualized and accounted for prior to releasing a program to the user. You have undoubtedly heard stories of program bugs that resulted in employees receiving million-dollar paychecks or, more commonly, in credit card customers being billed for merchandise they had already paid for, so it should not be surprising to find that debugging is very difficult. In fact, software testing cannot accomplish what we actually want—which is to prove that the program is bug-free. Instead, as testing uncovers errors, it shows the presence of bugs, not their absence. This limitation usually results in testing until the developer is reasonably confident that all serious bugs have been found. Then the user assumes the risk of undiscovered bugs interfering with daily operations.

As an example of how bugs can creep into a program, consider the square-root-routine flowchart shown in Fig. 3-6. This routine uses the *Newton algorithm* for

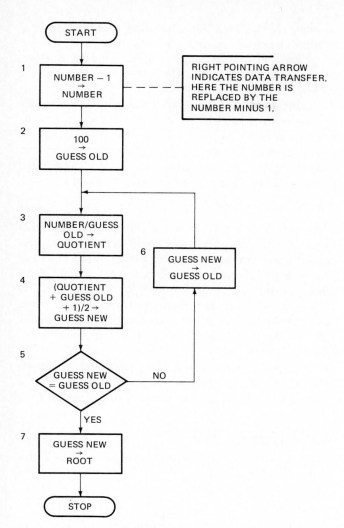

Fig. 3-6 Newton algorithm.

In the flowchart the boxes are labeled:

1. NUMBER − 1 → NUMBER

   RIGHT POINTING ARROW INDICATES DATA TRANSFER. HERE THE NUMBER IS REPLACED BY THE NUMBER MINUS 1.

2. 100 → GUESS OLD

3. NUMBER/GUESS OLD → QUOTIENT

4. (QUOTIENT + GUESS OLD + 1)/2 → GUESS NEW

6. GUESS NEW → GUESS OLD

5. GUESS NEW = GUESS OLD

   NO

   YES

7. GUESS NEW → ROOT

extracting a square root, which provides a faster solution by computer than the more familiar method you learned in your mathematics courses. Explanation of the algorithm will be clearest by means of an example. The algorithm finds the nearest integer square root of any positive number; that is, there is no decimal point in the answer. The nearest integer square root of 12 is 3 because 9 is the largest square less than 12.

The lack of a decimal point in the answer is not really a shortcoming, as the number could be multiplied by 100 or 10,000 prior to finding the root. This multiplication, also called *scaling*, would produce a root correct to one or two fractional positions, respectively. In this example the nearest integer square roots would be:

Number	Scale Factor	Nearest Integer Square Root
12	1	3
1200	100	34
120,000	10,000	346

The square root of 12 to two decimal places is 3.46. By first multiplying by 10,000 and then placing the decimal point in the proper position in the answer, the Newton algorithm can be used to find the root quite accurately.

Now let's return to the flowchart and follow the example through the process. Let the number be 12. (The steps in the flowchart are numbered so that we can easily refer to them.) In step 1 the number is reduced to 11. Then "guess old" in step 2 is set to 100. (If we had forgotten to *initialize* "guess old" in this manner, it would have had a zero value in the computer. Then step 3 would involve a division by 0, which is clearly the wrong approach.) The number is divided by "guess old" in step 3 and the answer is saved in a variable called "quotient"; carrying out this division gives us 0 for an answer [$(11/100) = 0$ because no fractional numbers are used by the algorithm]. Step 4 will then yield

$$\frac{0 + 100 + 1}{2} = 50$$

for a value of "guess new." The decision in box 5 is answered negatively, so we return to step 3 after replacing "guess old" by "guess new." The iterative, or *looping,* process continues until "guess old" is equal to "guess new." At that time the root has been found and the process terminates. You should continue to follow the flowchart for the case where the original number is 12 to convince yourself that the correct answer is produced. Table 3-1 summarizes partial results at key points of each iteration.

Although the algorithm worked in this case, there are actually two bugs in the flowchart as given. One way to find bugs prior to running on a computer is to use test cases, as stated above. The computer action is traced as we execute each step. We simulate the computer by not taking fractional quotients, for example. Obviously, every possible number could not be tested in this way because there is not enough time to make that many manual checks. Instead, a selected set of numbers is chosen. A good rule of thumb is to use the minimum and the maximum values an algorithm can accept, a value of 0, and a few values between these extreme cases. If we use 0 as an input, we see that step 1 results in a negative number. The answer will no longer con-

Table 3-1 Newton Algorithm Partial Results

Iteration	Guess Old	Quotient	Guess New
1	100	0	50
2	50	0	25
3	25	0	13
4	13	0	7
5	7	1	4
6	4	2	3
7	3	3	3 stop

verge to the root if the number becomes negative at this point. (In fact, division by 0 occurs in the ninth iteration, as you can prove by following the flowchart.) This error can be prevented by placing a decision at the beginning of the algorithm to check for a 0 input.

The second bug is slightly harder to detect, but a knowledge of arithmetic should lead the programmer to it. The error is that the square root of negative numbers is imaginary. We only want to use real numbers in our navigation routine, so this case must also be eliminated by a second decision at the beginning to prevent negative inputs. The corrected flowchart is shown in Fig. 3-7.

Having seen one example of debugging, let's consider one more. You will also have ample opportunity to practice your debugging skills in the experiments, as your programs will often not run correctly the first time you try them. This algorithm (see Fig. 3-8) computes the factorial of the input by using the equation

$$n! = (n)(n - 1)(n - 2) \cdots (1) \tag{3-2}$$

where n is the input number. First, check the algorithm by using 6 as an input. If you found that 6! is 720, you correctly traced the program operation. What bugs can you discover? Does the algorithm work for 0? With large positive numbers? With negative numbers? The answers to the first and third questions are no. In the case of either a 0 input or a negative input, the process will not terminate because the input will never decrement to 0 in the third process box. Checks at the beginning for a 0 input, setting the output to 1 (0! equals 1 by definition), and giving an error indication for a negative input should all be inserted in the flowchart.

Debugging Review

1. What does a right-pointing arrow in a process box mean?

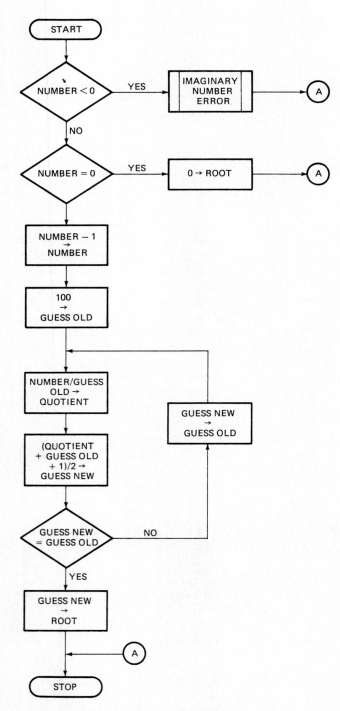

Fig. 3-7 Corrected Newton algorithm.

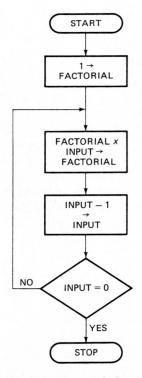

Fig. 3-8 Factorial algorithm.

2. Describe the use of tracing, test cases, and simulation to debug programs prior to running them on a computer.
3. What values should you use in test cases for an algorithm that allows a range of inputs of -100 to $+200$?

CHAPTER SUMMARY

1. A computer program is a logical sequence of instructions and data that produces a specified result after computer execution.
2. Routines are sets of instructions (portions of a larger program) that cause the computer to carry out frequently needed tasks.
3. A subroutine is a short instruction sequence that provides a solution to frequently encountered problems.
4. A bug is an error in a program.
5. A top-down approach to programming follows a disciplined series of actions.
6. The problem statement establishes exactly what the program is to do and what data is to be used in the operations.
7. After problem definition, the analysis surveys all methods of solution and selects the most suitable one in terms of development time, execution time, and memory available.
8. A problem model is a mathematical description of the program to be written.
9. Flowcharts graphically depict the process to be used in the computer solution.
10. Converting the flowchart to computer instructions takes place during the coding step.
11. Debugging a complicated program often takes more time than coding it.
12. Documentation is needed by the user to understand how to operate the program and by the programmers who must maintain the software after delivery.
13. The American National Standards Institute has established a set of symbols to be used in flowcharting computer programs.
14. Debugging can start prior to running the program on a computer by using test cases, tracing, and simulation.

KEY TERMS AND CONCEPTS

Program	Flowcharts	Connector
Routine	Coding	Predefined process
Subroutine	Listing	Decision
Bug	Documentation	Annotation
Problem statement	Terminal	Input/output (I/O)
Peripheral equipment	Process	Scaling
Analysis	Flowlines	Test cases, tracing, and simulation
Problem model		

PROBLEMS

3-1 Prepare a written statement of the problem, the analysis, and the model for a program that finds the roots to the second-degree quadratic equation

$$Ax^2 + Bx + C = 0$$

where the input parameters are A, B, and C. Use the formula

$$x = \frac{-B \pm \sqrt{B^2 - 4AC}}{2A}$$

3-2 Prepare a flowchart for the computer program of Prob. 3-1. Use the algorithm given below. Assume that all named subroutines have previously been programmed. (No flowcharts of those subroutines are to be drawn.)

STEP 1. Compute the value $B^2 - 4AC$, and if the result is negative, perform a subroutine called PROCESS IMAGINARY and then exit.

STEP 2. If $B^2 - 4AC$ is positive and A and B are 0, perform a predefined process called PROCESS TRIVIAL and then exit.

STEP 3. If $A = 0$ and $B \neq 0$, compute $-C/B$ and place the answer in variables called ROOT1 and ROOT2. Exit from the routine.

STEP 4. If $B^2 - 4AC$ is positive and A is not 0, send $B^2 - 4AC$ to a variable called SQUARE ROOT INPUT. Then perform the SQUARE ROOT subroutine.

STEP 5. Following Step 4, compute the value $-B$ + SQUARE ROOT OUTPUT. Divide this sum by $2A$ and place the result in ROOT1. Compute $-B$ − SQUARE ROOT OUTPUT and divide the difference by $2A$. Transfer the result to ROOT2 and then exit from the routine.

3-3 Prepare a flowchart of the following routine.

PROBLEM STATEMENT: This program is to compute the absolute values of the sums of the items in two lists and place these resulting values into corresponding positions in a third list.

INPUTS: List A and list B, each containing eight combinations of positive or negative numbers.

OUTPUT: List C, eight items long. Each item is equal to the absolute value of the sum of the two corresponding items in lists A and B.

ANALYSIS: The absolute value of a number is the magnitude of that number, regardless of the sign. This value is obtained in the computer by checking the number to see if it is negative or positive. If it is positive, then it is its own absolute value. If it is negative, then its 2's complement is the absolute value.

$$|A_i + B_i| \rightarrow C_i$$

where the symbol | | stands for absolute value.

PROBLEM MODEL: 1. Compute the sum $A + B$.
2. Complement the sum if it is negative.

3-4 Using the Newton algorithm, compute the nearest-integer square root of 26. Show partial results in a format similar to that of Table 3-1.

3-5 Repeat Prob. 3-4, computing the answer to two places to the right of the decimal point.

3-6 Change the flowchart shown in Fig. 3-7 to eliminate all bugs and to compute factorial values of positive integers greater than or equal to 0 and less than 1000π (where $\pi = 3.1415926$).

3-7 Prepare a problem model and a flowchart for this problem.

STATEMENT: Convert a 16-digit binary fraction into the BCD code equivalents of four decimal fractional digits, and pack these codes into an answer cell from right to left in reverse order of significance.

ANALYSIS: Use the explosion fractional base conversion algorithm.

INPUT: bit numbers

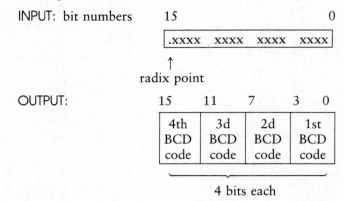

(*Note:* The rightmost BCD code is the most significant digit and the first generated. It will represent the decimal fractional digit next to the radix point.)

3-8 Given two lists of coordinates, each 10 items long, a program must be written to find the distance between each set of two points. The table layout is shown below.

	List 1			List 2	
Item 1	x_a	y_a	Item 1	x_b	y_b
2	x_a	y_a	2	x_b	y_b
⋮	⋮	⋮	⋮	⋮	⋮
10	x_a	y_a	10	x_b	y_b

Using the information from this chapter, draw a flowchart for the distance routine. The distance routine may use Fig. 3-6 as a subroutine.

3-9 The answer below is calculated to a specific precision by using scale factors. Complete the table to show the effects of scaling.

	Input		
Name	Value	Operation	Result
A	3.14	Scale up by 10^2	314
B	271828	Scale down by 10^3	271.828
D	0.107	$A - D \rightarrow A$	
—	—	$AB/0.22 \rightarrow B$	
—	—	Scale A by 10^{-2}	
—	—	Scale B by 10^{-3}	

3-10 Provide a flowchart for the following problem. Given: three tables called table C, table D, and table T, each of which is 100 items long. Table C starts at address CREDIT and contains 100 numbers. Table D starts at address DEBIT and contains 100 numbers. Table T starts at address TOTAL and contains 100 items that all are initially cleared to 0.

Add the first value of table C to the first value in table D, and place the sum in the first empty item in table T. Now add the second value from table C to the second value of table D and the first item you just placed in table T, and place this sum (subtotal) in the second item of table T. Continue in this fashion until all the items have been processed or until the subtotal in table T goes negative. Perform a subroutine called BANK-RUPT and exit the routine if table T does go negative.

If all items are processed and the subtotal never became negative, execute a predefined process called SUCCESS and exit the routine. (If the process SUCCESS were ever executed, table T would contain 100 values, and the last value would be the grand total of debits and credits.) For example:

Table C	Table D	Table T
4	−2	2
6	−3	5
2	−5	2
4	−4	2
⋮	⋮	⋮

8085 MICROPROCESSOR ARCHITECTURE

Now we will begin a detailed examination of a specific microprocessor, the 8085 and its supporting devices. When microprocessors that are compatible with the 8085 are included (that is, the 8080 and Z80), then over half the 8-bit microcomputers commercially available are based on this same architecture and instruction set. Many controllers used in industrial applications also use this family of microprocessors. Furthermore, the 16-bit 8086 family (80186 and 80286) share some of the features of the 8085. So by learning about this microprocessor, you will actually be covering the essential characteristics of a significant number of other microprocessors. Other devices in the 8085 family used for input/output and control are covered in Chaps. 13 and 14. A description of the 8080, its support chips, and the Z80 are provided in the Appendix.

CHAPTER OBJECTIVES

Upon completion of this chapter, you should be able to:

1. List the functions of the 8085 integrated circuit.
2. Discuss the programmable registers and stack of the 8085.
3. Discuss the functions of the ALU.
4. Explain the control and timing of the 8085 by use of timing diagrams.
5. Describe the interface between the 8085 and either ROM or RAM, and describe the methods of address mapping.
6. Define the purpose of bidirectional bus drivers in a microprocessor system.
7. List the types of instructions used in the 8085 and explain the timing diagrams of the instructions.

THE 8085 MICROPROCESSOR INTEGRATED CIRCUIT

The 8085 performs all the MPU functions needed in a computer system, including arithmetic and logic, control and timing, and programmable registers. The microprocessor provides and accepts TTL-compatible signals. A single +5-V power supply is all that is necessary to drive the chip. There are several manufacturers of the 8085, and slight functional differences are found among the versions; variations in maximum clock frequency, environmental conditions, and electrical parameters are typical of these differences. Because the particular 8085 model must suit the intended operating conditions, always consult the data sheets to ensure proper performance of that model in your application.

Data and Address Lines

The pin assignments for the 8085 are shown in Fig. 4-1. As you can see, the 8085 is housed in a 40-pin DIP. The purpose of each pin is described in Table 4-1. The lower 8 bits of the address bus and data bus of the 8085 are *multiplexed*; that is, the same lines carry two kinds of signals at different times. (A *bus* is a group of paths for related signals.) The lower 8 bits of the multiplexed address and data buses are denoted AD0 through AD7; at some times they represent addresses, and at others, data. The remaining bits of the 16-bit address bus (A8 through A15) carry only addresses. All of these lines are three-state. Addresses set on these lines indicate the binary location in memory of the data to be read or written. The address lines also designate a particular input/output (I/O) device to be used in data transfers external to the microprocessor. The address bus, because it consists of three-state logic, can *float* (switch to the high-impedance state) to allow other devices to exchange data on the bus without confusing the MPU; for example, an I/O device can put data directly into memory without involving the MPU.

The bidirectional lines AD0 through AD7 form the data bus for the 8 bits of information being sent or received by the microprocessor. Input/output data to or from the processor is transferred by means of this bus.

The type of information currently being multiplexed on the address and data buses is indicated by the address latch enable (ALE) signal. When the ALE signal is high, address information is on lines AD0 through AD7. When the ALE is low, these lines are being used for data transfer.

Table 4-1 8085 Signals

Signal Name*	Purpose	Type of Data	Other Characteristics
AD0–AD7	Address/data bus	Bidirectional	Three-state
A8–A15	Address bus	Output	Three-state
ALE	Address latch enable	Output	Three-state
$\overline{RD}$	Read control	Output	Three-state
$\overline{WR}$	Write control	Output	Three-state
$IO\overline{M}$	I/O memory switch	Output	Three-state
S0, S1	Bus state indicators	Output	
READY	Wait state indicator	Input	
SID	Serial input data	Input	
SOD	Serial output data	Output	
HOLD	Hold request	Input	
HLDA	Hold acknowledge	Output	
INTR	Interrupt request	Input	
TRAP	Nonmaskable interrupt	Input	
RST 5.5	Vectored interrupt	Input	
RST 6.5	Vectored interrupt	Input	
RST 7.5	Vectored interrupt	Input	
$\overline{INTA}$	Interrupt acknowledge	Output	
$\overline{RESETIN}$	System reset	Input	
$\overline{RESETOUT}$	Peripheral reset	Output	
X1, X2	Crystal contacts	Input	
CLK	System clock	Output	
V_{CC}	Power	Input	
V_{SS}	Ground	Input	

* The overbar indicates a signal that is true when low. The signal $IO\overline{M}$ means IO and $\overline{M}$ control.

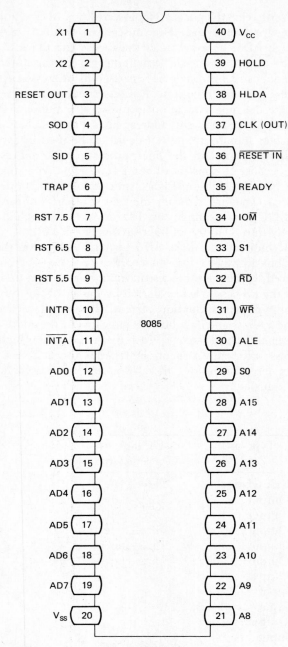

Fig. 4-1 8085 pin configuration.

Timing and Control Signals

The five signals used to indicate how the data and address lines are to be interpreted are listed in Table 4-2. The $\overline{RD}$ signal indicates when a read operation is being performed (the overbar means that the signal is true when low); the data can be obtained from memory or from an I/O port. The $\overline{WR}$ signal indicates when a write operation is being performed. When $\overline{WR}$ is low, data is being sent either to memory or to an I/O port. For the 8085 to distinguish between reading and writing to memory or to an I/O port, another signal is needed. The IO$\overline{M}$ (that is, IO and $\overline{M}$) signal is pulsed high when

Table 4-2 Control Signals

Signal	Purpose	Use
$\overline{RD}$	Memory or I/O read	Pulsed low for read operation
$\overline{WR}$	Memory or I/O write	Pulsed low for write operation
IO$\overline{M}$	I/O or memory access (used with $\overline{RD}$ and $\overline{WR}$)	Pulsed low for memory access Pulsed high for I/O access
S0	System bus status	See Table 4-3
S1	System bus status	See Table 4-3

the read or write involves an I/O port. During memory access for reading or writing, IO$\overline{M}$ is pulsed low.

The remaining two signals tell how the system buses are being used. These signals are listed in Table 4-3. When the MPU is halted, both S0 and S1 are 0. During write operations, S0 is 0 and S1 is 1. For a read, S0 is set to 1 and S1 is 0. Finally both of these signals are 1s for an instruction fetch operation.

Interrupt Control and I/O Signals

Six status lines (INTR, TRAP, RST 5.5, RST 6.5, RST 7.5, and $\overline{INTA}$) are used to coordinate exchange of interrupt status. All signals except $\overline{INTA}$ are set high by external devices to request an interrupt. The processor sets $\overline{INTA}$ low to reply. Chapter 13 discusses the use of interrupts in detail. The SID and SOD pins can be used for serial I/O data exchange, which is also described in Chap. 13.

Programmable Registers

There are 10 registers in the 8085 that are used by the programmer and controlled by use of processor instructions (see Fig. 4-2). The purpose of these registers is similar to those discussed in Chap. 1. A brief comment on each serves as a review.

The A register is the 8-bit primary accumulator. It is most commonly used in arithmetic, logical, and data transfer instructions. Certain aspects of arithmetic or logical results are shown by flag bits in the program status word (PSW) register. The meaning of each bit in

Table 4-3 System Bus Status Signals

Signal Level		
S0	S1	Meaning
0	0	Halt
0	1	Write operation
1	0	Read operation
1	1	Instruction fetch

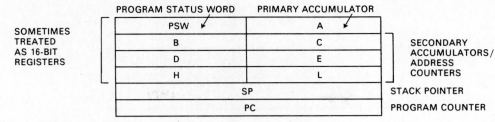

Fig. 4-2 Programmable registers

the status register is shown in Fig. 4-3. The sign, zero, parity, and carry flags were discussed in Chap. 1. The auxiliary carry is a new feature, though. This flag operates the same as the carry indicator, but the A_C bit reflects the carries out of bit position 3 into position 4 of the 8-bit sum. This status flag is often used in BCD operations (see Chap. 7). In some cases the A register is combined with the status register to form a 16-bit unit.

There are six scratchpad registers (secondary accumulators): B, C, D, E, H, and L. Each is an 8-bit register and can, in many cases, be used in the same manner as the A register. In addition, these registers can be linked to be 16-bit address counters. When used in this manner, they are referred to as the BC, DE, or HL registers. The HL register is used as the primary address counter. The use of the address counters is discussed in detail in Chap. 6.

You already know how the stack pointer (SP) is set to show the address for the top of the stack. The 8085 uses memory as the stack, so the programmer can have a stack of 64K locations long if desired; normally, much shorter stack lengths are called for. When the stack is popped, the content of the memory cell on top of the stack, as addressed by the SP register, is obtained. New data is also pushed on the stack by using the address given by the pointer register.

The final register in the 8085 of interest to programmers is the program counter (PC). The program counter holds the address of the next instruction to be executed. Recall that this register is incremented during the instruction fetching so that it always shows the proper memory location.

CLOCK AND CONTROL SIGNALS

The crystal on the X1 and X2 inputs drives the internal 8085 clock logic. A TTL-compatible clock signal is provided for external devices on the CLK output pin.

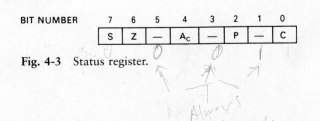

Fig. 4-3 Status register.

The clock signal delineates the clock periods, T, of Fig. 4-4. As Fig. 4-5 shows, the clock signal makes a transition from high to low at the beginning of each period. This type of clock signal consisting of a *single phase* is the simplest one possible. Other microprocessors may require two signals to form a two-phase clock; the 8080 MPU, for one, requires a two-phase clock.

Instruction Execution Timing

During any machine cycle (MC), clock periods T1 through T3 are reserved from memory references. The use of these clock periods is illustrated in Fig. 4-6a. The remaining time in the machine cycle, T4 and T5, is available for MPU functions not involving memory or for use by external logic to complete its operations.

In addition, there is a special meaning of MC1 for any instruction; it is during this machine cycle that the instruction is fetched. As Fig. 4-6b shows, T1, T2, and T3 are used to obtain the instruction. This timing is a special case of the basic rule that memory is referenced during the first three clock periods. It is in the T4 interval that the program counter will increment and the instruction be decoded. The remaining period T5 is optional; that is, for some instructions the MPU can use this time for other operations; otherwise, T5 is canceled.

Identifying Operations

With all the different tasks accomplished by the 8085, how can anyone keep track of what is happening? Actually, this seemingly complex problem is solved quite simply. One need only look at the signals on the control lines to tell what is happening. Refer back to Tables 4-2 and 4-3 to review those signals. Some signals indicate when to read or write, while others designate the source or destination of the data. Examples of each type of operation will be described in a series of timing diagrams, which follow.

In Fig. 4-7 you can see how the ALE signal tells when the multiplexed address and data lines contain an address. When ALE is high, the address is valid. Also, note that S0 and S1 are both high during MC1, which uniquely identifies this machine cycle as the one to fetch the next instruction.

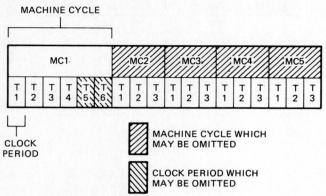

Fig. 4-4 8085 Timing.

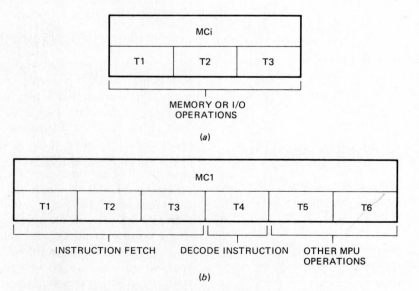

Fig. 4-5 Clock signal.

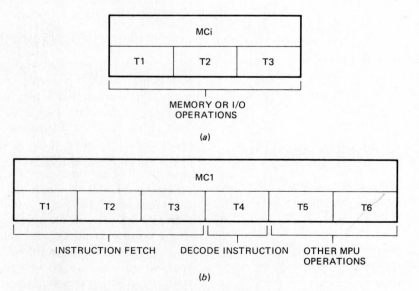

Fig. 4-6 Machine cycles: (a) other than MC1, (b) MC1.

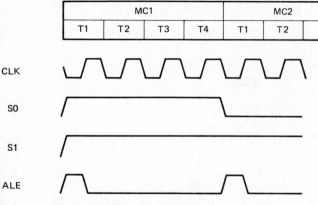

Fig. 4-7 Start of machine cycle timing.

Instruction Fetching

Let's analyze the instruction-fetching microprogram in more detail to gain a further understanding of the timing relationships in the MPU. Figure 4-8 shows the instruction-fetching cycle during MC1. During MC1, as previously explained, S0 and S1 both become high. The address of the instruction is placed on the higher address lines (A8 through A15) and the lower address lines (AD0 through AD7). Then ALE goes high to indicate that the address is valid. The trailing edge of ALE should

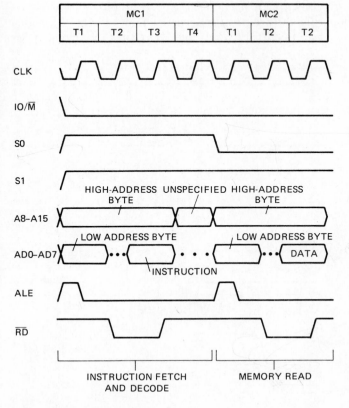

Fig. 4-8 Instruction fetching.

be used to latch the low-order byte of the address. The ALE signal then falls to the low level to show that the address is not a valid one after T1. The $\overline{RD}$ signal is pulsed low to signal the time to read the instruction from the specified memory address. That permits the instruction to be read in over lines AD0 through AD7, which are now being used to transfer data. During T4 the instruction is being decoded. At that time the content of the address bus is unspecified.

As was previously noted, the only difference between the instruction-fetching machine cycle and any other is the number of clock cycles. The instruction fetch can take either four or six clock cycles, while all other machine cycles are limited to three clock periods. The instruction is decoded on the fourth clock cycle of MC1. Clock cycles 5 and 6 must be used for subsequent internal operations; otherwise, these extra clock cycles are deleted. Regardless of the type of machine cycle, all memory operations take place in three clock cycles.

Reading Memory Data

The first two machine cycles of an instruction that reads memory data are shown in Fig. 4-8. The reading of data from memory takes place in MC2 following the instruction fetch of MC1. The only change in signals between the fetching of the instruction and the reading of the data is in S0 and S1. During MC1 both are high, but when data is read from memory, S0 is low. It takes three clock cycles to read the data. During the first cycle the address is placed on the upper and lower byte lines. The ALE signal is pulsed to indicate that the lower address byte is valid. During the second cycle, the $\overline{RD}$ signal goes low to signal that the data is to be obtained. During this entire process, the IO$\overline{M}$ line is held low to signal that the source of data is from memory. If this were an input from an external device, the IO$\overline{M}$ line would go high instead.

Writing Memory Data

Because the sequence of events to write data is the same as reading during MC1 (that is, the instruction must be fetched), only MC2 is shown in Fig. 4-9. Comparing this timing diagram with the previous one, we see that there are two major areas of difference. In the case of writing to memory, the $\overline{S0}$ line is held high and the S1 line goes low. Also, the $\overline{WR}$ line is pulsed low to signal the memory to accept the data word. Note that during T1 the ALE signal works in the normal manner to show when the lower address byte is valid on lines AD0 through AD7. Writing the data took three clock cycles. If this had been an output instruction, the IO$\overline{M}$ line would have gone high to signify that the data was intended for an external device.

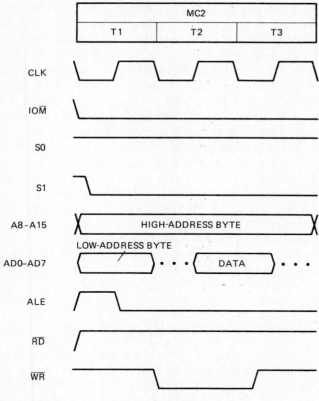

Fig. 4-9 Memory writing.

The Wait State

Some memories and I/O devices are too slow to respond to data transfers within three clock cycles. How can these components be made compatible with the 8085? The wait state is provided for this reason. By means of the wait state, the slow peripheral or memory can signal the processor to slow down. The delay is inserted in the instruction timing between clock cycles T2 and T3. The peripheral asks for the delay by setting the READY line low. The MPU samples the READY line during T2 of every machine cycle. Figure 4-10 shows the sequence of events. If READY is low, the MPU adds a wait clock cycle (T_W) following T2. Additional wait clock cycles are inserted until the READY line goes high. After the MPU senses that READY is high, T3 is allowed to occur.

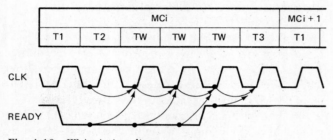

Fig. 4-10 Wait timing diagram.

The Hold State

Another responsibility of the MPU is to grant external devices an opportunity to gain control of memory. This change of control is usually associated with devices that can perform a direct memory access (DMA). Chapter 13 fully describes this operation, so here we will just cover how the 8085 provides this service. Another use for the hold state is to stop the processor between instructions. This periodic stop is useful in debugging and in performing maintenance.

Be careful to distinguish the wait state from the hold state. During the wait state the processor is held up in the middle of an instruction, but in the hold state the processor is between instructions. The device sets the HOLD input high to place the processor in the hold state. On receipt of the high HOLD signal, the processor floats both the data and address buses, allowing the device to use the buses at will. The 8085 sets the HLDA signal high to acknowledge the input signal. This output is used by the device to identify the beginning of the hold period.

The hold state is slightly different for four- and six-clock-cycle machine cycles. The difference is shown in Figs. 4-11 and 4-12. The HOLD line is sampled during T2 of a four-clock-cycle machine cycle (Fig. 4-12a). The 8085 inserts hold cycles (T_H) following T4 and sets HLDA high. In the six-clock-cycle case, the HOLD is sampled during T4 and the hold cycles are inserted following T6. The HOLD line is sampled on every cycle while the processor is suspended until the HOLD signal is dropped. The hold state terminates two clock cycles

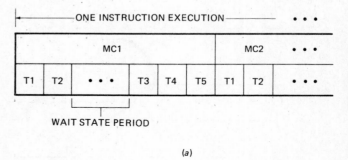

(a)

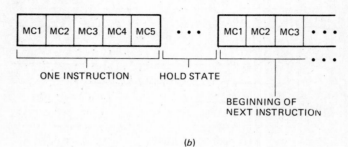

(b)

Fig. 4-11 Comparison of wait state and hold state: (*a*) wait state timing, (*b*) hold state timing.

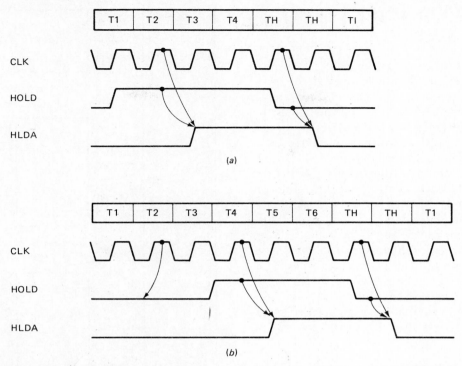

| T1 | T2 | T3 | T4 | TH | TH | TI |

CLK

HOLD

HLDA

(a)

| T1 | T2 | T3 | T4 | T5 | T6 | TH | TH | T1 |

CLK

HOLD

HLDA

(b)

Fig. 4-12 Hold timing diagram: *(a)* four-clock period machine cycle, *(b)* six-clock period machine cycle.

afterward. In this way an external device can suspend the operations of the MPU for as long as is needed.

The Halt State

The programmer can cause the 8085 to stop by executing a halt instruction. The processor stops all operations and pauses, with nothing to do until it is restarted. Almost every program written for the microprocessor will contain at least one halt instruction. When the 8085 stops, the programmer knows that the program has been completed.

When the halt instruction is executed, the microprocessor issues a series of idle clock periods. During this time, no operations take place. The S0 and S1 outputs are low. All three-state signals are floated. The halt state is terminated by either a reset or an interrupt. The microprocessor can be placed in the hold state while it is halted.

The Reset Signal

The microprocessor is reset by some external action that sets the $\overline{\text{RESETIN}}$ signal low. This signal is frequently used to restart the processor after a halt. Another time when a reset occurs is during the initial power-up sequence. When power is first applied, the $\overline{\text{RESETIN}}$ signal must be held low for at least 500 ns. The internal 8085 logic synchronizes the $\overline{\text{RESETIN}}$ signal with the

internal clock. In turn, the 8085 issues the $\overline{\text{RESETOUT}}$ signal for use by other devices to initialize themselves.

When the 8085 resets, the program counter is set to 0. This action means that the first instruction to be executed after restart must be placed in memory location 0000. In addition, the reset clears the instruction register. During the reset, all interrupts are also disabled and all three-state lines are floated.

Control Review

1. Distinguish between machine cycles, clock periods, and clock phases.
2. What is the purpose of T1 through T3 in any machine cycle? What is T4 used for during MC1?
3. In which clock period is an instruction fetched? When is it decoded so that the processor knows the action to complete?
4. List the sequence of signals used during MC1 to fetch an instruction. How does fetching data from memory differ from this sequence?
5. Discuss the differences between control signals used to write and to read memory data.
6. How does an external device request more time for a reply? What signal does the 8085 use to acknowledge that the request is granted?
7. Contrast the hold state with the halt state.
8. Why does the processor execute the instruction in memory location 0000_{16} after the $\overline{\text{RESETIN}}$ line goes low after being held high?

DEMULTIPLEXING AND BUFFERING THE SYSTEM BUSES

The complete set of signals for the 8085 is shown in Fig. 4-13. On the left are the power and control signals that affect processor operations. On the right are the address and data bus and the I/O control signals. Because the lower address lines and data lines are shared, interfacing with the MPU is inconvenient. The read and write signals apply to both memory and I/O data operations, which is another complication. One other problem to be resolved is that each of these lines can drive only one TTL load; often we want to route these signals to a number of devices.

All these problems can be solved by demultiplexing the buses and providing buffering to enable them to drive more than a single load. First, let us consider the address bus. We want to form a complete 16-bit address, so that no matter what the microprocessor is doing, the information on A0 through A16 is always an address. Figure 4-14 shows the approach to use. Two

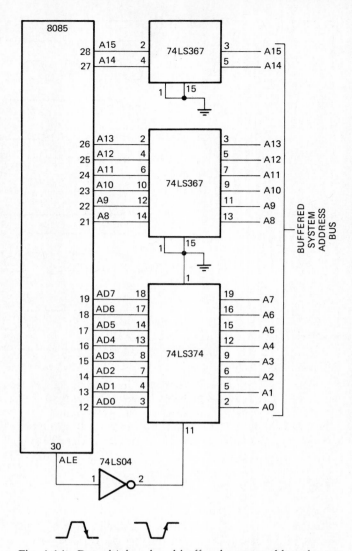

Fig. 4-14 Demultiplexed and buffered system address bus.

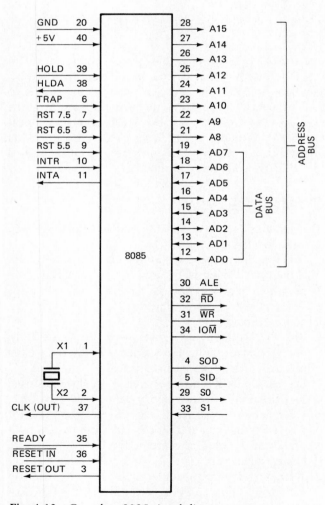

Fig. 4-13 Complete 8085 signal diagram.

types of integrated circuits (ICs) will be required. The 74LS367 is a three-state buffer that will drive multiple loads. The 74LS374 is a latch and buffer in a single device that will latch lines AD0 through AD7 when the address is placed on them.

Let us deal first with latching the lower address byte. As you may remember, the ALE signal indicates when the address is valid. The address is to be sampled on the transition from high to low of the ALE signal. As it happens, the 74LS374 latches on a signal transitioning from low to high. This difference means that the ALE signal must be inverted prior to applying it to the 74LS374. That is the purpose of the 74LS04 inverter in the diagram. Now when the ALE line indicates that the address is valid, the bits are latched, and outputs of the 74LS374 hold these values until the address is changed. These lower address lines are also buffered by this chip. The upper address lines are much simpler to deal with. In the case of A8 through A15, we must simply buffer

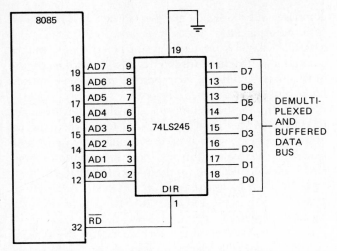

Fig. 4-15 Demultiplexed and buffered system data bus.

them with the 74LS367 ICs, as Fig. 4-14 shows. Now we have a full 16-bit buffered system address bus that can be routed to a variety of other devices.

The data bus is demultiplexed and buffered in the manner shown in Fig. 4-15. The 74LS245 bidirectional bus driver is selected. The theory of a bidirectional bus driver is provided in a subsequent section of this chapter. At this point it is sufficient to note that the device can buffer both input and output signals. The direction of the signal is provided to the driver by the direction (DIR) input on pin 1. We will use the $\overline{RD}$ output of the 8085 to indicate direction. When the signal is low, data

is to be received by the MPU. The MPU is sending data when the signal is high. With that input, the 74LS245 will route the signal in the proper direction and buffer it too. By this method we have produced a system data bus that is fully buffered and demultiplexed.

Did you note that in Figs. 4-14 and 4-15 it seems that lines AD0 through AD7 seem to be driving two loads (the 74LS374 in Fig. 4-14 and the 74LS245 in Fig. 4-15)? This seeming contradiction to the statement that only one load can be driven can be resolved by understanding the enabling signals for the two chips. The 74LS374 is only enabled by the high-to-low transition on the ALE signal. The 74LS245 is enabled by the $\overline{RD}$ signal being true. Because these two signals are true at different times, one or both of these chips are disabled at all times. So there is at most one load on lines AD0 through AD7.

The handling of the system control bus signals takes a little thought. An easily implemented control bus will indicate to the memory or I/O device the type of operation the processor wants and the direction of data transfer. This means that we would like to have four signals: read memory, write memory, input, and output. Figure 4-16 shows how these signals may be realized. The truth table in the figure shows how the three signals that the 8085 generates ($\overline{RD}$, $\overline{WR}$, and $\overline{IOM}$) can be converted to the four signals we want. Using that table, we may straightforwardly develop a combinatorial network to produce these signals. Trace the signals to verify that the truth table is correctly implemented.

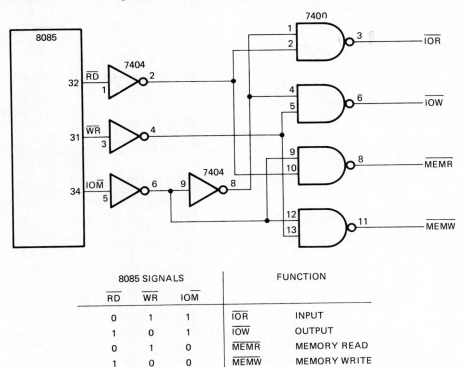

8085 SIGNALS				FUNCTION	
$\overline{RD}$	$\overline{WR}$	$\overline{IOM}$			
0	1	1	$\overline{IOR}$	INPUT	
1	0	1	$\overline{IOW}$	OUTPUT	
0	1	0	$\overline{MEMR}$	MEMORY READ	
1	0	0	$\overline{MEMW}$	MEMORY WRITE	

Fig. 4-16 Demultiplexed and buffered system control bus.

Demultiplexing and Buffering the System Buses Review

1. Why is demultiplexing of the address, data, and control buses desirable?
2. What would happen if the address, data, and control buses were not buffered?
3. Explain why the address lines AD0 through AD7 must be latched. Why do the upper address lines require no latching?
4. What is the purpose of the inverter in the address bus demultiplexer?
5. How are both input and output signals buffered on the data bus?
6. What are the I/O and memory control signals that are most easily used by external devices? How can these signals be generated from the signals the 8085 produces?

MEMORY

There are so many memory locations available for use with the 8085 that it may be difficult to grasp the overall organization. The *memory map* shown in Fig. 4-17 is an effective way of picturing the memory space in the computer. The 64K memory is shown in 1K *blocks*. (The notation "1K" actually means 1024 memory locations.) There is no requirement to equip the microcomputer with the entire 64K cells, so some of the blocks may be missing for a particular implementation. Eight blocks form a *memory bank*.

Furthermore, the memory in each block may be either ROM or RAM. Recall from Chap. 1 that the capacity of each memory IC will be the deciding factor in how many ICs are required in the total memory. For example, if 256 × 8 ROMs are used, four ROM ICs (a total of 1024 × 8) comprise one block. On the other hand, it would take eight 1K × 1 RAMs to form a block because there are 8 bits in each word.

A memory address does not depend on the type of memory used. The designer assigns the addresses in memory by laying out the memory configuration. Any address can be used for either ROM or RAM. In addition, it makes no difference whether the ROM is mask-programmed by the manufacturer or is a programmable fusible link ROM (PROM) or ultraviolet erasable programmable ROM (EPROM).

The address bits designate the bank and memory block, as indicated in Fig. 4-17. The process of selecting the correct block is a result of *address decoding*. For instance, let the address be $06BC_{16}$. Converting the

		ADDRESS BITS A12, A11, AND A10							
		000	001	010	011	100	101	110	111
000 BANK 0		BLOCK 0 0000–03FF	BLOCK 1 0400–07FF	BLOCK 2 0800–0BFF	BLOCK 3 0C00–0FFF	BLOCK 4 1000–13FF	BLOCK 5 1400–17FF	BLOCK 6 1800–1BFF	BLOCK 7 1C00–1FFF
001 BANK 1		BLOCK 8 2000–23FF	BLOCK 9 2400–27FF	BLOCK 10 2800–2BFF	BLOCK 11 2C00–2FFF	BLOCK 12 3000–33FF	BLOCK 13 3400–37FF	BLOCK 14 3800–3BFF	BLOCK 15 3C00–3FFF
010 BANK 2		BLOCK 16 4000–43FF	BLOCK 17 4400–47FF	BLOCK 18 4800–4BFF	BLOCK 19 4C00–4FFF	BLOCK 20 5000–53FF	BLOCK 21 5400–57FF	BLOCK 22 5800–5BFF	BLOCK 23 5C00–5FFF
011 BANK 3		BLOCK 24 6000–63FF	BLOCK 25 6400–67FF	BLOCK 26 6800–6BFF	BLOCK 27 6C00–6FFF	BLOCK 28 7000–73FF	BLOCK 29 7400–77FF	BLOCK 30 7800–7BFF	BLOCK 31 7C00–7FFF
100 BANK 4		BLOCK 32 8000–83FF	BLOCK 33 8400–87FF	BLOCK 34 8800–8BFF	BLOCK 35 8C00–8FFF	BLOCK 36 9000–93FF	BLOCK 37 9400–97FF	BLOCK 38 9800–9BFF	BLOCK 39 9C00–9FFF
101 BANK 5		BLOCK 40 A000–A3FF	BLOCK 41 A400–A7FF	BLOCK 42 A800–ABFF	BLOCK 43 AC00–AFFF	BLOCK 44 B000–B3FF	BLOCK 45 B400–B7FF	BLOCK 46 B800–BBFF	BLOCK 47 BC00–BFFF
110 BANK 6		BLOCK 48 C000–C3FF	BLOCK 49 C400–C7FF	BLOCK 50 C800–CBFF	BLOCK 51 CC00–CFFF	BLOCK 52 D000–D3FF	BLOCK 53 D400–D7FF	BLOCK 54 D800–DBFF	BLOCK 55 DC00–DFFF
111 BANK 7		BLOCK 56 E000–E3FF	BLOCK 57 E400–E7FF	BLOCK 58 E800–EBFF	BLOCK 59 EC00–EFFF	BLOCK 60 F000–F3FF	BLOCK 61 F300–F7FF	BLOCK 62 F800–FBFF	BLOCK 63 FC00–FFFF

(Left vertical label: ADDRESS BITS A15, A14, AND A13)

Fig. 4-17 64K memory map.

hexadecimal address to binary, we see that bits A15, A14, and A13 are all 0s, thus causing bank 0 to be selected. The column of the block on the map depends on bits A12, A11, and A10, which are 001_2, respectively. The intersection of the bank 0 row and the 001_2 column is block 1, which contains addresses in the range 0400_{16} to $07FF_{16}$. The remaining address bits (A0 through A9) select the specific cell within the memory block.

A decoding circuit that uses the 8205 decoder is shown in Fig. 4-18. The pin diagram and the logic table for the 8205 1-of-8 decoder are shown in Fig. 4-19. The 8205 has three address input pins (A0, A1, and A2) and three enabling pins ($\overline{E1}$, $\overline{E2}$, and E3). There are eight outputs, only one of which can be low at any time. When E3 is high and the other enable inputs are low, the level of the output line corresponding to the binary value on the address line is low and all others are high. For example, when levels A2 through A0 are low, high, and low, respectively (010_2), output line 2 is driven to its low state; all other outputs stay high.

Returning to Fig. 4-18, we see that the enable lines can be used to extend the addressing range of the 8205. Address bit 15 is ANDed with $\overline{MEMR}$ to synchronize the addressing of memory with the true state of the latter signal. (The inverters on the AND gate inputs produce an output of the correct level to enable E3

when both inputs are low.) Bits A14 through A10 are properly connected to select the eight blocks of memory bank 0. (The entire 64K memory will require eight 8205 decoders in all.) When all inputs to the 8205 are low, pin 15 (output 0) goes low, thus making chip select ($\overline{CS}$) true for bank 0. The remaining bits on the address bus (A0 through A9), are applied to the 10 address pins on the ROM to read one of its 1024 memory cells. The data is available on the ROM output lines (D0 through D7), which place the data on the system bus.

Sequencing and timing signals used to read the ROM are shown in Fig. 4-20. The microprocessor ensures that the address is stable on the address bus at the same time that $\overline{MEMR}$ is set low. The 8205 decodes the upper 6 bits of the address, thus causing $\overline{CS}$ to go low for one memory bank. Data is unstable on the output lines during ROM access time, but eventually the information levels stabilize and the data can be read.

Accessing RAM is accomplished in much the same manner as is accessing ROM, except that another control line must be provided to store data. Figure 4-21 shows another example of address decoding using 1K × 1 RAMs. Of course, the 8205 could also have been used with RAMs. Here, instead, the upper 6 bits for each block are decoded by a NAND gate for addresses in the range $FC00_{16}$ to $FFFF_{16}$. In all, 64 gates would be needed for a full 64K memory. Appropriate inverters

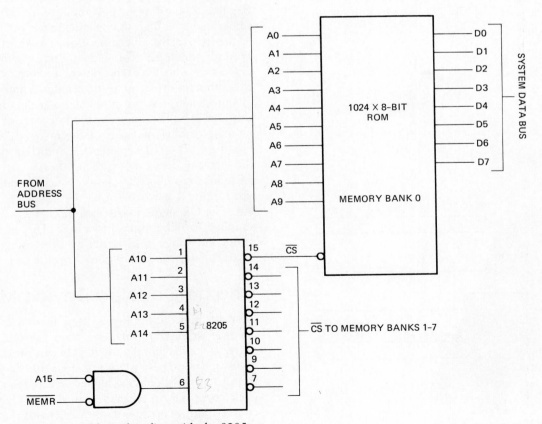

Fig. 4-18 Address decoding with the 8205.

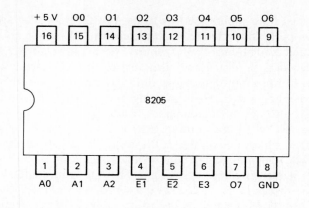

INPUTS						OUTPUTS							
ADDRESS			ENABLE										
A2	A1	A0	E3	$\overline{E2}$	$\overline{E1}$	7	6	5	4	3	2	1	0
L	L	L	H	L	L	H	H	H	H	H	H	H	L
L	L	H	H	L	L	H	H	H	H	H	H	L	H
L	H	L	H	L	L	H	H	H	H	H	L	H	H
L	H	H	H	L	L	H	H	H	H	L	H	H	H
H	L	L	H	L	L	H	H	H	L	H	H	H	H
H	L	H	H	L	L	H	H	L	H	H	H	H	H
H	H	L	H	L	L	H	L	H	H	H	H	H	H
H	H	H	H	L	L	L	H	H	H	H	H	H	H
X	X	X	L	L	L	H	H	H	H	H	H	H	H
X	X	X	L	L	H	H	H	H	H	H	H	H	H
X	X	X	L	H	L	H	H	H	H	H	H	H	H
X	X	X	L	H	H	H	H	H	H	H	H	H	H
X	X	X	H	L	H	H	H	H	H	H	H	H	H
X	X	X	H	H	L	H	H	H	H	H	H	H	H
X	X	X	H	H	H	H	H	H	H	H	H	H	H

Fig. 4-19 8205 1-of-8 decoder.

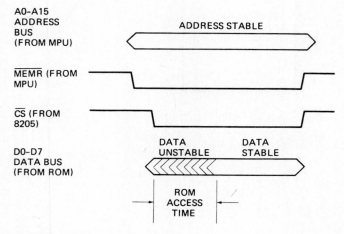

Fig. 4-20 ROM memory timing.

on the NAND perform the decoding function (0 bits in the address must be inverted). For example, if bits A15 through A10 for the address block to be selected were 110 101$_2$, address lines A13 and A11 must be inverted on the NAND inputs. Then the output of the gate ($\overline{CS}$) would be low only when the input was 110 101$_2$, and the proper memory block would be selected.

Each RAM in Fig. 4-21 provides 1 bit of the output data, so all 8 RAMs must be enabled by the same low $\overline{CS}$ signal. The RAM knows whether to read or write data from the settings of $\overline{MEMW}$ and $\overline{MEMR}$. The timing diagram for reading RAM is quite similar to that for ROM (see Fig. 4-22), but there are two differences in writing data into memory (see Fig. 4-23). First, the processor supplies the data that is placed on the system data bus. Second, the $\overline{MEMW}$ signal is set low as a command for the memory action to be performed.

Bus Contention

Because of the uncertainty in the time that data is stable on the system bus when reading ROM or RAM, bus contention can occur. In both Figs. 4-20 and 4-22 the output data is unstable when first strobed onto the output bus by the $\overline{CS}$ signal. During the memory access delay, information may be placed on the shared bus too early, and some other source may also be using the bus. This contention may result in the two drivers for a single bus line attempting to pull the level in opposite directions: that is, a high in one case and a low in the other. Those two drivers become almost a short for 5 V to ground, which sends a sharp pulse, or *glitch,* to other devices on the bus. The glitch, in turn, can produce random data errors or incorrect state changes.

Some memories are providing a means for avoiding this problem. Two pins are used in place of a single $\overline{CS}$ input. A timing diagram of these signals is shown in Fig. 4-24. The chip enable ($\overline{CE}$) pin is used to enable the memory device when the address is decoded and a particular memory IC is selected. The output enable ($\overline{OE}$) input is used to strobe the data onto the output bus. The $\overline{OE}$ signal to the memory is the $\overline{MEMR}$ signal supplied by the microprocessor. The narrower $\overline{OE}$ strobe eliminates the possibility of causing contention when the information is placed on the bus.

Charge-Coupled Device Memory

New memory technologies used in image processing (such as in satellite imagery) offer the user larger capacity than semiconductor RAMs can provide. One of these technologies is charge-coupled device (CCD) memories, which, having higher density than RAM, can pack more bits in a smaller area. The higher density comes about because only 30 percent of the CCD chip area needs to be dedicated to overhead circuitry, such

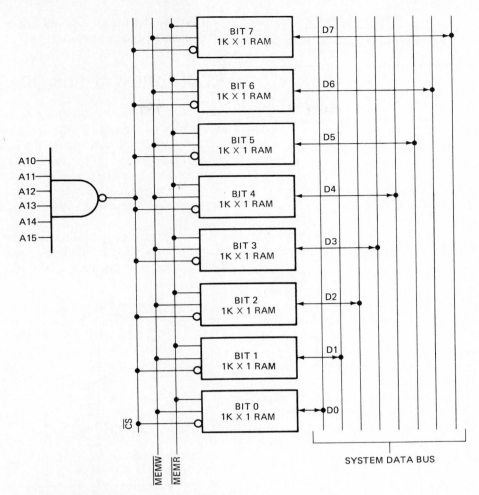

Fig. 4-21 Address decoding with a NAND gate.

as address decoding, while 50 percent of a RAM chip is needed for this purpose.

The CCD memories are inherently slower than RAM because of their internal structure. Actually, the CCD is a serial shift register, and data is continuously circulating through the device. In contrast to the random access of RAM, a CCD lends itself to block-oriented access in which data is read serially in large quantities. Transfer speed of 5 megabits per second (Mbits/s) can be achieved when data is properly organized. One characteristic that CCD memories share with RAM is their *volatility*; that is, memory content is lost when power is turned off.

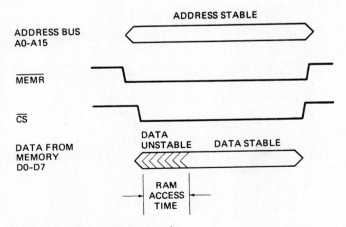

Fig. 4-22 RAM timing (read).

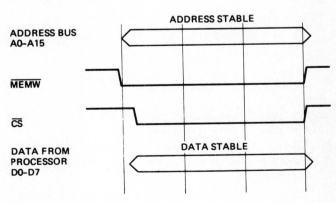

Fig. 4-23 RAM timing (write).

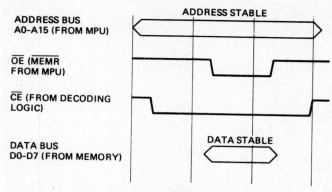

Fig. 4-24 Improved memory read timing.

Bubble Memory Devices

Bubble memory devices (BMDs) are IC packages containing all the components needed for storing data in the form of magnetic domains. Noted for ruggedness, BMDs may be used in military and industrial applications. The bubble memory chip, two magnetic field coils, and two permanent magnets are the components of the device. Using magnetic circuits, cylindrical magnetic domains, or "bubbles," can be formed. The magnetic domains can point up or down, so binary data can be represented by the bubble orientation. Bubbles are 2 to 20 microns in diameter, although manufacturers are working to reduce that size. The bubbles are circulated through the device by a magnetic field in the field coils.

Rotating magnetic fields generated by the coils (which are arranged at right angles to each other) cause the bubbles to move through the chip in a serial manner—much like a serial shift register. The permanent magnets stabilize the bubbles and make the memory nonvolatile, so no data is lost when power is removed.

The data input and output lines are TTL-compatible. In addition to nonvolatility, the bubble memories each have a large capacity and are very rugged. They appear to be attractive replacements for floppy disks as storage devices. As compared with RAMs, the bubble memories have a slower data rate and require more complex interfacing circuitry.

Memory Review

1. List the types of information displayed on a memory map.
2. What bank contains address $92AB_{16}$ in a 32K memory? Which block is that address in?
3. Describe the address decoding process.
4. Explain the use of an 8205 decoder in a microcomputer memory.
5. How can a NAND gate be used to perform a similar decoding function?

6. Describe the use of $\overline{CE}$ and $\overline{OE}$ memory signals in preventing bus contention.

BIDIRECTIONAL BUS DRIVERS

Most microprocessor ICs can drive only limited loads, so bus drivers are used to guarantee sufficient capacity. A three-state bus driver, such as the 8216 shown in Fig. 4-25 consists of two separate buffers; each is used to transmit data in its respective direction. The output of one buffer is tied to the input of the other, thus forming a system bus. For an 8-bit bus, two 8216 ICs would be used.

There are two control inputs to the driver. Chip selection is controlled by $\overline{CS}$ in a manner similar to the method used with memories. The direction of flow is

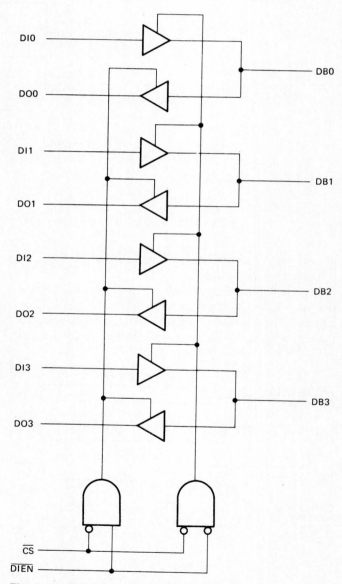

Fig. 4-25 8216 three-state bidirectional bus driver.

determined by $\overline{DIEN}$. When this signal is low, data flows from the inputs (DI0 through DI3) to the system bus interface (DB0 through DB3). When $\overline{DIEN}$ is high, data flow is in the opposite direction (from DB0 through DB3 to DO0 through DO3).

INTRODUCTION TO 8085 PROGRAMMING

Having studied the components of the microcomputer, let's now see how the processor can be programmed to perform calculations and process information. Instructions for the 8085 can be grouped into six functional areas:

Data transfer
Arithmetic
Logical
Branching
Input/output
Miscellaneous

Data transfer operations are those which involve moving data between the processor registers and memory. Arithmetic instructions allow us to add and subtract, and logical instructions execute boolean functions such as ANDing and ORing. When a program is to do one of two things based on the outcome of a decision, one or more branching instructions are used in making that choice. All data is sent or received by means of input and output instructions. The remaining instructions are used for stack operations and control, such as halting the processor.

Instructions can also be categorized by format. One, two, or three memory words may be used for an instruction (see Fig. 4-26). Single-byte instructions consist only of the *operation code (op code)*. The op code is an 8-bit number that tells the processor what to do,

such as data transfer, halt, input data, or perform addition. Every instruction, regardless of length, has the op code in its first byte.

The second word of a 2-byte instruction is used for either data or a device code. If the second byte is data, it is used as the *operand* of the instruction. For example, the data can be a number to be added to the accumulator. The 8 bits can be used for coded data as well as for numbers if the programmer desires. The data could represent two BCD digits or an ASCII code for an alphanumeric character. The processor can operate on decimal numbers or text in coded form as well as on binary digits. The device code is used only for I/O instructions. The code specifies the input or output equipment to be used in the operation. The 8 bits of the device code provide the capability for addressing 256 ($2^8 = 256$) different input devices and the same number of output devices. If a peripheral device is used for both input and output, such as a floppy-disk unit, then both input and output device codes must be assigned.

There are also two formats for the 3-byte instructions. One format provides for 2 data bytes. This type of instruction allows the processor to work on data as 16-bit words. The other format uses words 2 and 3 of the 3-byte instruction to indicate the memory address of the operand. Word 2 is called the *low-address byte*—the least significant 8 bits (bits A0 through A7) of the address. The *high-address byte*, of course, provides the most significant 8 bits of the address (bits A8 through A15).

Some Instructions

The instructions necessary to write a simple program are provided in this section. Aspects of the instructions that do not affect the outcome of this program will not be covered in this first exposure to programming. In the following chapters the full details of these instructions, together with the rest of the 8085 repertoire, will be discussed.

The description of each instruction will include the *mnemonic* code and the hexadecimal, or *machine*, code for the instruction. The instruction is also listed in binary form with data bytes, device codes, or address bytes indicated. An explanation of the changes that the instruction causes in the registers and on the system buses completes the description.

HALT INSTRUCTION The halt instruction causes the processor to increment the program counter and enter the halt state. No further processor activity takes place until some external actions occur. Four clock periods are used in execution. During the first three periods of MC1 the instruction is fetched from memory. The instruction is interpreted in T4 of MC1. By this time the address and data buses are floating. During T2 of MC2

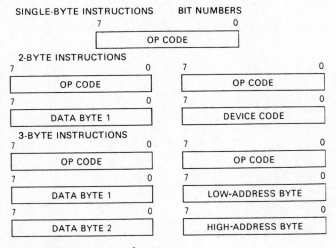

Fig. 4-26 Instruction formats.

the S0 and S1 control lines go low, at which point the processor has entered the halt state.

Mnemonic code   HLT
HLT machine code 76_{16}

	Bit number	
	7 6 5 4 3 2 1 0	
Word 1	0 1 1 1 0 1 1 0	

Most computer programs use the halt instruction to stop after all the data has been processed.

☐ **EXAMPLE**   Stop the processor.

Mnemonic	Address$_{16}$	Machine Code$_{16}$
HLT	0501	76

Before Execution	After Execution
Program counter 0501	Program counter 0502

MOVE IMMEDIATE TO ACCUMULATOR
The data *immediately* following the op code is stored in the primary accumulator. In a manner similar to the previous instruction, MC1 is used to fetch and interpret the instruction. The address for byte 2 of the instruction is set on the bus on the falling edge of the clock pulse for T1 of MC2. The data is read and stored in the A register in the following two clock periods.

Mnemonic code   MVI A
Machine code $3E_{16}$

	Bit number	
	7 6 5 4 3 2 1 0	
Word 1	0 0 1 1 1 1 1 0	
Word 2	Data byte	

☐ **EXAMPLE**   Set the A register to 1.

Mnemonic	Operand	Address$_{16}$	Machine Code$_{16}$
MVI A	01	1000	3E
		1001	01

Before Execution	After Execution
Program counter 1000	Program counter 1002
A register F2	A register 01

The original content of the accumulator (which could have been any value) is changed to 1, and the program counter is set to the address of the next instruction.

ADD IMMEDIATE TO ACCUMULATOR
The data byte is added to the contents of the accumulator by using 2's complement arithmetic. The timing for this instruction is the same as that for MVI A.

Mnemonic code   ADI
Machine code $C6_{16}$

	Bit number	
	7 6 5 4 3 2 1 0	
Word 1	1 1 0 0 0 1 1 0	
Word 2	Data byte	

☐ **EXAMPLE**   Add 22_{16} to the accumulator.

Mnemonic	Operand	Address$_{16}$	Machine Code$_{16}$
ADI	22	FF01	C6
		FF02	22

Before Execution	After Execution
Program counter FF01	Program counter FF03
A register 04	A register 26

STORE ACCUMULATOR DIRECT
The contents of the accumulator are placed in the memory location given by the high- and low-address bytes. Three accesses to memory are needed to read the instruction and the 2 address bytes. A fourth memory access is used to write the data. Altogether, four machine cycles, totaling 13 clock periods, are consumed by this instruction.

Mnemonic code   STA
Machine code 32_{16}

	Bit number	
	7 6 5 4 3 2 1 0	
Word 1	0 0 1 1 0 0 1 0	
Word 2	Low-address byte	
Word 3	High-address byte	

☐ **EXAMPLE**   Store the number in the A register in memory location $03FD_{16}$.

Mnemonic	Operand	Address$_{16}$	Machine Code$_{16}$
STA	03FD	DB01	32
		DB02	FD
		DB03	03

Before Execution	After Execution
Program counter DB01	Program counter DB04
A register A0	A register A0
Memory 03FD 03	Memory 03FD A0

Do not get confused between the address of the instruction (DB01) and the destination address for the accumulator contents (03FD). Note that the accumulator is unchanged after execution.

OUTPUT The contents of the accumulator are sent to the output device designated by the device code. The first two machine cycles are identical to those for previous instructions. The first is used to fetch and interpret the instruction, and the second is used to obtain the device code. Data is transmitted over the data lines during MC3. The devices on the system bus can determine which is to receive the data by decoding the address bus and comparing that device address with their own.

Mnemonic code   OUT
Machine code $D3_{16}$

Bit number

	7 6 5 4	3 2 1 0
Word 1	1 1 0 1	0 0 1 1
Word 2	Device code	

□ **EXAMPLE** Send the A register contents to output device 7.

Mnemonic	Operand	$Address_{16}$	Machine $Code_{16}$
OUT	07	200F	D3
		2010	07

Before Execution		After Execution	
Program counter	200F	Program counter	2011
A register	B7	A register	B7

A Simple Program

Now that you know a few of the instructions, let's put them to use in a simple program. The program will execute the following procedure:

1. Clear memory cell 0200_{16}.
2. Add 20_{16} to the accumulator.
3. Send the sum in the accumulator to output device 1.
4. Stop.

The first step will have to be split into two actions so that we can use the instructions to carry it out. First, the accumulator must be cleared, and then it will be stored in address 0200_{16}. The program is given in Table 4-4.

Go over the program line by line to be sure that you understand what each instruction is doing. Note how the values that represent the op code are almost impossible to decipher without the mnemonics and comments. Remember this problem when you are documenting your own programs.

8085 Programming Introduction Review

1. List the six functional groups of 8085 instructions.
2. Describe the instruction formats used in the 8085.
3. How are two 8-bit words used to represent a 16-bit address?
4. Why are four machine cycles required in the STA instruction when ADI only needs two?

CHAPTER SUMMARY

1. The 8085 is a 40-pin DIP with one power supply input, one ground, eight address lines, and eight multiplexed address and data lines. The remaining pins are used for control signals. The address and data buses use three-state logic.
2. A device can request the processor to wait for a data exchange by driving the READY input low. The 8085 then enters the wait state.
3. A high input on the HOLD line causes the processor to stop between instructions. The data and address buses are floated by the microprocessor, which indicates this action by setting the HLDA signal high.
4. A low $\overline{\text{RESETIN}}$ input clears the microprocessor

Table 4-4 Sample Program Listing

Mnemonic	Operand	$Address_{16}$	Machine $Code_{16}$	Comments
MVI A	0	0150	3E	Clear A
		0151	00	Data byte
STA	0200	0152	32	Store A
		0153	00	Low-address byte
		0154	02	High-address byte
ADI	20	0155	C6	Add to A
		0156	20	Data byte
OUT	01	0157	D3	Output
		0158	01	Device code
HLT		0159	76	Stop

registers and causes the instruction in cell 0000_{16} to be executed.

5. The situation on the data bus is signaled by $IO\overline{M}$, the $\overline{RD}$ strobe, and the $\overline{WR}$ strobe.

6. There are 10 programmable registers in the 8085. The A register is the primary accumulator. The status register provides flags of the results from the last operation. The six scratchpad registers can also be linked into 16-bit address counters. The stack pointer contains the top address on the stack. The program counter contains the address of the next instruction.

7. Timing for control of the microprocessor is based on a sequence of machine cycles that are subdivided into clock periods. The clock signal establishes the boundaries of clock periods. A low on S0 and S1 marks T1 during each machine cycle.

8. All memory references take place in T1 through T3 of any machine cycle. During MC1, T1 through T3 are used for instruction fetching and T4 for instruction interpretation.

9. The control signals inform all devices on the bus which operation will be performed.

10. The wait state permits external devices to request additional time in which to reply. The hold state causes the processor to pause between instructions.

11. On restart the 8085 can be initialized in a known state by use of the $\overline{RESETIN}$ signal.

12. The address and data buses can be demultiplexed and converted to system bus signals.

13. A memory map shows the organization of computer storage into banks and blocks. Address decoding logic in the memory selects the bank and block to be referenced. Address bits A13 through A15 designate the bank, and bits A10 through A12 designate the block within the bank.

14. Charge-coupled devices and bubble memories offer higher density, but slower speeds, than semiconductor RAM does.

15. Bidirectional bus drivers can produce sufficient current to provide reliable three-state signal levels. The driver is actually a matched set of buffers, one for each signal direction.

16. The instruction set of the 8085 provides for data transfer, arithmetic, boolean logic, branching, and I/O. Instruction formats use one, two, or three words.

KEY TERMS AND CONCEPTS

Microprocessor

Data bus

Address bus

Programmable registers (A, B, C, D, E, H, L, PSW, SP, PC)

Status flags (S, Z, A_C, P, C)

Secondary accumulators

Address counters (BC, DE, HL)

Machine cycles

Clock periods

Clock

Reading and writing memory data

Wait, hold, and halt states

Reset

Crystal oscillator

Demultiplexing the system buses

Memory map

Memory organization

Memory banks and blocks

Address decoding

Memory timing diagrams

Bus contention

Charge-coupled device (CCD) memory

Bubble memory devices (BMD)

Bidirectional bus drivers

Instruction formats

Operation code (op code)

Operand

Device code

High- and low-address bytes

PROBLEMS

4-1 How many memory banks are needed in a 24K memory? What is the range of addresses in the memory?

4-2 Draw a 16K memory map for a memory organized as follows.

Device	Address
256 × 8 ROM	2000–20FF
8 each 1K × 1 RAMs	3C00–3FFF
8 each 1K × 1 RAMs	3400–37FF
256 × 8 ROM	2200–22FF
8 each 1K × 1 RAMs	2C00–2FFF
1K × 8 ROM	3000–33FF
256 × 8 ROM	2300–23FF
8 each 1K × 1 RAMs	3800–3BFF
8 each 1K × 1 RAMs	2400–27FF
256 × 8 ROM	2100–21FF
1K × 8 ROM	0000–03FF

Indicate the type of memory used in each block. (Some blocks will be empty.)

4-3 Draw a circuit diagram using the 8205 decoder shown in Fig. 4-19 to decode addresses in memory bank 5. (Total memory capacity is 64K.) Your diagram will differ from Fig. 4-18 primarily in the possible use of inverters on pins 1 through 6.

4-4 Draw the circuit diagram for a NAND gate decoder, similar to that of Fig. 4-21, for addresses in the same block as $AC17_{16}$.

4-5 What memory block is referenced by the following instructions to obtain the operands?

a.
Address$_{16}$	Machine Code$_{16}$
1010	32
1011	A1
1012	B2

b.
Address$_{16}$	Machine Code$_{16}$
AC01	C6
AC02	0A

4-6 Show the changes in the registers and memory locations after the given program has been executed.

Address$_{16}$	Instruction
C716	MVI A
C717	10
C718	STA
C719	17
C71A	27
C71B	ADI
C71C	2
C71D	HLT

PC $\boxed{C716}$ A register $\boxed{4F}$

Memory
 1727 $\boxed{FF}$

 2717 $\boxed{00}$

C71A $\boxed{27}$

4-7 The following machine-code program has run to completion. What value is in the accumulator?

Address$_{16}$	Machine Code$_{16}$
5020	C6
5021	71
5022	3E
5023	12
5024	76
5025	D3

4-8 After the execution of the program below, what number is left in the A register?

Address$_{16}$	Instruction
7777	MVI A
7778	80
7779	ADI
777A	20
777B	ADI
777C	92
777D	HLT

4-9 What changes in memory are produced by this program?

Address	Instruction
F000	OUT
F001	03
F002	MVI A
F003	04
F004	STA
F005	FF
F006	08
F007	ADI
F008	A1
F009	ADI
F00A	F0
F00B	STA
F00C	0C
F00D	AA
F00E	HLT

4-10 Write a program, using only the instructions given in this chapter, that will do the following:

1. Zero memory cell $BB7D_{16}$.
2. Transmit the number $2E_{16}$ to device number 18_{10}.
3. Set the A register to 76_{16}.
4. Halt.

6800 MICROPROCESSOR ARCHITECTURE

The 6800 microprocessor and its supporting devices are widely used components. The 6800 design followed after the 8080 microprocessor. For that reason, the 6800 has added features that make it more easily and economically applied. The 6800 also is the introduction to a family of microprocessors. The 6802 shares the same instruction set, and the 6809 is upward-compatible with both. Even the 16/32-bit 68000 has similarities to the 6800. By learning about this microprocessor, you will become aware of the features of a number of others. Devices for input and output with the 6800 are covered in later chapters.

CHAPTER OBJECTIVES

Upon completion of this chapter, you should be able to:

1. List the functions of the 6800 integrated circuit.
2. Describe the programmable registers and stack of the 6800.
3. Discuss the functions of the ALU.
4. Explain the control and timing of the 6800 by use of timing diagrams.
5. Describe the interface between the 6800 and either ROM or RAM, and describe the methods of address mapping.
6. Define the purpose of bidirectional bus drivers in a microcomputer system.
7. List the types of instructions used in the 6800 and explain the timing diagrams of the instructions.

THE 6800 MICROPROCESSOR INTEGRATED CIRCUIT

The 6800 is characterized by its ability to perform all the MPU functions necessary in a computer system, including arithmetic and logic, control and timing, and programmable registers. The microprocessor provides and accepts TTL-compatible signals. The 6800 lines can drive a single load on each line. More loads will normally be necessary, so buffers or drivers are needed, as described later in this chapter. The 6800 requires a single +5-V power supply. There are several manufacturers of the 6800, and slight functional differences may be found in these versions; variations in maximum clock frequency, environmental conditions, and electrical parameters are typical of these differences. Because a particular 6800 must suit its intended operating conditions, always consult the data sheets to ensure proper performance or that model in your application.

Data and Address Lines

The pin diagram for the 6800 is shown in Fig. 5-1. The chip is a 40-pin DIP. The purpose of each pin is explained in Table 5-1. The address lines (A0 through A15) form a *three-state address bus*. The address bus is therefore 16 bits wide. The addresses of both memory locations and I/O devices appear on this bus. Unlike the 8085, the I/O in the 6800 is treated just like memory, as will be explained later in this chapter. Because this bus is three-state, it can float (switch to a high-impedance state) to allow users other than the MPU to exchange data on the bus without confusing the 6800.

The bidirectional lines D0 through D7 form the data bus for 8 bits of information being sent or received by the microprocessor. Input and output to or from the processor is also transferred on this bus. The data bus is also a three-state bus.

Control Signals

The various control signals coordinate activity on the data and address buses and indicate when significant events occur. As mentioned above, sometimes the three-state address bus must be floated to allow other devices to use it. A device that wants to use the address bus sets the three-state control (TSC) signal high to request the address bus. When the processor grants control and floats the address bus, the bus available (BA) output is set high. These signals are most often associated with direct memory access (DMA) operations, which are described in Chap. 13. If there is no need for DMA, the TSC signal is tied to ground and the BA signal is not connected. The data bus enable (DBE) is another input associated with DMA. This input requests that the MPU float the data bus.

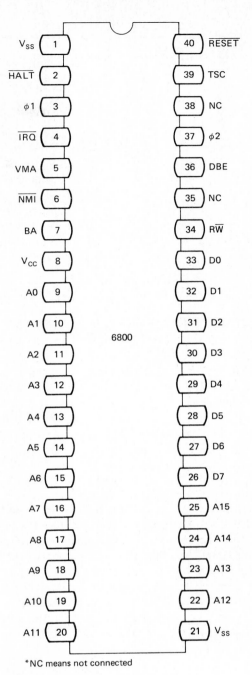

*NC means not connected

Fig. 5-1 6800 pin configurations.

The $\overline{\text{HALT}}$ signal is an input that stops the MPU. It is true when low (as the overbar indicates). The MPU will cease all operations when this signal is true. The data and address buses are both floated while the processor is halted.

When the system is initially started, registers must be cleared and various status conditions must be set to their starting values. The $\overline{\text{RESET}}$ signal provides the mechanism for this initialization. Other chips in the system can also be cleared by this signal.

Table 5-1 _6800 Signals_

Signal Name*	Purpose	Type of Data	Other Characteristics
A0–A15	Address lines	Output	Three-state
D0–D7	Data lines	Bidirectional	Three-state
$\overline{HALT}$	Halt	Input	
TSC	Three-state control	Input	
R$\overline{W}$	Read-write control	Output	Three-state
VMA	Valid memory address	Output	
DBE	Data bus enable	Input	
BA	Bus available	Output	
$\overline{IRQ}$	Interrupt request	Input	
RESET	Reset	Input	
$\overline{NMI}$	Nonmaskable interrupt	Input	
Φ1, Φ2	Clock signals	Input	
V_{SS}, V_{CC}	Power and ground	Input	

* An overbar (such as in $\overline{HALT}$) means that the pin is true when low.

INTERRUPT CONTROL AND I/O SIGNALS Three signals are used to coordinate the exchange of data. The main one is the R$\overline{W}$ signal. When this signal is high, the MPU is in the process of reading from the data bus. The signal is low (as indicated by the overbar) when the microprocessor writes data to the bus.

Two other lines are involved with the handshaking involving data transfers. The valid memory address (VMA) line becomes high to indicate that the address bus currently is sending a valid address. The other signal, BA, becomes high after the data and address buses are floating following the $\overline{HALT}$ input.

Two status lines coordinate the exchange of interrupts. The interrupt request ($\overline{IRQ}$) is sent by an external device. This signal is active when low. The microprocessor acknowledges the signal at the completion of the current instruction if the MPU is running and the interrupts are enabled. The nonmaskable interrupt ($\overline{NMI}$) line is an interrupt request that the processor cannot disable; typically, this signal would be an indicator of a power failure. Chapter 13 discusses these interrupt signals in more detail.

Programmable Registers

There are six registers in the 6800 that are used by the programmer and controlled by use of processor instruc-tions (see Fig. 5-2). The purpose of these registers is similar to those discussed in Chap. 1. A brief comment on each will serve as a review.

The A and B registers are 8-bit accumulators. They are commonly used in arithmetic, logical, and data transfer instructions. The main difference between them is that only the A register can be used to move the flags from the status register. Certain aspects of arithmetic or logical results are shown by flag bits in the program status word (PSW) register. The meaning of each bit in the status register is shown in Fig. 5-3. The sign, zero, and carry flags were discussed previously. The auxiliary carry is a new feature, though. This flag operates the same as the carry indicator, but the A_C bit reflects the carries out of bit position 3 into position 4 of the 8-bit sum. This status flag is often used in BCD operations (see Chap. 7). The overflow flag is set when results exceed the size of the register to contain them. The interrupt enable/disable flag is set to allow the $\overline{IRQ}$ line to interrupt the processor; otherwise, interrupts are ignored.

The index register (X) can be used to alter the address of an instruction, as was described in Chap. 1. You already know how the stack pointer (SP) is set to show the address at the top of the stack. The 6800 uses memory as the stack, so the programmer can have a stack 64K locations long if desired; normally, much

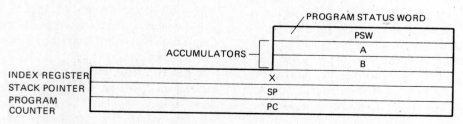

Fig. 5-2 Programmable registers.

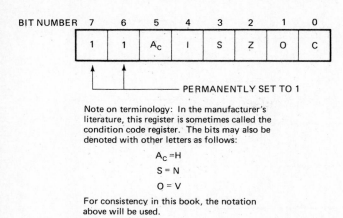

BIT NUMBER 7 6 5 4 3 2 1 0

| 1 | 1 | A_c | I | S | Z | O | C |

——— PERMANENTLY SET TO 1

Note on terminology: In the manufacturer's literature, this register is sometimes called the condition code register. The bits may also be denoted with other letters as follows:

$$A_c = H$$
$$S = N$$
$$O = V$$

For consistency in this book, the notation above will be used.

Fig. 5-3 Status register.

shorter stack lengths are called for. When the stack is popped, the content of the memory cell on top of the stack, as addressed by the SP register, is obtained. New data is also pushed on the stack by using the address given by the pointer register.

The final register in the 6800 of interest to programmers is the program counter (PC). The program counter gives the address of the next instruction to be executed. Recall that this register is incremented during instruction fetching, so that it always shows the proper memory location.

6800 Integrated Circuit Review

1. List the microprocessor functions performed by the 6800.
2. Describe the purpose and type of signal applied to or sent by each pin of the 6800.
3. Why are data lines and address lines three-state buses? Why are only the data lines bidirectional?
4. What signal does the processor use to indicate that the address is stable? How do external devices use the TSC signal to request control of the buses?
5. Describe the use of the programmable registers in the 6800.

CLOCK AND CONTROL SIGNALS

The control section of the 6800 executes instructions as timed by a sequence of machine cycles (MCs). There

are basically three types of operations that the 6800 executes: An *internal* instruction requires no activity on the status bus; a *read* instruction obtains data from memory or an external device; a *write* instruction sends data from the processor to memory or another device. Specific instructions are studied in this and following chapters to illustrate further how the processor timing is controlled by machine cycles.

The two clock signals, Φ_1 and Φ_2, are used by the microprocessor to delineate the machine cycles, as shown in Fig. 5-4. The combination of the two signals comprises each machine cycle. The clocks are generated by a two-phase clock generator, such as the 6871A (described later in this chapter). The beginning of each machine cycle is indicated by the leading edge of Φ_1.

Instruction Execution Timing

During each machine cycle an internal, read, or write operation can take place. Every instruction execution must begin with fetching the instruction from memory, which is just a special case of a read operation.

The timing for a typical read instruction is shown in Fig. 5-5. The two clock signals control the overall sequence of events. The address of the data is placed on the address bus and the VMA signal goes high. The read signal is used to strobe the data into the processor over lines D0 through D7. The write instruction timing shown in Fig. 5-6 is quite similar. The major difference is that the $R\overline{W}$ signal goes low (as we would expect) and that the DBE signal floats the data bus during the first part of the instruction. When data is to be placed on the bus, the DBE signal transitions to the high level. The processor indicates the destination of the information with the address bus and the VMA signal.

The Wait State

The wait state in the 6800 results from executing the wait-for-interrupt instruction. This instruction can be inserted in the program at any point. When the processor executes the instruction, the processor floats the system buses and awaits an interrupt. We will consider this instruction further when we discuss interrupt processing in Chap. 13. An interesting side effect of this instruction is that the registers are pushed on the stack as a result.

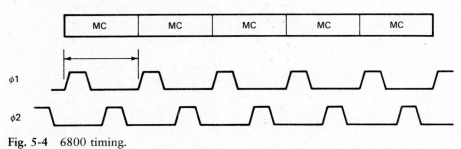

Fig. 5-4 6800 timing.

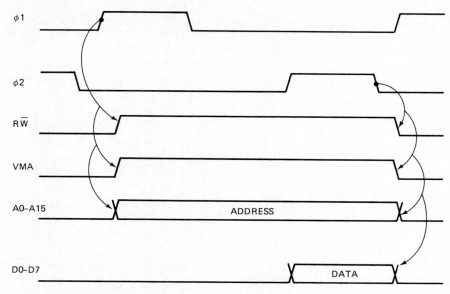

Fig. 5-5 Read instruction cycle.

The Hold State

A condition equivalent to the hold state can be created by the TSC and DBE signals. The system buses are floated during this state. If the TSC signal is held high as an input, the address bus and R$\overline{W}$ and line will be floated by the processor, as shown in Fig. 5-7. During this same period, the VMA and BA signals are held low. Note in the figure that the clock is stopped by holding Φ_1 high and Φ_2 low. This state can be maintained long enough to perform one DMA transfer, but the processor cannot be kept in the hold state longer than 5 μs without loss of data.

The DBE signal has the same effect on the data bus as the TSC has on the address bus. When the DBE is a low input, the MPU will float the data bus. The clock device (explained later in this chapter) can provide all of these timing features.

The Halt State

The halt state in the 6800 results from the $\overline{\text{HALT}}$ input becoming low. At the completion of the current instruction, the system bus is floated. As shown in Fig. 5-8, the BA signal becomes high and the VMA low. The halt state can also be used in a DMA operation.

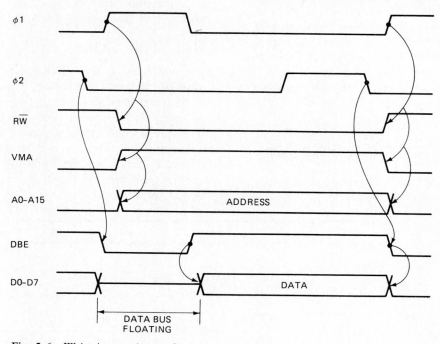

Fig. 5-6 Write instruction cycle.

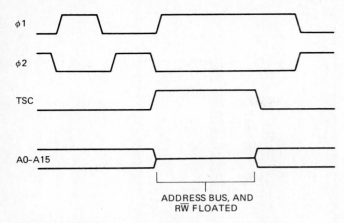

Fig. 5-7 TSC signal causes the address bus to float.

The Reset Signal

The microprocessor is reset by some external action that sets the $\overline{\text{RESET}}$ signal low. This signal is frequently used to restart the processor after a halt. Another time when reset occurs is during the initial power-up sequence. The $\overline{\text{RESET}}$ signal must be held low for a minimum of eight machine cycles. Also, the $\overline{\text{RESET}}$ signal must rise in less than 100 ns. This signal causes the contents of memory locations FFFE_{16} and FFFF_{16} to be placed in the program counter register. This, of course, should be the starting address of your program. The VMA and BA outputs are low during the reset, and $\overline{\text{RW}}$ is high.

Control Review

1. Distinguish between machine cycles and clock phases.
2. What types of operations does the 6800 perform?
3. What operation comes first in any instruction execution?
4. Discuss the differences between control signals used to write and to read memory data.

5. What two methods can an external device use to request time for a DMA operation?
6. Contrast the hold state with the halt state.
7. What instruction does the processor execute after a reset?

TIMING CONTROL

As mentioned earlier, the clock generation for the 6800 is accomplished by a device such as the 6871A shown in Fig. 5-9. The clock generator has a single +5-V power supply input and two grounds. The two clock signals for the 6800 are marked Φ_1 and Φ_2 (NMOS). Another TTL-level signal of the second clock phase is also provided. The MEMORY CLOCK selects memory devices. Two of the signals result in "stretching" the two clock phases for the hold state. The $\overline{\text{HOLD1}}$ signal is active low, while the MEMORY READY signal is active high. The $\overline{\text{HOLD1}}$ signal is important in DMA transfers. The MEMORY READY signal can slow the processor down to wait for slow memories. The double clock frequency output is sometimes handy to synchronize external logic.

DEMULTIPLEXING AND BUFFERING THE SYSTEM BUSES

The buses of the 6800 can only drive a single load. Often one load per signal is an inadequate amount; then buffering of the data and address buses is necessary to provide the additional drive needed. Also, the control signals of the 6800 are not the most convenient to work with. A better approach might be a set of signals that indicate whether memory or I/O is involved and whether the data is to be read or written. The purpose of this section is to show how the basic 6800 can be augmented to offer such capabilities.

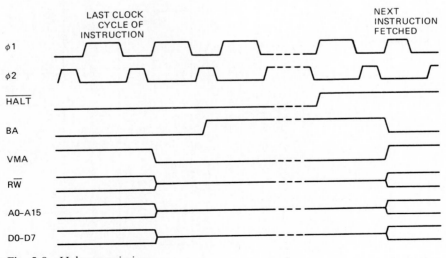

Fig. 5-8 Halt state timing.

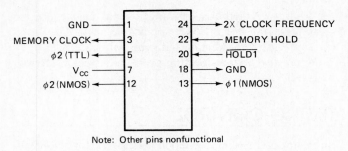

GND ——— 1   24 ——→ 2× CLOCK FREQUENCY

MEMORY CLOCK ←— 3   22 ——— MEMORY HOLD

φ2 (TTL) ←— 5   20 ←— $\overline{\text{HOLD1}}$

V_{cc} ——— 7   18 ——→ GND

φ2 (NMOS) ←— 12   13 ——→ φ1 (NMOS)

Note: Other pins nonfunctional

Fig. 5-9 6871A clock generator.

First, let us consider the address bus. We want to form a 16-bit address, so A0 through A15 will represent the bus. As Fig. 5-10 shows, the buffering can be accomplished with the 74LS367 buffer chip. Each chip can handle six lines, so three ICs are needed for the entire 16 bits. The 74LS367 is a three-state buffer that can drive multiple loads.

The data bus is buffered in the manner shown in Fig. 5-11. Here, we use the 74LS245 bidirectional bus driver. The theory of a bidirectional bus driver is provided in a subsequent section of this chapter. At this point it is

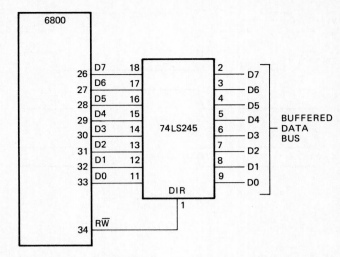

Fig. 5-11 Buffered data bus.

sufficient to note that the device can buffer both input and output signals. The direction of the signal is provided to the driver by the direction (DIR) signal input on pin 1. We will use the $R\overline{W}$ output of the 6800 to indicate the direction. The MPU is reading data when this signal is high. With this input the 74LS245 will route the data in the proper direction and buffer it as well. By this method we have produced a system data bus that is fully buffered.

The handling of the system control bus signals takes a little thought. An easily implemented control bus will indicate to the memory or I/O device the type of operation the processor wants and the direction of data transfer. This means that we would like to have four signals: read memory, write memory, input, and output. Figure 5-12 shows the general concept and Fig. 5-13

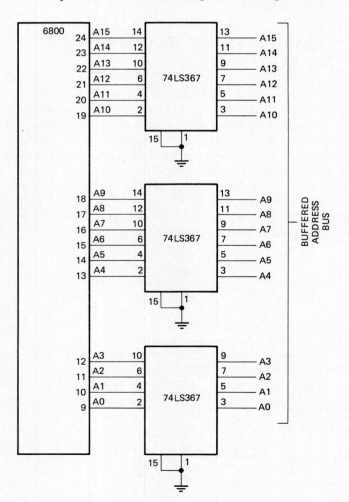

Fig. 5-10 Buffered address bus.

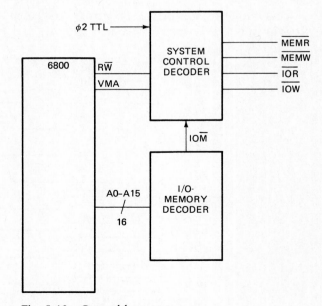

Fig. 5-12 Control bus strategy.

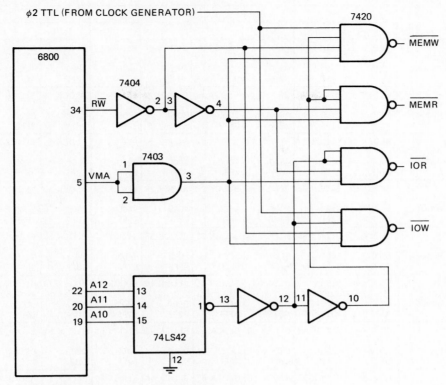

Fig. 5-13 Control bus implementation.

MEMORY

shows one way of implementing this scheme for the 6800.

There are so many memory locations available for use with the 6800 that it may be difficult to grasp the overall organization. The memory map as shown in Fig. 5-14 is an effective way of picturing the memory space in the computer. The 64K memory is shown in 1K blocks. (The notation "1K" actually means 1024 memory locations.) There is no requirement to equip the microcomputer with the entire 64K cells, so some of the blocks may be missing for a particular implementation. Eight blocks form a memory bank.

Furthermore, the memory in each block may be either ROM or RAM. Recall from Chap. 1 that the capacity of each memory IC will be the deciding factor in how many ICs are required in the total memory. For example, if 256×8 ROMs are used, four ROM ICs (a total of 1024×8) comprise one block. On the other hand, it would take eight $1K \times 1$ RAMs to form a block because there are 8 bits in each word.

A memory address does not depend on the type of memory used. The designer assigns the addresses in memory by laying out the memory configuration. Any address can be used for either ROM or RAM. In addition, it makes no difference whether the ROM is mask-programmed by the manufacturer or is a pro-grammable fusible link ROM (PROM) or ultraviolet erasable programmable ROM (EPROM).

The address bits designate the bank and memory block, as indicated in Fig. 5-14. The process of selecting the correct block is a result of address decoding. For instance, let the address be $06BC_{16}$. Converting the hexadecimal address to binary, we see that bits A15, A14, and A13 are all 0s, thus causing bank 0 to be selected. The column of the block on the map depends on bits A12, A11, and A10, which are 001_2, respectively. The intersection of the bank 0 row and the 001_2 column is block 1, which contains addresses in the range of 0400_{16} to $07FF_{16}$. The remaining address bits (A0 through A9) select the specific cell within the memory block.

A decoding circuit that uses the 8205 decoder is shown in Fig. 5-15. The pin diagram and the logic table for the 8205 1-of-8 decoder are shown in Fig. 5-16. The 8205 has three address input pins (A0, A1, and A2) and three enabling pins ($\overline{E1}$, $\overline{E2}$, and E3). There are eight outputs, only one of which can be low at any time. When E3 is high and the other enable inputs are low, the level of the output line corresponding to the binary value on the address lines is low and all others are high. For example, when levels A2 through A0 are low, high, and low, respectively (010_2), output line 2 is driven to its low state; all other outputs stay high.

Returning to Fig. 5-15, we see that the enable lines can be used to extend the addressing range of the 8205.

		ADDRESS BITS A12, A11, AND A10							
		000	001	010	011	100	101	110	111
000 BANK 0		BLOCK 0 0000–03FF	BLOCK 1 0400–07FF	BLOCK 2 0800–0BFF	BLOCK 3 0C00–0FFF	BLOCK 4 1000–13FF	BLOCK 5 1400–17FF	BLOCK 6 1800–1BFF	BLOCK 7 1C00–1FFF
001 BANK 1		BLOCK 8 2000–23FF	BLOCK 9 2400–27FF	BLOCK 10 2800–2BFF	BLOCK 11 2C00–2FFF	BLOCK 12 3000–33FF	BLOCK 13 3400–37FF	BLOCK 14 3800–3BFF	BLOCK 15 3C00–3FFF
010 BANK 2		BLOCK 16 4000–43FF	BLOCK 17 4400–47FF	BLOCK 18 4800–4BFF	BLOCK 19 4C00–4FFF	BLOCK 20 5000–53FF	BLOCK 21 5400–57FF	BLOCK 22 5800–5BFF	BLOCK 23 5C00–5FFF
011 BANK 3		BLOCK 24 6000–63FF	BLOCK 25 6400–67FF	BLOCK 26 6800–6BFF	BLOCK 27 6C00–6FFF	BLOCK 28 7000–73FF	BLOCK 29 7400–77FF	BLOCK 30 7800–7BFF	BLOCK 31 7C00–7FFF
100 BANK 4		BLOCK 32 8000–83FF	BLOCK 33 8400–87FF	BLOCK 34 8800–8BFF	BLOCK 35 8C00–8FFF	BLOCK 36 9000–93FF	BLOCK 37 9400–97FF	BLOCK 38 9800–9BFF	BLOCK 39 9C00–9FFF
101 BANK 5		BLOCK 40 A000–A3FF	BLOCK 41 A400–A7FF	BLOCK 42 A800–ABFF	BLOCK 43 AC00–AFFF	BLOCK 44 B000–B3FF	BLOCK 45 B400–B7FF	BLOCK 46 B800–BBFF	BLOCK 47 BC00–BFFF
110 BANK 6		BLOCK 48 C000–C3FF	BLOCK 49 C400–C7FF	BLOCK 50 C800–CBFF	BLOCK 51 CC00–CFFF	BLOCK 52 D000–D3FF	BLOCK 53 D400–D7FF	BLOCK 54 D800–DBFF	BLOCK 55 DC00–DFFF
111 BANK 7		BLOCK 56 E000–E3FF	BLOCK 57 E400–E7FF	BLOCK 58 E800–EBFF	BLOCK 59 EC00–EFFF	BLOCK 60 F000–F3FF	BLOCK 61 F300–F7FF	BLOCK 62 F800–FBFF	BLOCK 63 FC00–FFFF

(ADDRESS BITS A15, A14, AND A13 label on left for rows 000–111)

Fig. 5-14 64K memory map.

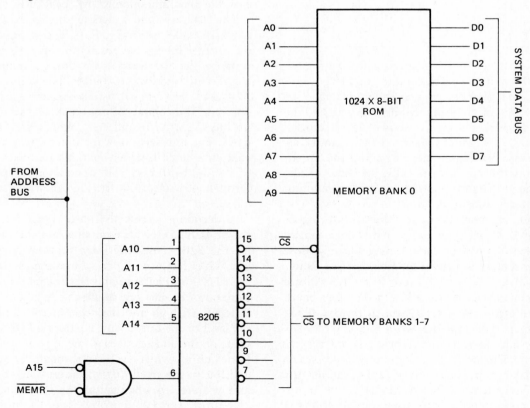

Fig. 5-15 Address decoding with 8205.

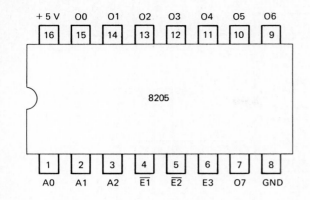

INPUTS						OUTPUTS							
ADDRESS			ENABLE										
A2	A1	A0	E3	$\overline{E2}$	$\overline{E1}$	7	6	5	4	3	2	1	0
L	L	L	H	L	L	H	H	H	H	H	H	H	L
L	L	H	H	L	L	H	H	H	H	H	H	L	H
L	H	L	H	L	L	H	H	H	H	H	L	H	H
L	H	H	H	L	L	H	H	H	H	L	H	H	H
H	L	L	H	L	L	H	H	H	L	H	H	H	H
H	L	H	H	L	L	H	H	L	H	H	H	H	H
H	H	L	H	L	L	H	L	H	H	H	H	H	H
H	H	H	H	L	L	L	H	H	H	H	H	H	H
X	X	X	L	L	L	H	H	H	H	H	H	H	H
X	X	X	L	L	H	H	H	H	H	H	H	H	H
X	X	X	L	H	L	H	H	H	H	H	H	H	H
X	X	X	L	H	H	H	H	H	H	H	H	H	H
X	X	X	H	L	H	H	H	H	H	H	H	H	H
X	X	X	H	H	L	H	H	H	H	H	H	H	H
X	X	X	H	H	H	H	H	H	H	H	H	H	H

Fig. 5-16 8205 1-of-8 decoder.

Address bit 15 is ANDed with $\overline{\text{MEMR}}$ to synchronize the addressing of memory with the true state of the latter signal. (The inverters on the AND gate inputs produce an output of the correct level to enable E3 when both inputs are low.) Bits A14 through A10 are properly connected to select the eight blocks of memory bank 0. (The entire 64K memory will require eight 8205 decoders in all.) When all inputs to the 8205 are low, pin 15 (output 0) goes low, thus making chip select ($\overline{\text{CS}}$) true for bank 0. The remaining bits on the address bus (A0 through A9), are applied to the 10 address pins on the ROM to read one of its 1024 memory cells. The data is available on the ROM output lines (D0 through D7), which place the data on the system bus.

Sequencing and timing signals used to read the ROM are shown in Fig. 5-17. The microprocessor ensures that

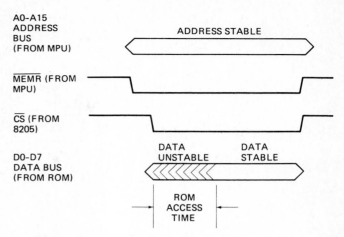

Fig. 5-17 ROM memory timing.

the address is stable on the address bus at the same time that $\overline{\text{MEMR}}$ is set low. The 8205 decodes the upper 6 bits of the address, thus causing $\overline{\text{CS}}$ to go low for one memory bank. Data is unstable on the output lines during ROM access time, but eventually the information levels stabilize and the data can be read.

Accessing RAM is accomplished in much the same manner as is accessing ROM, except another control line must be provided to store data. Figure 5-18 shows another example of address decoding using 1K × 1 RAMs. Of course, the 8205 could also have been used with RAMs. Here, instead, the upper 6 bits for each block are decoded by a NAND gate for addresses in the range $FC00_{16}$ to $FFFF_{16}$. In all, 64 gates would be needed for a full 64K memory. Appropriate inverters on the NAND perform the decoding function (0 bits in the address must be inverted). For example, if bits A15 through A10 for the address block to be selected were $110\ 101_2$, address lines A13 and A11 must be inverted on the NAND inputs. Then the output of the gate ($\overline{\text{CS}}$) would be low only when the input was $110\ 101_2$, and the proper memory block would be selected.

Each RAM in Fig. 5-18 provides 1 bit of the output data, so all 8 RAMs must be enabled by the same low $\overline{\text{CS}}$ signal. The RAM knows whether to read or write data from the settings of $\overline{\text{MEMW}}$ and $\overline{\text{MEMR}}$. The timing diagram for reading RAM is quite similar to that for ROM (see Fig. 5-19), but there are two differences in writing data into memory (see Fig. 5-20). First, the processor supplies the data that is placed on the system data bus. Second, the $\overline{\text{MEMW}}$ signal is set low as a command for the memory action to be performed.

Bus Contention

Because of the uncertainty in the time that data is stable on the system bus when reading ROM or RAM, bus contention can occur. In both Figs. 5-17 and 5-19 the output data is unstable when first strobed onto the

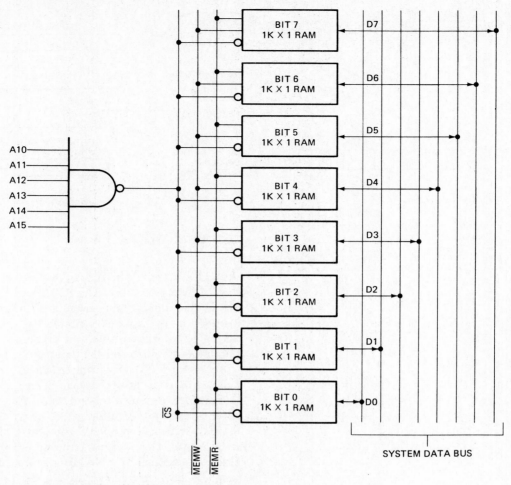

Fig. 5-18 Address decoding with a NAND gate.

output bus by the $\overline{CS}$ signal. During the memory access delay, information may be placed on the shared bus too early, and some other source may also be using the bus. This contention may result in the two drivers for a single bus line attempting to pull the level in opposite directions; that is, a high in one case and a low in the other. Those two drivers become almost a short for 5 V to

ground, which sends a sharp pulse, or glitch, to other devices on the bus. The glitch, in turn, can produce random data errors or incorrect state changes.

Some new memories are providing a means for avoiding this problem. Two pins are used in place of a single $\overline{CS}$ input. A timing diagram of these signals is shown in Fig. 5-21. The chip enable ($\overline{CE}$) pin is used to enable the memory device when the address is decoded and a particular memory IC is selected. The output enable

Fig. 5-19 RAM timing (read).

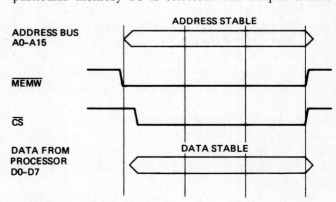

Fig. 5-20 RAM timing (write).

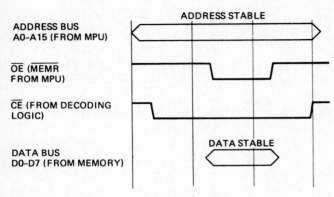

ADDRESS BUS
A0–A15 (FROM MPU)

ADDRESS STABLE

OE (MEMR
FROM MPU)

CE (FROM DECODING
LOGIC)

DATA BUS
D0–D7 (FROM MEMORY)

DATA STABLE

Fig. 5-21 Improved memory read timing.

($\overline{OE}$) input is used to strobe the data onto the output bus. The $\overline{OE}$ signal to the memory is the $\overline{MEMR}$ signal supplied by the microprocessor. The narrower $\overline{OE}$ strobe eliminates the possibility of causing contention when the information is placed on the bus.

Charge-Coupled Device Memory

New memory technologies used in image processing (such as in satellite imagery) offer the user larger capacity than semiconductor RAMs can provide. One of these technologies is charge-coupled device (CCD) memories, which, having higher density than RAM, can pack more bits in a smaller area. The higher density comes about because only 30 percent of the CCD chip area needs to be dedicated to overhead circuitry, such as address decoding, while 50 percent of a RAM chip is needed for this purpose.

The CCD memories are inherently slower than RAM because of their internal structure. Actually, the CCD is a serial shift register, and data is continuously circulating through the device. In contrast to the random access of RAM, a CCD lends itself to block-oriented access in which data is read serially in large quantities. Transfer speed of 5 Mbits/s can be achieved when data is properly organized. One characteristic that CCD memories share with RAM is their volatility; that is, memory content is lost when power is turned off.

Bubble Memory Devices

Bubble memory devices (BMDs) are IC packages containing all the components needed for storing data in the form of magnetic domains. Noted for ruggedness, BMDs may be used in military and industrial applications. The bubble memory chip, two magnetic field coils, and two permanent magnets are the components of the device. Using magnetic circuits, cylindrical magnetic domains, or "bubbles," can be formed. The magnetic domains can point up or down, so binary data can be represented by the bubble orientation. Bubbles are 2 to 20 microns in diameter, although manufacturers

are working to reduce that size. The bubbles are circulated through the device by a magnetic field in the field coils.

Rotating magnetic fields generated by the coils (which are arranged at right angles to each other) cause the bubbles to move through the chip in a serial manner—much like a serial shift register. The permanent magnets stabilize the bubbles and make the memory nonvolatile, so no data is lost when power is removed.

The data input and output lines are TTL-compatible. In addition to nonvolatility, the bubble memories each have a large capacity and are very rugged. They appear to be attractive replacements for floppy disks as storage devices. As compared with RAMs, the bubble memories have a slower data rate and require more complex interfacing circuitry.

Memory Review

1. List the types of information displayed on a memory map.
2. What bank contains address $92AB_{16}$ in a 32K memory? Which block is that address in?
3. Describe the address decoding process.
4. Explain the use of an 8205 decoder in a microcomputer memory.
5. How can a NAND gate be used to perform a similar decoding function?
6. Describe the use of $\overline{CE}$ and $\overline{OE}$ memory signals in preventing bus contention.

BIDIRECTIONAL BUS DRIVERS

Most microprocessor ICs can drive only limited loads, so bus drivers are used to guarantee sufficient capacity. A three-state bus driver, such as the 8216 shown in Fig. 5-22 consists of two separate buffers; each is used to transmit data in its respective direction. The output of one buffer is tied to the input of the other, thus forming a system bus. For an 8-bit bus, two 8216 ICs would be used.

There are two control inputs to the driver. Chip selection is controlled by $\overline{CS}$ in a manner similar to the method used with memories. The direction of flow is determined by $\overline{DIEN}$. When this signal is low, data flows from the inputs (DI0 through DI3) to the system bus interface (DB0 through DB3). When $\overline{DIEN}$ is high, data flow is in the opposite direction (from DB0 through DB3 to DO0 through DO3).

INTRODUCTION TO 6800 PROGRAMMING

Having studied the components of the microcomputer, let's now see how the processor can be programmed to

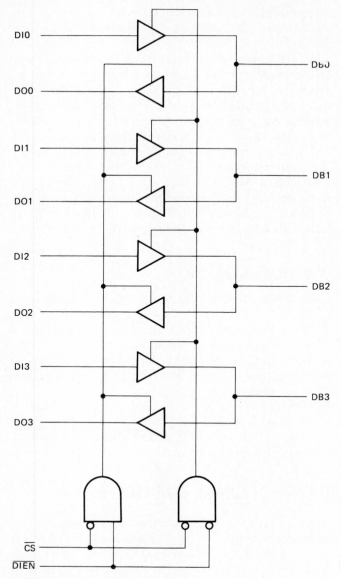

Fig. 5-22 8216 three-state bus controller.

perform calculations and process information. Instructions for the 6800 can be grouped into six functional areas:

Data transfer
Arithmetic
Logical
Branching
Input/output
Miscellaneous

Data transfer operations are those which involve moving data between the processor registers and memory. Arithmetic instructions allow us to add and subtract, and logical instructions execute boolean functions such as ANDing and ORing. When a program is to do one of two things based on the outcome of a decision, one

or more branching instructions are used in making that choice. All data is sent or received by means of input and output instructions. The remaining instructions are used for stack operations and control, such as halting the processor.

Instructions can also be categorized by format. One, two, or three memory words may be used for an instruction (see Fig. 5-23). Single-byte instructions consist only of the operation code (op code). The op code is an 8-bit number that tells the processor what to do, such as data transfer, halt, input data, or perform addition. Every instruction, regardless of length, has the op code in its first byte.

The second word of a 2-byte instruction is used for either data or an address. If the second byte is data, it is used as the operand of the instruction. For example, the data can be a number to be added to the accumulator. The 8 bits can be used for coded data as well as for numbers if the programmer desires. The data could represent two BCD digits or an ASCII code for an alphanumeric character. The processor can operate on decimal numbers or text in coded form as well as on binary digits.

There are two formats for the 3-byte instructions. One format provides for 2 data bytes. This type of instruction allows the processor to work on data as 16-bit words. The other format uses words 2 and 3 of the 3-byte instruction to indicate the memory address of the operand. Word 2 is called the high-address byte—the most significant 8 bits (bits A8 through A15) of the address. The low-address byte provides the least significant 8 bits of the address (bits A0 through A7).

Some Instructions

The instructions necessary to write a simple program are provided in this section. Aspects of the instructions

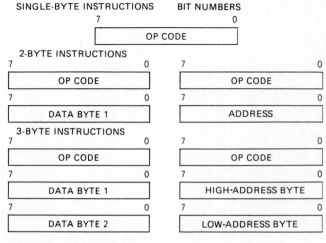

Fig. 5-23 Instruction formats.

that do not affect the outcome of the program will not be covered in this first exposure to programming. In the following chapters the full details of these instructions, together with the rest of the 6800 repertoire, will be discussed.

The description of each instruction will include the mnemonic code and the hexadecimal, or machine, code for the instruction. The instruction is also listed in binary form with data bytes or address bytes indicated. An explanation of the changes the instruction causes in the registers and on the system buses completes the description.

WAIT-FOR-INTERRUPT INSTRUCTION

WAIT-FOR-INTERRUPT INSTRUCTION The wait-for-interrupt instruction causes the processor to increment the program counter and then push the program counter, index, status, A and B registers on the stack. Operation is then suspended until an interrupt arrives. No further processor activity takes place until some external action occurs. Nine machine cycles are used in execution.

Mnemonic code   WAI
Machine code $3E_{16}$

	Bit number	
	7 6 5 4 3 2 1 0	
Word 1	0 0 1 1 1 1 1 0	

Many computer programs use the wait-for-interrupt instruction to stop after all data is processed to await the new data.

☐ EXAMPLE   Stop the processor.

Mnemonic	Address$_{16}$	Machine Code$_{16}$
WAI	0501	3E

Before Execution	After Execution
Program counter 0501	Program counter 0502

LOAD ACCUMULATOR IMMEDIATE

LOAD ACCUMULATOR IMMEDIATE The data *immediately* following the op code is stored in accumulator A. During the first machine cycle the op code is fetched from memory and interpreted. The second machine cycle is used to read the data from memory and place it in the A register.

Mnemonic code   LDAA
Machine code 86_{16}

	Bit number	
	7 6 5 4 3 2 1 0	
Word 1	1 0 0 0 0 1 1 0	
Word 2	Data byte	

☐ EXAMPLE   Set the A register to 1.

Mnemonic	Operand	Address$_{16}$	Machine Code$_{16}$
LDAA	01	1000	86
		1001	01

Before Execution	After Execution
Program counter 1000	Program counter 1002
A register F2	A register 01

The original content of the A accumulator (which could have been any value) is changed to 1, and the program counter is set to the address of the next instruction.

ADD WITHOUT CARRY IMMEDIATE

ADD WITHOUT CARRY IMMEDIATE The data byte is added to the contents of the accumulator by using 2's complement arithmetic. The timing of this instruction is the same as that for the LDAA instruction.

Mnemonic code   ADDA
Machine code $8B_{16}$

	Bit number	
	7 6 5 4 3 2 1 0	
Word 1	1 0 0 0 1 0 1 1	
Word 2	Data byte	

☐ EXAMPLE   Add 22_{16} to accumulator A.

Mnemonic	Operand	Address$_{16}$	Machine Code$_{16}$
ADDA	22	FF01	8B
		FF02	22

Before Execution	After Execution
Program counter FF01	Program counter FF03
A register 04	A register 26

The value in the A register has been increased by 22_{16}.

STORE ACCUMULATOR EXTENDED

STORE ACCUMULATOR EXTENDED The contents of the accumulator are placed in the memory location given by the high- and low-address bytes. Three machine cycles and three accesses to memory are needed to read the op code and the 2 address bytes. A fourth machine cycle is used to obtain the accumulator value. A fifth machine cycle and a fourth memory access are used to write the data.

Mnemonic code   STAA
Machine code $B7_{16}$

	Bit number	
	7 6 5 4 3 2 1 0	
Word 1	1 0 1 1 0 1 1 1	
Word 2	High-address byte	
Word 3	Low-address byte	

□ **EXAMPLE** Store the number in the A register in memory location 03FD₁₆.

Mnemonic	Operand	Address₁₆	Machine Code₁₆
STAA	03FD	DB01	B7
		DB02	03
		DB03	FD

Before Execution		After Execution	
Program counter	DB01	Program counter	DB04
A register	A0	A register	A0
Memory 03FD	03	Memory 03FD	A0

Do not get confused between the address of the instruction (DB01) and the destination address for the accumulator contents (03FD). Note that the accumulator contents are unchanged after execution.

A Simple Program

Now that you know a few of the instructions, let's put them to use in a simple program. The program will execute the following procedure:

1. Clear memory cell 0200₁₆.
2. Add 20₁₆ to accumulator A.
3. Store the sum in memory cell 0230₁₆.
4. Stop (wait for interrupt).

The first step will have to be divided into two actions so that we can use the computer instructions to carry it out. First the accumulator will be cleared, and then the data will be stored in address 0200₁₆. The program is given in Table 5-2.

6800 Programming Introduction Review

1. List the six functional groups of 6800 instructions.

2. Describe the instruction formats used in the 6800.
3. How are two 8-bit words used to represent a 16-bit address?
4. Why are five machine cycles required in the STAA instruction when LDAA only needs two?

CHAPTER SUMMARY

1. The 6800 microprocessor is usually used together with the 6871A, or equivalent, clock generator.
2. The 6800 is a 40-pin DIP with one power supply input, one ground, 16 address lines, and eight data lines. The remaining pins are used for control signals. The address and data buses use three-state logic.
3. A device can request the processor to wait by setting the $\overline{\text{HALT}}$ line low. The 6800 enters the halt state and floats the system buses.
4. A high on the TSC and DBE lines causes the processor to enter the hold state. The processor should not be kept in this condition longer than 5 μs.
5. A low $\overline{\text{RESET}}$ signal clears the microprocessor registers and causes the address in cells FFFE₁₆ and FFFF₁₆ to be placed in the program counter register.
6. The situation on the data bus is signaled by the $R\overline{W}$ signal.
7. There are six programmable registers on the 6800. The A and B registers are accumulators. The status register provides flags of the results of the last operation. The stack pointer contains the top address of the stack. The index register can be used to alter the address of the instruction. The program counter contains the address of the next instruction.
8. The timing and control of the microprocessor are based on a sequence of machine cycles. The two clock phases establish the boundaries of machine cycles.
9. The control signals inform all devices on the status bus which operation will be performed.

Table 5-2 Sample Program Listing

Mnemonic	Operand	Address₁₆	Machine Code₁₆	Comments
LDAA	0	0150	86	Clear A
		0151	00	Data byte
STAA	0200	0152	B7	Store A
		0153	02	High-address byte
		0154	00	Low-address byte
ADDA	20	0155	8B	Add to A
		0156	20	Data byte
STAA	0230	0157	B7	Store A
		0158	02	High-address byte
		0159	30	Low-address byte
WAI		015A	3E	Stop

10. On restart the 6800 can be initialized in a known state by use of the reset signal.
11. The 6871A generates the two-phase clock signal as well as other timing signals.
12. The address and data buses can be buffered, and the control bus can be converted to a universal I/O control system bus.
13. A memory map shows the organization of computer storage into banks and blocks. Address decoding logic in the memory selects the bank and block to be referenced. For example, address bits A13 through A15 can designate a bank, and bits A10 through A12 can designate the block within the bank.
14. Charge-coupled devices and bubble memories offer higher density, but slower speeds, than semiconductor RAM does.
15. Bidirectional bus drivers can produce sufficient current to provide reliable three-state signal levels. The driver is actually a matched set of buffers, one for each signal direction.
16. The instruction set of the 6800 provides for data transfer, arithmetic, boolean logic, branching, and I/O. Instruction formats use one, two, or three words.

KEY TERMS AND CONCEPTS

Microprocessor

Data bus

Address bus

Programmable register (A, B, S, X, PC, SP)

Status flags (S, Z, A_C, O, C, and I)

Machine cycle (MC)

Clock phases

Memory banks and blocks

Memory timing diagrams

Charge-coupled devices (CCD)

Bidirectional bus drivers

Operation code (op code)

High- and low-address bytes

Reading and writing memory data

Hold, wait, and halt states

Reset

Crystal oscillator

Buffering the system buses

Memory map

Memory organization

Address decoding

Bus contention

Bubble memory device (BMD)

Instruction formats

Operand

P R O B L E M S

5-1 How many memory banks are needed in a 24K memory? What is the range of addresses in the memory?

5-2 Draw a 16K memory map for a memory organized as follows.

Device	Address
256 × 8 ROM	2000–20FF
8 each 1K × 1 RAMs	3C00–3FFF
8 each 1K × 1 RAMs	3400–37FF
256 × 8 ROM	2200–22FF
8 each 1K × 1 RAMs	2C00–2FFF
1K × 8 ROM	3000–33FF
256 × 8 ROM	2300–23FF
8 each 1K × 1 RAMs	3800–3BFF
8 each 1K × 1 RAMs	2400–27FF
256 × 8 ROM	2100–21FF
1K × 8 ROM	0000–03FF

Indicate the type of memory used in each block. (Some blocks will be empty.)

5-3 Draw a circuit diagram using the 8205 decoder shown in Fig. 5-16 to decode addresses in memory bank 5. (Total memory capacity is 64K.) Your diagram will differ from Fig. 5-15 primarily in the possible use of inverters on pins 1 through 6.

5-4 Draw the circuit diagram for a NAND gate decoder, similar to that of Fig. 5-18, for addresses in the same block as $AC17_{16}$.

5-5 What memory block is referenced by the following instructions to obtain the operands?

a. Address$_{16}$	Machine Code$_{16}$
1010	B7
1011	A1
1012	B2

b.

Address$_{16}$	Machine Code$_{16}$
AC01	8B
AC02	0A

5-6 Show the changes in the registers and memory locations below after the program has been executed.

Address$_{16}$	Instruction
C716	LDAA
C717	10
C718	STAA
C719	17
C71A	27
C71B	ADDA
C71C	2
C71D	WAI

PC $\boxed{\text{C716}}$ A register $\boxed{\text{4F}}$

Memory

1727 $\boxed{\text{FF}}$

2717 $\boxed{\text{00}}$

C71A $\boxed{\text{27}}$

5-7 The following machine-code program has run to completion. What value is in the A accumulator?

Address$_{16}$	Instruction
5020	22
5021	88
5022	8B
5023	6B
5024	22
5025	16

5-8 After execution of the program below, what number is left in the A register?

Address$_{16}$	Instruction
7777	LDAA
7778	80
7779	ADDA
777A	20
777B	ADDA
777C	92

5-9 What changes in memory are produced by this program?

Address$_{16}$	Instruction
F000	LDAA
F001	03
F002	LDAA
F003	04
F004	STAA
F005	FF
F006	08
F007	ADDA
F008	A1
F009	ADDA
F00A	F0
F00B	STAA
F00C	AA
F00D	0C

5-10 Write a program, using only instructions given in this chapter, that will do the following:

1. Zero memory cell BB7D$_{16}$.
2. Set the A register to 76$_{16}$.
3. Add 7 to the A register.
4. Halt.

AN INTRODUCTION TO THE INSTRUCTION REPERTOIRE

Having studied the registers, data paths, and control timing of a microprocessor, we can now proceed to a more detailed look at the instructions. The 8085 MPU can perform a total of 80 instructions, and the 6800 can perform 97 instructions. By use of these instructions, the programmer can move data between memory locations and registers, perform arithmetic and logical operations, control the program sequence, and communicate by using input and output transactions.

CHAPTER OBJECTIVES

Upon completion of this chapter, you should be able to:

1. List the instruction notation used for working registers and memory.
2. Describe the three methods of addressing memory.
3. Distinguish among register, immediate, and direct addressing modes.
4. Encode and decode instructions by properly interpreting the operation code and operand fields.
5. Describe the operations performed by the data transfer instructions.
6. Control computer operations which involve the program counter registers that stop the computer.

80 8085 MEMORY, REGISTER, AND I/O DEVICE NOTATION

The 8085 is a *stored-program* computer (as is the 6800). The term "stored-program" means that all the instructions and data are stored in memory. The program informs the processor which cells are to be treated as containing instructions and which cells hold the information to be manipulated. Remember that every memory location simply represents an 8-bit number to the processor. The number $2A_{16}$ could indicate the necessity to execute a particular operation; on the other hand, it could be just a hexadecimal quantity or even the ASCII code for an asterisk. The processor treats that number precisely as the program dictates. This literal nature of the computer, which is incapable of such a simple act as distinguishing between data and instructions, can easily lead to a bug (mistake) in the program if the operator is careless.

80 8085 Working Registers

Recall from Chap. 4 that there are seven working registers in the 8085 MPU: the accumulator and six *scratchpad* registers. Each register is 1 byte in length. The registers were referred to as the A (accumulator), B, C, D, E, H, and L registers. When these registers are used in carrying out some processor action, the MPU must be told which register to use. The registers are assigned numbers (listed in Table 6-1) which inform the processor that a particular register is involved in the instruction. For example, an instruction that is to move data to the accumulator provides the number 7 to specify the destination for the data. As you know, an operation may alternatively involve a memory cell rather than a register. The number 6 has been reserved for this purpose, as Table 6-1 shows. (The particular memory cell to be addressed must be indicated as well. The method used is described in the following section.)

Table 6-1 8085 Working Registers and Memory Designation

Register	Numerical Designation
B	0
C	1
D	2
E	3
H	4
L	5
M (memory)	6
A	7

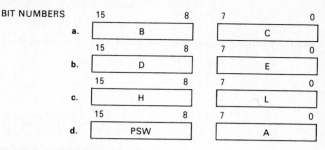

Fig. 6-1 8085 register pairs.

80 Register Pairs

Recall from Chap. 4 that the registers could be linked to form a 16-bit-capacity register. When the registers are linked, there are three ways to refer to them. Table 6-2 lists these options. The double-length BC register (see Fig. 6-1*a*) has its least significant 8 bits in the C register and its most significant 8 bits in the B register. The register pair is also referenced by the most significant register alone in some instruction manuals, that is, by the "B register pair." As Table 6-2 indicates, the DE pair is also known as the "D" or "1" pair and the HL pair as just "H" or "2."

The last row in Table 6-2 requires a little more explanation. When the program status word (PSW) is linked to the accumulator, the two registers are designated as the number 3 register pair in an instruction. The stack pointer (SP) is also sometimes given the same designator. Could the assignment of the same number cause confusion in the processor? The answer is no, because only instructions dealing with stack addressing refer to the stack pointer; other instructions involve only the PSW and the A register. (Even though the processor will not be confused by the assignment of the same designator to two register pairs, programmers may be. In the explanations to follow, carefully note which pair is specified in the descriptions for each instruction.)

80 Memory Designation

The program can read the contents of any memory cell and write in any location in RAM. The contents of a ROM location cannot be altered by program action, but a bug will result if writing into ROM is attempted. Let's consider an example. Say that a programmer

Table 6-2 8085 Register Pair Designation

Register Pair	Single-Letter Designation	Numerical Designation
BC	B	0
DE	D	1
HL	H	2
PSW/A or SP	—	3

meant to store the results of a calculation at memory location 1400_{16}, which is a RAM cell. By mistake, the address of the storage location in the program was altered to 0400_{16}, a ROM location. (Such an error could result from a bad input from the peripheral device that read the program, from human error, or from a malfunction in the I/O circuitry.) When that instruction is executed, the processor will attempt to store data at memory location 0400_{16}. As a result, *no* error indication is generated, but three errors have been committed:

1. The contents of cell 0400_{16} do not change in spite of the store action.
2. Cell 1400_{16} does not contain the correct value.
3. The calculation's answer is lost.

Obviously, in programming, writing into ROM must be avoided.

The entire memory address range of 65,536 cells (0000_{16} through $FFFF_{16}$) can be reached by the instructions. Consequently, another memory-addressing error that can occur is the referencing of a nonexistent location. If the computer is not supplied with a full 64K memory, some locations are illegal. If the memory is actually only 32K in length (0000_{16} through $7FFF_{16}$), attempts to read location 8000_{16} or above would be wrong. Again the processor does not give any indication of this mistake, so it is the responsibility of the programmer to prevent it.

80 Memory-Addressing Procedures

There are three ways of providing the processor with the 16-bit address of a memory cell. The memory address may be specified by 2 bytes of an instruction, the contents of a register pair, or the stack pointer.

ADDRESS SPECIFICATION BY INSTRUCTION

Many instructions supply the address explicitly and require 3 bytes to indicate the operation as well as the data address. Figure 6-2a shows the 3-byte format (which we briefly studied in Chap. 4). The operation code (op code) can be placed in any memory cell, say memory cell 2020_{16}. The least significant address byte must be located at cell 2021_{16}. The upper byte of the address then occupies cell 2022_{16}. (This somewhat cumbersome address designation is a carryover from the 8008 design. The designers wanted to maintain some downward compatibility between the 8085 and its predecessor.)

ADDRESS SPECIFICATION BY REGISTER PAIR

The main purpose for linking registers into pairs is to allow them to hold a 2-byte address, as shown in Fig. 6-2b. The HL pair is most frequently used, but the BC or DE pairs are also employed in some cases. The first register of the pair always holds the most significant address byte, as was shown in Fig. 6-1.

ADDRESS SPECIFICATION BY STACK POINTER

The 16-bit stack pointer can also provide the address. Only two instructions permit us to use the stack pointer in this manner: PUSH and POP. Figure 6-2c shows the use of the stack pointer. If the contents of the stack pointer are $7E2A_{16}$, the most significant byte of the specified address is in the stack at location $7E29_{16}$, and the least significant is at $7E28_{16}$. The use of the stack pointer will be fully discussed in Chap. 11.

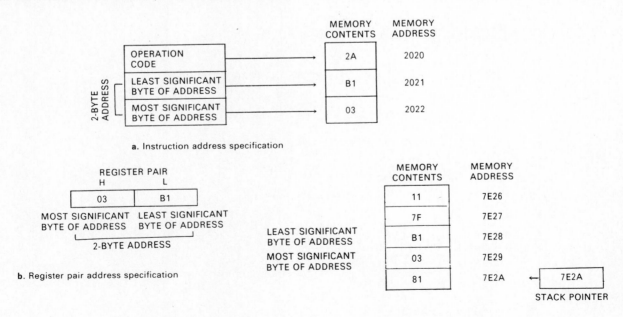

a. Instruction address specification

b. Register pair address specification

c. Stack pointer address specification

Fig. 6-2 8085 memory cell addressing.

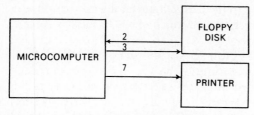

Fig. 6-3 8085 input/output port example.

80 I/O Devices

The 8085 can specify up to 256 independent input devices and the same number of output devices. The input ports are numbered 00_{16} through FF_{16}. The output ports are identically designated. To demonstrate the use of I/O port designators, consider the peripheral equipment configuration shown in Fig. 6-3.

If the program were to send an output on port 3, the information would be written on the floppy disk. An output command to port 7 would cause a printer action. If only one input port is provided, port 3 can be used to read from the disk.

All other port numbers are invalid, but no error indication is generated by the processor if a program attempts to use them.

80 8085 Memory, Register, and I/O Device Notation Review

1. List the 8085 microprocessor working registers and their respective numerical designations.
2. What does the register designation "6" signify?

3. Which register pair has a numerical designation of 2? What is the single letter for the pair?
4. Which registers would the processor use if an instruction specifies register pair 3?
5. What happens if the processor attempts to store data in ROM?
6. Distinguish between instruction address specification and register-pair address specification.
7. Why does the floppy disk in Fig. 6-3 require two address ports?

80 8085 ADDRESSING MODES

Now that we know how memory addresses are indicated, let's see how the address may be used. The mode of addressing depends on the instruction format of each instruction. The addressing mode we select must be either a direct address, a register, or an immediate address. Figure 6-4 illustrates each of the addressing modes. Every instruction is limited to the use of only one of these three modes. As you read the descriptions below, note whether the instruction provides the data immediately or just points to the data by means of an address.

80 Direct Addressing

Direct addressing is used by instructions which transfer data from memory to a particular register or from a register into memory. The instruction supplies the specific address to be used. When the diirect addressing mode is used, the instruction always occupies 3 memory bytes (refer to Fig. 6-2a). The address is in the two memory cells following the operation code.

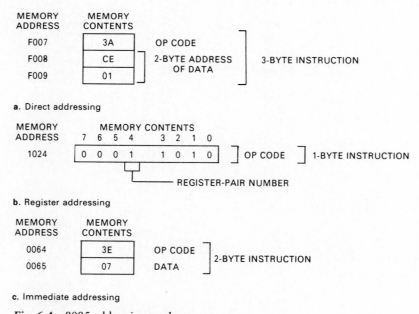

Fig. 6-4 8085 addressing modes.

80 Register Addressing

Some instructions involve only the data in a single register, such as adding data to a register. Others use a register pair to hold an address. If a single register is involved, the number of the register (see Table 6-1) will be included in the instruction. Other instructions specify the register pair that contains the address. Instructions that use two registers (moving data from one to the other, for example) must specify the register sending the information and the one receiving; the former is the *source register,* and the latter is the *destination register.*

80 Immediate Addressing

The instruction may include the value to be used in the operation. In the immediate addressing mode, the byte following the op code is the quantity that will be used in executing the command. The data is obtained in conjunction with fetching the instruction.

80 8085 Addressing Modes Review

1. Define the terms "direct addressing" and "immediate addressing."
2. Why are 3 bytes required for the instruction in Fig. 6-4*a* and only one for that in Fig. 6-4*b*?
3. How is the register pair designated in the instruction of Fig. 6-4*b*?

80 ENCODING AND DECODING 8085 INSTRUCTIONS

Before we begin our study of specific instructions, we will consider the coded method used in writing an instruction. Because we are using machine code, every instruction will be an 8-bit binary string. We will write the code in hexadecimal for compactness. Every instruction must include two parts, or fields.

80 Operation Code Field

The operation code (or op code) field uniquely identifies the machine function to be performed, as we have seen. In addition to the numerical op code, each instruction has a mnemonic associated with it. A *mnemonic* is a three- or four-letter abbreviation for the instruction intended to help the programmer remember the operation and document the program, but the computer cannot interpret the mnemonic. Examples of mnemonics are ADD for addition and LDA for load accumulator direct. If an assembler is used to generate programs, the mnemonics can be used as inputs to the assembler directly. In this book, mnemonics are used only to document the routines.

80 Operand Field

The second part of the instruction is the operand field. The operand field designates the data to be manipulated as a result of the computer decoding the operation and executing the instruction. The operand field may specify that data is:

1. Immediate (part of the instruction).
2. Contained in some register.
3. Contained in the memory cell indicated by a 16-bit memory address.
4. Contained in the address indicated by a register pair.
5. Contained in the address indicated by the stack pointer.

The operand can be any value represented by binary numbers. Examples of operands include hexadecimal values, hexadecimal I/O device codes, hexadecimal addresses, ASCII codes, and BCD codes.

80 Label Field

The programmer can simplify the coding process by assigning optional names to certain addresses in the program. These names, called *symbolic addresses,* are useful only to human beings. They appear on the coding sheet but are not meaningful to the computer. They help someone reading the program keep track of what is happening.

Examples of two instructions, with all the fields described in this section, are given at the bottom of this page. The first instruction requires 3 bytes: 1 byte for the op code and 2 bytes to specify the address of the operand (memory location 1000_{16}). The second instruction uses only 1 byte because the halt operation does not need any data. Memory location 2000_{16} is given the label START, and cell 2003_{16} is labeled STOP. The mnemonics remind us that the first instruction means to load the accumulator using the direct addressing mode and that the second halts the processor.

Label Field	Mnemonic	Memory Address	Operation Code Field		Operand Field
START	LDA	2000	3A	—	First instruction
		2001	—	00	
		2002	—	10	
STOP	HLT	2003	76	—	Second instruction

Encoding and Decoding 8085 Instructions Review

1. What is the purpose of the operation code field?
2. Define the term "mnemonic." How does the use of mnemonics help the programmer?
3. List the locations that the operand field can designate as the source of data.
4. Which of the following cannot be operands for a computer instruction: I/O device codes, BCD codes, letters, binary numbers, and decimal numbers?
5. What is the purpose of the label field?

80 INTRODUCTION TO 8085 INSTRUCTIONS

This section presents 14 instructions that will allow you to transfer data from one location to another and to control the instruction sequence. The explanation for each instruction code will describe what the instruction does and the addressing mode it uses, the execution time (in clock periods), and the effect on the status register. A complete discussion of the status register is provided in Chap. 7 (where it is more appropriate, as none of the instructions explained here has any effect on the status flags). Examples of how the instruction might be used follow the description.

80 No Operation

The *no operation* instruction is the simplest one in the 8085 repertoire. It does just what the name says—nothing. One of its purposes is to fill unused memory cells, which are being reserved for adding instructions at a later time. The no operation can also be used to create a time delay, as its execution takes four clock periods. The instruction uses a single-byte format.

Operation code   00
Mnemonic   NOP
Addressing mode   none
Status bits affected none
Clock periods   4
Format

```
                          Bit number
                       7 6 5 4   3 2 1 0
    Memory cell    m  0 0 0 0   0 0 0 0
```

☐ EXAMPLE

Before Execution		After Execution	
Program counter	3000	Program counter	3001
Memory 3000	00	Memory 3000	00

The only change apparent as a result of executing the instruction is that the program counter has been incremented.

80 Load Instructions

There are four instructions for loading registers (that is, for moving information from memory to one of the working registers). The loading operation is usually a preliminary to a longer sequence, such as an arithmetic function or establishing the operand address.

LOAD ACCUMULATOR DIRECT This instruction moves 1 byte from the memory cell specified by the direct address into the A register. The previous contents of the register are lost.

Operation code   3A
Mnemonic   LDA
Addressing mode   direct
Status bits affected none
Clock periods   13
Format

```
                          Bit number
                       7 6 5 4   3 2 1 0
    Memory cell  m     0 0 1 1   1 0 1 0
                 m + 1   Low-address byte
                 m + 2   High-address byte
```

☐ EXAMPLE

Before Execution			After Execution		
Program counter		1050	Program counter		1053
A register		47	A register		BB
Memory	1050	3A	Memory	1050	3A
	1051	26		1051	26
	1052	17		1052	17
	1726	BB		1726	BB

This instruction is frequently used to set the accumulator to the value of a constant stored in memory.

LOAD ACCUMULATOR REGISTER The value in the memory cell, specified by the contents of a register pair, replaces the number in the accumulator on completion of the instruction. The register pair can be either BC or DE. The address in the register pair is unchanged after instruction execution. Bit 4 of the operation code selects the register pair; if that bit is 0, BC is designated, but setting the bit to 1 results in the use of DE.

Operation codes   0A   1A
Mnemonic   LDAX B   LDAX D
Addressing mode   register
Status bits affected none
Clock periods   7

Format

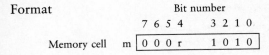

Bit number

7 6 5 4   3 2 1 0

Memory cell   m | 0 0 0 r | 1 0 1 0 |

If r = 0, use register pair BC
If r = 1, use register pair DE

□ EXAMPLE 1

Before Execution		After Execution	
Program counter	B0C1	Program counter	B0C2
A register	14	A register	00
B register	26	B register	26
C register	01	C register	01
D register	00	D register	00
E register	14	E register	14
Memory 0014	FF	Memory 0014	FF
2601	00	2601	00
B0C1	0A	B0C1	0A

The instruction at location $B0C1_{16}$ (indicated by the program counter) specifies that register pair BC points to the address of the data that will replace the present value in the accumulator. The memory cell (2601_{16}) value is 0, so the accumulator is cleared after the instruction has been completed.

□ EXAMPLE 2

Before Execution		After Execution	
Program counter	30C0	Program counter	30C1
A register	14	A register	FF
B register	26	B register	26
C register	01	C register	01
D register	00	D register	00
E register	14	E register	14
Memory 0014	FF	Memory 0014	FF
2601	00	2601	00
30C0	1A	30C0	1A

The instruction at $30C0_{16}$ causes the value in cell 0014_{16} (the DE register pair indicates the address) to be transferred to the accumulator. The program counter increments to reference the next instruction.

LOAD H AND L REGISTER PAIR DIRECT

The H and L register pair can be loaded with the information in two consecutive memory locations with a single instruction. The usual reason for this operation is to set up an address in HL to be used by another instruction.

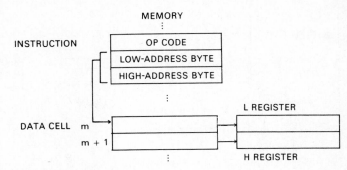

Fig. 6-5 Load H and L register pair direct.

The byte in the memory cell addressed is transferred to the L register; the byte in the next successive memory cell goes to the H register. Figure 6-5 depicts the instruction operation.

Operation code   2A
Mnemonic   LHLD
Status bits affected none
Clock periods   16
Format

Bit number

7 6 5 4   3 2 1 0

Memory cell   m | 0 0 1 0 | 1 0 1 0 |
                m + 1 | Low-address byte |
                m + 2 | High-address byte |

□ EXAMPLE

Before Execution		After Execution	
Program counter	4000	Program counter	4003
A register	77	A register	77
H register	01	H register	6D
L register	00	L register	21
Memory 4000	2A	Memory 4000	2A
4001	07	4001	07
4002	AB	4002	AB
AB07	21	AB07	21
AB08	6D	AB08	6D

The direct address in the instruction is $AB07_{16}$, which holds the value 21_{16}. The L register is therefore set equal to 21_{16}. The next cell ($AB08_{16}$) has $6D_{16}$ in it. This number is transferred to the H register. After execution, the contents of two memory cells have been moved to fill the register pair.

LOAD REGISTER PAIR IMMEDIATE

There are several similarities between this instruction and LHLD. The instruction requires 3 bytes, but in this case the op code is followed by 2 bytes of immediate data. The instruction is illustrated by Fig. 6-6. Byte 2 of the instruction is moved to the second register of the specified pair, and

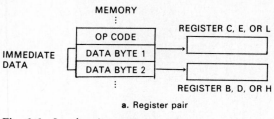

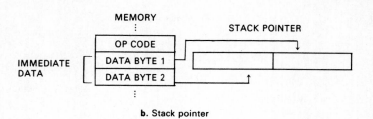

a. Register pair   b. Stack pointer

Fig. 6-6 Load register pair immediate.

the third byte to the first register of the pair. (There is an exception in the case of the stack pointer, where byte 2 fills the least significant byte of the pointer and byte 3 fills the most significant byte.)

Operation codes	01	11	21	31
Mnemonics	LXI B	LXI D	LXI H	LXI SP
Addressing mode	immediate			
Status bits affected	none			
Clock periods	10			
Format				

Bit number

7 6 5 4   3 2 1 0

Memory cell	m	0 0 r r 0 0 0 1
	m + 1	Data byte 1
	m + 2	Data byte 2

rr	Register Pair
00	BC
01	DE
10	HL
11	SP

☐ EXAMPLE 1

Before Execution		After Execution	
Program counter	5110	Program counter	5113
H register	76	H register	AF
L register	00	L register	02
Stack pointer	1658	Stack pointer	1658
Memory 5110	21	Memory 5110	21
5111	02	5111	02
5112	AF	5112	AF

Here the value of rr was 2, so HL is the register pair. The immediate data byte 1 (02_{16}) is sent to L, and data byte 2 (AF_{16}) is sent to the H register.

☐ EXAMPLE 2

Before Execution		After Execution	
Program counter	65BC	Program counter	65BF
H register	76	H register	76

Before Execution		After Execution	
L register	32	L register	32
Stack pointer	1658	Stack pointer	2211
Memory 65BC	31	Memory 65BC	31
65BD	11	65BD	11
65BE	22	65BE	22

Changing rr to 3 specifies the stack pointer as the data destination. The pointer's lower byte is obtained from immediate data byte 1, and the upper byte of the pointer is found in immediate data byte 2.

80 Move Instructions

Move instructions are a lot like the load instructions, except that data can be moved to memory locations as well as to registers. There are two types of move instruction in the 8085 repertoire.

Operation codes	06	0E	16	1E
Mnemonuic	MVI B	MVI C	MVI D	MVI E
Operation codes	26	2E	36	3E
Mnemonic	MVI H	MVI L	MVI M	MVI A
Addressing mode	immediate			
Status bits affected	none			
Clock periods	7 (10 for memory)			
Format				

Bit number

7 6 5 4   3 2 1 0

Memory cell	m	0 0 r r r 1 1 0
	m + 1	Data byte

rrr	Register
000	B
001	C
010	D
011	E
100	H
101	L
110	memory
111	A

MOVE IMMEDIATE One byte of immediate data is transferred to either a register or a memory location. The memory location's address must first be placed in the linked HL registers. Figure 6-7 shows the operation.

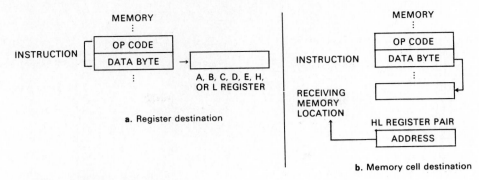

Fig. 6-7 Move immediate.

☐ EXAMPLE 1

Before Execution		After Execution	
Program counter	1700	Program counter	1702
A register	42	A register	0F
H register	00	H register	00
L register	CB	L register	CB
Memory 1700	3E	Memory 1700	3E
1701	0F	1701	0F
00CB	AA	00CB	AA

With op code $3E_{16}$, the register bits rrr are 7, so the A register will be set to the value of the immediate data byte.

☐ EXAMPLE 2

Before Execution		After Execution	
Program counter	1800	Program counter	1802
A register	42	A register	42
H register	00	H register	00
L register	CB	L register	CB
Memory 1800	36	Memory 1800	26
1801	0F	1801	0F
00CB	AA	00CB	0F

Now with rrr of 6, a memory location will receive the data. The value of the HL pair is examined, and it is found that the contents of cell $00CB_{16}$ will be changed to equal the immediate data byte.

TRANSFER DATA When a programmer wants to move 1 byte from a source register or memory location to a destination register or location, the transfer instruction can be used. The source and destination are indicated by using the standard number code for registers and memory. If memory is specified as either the source or the destination, the location is the contents of register pair HL. When the source and destination registers are the same, the instruction is essentially the same as a no operation. (A memory cell cannot be both a source and a destination.) Table 6-3 describes each of the op codes for each of these instructions.

Mnemonic   MOV d, s

where d = A, B, C, D, E, H, L, or M

            s = A, B, C, D, E, H, L, or M

Addressing mode   register
Status bits affected   none
Clock periods   4 (7 if memory is used)

Format

                           Bit number

                    7 6 5 4   3 2 1 0

Memory cell   m | 0 1 d d   d s s s |

ddd	sss	Register
000	000	B
001	001	C
010	010	D
011	011	E
100	100	H
101	101	L
110	110	Memory
111	111	A

Table 6-3 Transfer Op Codes

		Source							
		B	**C**	**D**	**E**	**H**	**L**	**M**	**A**
Destination	**B**	40	41	42	43	44	45	46	47
	C	48	49	4A	4B	4C	4D	4E	4F
	D	50	51	52	53	54	55	56	57
	E	58	59	5A	5B	5C	5D	5E	5F
	H	60	61	62	63	64	65	66	67
	L	68	69	6A	6B	6C	6D	6E	6F
	M	70	71	72	73	74	75	*	77
	A	78	79	7A	7B	7C	7D	7E	7F

* Op code 76 is reserved for the halt instruction.

□ EXAMPLE 1

Before Execution		After Execution	
Program counter	2000	Program counter	2001
A register	00	A register	FF
B register	FF	B register	FF
Memory 2000	78	Memory 2000	78

The source is the B register. Its contents are moved to the destination, the A register.

□ EXAMPLE 2

Before Execution		After Execution	
Program counter	3500	Program counter	3501
A register	00	A register	00
H register	10	H register	10
L register	00	L register	00
Memory 1000	B0	Memory 1000	00
3500	77	3500	77

The contents of the A register (source) clear memory cell 1000_{16}. The address for the memory cell was found in register pair HL.

80 Exchange Instruction

One instruction allows us to swap the values in the DE and HL register pairs. The 8 bits from the H and the D registers are interchanged, as are the 8 bits from the L and the E registers. Figure 6-8 shows the operation.

Operation code	EB
Mnemonic	XCHG
Addressing mode	none
Status bits affected	none
Clock periods	4
Format	

Bit number

7 6 5 4   3 2 1 0

Memory cell   m | 1 1 1 0   1 0 1 1 |

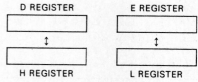

Fig. 6-8 Exchange.

□ EXAMPLE

Before Execution		After Execution	
Program counter	7600	Program counter	7600
D register	11	D register	33
E register	22	E register	44
H register	33	H register	11
L register	44	L register	22
Memory 7600	EB	Memory 7600	EB

The 16 bits that were in HL are now in DE, and vice versa.

80 Store Instructions

The store instructions are reverse operations to the load commands. Data is transferred from a register to memory. There is no change in the originating register contents when the data is written into memory. The 8085 provides three store instructions.

STORE ACCUMULATOR DIRECT   The value in the A register is moved to the memory cell addressed by the immediate data address bytes. The most significant byte of the memory address is data byte 2, and the least significant byte is data byte 1.

Operation code	32
Mnemonic	STA
Addressing mode	direct
Status bits affected	none
Clock periods	13
Format	

Bit number

7 6 5 4   3 2 1 0

Memory cell	m	0 0 1 1 0 0 1 0
	m + 1	Low-address byte
	m + 2	High-address byte

□ EXAMPLE

Before Execution		After Execution	
Program counter	7700	Program counter	7703
A register	EE	A register	EE
Memory 7700	32	Memory 7700	32
7701	00	7701	00
7702	FE	7702	FE
FE00	00	FE00	EE

The number in the accumulator has been stored in the directly addressed memory location.

STORE ACCUMULATOR This instruction is identical to the previous one, except that the address is specified by either the BC or the DE register pairs.

Operation codes	02	12
Mnemonics	STAX B	STAX D
Addressing mode	register	
Status bits affected	none	
Clock periods	7	

Format

		Bit number
		7 6 5 4 3 2 1 0
Memory cell	m	0 0 0 r 0 0 1 0

If r = 0, BC holds the address
If r = 1, DE holds the address

☐ EXAMPLE

Before Execution			After Execution		
Program counter		8100	Program counter		8101
A register		1F	A register		1F
B register		F0	B register		F0
C register		FB	C register		FB
Memory	8100	02	Memory	8100	02
	F0FB	00		F0FB	1F

The address is to be found in register pair BC because the r field in the op code is 0. The contents of the A register are written into memory cell F0FB.

STORE H AND L DIRECT This instruction stores the L register contents in the directly addressed memory cell. The result of executing the instruction is shown in Fig. 6-9. The L register is stored at the cell addressed by data bytes 1 and 2, while the H register is stored in the next-higher memory location.

Operation code	22
Mnemonic	SHLD
Addressing mode	direct
Status bits affected	none

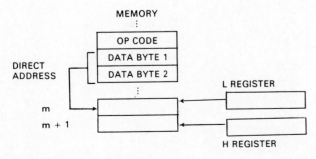

Fig. 6-9 Store H and L direct.

Clock periods	16

Format

		Bit number
		7 6 5 4 3 2 1 0
Memory cell	m	0 0 1 1 0 0 1 1
	m + 1	Low-address byte
	m + 2	High-address byte

☐ EXAMPLE

Before Execution			After Execution		
Program counter		2900	Program counter		2903
H register		46	H register		46
L register		00	L register		00
Memory	2900	22	Memory	2900	22
	2901	03		2901	03
	2902	29		2902	29
	2903	FA		2903	00
	2904	BE		2904	46

80 Jump Instructions

After a series of instructions has been completed, a change to a different sequence is sometimes required. Instead of selecting the next consecutive instruction, the microprocessor must transfer control to the instruction in a memory address far removed from the current one. This transfer of control is accomplished with some form of *jump* command. In this section we will investigate two types of jumps. Other jump options will be considered in Chap. 8.

JUMP This instruction causes program control to transfer to the direct address in the 2 data bytes. Program execution continues from that memory address. In effect, the jump instruction changes the value of the program counter.

Operation code	C3
Mnemonic	JMP
Addressing mode	direct
Status bits affected	none
Clock periods	10

Format

		Bit number
		7 6 5 4 3 2 1 0
Memory cell	m	1 1 0 0 0 0 1 1
	m + 1	Low-address byte
	m + 2	High-address byte

☐ EXAMPLE

Before Execution		After Execution	
Program counter	5027	Program counter	4400

Before Execution			After Execution		
Memory	5027	C3	Memory	5027	C3
	5028	00		5028	00
	5029	44		5029	44

Normally, the program counter would be set to $502A_{16}$ after executing the 3-byte instruction, but the JMP instruction forces the program counter to select the next instruction from cell 4400_{16}.

LOAD PROGRAM COUNTER
The effect of this instruction is similar to that of the JMP instruction, except that the source of the address is the HL register pair. The H register holds the high-address byte, and the L register holds the low-address byte. The value in the HL pair is transferred to the program counter, and program execution continues from that address.

Operation code	E9
Mnemonic	PCHL
Addressing mode	register
Status bits affected	none
Clock periods	6
Format	

Bit number

Memory cell	m	1 1 1 0	1 0 0 1

□ EXAMPLE

Before Execution		After Execution	
Program counter	3000	Program counter	0014
H register	00	H register	00
L register	14	L register	14
Memory 3000	E9	Memory 3000	E9

The address in the program counter is forced to 0014_{16}, the contents of the HL register pair.

80 Halt Instruction

After a program has run to completion, the computer must be stopped. The halt instruction brings this action about. Before stopping, the processor increments the program counter to the next sequential instruction. The MPU is halted until an interrupt arrives. (An *interrupt* is a break in the normal signal flow. Chapter 13 provides a full description of interrupts and their effects on the microcomputer.)

Operation code	76
Mnemonic	HLT
Addressing mode	none
Status bits affected	none
Clock periods	5

Format

Bit number

Memory cell	m	0 1 1 1	0 1 1 0

□ EXAMPLE

Before Execution		After Execution	
Program counter	1050	Program counter	1051
Memory 1050	76	Memory 1050	76

After completing the instruction and incrementing the program counter, the processor stops executing the program.

80 Summary of 8085 Instructions

The instructions described in this chapter are summarized in Table 6-4. For each instruction, the mnemonic, operation code, and number of bytes in length are listed. None of these instructions changes the status bit settings.

80 8085 PROGRAMMING EFFICIENCY

Even with the limited number of instructions you know, it may seem that several instructions do the same thing. This apparent redundancy of op codes is actually misleading. It is rather an indication of the flexibility that a large repertoire can offer.

We will examine four rather similar instructions to show how they differ and the way that choosing an instruction can affect the program execution time (in clock periods) and memory requirements. The instruc-

Table 6-4 Summary of 8085 Instructions

Mnemonic	Op Code	Bytes
HLT	76	1
JMP	C3	3
LDA	3A	3
LDAX	0A, 1A	1
LHLD	2A	3
LXI	01, 11, 21, 31	3
MVI	06, 0E, 16, 0E, 26, 2E, 36, 3E	2
MOV	See Table 6-3	1
NOP	00	1
PCHL	E9	1
SHLD	22	3
STA	32	3
STAX	02, 12	1
XCHG	EB	1

tions we are interested in are listed in Table 6-5. As you can see just by selecting one instruction or the other, we can seemingly get execution times ranging from 7 to 13 clock periods and use 1 to 3 bytes of memory. These obvious differences are not the whole effect, though, because instructions are never used in isolation. They must be combined to do a certain task. Let us assume that the job we want to do is to clear the accumulator. We will write programs using each of the instructions in Table 6-5 to accomplish this function.

Program 1

Memory Address	Machine Code	Comments
1000	3E	MVI A
1001	00	Data

Program 2

Memory Address	Machine Code	Comments
1000	2A	LHLD (Load HL with memory address)
1001	05	Address of data
1002	10	
1003	7E	MOV A, M
1004	00	Data
1005	04	Address of
1006	10	data

Program 3

Memory Address	Machine Code	Comments
1000	3A	LDA
1001	03	Address of data
1002	10	
1003	00	Data

Program 4

Memory Address	Machine Code	Comments
1000	01	LXI B (Load BC with memory address)
1001	04	Address of data
1002	10	
1003	0A	LDAX B
1004	00	Data

Table 6-5 Instruction Comparison

Mnemonic	Clock Periods*	Bytes
MVI	10	2
MOV	7	1
LDA	13	3
LDAX	7	1

* Execution times for memory data.

Now we will tabulate the time and the memory needed for each program. The results are shown in Table 6-6.

It is more obvious now that proper selection of instructions can significantly decrease both the execution time and the memory space needed for a program. There are no general rules for instruction selection, but as you become more familiar with the repertoire, finding the most appropriate instruction will get easier.

🔟 Some Problems to Avoid in Programming the 8085

After you enter programs into the computer, you may find that they do not run properly. This failure is often the result of just not entering the program as written. Simple mistakes are easy to make, while the use of machine language instructions is a new experience. If your program does not run correctly, you must debug it to find the error. Inspecting memory contents and comparing them to the program listing is a good way to proceed. The results of two common errors are described so that you will have an idea of the problems that seemingly trivial mistakes can cause.

🔟 8085 Examples

JUMPING TO A DATA CELL A partial listing is provided in Table 6-7. The computer is to clear the accumulator and jump to the halt. By mistake, the program has a jump address of 1000_{16} instead of 0100_{16}. (The single-bit oversight in entering the program caused the error.) The program will clear the accumulator and then jump to cell 1000_{16}, where it will treat the data as an instruction. This data will be interpreted as a command to load the program counter with whatever value is in the HL register pair, because the data is the op code for a PCHL instruction. Now the processor is completely out of control and will randomly execute instructions in a manner not intended by the operator. The lesson is that even a single-bit mistake can totally disrupt a program. On the other hand, no real harm was done; it is impossible to damage a processor by disrupt a program. On the other hand, no real harm was done; it is impossible to damage a processor by putting in a bad program. That means that the price of

Table 6-6 Time and Memory Comparison

Instruction	Clock Periods	Memory (bytes)
MVI	10	2
MOV	23	5
LDA	13	4
LDAX	17	5

Table 6-7 8085 Erroneous Jump

Location	Machine Code	Comments
0100	76	HLT
⋮		
1000	E9	Data
⋮		
10AE	3E	MVI A (clear A)
10AF	00	Data
10B0	C3	JMP
10B1	00	Incorrect address
10B2	10	

experimentation is quite reasonable, because no hardware can be destroyed.

INCORRECT INSTRUCTION LENGTH Another easy trap to fall into is to put in an instruction with the wrong length. The purpose of the program given in Table 6-8 is to set the A register value to the number in memory cell $07FF_{16}$ and then exchange the contents of the DE and HL register pairs. When the processor executes cell 0700_{16}, it must take the contents of the next two locations as an address. The result is that the accumulator is loaded with the contents of cell $EBFF_{16}$ and the register pair exchange never takes place. Another simple omission has produced two incorrect actions. The impact of these actions will depend on the remainder of the program.

This section has provided just a small sample of the various things that can go wrong because of software errors. Remember that the computer is a very literal device—it cannot differentiate between a correct and an incorrect program. Only the human being doing the programming can.

🔲80 8085 Programming Efficiency Review

1. Why are the memory lengths in Table 6-5 misleading for evaluating efficiency?
2. Which instruction made the MOV execution time

Table 6-8 8085 Instruction Length Error

Location	Machine Code	Comments
0700	3A	LDA
0701	FF	Data (high-address byte was omitted)
0702	EB	XCHG

results in Table 6-6 so much longer than the other instruction sequences?
3. After the program in Table 6-7 is corrected, what is the value in the program counter when the processor stops?

🔲68 6800 MEMORY, REGISTER, AND I/O DEVICE NOTATION

The 6800, like the 8085, is a stored-program computer. Again, the term "stored program" means that all the instructions and data are stored in memory. The program informs the processor which cells are to be treated as containing instructions and which cells hold the information to be manipulated. Remember that every memory location simply represents an 8-bit number to the processor. The number $2A_{16}$ could indicate the necessity to execute a particular operation; on the other hand, it could be just a hexadecimal quantity or even the ASCII code for an asterisk. The processor treats that number precisely as the program dictates. This literal nature of the computer, which is incapable of such a simple act as distinguishing between data and instructions, can easily lead to a bug (mistake) in the program if the operator is careless.

🔲68 Working Registers

Recall from Chap. 5 that there are four working registers in the 6800 MPU: the A and B accumulators, the index register, and the stack pointer. The A and B registers are 1 byte in length, while the index register and stack pointer are 2 bytes long. The registers were referred to as the A, B, X, and SP registers, respectively. When these registers are used in carrying out some processor action, the MPU must be told which register to use. In some cases the type of instruction designates the register. At other times the registers are assigned numbers (listed in Table 6-9), which inform the processor that a particular register is involved in an instruction.

🔲68 Memory Designation

The program can read the contents of any memory cell and write in any location in RAM. The contents of a

Table 6-9 6800 Working Register Designation

Register	Numerical Designation
A	0
B	1

ROM location cannot be altered by program action, but a bug will result if writing into ROM is attempted. Let's consider an example. Say that a programmer meant to store the results of a calculation at memory location 1400_{16}, which is a RAM cell. By mistake, the address of the storage location in the program was altered to 0400_{16}, a ROM location. (Such an error could result from a bad input from the peripheral device that read the program, from human error, or from a malfunction in the I/O circuitry.) When that instruction is executed, the processor will attempt to store data at memory location 0400_{16}. As a result, *no* error indication is generated, but three errors have been committed:

1. The contents of cell 0400_{16} do not change in spite of the store action.
2. Cell 1400_{16} does not contain the correct value.
3. The calculation's answer is lost.

Obviously, in programming, writing into ROM must be avoided.

The entire memory address range of 65,536 cells (0000_{16} through $FFFF_{16}$) can be reached by the instructions. Consequently, another memory-addressing error that can occur is the referencing of a nonexistent location. If the computer is not supplied with a full 64K memory, some locations are illegal. If the memory is actually only 32K in length (0000_{16} through $7FFF_{16}$), attempts to read location 8000_{16} or above would be wrong. Again the processor does not give any indication of this mistake, so it is the responsibility of the programmer to prevent it.

68 Memory-Addressing Procedure

There are three ways of providing the processor with the 16-bit address of the memory cell. The memory address may be specified by 1 or 2 bytes of an instruction, the contents of the index register, or the stack pointer.

ADDRESS SPECIFICATION BY INSTRUCTION

Many instructions supply the address explicitly and require 2 or 3 bytes to indicate the operation code as well as the data address. Figure 6-10*a* shows the 2-byte format. The operation code is placed in any memory cell, say memory cell 2020_{16}. The address byte must be located at cell 2021_{16}. Because the address is only 1 byte long, the location must be in cells 0000_{16} to $00FF_{16}$.

Figure 6-10*b* shows the 3-byte format. The operation code in this case is in cell 2020_{16}. The most significant address byte must be located in cell 2021_{16}. The lower byte of the address then occupies cell 2022_{16}.

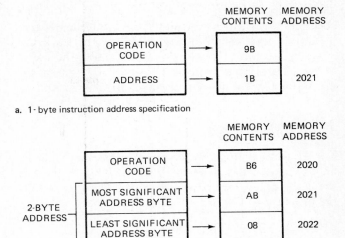

a. 1-byte instruction address specification

b. 2-byte instruction address specification

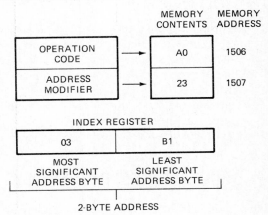

c. Index register address specification

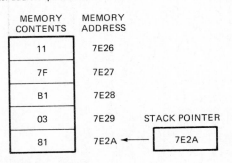

d. Stack pointer address specification

Fig. 6-10 6800 memory cell addressing.

ADDRESS SPECIFICATION BY INDEX REGISTER

The index register can contain a 16-bit address. The effective address of the instruction is formed by adding the address modifier (the second byte of the instruction) to the contents of the index register. For the example in Fig. 6-10*c*:

Address modifier byte	23_{16}
Index register	$03B1_{16}$
Effective address	$03D4_{16}$

ADDRESS SPECIFICATION BY STACK POINTER

The 16-bit stack pointer can also provide the address. Only two instructions permit us to use the stack this way: PUSH and PULL. Figure 6-10*d* shows the use of the stack pointer to indicate an address. The use of the stack pointer will be fully discussed in Chap. 11.

68 I/O Devices

The 6800 treats I/O devices just like memory; that is, an I/O device has a 16-bit address. This method is therefore called *memory-mapped I/O*. Further details are provided in Chap. 12.

68 6800 Memory, Register, and I/O Device Review

1. List the 6800 microprocessor working registers and their respective numerical designations.
2. Which registers can specify a 16-bit address?
3. What happens if the processor attempts to store data in ROM?
4. What are the ways that a memory address can be specified in an instruction?
5. How does the 6800 identify I/O devices?

68 6800 ADDRESSING MODES

Now that we know how memory addresses are indicated, let's see how the address may be used. The mode of addressing depends on the instruction format. The addressing mode we select must be either direct address, immediate address, indexed address, extended address, or inherent address. (The relative address mode is discussed in Chap. 8.) Figure 6-11 illustrates each of these five addressing modes. Every instruction is limited to the use of only one of these modes. As you read the descriptions below, note whether the instruction provides the data immediately or just points to the data by means of an address.

68 Direct Addressing

Direct addressing is used by instructions that transfer data from lower memory (addresses 0000_{16} to $00FF_{16}$) to a particular register or is used to write data from a register to lower memory. The instruction supplies the specific address to be used. When the direct addressing mode is employed, the instruction always occupies 2 memory bytes (see Fig. 6-11*a*). The address is in the memory cell following the op code.

68 Immediate Addressing

The instruction may include the value to be used in the operation (see Fig. 6-11*b*). In the immediate addressing mode, the byte (or bytes) following the op code is (are) the quantity that will be used in executing the command. The data is obtained in conjunction with fetching the op code by reading the successive memory location(s).

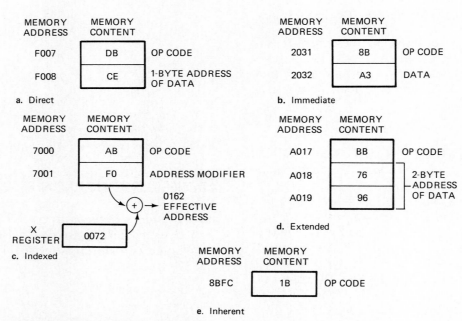

Fig. 6-11 6800 addressing modes.

68 Indexed Addressing

This form of addressing uses the second byte of the instruction to modify the index register contents to form the effective address. As Fig. 6-11c shows, these two quantities are added to produce a 16-bit address.

68 Extended Addressing

Extended addressing is quite similar to direct addressing. The address follows the op code, as shown in Fig. 6-11d. Here the address requires 2 bytes to cover the entire 64K memory range of addresses. The byte following the op code is the upper half of the address. The lower half of the address is in the second byte after the op code.

68 Inherent Addressing

Some instructions state the address involved by their nature; for example, the operation may involve one or two accumulators. Another case involves some of the stack instructions; because the instructions imply the address, only the op code need be specified.

68 6800 Addressing Modes Review

1. Define the terms "direct addressing" and "immediate addressing."
2. How does extended addressing differ from direct addressing?
3. Why are 3 bytes required in the instruction of Fig. 6-11d but only 2 bytes required in that of Fig. 6-11c?

68 ENCODING AND DECODING 6800 INSTRUCTIONS

Before we begin our study of specific instructions, we will consider the coded method used in writing an instruction. Because we are using machine code, every instruction will be an 8-bit binary string. We will write the code in hexadecimal for compactness. Every instruction must include two parts, or fields.

68 Operation Code Field

The operation code (or op code) field uniquely identifies the machine function to be performed, as we have seen.

In addition to the numerical op code, each instruction has a mnemonic associated with it. A mnemonic is a three- or four-letter abbreviation for the instruction intended to help the programmer remember the operation and document the program, but the computer cannot interpret the mnemonic. Examples of mnemonics are ADDA for addition and LDAA for load accumulator direct. If an assembler is used to generate programs, the mnemonics can be used as inputs to the assembler directly. In this book, mnemonics are used only to document the routines.

68 Operand Field

The second part of the instruction is the operand field. The operand field designates the data to be manipulated as a result of the computer decoding the operation and executing the instruction. The operand field may specify that data is:

1. Immediate (part of the instruction).
2. Contained in some register.
3. Contained in the memory cell indicated by an 8-bit or 16-bit memory address.
4. Contained in the address indicated by the index register.
5. Indicated by the stack pointer.

The operand can be any value represented by binary numbers. Examples of operands include hexadecimal values, hexadecimal I/O device codes, hexadecimal addresses, ASCII codes, and BCD codes.

68 Label Field

The programmer can simplify the coding process by assigning optional names to certain addresses in the program. These names, called symbolic addresses, are useful only to human beings. They appear on the coding sheet but are not meaningful to the computer. They help someone reading the program keep track of what is happening. Examples of two instructions, with all the fields described in this section, are given at the bottom of this page. The first instruction requires 3 bytes: 1 byte for the op code and 2 bytes to specify the address of the operand (memory location 1000_{16}). The second instruction uses 2 bytes because data follows the op code.

Label Field	Mnemonic	Memory Address	Operation Code Field	Operand Address
START	LDAA	2000	B6	—
		2001	—	10
		2002	—	00
NEXT	ADDA	2003	8B	—
		2004	—	06

Encoding and Decoding 6800 Instructions Review

1. What is the purpose of the operation code field?
2. Define the term "mnemonic." How does the use of mnemonics help the programmer?
3. List the locations that the operand field can designate as the source of data.
4. Which of the following cannot be operands for a computer instruction: I/O device codes, BCD codes, letters, binary numbers, and decimal numbers?
5. What is the purpose of the label field?

68 INTRODUCTION TO 6800 INSTRUCTIONS

This section presents 12 instructions that will allow you to transfer data from one location to another and to control the instruction sequence. The explanation for each instruction code will describe what the instruction does, the addressing mode it uses, the effect on the status register, and the execution time (in machine cycles). A complete discussion of the effect the instructions have on the status register is delayed until Chap. 7 (where it is more appropriate). Examples of how the instruction might be used follow the description.

The general format of a 6800 instruction op code word is shown in Fig. 6-12. Bits 0 through 3 and bit 7 are the actual op code value. Whether the A or B accumulator is to be used in the instruction is identified in bit 6. Finally, bits 4 and 5 give the addressing mode.

68 No Operation

The no operation instruction is the simplest one in the 6800 repertoire. It does just what the name says—nothing. One of its purposes is to fill unused memory cells, which are being reserved for adding instruction at a

later time. The no operation can also be used to create a time delay, as its execution takes two machine cycles. The instruction uses a single-byte format.

Operation code	01
Mnemonic	NOP
Addressing mode	none
Status bits affected	none
Machine cycles	2
Format	

Bit number

7 6 5 4   3 2 1 0

Memory cell   m | 0 0 0 0   0 0 0 1 |

☐ EXAMPLE

Before Execution		After Execution	
Program counter	3000	Program counter	3001
Memory 3000	01	Memory 3000	01

The only change as a result of executing this instruction is that the program counter has been incremented.

68 Load Accumulator Instructions

There are two instructions for loading accumulator registers (that is, for moving information from memory to one of the accumulators). Each instruction provides for four addressing modes: immediate, direct, indexed, or extended. Altogether, we then have eight variations. The loading operation is usually a preliminary to a longer sequence, such as an arithmetic function. All of these instructions load the value of the specified memory cell into the A or B register.

LOAD ACCUMULATOR IMMEDIATE   These two instructions move 1 byte from the memory cell following the op code into the A or B register. The previous contents of the register involved are lost.

	A Register	B Register
Operation code	86	C6
Mnemonic	LDAA	LDAB
Addressing mode	immediate	immediate
Status bits affected	sign and zero bits	
Machine cycles	2	
Format		

Bit number

7 6 5 4   3 2 1 0

| Memory cell   m | 1 r 0 0   0 1 1 0 |
| m + 1 | Data byte |

where r = 0 for A accumulator
r = 1 for B accumulator

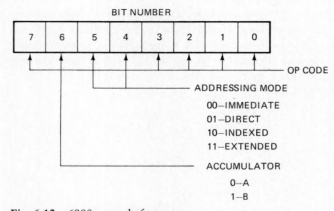

Fig. 6-12   6800 op code format.

BIT NUMBER

| 7 | 6 | 5 | 4 | 3 | 2 | 1 | 0 |

—— OP CODE

ADDRESSING MODE

00—IMMEDIATE
01—DIRECT
10—INDEXED
11—EXTENDED

ACCUMULATOR

0—A
1—B

□ EXAMPLE

Before Execution		After Execution	
Program counter	1050	Program counter	1052
B register	47	B register	BB
Memory 1050	C6	Memory 1050	C6
1051	BB	1051	BB

This instruction is frequently used to set the accumulator to an initial value.

LOAD ACCUMULATOR DIRECT The value in the memory cell specified by the address byte is placed in the A or B register. The previous contents of the register involved are lost.

	A Register	B Register
Operation code	96	D6
Mnemonic	LDAA	LDAB
Addressing mode	direct	direct
Status bits affected	sign and zero bits	
Machine cycles	3	
Format	Bit number	

```
            7 6 5 4   3 2 1 0
Memory cell  m  | 1 r 0 1   0 1 1 0 |
          m + 1  | Address byte |
```

where r = 0 for A accumulator
r = 1 for B accumulator

□ EXAMPLE

Before Execution		After Execution	
Program counter	B0C1	Program counter	B0C3
A register	14	A register	00
Memory 002E	00	Memory 002E	00
B0C1	96	B0C1	96
B0C2	2E	B0C2	2E

The instruction at location $B0C1_{16}$ (indicated by the program counter) specifies that the contents of address $002E_{16}$ will replace the present value in the A register. The memory cell $002E_{16}$ contains the value 0, which causes the A register to be cleared after the instruction is completed.

LOAD ACCUMULATOR INDEXED The value in the memory cell, specified by the sum of the index register and the address modifier byte, replaces the number in the A or B accumulator upon completion of the instruction. The address in the index register is unchanged after instruction execution.

	A Register	B Register
Operation code	A6	E6
Mnemonic	LDAA	LDAB
Addressing mode	indexed	indexed
Status bits affected	sign and zero bits	
Machine cycles	5	
Format	Bit number	

```
            7 6 5 4   3 2 1 0
Memory cell  m  | 1 r 1 0   0 1 1 0 |
          m + 1  | Address modifier byte |
```

where r = 0 for A accumulator
r = 1 for B accumulator

□ EXAMPLE

Before Execution		After Execution	
Program counter	30C0	Program counter	30C2
A register	26	A register	77
X register	2073	X register	2073
Memory 2139	77	Memory 2139	77
30C0	A6	30C0	A6
30C1	C6	30C1	C6

The address modifier byte in cell $30C1_{16}$ ($C6_{16}$) is added to the contents of the index register (2073_{16}) to form the address that will be the source of the data. The data address is therefore 2139_{16}. The contents of the A register are then replaced by 77_{16}.

LOAD ACCUMULATOR EXTENDED The contents of the memory byte identified by the two word address following the op code will be placed in the appropriate accumulator.

	A Register	B Register
Operation code	B6	F6
Mnemonic	LDAA	LDAB
Addressing mode	extended	extended
Status bits affected	sign and zero bits	
Machine cycles	4	
Format	Bit number	

```
            7 6 5 4   3 2 1 0
Memory cell  m  | 1 r 1 1   0 1 1 0 |
          m + 1  | High-address byte |
          m + 2  | Low-address byte |
```

where r = 0 for A accumulator
r = 1 for B accumulator

□ EXAMPLE

	Before Execution		After Execution	
Program counter	4000	Program counter	4003
A register	77	A register	6D

Memory	4000	B6	Memory	4000	B6
	4001	AB		4001	AB
	4002	08		4002	08
	AB08	6D		AB08	6D

The extended address in the instruction is $AD08_{16}$, which holds the value $6D_{16}$. The A register is set equal to $6D_{16}$.

68 Transfer Accumulator Instructions

These two instructions allow us to move the contents of accumulator A to accumulator B, or vice versa. Moving data in this fashion is often necessary in order to set up the contents prior to arithmetic operations. Because no memory is involved, these instructions use inherent addressing; hence, their length is just 1 byte.

	Move A Register to B Register	Move B Register to A Register
Operation code	16	17
Mnemonic	TAB	TBA
Addressing mode	inherent	inherent
Status bits affected	sign, zero, and overflow bits	
Machine cycles	2	
Format	Bit number	

Memory cell m

```
Bit number
7 6 5 4   3 2 1 0
0 0 0 1   0 1 1 r
```

where r = 0 for A accumulator
r = 1 for B accumulator

□ EXAMPLE

	Before Execution		After Execution	
Program counter	5110	Program counter	5111
A register	76	A register	00
B register	00	B register	00
Memory 5110	17	Memory 5110	17

The A register is set to the value of the B register. The B register is unchanged by this instruction.

68 Load Index Register

The contents of two consecutive memory locations are loaded into the index register. The first memory cell's contents are placed in the upper byte of the index register, and the second cell's go in the lower byte of the index register. All of the addressing modes described for the load accumulator instructions are also available for this instruction. In the immediate addressing mode, the two memory locations following the op code form the new contents of the index register.

Addressing Mode	Operation Code
Immediate	CE
Direct	DE
Indexed	EE
Extended	FE

Mnemonic	LDX
Addressing mode	immediate, direct, indexed, extended
Status bits affected	sign, zero, and overflow bits
Machine cycles	3, 4, 6, 5, depending on respective addressing mode above
Format	immediate addressing

```
                         Bit number
                       7 6 5 4   3 2 1 0
Memory cell   m        1 1 0 0   1 1 1 0
             m + 1        Data byte 1
             m + 2        Data byte 2
```

Format — direct addressing

```
                         Bit number
                       7 6 5 4   3 2 1 0
Memory cell   m        1 1 0 1   1 1 1 0
             m + 1        Address byte
```

Format — indexed addressing

```
                         Bit number
                       7 6 5 4   3 2 1 0
Memory cell   m        1 1 1 0   1 1 1 0
             m + 1      Address modifier byte
```

Format — extended addressing

```
                         Bit number
                       7 6 5 4   3 2 1 0
Memory cell   m        1 1 1 1   1 1 1 0
             m + 1       High-address byte
             m + 2       Low-address byte
```

Before Execution		After Execution	
Program counter	30C0	Program counter	30C3
X register	2601	X register	21AF
Memory	30C0 FE	Memory	30C0 FE
	30C1 40		30C1 40
	30C2 00		30C2 00
	4000 21		4000 21
	4001 AF		4001 AF

The memory cell specified by the extended address is 4000_{16}. The byte in that cell (21_{16}) is placed in the upper half of the X register. The byte in cell 4001_{16} (AF_{16}) is placed in the lower half of the X register.

68 Load Stack Pointer

This instruction provides a means of initializing the stack pointer. Before the stack is used, the pointer must be set to the top location. The contents of two consecutive memory cells form the value. The first memory cell is the upper byte of the stack pointer, and the following cell forms the lower byte of the stack pointer. All the addressing modes described for the load accumulator instructions are also available for this instruction.

Addressing Mode	Operation Code
Immediate	8E
Direct	9E
Indexed	AE
Extended	BE

Mnemonic	LDS
Addressing mode	immediate, direct, indexed, extended
Status bits affected	sign, zero, and overflow bits
Machine cycles	3, 4, 6, 5, depending on respective addressing mode above
Format	immediate addressing

Bit number

		7 6 5 4	3 2 1 0
Memory cell	m	1 0 0 0	1 1 1 0
	m + 1	Data byte 1	
	m + 2	Data byte 2	

Format	direct addressing

Bit number

		7 6 5 4	3 2 1 0
Memory cell	m	1 0 0 1	1 1 1 0
	m + 1	Address byte	

Format	indexed addressing

Bit number

		7 6 5 4	3 2 1 0
Memory cell	m	1 0 1 0	1 1 1 0
	m + 1	Address modifier byte	

Format	extended addressing

Bit number

		7 6 5 4	3 2 1 0
Memory cell	m	1 0 1 1	1 1 1 0
	m + 1	High-address byte	
	m + 2	Low-address byte	

□ EXAMPLE

Before Execution		After Execution	
Program counter	5110	Program counter	5113
SP register	6D21	SP register	1658
Memory	5110 8E	Memory	5110 8E
	5111 16		5111 16
	5112 58		5112 58

Because immediate addressing is required by the op code, the contents of the two following memory cells (1658_{16}) are moved to the stack pointer.

68 Transfer the Stack Pointer to the Index Register

The 2-byte contents of the stack pointer are *incremented* by 1 and placed in the index register. The stack pointer retains its original value after execution.

Operation code	30
Mnemonic	TSX
Addressing mode	inherent
Status bits affected	none
Machine cycles	4
Format	

Bit number

		7 6 5 4	3 2 1 0
Memory cell	m	0 0 1 1	0 0 0 0

□ EXAMPLE

Before Execution		After Execution	
Program counter	1800	Program counter	1801
X register	36AA	X register	42CD
SP register	42CC	SP register	42CC
Memory	1800 30	Memory	1800 30

The reason that the value of the stack pointer is incremented before the transfer is to set the index register to point to the top of the stack.

68 Transfer Index Register to the Stack Pointer

The value of the index register is *decremented* by 1 and placed in the stack pointer.

Operation code	35
Mnemonic	TXS
Addressing mode	inherent
Status bits affected	none
Machine cycles	4
Format	

Bit number

7 6 5 4   3 2 1 0

Memory cell   m   `0 0 1 1   0 1 0 1`

☐ EXAMPLE

Before Execution		After Execution	
Program counter	2000	Program counter	2001
X register	FF00	X register	FF00
SP register	AA11	SP register	FEFF
Memory 2000	35	Memory 2000	35

Subtracting 1 from the index register gives $FEFF_{16}$. The value is placed in the stack pointer.

68 Store Accumulator

The store accumulator instructions are reverse operations to the load commands. Data is transferred from the A or B register to memory. There is no change in the source register contents when the data is written into memory. The 6800 provides direct, indexed, and extended addressing modes for this instruction.

Addressing Mode	Operation Code	
	A Register Source	B Register Source
Direct	97	D7
Indexed	A7	E7
Extended	B7	F7

Mnemonic	STAA STAB
Status bits affected	sign, zero, and overflow bits
Machine cycles	4, 6, 5, depending on respective addressing mode above

For each format below r = 0 for A accumulator

r = 1 for B accumulator

Format   direct addressing

Bit number

7 6 5 4   3 2 1 0

Memory cell   m   `1 r 0 1   0 1 1 1`
           m + 1   `Address byte`

Format   indexed addressing

Bit number

7 6 5 4   3 2 1 0

Memory cell   m   `1 r 1 0   0 1 1 1`
           m + 1   `Address modifier byte`

Format   extended addressing

Bit number

7 6 5 4   3 2 1 0

Memory cell   m   `1 r 1 1   0 1 1 1`
           m + 1   `High-address byte`
           m + 2   `Low-address byte`

☐ EXAMPLE

Before Execution		After Execution	
Program counter	8100	Program counter	8103
B register	C2	B register	C2
Memory 8100	F7	Memory 8100	F7
8101	F0	8101	F0
8102	FB	8102	FB
F0FB	00	F0FB	C2

The value in the B register is moved to cell $F0FB_{16}$.

68 Store Stack Pointer

The stack pointer is stored in two consecutive memory bytes. The upper half of the SP register is stored in the cell addressed by the instruction. The lower half of the register is stored in the following cell. The direct, indexed, and extended addressing modes are provided.

Addressing Mode	Operation Code
Direct	9F
Indexed	AF
Extended	BF

Mnemonic	STS
Status bits affected	sign, zero, and overflow bits
Machine cycles	5, 7, 6, depending on respective addressing mode above

Format   direct addressing

Bit number

7 6 5 4   3 2 1 0

Memory cell	m	1 0 0 1 1 1 1 1
	m + 1	Address byte

Format   indexed addressing

Bit number

7 6 5 4   3 2 1 0

Memory cell	m	1 0 1 0 1 1 1 1
	m + 1	Address modifier byte

Format   extended addressing

Bit number

7 6 5 4   3 2 1 0

Memory cell	m	1 0 1 1 1 1 1 1
	m + 1	High-address byte
	m + 2	Low-address byte

□ **EXAMPLE**

Before Execution			After Execution		
Program counter		7700	Program counter		7702
SP register		4433	SP register		4433
Memory	003D	00	Memory	003D	44
	003E	00		003E	33
	7700	9F		7700	9F
	7701	3D		7701	3D

Because direct addressing is called for, the stack upper byte is stored in memory at $003D_{16}$. The lower byte of the stack is placed in cell $003E_{16}$.

68 Store Index Register

This instruction is quite similar to the store stack pointer instruction, except that the index register is stored. The direct, indexed, and extended addressing modes are available.

Addressing Mode	Operation Code
Direct	DF
Indexed	EF
Extended	FF

Mnemonic	STX
Status bits affected	sign, zero, and overflow bits
Machine cycles	5, 7, 6, depending on respective addressing mode above

Format   direct addressing

Bit number

7 6 5 4   3 2 1 0

Memory cell	m	1 1 0 1 1 1 1 1
	m + 1	Address byte

Format   indexed addressing

Bit number

7 6 5 4   3 2 1 0

Memory cell	m	1 1 1 0 1 1 1 1
	m + 1	Address modifier byte

Format   extended addressing

Bit number

7 6 5 4   3 2 1 0

Memory cell	m	1 1 1 1 1 1 1 1
	m + 1	High-address byte
	m + 2	Low-address byte

□ **EXAMPLE**

Before Execution			After Execution		
Program counter		3500	Program counter		3502
X register		F000	X register		F000
Memory	3500	EF	Memory	3500	EF
	3501	0B		3501	0B
	FF0B	02		FF0B	F0
	FF0C	1F		FF0C	00

Be careful to avoid confusion on an indexed addressing instruction that involves the index register. When we understand its execution a step at a time, the instruction is quite simple. First, we form the effective address by adding the modifier byte to the index register value (note that this operation does not change the index register):

Index register	$F000_{16}$
Address modifier	$+\ 0B_{16}$
Sum	$F00B_{16}$

Cell $F00B_{16}$ is then the destination for the upper half of the index register. The lower half of the index register gets stored in cell $F00C_{16}$.

68 Jump Instruction

After a series of instructions has been completed, a change to a different sequence is sometimes required. Instead of selecting the next consecutive instruction, the microprocessor must transfer control to the instruction in a memory address far removed from the current one. This transfer of control is accomplished with some form of jump command. Here we will consider one type of jump (other options will be examined in Chap. 8).

The jump instruction causes program control to transfer to the indexed or extended address in the instruction. Program execution continues from that memory address. In effect, the jump instruction just changes the value of the program counter.

Addressing Mode	Operation Code
Indexed	6E
Extended	7E

Mnemonic	JMP
Status bits affected	none
Machine cycles	4 or 3, depending on respective addressing mode above
Format	indexed addressing

Bit number

7 6 5 4   3 2 1 0

Memory cell	m	0 1 1 0 1 1 1 0
	m + 1	Address modifier byte

Format	extended addressing

Bit number

7 6 5 4   3 2 1 0

Memory cell	m	0 1 1 1 1 1 1 0
	m + 1	High-address byte
	m + 2	Low-address byte

□ EXAMPLE

Before Execution	After Execution
Program counter 5027	Program counter 4400

Before Execution				After Execution		
Memory	5027	7E	Memory	5027	7E
	5028	44		5028	44
	5029	00		5029	00

Normally the program counter would be set to $502A_{16}$ after executing the 3-byte instruction, but the JMP instruction forces the program counter to select the next instruction from cell 4400_{16}.

68 Summary of 6800 Instructions

The instructions described in this chapter are summarized in Table 6-10. For each instruction, the mnemonic, operation code, number of bytes in length, and execution time are listed.

68 6800 PROGRAMMING EFFICIENCY

Even with the limited number of instructions you know, it may seem that several instructions do the same thing. This apparent redundancy of op codes is actually misleading. It is rather an indication of the flexibility that a large repertoire can offer.

We will examine four rather similar instructions to show how they differ and the way that choosing an instruction can affect the program execution time and memory requirements. The instructions we are interested in are listed in Table 6-11. As you can see just by selecting one addressing mode or another, we can seemingly get execution times ranging from two to five machine cycles and use 2 or 3 bytes of memory. These obvious differences are not the whole story, though, because instructions are never used in isolation. They must be combined to do a certain task. Let us assume

Table 6-10 Summary of 6800 Instructions

Mnemonic	Operation Code	Bytes	Execution Time (machine cycles)
JMP	6E, 7E	2, 3	4, 3
LDAA	86, 96, A6, B6	2, 2, 2, 3	2, 3, 5, 4
LDAB	C6, D6, E6, F6	2, 2, 2, 3	2, 3, 5, 4
LDS	8E, 9E, AE, BE	3, 2, 2, 3	3, 4, 6, 5
LDX	CE, DE, EE, FE	3, 2, 2, 3	3, 4, 6, 5
NOP	01	1	2
STAA	97, A7, B7	2, 2, 3	4, 6, 5
STAB	D7, E7, F7	2, 2, 3	4, 6, 5
STS	9F, AF, BF	2, 2, 3	5, 7, 6
STX	DF, EF, FF	2, 2, 3	5, 7, 6
TAB	16	2	1
TBA	17	2	1
TSX	30	4	1
TXS	35	4	1

Table 6-11 LDAA Instruction Comparison

Addressing Mode	Execution Time (machine cycles)	Bytes
Immediate	2	2
Direct	3	2
Indexed	5	2
Extended	4	3

that the job we want to do is to clear the accumulator. We will write programs using each of the instructions in Table 6-11 to accomplish this task.

Program 1

Memory Address	Machine Code	Comments
1000	86	LDAA (immediate)
1001	00	Data

Program 2

Memory Address	Machine Code	Comments
1000	96	LDAA (direct)
1001	1F	Address of data

Program 3

Memory Address	Machine Code	Comments
1000	CE	LDX
1001	30	Address of data
1002	00	
1003	A6	LDAA (indexed)
1004	00	Address modifier

Program 4

Memory Address	Machine Code	Comments
1000	B6	LDAA (extended)
1001	30	Data address
1002	00	

Now we need to tabulate the time and memory needed for each program. The results are shown in Table 6-12. It is even more obvious now that proper selection of instructions can significantly decrease the

Table 6-12 Time and Memory Comparison

Addressing Mode	Time (machine cycles)	Memory (bytes)
Immediate	2	2
Direct	3	2
Indexed	8	5
Extended	4	3

execution time and memory space needed for a program. There are no general rules for instruction selection, but as you become more familiar with the repertoire, finding the most appropriate instruction will get easier.

[68] Some Problems to Avoid in Programming the 6800

After you enter programs into the computer, you may find that they do not run properly. This failure is often the result of just not entering the program as written. Simple mistakes are easy to make, while the use of machine language instructions is a new experience. If your program does not run correctly, you must debug it to find the error. Inspecting memory contents and comparing them to the program listing is a good way to proceed. The results of two common errors are described so that you will have an idea of the problems that seemingly trivial mistakes can cause.

[68] 6800 Examples

JUMPING TO A DATA CELL A partial listing is provided in Table 6-13. The computer is to clear accumulator A and jump to load the index register. By mistake, the program has a jump address of 1000_{16} instead of 0100_{16}. (The oversight in just this single set of bits in entering the program generates the error.) The program will clear accumulator A and then jump to address 1000_{16}, where it will treat the data as an op code.

This data will be interpreted as a TAB (op code is 16) instruction. Now the processor is completely out of control and will randomly execute instructions in a manner not intended by the operator. The lesson is that even a single-bit mistake can totally disrupt a program. On the other hand, no real harm was done; it is im-

Table 6-13 6800 Erroneous Jump

Location	Machine Code	Comments
0100	CE	Load index register
0101	03	Data
0102	00	Data
⋮		
1000	16	Data
⋮		
10AF	86	Load A register
10B0	00	Data
10B1	7E	Jump
10B2	10	Incorrect address
10B3	00	

Table 6-14 6800 Instruction Length Error

Location	Machine Code	Comments
0700	E6	LDAB
0701	07	High-address byte
0702	17	TBA (note that the low-address byte for the previous instruction is missing)

possible to damage a processor by putting in a bad program. That means that the price of experimentation is quite reasonable, because no hardware can be destroyed.

INCORRECT INSTRUCTION LENGTH Another easy trap to fall into is to put in an instruction with the wrong length. The purpose of the program given in Table 6-14 is to set the B register to the number in memory cell $07FF_{16}$. When the processor executes cell 0700_{16}, it must take the contents of the next two locations as an address because extended addressing is specified. The result is that accumulator B is loaded with the contents of cell 0717_{16} and the next instruction (which should have been TBA) never takes place. Another simple omission has produced two incorrect actions. The impact of these errors will depend on the remainder of the program.

This section has provided just a small sample of the various things that can go wrong because of software errors. Remember that the computer is a very literal device—it cannot differentiate between a correct and an incorrect program. Only the human being doing the programming can.

68 6800 Programming Efficiency Review

1. Why are the memory lengths in Table 6-12 misleading for evaluating efficiency?
2. Which instruction made the indexed addressing execution time so much longer than the other times in Table 6-12?
3. After the program in Table 6-13 is corrected, what is the value in the program counter after the index register is loaded?

CHAPTER SUMMARY

1. Any memory address can be either written or read. It is the programmer's responsibility to prevent attempts to write in ROM or to read nonexistent locations.

2. The no operation instruction occupies a memory cell but does not cause any change in microprocessor state, except for incrementing the program counter.
3. The store instructions write data into memory.
4. Jumps allow the programmer to change the sequence of instruction execution from the normal, consecutive order.
5. The halt instruction stops the execution of the program.
6. Proper choice of instructions can minimize the amount of time needed to run the program or the number of memory cells needed to store it. Usually only one of these two goals can be achieved; running time can be reduced only at the expense of more memory, and vice versa.

80 8085 Unique Items

7. The working registers and the memory to be used in many instructions are indicated by a 3-bit code.
8. Register pairs are referred to by a single letter in many instruction manuals and by a 2-bit designator in some instructions.
9. A memory address for an instruction can be supplied by the data in an instruction, a register pair, or the stack pointer.
10. A maximum of 256 independent input and output ports is available. The user must avoid referencing nonexistent ports because no error notification is provided by the processor.
11. Three addressing modes are used by the 8085. Direct addressing supplies the location as part of the 3-byte instruction. When a register pair holds the address, or when only a single register is involved in the instruction, the register addressing mode is used. Immediate addressing uses a format that includes data with the instruction.
12. Load instructions move data into the working registers or the stack pointer.
13. Move instructions are quite similar to load instructions except in terms of destination, for data can be moved to memory locations as well as to registers.
14. The exchange instruction completely replaces the HL register pair content with the DE pair and then replaces the original DE value with that of HL. The result is an interchange of the register contents.

68 6800 Unique Items

15. The working registers are indicated by a 1-bit code.
16. A memory address for an instruction can be supplied by data in the instruction, the index register, or the stack pointer.

17. In a method called memory-mapped I/O, I/O devices are treated just like memory.
18. There are five addressing modes for the 6800: Direct addressing supplies a low memory address as part of the 2-byte instruction. When the data is part of the instruction, we have immediate addressing. With indexed addressing, the index register holds the address. Extended addressing provides a 16-bit address as part of the 3-byte instruction. Some instructions provide the address inherently.
19. Load instructions move data into accumulators, the index register, or stack pointer.
20. Transfer accumulator instructions allow data to be exchanged between registers.

KEY TERMS AND CONCEPTS

Register notation	Label field	Store instructions
Direct addressing	No operation	Jump instructions
Register addressing	Load instructions	Halt instruction
Immediate addressing	Move instructions	Indexed addressing
Operation (op) code field	Source and destination registers and memory	Extended addressing
Mnemonic		Inherent addressing
Operand field	Exchange instruction	Transfer instructions

P R O B L E M S

The initial conditions for Probs. 6-1 through 6-10 are given in the following table. That is, the register and memory locations are to be set to the given values before the instructions in Probs. 6-1 through 6-10 are executed.

Program Counter	4090	Stack Pointer	2000

Registers		Memory	
A	0F	0000	00
B	00	0001	50
C	01	0002	AA
D	02	0003	7B
E	A0	02A0	00
H	0F	0B0F	50
L	0B	A002	20
		0F0B	00
		0F0C	07

For each problem, record only the *changes* in any register or memory location *after* the problem's instructions have been executed. Problems 6-1 through 6-10 refer to the 8085.

6-1

Location	Contents
4090	3A
4091	02
4092	00
4093	76

6-2

Location	Contents
4090	2A
4091	01
4092	00
4093	EB
4094	76

6-3

Location	Contents
4090	21
4091	95
4092	40
4093	E9
4094	76
4095	EB
4096	76

6-4

Location	Contents
4090	0A
4091	32
4092	00
4093	00
4094	00
4095	76

6-5

Location	Contents
4090	06
4091	FF
4092	32
4093	0B
4094	0F
4095	76

6-6

Location	Contents
4090	66
4091	00
4092	2A
4093	0B
4094	0F
4095	76

6-7

Location	Contents
4090	22
4091	02
4092	00
4093	32
4094	03
4095	00
4096	76

6-8

Location	Contents
4090	02
4091	2A
4092	01
4093	00
4094	00
4095	76
4096	00
4097	1A

6-9

Location	Contents
4090	C3
4091	94
4092	40
4093	76
4094	0A
4095	75
4096	00
4097	C3
4098	93
4099	40
409A	76

6-10 What is the bug in the following program? (Do not record changes in memory or registers.)

Location	Contents
4090	3A
4091	03
4092	00
4093	00
4094	31
4095	76
4096	76
4097	C3
4098	90
4099	40
409A	76

Problems 6-11 through 6-20 refer to the 6800. The initial conditions for these problems are given in the following table; that is, the register and memory locations are to be set to the given values before the instructions in the problems are executed. For each problem, record only the *changes* in any register or memory location *after* the problem's instructions have been executed.

Program Counter	5043	Stack Pointer	3000

Registers		Memory	
A	0F	0000	50
B	A0	0001	00
X	0B00	0002	AA
		0003	7B
		02A0	00
		0B00	35
		3000	07
		3001	00

6-11

Location	Contents
5043	B6
5044	02
5045	A0
5046	01

6-12

Location	Contents
5043	16
5044	97
5045	01
5046	17

6-13

Location	Contents
5043	30
5044	AF
5045	00
5046	C6
5047	14

6-14

Location	Contents
5043	97
5044	02
5045	6E
5046	00
5047	00

6-15

Location	Contents
5043	F7
5044	02
5045	A0
5046	A7
5047	00

6-16

Location	Contents
5043	00
5044	DF
5045	01
5046	35
5047	8E
5048	80
5049	FF

6-17

Location	Contents
5043	FF
5044	12
5045	00

Location	Contents
5046	FE
5047	01
5048	00
5049	00

6-18

Location	Contents
5043	DF
5044	01
5045	8E
5046	11
5047	AC
5048	D7
5049	00

6-19

Location	Contents
5043	EE
5044	00
5045	7E
5046	50
5047	48
5048	86
5049	7F

6-20 What is the bug in the following program? (Do not record changes in memory or registers.)

Location	Contents
5043	CE
5044	14
5045	7E
5046	D7
5047	02
5048	7E
5049	43

ARITHMETIC AND LOGIC

Most people think of a computer as a fast arithmetic processor. In fact, computers were invented primarily to perform mathematical computations that would have taken years to do by hand. The ENIAC computer built in 1946 took only 2 hours to do calculations that took 100 engineers a full year. The ENIAC computer filled an entire building, yet today's microprocessors, like the 8085 and 6800, can do all that and more. In this chapter we will concentrate on the arithmetic and boolean instructions of the microprocessor. Our study will require a detailed examination of the status register and how the operations change the flag bits to signify various conditions.

CHAPTER OBJECTIVES

Upon completion of this chapter, you should be able to:

1. Describe the meaning and application of the status indicators.
2. List two ways for directly controlling the carry status bit.
3. Explain how registers and memory cells can be incremented or decremented.
4. Describe how to complement the accumulator.
5. Distinguish between the various addition and subtraction instructions in the repertoire.
6. Describe the effects of boolean AND, OR, and exclusive OR operations.
7. Demonstrate the use of boolean instructions for masking specific bits in a register or memory.
8. Show how the microprocessor can perform direct BCD additions.
9. Explain the use of compare instructions to determine the relative magnitudes of memory cell or register contents.

THE STATUS REGISTER IN DETAIL

The status register was briefly discussed in Chaps. 4 and 5. Remember that the flag bits in the status register show the conditions met by the data in the accumulator. The settings of all status flags (except the auxiliary carry) can be tested by computer instructions. The instructions used to test these bits are described in Chaps. 8 and 11. Here we are mainly interested in the meaning of the status bits and how they are set or cleared. Almost every arithmetic and logical instruction will have some effect on the status register. In the descriptions to follow, note which bits are changed by the instructions and whether these bit conditions can influence the operation of the processor.

Carry (C) Bit

The carry bit can be changed by addition, subtraction, shifting, and logical instructions. When adding, a carry from the high-order bit will set the carry status to 1. If no carry out is generated, the bit will be reset (that is, set to 0). Although it may seem a little strange, subtraction reverses the process (except for the 6800). If a carry out is produced, it means that no borrow was required from the most significant bit (MSB); therefore, it makes sense to reset the carry status for that case. Unlike the 8085 and Z80, the 6800 C bit is set if a borrow occurs, just as it is set for a carry in addition. Details are provided in the instruction explanations to clarify how the carry status is used for each one. Before beginning those explanations, let us look at some examples of how the carry status works.

□ **EXAMPLE 1**   Addition with no carry.

$$
\begin{array}{r}
2A_{16} = \quad 0010 \quad 1010_2 \\
+ 56_{16} = +0101 \quad 0110_2 \\
\hline
80_{16} = \boxed{0}1000 \quad 0000_2 \\
\uparrow \\
\text{No carry}
\end{array}
$$

Because the carry out is 0, the status bit will be reset.

□ **EXAMPLE 2**   Addition with carry.

$$
\begin{array}{r}
E7_{16} = \quad 1110 \quad 0111_2 \\
+ 7C_{16} = +0111 \quad 1100_2 \\
\hline
163_{16} = \boxed{1}0110 \quad 0011_2 \\
\uparrow \\
\text{Carry}
\end{array}
$$

There is a carry from the MSB position, so the status bit will be set.

□ **EXAMPLE 3**   Subtraction with no borrow.

$$
\begin{array}{r}
04_{16} = \quad 0000 \quad 0100_2 \\
- 02_{16} = +1111 \quad 1110_2 \leftarrow \text{2's complement} \\
\hline
02_{16} = \boxed{1}0000 \quad 0010_2 \\
\uparrow \\
\text{Carry indicates no borrow}
\end{array}
$$

The MSB did not require a borrow, so the carry status will be reset.

□ **EXAMPLE 4**   Carry with borrow.

$$
\begin{array}{r}
04_{16} = \quad 0000 \quad 0100_2 \\
- 07_{16} = \quad 1111 \quad 1001_2 \\
\hline
- 03_{16} = \boxed{0}1111 \quad 1101_2 \\
\uparrow \\
\text{No carry}
\end{array}
$$

The MSB produces no carry, thus indicating that a borrow was necessary (the negative difference shows this borrow also); the carry status will be set.

Auxiliary Carry (A$_C$) Bit

The purpose of this status bit is to allow one instruction (decimal adjust accumulator) to perform its function. The use of this bit will be explained with that instruction description. For the time being, we will just examine situations that cause the bit to be set or cleared.

Any operation that produces a carry from bit position 3 while adding, subtracting, incrementing, decrementing, or comparing will set the bit; otherwise, it will be reset.

□ **EXAMPLE**

Carry from MSB → $\boxed{0}$ $\boxed{1}$ ← Carry from position 3

$$
\begin{array}{r}
2A_{16} = \quad 0010 \quad 1010_2 \\
+ 56_{16} = \quad 0101 \quad 0110_2 \\
\hline
80_{16} = \quad 1000 \quad 0000_2
\end{array}
$$

The auxiliary carry will be set to 1 because bit position 3 generated a carry. The carry status bit (explained above) is independent of the auxiliary carry. In this case there is no carry from the MSB, so the carry status bit is reset.

Sign (S) Bit

Bit 7 of the accumulator always represents the sign of the number in that register. At the completion of arithmetic and logical operations, the sign status is set equal to bit 7.

EXAMPLE

Sign bit
↓

A register 92_{16} = 1 0 0 1   0 0 1 0$_2$

The sign status flag will be set to 1, meaning that the number is negative.

Zero (Z) Bit

If the accumulator value is 0 as the result of certain operations, this status flag is set. A nonzero number causes the flag to be reset. A special situation can result if the answer overflows the A register, and although the answer is not 0, the portion remaining in the accumulator is 0.

EXAMPLE

$\boxed{1}$ ← Carry

$A7_{16}$ = 1 0 1 0   0 1 1 1$_2$
+ 59_{16} = 0 1 0 1   1 0 0 1$_2$
───────────────────────────────
100_{16} = $\boxed{0 0 0 0 \ \ 0 0 0 0_2}$ ← Final accumulator value

The accumulator can only hold the 8 least significant bits (LSBs). (Bit 9 is 1, but it will not fit into the register.) As a result, the Z bit is set to indicate that the accumulator contents are 0. (In this example, the carry bit will also be set. The overflow bit of the 6800 will be set as well.)

80 8085 Parity (P) Bit

The quantity of set bits (1s) in the accumulator is counted. Should this count be an odd number, the parity bit is cleared; if even, the bit is set.

EXAMPLE

96_{16} = 1 0 0 1   0 1 1 0$_2$

4 bits are set (even):
parity bit = 1

BF_{16} = 1 0 1 1   1 1 1 1$_2$

7 bits are set (odd):
parity bit = 0

68 6800 Overflow (O) Bit

If the result of an operation exceeds the capacity of the accumulator, the overflow bit is set in the 6800. When the processor is initially started after a reset, this bit is cleared. The overflow status indicator can be a good way to catch errors.

EXAMPLE

$E4_{16}$
+ $4 C_{16}$
─────────
130_{16}

The result exceeds the 8-bit length of the accumulator, so the overflow bit will be set.

80 8085 Status Register Configuration

The bit assignments for the status register were described in Chap. 4, but it would be appropriate to review those assignments and to note a few details, not previously covered, before discussing the use of the status register in instructions.

As was previously explained, bits 1, 3, and 5 have no meaning attached to their condition, so their states are "don't care" values. Should you ever examine the register, however, knowledge of those bit states will avoid confusion. As Fig. 7-1 shows, bit 1 is always set and bits 3 and 5 are always reset. Figure 7-1 also shows the positions for the sign, zero, auxiliary carry, parity, and carry bits.

68 6800 Status Register Configuration

The bit assignments for the status register were described in Chap. 5, but it would be appropriate to review these assignments and to note a few details, not previously covered, before discussing the use of the status register in instructions.

As was previously explained, bits 6 and 7 have no meaning attached to their condition, so their states are don't care values. In fact, these bits are always set to 1. Should you examine the register, knowledge of those bit states will avoid confusion. As Fig. 7-2 shows, the auxiliary carry is bit 5, the interrupt mask is bit 4, the sign status is bit 3, the zero status is bit 2, the overflow status is bit 1, and the carry is bit 0.

Status Register Review

1. List the conditions that set the carry bit as a result of addition or subtraction.

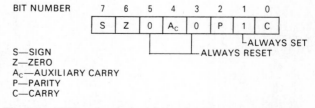

Fig. 7-1 8085 status register bit assignments.

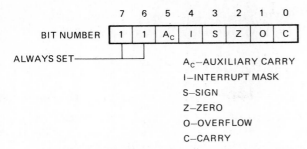

BIT NUMBER 7 6 5 4 3 2 1 0
            [1 1 Ac I S Z O C]

ALWAYS SET ———

Ac—AUXILIARY CARRY
I—INTERRUPT MASK
S—SIGN
Z—ZERO
O—OVERFLOW
C—CARRY

Fig. 7-2 6800 status register bit assignments.

2. Compare the auxiliary carry and carry bits. How are they similar? In what ways do they differ?
3. If the number in the accumulator is $C2_{16}$, is the sign bit set or cleared?
4. Given that the 8085 status register contains the value 83_{16}, what can you conclude about the parity of the accumulator value? Is the number nonzero?

80 8085 CARRY BIT MODIFICATION

Two instructions in the repertoire directly affect the condition of the status register carry bit. The use of these instructions in computer arithmetic will be demonstrated in later chapters.

80 Set Carry Bit

The carry bit can be unconditionally set to 1 with this operation. None of the other status bits is changed after a set carry bit instruction. If the carry bit had been set before this instruction is executed, the effect is the same as a no operation instruction.

Operation code   37
Mnemonic   STC
Addressing Mode   none
Status bits affected   carry bit set
Clock periods   4
Format

Bit number
7 6 5 4   3 2 1 0
Memory cell   m [0 0 1 1   0 1 1 1]

☐ EXAMPLE

Before Execution		After Execution	
Program counter	5780	Program counter	5781
Status register	82	Status register	83
Memory 5780	37	Memory 5780	37

The carry bit is set. The previously set sign bit (bit 7) and the don't care bit (bit 1) are not altered.

80 Complement Carry Bit

The state of the carry bit can be inverted with this instruction. If the bit was previously 1, it becomes 0, and if 0, the bit will be set to 1. Again, no bits other than the carry condition bit will be modified.

Operation code   3F
Mnemonic   CMC
Addressing mode   none
Status bits affected   carry bit complemented
Clock periods   4
Format

Bit number
7 6 5 4   3 2 1 0
Memory cell   m [0 0 1 1   1 1 1 1]

☐ EXAMPLE 1

Before Execution		After Execution	
Program counter	3300	Program counter	3301
Status register	02	Status register	03
Memory 3300	3F	Memory 3300	3F

The carry bit (bit 0) was changed from the 0 condition to a 1.

☐ EXAMPLE 2

Before Execution		After Execution	
Program counter	4CF0	Program counter	4CF1
Status register	83	Status register	82
Memory 4CF0	3F	Memory 4CF0	3F

Because the carry bit was set, it becomes 0 after the complement instruction has been executed.

68 6800 CARRY BIT MODIFICATION

Two instructions in the repertoire directly affect the condition of the status register carry bit. The use of these instructions in computer arithmetic will be demonstrated in later chapters.

68 Set Carry Bit

The carry bit can be unconditionally set to 1 with this operation. None of the other status bits is changed after a set carry instruction. If the carry bit had been set before this operation is executed, the effect is the same as a no operation instruction.

Operation code   0D
Mnemonic   SEC

Addressing mode   inherent
Status bits affected   carry bit set
Clock periods   2
Format

Bit number

7 6 5 4   3 2 1 0

Memory cell   m | 0 0 0 0   1 1 0 1 |

□ EXAMPLE

Before Execution		After Execution	
Program counter	5780	Program counter	5781
Status register	C0	Status register	C1
Memory 5780	0D	Memory 5780	0D

The carry bit is set. The previously set don't care bits (6 and 7), auxiliary carry, and interrupt mask are not altered.

68 Clear Carry Bit

The carry bit can be unconditionally cleared to 0 with this operation. None of the other status bits is changed after a clear carry instruction. If the carry bit had been cleared before this operation is executed, the effect is the same as a no operation instruction.

Operation code   0C
Mnemonic   CLC
Addressing mode   inherent
Status bits affected   carry bit cleared
Clock periods   2
Format

Bit number

7 6 5 4   3 2 1 0

Memory cell   m | 0 0 0 0   1 1 0 0 |

□ EXAMPLE

Before Execution		After Execution	
Program counter	5780	Program counter	5781
Status register	C1	Status register	C0
Memory 5780	0C	Memory 5780	0C

The carry bit is cleared. The previously set don't care bits (6 and 7), auxiliary carry, and interrupt mask are not altered.

Carry Bit Modification Review

1. Describe the action of the set carry instruction when the carry bit was clear prior to execution. When was it set prior to execution?
2. When is the set carry bit instruction equivalent to a no operation?

3. Explain the result of complementing the carry bit in the 8085 depending on its initial condition.

68 6800 OVERFLOW BIT MODIFICATION

Two instructions in the repertoire directly affect the condition of the status register overflow bit. The use of these instructions is illustrated below.

68 Set Overflow Bit

The overflow bit can be unconditionally set to 1 with this operation. None of the other status bits is changed after a set overflow instruction. If the overflow bit had been set before this operation is executed, the effect is the same as a no operation instruction.

Operation code   0B
Mnemonic   SEV
Addressing mode   inherent
Status bits affected   overflow bit set
Clock periods   2
Format

Bit number

7 6 5 4   3 2 1 0

Memory cell   m | 0 0 0 0   1 0 1 1 |

□ EXAMPLE

Before Execution		After Execution	
Program counter	5780	Program counter	5781
Status register	C0	Status register	C2
Memory 5780	0B	Memory 5780	0B

The overflow bit is set. The previously set don't care bits (6 and 7), auxiliary carry, and interrupt mask are not altered.

68 Clear Overflow Bit

The overflow bit can be unconditionally cleared to 0 with this operation. None of the other status bits is changed after a clear overflow instruction. If the overflow bit had been cleared before this operation is executed, the effect is the same as a no operation instruction.

Operation code   0A
Mnemonic   CLV
Addressing mode   inherent
Status bits affected   overflow bit cleared
Clock periods   2
Format

Bit number

7 6 5 4   3 2 1 0

Memory cell   m | 0 0 0 0   1 0 1 0 |

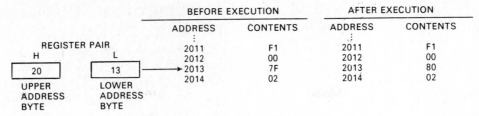

	BEFORE EXECUTION		AFTER EXECUTION	
	ADDRESS	CONTENTS	ADDRESS	CONTENTS
	⋮		⋮	
	2011	F1	2011	F1
	2012	00	2012	00
→	2013	7F	2013	80
	2014	02	2014	02

Fig. 7-3 Increment memory.

□ EXAMPLE

Before Execution		After Execution	
Program counter	5780	Program counter	5781
Status register	C2	Status register	C0
Memory 5780	0A	Memory 5780	0A

The overflow bit is cleared. The previously set don't care bits (6 and 7), auxiliary carry, and interrupt mask are not altered.

🔲 8085 REGISTER INSTRUCTIONS

Several instructions are provided in the repertoire to assist in counting and in altering the values of registers or memory. This group of commands is especially useful for incrementing or decrementing a value used as an index.

🔲 Increment Register or Memory

A very straightforward command, the increment instruction increases the count contained in the designated register or memory cell by 1. The register is indicated by means of the standard numerical designator. If a memory cell is to be incremented, the address must have been entered in the HL register pair beforehand, as shown in Fig. 7-3.

Operation Code	Mnemonic
04	INR B
0C	INR C
14	INR D
1C	INR E
24	INR H

Operation Code	Mnemonic
2C	INR L
34	INR M
3C	INR A

Addressing mode — register
Status bits affected — zero, sign, parity, and auxiliary carry bits
Clock periods — 5 (10 for memory reference)
Format

	Bit number	
	7 6 5 4	3 2 1 0
Memory cell m	0 0 r r	r 1 0 0

rrr	Register
000	B
001	C
010	D
011	E
100	H
101	L
110	memory
111	A

□ EXAMPLE

Before Execution		After Execution	
Program counter	4010	Program counter	4011
B register	03	B register	04
Memory 4010	04	Memory 4010	04

To see how the instruction may be combined with others you have studied, consider the task of saving the E register in two memory cells ($10FE_{16}$ and $10FF_{16}$) for later use. The program at the bottom of this page will accomplish the required storage.

Address	Machine Code	Instruction	Comments
0100	21	LXI H, 10FE	Load HL register pair with first address
0101	FE		
0102	10		
0103	73	MOV M, E	Store contents of E in 10FE
0104	2C	INR L	Increment lower half of destination address (new address will be 10FF)
0105	73	MOV M, E	Store contents of E in 10FF

After the address has been established in HL, it would be a simple matter to store the E register in several consecutive memory locations by using the same technique.

80 Increment Register Pair

In the short program above, what changes would be necessary if the addresses to be used for storage ranged from 10FE through 1104? After examination, we conclude that the H register must be increased, as well as the L register, in going from 10FF to 1100. Although we could have carried the operation out using an INR instruction, the increment register-pair command is much more practical. In this case the register pair is treated as a 16-bit quantity. If a carry is produced when the lower 8 bits (contained in the least significant register) are incremented, then the most significant byte is also incremented.

Operation Code	Mnemonic	Register Pair
03	INX B	BC
13	INX D	DE
23	INX H	HL
33	INX SP	Stack pointer

Addressing mode   register
Status bits affected   none
Clock periods   5
Format

```
                        Bit number
                    7 6 5 4   3 2 1 0
Memory cell   m  | 0 0 r r   0 0 1 1 |
```

rr	Register Pair
00	BC
01	DE
10	HL
11	SP

☐ EXAMPLE

Before Execution		After Execution	
Program counter	0250	Program counter	0251
D register	00	D register	01
E register	FF	E register	00
Memory 0250	13	Memory 0250	13

The previous program used with the INR instruction would perform as well if the instruction in cell 0104_{16} were changed to 23_{16}. The only effect is that the HL register pair would be incremented as a 2-byte quantity. The results would be identical.

80 Decrement Register or Memory

This instruction is a direct analog to INR. The two differ only in that this instruction decreases the register or memory value by 1. Two's complement arithmetic is used in the subtraction. As we have seen before, the linked H and L registers provide the address if a memory cell is involved.

Operation Code	Mnemonic
05	DCR B
0D	DCR C
15	DCR D
1D	DCR E
25	DCR H
2D	DCR L
35	DCR M
3D	DCR A

Addressing mode   register
Status bits affected   zero, sign, parity, and auxiliary carry bits
Clock periods   5 (10 for memory reference)
Format

```
                        Bit number
                    7 6 5 4   3 2 1 0
Memory cell   m  | 0 0 r r   r 1 0 1 |
```

rrr	Register
000	B
001	C
010	D
011	E
100	H
101	L
110	memory
111	A

☐ EXAMPLE

Before Execution		After Execution	
Program counter	35D3	Program counter	35D4
H register	20	H register	20
L register	14	L register	14
Memory 2014	00	Memory 2014	FF
35D3	35	35D3	35

The op code indicates that a memory cell is to be decremented. The address from the HL pair is 2014_{16}. By use of 2's complement subtraction, the original contents (00_{16}) are reduced by 1 to FF_{16} (-1).

80 Decrement Register Pair

Another instruction that is closely related to the previous register-pair command is the decrement register pair. This operation decreases the quantity but otherwise works like the INX series of op codes. The register pair is a 16-bit number and is reduced in value by 1. The result is expressed in 2's complement terms.

Operation Code	Mnemonic	Register Pair
0B	DCX B	BC
1B	DCX D	DE
2B	DCX H	HL
3B	DCX SP	Stack pointer

Addressing mode   register
Status bits affected   none
Clock periods   6
Format

Bit number
7 6 5 4   3 2 1 0

Memory cell   m | 0 0 r r   1 0 1 1 |

rr	Register Pair
00	BC
01	DE
10	HL
11	SP

☐ EXAMPLE

Before Execution		After Execution	
Program counter	D100	Program counter	D101
B register	FE	B register	FD
C register	00	C register	FF
Memory D100	0B	Memory D100	0B

The value in the two registers is $FE00_{16}$. Subtracting one produces a difference of $FDFF_{16}$.

80 Complement Accumulator

The 8085 normally employs 2's complement arithmetic, but 1's complement arithmetic may be needed for special purposes. This instruction supplies that capability. Execution of the instruction will cause each bit of the accumulation to reverse its state.

Operation code   2F
Mnemonic   CMA
Addressing mode   none
Status bits affected   none
Clock periods   4

Format

Bit number
7 6 5 4   3 2 1 0

Memory cell   m | 0 0 1 0   1 1 1 1 |

☐ EXAMPLE

Before Execution		After Execution	
Program counter	AA01	After execution	AA02
A register	00	A register	FF
Memory AA01	2F	Memory AA01	2F

The original value of 00_{16} in the accumulator has been changed to its 1's complement equivalent. (In 1's complement, FF_{16} is negative 0.)

80 8085 Register Instructions Review

1. Explain how the register affected in the INR instruction is indicated by the op code. Where is the address found if a memory cell is to be incremented?
2. Why is the INX instruction needed in addition to the INR instruction? When can INR be substituted for INX?
3. If the E register containing $7F_{16}$ is incremented, the value becomes a negative number. Explain this contradiction.
4. Distinguish between the effects that the DCR and the DCX instructions have on the condition of the status flags.
5. Explain how 1's complement numbers can be introduced into the 8085, which normal processes only 2's complements.

68 6800 REGISTER AND MEMORY INSTRUCTIONS

Several instructions are provided in the repertoire to assist in counting and in altering the values of registers or memory. This group of commands is especially useful for incrementing or decrementing a value used as an index.

68 Increment Register or Memory

This command is very straightforward. The increment instruction increases the count contained in the designated register or memory cell by 1. There are instructions to increment the A or B accumulator, stack pointer, index register, or memory. Each form of the instruction is described below.

Operation Code	Mnemonic	Addressing Mode	Clock Periods	Register or Memory
4C	INCA	Inherent	2	A
5C	INCB	Inherent	2	B
6C	INC	Indexed	7	memory
7C	INC	Extended	6	memory
08	INX	Inherent	4	X
31	INS	Inherent	4	SP

Status bits affected   zero and sign bits

INCREMENT A REGISTER

Format   Bit number

                                   7 6 5 4   3 2 1 0

Memory cell   m | 0 1 0 0   1 1 0 0 |

☐ EXAMPLE

Before Execution		After Execution	
Program counter	4010	Program counter	4011
A register	03	A register	04
Status register	C0	Status register	C0
Memory 4010	4C	Memory 4010	4C

INCREMENT B REGISTER

Format   Bit number

                                   7 6 5 4   3 2 1 0

Memory cell   m | 0 1 0 1   1 1 0 0 |

☐ EXAMPLE

Before Execution		After Execution	
Program counter	4010	Program counter	4011
B register	78	B register	79
Status register	C0	Status register	C0
Memory 4010	5C	Memory 4010	5C

INCREMENT MEMORY

Format   indexed addressing
                                Bit number
                          7 6 5 4   3 2 1 0

Memory cell   m | 0 1 1 0   1 1 0 0 |
            m + 1 | Address modifier byte |

Format   extended addressing
                                Bit number
                          7 6 5 4   3 2 1 0

Memory cell   m | 0 1 1 1   1 1 0 0 |
            m + 1 | High-address byte |
            m + 2 | Low-address byte |

☐ EXAMPLE

Before Execution		After Execution	
Program counter	4010	Program counter	4013
Status register	C0	Status register	C4
Memory 4010	7C	Memory 4010	7C
4011	73	4011	73
4012	2C	4012	2C
732C	7F	732C	80

Note that incrementing the memory cell produced a negative number and caused the sign status bit to be set.

INCREMENT X REGISTER

Format   Bit number

                                   7 6 5 4   3 2 1 0

Memory cell   m | 0 0 0 0   1 0 0 0 |

☐ EXAMPLE

Before Execution		After Execution	
Program counter	4010	Program counter	4011
X register	0000	X register	0001
Status register	C0	Status register	C0
Memory 4010	08	Memory 4010	08

INCREMENT SP REGISTER

Format   Bit number

                                   7 6 5 4   3 2 1 0

Memory cell   m | 0 0 1 1   0 0 0 1 |

□ EXAMPLE

Before Execution		After Execution	
Program counter	4010	Program counter	4011
SP register	000F	SP register	0010
Status register	C0	Status register	C0
Memory 4010	31	Memory 4010	31

68 Decrement Register or Memory

The decrement instruction decreases the count contained in the designated register or memory cell by 1. There are instructions to decrement the A or B accumulator, stack pointer, index register, or memory. Each form of the instruction is described below.

Operation Code	Mnemonic	Addressing Mode	Clock Periods	Register or Memory
4A	DECA	Inherent	2	A
5A	DECB	Inherent	2	B
6A	DEC	Indexed	7	memory
7A	DEC	Extended	6	memory
09	DEX	Inherent	4	X
34	DES	Inherent	4	SP

Status bits affected   zero and sign bits

DECREMENT A REGISTER

Format
Bit number

		7 6 5 4	3 2 1 0
Memory cell	m	0 1 0 0	1 0 1 0

□ EXAMPLE

Before Execution		After Execution	
Program counter	4010	Program counter	4011
A register	03	A register	02
Status register	C0	Status register	C0
Memory 4010	4A	Memory 4010	4A

DECREMENT B REGISTER

Format
Bit number

		7 6 5 4	3 2 1 0
Memory cell	m	0 1 0 1	1 0 1 0

□ EXAMPLE

Before Execution		After Execution	
Program counter	4010	Program counter	4011
B register	78	B register	77
Status register	C0	Status register	C0
Memory 4010	5A	Memory 4010	5A

DECREMENT MEMORY

Format   indexed addressing
Bit number

		7 6 5 4	3 2 1 0
Memory cell	m	0 1 1 0	1 0 1 0
	m + 1	Address modifier byte	

Format   extended addressing
Bit number

		7 6 5 4	3 2 1 0
Memory cell	m	0 1 1 1	1 0 1 0
	m + 1	High-address byte	
	m + 2	Low-address byte	

□ EXAMPLE

Before Execution			After Execution		
Program counter		4010	Program counter		4013
Status register		C4	Status register		C0
Memory	4010	7A	Memory	4010	7A
	4011	73		4011	73
	4012	2C		4012	2C
	732C	80		732C	7F

Note that decrementing the memory cell produced a positive number and caused the sign status bit to be cleared.

DECREMENT X REGISTER

Format
Bit number

		7 6 5 4	3 2 1 0
Memory cell	m	0 0 0 0	1 0 0 1

□ EXAMPLE

Before Execution		After Execution	
Program counter	4010	Program counter	4011
X register	0000	X register	FFFF
Status register	C0	Status register	C4
Memory 4010	09	Memory 4010	09

Why does the sign bit become set?

DECREMENT SP REGISTER

Format

```
                          Bit number
                      7 6 5 4   3 2 1 0
Memory cell    m  | 0 0 1 1   0 1 0 0 |
```

□ EXAMPLE

Before Execution		After Execution	
Program counter	4010	Program counter	4011
SP register	000F	SP register	000E
Status register	C0	Status register	C0
Memory 4010	34	Memory 4010	34

68 Complement Register or Memory

The 6800 normally employs 2's complement arithmetic, but 1's complement arithmetic may be needed for special purposes. A set of instructions supplies this capability; execution of one of these instructions will cause each bit of the accumulator to reverse its state. Instructions are also available to the 2's complement, or the negative, of an accumulator or memory cell.

1'S COMPLEMENT

Operation Code	Mnemonic	Addressing Mode	Clock Periods	Register or Memory
43	COMA	Inherent	2	A
53	COMB	Inherent	2	B
63	COM	Indexed	7	memory
73	COM	Extended	6	memory

Status bits affected — zero, sign, overflow, and carry bits always set

COMPLEMENT A REGISTER

Format

```
                          Bit number
                      7 6 5 4   3 2 1 0
Memory cell    m  | 0 1 0 0   0 0 1 1 |
```

□ EXAMPLE

Before Execution		After Execution	
Program counter	AA01	Program counter	AA02
A register	0F	A register	F0
Status register	C0	Status register	C9
Memory AA01	4A	Memory AA01	4A

The sign and carry bits are set as a result.

COMPLEMENT MEMORY

Format — indexed addressing

```
                          Bit number
                      7 6 5 4   3 2 1 0
Memory cell    m      | 0 1 1 0   0 0 1 1 |
               m + 1  | Address modifier byte |
```

Format — extended addressing

```
                          Bit number
                      7 6 5 4   3 2 1 0
Memory cell    m      | 0 1 1 1   0 0 1 1 |
               m + 1  | High-address byte |
               m + 2  | Low-address byte |
```

□ EXAMPLE

Before Execution		After Execution	
Program counter	AA01	Program counter	AA04
Status register	C4	Status register	C1
Memory AA01	73	Memory AA01	73
AA02	9B	AA02	9B
AA03	2C	AA03	2C
9B2C	80	9B2C	7F

The carry bit is set by the instruction and the sign bit it cleared.

2'S COMPLEMENT

Operation Code	Mnemonic	Addressing Mode	Clock Periods	Register or Memory
40	NEGA	Inherent	2	A
50	NEGB	Inherent	2	B
60	NEG	Indexed	7	memory
70	NEG	Extended	6	memory

Status bits affected   zero, sign, overflow, and carry bits

NEGATE B REGISTER

Format

Bit number

		7 6 5 4	3 2 1 0
Memory cell	m	0 1 0 1	0 0 0 0

☐ EXAMPLE

Before Execution		After Execution	
Program counter	AA01	Program counter	AA02
B register	0F	B register	F1
Status register	C0	Status register	C9
Memory AA01	40	Memory AA01	40

The sign bit is set as a result.

NEGATE MEMORY

Format   indexed addressing

Bit number

		7 6 5 4	3 2 1 0
Memory cell	m	0 1 1 0	0 0 0 0
	m +	Address modifier byte	

Format   extended addressing

Bit number

		7 6 5 4	3 2 1 0
Memory cell	m	0 1 1 1	0 0 0 0
	m + 1	High-address byte	
	m + 2	Low-address byte	

☐ EXAMPLE

Before Execution		After Execution	
Program counter	AA01	Program counter	AA04
Status register	C4	Status register	C4

Before Execution		After Execution	
Memory	AA01	70	Memory	AA01	70

Before Execution			After Execution		
Memory	AA01	70	Memory	AA01	70
	AA02	9B		AA02	9B
	AA03	2C		AA03	2C
	9B2C	80		9B2C	80

Remember that the 2's complement of 80_{16} in an 8-bit word is 80_{16}. The sign bit is set by the instruction.

Clear Register or Memory

With these instructions, the contents of either the accumulator or a memory cell can be set to 0. These instructions provide an efficient means of accomplishing this operation.

Operation Code	Mnemonic	Addressing Mode	Clock Periods	Register or Memory
4F	CLRA	Inherent	2	A
5F	CLRB	Inherent	2	B
6F	CLR	Indexed	7	memory
7F	CLR	Extended	6	memory

Status bits affected   sign, overflow, and carry bits reset; zero bit set

CLEAR A REGISTER

Format

Bit number

		7 6 5 4	3 2 1 0
Memory cell	m	0 1 0 0	1 1 1 1

☐ EXAMPLE

Before Execution		After Execution	
Program counter	AA01	Program counter	AA02
A register	3D	A register	00
Status register	C0	Status register	C4
Memory AA01	4F	Memory AA01	4F

The sign, overflow, and carry status bits are reset and the zero status is set.

CLEAR MEMORY

Format   indexed addressing

Bit number

		7 6 5 4	3 2 1 0
Memory cell	m	0 1 1 0	1 1 1 1
	m + 1	Address modifier byte	

Format   extended addressing
                               Bit number
                            7 6 5 4   3 2 1 0

Memory cell   m | 0 1 1 1   1 1 1 1 |
               m + 1 | High-address byte |
               m + 2 | Low-address byte |

☐ EXAMPLE

Before Execution   **After Execution**

Program counter | AA01 | Program counter | AA04 |

Status register | C8 | Status register | C4 |

Memory   AA01 | 7F | Memory   AA01 | 7F |
          AA02 | 9B | AA02 | 9B |
          AA03 | 2C | AA03 | 2C |
          9B2C | 80 | 9B2C | 00 |

Explain why the sign status gets reset and the zero is set.

68 6800 Register and Memory Instructions Review

1. What is the result of executing an instruction to find the 2's complement of 80_{16} contained in a memory cell?
2. If the B register containing $7F_{16}$ is incremented, the value becomes a negative number. Explain this apparent contradiction.
3. Explain the different effects that the NEG and COM have on the status flags.
4. Explain how 1's complement numbers can be introduced into the 6800, which normally processes only 2's complements.

ADDITION

This section and the following one on subtraction introduce arithmetic processing within the microprocessor. The capabilities of the microprocessor to calculate mathematical results depend not only on the basic arithmetic instructions but also on instructions that can sense the outcome of these processes. By combining several instructions into a routine, the processor can handle multibyte arithmetic and even multiply and divide. Some of these routines will be covered in Chaps. 8 and 9. In this chapter the discussion will concentrate on basic functions.

80 8085 Addition

ADD REGISTER OR MEMORY TO ACCUMULATOR
The byte, specified by the register designator, will be added to the present contents of the accumulator

using 2's complement arithmetic. The resulting sum is placed in the accumulator, thus destroying the initial value. If memory is the origin for the byte to be added, the address is established by the HL register pair.

Operation Code	Mnemonic
80	ADD B
81	ADD C
82	ADD D
83	ADD E
84	ADD H
85	ADD L
86	ADD M
87	ADD A

Addressing mode   register
Status bits affected   carry, sign, zero, parity, and
                        auxiliary carry bits
Clock periods   4 (7 for memory reference)
Format   Bit number
                          7 6 5 4   3 2 1 0

Memory cell   m | 1 0 0 0   0 r r r |

rrr	Register
000	B
001	C
010	D
011	E
100	H
101	L
110	memory
111	A

☐ EXAMPLE 1   Add $3E_{16}$ to $7B_{16}$.

Before Execution   **After Execution**

Program counter | 5030 | Program counter | 5031 |

A register | 7B | A register | B9 |

H register | 10 | H register | 10 |

L register | 00 | L register | 00 |

Status register | 02 | Status register | 92 |

Memory   1000 | 3E | Memory   1000 | 3E |
         5030 | 87 | 5030 | 87 |

Binary addition

     No
| 0 | carry | 1 | Carry out of bit 3

$3E_{16}$ = 0 0 1 1   1 1 1 0_2
+ $7B_{16}$ = 0 1 1 1   1 0 1 1_2
$B9_{16}$ = 1 0 1 1   1 0 0 1_2

Several effects of this addition are worth noting. First, the A register value is changed to the resulting sum. The sum is negative and a carry was produced from bit position 3, so the sign and the auxiliary carry bits are set. The result is nonzero with odd parity, and no carry was generated from the MSB, so those respective status bits are reset. By examining the augend and addend, we see that they were both positive (sign bit is 0), but the sum is negative. How could the addition of two positive numbers produce a negative sum? The answer to this puzzle is that the accumulator overflowed. Bit 7 is actually the MSB of the sum, but the computer interprets it as a negative number. All further computer operations on that value will treat it as a 2's complement negative number (-47_{16} in this case). Overflowing an 8-bit register is an easy mistake to make; the only way to prevent it is to be sure that the range of numbers to be added will not cause overflow. If larger numbers must be added, multibyte addition (also called *double precision addition*) will be needed.

□ EXAMPLE 2   Double the accumulator.

Before Execution		After Execution	
Program counter	20B0	Program counter	20B1
A register	04	A register	08
Status register	02	Status register	02
Memory 20B0	87	Memory 20B0	87

By use of the ADD A (op code 87_{16}) instruction, the contents of the accumulator can be doubled. In this case, the final conditions of the status flags are the same as the initial ones because there was no change in sign, zero status, or carry, and the parity of both the initial and the final values is odd.

ADD IMMEDIATE
The immediate data byte is added to the accumulator, and then the sum is placed in the accumulator. Other than the fact that the instruction uses immediate data, the 2's complement addition carried out by an add immediate is the same as that of the add instruction.

Operation code   C6
Mnemonic   ADI
Addressing mode   immediate
Status bits affected carry, sign, zero, parity, and
                      auxiliary carry bits
Clock periods   7
Format

		Bit number	
		7 6 5 4 3 2 1 0	
Memory cell	m	1 1 0 0 0 1 1 0	
	m + 1	Immediate data byte	

□ EXAMPLE

Before Execution		After Execution	
Program counter	0730	Program counter	0732
A register	D2	A register	8E
Status register	87	Status register	87
Memory 0730	C6	Memory 0730	C6
0731	BC	0731	BC

Binary addition

$\boxed{1}$ Carry $\boxed{0}$ No carry

$$
\begin{array}{rl}
D2_{16} = & 1101\ 0010_2 \\
+\ BC_{16} = & 1011\ 1100_2 \\
\hline
\boxed{1}8E_{16} = & 1000\ 1110_2
\end{array}
$$

Although there was a carry out of the MSB, no overflow occurred in this problem. The sum is negative (as expected from adding two negative numbers). By converting to the 2's complement, we can verify that the final A register value is correct.

$$
\begin{array}{rl}
D2_{16} = & -\ 2E_{16} \\
BC_{16} = & -\ 44_{16} \\
\hline
& -\ 72_{16} = 8E_{16}
\end{array}
$$

Remember that a carry out in the case of subtraction (or addition of a negative number) means that no borrow was needed from the high-order bit. In this problem the carry status will be set because an add instruction is used. (Compare this result with that of the subtraction instruction.) The sign status and parity bits remain set. No carry was produced from bit 3, so the auxiliary carry status is 0.

ADD REGISTER OR MEMORY TO ACCUMULATOR WITH CARRY
This instruction differs from a normal add in that the value of the carry status bit is added to the sum. The addition uses 2's complement arithmetic. If referenced, the memory address must be placed in the HL pair prior to executing the instruction.

Operation Code	Mnemonic
88	ADC B
89	ADC C
8A	ADC D
8B	ADC E
8C	ADC H
8D	ADC L
8E	ADC M
8F	ADC A

Addressing mode   register

Status bits affected	carry, sign, zero, parity, and auxiliary carry bits
Clock periods	4 (7 for memory reference)
Format	Bit number

		7 6 5 4	3 2 1 0
Memory cell	m	1 0 0 0	0 r r r

rrr	Register
000	B
001	C
010	D
011	E
100	H
101	L
110	memory
111	A

☐ **EXAMPLE**

Before Execution		After Execution	
Program counter	1150	Program counter	1151
A register	17	A register	50
B register	38	B register	38
Status register	07	Status register	12
Memory 1150	88	Memory 1150	88

Binary addition

$$17_{16} = 0001 \quad 0111_2$$
$$+\ 38_{16} = 0011 \quad 1000_2$$
$$\overline{4F = 0100 \quad 1111_2}$$

$$\boxed{0}\ \text{No carry} \qquad \boxed{1}\ \text{Carry}$$

	4F	0100 1111$_2$
Carry status	+ 1	+ 1
	50$_{16}$	0101 0000$_2$

The original carry bit was set, so 1 is added to the sum of the A and B register contents, and the final addition causes a carry from bit 3, so the auxiliary carry is set.

ADD IMMEDIATE WITH CARRY This instruction is a simple extension of the add immediate instruction. The carry status existing prior to execution is added to the sum of the accumulator and the immediate data in computing the result.

Operation code	CE
Mnemonic	ACI
Addressing mode	immediate

Status bits affected	carry, sign, zero, parity, and auxiliary carry bits
Clock periods	7
Format	Bit number

		7 6 5 4	3 2 1 0
Memory cell	m	1 1 0 0	1 1 1 0
	m + 1	Immediate data byte	

☐ **EXAMPLE**

Before Execution		After Execution	
Program counter	0910	Program counter	0912
A register	0D	A register	00
Status register	03	Status register	57
Memory 0910	CE	Memory 0910	CE
0911	F2	0911	F2

Binary addition

$$0D_{16} \quad 0000 \quad 1101_2$$
$$+\ F2_{16} \quad 1111 \quad 0010_2$$

$$\boxed{1}\ \text{Carry} \quad \boxed{1}\ \text{Carry}$$

	FF$_{16}$	1111	1111$_2$
Carry status	+ 1		+ 1
	$\boxed{1}$00$_{16}$	0000	0000$_2$

The 0 sum sets the zero and even-parity flags. As a result of carries from bits 3 and 7, both carry status bits are set as well.

DOUBLE ADD The double byte in a register pair on the stack pointer can be added to the contents of the HL register pair by using the double-add instruction. The addition is done in 2's complement form, and the final sum is placed in the HL pair.

Operation Code	Mnemonic	Register Pair
09	DAD B	BC
19	DAD D	DE
29	DAD H	HL
39	DAD SP	SP

Addressing mode	register
Status bits affected	carry bit
Clock periods	10
Format	Bit number

		7 6 5 4	3 2 1
Memory cell	m	0 0 r r	1 0 0 1

rr	Register Pair
00	BC
01	DE
10	HL
11	SP

□ EXAMPLE

Before Execution		After Execution	
Program counter	0778	Program counter	0779
B register	3F	B register	3F
C register	BA	C register	BA
H register	02	H register	42
L register	46	L register	00
Status register	17	Status register	16
Memory 0778	09	Memory 0778	09

Binary addition

$$\boxed{0} \text{ No carry}$$

$$
\begin{array}{rl}
3FBA_{16} = & 0011\ \ 1111\ \ 1011\ \ 1010_2 \\
+\ 0246_{16} = & +0000\ \ 0010\ \ 0100\ \ 0110_2 \\
\hline
4200_{16} = & 0100\ \ 0010\ \ 0000\ \ 0000_2
\end{array}
$$

The double-byte sum is stored in the HL register pair. The carry bit is reset because there was no carry from the MSB. Other status bits are unchanged. The double-add instruction op code 29_{16} doubles the value in the HL register.

68 6800 Addition

ADD REGISTER OR MEMORY TO ACCUMULATOR

A byte in memory can be added to the present contents of the designated accumulator using 2's complement arithmetic. The resulting sum is placed in the accumulator. Alternatively, the A and B accumulators can be added together. The sum replaces the initial value of the A register.

Mnemonic	Addressing Mode	Operation Code	Machine Cycles
ADDA	Immediate	8B	2
	Direct	9B	3
	Indexed	AB	5
	Extended	BB	4
ADDB	Immediate	CB	2
	Direct	DB	3
	Indexed	EB	5
	Extended	FB	4
ABA	Inherent	1B	2

Status bits affected	auxiliary carry, sign, zero, overflow, and carry bits
Format	standard for addressing mode

□ EXAMPLE 1   Add memory to accumulator A.

Before Execution		After Execution	
Program counter	5030	Program counter	5033
A register	7A	A register	15
Status register	C0	Status register	E3
Memory 5030	BB	Memory 5030	BB
5031	C0	5031	C0
5032	00	5032	00
C000	9B	C000	9B

The addition is performed as follows:

$$
\begin{array}{rl}
7A_{16} = & 0111\ \ 1010_2 \\
+\ 9B_{16} = & 1001\ \ 1011_2 \\
\hline
115_{16} = 1 & 0001\ \ 0101_2
\end{array}
$$

The sum is 115_{16}, which overflows the register. The overflow flag is set. There are also carries from bits 3 and 7, causing both carry bits to be set.

□ EXAMPLE 2   Add accumulators.

Before Execution		After Execution	
Program counter	1073	Program counter	1074
A register	9C	A register	76
B register	DB	B register	DB
Status register	C8	Status register	E1
Memory 1073	1B	Memory 1073	1B

This addition involves negative numbers (the sign bits for both are set).

$$
\begin{array}{rl}
9C_{16} = & 1001\ \ 1100_2 \\
+\ DB_{16} = & 1101\ \ 1011_2 \\
\hline
77_{16} = & 0111\ \ 0111_2
\end{array}
$$

Here, too, there were carries from bits 3 and 7.

ADD REGISTER OR MEMORY TO ACCUMULATOR WITH CARRY

These instructions differ from a normal add in that the value of the carry status bit is added to the sum. The addition uses 2's complement arithmetic.

Mnemonic	Addressing Mode	Operation Code	Machine Cycles
ADCA	Immediate	89	2
	Direct	99	3

Mnemonic	Addressing Mode	Operation Code	Machine Cycles
	Indexed	A9	5
	Extended	B9	4
ADCB	Immediate	C9	2
	Direct	D9	3
	Indexed	E9	5
	Extended	F9	4

Status bits affected   auxiliary carry, sign, zero, overflow, and carry bits

Format   standard for addressing mode

□ **EXAMPLE**   Add memory to accumulator B with carry.

Before Execution		After Execution	
Program counter	1150	Program counter	1152
A register	17	A register	50
Status register	C1	Status register	E0
Memory 1150	C9	Memory 1150	C9
1151	38	1151	38

The number to be added is in the immediate data byte.

$$17_{16} = 0001\ 0111_2$$
$$+\ 38_{16} = 0011\ 1000_2$$
$$\overline{4F_{16} = 0100\ 1111_2}$$

Now we add the carry status that was present prior to the instruction execution:

$$4F_{16}$$
$$+\ 1 \quad \text{carry status}$$
$$\overline{50_{16}}$$

When the carry status was added, it caused a carry from bit 3, which is reflected in the final carry status.

Addition Review

1. Using any above example of the add instruction, explain the reason for the final value of each bit in the status register.
2. Distinguish between the add and add-with-carry operations.
3. How was the overflow in the ADD instruction detected?
4. Explain the significance of the carry bit being set in addition.

SUBTRACTION

The subtraction instructions have a one-to-one correspondence with the addition instructions just discussed. That is, subtraction operands can be in registers, memory cells, or immediate data bytes. There is, however,

no double-register subtraction instruction. A subtle difference between addition and subtraction to watch for is the setting of the carry bit. The examples in this section will provide more insight into the meaning of that status flag.

▓ 8085 Subtraction

SUBTRACT REGISTER OR MEMORY FROM ACCUMULATOR
This instruction subtracts the designated byte from the A register using 2's complement arithmetic. The difference is placed in the accumulator. If the memory cell contents are the operand, the address must be put into the HL register pair.

Operation Code	Mnemonic
90	SUB B
91	SUB C
92	SUB D
93	SUB E
94	SUB H
95	SUB L
96	SUB M
97	SUB A

Addressing mode   register

Status bits affected   carry, sign, zero, parity, and auxiliary carry bits

Clock periods   4 (7 for memory reference)

Format

	Bit number
	7 6 5 4 3 2 1 0
Memory cell m	1 0 0 1 0 r r r

rrr	Register
000	B
001	C
010	D
011	E
100	H
101	L
110	memory
111	A

□ **EXAMPLE**   Clear the accumulator and reset the carry bit.

Before Execution		After Execution	
Program counter	6700	Program counter	6701
A register	7B	A register	00
Status register	06	Status register	56
Memory 6700	97	Memory 6700	97

In this example we are subtracting the accumulator from itself.

Binary subtraction

$$
\begin{array}{r}
\boxed{1}\ \text{Carry} \quad \boxed{1}\ \text{Carry} \\
7B_{16} = \quad 0\ 1\ 1\ 1 \quad 1\ 0\ 1\ 1_2 \\
-\ 7B_{16} = +\ 1\ 0\ 0\ 0 \quad 0\ 1\ 0\ 1_2 \quad \text{(2's complement} \\
\hline
00_{16} = \quad 0\ 0\ 0\ 0 \quad 0\ 0\ 0\ 0_2 \quad \text{is added)}
\end{array}
$$

Because the rules for subtraction are used, the carry from bit 7 will reset the carry status bit. Because of the carry from bit 3, the auxiliary carry bit is set. The parity and zero bits will also be set. Thus the subtract accumulator instruction will zero that register and the carry status bit.

SUBTRACT IMMEDIATE FROM ACCUMULATOR

Using the accumulator value as the minuend and the immediate data as the subtrahend, a 2's complement difference is generated and sent to the accumulator. The example for this instruction uses the same values as the add immediate in the previous section, "Addition." The treatment of the carry bit for the two operations is compared below.

Operation code	D6
Mnemonic	SUI
Addressing mode	immediate
Status bits affected	carry, sign, zero, parity, and auxiliary carry bits
Clock periods	7
Format	

Bit number

		7 6 5 4	3 2 1 0
Memory cell	m	1 1 0 1	0 1 1 0
	m + 1	Immediate data byte	

☐ EXAMPLE

Before Execution		After Execution	
Program counter	0730	Program counter	0732
A register	D2	A register	8E

Before Execution		After Execution	
Status register	87	Status register	82
Memory	0730 D6	Memory	0730 D6
	0731 44		0731 44

The immediate data is 44_{16}.

Binary subtraction

$$
\begin{array}{r}
\boxed{1}\ \text{Carry} \quad \boxed{0}\ \text{No carry} \\
D2_{16} = \quad 1\ 1\ 0\ 1 \quad 0\ 0\ 1\ 0_2 \\
-\ 44_{16} = +\ 1\ 0\ 1\ 1 \quad 1\ 1\ 0\ 0_2 \quad \text{(2's complement} \\
\hline
8E_{16} = \quad 1\ 0\ 0\ 0 \quad 1\ 1\ 1\ 0_2 \quad \text{is added)}
\end{array}
$$

The difference is identical to that of the former example. Although the carry from bit 7 took place in both cases, this time the carry status is reset. Table 7-1 summarizes the way in which the carry status and the auxiliary carry status are used in addition and subtraction.

SUBTRACT REGISTER OR MEMORY FROM ACCUMULATOR WITH BORROW
The primary purpose for this instruction is multibyte subtraction, which is explained in Chap. 8. Here we will show the single-byte use of the instruction. The subtract-with-borrow instruction first adds the carry status bit value to the contents of the appropriate memory cell or register. Then that sum is subtracted from the accumulator. The results are put into the A register. Two's complement arithmetic is used. As usual with memory operands, the memory address corresponds to the HL register value.

Operation Code	Mnemonic
98	SBB B
99	SBB C
9A	SBB D
9B	SBB E
9C	SBB H
9D	SBB L
9E	SBB M
9F	SBB A

Table 7-1 Carry Status Bits

Operation	Carry		Auxiliary Carry	
	Condition	Meaning	Condition	Meaning
Addition	Set	Carry from MSB	Set	Carry from bit 3
	Reset	No carry from MSB	Reset	No carry from bit 3
Subtraction	Set	Borrow to MSB	Set	Same as for addition
	Reset	No borrow to MSB	Reset	Same as for addition

Addressing mode register
Status bits affected carry, sign, zero, parity, and
        auxiliary carry bits
Clock periods   4 (7 for memory reference)
Format

Bit number

7 6 5 4 3 2 1 0

Memory cell m | 1 0 0 1 1 r r r |

rrr	Register
000	B
001	C
010	D
011	E
100	H
101	L
110	memory
111	A

□ EXAMPLE

Before Execution   **After Execution**

Before Execution		After Execution	
Program counter	1805	Program counter	1806
A register	2C	A register	FC
C register	30	C register	30
Status register	02	Status register	87
Memory 1805	99	Memory 1805	99

STEPS IN EXECUTION

STEP 1. Adding the carry status to the subtrahend.

C register 30_{16}
Carry $+\ 0_{16}$
      30_{16}

STEP 2. Binary subtraction.

   No   No
  | 0 | carry | 0 | carry

$2C_{16} =$ 0 0 1 0   1 1 0 0_2
$-\ 30_{16} =$ $+$ 1 1 0 1   0 0 0 0   (2's complement
$-\ 4_{16} =$ 1 1 1 1   1 1 0 $0_2 = FC_{16}$ is added)

The 2's complement of the binary difference (1111 $1100_2 = FC_{16}$) is -4_{16}; thus the result is correct. There was no carry from the MSB, so the carry status bit will be set. The sign and parity bits will be set as well.

SUBTRACT IMMEDIATE WITH BORROW The immediate data byte is added to the carry status bit. That result is subtracted from the accumulator, and the difference replaces the initial accumulator quantity.

Operation code   DE
Mnemonic   SBI
Addressing mode immediate
Status bits affected carry, zero, parity, and auxiliary
        carry bits
Clock periods   7
Format

Bit number

7 6 5 4 3 2 1 0

Memory cell m | 1 1 0 1 1 1 1 0 |
      m + 1 | Immediate data byte |

□ EXAMPLE

Before Execution		After Execution	
Program counter	1220	Program counter	1222
A register	20	A register	11
Status register	03	Status register	06
Memory 1220	DE	Memory 1220	DE
1221	0E	1221	0E

STEPS IN EXECUTION

STEP 1. Adding the carry status to the subtrahend.

Immediate data $0E_{16}$
Carry status $+\ 1$
       $0F_{16}$

STEP 2. Binary subtraction.

  | 1 | Carry | 0 | No carry

$20_{16} =$ 0 0 1 0   0 0 0 0_2 (2's complement is
$-\ 0F_{16} =$ $+$ 1 1 1 1   0 0 0 1_2 added)
$11_{16} =$ 0 0 0 1   0 0 0 1_2

The 2's complement addition is straightforward. The carry status will be reset. Parity is even.

68 6800 Subtraction

SUBTRACT REGISTER OR MEMORY FROM ACCUMULATOR A byte in memory can be subtracted from the present contents of the designated accumulator using 2's complement arithmetic. The resulting difference is placed in the accumulator. Alternatively, the B accumulator can be subtracted from the A accumulator. The difference replaces the initial value of the A register.

Mnemonic	Addressing Mode	Operation Code	Machine Cycles
SUBA	Immediate	80	2
	Direct	90	3
	Indexed	A0	5
	Extended	B0	4
SUBB	Immediate	C0	2
	Direct	D0	3
	Indexed	E0	5
	Extended	F0	4
SBA	Inherent	10	2

Status bits affected   sign, zero, overflow, and carry bits

Format   standard for addressing mode

☐ **EXAMPLE 1**   Subtract memory from accumulator A.

Before Execution		After Execution	
Program counter	5030	Program counter	5033
A register	7A	A register	15
Status register	C0	Status register	C9
Memory	5030 B0	Memory	5030 B0
	5031 C0		5031 C0
	5032 00		5032 00
	C000 9B		C000 9B

The addition is performed as follows:

$$\begin{array}{r} 7A_{16} = 0\,1\,1\,1\ \ 1\,0\,1\,0_2 \\ -\ 9B_{16} = 1\,0\,0\,1\ \ 1\,0\,1\,1_2 \\ \hline DF_{16} = 1\,1\,0\,1\ \ 1\,1\,1\,1_2 \end{array}$$

The difference is DF_{16}. The sign bit is set, and the carry bit is set because a borrow occurred.

☐ **EXAMPLE 2**   Subtract accumulator B from accumulator A.

Before Execution		After Execution	
Program counter	1073	Program counter	1074
A register	9C	A register	76
B register	DB	B register	DB
Status register	C8	Status register	C8
Memory	1073 10	Memory	1073 10

This subtraction involves negative numbers (the sign bits for both are set).

$$\begin{array}{r} 9C_{16} = 1\,0\,0\,1\ \ 1\,1\,0\,0_2 \\ -\ DB_{16} = 1\,1\,0\,1\ \ 1\,0\,1\,1_2 \\ \hline C1_{16} = 1\,1\,0\,0\ \ 0\,0\,0\,1_2 \end{array}$$

Here, too, the sign bit is set in the status register.

SUBTRACT REGISTER OR MEMORY FROM ACCUMULATOR WITH BORROW

These instructions differ from a normal subtraction in that the value of the carry (borrow) status bit is subtracted from the difference. The subtraction uses 2's complement arithmetic. The auxiliary carry bit is not affected by subtraction. The meaning of the carry bit in addition and subtraction is summarized in Table 7-2.

Mnemonic	Addressing Mode	Operation Code	Machine Cycles
SBCA	Immediate	82	2
	Direct	92	3
	Indexed	A2	5
	Extended	B2	4
SBCB	Immediate	C2	2
	Direct	D2	3
	Indexed	E2	5
	Extended	F2	4

Status bits affected   sign, zero, overflow, and carry bits

Format   standard for addressing mode

☐ **EXAMPLE**   Subtract memory from accumulator B with carry.

Before Execution		After Execution	
Program counter	1150	Program counter	1152
A register	17	A register	50
Status register	C1	Status register	C8
Memory	1150 C2	Memory	1150 C2
	1151 38		1151 38

The number to be subtracted is in the immediate data byte.

$$\begin{array}{r} 17_{16} = 0\,0\,0\,1\ \ 0\,1\,1\,1_2 \\ -\ 38_{16} = 0\,0\,1\,1\ \ 1\,0\,0\,0_2 \\ \hline DF_{16} = 1\,1\,0\,1\ \ 1\,1\,1\,1_2 \end{array}$$

Table 7-2   Carry Status Bit

Operation	Condition	Meaning
Addition	Set	Carry from MSB
	Clear	No carry from MSB
Subtraction	Set	Borrow from MSB
	Clear	No borrow from MSB

Now we subtract the carry status that was present prior to the instruction execution:

$$\begin{array}{r} DF_{16} \\ -\ 1 \quad \text{carry status} \\ \hline DE_{16} \end{array}$$

The difference is negative, thus setting the sign bit.

Subtraction Review

1. Explain how to clear the carry status flag and the accumulator using a single instruction.
2. Compare the way in which the carry bit is set or cleared in subtraction with the handling of that bit in addition.
3. What effect does the group of subtraction instructions have on the auxiliary carry?

BOOLEAN OPERATIONS

The MPU can perform logical AND, OR, and exclusive OR operations. You are probably well acquainted with these functions from your experience with combinatorial circuits. Tables 7-3 through 7-5 give the boolean truth tables for these operators. In these operations, the logical combination of the two 8-bit inputs is done on a bit-by-bit basis. The example in Fig. 7-4 shows how.

A frequently used capability provided by logical instructions is the *masking* of certain bits in a word. By using a suitable mask together with the proper instruction, a single bit can be read, set, cleared, or complemented. (The use of this masking capability in boolean instructions will be discussed beginning on page 144 of this section.)

Table 7-3 AND Truth Table

Input Bits		
A	B	Result
0	0	0
0	1	0
1	0	0
1	1	1

Table 7-4 OR Truth Table

Input Bits		
A	B	Result
0	0	0
0	1	1
1	0	1
1	1	1

Table 7-5 Exclusive OR Truth Table

Input Bits		
A	B	Result
0	0	0
0	1	1
1	0	1
1	1	0

BYTE X	x_7	x_6	x_5	x_4	x_3	x_2	x_1	x_0
BYTE Y	y_7	y_6	y_5	y_4	y_3	y_2	y_1	y_0
RESULT	r_7	r_6	r_5	r_4	r_3	r_2	r_1	r_0

WHERE
$r_0 = x_0 \text{ AND } y_0$ $r_4 = x_4 \text{ AND } y_4$
$r_1 = x_1 \text{ AND } y_1$ $r_5 = x_5 \text{ AND } y_5$
$r_2 = x_2 \text{ AND } y_2$ $r_6 = x_6 \text{ AND } y_6$
$r_3 = x_3 \text{ AND } y_3$ $r_7 = x_7 \text{ AND } y_7$

Fig. 7-4 Bit-by-bit AND example.

80 8085 Boolean Operations

AND REGISTER OR MEMORY WITH ACCUMULATOR The specified byte from the register or memory cell is bit-by-bit ANDed with the accumulator. The carry bit is always reset. The result will replace the original A register contents. The HL register pair represents the memory cell address if the operand is located in memory.

Operation Code	Mnemonic
A0	ANA B
A1	ANA C
A2	ANA D
A3	ANA E
A4	ANA H
A5	ANA L
A6	ANA M
A7	ANA A

Addressing mode   register
Status bits affected   carry, zero, sign, and parity bits
Clock periods   4 (7 for memory reference)
Format

Bit number
7 6 5 4   3 2 1 0

Memory cell   m | 1 0 1 0 | 0 r r r |

rrr	Register
000	B
001	C
010	D
011	E
100	H
101	L
110	memory
111	A

☐ EXAMPLE

Before Execution		After Execution	
Program counter	2AE0	Program counter	2AE1
A register	B7	A register	25
L register	65	L register	65
Status register	97	Status register	12
Memory 2AE0	A5	Memory 2AE0	A5

Binary AND

$$B7_{16} = 1011\ 0111_2$$
$$65_{16} = 0110\ 0101_2$$
$$25_{16} = 0010\ 0101_2$$

The sign of the result is positive and the parity is odd, so those condition bits are reset. The auxiliary carry, which was set prior to execution, remains unchanged.

AND IMMEDIATE   This instruction is directly analogous to the previous one, except that the operand is immediate data. The carry bit is always reset at the completion of the operation.

Operation code	E6
Mnemonic	ANI
Addressing mode	immediate
Status bits affected	carry, zero, sign, and parity bits
Clock periods	7
Format	

Bit number

		7 6 5 4	3 2 1 0
Memory cell	m	1 1 1 0	0 1 1 0
	m + 1	Immediate data byte	

□ **EXAMPLE**

Before Execution		After Execution	
Program counter	0672	Program counter	0674
A register	6D	A register	01
Status register	02	Status register	02
Memory 0672	E6	Memory 0672	E6
0673	81	0673	81

Binary AND

$$6D_{16} = 0110\ 1101_2$$
$$81_{16} = 1000\ 0001_2$$
$$01_{16} = 0000\ 0001_2$$

OR REGISTER OR MEMORY WITH ACCUMULATOR   The selected byte will be ORed with the accumulator and the results placed in the latter register. Memory cell addresing is accomplished by means of the HL pair. The carry status is always reset.

Operation Code	Mnemonic
B0	ORA B
B1	ORA C
B2	ORA D
B3	ORA E
B4	ORA H
B5	ORA L
B6	ORA M
B7	ORA A

Addressing mode	register
Status bits affected	carry, zero, sign, and parity bits
Clock periods	4 (7 for memory reference)
Format	

Bit number

		7 6 5 4	3 2 1 0
Memory cell	m	1 0 1 1	0 r r r

rrr	Register
000	B
001	C
010	D
011	E
100	H
101	L
110	memory
111	A

□ **EXAMPLE**

Before Execution		After Execution	
Program counter	01A0	Program counter	01A1
A register	E3	A register	F3
H register	32	H register	32
Status register	87	Status register	82
Memory 01A0	B4	Memory 01A0	B4

Binary OR

$$E3_{16} = 1110\ 0011_2$$
$$32_{16} = 0011\ 0010_2$$
$$F3_{16} = 1111\ 0011_2$$

The carry, parity, and zero bits are reset to 0. The sign bit remains set.

OR IMMEDIATE   The immediate byte is ORed with the accumulator. The carry status is always reset.

Operation code	F6
Mnemonic	ORI
Addressing mode	immediate
Status bits affected	carry, zero, sign, and parity bits
Clock periods	7
Format	

Bit number

		7 6 5 4	3 2 1 0
Memory cell	m	1 1 1 1	0 1 1 0
	m + 1	Immediate data byte	

□ EXAMPLE

Before Execution		After Execution	
Program counter	0336	Program counter	0338
A register	00	A register	58
Status register	46	Status register	02
Memory 0336	F6	Memory 0336	F6
0337	58	0337	58

Binary OR

$$
\begin{aligned}
00_{16} &= 0000\ \ 0000_2 \\
\underline{58_{16}} &= \underline{0101\ \ 1000_2} \\
58_{16} &= 0101\ \ 1000_2
\end{aligned}
$$

EXCLUSIVE OR REGISTER OR MEMORY WITH ACCUMULATOR

An 8-bit quantity obtained from a register or a memory location is exclusive ORed with the accumulator. The accumulator holds the final result. If a memory cell is to be referenced, the address must be in HL. The carry bit will be reset. The exclusive OR can be used to zero the accumulator, to set the accumulator to the 1's complement of any register or memory cell, and to test for a change in the value of any memory location. Examples of these applications are given below.

Operation Code	Mnemonic
A8	XRA B
A9	XRA C
AA	XRA D
AB	XRA E
AC	XRA H
AD	XRA L
AE	XRA M
AF	XRA A

Addressing mode	register
Status bits affected	carry, zero, sign, and parity bits
Clock periods	4 (7 for memory reference)
Format	

Bit number

		7 6 5 4	3 2 1 0
Memory cell	m	1 0 1 0	1 r r r

rrr	Register
000	B
001	C
010	D
011	E
100	H
101	L
110	memory
111	A

□ EXAMPLE 1 Zero the accumulator.

Before Execution		After Execution	
Program counter	0200	Program counter	0201
A register	FF	A register	00
Status register	86	Status register	46
Memory 0200	AF	Memory 0200	AF

Binary Exclusive OR

$$
\begin{aligned}
FF_{16} &= 1111\ \ 1111_2 \\
\underline{FF_{16}} &= \underline{1111\ \ 1111_2} \\
00_{16} &= 0000\ \ 0000_2
\end{aligned}
$$

The carry status bit is also reset as a result of this instruction.

□ EXAMPLE 2 Obtain the 1's complement of a memory cell.

Before Execution		After Execution	
Program counter	0200	Program counter	0201
A register	FF	A register	4C
H register	05	H register	05
L register	00	L register	00
Status register	86	Status register	02
Memory 0200	AF	Memory 0200	AF
0500	B3	0500	B3

Binary exclusive OR

$$
\begin{aligned}
FF_{16} &= 1111\ \ 1111_2 \\
\underline{B3_{16}} &= \underline{1011\ \ 0011_2} \\
4C_{16} &= 0100\ \ 1100_2
\end{aligned}
$$

The 1's complement of $B3_{16}$ is $4C_{16}$. The A register contains that value.

□ EXAMPLE 3 Test for a change in value.

Assume that the initial value of a variable was stored in memory cell 0100_{16} and that the present value is in the accumulator.

Before Execution		After Execution	
Program counter	0200	Program counter	0201
A register	47	A register	11
H register	01	H register	01
L register	00	L register	00
Status register	06	Status register	06
Memory 0100	56	Memory 0100	56
0200	AE	0200	AE

Binary exclusive OR

New value	47_{16} =	0 1 0 0 0 1 1 1$_2$
Original value	56_{16} =	0 1 0 1 0 1 1 0$_2$
	11_{16} =	0 0 0 1 0 0 0 1$_2$

$$\uparrow \qquad\qquad \uparrow$$

Bit positions that
changed in value

Two bits have changed in the variable. Bit 0 has gone from a 0 to a 1, and bit 4 has gone from a 1 to a 0. The 2-bit positions that have been altered are indicated by 1s in the result.

EXCLUSIVE OR IMMEDIATE This instruction produces the exclusive OR of the immediate data byte and the accumulator; the result resides in the accumulator. The carry bit is always reset.

Operation code	EE
Mnemonic	XRI
Addressing mode	immediate
Status bits affected	carry, zero, sign, and parity bits
Clock periods	7
Format	

Bit number

7 6 5 4	3 2 1 0

Memory cell	m	1 1 1 0 1 1 1 0
	m + 1	Immediate data byte

□ EXAMPLE

Before Execution		After Execution	
Program counter	00A3	Program counter	00A5
A register	00	A register	C2
Status register	46	Status register	02
Memory 00A3	EE	Memory 00A3	EE
00A4	C2	00A4	C2

Binary exclusive OR

00_{16} =	0 0 0 0 0 0 0 0$_2$
$C2_{16}$ =	1 1 0 0 0 0 1 0$_2$
$C2_{16}$ =	1 1 0 0 0 0 1 0$_2$

68 6800 Boolean Operations

AND MEMORY WITH ACCUMULATOR The specified byte from a memory cell is bit-by-bit ANDed with the A or B register. The overflow bit is always reset. The sign and zero bits are also affected. The result will replace the original register contents.

Mnemonic	Addressing Mode	Operation Code	Machine Cycles
ANDA	Immediate	84	2
	Direct	94	3
	Indexed	A4	5
	Extended	B4	4
ANDB	Immediate	C4	2
	Direct	D4	3
	Indexed	E4	5
	Extended	F4	4

Status bits affected	sign, zero, and overflow bits
Format	standard for addressing mode

Figure 7-4 shows an example of bit-by-bit ANDing.

□ EXAMPLE

Before Execution		After Execution	
Program counter	2AE0	Program counter	2AE2
A register	B7	A register	25
Status register	C1	Status register	C0
Memory 2AE0	84	Memory 2AE0	84
2AE1	65	2AE1	65

Binary AND

$B7_{16}$ =	1 0 1 1 0 1 1 1$_2$
65_{16} =	0 1 1 0 0 1 0 1$_2$
25_{16} =	0 0 1 0 0 1 0 1$_2$

The sign of the result is positive, so the sign and zero status bits are reset. The overflow bit is always reset.

BIT TEST These instructions AND the contents of the A or B register with the selected memory cell and to set the status flags accordingly. Neither the contents of the register nor the memory byte are altered by these instructions. The overflow bit is always reset.

Mnemonic	Addressing Mode	Operation Code	Machine Cycles
BITA	Immediate	85	2
	Direct	95	3
	Indexed	A5	5
	Extended	B5	4
BITB	Immediate	C5	2
	Direct	D5	3
	Indexed	E5	5
	Extended	F5	4

Status bits affected	sign, zero, and overflow bits
Format	standard for addressing mode

□ EXAMPLE

Before Execution			After Execution		
Program counter		2AE0	Program counter		2AE3
B register		F0	B register		F0
Status register		C1	Status register		C0
Memory	2AE0	F5	Memory	2AE0	F5
	2AE1	78		2AE1	78
	2AE2	54		2AE2	54
	7854	91		7854	91

Binary AND

$$F0_{16} = 1111\ 0000_2$$
$$91_{16} = 1001\ 0001_2$$
$$90_{16} = 1001\ 0000_2$$

The sign of the result is negative, so the sign bit is set and the zero status bit is reset. The overflow bit is always reset.

OR ACCUMULATOR WITH MEMORY
The selected byte will be ORed with the A or B accumulator, and the result will be placed in the register. The overflow status is always reset.

Mnemonic	Addressing Mode	Operation Code	Machine Cycles
ORAA	Immediate	8A	2
	Direct	9A	3
	Indexed	AA	5
	Extended	BA	4
ORAB	Immediate	CA	2
	Direct	DA	3
	Indexed	EA	5
	Extended	FA	4

Status bits affected — sign, zero, and overflow bits
Format — standard for addressing mode

□ EXAMPLE

Before Execution			After Execution		
Program counter		10E0	Program counter		10E2
A register		F0	A register		F0
Status register		C1	Status register		C8
Memory	10E0	8A	Memory	10E0	8A
	10E1	73		10E1	73

Binary OR

$$F0_{16} = 1111\ 0000_2$$
$$73_{16} = 0111\ 0011_2$$
$$F3_{16} = 1111\ 0011_2$$

The sign of the result is negative, so the sign bit is set and the zero status bit is reset. The overflow bit is always reset.

EXCLUSIVE OR MEMORY WITH ACCUMULATOR
This instruction performs an exclusive OR of memory with the A or B accumulator, and the result will be placed in the register. The overflow status is always reset.

Mnemonic	Addressing Mode	Operation Code	Machine Cycles
EORA	Immediate	88	2
	Direct	98	3
	Indexed	A8	5
	Extended	B8	4
EORB	Immediate	C8	2
	Direct	D8	3
	Indexed	E8	5
	Extended	F8	4

Status bits affected — sign, zero, and overflow bits
Format — standard for addressing mode

□ EXAMPLE

Before Execution			After Execution		
Program counter		10E0	Program counter		10E2
B register		9D	B register		F0
Status register		C1	Status register		C8
Memory	00A4	C2	Memory	00A4	C2
	10E0	D8		10E0	D8
	10E1	A4		10E1	A4

Binary exclusive OR

$$9D_{16} = 1001\ 1101_2$$
$$C2_{16} = 1100\ 0010_2$$
$$5F_{16} = 0101\ 1111_2$$

The sign of the result is negative, so the sign bit is set and the zero status bit is reset. The overflow bit is always reset.

Masking

Data is often packed into fields of memory cells to conserve space. A *field* is a grouping of bits used to hold one item of information. As an example, consider Fig. 7-5. Field 1 (bits 3 through 7) represents the size of a family residing in a house. Field 2 is set if the occupant is a renter, but if the bit is clear, the occupant is a home owner. Bits 0 and 1 are unused but are always set. Assume that the contents of that memory cell have been placed in the accumulator and that on different

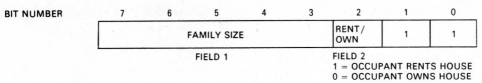

BIT NUMBER	7	6	5	4	3	2	1	0
			FAMILY SIZE			RENT/OWN	1	1
			FIELD 1			FIELD 2		

FIELD 2
1 = OCCUPANT RENTS HOUSE
0 = OCCUPANT OWNS HOUSE

Fig. 7-5 Packed data.

occasions the information is to be retrieved or altered. The use of masking to satisfy those requirements is shown below.

SELECTIVELY READING A FIELD
The following example demonstrates how only the family size can be read. Remember that the packed data word has already been fetched from memory and is in the A register.

☐ **EXAMPLE**

	8085	6800
A register	37	37
Instruction	ANI F8	ANDA F8
Result of ANDing		These bits are to be read

$$\begin{array}{l}
\text{A register} \quad 37_{16} = 0110\ 0111_2 \\
\text{Immediate data (mask)} \quad F8_{16} = \underline{1111\ 1000_2} \\
\qquad\qquad\qquad\qquad\quad \boxed{0011\ 0}000
\end{array}$$

Family size = 6

The immediate data byte is the mask. The 1s in that byte correspond to the bits in the data to be read.

SELECTIVELY CLEARING BITS IN A FIELD
New data has arrived that says the home is now owned by the occupant. Alter field 2 to reflect this change.

☐ **EXAMPLE**

	8085	6800
A register	37	37
Instruction	ANI FB	ANDA FB
Result of ANDing		This bit will be cleared

$$\begin{array}{l}
\text{Immediate data (mask)} \quad FB_{16} = 1111\ 1011_2 \\
\text{A register} \quad 37_{16} = \underline{0011\ 0111_2} \\
\qquad\qquad\qquad\qquad\qquad 0011\ 0\boxed{0}11
\end{array}$$

The rent-own code is now 0

SELECTIVELY COMPLEMENTING BITS IN A FIELD
If we had known that the previous value of the rent-own field was 1, we could have changed the bit status

with a complement operation instead. The result would have been identical to clearing the field selectively.

☐ **EXAMPLE**

	8085	6800
A register	37	37
Instruction	XRI 04	EORA 04
Result of exclusive ORing		This bit will be complemented

$$\begin{array}{l}
\text{Immediate data (mask)} \quad 04_{16} = 0000\ 0100_2 \\
\text{A register} \quad 37_{16} = \underline{0011\ 0111_2} \\
\qquad\qquad\qquad\qquad\qquad 1111\ 0\boxed{0}11
\end{array}$$

The rent-own status has been complemented

SELECTIVELY SETTING BITS IN A FIELD
The family size has increased to seven members. The contents of field 1 must be updated to the new number.

☐ **EXAMPLE**

	8085	6800
A register	37	37
Instruction	ORI 38	ORRA 38
Result of ORing		These bits will be set

$$\begin{array}{l}
\text{Immediate data (mask)} \quad 38_{16} = 0011\ 1000_2 \\
\text{A register} \quad 37_{16} = \underline{0011\ 0111_2}
\end{array}$$

New family size is 7 → $\boxed{0011\ 1}111$

These bits are unaltered

Boolean Operations Review

1. What can be said about the carry status bit in the 8085 and the overflow status bit in the 6800 at the completion of any boolean instruction?
2. What would be the result of an OR instruction if the accumulator contained 72_{16} and the memory data were 83_{16}?
3. List three applications for the exclusive OR instruction.
4. Explain how masking can be used to read, set, clear, or complement selected bits in a word.

INTRODUCTION TO BCD ARITHMETIC

The 8085 and 6800 will support BCD as well as binary arithmetic. This section presents the general concepts and explains the key instructions used for the operation. Chapter 8 completes the explanation for using the microprocessor for BCD addition and subtraction.

The problem of adding BCD numbers may not be immediately obvious. Let us examine the situation by looking at some specific cases. In some situations BCD addition is the same as binary addition.

☐ **EXAMPLE 1**   Add the BCD quantities 62 and 13.

Decimal addition	BCD equivalent	Binary addition
62_{10}	→	0 1 1 0 0 0 1 0
$+ 13_{10}$	→	0 0 0 1 0 0 1 1
75_{10}	→	0 1 1 1 0 1 0 1 = 75 BCD

A problem arises, however, when the sum of the least significant BCD digit (LSD) is greater than 9.

☐ **EXAMPLE 2**   Add the BCD quantities 28 and 36.

Decimal addition	BCD equivalent	Binary addition
28_{10}	→	0 0 1 0 1 0 0 0
$+ 36_{10}$	→	0 0 1 1 0 1 1 0
64_{10}	?	0 1 0 1 1 1 1 0

The result of the binary addition has no BCD equivalent. This problem can be resolved, however, by use of an algorithm.

BCD ADDITION ALGORITHM

STEP 1.   Add the numbers by use of binary arithmetic.

STEP 2.   If the least significant digit is equal to or less than 9 (1001_2), the BCD equivalent of the binary sum is the answer; otherwise, go to Step 3.

STEP 3.   Add 6 to the LSD, thus generating a carry of 1 into the most significant digit position. The binary sum is now the BCD equivalent.

Our examples above illustrated both possibilities of the algorithm. Example 1 has an LSD of 5, which is less than 9. The BCD code for the binary sum is the answer. Example 2 requires that we go to algorithm Step 3. We will continue that example by following the procedure of the algorithm as Step 3.

☐ **EXAMPLE 2** *(cont'd)*

decimal addition	Binary addition
28_{10}	0 0 1 0 1 0 0 0
$+ 36_{10}$	0 0 1 1 0 1 1 0
64_{10}	

1 Carry

0 1 0 1   1 1 1 0   Greater than 9,
     + 0 1 1 0   so add 6
0 1 1 0   0 1 0 0   = 64 BCD

Now the sum does represent the proper BCD result. The following instruction implements this BCD addition algorithm.

Decimal Adjust Accumulator

The decimal adjust accumulator command is used only for BCD arithmetic. It is unique in that this is the only instruction in the 6800 and 8085 repertoires that is affected by the condition of the auxiliary carry bit. The method used to implement the BCD addition algorithm is as follows. The accumulator is adjusted to form a proper two-digit BCD sum by:

1. Testing the least significant BCD digit in the accumulator.
   a. If the LSD is greater than 9 or if A_C is set, the accumulator is incremented by 6. If this addition generates a carry from bit position 3, the auxiliary carry bit is set; otherwise, it is reset.
   b. If the LSD is less than or equal to 9 and A_C is 0, there is no incrementing.
2. Testing the most significant digit.
   a. If the MSD is now greater than 9 or if the carry bit is set, the MSD of the accumulator is incremented by 6. If a carry is generated from bit position 7, the carry status is set; otherwise, it is reset.
   b. If the MSD is less than or equal to 9 and the carry bit is 0, there is no incrementing.

The proper sum is now held in the accumulator.

Before studying the instruction itself, we will trace the instruction execution through examples.

☐ **EXAMPLE 3**   Add 19_{10} to 62_{10}.

Decimal addition	Binary addition
	No carry No carry
	0 0
62_{10}	0 1 1 0 0 0 1 0$_2$
$+ 19_{10}$	0 0 0 1 1 0 0 1$_2$
81_{10}	0 1 1 1 1 0 1 1$_2$

STEP 1. $A_C = 0$, but LSD > 9. Add 6 to LSD.

$$\boxed{0}\ \overset{\text{No}}{\text{carry}} \qquad \boxed{1}\ \text{Carry}$$

$$
\begin{array}{cc}
0\ 1\ 1\ 1 & 1\ 0\ 1\ 1_2 \\
 & 0\ 1\ 1\ 0_2 \\
\hline
1\ 0\ 0\ 0 & 0\ 0\ 0\ 1_2 = 81\ \text{BCD}
\end{array}
$$

STEP 2. $C = 0$ and MSD $\leq$ 9. No incrementing.

Final result: $A = 81$, $A_C = 1$, $C = 0$ (carry status).

□ **EXAMPLE 4**   Add 19_{10} to 82_{10}.

Decimal
addition   Binary addition

$$\boxed{0}\ \overset{\text{No}}{\text{carry}} \qquad \boxed{0}\ \overset{\text{No}}{\text{carry}}$$

$$
\begin{array}{rcc}
82_{10} & 1\ 0\ 0\ 0 & 0\ 0\ 1\ 0_2 \\
+\ 19_{10} & 0\ 0\ 0\ 1 & 1\ 0\ 0\ 1_2 \\
\hline
101_{10} & 1\ 0\ 0\ 1 & 1\ 0\ 1\ 1_2
\end{array}
$$

STEP 1. LSD > 9. Add 6 to LSD.

$$\boxed{0}\ \overset{\text{No}}{\text{carry}} \qquad \boxed{1}\ \text{Carry}$$

$$
\begin{array}{cc}
1\ 0\ 0\ 1 & 1\ 0\ 1\ 1_2 \\
 & 0\ 1\ 1\ 0 \\
\hline
1\ 0\ 1\ 0 & 0\ 0\ 0\ 1_2
\end{array}
$$

STEP 2. MSD > 9. Add 6 to MSD.

$$\boxed{1}\ \text{Carry}$$

$$
\begin{array}{c}
1\ 0\ 1\ 0 \quad 0\ 0\ 0\ 1_2 \\
0\ 1\ 1\ 0 \\
\hline
0\ 0\ 0\ 0 \quad 0\ 0\ 0\ 1_2
\end{array}
$$

Final result: $A = 01$, $A_C = 1$, $C = 1$ (carry status).

The 9-bit sum is too large for the 8-bit register. The set carry status bit is an indication of this error. When the numbers are longer than two BCD digits, multibyte arithmetic is required, as the next example shows.

Multibyte BCD Addition Procedures

A series of 8085 and 6800 instructions can be used for multibyte BCD arithmetic. (The specifics of the technique are provided in Chap. 8.) Repeated use of the decimal adjust accumulator provides the microprocessor with the capacity to handle the longer numbers.

□ **EXAMPLE 5**   Add 5625_{10} to 1498_{10}.

Decimal addition

$$
\begin{array}{r}
5625_{10} \\
+\ 1498_{10} \\
\hline
7123_{10}
\end{array}
$$

Clear the carry bit.

Add the two lower-order digits.

$$\boxed{0} \qquad\quad \boxed{0}$$

$$
\begin{array}{rcc}
25 \rightarrow & 0\ 0\ 1\ 0 & 0\ 1\ 0\ 1 \\
+\ 98 \rightarrow & 1\ 0\ 0\ 1 & 1\ 0\ 0\ 0 \\
\hline
 & 1\ 0\ 0\ 1 & 1\ 1\ 0\ 1
\end{array}
$$

Status bits
$C = 0$
$A_C = 0$

Decimal adjust.

The LSD is greater than 9, so increment by 6.

$$\boxed{0} \qquad\quad \boxed{1}$$

$$
\begin{array}{cc}
1\ 0\ 1\ 1 & 1\ 1\ 0\ 1 \\
 & +\ 1\ 1\ 0 \\
\hline
1\ 1\ 0\ 0 & 0\ 0\ 1\ 1
\end{array}
$$

Status bits
$A_C = 0$
$C = 0$

The MSD is greater than 9, so increment by 6.

$$\boxed{1}$$

$$
\begin{array}{c}
1\ 1\ 0\ 0 \quad 0\ 0\ 1\ 1 \\
+\ 1\ 1\ 0 \\
\hline
0\ 0\ 1\ 0 \quad 0\ 0\ 1\ 1
\end{array}
$$

Status bits
$A_C = 1$
$C = 1$

Result = 23.

Store lower-order digits.

Add two higher-order digits with the carry status.

$$\boxed{0} \qquad\quad \boxed{0}$$

$$
\begin{array}{rcc}
56 \rightarrow & 0\ 1\ 0\ 1 & 0\ 1\ 1\ 0 \\
14 \rightarrow & 0\ 0\ 0\ 1 & 0\ 1\ 0\ 0 \\
\text{Carry} \rightarrow & & +\ 1 \\
\hline
 & 0\ 1\ 1\ 0 & 1\ 0\ 1\ 1
\end{array}
$$

Status bits
$A_C = 0$
$C = 0$

Decimal adjust.

The LSD is greater than 9, so increment

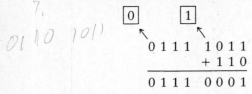

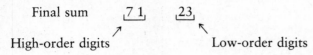

$$\begin{array}{r} 0111\ 1011 \\ +\ 110 \\ \hline 0111\ 0001 \end{array}$$

The MSD is equal to or less than 9, so do not increment.

Result: A = 71, A_C = 1, C = 0.

Store higher-order digits.

Final sum   71   23

High-order digits   Low-order digits

See Chap. 8 for the program listing specific instructions for this multibyte BCD addition. Next we will look at the instruction format.

80 8085 FORMAT

Operation code	27
Mnemonic	DAA
Addressing mode	none
Status bits affected	zero, sign, parity, carry, and auxiliary carry bits
Clock periods	4
Format	

Bit number

7 6 5 4   3 2 1 0

Memory cell   m | 0 0 1 0   0 1 1 1 |

□ EXAMPLE

Before Execution		After Execution	
Program counter	0230	Program counter	0231
A register	3C	A register	42
Status register	02	Status register	16
Memory 0230	27	Memory 0230	27

68 6800 FORMAT

Operation code	19
Mnemonic	DAA
Addressing mode	inherent
Status bits affected	sign, zero, overflow, and carry bits
Machine cycles	2
Format	

Bit number

7 6 5 4   3 2 1 0

Memory cell   m | 0 0 0 1   1 0 0 1 |

□ EXAMPLE

Before Execution		After Execution	
Program counter	0230	Program counter	0231
A register	39	A register	66
Status register	C0	Status register	C4
Memory 0230	27	Memory AA01	27

The sign, overflow, zero, and carry status bits are reset.

BCD Arithmetic Review

1. List the steps in the BCD addition algorithm.
2. When does binary addition produce a correct BCD result?
3. Explain how the decimal adjust accumulator implements the algorithm.
4. What is the meaning of the carry bit condition at the completion of Example 4?
5. How is the carry bit generated in Example 5 used? What error would have resulted had that carry been ignored?

COMPARE INSTRUCTIONS

There are many occasions when the relative magnitudes of two numbers are important. Knowing if two numbers are equal, or which is the larger, allows the processor to make decisions based on the relationships between variables. Instructions in the 8085 and 6800 compare quantities and set the status bits to indicate the outcome of that comparison.

80 8085 Compare Register or Memory With Accumulator

The byte in the specified register or memory cell is compared with the accumulator value. (Actually an internal subtraction is performed, but the final contents of the accumulator are the same as the initial values.) The results control the zero and carry status bits, as shown in Table 7-6. The use of parentheses in Table 7-6 means that it is the *contents* of that register or cell which are being compared. As Table 7-6 shows for unequal values, the interpretation of the status bits depends on whether the accumulator and the register (or memory cell) being compared have the same sign. As we have seen, the HL register pair contains the memory address.

Table 7-6 8085 Compare Status Bit Conditions

Condition	Status Bits		Meaning*
	Zero	Carry	
Equality	1	X	(A) = (Register)
Accumultor and register have the same sign	0 0	1 0	(A) < (Register) (A) > (Register)
Accumulator and register have opposite signs	0 0	1 0	(A) > (Register) (A) < (Register)

X is a don't care setting.
* Parentheses refer to the contents of the register or memory cell.

Operation Code	Mnemonic
B8	CMP B
B9	CMP C
BA	CMP D
BB	CMP E
BC	CMP H
BD	CMP L
BE	CMP M
BF	CMP A

Addressing mode   register
Status bits affected   carry, zero, sign, parity, and auxiliary carry bits
Clock periods   4 (7 for memory reference)
Format

Bit number

7 6 5 4   3 2 1 0

Memory cell   m | 1 0 1 1   1 r r r |

rrr	Register
000	B
001	C
010	D
011	E
100	H
101	L
110	memory
111	A

☐ EXAMPLE

Before Execution

Program counter	0245
A register	38
C register	72
Status register	06
Memory 0245	B9

After Execution

Program counter	0245
A register	38
C register	72
Status register	13
Memory 0245	B9

The zero status bit is reset and the carry is set. The quantities are unequal and have the same sign. From Table 7-6 we see that the set carry bit indicates that the accumulator value is less than that of the C register.

80   8085 Compare Immediate

The immediate data byte is compared with the contents of the accumulator (by means of an internal subtraction). The final value in the A register is the same as the initial value. If the quantities are equal, the zero status bit is set. If they are not equal, the carry status bit indicates the larger by its setting. The meaning of the carry bit depends on whether the accumulator and the immediate data have the same or opposite signs, as shown in Table 7-7.

Table 7-7 8085 Compare Immediate Status Bit Conditions

Condition	Status Bits		Meaning*
	Zero	Carry	
Equality	1	X	(A) = (data byte)
Accumulator and data byte have the same sign	0 0	1 0	(A) < (data byte) (A) > (data byte)
Accumulator and data byte have opposite signs	0 0	1 0	(A) > (data byte) (A) < (data byte)

X is don't care setting.
* Parentheses refer to the contents of the register or memory cell.

Operation code	FE		
Mnemonic	CPI		
Addressing mode	immediate		
Status bits affected	carry, zero, sign, parity, and auxiliary carry bits		
Clock periods	7		
Format			

```
                        Bit number
                    7 6 5 4   3 2 1 0
Memory cell   m     [ 1 1 1 1   1 1 1 0 ]
              m + 1 [   Immediate data byte   ]
```

□ EXAMPLE

Before Execution		After Execution	
Program counter	0083	Program counter	0085
A register	73	A register	73
Status register	02	Status register	12
Memory 0083	FE	Memory 0083	FE
0084	5A	0084	5A

The quantities are unequal, so the zero bit is cleared. The A register value is the larger, as indicated by a resetting of the carry bit. Note that the auxiliary carry and parity bits reflect the value of the difference resulting from the internal subtraction; these bits should be ignored.

68 6800 Compare Memory With Accumulator or Index Register

The byte in the specified memory cell is compared with the A or B accumulator. Alternatively, the bytes in two consecutive memory cells are compared with the index register. The results control the zero and carry status bits, as shown in Table 7-8. The use of parentheses in this table mean that it is the *contents* of that register or cell which are being compared. As Table 7-8 shows for unequal values, the status bits depend on whether the register and the memory cell being compared have the same sign.

Mnemonic	Addressing Mode	Operation Code	Machine Cycles
CMPA	Immediate	81	2
	Direct	91	3
	Indexed	A1	5
	Extended	B1	4
CMPB	Immediate	C1	2
	Direct	D1	3
	Indexed	E1	5
	Extended	F1	4
CBA	Inherent	11	2

Status bits affected	sign, zero, overflow, and carry bits
Format	standard for addressing mode

□ EXAMPLE 1   Compare memory to accumulator A.

Before Execution		After Execution	
Program counter	5030	Program counter	5033
A register	38	A register	38
Status register	C0	Status register	C4
Memory 5030	B1	Memory 5030	B1
5031	C0	5031	C0
5032	00	5032	00
C000	38	C000	38

Because the values are equal, the zero bit is set.

□ EXAMPLE 2   Compare accumulator A with accumulator B.

Before Execution		After Execution	
Program counter	5030	Program counter	5031
A register	74	A register	74
B register	9B	B register	9B
Status register	C0	Status register	C1
Memory 5030	11	Memory 5030	11

The values are unequal. The A register is larger (more positive), as indicated by the status register and Table 7-8.

Table 7-8   6800 Compare Status Bit Conditions

Condition	Status Bits		Meaning*
	Zero	Carry	
Equality	1	X	(Register) = (Memory)
Register and memory have the same sign	0	1	(Register) < (Memory)
	0	0	(Register) > (Memory)
Register and memory have opposite signs	0	1	(Register) > (Memory)
	0	0	(Register) < (Memory)

X is a don't care setting.
* Parentheses refer to the contents of the register or memory cell.

⑱ 6800 Test the Contents of Accumulator or Memory

The instruction sets the sign and zero flags to agree with the value in the specified accumulator or memory byte. The overflow and carry bits are always reset.

Mnemonic	Addressing Mode	Operation Code	Machine Cycles
TST	Indexed	6D	7
	Extended	7D	6
TSTA	Inherent	4D	2
TSTB	Inherent	5D	2

Status bits affected   sign, zero, overflow, and carry bits
Format   standard for addressing mode

☐ EXAMPLE

Before Execution		After Execution	
Program counter	2045	Program counter	2046
A register	A2	A register	A2
Status register	C0	Status register	C8
Memory 2045	4D	Memory 2045	4D

Because the value is negative, the sign bit is set. All other status bits are reset.

Compare Instructions Review

1. Explain how the compare instructions permit the programmer to decide the relative magnitudes of numbers in the accumulator and in a memory cell.
2. What does the resetting of the zero bit, after the comparison, mean?
3. What other information is needed, in addition to the zero and carry bit settings, to determine which quantity is greater after a compare instruction is examined?
4. Discuss the meaning of the parity and the auxiliary carry conditions following a compare instruction.

CHAPTER SUMMARY

1. The instructions discussed in this chapter are listed in Tables 7-9 and 7-10 (see pages 152 and 153). Operation code, length, and effect on the status bits are given for each.
2. The status register bits reflect the results calculated in arithmetic and logical operations. The carry bit indicates a carry from the MSB in addition, or a borrow from the MSB in subtraction. The auxiliary carry is set whenever there is a carry from bit position 3. The sign bit of the accumulator and the sign status bit are always equal. The zero condition bit is set to 1 if the accumulator contains a 0 value.
3. The carry bit can be set or complemented directly by microprocessor instructions.
4. Memory cells and registers can be incremented or decremented on command. Registers can also be incremented or decremented.
5. A 1's complement can be introduced by means of the complement accumulator instruction.
6. Addition and subtraction instructions perform the basic arithmetic operations. More complex arithmetic requires instruction sequences.
7. The boolean operations of AND, OR, and exclusive OR are provided in the logical instructions group.
8. In a routine, use of the decimal adjust accumulator instruction implements the BCD addition algorithm.
9. The relative magnitude of the accumulator value and that of a register or a memory cell can be determined by use of the compare instructions. The outcome can be found from the settings of the zero and carry bits.

KEY TERMS AND CONCEPTS

Status register	Increment instruction	Field
Carry (C) bit	Decrement instruction	Selective read
Auxiliary carry (A_C) bit	Complement accumulator	Selective clear
Sign (S) bit	Addition	Selective complement
Zero (Z) bit	Subtraction	Selective set
Parity (P) bit	Boolean (logical) instructions	BCD arithmetic
Overflow (O) bit		
Setting and complementing the carry bit	Masking	Multibyte BCD addition
		Compare

Table 7-9 8085 Arithmetic and Logical Instructions

Mnemonic	Operation Code	Bytes	Status*				
			C	A_C	Z	S	P
ACI	CE	2	X	X	X	X	X
ADC	88, 89, 8A, 8B, 8C, 8D, 8E, 8F	1	X	X	X	X	X
ADD	80, 81, 82, 83, 84, 85, 86, 87	1	X	X	X	X	X
ADI	C6	2	X	X	X	X	X
ANA	A0, A1, A2, A3, A4, A5, A6, A7	1	0	X	X	X	X
ANI	E6	2	0	0	X	X	X
CMA	2F	1					
CMC	3F	1	X				
CMP	B8, B9, BA, BB, BC, BD, BE, BF	1	X	X	X	X	X
CPI	FE	2	X	X	X	X	X
DAA	27	1	X	X	X	X	X
DAD	09, 19, 29, 39	1	X				
DCR	05, 0D, 15, 1D, 25, 2D, 35, 3D	1		X	X	X	X
DCX	0B, 1B, 2B, 3B	1					
INR	04, 0C, 14, 1C, 24, 2C, 34, 3C	1		X	X	X	X
INX	03, 13, 23, 33	1					
ORA	B0, B1, B2, B3, B4, B5, B6, B7	1	0	1	X	X	X
ORI	F6	2	0	0	X	X	X
SBB	98, 99, 9A, 9B, 9C, 9D, 9E, 9F	1	X	X	X	X	X
SBI	DE	2	X	X	X	X	X
STC	37	1	1				
SUB	90, 91, 92, 93, 94, 95, 96, 97	1	X	X	X	X	X
SUI	D6	2	X	X	X	X	X
XRA	A8, A9, AA, AB, AC, AD, AE, AF	1	0	1	X	X	X
XRI	EE	2	0	0	X	X	X

* Code: X indicates that bit is changed; 1 indicates that bit is always set; 0 indicates that bit is always cleared.

P R O B L E M S

7-1 The accumulator is set to 56_{16}. Write a single instruction that will clear the carry bit without altering the accumulator.

7-2 Assume that the accumulator contains 27_{16}. Subtract 40_{16} from that register with one instruction. What is the final accumulator and status register configuration?

7-3 Write a two-instruction sequence that will result in the 1's complement of memory location 2000_{16} being placed in the accumulator. The accumulator and carry status have starting values of 0.

7-4 When the microcomputer was first started, the status register contents were obtained and stored in memory cell $701A_{16}$. The latest value of the status register is stored at $02FB_{16}$. Write an instruction sequence that will show if the carry status bit differs between the two stored values.

7-5 Write a program to perform the following steps:

a. Set a register to $A7_{16}$.
b. Add $3C_{16}$.
c. Read the odd-numbered bits and store the result in cell 2000_{16}.

Table 7-10 6800 Arithmetic and Logic Instructions

Mnemonic	Operation Code	Bytes	Status* A_C	S	Z	O	C
ABA	1B	1	X	X	X	X	X
ADCA	89, 99, A9, B9	2, 3	X	X	X	X	X
ADCB	C9, D9, E9, F9	2, 3	X	X	X	X	X
ADDA	8B, 9B, AB, BB	2, 3	X	X	X	X	X
ADDB	CB, DB, EB, FB	2, 3	X	X	X	X	X
ANDA	84, 94, A4, B4	2, 3		X	X	0	
ANDB	C4, D4, E4, F4	2, 3		X	X	0	
BITA	85, 95, A5, B5	2, 3		X	X	0	
BITB	C5, D5, E5, F5	2, 3		X	X	0	
CLC	0C	1					0
CLR	6F, 7F	2, 3		0	1	0	0
CLRA	4F	1		0	1	0	0
CLRB	5F	1		0	1	0	0
CLV	0A	1				0	
COM	63, 73	2, 3		X	X	0	1
COMA	43	1		X	X	0	1
COMB	53	1		X	X	0	1
DAA	19	1		X	X	X	X
DEC	6A, 7A	2, 3		X	X	X	
DECA	4A	1		X	X	X	
DECB	5A	1		X	X	X	
DES	34	1					
DEX	09	1			X		
EORA	88, 98, A8, B8	2, 3		X	X	0	
EORB	C8, D8, E8, F8	2, 3		X	X	0	
INC	6C, 7C	2, 3		X	X	X	X
INCA	4C	1		X	X	X	X
INCB	5C	1		X	X	X	X
INS	31	1					
INX	08	1			X		
NEG	60, 70	2, 3		X	X	X	X
NEGA	40	1		X	X	X	X
NEGB	50	1		X	X	X	X
ORAA	8A, 9A, AA, BA	2, 3		X	X	0	
ORAB	CA, DA, EA, FA	2, 3		X	X	0	
SBA	10	1		X	X	X	X
SBCA	82, 92, A2, B2	2, 3		X	X	X	X
SBCB	C2, D2, E2, F2	2, 3		X	X	X	X
SEC	0D	1					1
SEV	0B	1				1	
SUBA	80, 90, A0, B0	2, 3		X	X	X	X
SUBB	C0, D0, E0, F0	2, 3		X	X	X	X

* Code: X indicates that bit is changed; 1 indicates that bit is always set; 0 indicates that bit is always cleared.

7-6 How would you program the requirement to add 7_{16} to the lower 4 bits in cell $76BB_{16}$?

7-7 Write the instructions to add the BCD number in cell 6345_{16} to the one in cell $4F21_{16}$.

7-8 What bits would be set in the status register if the A register is 68_{16} and the data byte in a compare instruction is $E7_{16}$?

7-9 Write a program to evaluate the following boolean algebra expression:

(K OR L) AND (M exclusive OR P)

if the variables are located in these memory cells

K	1000
L	1001
M	1002
P	1003

7-10 Form the 1's complement of $7B_{16}$ and add it to the 2's complement of $A1_{16}$ using the instructions you have learned so far.

JUMPS

Most of the processor decision-making capability involves the use of instructions that can choose between two alternatives. In a program, those alternatives will be characterized by two instruction strings. By using jump commands, the execution of the program can be diverted from the next successive address to a completely different sequence. This chapter presents the unconditional and conditional jump instructions of the microprocessor and demonstrates how the instructions allow the processor to make decisions.

CHAPTER OBJECTIVES

Upon completion of this chapter, you should be able to:

1. Distinguish between conditional and unconditional jumps.
2. Describe the operation of all jump instructions.
3. Explain how conditional jumps are used to implement multibyte addition and subtraction algorithms.
4. Write multibyte BCD addition or subtraction routines.

UNCONDITIONAL AND CONDITIONAL JUMPS

The purpose of a jump instruction is to alter the normal sequence of operations in the processor. Rather than allowing the program counter to increment in a normal manner, a jump forces the counter to a particular value. Once that value has been entered in the program counter, the next instruction will be obtained from that address.

An *unconditional jump* always causes the program counter value to change. The instructions described in Chap. 6 were examples of unconditional jumps. In contrast, the *conditional jump* instruction transfers control only when a specified condition is true. If false, the jump is not taken; instead, the next sequential instruction is executed. Thus a conditional jump is like a decision block on a flowchart. (Examples of such conditions include a zero sum after addition or an odd parity resulting from a boolean instruction.) Figure 8-1 depicts the operation of the two types of jumps.

Even though the conditional jump instructions can sense the value of a status condition, no jump instruction can alter the status register. In the examples that follow, you will see some of the techniques used to set the status bits properly prior to executing a conditional jump instruction.

80 Review of 8085 Unconditional Jump Instructions

The instructions covered in Chap. 6 are briefly listed below by way of review. (Refer to Chap. 6 for examples and more details.)

JUMP Unconditional transfer to a memory address.

Operation code	C3
Mnemonic	JMP
Addressing mode	direct
Status bits affected	none
Clock periods	10

Format

			Bit number	
			7 6 5 4	3 2 1 0
Memory cell	m		1 1 0 0	0 0 1 1
	m + 1		Low-address byte	
	m + 2		High-address byte	

LOAD PROGRAM COUNTER Load the program counter with the value in the HL register pair. The H register contains the high-order address byte.

Operation code	E9
Mnemonic	PCHL
Addressing mode	none
Status bits affected	none
Clock periods	6

Format

			Bit number	
			7 6 5 4	3 2 1 0
Memory cell	m		1 1 1 0	1 0 0 1

68 6800 Unconditional Jump and Branch Instructions

One of these instructions has previously been covered on page 101 and is briefly listed below for completeness. Refer to Chap. 6 for more information and examples.

JUMP Unconditional transfer to a memory address.

Operation codes	6E, 7E
Mnemonic	JMP
Addressing mode	indexed, extended
Status bits affected	none
Clock periods	4, 3
Format	standard for addressing mode

BRANCH The *unconditional branch* is a transfer to a memory address. It differs from a jump only in that the range of addresses is limited. The address in a branch is determined by adding the contents of the byte following the branch operation code (called the *dis-*

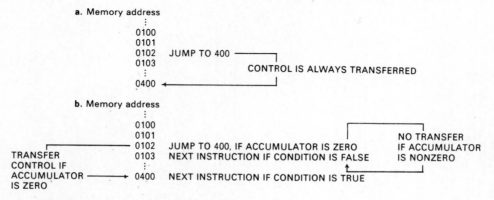

Fig. 8-1 Jumps: (a) Unconditional, (b) Conditional.

placement) to the program counter plus 2. In equation form:

$$BA = (PC) + 2 + d$$

where BA = absolute branch address

(PC) = contents of program counter register

d = displacement

For example, let the PC contain an address of $6C3B_{16}$ and let the displacement be $9E_{16}$. The branch address is therefore:

```
  6C3B
 +  2
  6C3D
 + 9E
  6CDB
```

The next instruction will be fetched from cell $6CDB_{16}$. The displacement can be a positive or negative 2's complement number. Bit 7 is the sign bit, and if it is set, the displacement is considered negative. In that case the next instruction is fetched from a memory cell preceding that of the branch instruction. For example, let the PC have a value of $78F2_{16}$ and the displacement byte equal 93_{16}.

```
  78F2
 +  2
  78F4
 + FF93
  7887
```

The address of the next instruction is 7887_{16}, which is less than the previous PC value. Because the displacement is limited to 8 bits, the branch address must be within $+127$ or -126 cell locations from the branch instruction.

Operation code	20	
Mnemonic	BRA	
Addressing mode	relative	
Status bits affected	none	
Clock periods	4	
Format		Bit number

		7 6 5 4 3 2 1 0
Memory cell	m	0 0 1 0 0 0 0 0
	m + 1	Displacement

Unconditional and Conditional Jumps Review

1. Define the term "conditional jump."
2. Under what conditions is a conditional jump the same as an unconditional jump? When would a con-

ditional jump be the same as a no operation instruction?
3. How does the setting of the status bits affect the conditional jump decision?
4. Which status bits can be changed by unconditional jumps?

80 8085 CONDITIONAL JUMP INSTRUCTIONS

Each of the instructions that follows will decide the next address based on the setting of a status bit. The carry, parity, zero, or sign bit can be used as the deciding factor. (The auxiliary carry status is excluded from the conditions that can be tested.)

80 Jump if Carry

If the carry bit is set, the immediate address following the op code is placed into the program counter. The program sequence continues from that point. Should the carry bit be reset, however, this instruction is essentially a no operation. The next sequential instruction will be selected in the latter case. (In all conditional jump instructions to follow, the first number for "clock periods" is the case if the condition is satisfied; the second number applies if the condition is false.)

Operation code	DA	
Mnemonic	JC	
Addressing mode	direct	
Status bits affected	none	
Clock periods	10, 7	
Format		Bit number

		7 6 5 4 3 2 1 0
Memory cell	m	1 1 0 1 1 0 1 0
	m + 1	Low-address byte
	m + 2	High-address byte

☐ EXAMPLE

Before Execution		After Execution	
Program counter	0420	Program counter	0501
Status register	83	Status register	83
Memory 0420	DA	Memory 0402	DA
0421	01	0421	01
0422	05	0422	05

The carry status (bit 0) is set, so the jump condition is true. The program counter is set equal to the immediate address contained in memory cells 0421_{16} and 0422_{16}. In this example the next address will be 0501_{16}.

80 Jump if No Carry

This instruction performs a comparison that is the converse of the previous one. If the carry bit is 0, the jump is taken; otherwise, the next instruction in the normal order will be executed.

Operation code	D2
Mnemonic	JNC
Addressing mode	direct
Status bits affected	none
Clock periods	10, 7
Format	

Bit number

		7 6 5 4	3 2 1 0
Memory cell	m	1 1 0 0	0 0 1 0
	m + 1	Low-address byte	
	m + 2	High-address byte	

□ EXAMPLE

Before Execution			After Execution		
Program counter		1040	Program counter		1043
Status register		03	Status register		03
Memory	1040	D2	Memory	1040	D2
	1041	11		1041	11
	1042	66		1042	66

The status register shows that the carry bit is set, so the jump is not taken. The program counter is set to fetch the next instruction of the original sequence.

80 Jump if Zero

The zero status bit controls the decision for this jump. If the bit is set (indicating that the accumulator contains a 0), the jump is selected.

Operation code	CA
Mnemonic	JZ
Addressing mode	direct
Status bits affected	none
Clock periods	10, 7
Format	

Bit number

		7 6 5 4	3 2 1 0
Memory cell	m	1 1 0 0	1 0 1 0
	m + 1	Low-address byte	
	m + 2	High-address byte	

□ EXAMPLE

Before Execution		After Execution	
Program counter	0560	Program counter	0700
Status register	47	Status register	47

Before Execution			After Execution		
Memory	0560	CA	Memory	0560	CA
	0561	00		0561	00
	0562	07		0562	07

Bit 6 in the status register is set, so the A register value is 0. The jump is activated.

80 Jump if Not Zero

If the zero status bit is 0 (meaning that the A register is nonzero), the next instruction will be executed at the direct-address location. Should the status bit be set, the jump is ignored.

Operation code	C2
Mnemonic	JNZ
Addressing mode	direct
Status bits affected	none
Clock periods	10, 7
Format	

Bit number

		7 6 5 4	3 2 1 0
Memory cell	m	1 1 0 0	0 0 1 0
	m + 1	Low-address byte	
	m + 2	High-address byte	

□ EXAMPLE

Before Execution			After Execution		
Program counter		0250	Program counter		0253
Status register		42	Status register		42
Memory	0250	C2	Memory	0250	C2
	0251	08		0251	08
	0252	06		0252	06

The zero condition bit is set, so there is no jump.

80 Jump if Minus

If the accumulator value is negative, the processor will take the jump. The sign bit being set indicates this condition. If the sign bit is clear, there will be no jump.

Operation code	FA
Mnemonic	JM
Addressing mode	direct
Status bits affected	none
Clock periods	10, 7
Format	

Bit number

		7 6 5 4	3 2 1 0
Memory cell	m	1 1 1 1	1 0 1 0
	m + 1	Low-address byte	
	m + 2	High-address byte	

☐ EXAMPLE

Before Execution		After Execution	
Program counter	0110	Program counter	0630
Status register	83	Status register	83
Memory 1010	FA	Memory 1010	FA
1011	30	1011	30
1012	06	1012	06

The number in the A register is negative, so the jump address is placed into the program counter.

So far in this discussion of the conditional jumps, we have not concerned ourselves with how the status bits become set. Before any of the tests for a conditional jump are made, a deliberate effort is required to set the status bits to reflect the present value in the accumulator. The arithmetic and logical instructions cause the status bits to change, so generally an instruction from that group must precede a comparison by means of a conditional jump. In the two examples below, the sign bit is changed in preparation for a jump on minus condition.

☐ EXAMPLE 1 Checking the results of addition.

Address	Machine Code	Comments
1000	86	Add memory contents to A
1001	FA	Jump to 0200_{16} if the sign bit is set
1002	00	
1003	02	

☐ EXAMPLE 2 Testing a memory cell for a negative number.

Address	Machine Code	Comments
0500	7E	Move the memory contents to A.
0501	E6	AND immediate, to mask only the sign bit into A. (Set all status bits except carry.)
0502	80	
0503	FA	Jump to 0200_{16} if the sign bit is set.
0504	00	
0505	02	

An alternate, equally effective sequence for the conditional jump in Example 2 would be:

0503	C2	Jump if A is not zero. (If the sign bit were set by the masking, the register would contain a nonzero quantity.)
0504	00	
0505	02	

80 Jump if Plus

With this instruction we can test for a positive result in the accumulator. The processor will jump only if the sign status bit is 0 (positive).

Operation code	F2
Mnemonic	JP
Addressing mode	direct
Status bits affected	none
Clock periods	10, 7
Format	

	Bit number 7 6 5 4 3 2 1 0
Memory cell m	1 1 1 1 0 0 1 0
m + 1	Low-address byte
m + 2	High-address byte

☐ EXAMPLE

Before Execution		After Execution	
Program counter	0025	Program counter	0028
Status register	86	Status register	86
Memory 0025	F2	Memory 0025	F2
0026	80	0026	80
0027	06	0027	06

The sign is negative, so there will be no jump.

80 Jump if Parity Even

The parity status bit is used to decide the conditional jump selection. If the bit is 1, for even parity, the jump will happen. If the bit is 0, there is no jump.

Operation code	EA
Mnemonic	JPE
Addressing mode	direct
Status bits affected	none
Clock periods	10, 7
Format	

	Bit number 7 6 5 4 3 2 1 0
Memory cell m	1 1 1 0 1 0 1 0
m + 1	Low-address byte
m + 2	High-address byte

☐ EXAMPLE

Before Execution		After Execution	
Program counter	00E0	Program counter	0A10
Status register	07	Status register	07
Memory 00E0	EA	Memory 00E0	EA
00E1	10	00E1	10
00E2	0A	00E2	0A

Because the parity is even (bit 2 is set), the jump occurs.

80 Jump if Parity Odd

An odd parity (that is, with the status bit 0), this instruction will cause a jump. If the parity is even, there will be no jump.

Operation code   E2
Mnemonic   JPO
Addressing mode   direct
Status bits affected   none
Clock periods   10, 7
Format

		Bit number
		7 6 5 4 3 2 1 0
Memory cell	m	1 1 1 0 0 0 1 0
	m + 1	Low-address byte
	m + 2	High-address byte

☐ EXAMPLE

Before Execution			After Execution		
Program counter		04B0	Program counter		14B3
Status register		87	Status register		87
Memory	04B0	E2	Memory	04B0	E2
	04B1	00		04B1	00
	04B2	0D		04B2	0D

No jump is executed because the parity status is set, thus indicating even parity.

80 8085 Conditional Jump Instructions Review

1. If the condition is true, where is the new address (that is, the address to jump to) found?
2. How can you be sure that the status register properly reflects the condition being tested? Give an example.
3. If you wanted to write a program that checks the result of a boolean operation, which two instructions would you use to jump to address 0140_{16} if the answer were 0 and to 0150_{16} if the answer had odd parity? Does it matter which test is performed first?

68 6800 CONDITIONAL JUMP AND BRANCH INSTRUCTIONS

Each of the instructions that follows will decide the next address based on the setting of one or more status bits. The carry, zero, sign, or overflow bits can be used as deciding factors. (The auxiliary carry bit is excluded from the conditions that can be tested.)

68 Branch if Carry Set

If the carry bit is set, the displacement is added to the program counter plus 2, as was explained for the un-conditional branch. The program continues execution from that cell. Should the carry bit be clear, the instruction is essentially a no operation. The next sequential instruction will be selected in that case.

Operation code   25
Mnemonic   BCS
Addressing mode   relative
Status bits affected   none
Clock periods   4
Format

		Bit number
		7 6 5 4 3 2 1 0
Memory cell	m	0 0 1 0 0 1 0 1
	m + 1	Displacement

☐ EXAMPLE

Before Execution			After Execution		
Program counter		1040	Program counter		106B
Status register		C1	Status register		C1
Memory	1040	25	Memory	1040	25
	1041	29		1041	29

The carry status bit is set, so the next instruction will be the one at $106B_{16}$.

68 Branch if Carry Clear

If the carry bit is clear, the displacement is added to the program counter plus 2, as was explained for the un-conditional branch. The program continues execution from that cell. Should the carry bit be set, the instruction is essentially a no operation. The next sequential instruction will be selected in that case.

Operation code   24
Mnemonic   BCC
Addressing mode   relative
Status bits affected   none
Clock periods   4
Format

		Bit number
		7 6 5 4 3 2 1 0
Memory cell	m	0 0 1 0 0 1 0 0
	m + 1	Displacement

☐ EXAMPLE

Before Execution			After Execution		
Program counter		1040	Program counter		1042
Status register		C1	Status register		C1
Memory	1040	24	Memory	1040	24
	1041	29		1041	29

The carry status bit is set, so the branch is not taken and the next instruction will be the one at 1042_{16}.

68 Branch if Zero Set

If the zero bit is set, the displacement is added to the program counter plus 2, as was explained for the unconditional branch. The program continues execution from that cell. Should the zero bit be clear, the instruction is essentially a no operation. The next sequential instruction will be selected in that case.

Operation code	27
Mnemonic	BEQ
Addressing mode	relative
Status bits affected	none
Clock periods	4
Format	

		Bit number
		7 6 5 4 3 2 1 0
Memory cell	m	0 0 1 0 0 1 1 1
	m + 1	Displacement

□ EXAMPLE

Before Execution		After Execution	
Program counter	4420	Program counter	4488
Status register	C4	Status register	C4
Memory 4420	27	Memory 4420	27
4421	66	4421	66

The zero status bit is set, so the branch is taken and the next instruction will be the one at 4488_{16}.

68 Branch if Greater Than or Equal to Zero

If the exclusive OR of the sign and overflow bits is 0, the displacement is added to the program counter plus 2, as was explained for the unconditional branch. The program continues execution from that cell. Should the exclusive OR of the sign with the overflow bit be nonzero, the instruction is essentially a no operation. The next sequential instruction will be selected in that case.

Operation code	2C
Mnemonic	BGE
Addressing mode	relative
Status bits affected	none
Clock periods	4
Format	

		Bit number
		7 6 5 4 3 2 1 0
Memory cell	m	0 0 1 0 1 1 0 0
	m + 1	Displacement

□ EXAMPLE

Before Execution		After Execution	
Program counter	4420	Program counter	4422

Before Execution		After Execution	
Status register	CC	Status register	CC
Memory 4420	2C	Memory 4420	2C
4421	A7	4421	A7

The exclusive OR of the sign and overflow bits is:

sign (exclusive OR) overflow = 1 (exclusive OR) 0 = 1

so the branch is not taken and the next instruction will be the one at 4422_{16}.

68 Branch if Greater Than Zero

If the zero bit is cleared and the sign and overflow bits have the same value (that is, either both are 1 or both are 0), the displacement is added to the program counter plus 2, as was explained for the unconditional branch. The program continues execution from that cell. Should the conditions not be met, the instruction is essentially a no operation. The next sequential instruction will be selected in that case.

Operation code	2E
Mnemonic	BGT
Addressing mode	relative
Status bits affected	none
Clock periods	4
Format	

		Bit number
		7 6 5 4 3 2 1 0
Memory cell	m	0 0 1 0 1 1 1 0
	m + 1	Displacement

□ EXAMPLE

Before Execution		After Execution	
Program counter	4420	Program counter	4472
Status register	C0	Status register	C0
Memory 4420	2E	Memory 4420	2E
4421	50	4421	50

The zero status bit is cleared, and both the sign and overflow bits are 0, so the branch is taken and the next instruction will be the one at 4472_{16}.

68 Branch if Higher

If the zero and carry bits are both cleared, the displacement is added to the program counter plus 2, as was explained for the unconditional branch. The program continues execution from that cell. Should the conditions not be met, the instruction is essentially a no operation. The next sequential instruction will be selected in that case.

Operation code	22
Mnemonic	BHI
Addressing mode	relative
Status bits affected	none
Clock periods	4
Format	

```
                        Bit number
                    7 6 5 4    3 2 1 0
Memory cell    m    0 0 1 0    0 0 1 0
              m + 1     Displacement
```

□ **EXAMPLE**

Before Execution		After Execution	
Program counter	4420	Program counter	4472
Status register	CA	Status register	CA
Memory 4420	22	Memory 4420	22
4421	50	4421	50

Both status bits are clear, so the branch is taken and the next instruction will be the one at 4472_{16}.

68 Branch if Less Than or Equal to Zero

If the zero bit is set or the exclusive OR of the overflow and sign bits is 1, the displacement is added to the program counter plus 2, as was explained for the unconditional branch. The program continues execution from that cell. Should the conditions not be met, the instruction is essentially a no operation. The next sequential instruction will be selected in that case.

Operation code	2F
Mnemonic	BLE
Addressing mode	relative
Status bits affected	none
Clock periods	4
Format	

```
                        Bit number
                    7 6 5 4    3 2 1 0
Memory cell    m    0 0 1 0    1 1 1 1
              m + 1     Displacement
```

□ **EXAMPLE**

Before Execution		After Execution	
Program counter	5674	Program counter	567D
Status register	C2	Status register	C2
Memory 5674	2F	Memory 5674	2F
5675	07	5675	07

The zero status bit is cleared, so the condition is not satisfied. However, the exclusive OR of the sign and

overflow bits is 1. The branch is taken and the next instruction will be the one at $567D_{16}$.

68 Branch if Lower or Same

If either the carry or the zero bit is set, the displacement is added to the program counter plus 2, as was explained for the unconditional branch. The program continues execution from that cell. Should the conditions not be met, the instruction is essentially a no operation. The next sequential instruction will be selected in that case.

Operation code	23
Mnemonic	BLS
Addressing mode	relative
Status bits affected	none
Clock periods	4
Format	

```
                        Bit number
                    7 6 5 4    3 2 1 0
Memory cell    m    0 0 1 0    0 0 1 1
              m + 1     Displacement
```

□ **EXAMPLE**

Before Execution		After Execution	
Program counter	5674	Program counter	5676
Status register	CA	Status register	CA
Memory 5674	23	Memory 5674	23
5675	07	5675	07

Both the zero and the carry status bits are cleared, so the condition is not satisfied. The branch is not taken and the next instruction will be the one at 5676_{16}.

68 Branch if Less Than Zero

If the exclusive OR of the sign and overflow bits is 1, the displacement is added to the program counter plus 2, as was explained for the unconditional branch. The program continues execution from that cell. Should the conditions not be met, the instruction is essentially a no operation. The next sequential instruction will be selected in that case.

Operation code	2D
Mnemonic	BLT
Addressing mode	relative
Status bits affected	none
Clock periods	4
Format	

```
                        Bit number
                    7 6 5 4    3 2 1 0
Memory cell    m    0 0 1 0    1 1 0 1
              m + 1     Displacement
```

EXAMPLE

Before Execution		After Execution	
Program counter	E003	Program counter	DFF5
Status register	C8	Status register	C8
Memory E003	2D	Memory E003	2D
E004	F0	E004	F0

The exclusive OR of the sign and overflow bits is 1, so the condition is satisfied. The branch is taken and the next instruction will be the one at DFF5$_{16}$.

68 Branch if Minus

If the sign bit is 1, the displacement is added to the program counter plus 2, as was explained for the unconditional branch. The program continues execution from that cell. Should the condition not be met, the instruction is essentially a no operation. The next sequential instruction will be selected in that case.

Operation code   2B
Mnemonic   BMI
Addressing mode   relative
Status bits affected none
Clock periods   4
Format   Bit number

		7 6 5 4	3 2 1 0
Memory cell	m	0 0 1 0	1 0 1 1
	m + 1	Displacement	

EXAMPLE

Before Execution		After Execution	
Program counter	E003	Program counter	E005
Status register	C7	Status register	C7
Memory E003	2B	Memory E003	2B
E004	F0	E004	F0

The bit is cleared, so the condition is not satisfied. The branch is not taken and the next instruction will be the one at E005$_{16}$.

68 Branch if Not Equal Zero

If the zero bit is 0, the displacement is added to the program counter plus 2, as was explained for the unconditional branch. The program continues execution from that cell. Should the condition not be met, the instruction is essentially a no operation. The next sequential instruction will be selected in that case.

Operation code   26
Mnemonic   BNE

Addressing mode   relative
Status bits affected none
Clock periods   4
Format   Bit number

		7 6 5 4	3 2 1 0
Memory cell	m	0 0 1 0	0 1 1 0
	m + 1	Displacement	

EXAMPLE 1

Before Execution		After Execution	
Program counter	2578	Program counter	259D
Status register	C3	Status register	C3
Memory 2578	26	Memory 2578	26
2579	23	2579	23

The bit is cleared, so the condition is satisfied. The branch is taken and the next instruction will be the one at 259D$_{16}$. Let's consider a program fragment that might cause the not equal condition to be created.

EXAMPLE 2   Check the results of addition.

Address	Machine Code	Comments
1000	8B ⎫	Add immediate to A
1001	40 ⎭	
1002	26 ⎫	Branch if the sum is not
1003	5C ⎭	zero

68 Branch if Overflow Is Clear

If the overflow bit is cleared, the displacement is added to the program counter plus 2, as was explained for the unconditional branch. The program continues execution from that cell. Should the condition not be met, the instruction is essentially a no operation. The next sequential instruction will be selected in that case.

Operation code   28
Mnemonic   BVC
Addressing mode   relative
Status bits affected none
Clock periods   4
Format   Bit number

		7 6 5 4	3 2 1 0
Memory cell	m	0 0 1 0	1 0 0 0
	m + 1	Displacement	

EXAMPLE

Before Execution		After Execution	
Program counter	4B67	Program counter	4600
Status register	C1	Status register	C1

Memory	4B67	28	Memory	4B67	28
	4B68	97		4B68	97

The bit is cleared, so the condition is satisfied. The branch is taken and the next instruction will be the one at 4600_{16}.

[68] Branch if Overflow Is Set

If the overflow bit is set, the displacement is added to the program counter plus 2, as was explained for the unconditional branch. The program continues execution from that cell. Should the condition not be met, the instruction is essentially a no operation. The next sequential instruction will be selected in that case.

Operation code	29
Mnemonic	BVS
Addressing mode	relative
Status bits affected	none
Clock periods	4
Format	

```
                              Bit number
                        7 6 5 4    3 2 1 0
   Memory cell   m     | 0 0 1 0    1 0 0 1 |
                m + 1  |     Displacement    |
```

□ EXAMPLE

Before Execution   **After Execution**

Program counter	4B67	Program counter	4B69
Status register	C1	Status register	C1

Memory	4B67	29	Memory	4B67	29
	4B68	97		4B68	97

The bit is cleared, so the condition is not satisfied. The branch is not taken and the next instruction will be the one at $4B69_{16}$.

[68] Branch if Plus

If the sign bit is cleared, the displacement is added to the program counter plus 2, as was explained for the unconditional branch. The program continues execution from that cell. Should the condition not be met, the instruction is essentially a no operation. The next sequential instruction will be selected in that case.

Operation code	2A
Mnemonic	BPL
Addressing mode	relative
Status bits affected	none
Clock periods	4
Format	

```
                              Bit number
                        7 6 5 4    3 2 1 0
   Memory cell   m     | 0 0 1 0    1 0 1 0 |
                m + 1  |     Displacement    |
```

□ EXAMPLE

Before Execution   **After Execution**

Program counter	1493	Program counter	14A7
Status register	C1	Status register	C1

Memory	1493	2A	Memory	1494	2A
	1494	12		1495	12

The bit is cleared, so the condition is satisfied. The branch is taken and the next instruction will be the one at $14A7_{16}$.

[68] 6800 Conditional Jump and Branch Instructions Review

1. If the condition is true, where is the new address (that is, the address to jump or branch to) found?
2. How can you be sure that the status register properly reflects the condition being tested? Give an example.
3. If you wanted to write a program that checks the result of a boolean operation, which two instructions would you use to jump to address 0140_{16} if the answer were 0 and to 0150_{16} if the answer had odd parity? Does it matter which test is performed first?

MULTIBYTE ADDITION

Chapter 7 gave examples of overflow caused by arithmetic operations that used too short a word length for the quantities included. This section will show how the conditional jumps, together with other instructions, can provide a multibyte addition capability. If the number length selected is 2 bytes, the operation is called *double-precision arithmetic;* 3 bytes is *triple-precision,* and so on. The method discussed here allows the arithmetic to be carried out to whatever level of precision is desired.

Multibyte Addition Algorithm

The technique for multibyte arithmetic is based on the algorithm which follows. Two indices, or subscripts, are used by the algorithm. One index, i, indicates the number of bytes of precision in the operation. (That index is set to 2 for double precision, for example.) The other index, j, is used to fetch data and to store results. The numbers to be added are designated x and y. Bytes are numbered by subscript, with byte 0 being least significant. The sum will replace the initial value for x.

MULTIBYTE ADDITION ALGORITHM

STEP 1. Clear the carry status bit.

STEP 2. Set index i to the number of bytes. Set the address into index j.

STEP 3. Add *with carry* byte x_j to byte y_j.

STEP 4. Store results in x_j.

STEP 5. Decrement index i; increment index j.

STEP 6. Does $i = 0$? If so, stop.

STEP 7. If not, go to Step 3.

We will use the algorithm for a triple-precision addition to show how it works.

☐ **EXAMPLE** Triple-precision addition. Use the algorithm for the problem below.

$$x = 28EB9C_{16}$$
$$y = 79BADF_{16}$$
$$sum = A2A67B_{16}$$

FIRST ITERATION

STEP 1. Clear the carry bit.

STEP 2. Set i to 3, j to 0.

STEP 3. Byte 0 addition with carry

Byte x_0	9C
Byte y_0	DF
Carry	0

$\boxed{1}\,7B$

└─new carry

STEP 4. Store 7B in place of byte x_0.

STEP 5. $i = 2$, $j = 1$.

STEP 6. i is not 0.

STEP 7. Go to Step 3 (second iteration).

SECOND ITERATION

STEP 3. Byte 1 addition with carry.

Byte x_1	EB
Byte y_1	BA
Carry	1

$\boxed{1}\,A6$

└─new carry

STEP 4. Store A6 in place of byte x_1.

STEP 5. $i = 1$, $j = 2$.

STEP 6. i is not 0.

STEP 7. Go to Step 3 (third iteration).

THIRD ITERATION

STEP 3. Byte 2 addition with carry.

Byte x_2	28
Byte y_2	79
Carry	1

$\boxed{0}\,A2$

└─new carry

STEP 4. Store A2 in place of byte x_2.

STEP 5. $i = 0$, $j = 3$.

STEP 6. i does equal 0, so stop.

The sum that was generated in this example is A2A6 $7B_{16}$, which is the correct answer. The sum has replaced the bytes of x.

Multibyte Addition Routine

Next we will consider a program that performs the steps of the multibyte addition algorithm. Figure 8-2 is a memory map of the situation. A flowchart of the program is shown in Fig. 8-3.

LABEL	ADDRESS	CONTENTS	NOTES
NUMBX	0200	9C	BYTE x_0 ←
	0201	EB	BYTE x_1 ← LOCATION OF SUM AFTER EXECUTING THE PROGRAM
	0202	28	BYTE x_2 ←
	⋮		
NUMBY	0210	DF	BYTE y_0
	0211	BA	BYTE y_1
	0212	79	BYTE y_2

Fig. 8-2 Memory map for multibyte addition.

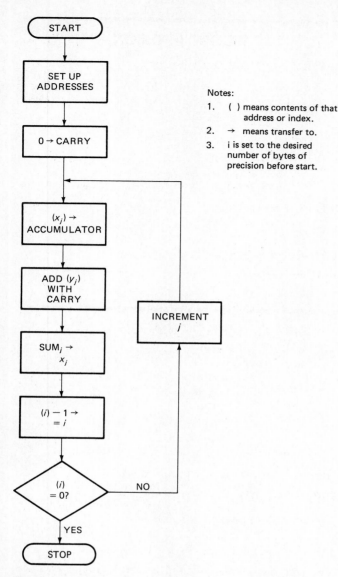

Notes:

1. ( ) means contents of that address or index.
2. → means transfer to.
3. i is set to the desired number of bytes of precision before start.

Fig. 8-3 Multibyte addition flowchart.

The 8085 example is shown in Table 8-1. The C register is used as index i; it must be set to the number of bytes desired for the final sum. The DE and HL register pairs operate as the j index. The numbers x and y are stored from the low-order byte to the high-order byte starting at memory locations labeled NUMBX and NUMBY, respectively. The sum is stored in the same order, starting at address NUMBX.

The 6800 example is shown in Table 8-2. The B register is used for the index i; it must be set to the number of bytes desired for the final sum before the routine starts. The X register operates as the j index. The numbers x and y are stored from the low-order byte to the high-order byte at memory locations labeled NUMBX and NUMBY, respectively. The sum is stored in the same order, starting at location NUMBX.

Multibyte Addition Review

1. Define the term "double-precision arithmetic."
2. Why must the add with carry instruction be used in Step 3 of the algorithm rather than just simple addition?
3. What is the purpose of the two indices used in the algorithm?
4. Draw a memory map similar to Fig. 8-2 for the situation after the program has run to completion.

MULTIBYTE SUBTRACTION

There is, of course, a multibyte subtraction algorithm corresponding to the one for addition in the previous section. Only a minor change to the addition algorithm is needed for this operation. At Step 3 we substitute a subtract with borrow operation for the addition. The algorithm and an example of its use are given below.

MULTIBYTE SUBTRACTION ALGORITHM

STEP 1. Clear carry bit.

STEP 2. Set index i to number of bytes. Set address into index j.

STEP 3. Subtract byte y_j from byte x_j *with borrow*.

STEP 4. Store results in x_j.

STEP 5. Decrement index i; increment index j.

STEP 6. Does $i = 0$? If so, stop.

STEP 7. If not, jump to Step 3.

☐ **EXAMPLE** Double-precision subtraction.

$$x = 3807_{16}$$
$$y = 15AD_{16}$$
$$\text{difference} = 225A_{16}$$

FIRST ITERATION

STEP 1. Clear carry bit.

STEP 2. Set $i = 2$, $j = 0$.

STEP 3. Subtract byte y_0 from byte x_0 with borrow.

		new borrow
Byte x_0	1	07
Byte y_0	−	AD
Borrow	−	0
		5A

Table 8-1 8085 Multibyte Addition Routine

Label	Mnemonic	Operand	Address	Machine Code	Comments
	LXI D	NUMBX	0300	11	NUMBX address →
			0301	00	register pair DE
			0302	02	
	LXI H	NUMBY	0303	21	NUMBY address →
			0304	10	register pair HL
			0305	02	
	XRA	A	0306	AF	Clear carry (XOR A register with itself)
AGAIN	LDAX	D	0307	1A	Byte x_j → A
	ADC	M	0308	8E	Add byte y_j with carry (HL contains address)
	STAX	D	0309	12	Sum_j → memory location x_j
	DCR	C	030A	0D	Decrement i
	JZ	STOP	030B	CA	If $i = 0$, jump
			030C	13	
			030D	03	
	INX	D	030E	13	Otherwise, increment address in DE in preparation for fetching next byte of x
	INX	H	030F	23	Increment address in HL in preparation for fetching next byte of y
	JMP	AGAIN	0310	C3	Go to next iteration
			0311	07	
			0312	03	
STOP	HLT		0313	76	Stop

Table 8-2 6800 Multibyte Addition Routine

Label	Mnemonic	Operand	Address	Machine Code	Comments
	LDX	NUMBX	0300	CE	Initialize j to point to NUMBX
			0301	20	
			0302	00	
	CLC		0303	0C	Clear carry
AGAIN	LDAA	NUMBX	0304	A6	Byte x_i → A
			0305	00	
	ADCA	NUMBY	0306	A9	Add byte y_i with carry
			0307	10	
	STAA	NUMBX	0308	A7	Store sum_i
			0309	00	
	INX		030A	08	Increment j
	DECB		030B	5A	Decrement i
	BNE	AGAIN	030C	26	Go to next iteration
			030D	F6	

FIRST ITERATION (cont'd)

STEP 4. Store difference in x_0.

STEP 5. $i = 1, j = 1$.

STEP 6. i is not 0.

STEP 7. Go to Step 3 (second iteration).

SECOND ITERATION

STEP 3. Subtract byte y_1 from byte x_1 with borrow.

$$
\begin{array}{lr}
& \text{new borrow} \\
\text{Byte } x_1 & \boxed{0} \quad 38 \\
\text{Byte } y_1 & - 15 \\
\text{Borrow} & - 1 \\
\hline
& 22
\end{array}
$$

SECOND ITERATION *(cont'd)*

STEP 4. Store difference in x_1.

STEP 5. $i = 0, j = 2$.

STEP 6. i is equal to 0, so stop.

The final difference is $225A_{16}$. Programs for this algorithm are listed in Tables 8-3 and 8-4. All registers and memory allocations correspond to those of the addition program.

Multibyte Subtraction Review

1. Explain how a modification of the addition algorithm converts it to a multibyte subtraction algorithm.

2. Why is it necessary to clear the carry bit in Step 1 if we are doing subtraction?

3. Where is the difference stored?

Table 8-3 8085 Multibyte Subtraction Routine

Label	Mnemonic	Operand	Address	Machine Code	Comments
	LXI D	NUMBX	0300	11	NUMBX address → DE
			0301	00	
			0302	02	
	LXI H	NUMBY	0303	21	NUMBY address → HL
			0304	10	
			0305	02	
	XRA	A	0306	AF	Clear carry
AGAIN	LDAX	D	0307	1A	Byte x_j → A
	SBB	M	0308	9E	Subtract byte y_j with borrow
	STAX	D	0309	12	Difference$_j$ → memory location x_j
	DCR	C	030A	0D	Decrement i
	JZ	STOP	030B	CA	If $i = 0$, jump to stop
			030C	13	
			030D	03	
	INX	D	030E	13	Otherwise, increment address in DE
	INX	H	030F	23	Increment address in HL
	JMP	AGAIN	0310	C3	Go to next iteration
			0311	07	
			0312	03	
STOP	HLT		0313	76	Stop

Table 8-4 6800 Multibyte Subtraction Routine

Label	Mnemonic	Operand	Address	Machine Code	Comments
	LDX	NUMBX	0300	CE	Initialize j to point to NUMBX
			0301	20	
			0302	00	
	CLC		0303	0C	Clear carry
AGAIN	LDAA	NUMBX	0304	A6	Byte x_i → A
			0305	00	
	SBCA	NUMBY	0306	A2	Subtract byte y_i with carry
			0307	10	
	STAA	NUMBX	0308	A7	Store difference$_i$
			0309	00	
	INX		030A	08	Increment j
	DECB		030B	5A	Decrement i
	BNE	AGAIN	030C	26	Go to next iteration
			030D	F6	

Table 8-5 8085 Multibyte BCD Addition Routine

Label	Mnemonic	Operand	Address	Machine Code	Comments
	LXI D	NUMBX	0300	11	NUMBX address $\rightarrow$ DE
			0301	00	
			0302	02	
	LXI H	NUMBY	0303	21	NUMBY address $\rightarrow$ HL
			0304	10	
			0305	02	
	XRA	A	0306	AF	Clear carry
AGAIN	LDAX	D	0307	1A	Byte $x_j \rightarrow$ A
	ADC	M	0308	8E	Add byte y_i with carry
	DAA		0309	27	Decimal adjust accumulator
	STAX	D	030A	12	Sum$_j \rightarrow$ memory location x_j
	DCR	C	030B	0D	Decrement j
	JZ	STOP	030C	CA	If $j = 0$, jump to stop
			030D	14	
			030E	03	
	INX	D	030F	13	Increment DE
	INX	H	0310	23	Increment HL
	JMP	AGAIN	0311	C3	Go to next iteration
			0312	07	
			0313	03	
	HLT		0314	76	Stop

MULTIBYTE BCD ADDITION

The algorithm for multibyte BCD addition was presented in Chap. 7. As you recall, the DAA instruction is the key element in providing that function. Because the algorithm was thoroughly discussed before, only the listing for the routine is given in Tables 8-5 and 8-6. You may wish to review the earlier material to understand the instruction sequence better. It is identical to the previous multibyte addition program, except a DAA instruction is inserted after the add with carry.

MULTIBYTE BCD SUBTRACTION

The final algorithm in this chapter combines our previous knowledge of arithmetic and conditional jumps with new concept to perform a BCD subtraction. We will be using the 9's complement of a decimal number,

Table 8-6 6800 Multibyte BCD Addition Routine

Label	Mnemonic	Operand	Address	Machine Code	Comments
	LDX	NUMBX	0300	CE	Initialize j to point to NUMBX
			0301	20	
			0302	00	
	CLC		0303	0C	Clear carry
AGAIN	LDAA	NUMBX	0304	A6	Byte $x_i \rightarrow$ A
			0305	00	
	ADCA	NUMBY	0306	A9	Add byte y_i with carry
			0307	10	
	DAA		0308	19	Decimal adjust
	STAA	NUMBX	0309	A7	Store sum$_i$
			030A	00	
	INX		030B	08	Increment j
	DECB		030C	5A	Decrement i
	BNE	AGAIN	030D	26	Go to next iteration
			030E	F5	

which corresponds to the 1's complement in binary. The reason for using the 9's complement is to adjust the auxiliary carry status bit setting properly prior to using the DAA instruction.

BCD SUBTRACTION ALGORITHM

STEP 1. Set the carry bit. (This will simulate no borrow for the first iteration.)

STEP 2. Set the accumulator to 99 (the 9's complement of 0).

STEP 3. Add 0 to the accumulator with carry. (The sum will be either 99_{16} or $9A_{16}$.)

STEP 4. Subtract the subtrahend byte from the accumulator.

STEP 5. Add the minuend byte to the accumulator.

STEP 6. Use DAA to obtain the BCD format and properly set the carry status (1 = no borrow, 0 = borrow). Store the difference byte.

STEP 7. If there are more bytes, go to Step 2; otherwise, stop.

☐ **EXAMPLE**   Multibyte BCD subtraction.

$$
\begin{array}{ll}
\text{Minuend} & 5829 \\
\text{Subtrahend} & -\ 3289 \\
\hline
& 2540
\end{array}
$$

FIRST ITERATION

STEP 1. Set carry = 1.

STEP 2. Set A to 99_{16}.

STEP 3. Add 0 to A with carry.

$$
\begin{array}{r}
99 \\
+\ 0 \\
+\ 1 \leftarrow \text{carry} \\
\hline
9A
\end{array}
$$

STEP 4. Subtract subtrahend's least significant byte.

Auxiliary carry

1 Carry 0

$$
\begin{array}{lll}
9A_{16} = & 1001\ 1010 \\
-\ 89_{16} = & +\ 0111\ 0111 & \text{(2's complement)} \\
\hline
11_{16} = & 0001\ 0001
\end{array}
$$

STEP 5. Add minuend's least significant byte.

0   0

$$
\begin{array}{lll}
11_{16} = & 0001\ 0001_2 \\
+\ 29_{16} = & +\ 0010\ 1001_2 \\
\hline
3A_{16} = & 0011\ 1010_2
\end{array}
$$

STEP 6. Decimal adjust.

0   1

$$
\begin{array}{lll}
3A_{16} = & 0011\ 1010 \\
+\ 6_{16} = & +\ 0110_2 \\
\hline
40_{16} = & 0100\ 0000_2
\end{array}
$$

STEP 7. Store the least significant byte of the difference. There are more bytes, so go to Step 2 (second iteration).

SECOND ITERATION

STEP 2. Set A to 99_{16}.

STEP 3. Add 0 with carry.

$$
\begin{array}{r}
99 \\
+\ 0 \\
+\ 0 \leftarrow \text{Carry from Step 6 of first iteration} \\
\hline
99
\end{array}
$$

STEP 4. Subtract subtrahend's most significant byte.

1   1

$$
\begin{array}{lll}
99_{16} = & 1001\ 1001_2 \\
-\ 32_{16} = & +\ 1100\ 1110_2 & \text{(2's complement)} \\
\hline
67_{16} = & 0110\ 0111_2
\end{array}
$$

STEP 5. Add minuend's most significant byte.

0   0

$$
\begin{array}{lll}
67_{16} = & 0110\ 0111_2 \\
+\ 58_{16} = & +\ 0101\ 1000_2 \\
\hline
BF_{16} & 1011\ 1111_2
\end{array}
$$

STEP 6. Decimal adjust.

0   1

$$
\begin{array}{lll}
BF_{16} = & 1011\ 1111_2 \\
+\ 6_{16} = & +\ 0110_2 \\
\hline
C5_{16} = & 1100\ 0101_2
\end{array}
$$

1

$$
\begin{array}{lll}
C5_{16} = & 1100\ 0101_2 \\
+\ 60_{16} = & +\ 0110\ 0000_2 \\
\hline
25_{16} = & 0010\ 0101_2
\end{array}
$$

STEP 7. Store the most significant byte of the difference. There are no more bytes, so stop.

Table 8-7 8085 Multibyte BCD Subtraction Routine

Label	Mnemonic	Operand	Address	Machine Code	Comments
	LXI D	MINU	0500	11	Minuend address → register pair DE
			0501	00	
			0502	02	
	LXI H	SBTRA	0503	21	Subtrahend address → register pair HL
			0504	10	
			0505	02	
	STC		0506	37	Set carry bit
AGAIN	MVI A	99	0507	3E	99_{16} → A (1's complement of 0)
			0508	99	
	ACI	0	0509	CE	
			050A	00	
	SUB	M	050B	96	Subtract subtrahend byte
	XCHG		050C	EB	Interchange contents of DE and HL
	ADD	M	050D	86	Add minuend byte
	DAA		050E	27	Decimal adjust accumulator
	MOV	M, A	050F	77	Store difference byte
	DCR	C	0510	0D	Decrement counter
	JZ	STOP	0511	CA	Jump to stop if 0
			0512	1A	
			0513	05	
	XCHG		0514	EB	Interchange contents of DE and HL
	INX	D	0515	13	Increment address of minuend byte
	INX	H	0516	23	Increment address of subtrahend byte
	JMP	AGAIN	0517	C3	Jump to next iteration
			0518	07	
			0519	05	
	STOP	HLT	051A	76	Stop

Table 8-8 6800 Multibyte BCD Subtraction Routine

Label	Mnemonic	Operand	Address	Machine Code	Comments
	LDX	MINU	0300	CE	Initialize j to point to MINU
			0301	20	
			0302	00	
	SEC		0303	0D	Set carry 99_{16} → A
AGAIN	LDAA	99	0304	86	
			0305	99	
	ADCA	0	0306	89	Add 0 with carry
			0307	00	
	SBCA	SBTRA	0308	A0	Subtract subtrahend
			0309	10	
	ADCA	MINU	030A	A9	Add minuend
			030B	00	
	DAA		030C	19	Decimal adjust
	STAA	MINU	030D	A7	Store sum_i
			030E	00	
	INX		030F	08	Increment j
	DECB		0310	5A	Decrement i
	BNE	AGAIN	0311	26	Go to next iteration
			0312	F1	

LABEL	ADDRESS	CONTENTS	NOTES	
MINU	0200	29	MINUEND BYTE 0	← LOCATION OF DIFFERENCE AFTER
	0201	58	MINUEND BYTE 1	← EXECUTING THE PROGRAM
	⋮			
SBTRA	0210	89	SUBTRAHEND BYTE 0	
	0211	32	SUBTRAHEND BYTE 1	

Fig. 8-4 Multibyte BCD subtraction memory map.

Multibyte BCD Subtraction Routine

The programs in Tables 8-7 and 8-8 perform BCD subtraction on numbers of arbitrary length. The minuend is stored with the least significant byte first, starting at the address labeled MINU. The subtrahend is similarly stored, starting at address SBTRA. The bytes of the difference will replace the corresponding bytes in the minuend. Figure 8-4 is a memory map for this situation. A flowchart for the program is given in Fig.

8-5. Before program execution, the C register (in the 8085) must be set equal to the number of bytes in the numbers.

A few comments on this routine will clarify some steps that may seem obscure. The routine relies on register addressing for the arithmetic instruction (addresses $050B_{16}$ and $050D_{16}$). Therefore, the operand address must be in the HL register pair prior to the arithmetic operation. The address of the subtrahend is initially in HL, but the exchange instruction at $050C_{16}$ swaps that for the address of the minuend. The second exchange,

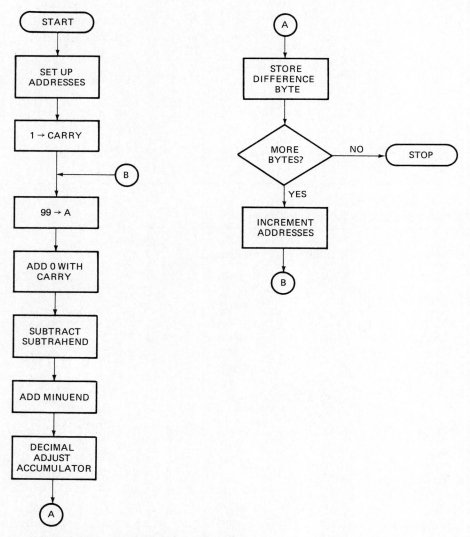

Fig. 8-5 Multibyte BCD subtraction flowchart.

at 0514_{16}, restores the original order for the next iteration. The C register is used as the index for the size of the numbers. When it decrements to 0, all bytes have been processed.

Multibyte BCD Subtraction Review

1. Explain why the 9's complement must be used for BCD subtraction.

2. What is the purpose of Step 6 in the BCD subtraction algorithm?

3. Distinguish between the operations performed in iterations 1 and 2 for Step 6 of the example.

4. How are the addresses specified by the memory map for the minuend, the subtrahend, and the difference initialized in the BCD subtraction routine?

5. What error would occur if the flowchart for this routine were altered and the connector labeled "B" reentered the flow above the "1 → carry" process box?

CHAPTER SUMMARY

1. Jump and branch instructions transfer control to an instruction that is not in the normal sequence. Unconditional jumps and branches always transfer control. Conditional jumps and branches make the transfer only if the tested condition is true.

Table 8-9 8085 Jump Instruction Summary*

Instruction	Machine Code	Number of Bytes
JC	DA	3
JM	FA	3
JMP	C3	3
JNC	D2	3
JNZ	C2	3
JP	F2	3
JPE	EA	3
JPO	E2	3
JZ	CA	3
PCHL	E9	1

* Status bits not affected by jump instructions.

Table 8-10 6800 Jump and Branch Instruction Summary*

Instruction	Machine Code	Number of Bytes	Addressing Mode
BRA	20	2	Relative
BCC	24	2	Relative
BCS	25	2	Relative
BEQ	27	2	Relative
BGE	2C	2	Relative
BGT	2E	2	Relative
BHI	22	2	Relative
BLE	2F	2	Relative
BLS	23	2	Relative
BLT	2D	2	Relative
BMI	2B	2	Relative
BNE	26	2	Relative
BVC	28	2	Relative
BVS	29	2	Relative
BPL	2A	2	Indexed
JMP	6E, 7E	2, 3	Extended

* Status bits not affected by jump and branch instructions.

2. The conditional jumps can test the condition of the carry, zero, sign, or parity bits. Prior to executing the jump instruction, the status bits must be correctly set. Usually this action is the result of an arithmetic or a logical instruction.

3. Multiple-precision arithmetic is necessary to prevent overflow of large numbers. The multibyte addition algorithm relies on the add with carry instruction to produce sums of more than 1 byte. The algorithm permits the summing of numbers of any size.

4. Multibyte subtraction is a simple modification of the addition algorithm. A subtract with borrow operation replaces the add with carry in this process.

5. Multibyte BCD addition and subtraction are also possible. The decimal adjust accumulator instruction is the key to these functions. The subtraction algorithm depends on the 9's complement because the auxiliary carry status bit is not correctly set after subtraction.

6. A summary of all 8085 jump instructions is presented in Table 8-9.

7. A summary of all 6800 jump and branch instructions is presented in Table 8-10.

KEY TERMS AND CONCEPTS

Unconditional jump

Conditional jump

Jump if carry

Jump if no carry

Jump if zero

Jump if not zero

Jump if minus

Jump if plus

Jump if parity even

Jump if parity odd

Unconditional branch

Conditional branch

Branch if carry set

Branch if carry clear

Branch if zero

Branch if greater than or equal to zero

Branch if greater than zero

Branch if higher

Branch if less than or equal to zero

Branch if lower or same

Branch if less than zero

Branch if minus

Branch if not zero

Branch if overflow clear

Branch if overflow set

Branch if plus

Double-precision arithmetic

Multibyte addition

Multibyte subtraction

Multibyte BCD addition

Multibyte BCD subtraction

PROBLEMS

8-1 Draw a flowchart for the multibyte subtraction algorithm.

8-2 Demonstrate the use of the multibyte addition algorithm, in a manner similar to Example 3 of Chap. 7, for the following problem:

$$\begin{array}{r} 6A \quad B2 \quad DD_{16} \\ + \ 72 \quad 97 \quad F0_{16} \end{array}$$

8-3 Draw a memory map and list the final contents of the accumulator registers for either the 8085 or the 6800, the program counter, and the status register after the multibyte subtraction routine has run to completion for the following problem:

$$\begin{array}{r} 9A \quad 1F_{16} \\ - \ 62 \quad BC_{16} \end{array}$$

8-4 For the BCD addition below, show the iterations of the algorithm necessary to produce the correct sum.

$$\begin{array}{r} 1 \ 9 \ 5 \ 6 \\ + \ 3 \ 8 \ 7 \ 5 \end{array}$$

8-5 In a manner similar to Example 5 of Chap. 7, record the steps for each iteration of this BCD subtraction.

$$\begin{array}{r} 6 \ 3 \ 1 \ 2 \ 0 \ 4 \\ - \ 5 \ 8 \ 9 \ 5 \ 3 \ 7 \end{array}$$

8-6 Write a routine that will branch to address 5600_{16} after reading a number that is equal to 0 from memory cell 0111_{16}. (The routine must first fetch that information prior to attempting to examine it.)

8-7 Write a routine that will make a decision based on the sign of a number stored in memory:

If the number is positive, go to address 0100_{16}.
If the number is negative, go to address 0200_{16}.
If the number is 0, go to address 0300_{16}.

The quantity of interest is stored at location 0513_{16}.

8-8 Write a routine that will exclusively OR $F0_{16}$ with the number in cell 0500_{16} if it is positive and exclusively OR $0F_{16}$ with the number if it is negative.

8-9 Write a routine to compute the number of years between any 2 years in the first to the ninety-ninth century. Your routine should check that the years involved are between 1 and 9999_{10}.

8-10 A program that compares the number in two memory cells must be written. If the number in the lower address is the smaller, set that address to 0. If the numbers are equal, set the higher address to 1.

CHAPTER 9

SHIFTING

The processor can function as a shift register by use of the group of shift commands. These operations, also called *rotate the accumulator* instructions, are handy for manipulating individual bits in a data word and also provide the means for multiplying or dividing numbers in the MPU.

CHAPTER OBJECTIVES

Upon completion of this chapter you should be able to:

1. Show how shift instructions can be used for scaling.
2. Explain the rotate accumulator instructions.
3. Distinguish between a normal rotation and a rotation-through-carry operation.
4. Write a multiplication routine based on shift instructions.
5. Describe the function of shift instructions in a division routine.

SHIFTING CONCEPTS

Shifting a register causes each bit in that register to move left or right one position. Before examining the actual shifting methods, let's consider a simplified form of shifting. Figure 9-1*a* shows the result of left-shifting an 8-bit register: Each bit has replaced the one in the next higher-order position; that is, bit 0 becomes bit 1, bit 1 becomes bit 2, and so on. The most significant bit (MSB) is discarded, and a 0 enters from the right. In a right shift (Fig. 9-1*b*), the bits move down one order; the least significant bit (LSB) is lost, and a 0 is entered as the most significant bit.

Another effect of shifting that can be seen in Fig. 9-1 is multiplication or division by 2. By left-shifting the number, we have multiplied it by 2 ($97_{16} \times 2_{16} = 12E_{16}$). Because of overflow, the most significant digit has been lost in this example. By performing multiple left shifts, we multiply by powers of 2. After n shifts, the original number is multiplied by 2^n. Care must be exercised to prevent overflow when this technique is used. Right shifting produces the opposite effect. A right shift divides by 2, as Fig. 9-1*b* demonstrates:

$$\frac{AD_{16}}{2_{16}} = 56_{16}$$

Shifting to produce binary multiplications or divisions is sometimes called *scaling*. Numbers may be scaled down to avoid overflow or scaled up to obtain greater precision. Scaling is often used with double-precision arithmetic.

As an example of scaling, consider the problem of adding 1.6_{16} to 5_{16}. There is no way of representing a radix point directly because all numbers are treated as integers. The programmer, however, can use scaling to overcome this difficulty. The person writing the program must remember to treat the scaled numbers properly from then on. By examining the numbers, we note that the smaller number must be scaled up at least four binary places to preserve its full significance.

$$1.6_{16} = 0001.\ 0110_2$$

Four places / Last position of significance / Radix point

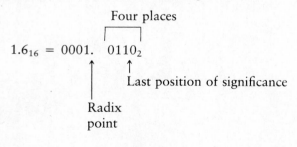

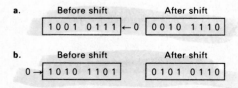

Fig. 9-1 Shifting: (a) left shift, (b) right shift.

In scaling, we must always balance preserving significance against preventing overflow. We can check for overflow by seeing how many places the larger number can be scaled without producing an overflow in the sum.

These bits can be shifted off

$$05_{16} = 0000\ 0101._2$$

Radix point
A 0 must be kept in the sign bit position

The final scaling and sum would look like this:

$$\begin{array}{ll} 1.6_{16}\text{ scaled up four places} = & 0001\quad 0110_2 \\ 5_{16}\text{ scaled up four places} = & +\,0101\quad 0000_2 \\ \hline & 0110\quad 0110_2 \end{array}$$

We must remember the implicit radix point in the sum. It must be treated as 6.6_{16}, not as 66_{16}.

Every scaling situation requires that the magnitude of the numbers involved be examined. Many times a single-byte word length is inadequate, so double precision is needed. What would have happened in the scaling example above if we had wanted to add 1.6_{16} to 7_{16}? By using the same 4 bits of scaling, we have:

$$\begin{array}{ll} 1.6_{16}\text{ scaled} = & 0001\quad 0110_2 \\ 7_{16}\text{ scaled} = & +\,0111\quad 0000_2 \\ \hline & 1000\quad 0110_2 \end{array}$$

Overflow
Sum is negative

The sum overflowed the 8-bit length. Now we may choose either to decrease the precision (to 3 bits, for instance) or to employ multibyte arithmetic.

To show that scaling need not always be in 4-bit increments, we will work this problem with 3 bits of precision. The digits will no longer be directly recognizable in hexadecimal because of the shifting, but the correct answer can be retrieved in spite of this complication (by writing the number in binary).

$$\begin{array}{ll} 1.6_{16}\text{ scaled 3 bits} = & 0000\quad 1011_2 \\ 7_{16}\text{ scaled 3 bits} = & +\,0100\quad 1000_2 \\ \hline & 0100\quad 0011_2 \end{array}$$

(The augend appears to be $0B_{16}$ and the addend 38_{16}.) The LSB of 1.6_{16} has been lost. The answer appears to be 43_{16}, but properly scaled, the correct sum appears:

$$0100\quad 0011_2\ =\ 0\ 1000.\ 0110_2$$

Radix point   Zero brought in
$$= 8.6_{16}$$

The trailing 0 had to be reinserted in the LSB position.

Shifting Concepts Review

1. Explain why a left shift can be considered to be equivalent to multiplication by 2.
2. What happens to the MSB in a right shift? The LSB?
3. What two errors must you guard against when using scaling?
4. Why did the sum appear to be 43_{16} in the 3-bit scaling example? How was that problem resolved?

🔲 8085 ROTATE ACCUMULATOR INSTRUCTIONS

These are four instructions that rotate, or shift, the accumulator in the 8085. All the instructions use the carry status bit together with the accumulator for the rotation. The carry bit may be thought of as an independent single-bit register in conjunction with the shift operation.

🔲 Rotate Accumulator Left

This instruction places the MSB of the accumulator in the carry bit. The accumulator is shifted left, and the previous MSB is also put in the LSB position of the register. Figure 9-2 shows the movement of the bits. This instruction may be thought of as a circular left shift, in that the accumulator content is circulated out the left side of the register and into the right side.

Operation code	07
Mnemonic	RLC
Addressing mode	none
Status bits affected	carry
Clock periods	4
Format	Bit number

```
                      7 6 5 4   3 2 1 0
Memory cell   m  | 0 0 0 0   0 1 1 1 |
```

🔲 EXAMPLE

Before Execution		After Execution	
Program counter	0400	Program counter	0401
A register	B7	A register	6F
Status register	02	Status register	03
Memory 0400	07	Memory 0400	07

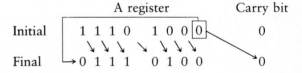

Fig. 9-2 8085 rotate accumulator left.

The A register is shifted left. The MSB causes the carry bit to be set. These changes may be more easily seen in a binary format:

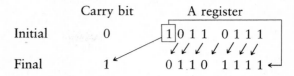

🔲 Rotate Accumulator Right

This instruction causes the LSB of the accumulator to be moved to the carry bit and to the MSB of the register. The remaining bits in the register are right-shifted. Figure 9-3 shows the result of executing the instruction.

Operation code	0F
Mnemonic	RRC
Addressing mode	none
Status bits affected	carry
Clock periods	4
Format	Bit number

```
                      7 6 5 4   3 2 1 0
Memory cell   m  | 0 0 0 0   1 1 1 1 |
```

🔲 EXAMPLE

Before Execution		After Execution	
Program counter	0370	Program counter	0371
A register	E8	A register	74
Status register	06	Status register	06
Memory 0370	0F	Memory 0370	0F

There is no change in the status register because the LSB of the A register is 0.

```
                  A register           Carry bit
Initial    1 1 1 0   1 0 0 0              0
Final      0 1 1 1   0 1 0 0              0
```

🔲 Rotate Accumulator Left Through Carry

Rotating through the carry is equivalent to a 9-bit shift. The carry bit is moved into the LSB of the accumulator,

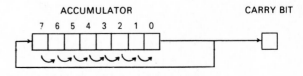

Fig. 9-3 8085 rotate accumulator right.

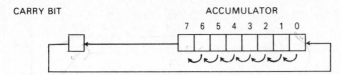

Fig. 9-4   8085 rotate accmulator left through carry.

the accumulator is shifted left, and the MSB of the register goes to the carry bit. Figure 9-4 shows this operation.

Operation code	17
Mnemonic	RAL
Addressing mode	none
Status bits affected	carry
Clock periods	4
Format	Bit number

		7 6 5 4	3 2 1 0
Memory cell	m	0 0 0 1	0 1 1 1

□ EXAMPLE

Before Execution		After Execution	
Program counter	0A10	Program counter	0A11
A register	CA	A register	94
Status register	82	Status register	83
Memory 0A10	17	Memory 0A10	17

The MSB of A sets the carry condition bit.

	Carry bit	A register
Initial	0	1 1 0 0 1 0 1 0
Final	1	1 0 0 1 0 1 0 0

⑧⓪ Rotate Accumulator Right Through Carry

This instruction right-circular-shifts the accumulator and the carry status as a 9-bit entity. The carry status goes to the MSB of the register, the accumulator is right-shifted, and the LSB is transferred to the carry bit. Figure 9-5 illustrates the rotation.

Operation code	1F
Mnemonic	RAR
Addressing mode	none

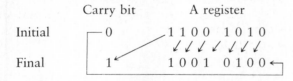

Fig. 9-5   8085 rotate accumulator right through carry.

Status bits affected	carry
Clock periods	4
Format	Bit number

		7 6 5 4	3 2 1 0
Memory cell	m	0 0 0 1	1 1 1 1

□ EXAMPLE

Before Execution		After Execution	
Program counter	0880	Program counter	0881
A register	6F	A register	87
Status register	03	Status register	03
Memory 0880	1F	Memory 0880	1F

The carry status remains unchanged because the LSB of the accumulator is 1.

	A register	Carry
Initial	0 1 1 0 1 1 1 1	1 ←
Final	1 0 1 1 0 1 1 1	1

⑧⓪ 8085 Rotate Accumulator Instructions Review

1. Explain why the rotate accumulator right instruction may be called a "circular shift."
2. Distinguish between the rotate accumulator left and the rotate acccumulator left through carry instructions.
3. In the example for the RRC instruction, why is the carry bit 0 after execution?
4. If the instruction sequence RLC and then RAR were executed, what change, if any, would occur in the A register and the carry register contents?

⑥⑧ 6800 ROTATE ACCUMULATOR AND MEMORY INSTRUCTIONS

There are five sets of instructions that rotate, or shift, the A or B accumulators or a memory cell in the 6800. All the instructions use the carry status bit with the accumulator for the rotation. The carry bit may be thought of as an independent single-bit register in conjunction with the shift operation.

⑥⑧ Arithmetic Shift Accumulator or Memory Left

This instruction places the MSB of the accumulator or memory cell in the carry bit. The accumulator or memory cell is shifted left, and the LSB is set to 0. The zero,

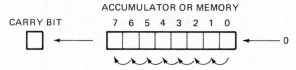

Fig. 9-6 6800 shift left.

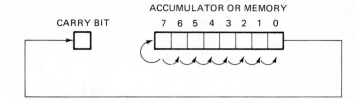

Fig. 9-7 6800 shift right.

overflow, and sign status bits are set according to the result. Figure 9-6 shows the movement of the bits.

Addressing Mode	Mnemonic	Operation Code	Clock Periods
Indexed	ASL	68	7
Extended	ASL	78	6
Inherent	ASLA	48	2
Inherent	ASLB	58	2

Status bits affected	sign, zero, overflow, and carry bits
Format	standard for addressing mode

☐ EXAMPLE

Before Execution		After Execution	
Program counter	0400	Program counter	0401
A register	B7	A register	6E
Status register	C8	Status register	C3
Memory 0400	48	Memory 0400	48

The A register is shifted left and the MSB causes the carry bit to be set. The sign bit is reset. The overflow bit becomes set. These changes become more obvious in binary format:

```
        Carry bit        A register
Initial     0         1 0 1 1  0 1 1 1   Original num-
                       / / / / / / / /    ber is negative
Final       1         0 1 1 0  1 1 1 0   Positive num-
                                          ber; overflow
                                          has occurred
```

68 Arithmetic Shift Accumulator or Memory Right

This instruction places the LSB of the accumulator or memory cell in the carry bit. The accumulator or memory cell is shifted right, and the MSB remains unchanged. The zero, overflow, and sign status bits are set according to the result. Figure 9-7 shows the movement of the bits.

Addressing Mode	Mnemonic	Operation Code	Clock Periods
Indexed	ASR	67	7
Extended	ASR	77	6
Inherent	ASRA	47	2
Inherent	ASRB	57	2

Status bits affected	sign, zero, overflow, and carry bits
Format	standard for addressing mode

☐ EXAMPLE

Before Execution		After Execution	
Program counter	0380	Program counter	0383
Status register	C9	Status register	C8
Memory 0380	77	Memory 0380	77
0381	05	0381	05
0382	00	0382	00
0500	E8	0500	F4

The memory cell is shifted right and the LSB causes the carry bit to be reset. The sign bit remains set because the sign stays negative. These changes become more obvious in binary format:

```
         Carry bit    Memory cell 0500
Initial      1        1 1 1 0  1 0 0 0   Original num-
                      ↓↓↓↓  ↘ ↓↓↓        ber is negative
Final        0        1 1 1 1  0 1 0 0   Negative
                                          number
```

68 Logical Shift Accumulator or Memory Right

This instruction places the LSB of the accumulator or memory cell in the carry bit. The accumulator or memory cell is shifted right, and the MSB is set to 0. The zero, overflow, and sign status bits are set according to the result. Figure 9-8 shows the movement of the bits.

Addressing Mode	Mnemonic	Operation Code	Clock Periods
Indexed	LSR	64	7
Extended	LSR	74	6
Inherent	LSRA	44	2
	LSRB	54	2

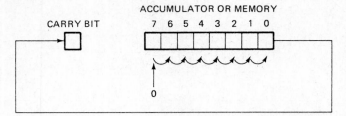

Fig. 9-8   6800 logical shift right.

Status bits affected — sign, zero, overflow, and carry bits

Format — standard for addressing mode

☐ EXAMPLE

Before Execution		After Execution	
Program counter	0100	Program counter	0101
B register	C9	B register	64
Status register	C8	Status register	C3
Memory 0100	54	Memory 0100	54

The B register is shifted right, and the LSB causes the carry bit to be set. The sign bit is reset. The overflow bit becomes set. These changes become more obvious in binary format:

	Carry bit	B register	
Initial	0	1 1 0 0 1 0 0 1	Original number is negative
Final	1	0 1 1 0 0 1 0 0	Positive number; overflow has occurred

68 Rotate Accumulator or Memory Left

This instruction places the MSB of the accumulator or memory cell in the carry bit. The accumulator or memory cell is shifted left, and the MSB is set to the original carry bit. The zero, overflow, and sign status bits are set according to the result. Figure 9-9 shows the movement of the bits.

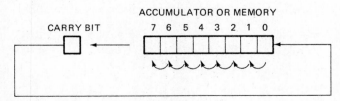

Fig. 9-9   6800 rotate left.

Addressing Mode	Mnemonic	Operation Code	Clock Periods
Indexed	ROL	69	7
Extended	ROL	79	6
Inherent	ROLA	49	2
	ROLB	59	2

Status bits affected — sign, zero, overflow, and carry bits

Format — standard for addressing mode

☐ EXAMPLE

Before Execution		After Execution	
Program counter	0A10	Program counter	0A11
A register	CA	A register	95
Status register	C9	Status register	C9
Memory 0A10	49	Memory 0A10	49

The A register is shifted left, and the MSB causes the carry bit to remain set. The sign bit also remains set. These changes become more obvious in binary format:

	Carry bit	A register	
Initial	1	1 1 0 0 1 0 1 0	Original number is negative
Final	1	1 0 0 1 0 1 0 1	Negative number

68 Rotate Accumulator or Memory Right

This instruction places the LSB of the accumulator or memory cell in the carry bit. The accumulator or memory cell is shifted right, and the MSB is set equal to the original carry bit. The zero, overflow, and sign status bits are set according to the result. Figure 9-10 shows the movement of the bits.

Addressing Mode	Mnemonic	Operation Code	Clock Periods
Indexed	ROR	66	7
Extended	ROR	76	6
Inherent	RORA	46	2
Inherent	RORB	56	2

Status bits affected — sign, zero, overflow, and carry bits

Format — standard for addressing mode

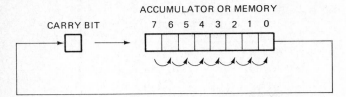

CARRY BIT   ACCUMULATOR OR MEMORY
7 6 5 4 3 2 1 0

Fig. 9-10   6800 rotate right.

☐ EXAMPLE

Before Execution		After Execution	
Program counter	0880	Program counter	0883
Status register	C1	Status register	CB
Memory 0880	76	Memory 0880	76
0881	0F	0881	0F
0882	01	0882	01
0F01	6F	0F01	B7

The memory cell is shifted right, and the LSB causes the carry bit to be set. The sign bit becomes set because the sign becomes negative. These changes become more obvious in binary format:

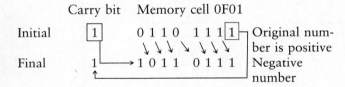

	Carry bit	Memory cell 0F01	
Initial	1	0 1 1 0 1 1 1 1	Original number is positive
Final	1	1 0 1 1 0 1 1 1	Negative number

⑥⑧ 6800 Rotate Accumulator and Memory Instructions Review

1. Why are rotate instructions sometimes called circular shifts?
2. How does the right-shift instruction differ from the logical right shift?
3. Which of the shift and rotate instructions leave the original sign bit of the number unchanged?
4. True or false? A rotate left instruction followed by a rotate right instruction restores the value of the original number.

SOFTWARE MULTIPLICATION

Combining rotations with other instructions will allow us to multiply numbers in the microprocessor. While relying on a program cannot duplicate the speed of high-speed multiplication circuits, software can adequately satisfy the needs for many applications. The algorithm in this section will multiply two unsigned 8-bit quantities and produce a 16-bit product. (In general, multiplying two numbers m bits long will generate a product $2m$ bits in length.)

There are two approaches to solving the problem of multiplication. We could use repetitive addition, such as adding $2A_{16}$ to itself 59_{16} times to find $2A_{16} \times 59_{16}$. A faster method relies on a combination of shifting and adding. Our algorithm uses the latter procedure.

MULTIPLICATION ALGORITHM

STEP 1.   Clear the product storage area.

STEP 2.   If the LSB of the multiplier is 0, go to Step 3; otherwise, add the multiplicand to the most significant byte of the product.

STEP 3.   Right-shift the multiplier and the 2-byte product. Have all 8 bits of the multiplier been examined? If not, go to Step 2.

An example showing all steps of the algorithm to calculate

$$\begin{array}{r} 4F_{16} \quad \text{Multiplicand} \\ \times \ 3D_{16} \quad \text{Multiplier} \\ \hline 12D3_{16} \quad \text{Product} \end{array}$$

is given in Table 9-1. You should trace the algorithm through each iteration to assure your understanding of the addition and shifting concept.

In iteration 1 of Table 9-1, the LSB of the multiplier is 1, so the multiplicand is added to the most significant byte of the product. There is no addition of the multiplicand in iteration 2 because the multiplier is $1E_{16}$. Addition does take place for iterations 3 through 6. From that point on the multiplier is 0, so no more additions are needed. Each pass through the algorithm results in a right shift of the double-byte product and of the multiplier.

Before examining the program for multiplication, let's discuss the technique to be used in shifting the 2-byte product. As Fig. 9-11 shows, the shifting requires two operations. In the first operation the most significant byte is right-shifted through the carry. Then the least significant byte is rotated right through the carry. Because only the accumulator can be used for shifting,

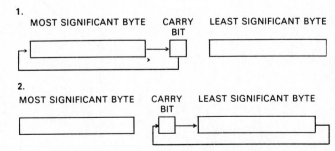

1.
MOST SIGNIFICANT BYTE   CARRY BIT   LEAST SIGNIFICANT BYTE

2.
MOST SIGNIFICANT BYTE   CARRY BIT   LEAST SIGNIFICANT BYTE

Fig. 9-11   Shifting a double length product.

Table 9-1 Multiplication Algorithm Example

Iteration	Step	Multiplier		Product			
				Most Significant Byte		Least Significant Byte	
1	1	0011	1101	0000	0000	0000	0000
	2	0011	1101	0100	1111	0000	0000
	3	0001	1110	0010	0111	1000	0000
2	2	0001	1110	0010	0111	1000	0000
	3	0000	1111	0001	0011	1100	0000
3	2	0000	1111	0110	0010	1100	0000
	3	0000	0111	0011	0001	0110	0000
4	2	0000	0111	1000	0000	0110	0000
	3	0000	0011	0100	0000	0011	0000
5	2	0000	0011	1000	1111	0011	0000
	3	0000	0001	0100	0111	1001	1000
6	2	0000	0001	1001	0110	1001	1000
	3	0000	0000	0100	1011	0100	1100
7	2	0000	0000	0100	1011	0100	1100
	3	0000	0000	0010	0101	1010	0110
8	2	0000	0000	0010	0101	1010	0110
	3	0000	0000	0001	0010	1101	0011

Table 9-2 8085 Multiplication Routine

Label	Mnemonic	Operand	Address	Machine Code	Comments
	MVI B	0	1000	06	Zero the most significant half (MSH) of the product
			1001	00	Set counter for eight iterations
	MVI E	9	1002	1E	
			1003	09	
STEP 2	MOV	A, C	1004	79	Rotate bit of multiplier to carry and shift
	RAR		1005	1F	
	MOV	C, A	1006	4F	Restore register
	DCR	E	1007	1D	Decrement counter
	JZ	STOP	1008	CA	Jump to stop if eight iterations have been completed
			1009	15	
			100A	10	
	MOV	A, B	100B	78	If not, MSH of product → A
	JNC	STEP 3	100C	D2	If bit of multiplier is 0, skip addition
			100D	10	
			100E	10	
	ADD	D	100F	82	Add multiplicand to MSH of product
STEP 3	RAR		1010	1F	Shift MSH of product
	MOV	B, A	1011	47	Restore register
	JMP	STEP 2	1012	C3	Jump to next iteration
			1013	04	
			1014	10	
STOP	HLT		1015	76	Halt

other registers must be used for temporary storage of the data in between shifts. The 8085 program will use the B and C registers for that purpose.

The 8085 multiplication program in Table 9-2 uses three registers to hold the values involved in the process. The C register must be set to the multiplier value before starting into the routine, and the D register is initially set to the multiplicand. The double-length product will be developed in the BC register pair, with the B register holding the most significant byte. By using the C register for both the multiplier and the least significant half (LSH) of the product, both quantities can be shifted by using a single instruction.

The instruction at address 1000_{16} simply clears the most significant byte of the product. Next, the index (E register) is set to stop the process after nine iterations. Starting into the main body of the routine, the multiplier and least significant product byte are rotated through the carry. After the counter has been decremented and nine iterations have been completed, the process examines the LSB of the multiplier (which had been moved to the carry bit by the instruction at 1005_{16}). If the bit is a 1, the multiplicand (in the D register) is added to the upper product. The routine then jumps to the next iteration. After eight times through the main program, the process is halted. Now we can understand why the index had to be set to 9, although only eight iterations were needed. A final right shift of the least significant byte of the product was needed after the last pass through the routine.

The 6800 multiplication program in Table 9-3 uses three registers and two memory cells to hold the values involved in the process. The A register will hold the most significant half (MSH) of the product, and the B register the LSH. The X register counts the iterations. The multiplicand must be stored in cell 1151_{16} prior to starting this routine; likewise, the multiplier must have been prestored in 1150_{16}.

The first two instructions just clear the product storage registers. Then the counter is set for eight iterations. The first bit of the multiplier is shifted into the carry. Each bit is checked to see if it is a 1; if it is, the multiplicand is added to the product. Then the counter is decremented and the process repeated until all bits are examined.

Software Multiplication Review

1. Explain why the algorithm works only with unsigned numbers.
2. Why is an add and shift multiplication algorithm more efficient than repetitive addition?
3. In Table 9-1, why does the upper product change at Step 2 of iteration 3? At Step 3 of iteration 3?
4. Discuss the procedure for shifting a double-length product by means of two rotations.

SOFTWARE DIVISION

It is also possible to divide numbers by using a program. The unsigned 16-bit divisor, an 8-bit quotient, and the 8-bit remainder are provided by the algorithm. A se-

Table 9-3 6800 Multiplication Routine

Label	Mnemonic	Operand	Address	Machine Code	Comments
	CLRA		1000	4F	Zero MSH of product
	CLRB		1001	5F	Zero LSH of product
	LDX	8	1002	CE	Set counter for eight iterations
			1003	00	
			1004	08	
SHIFT	ASLB		1005	58	Rotate bit of multiplier to carry and shift
	ROLA		1006	49	
	ASL	MPLR	1007	78	Shift multiplier to check next bit
			1008	11	
			1009	50	
	BCC	DECR	100A	24	If bit of multiplier is 0, skip addition
			100B	05	
	ADDB	MCAND	100C	FB	Add multiplicand to product
			100D	11	
			100E	51	
	ADCA		100F	89	
			1010	00	
DECR	DEX		1011	09	Decrement counter
	BNE	SHIFT	1012	26	Jump to next iteration
			1013	F1	

quence of subtractions and shifts is used to perform the operation; the rotate left instructions are used in shifting.

DIVISION ALGORITHM

STEP 1. Obtain the next MSB of the dividend by left shifting. Subtract the divisor from the partial dividend.

STEP 2. Did a borrow from the MSB position occur? If so, add the divisor back to the result.

STEP 3. Left-shift the borrow (carry) bit into the quotient.

STEP 4. Have eight iterations been completed? If not, go to Step 1.

STEP 5. Complement the value in the quotient.

A few comments should clarify the algorithm. We will use a simple binary division problem to illustrate key points.

$$11_2 \overline{)\,110_2} \quad 010_2$$

In Step 1 the leftmost bit of the dividend is obtained, and then the divisor is subtracted from it. In our example we obtain the first partial dividend by left-shifting 110_2 one bit:

$$\boxed{1}\;\text{Carry bit}$$

Partial dividend $\quad 0000\quad 0001_2$
Divisor $\qquad\quad -\ 0000\quad 0011_2$
$$\overline{\qquad\qquad 1111\quad 1110_2}\quad \text{(2's complement)}$$

The carry bit is set by the SUB instruction whenever a borrow occurs. (Review the instruction if your memory is hazy on this point.) The divisor "won't go into the partial dividend." The divisor must be added back to restore the original dividend value.

Next time through the algorithm, we have a different situation. Left-sharing 110_2 another bit gives a new partial dividend:

$$\boxed{0}\;\text{Carry bit}$$

Partial dividend $\quad 0000\quad 0011_2$
Divisor $\qquad\quad -\ 0000\quad 0011_2$
$$\overline{\qquad\qquad 0000\quad 0000_2}$$

Now the carry bit is cleared, thus indicating the fact that the divisor can be divided into the partial dividend. After all 8 bits have been examined, the quotient that has been generated must be complemented. The reason for this step is clearly shown in the two examples above. In the first subtraction the carry (acting as a borrow bit) is set, but the quotient bit should be 0. The second subtraction cleared the carry, but the quotient should be 1. Because the carry is always the complement of the quotient, taking a 1's complement of the final value will produce the correct result.

The 8085 division routine is listed in Table 9-4. The most significant part of the dividend must have been placed in the B register, and the least significant part in the C register. The divisor is in D. After nine cycles of the routine have been completed, the quotient will be in the C register and the remainder will be in the B register.

The 6800 division routine is given in Table 9-5. The divisor is prestored in cell 1151_{16}. Also, the dividend must be placed in the B register prior to starting the routine. The quotient is in the B register at the completion of the program. The process is completed in nine iterations.

Software Division Review

1. What does a borrow at Step 2 of the algorithm signify?
2. How does the algorithm compensate for the fact that the borrow bit is always the complement of the quotient bit?
3. Why is it sometimes necessary to add the divisor back to the partial dividend?
4. Where are the quotient and the remainder to be found after the division routine has halted?

CHAPTER SUMMARY

1. Shifting can move bits in a register either left or right. A single-bit left shift is equivalent to multiplication by 2; a right shift is the same as division by 2.
2. Scaling is used to maintain precision of numbers. Scaling a value too many bits can lead to overflow.
3. Instructions that rotate the accumulator left or right are also referred to as circular shifts.
4. Rotating through the carry status bit effectively produces a 9-bit shift. The two rotate through carry instructions are often used for multibyte shifting functions.
5. Two unsigned 8-bit numbers can be multiplied by using an algorithm. The product will consist of 16 bits. A series of right shifts and additions is the basis for the algorithm.

Table 9-4 8085 Division Routine

Label	Mnemonic	Operand	Address	Machine Code	Comments
	MVI H	9	1000	26	Preset the counter
			1001	09	
	MOV	A, B	1002	78	Initialization
STEP 3	MOV B	A	1003	47	Store partial result
	MOV	A, C	1004	79 ⎫	Shift carry into LSB of quotient; MSB of lower-
	RAL		1005	17 ⎬	half dividend → carry
	MOV	C, A	1006	4F ⎭	Save partial lower dividend
	DCR	H	1007	25	Are all bits processed?
	JZ	STEP 5	1008	CA	Yes, so go to final step
			1009	15	
			100A	10	
	MOV	A, B	100B	78	No, so obtain upper-half dividend
	RAL		100C	17	Shift bit from lower half to upper half
	SUB	D	100D	92	Subtract divisor
	JNC	STEP 3	100E	D2	If no borrow (divisor < dividend), go to Step 3
			100F	03	
			1010	10	
	ADD	D	1011	82	Otherwise, restore original dividend
	JMP	STEP 3	1012	C3	Go to Step 3
			1013	03	
			1014	10	
STEP 5	RAL		1015	17	Final shift
	MOV	E, A	1016	5F	Temporary storage
	MVI A	FF	1017	3E ⎫	
			1018	FF ⎬	Complement the quotient
	XRA	C	1019	A9 ⎭	
	MOV	C, A	101A	4F	
	MOV	A, E	101B	73	
	RAR		101C	1F	
	HLT		101D	76	Stop

Table 9-5 6800 Division Routine

Label	Mnemonic	Operand	Address	Machine Code	Comments
	LDX	8	1000	CE	Set number of iterations
			1001	00	
			1002	08	
	CLRA		1003	4F	Initialize
DIVD	ASLB		1004	58	Shift dividend and quotient
	ROLA		1005	49	
	CMPA	DIVISOR	1006	B1	Check borrow
			1007	11	
			1008	51	
	BCS	DECR	1009	25	Skip if no borrow
			100A	04	
	SUBA	DIVISOR	100B	B0	Subtract divisor
			100C	11	
			100D	51	
	INCB		100E	5C	
DECR	DEX		100F	09	Decrement counter
	BNE	DIVD	1010	26	Repeat until all bits are processed
			1011	F2	

Table 9-6 8085 Shift Instruction Summary

Mnemonic	Machine Code	Number of Bytes
RAL	17	1
RAR	1F	1
RLC	07	1
RRC	0F	1

Note: The carry bit only is affected by each shift instruction.

6. A similar routine for division can be derived. In this case a series of subtractions and left shifts is used. The quotient must be complemented as a final step in the process.

Table 9-7 6800 Shift Instruction Summary

Mnemonic	Machine Code	Number of Bytes
ASL, ASLA, ASLB	68, 78, 48, 58	2, 3, 1, 1
ASR, ASRA, ASRB	67, 77, 47, 57	2, 3, 1, 1
LSR, LSRA, LSRB	64, 74, 44, 54	2, 3, 1, 1
ROL, ROLA, ROLB	69, 79, 49, 59	2, 3, 1, 1
ROR, RORA, RORB	66, 76, 46, 56	2, 3, 1, 1

Note: All status bits, except A_C, are affected by these instructions.

7. Tables 9-6 and 9-7 list the shift instructions. The only status condition possibly changed by these instructions is the carry bit.

KEY TERMS AND CONCEPTS

Shifting

Scaling

Rotate accumulator left or right

Circular shifts

Rotate accumulator or memory through carry

Software multiplication and division

PROBLEMS

9-1 The initial contents of the accumulator are 93_{16}, and the status register is 03_{16}. How would these values be changed after the following instructions have been executed?

a. RAL
b. RAR
c. RLC
d. RRC

9-2 Write three instructions that perform the series of operations listed. (Overflow will not occur.)

Multiply the A register contents by 2.
Add 6 to that value.
Divide the result by 4.

9-3 Prepare a two-instruction sequence that will subtract $1.A_{16}$ from 7_{16}. (Choose the scaling that will preserve the precision of the difference but not cause overflow.)

9-4 In the addition problem below, the numbers have been scaled up 2 bits. Express the sum with the radix point in the proper position.

$$63_{16}$$
$$+ \ 1B_{16}$$

9-5 Prepare a table similar to Table 9-1, showing the step-by-step changes in the multiplier and product when the multiplication algorithm is used to calculate

$$5E_{16}$$
$$\times \ 47_{16}$$

9-6 Prepare a step-by-step table for the first and second iterations of the division algorithm when the dividend is $DB04_{16}$ and the divisor 3_{16}.

9-7 The carry bits resulting from all iterations of the division algorithm are listed below. What is the quotient?

Iteration	1	2	3	4	5	6	7	8
Carry	0	1	1	1	0	0	1	0

9-8 The division routine has been used to solve

$$\frac{19BC_{16}}{25_{16}}$$

What will the final contents of the registers be? (You do not have to use the division algorithm to solve this problem.)

9-9 Explain how negative numbers must be processed in order for the multiplication routine to work correctly.

9-10 Show how the division routine must be modified to work correctly with negative numbers.

LOOPS AND INDEXING

The processor is well suited for performance of repetitive tasks. It never gets bored or tired, so every iteration will be the same as the last. The multibyte arithmetic routines in the preceding chapters were examples of such repetitive, or *looping,* processes. This chapter will further our study of loops, primarily to develop a full understanding of the concept and to learn how loops may be implemented by using the 8085 and 6800 instructions. Our study will not include advanced applications of loops, however, because such topics are more appropriate in a programming course.

CHAPTER OBJECTIVES

Upon completion of this chapter, you should be able to:

1. List the component functions required in every loop.
2. Calculate the initial and the final values for all counting loop configurations.
3. Explain noncounting loop constructions.
4. Use timing loops to introduce delays in a program.
5. Describe the operation of address modification loops.
6. Show how loops can be combined by nesting.

LOOP FUNCTIONS

Although loops can become quite complicated sequences, every one must have certain essential parts. The looping process, also called *recursion*, depends on the processor being able to (1) complete a sequence of instructions over and over again and (2) stop the iterations at the proper time. Consider the flowchart in Fig. 10-1a, for example. This process will add 1 to the contents of the variable x and place the answer back in the same variable. The loop is shown on a flowchart by a process arrow leading back to the process that is to be repeated. Unfortunately, this loop has a fatal flaw; it never stops. Once the processor begins to execute the loop, it can only be halted by the intervention of the operator.

Figure 10-1b corrects this problem. The decision operation checks the value of x at each pass through the loop. Once x exceeds 10, the processor no longer takes the flow path back to the addition process. Instead, it exits the loop routine.

Even this loop has a problem. Can you spot it? We are using a register or memory cell to hold x. When the processor is first started, we have no way of telling what

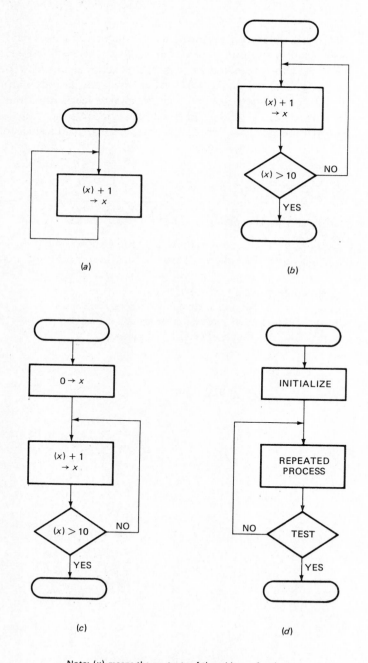

Note: (x) means the contents of the address of register x

Fig. 10-1 Loop examples.

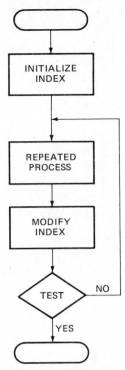

Fig. 10-2 Counting loop.

the value of x is. To ensure that x starts from the correct value, that variable must be initialized (see Fig. 10-1c). What would happen if the initial value of x had been 96_{16} and we had forgotten to set it to 0? Would the test have worked correctly?

A generalized loop structure is shown in Fig. 10-1d. As you can see, every loop must contain three operations. *Initialization* occurs before the actual loop logic is entered to ensure the proper starting point. The repeated *processing* is the working portion of the loop. Whether the loop is to be terminated or repeated is decided in the *test* portion. Analysis of any looping routine requires identification of its component parts. Look for them in the tables that follow.

Loop Functions Review

1. List the three parts of any loop.
2. What two errors were made in the loop of Fig. 10-1a?
3. Explain what would happen in Fig. 10-1c if the flowline from the "no" exit of the decision reentered the diagram above the "$0 \rightarrow x$" block. Would the loop's operation be satisfactory?

COUNTING LOOPS

Loops that count the number of passes are a simple extension of the basic loop. As Fig. 10-2 shows, a counting loop adds a fourth component to modify a variable

called the *index*. The index is simply a register or memory cell that holds the count of the number of times the loop has been executed. When the proper count has been reached, the "yes" branch from the test block is taken.

Let's write a counting loop, using the 8085 and 6800 instructions to illustrate more clearly how a counting loop works. The flowchart is shown in Fig. 10-3. This routine will multiply an unsigned 8-bit number by 3, using repeated addition. The 8085 and 6800 programs, corresponding to that flowchart, are listed in Tables 10-1 and 10-2. (For the 8085, the B register contains the index, and the answer is stored in D.) A step-by-step analysis of the program is shown in Table 10-3. After initialization, the number is placed in both the A and the C registers to facilitate addition. After addition, the partial product is put into the answer register. Next, a comparison is made to see if the index equals 3. (Remember that the compare instruction does an internal subtraction and sets the zero status if the two numbers are equal.) In the first iteration the count is not satisfied, so the loop is repeated. When the comparison is made again (Table 10-3, iteration 2, step 8), the values are equal, so the jump-on-zero condition does get executed and the processor halts.

In the 6800 routine shown in Table 10-2, the index is stored in the X register. The product is developed in

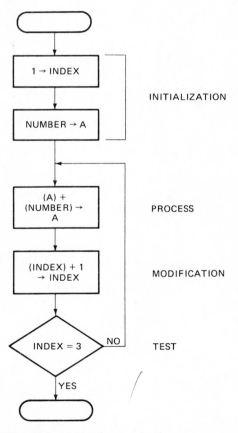

Fig. 10-3 A simple counting loop.

Table 10-1 8085 Multiplication by Repetitive Addition

Step	Label	Mnemonic	Operand	Address	Machine Code	Comments
1		MVI	B, 1	0200	06	1 → index
				0201	01	
2		LDA	NUMBR	0202	3A	(Number) → A
				0203	00	
				0204	03	
3		MOV	C, A	0205	4F	(A) → C
4	LOOP	ADD	C	0206	81	(A) + (C) → A
5		MOV	D, A	0207	57	Temporary storage
6		INR	B	0208	04	(Index) + 1 → Index
7		MVI A	3	0209	3E	Test count → A
				020A	03	
8		CMP	B	020B	B8	Compare index with test count
9		JZ	DONE	020C	CA	Jump to DONE if index equals 3
				020D	13	
				020E	02	
10		MOV	A, D	020F	7A	Otherwise, restore A value
11		JMP	LOOP	0210	C3	Go to next iteration
				0211	06	
				0212	02	
12	DONE	HLT		0213	76	Stop

accumulator A. After initialization, the number is placed in the A and B registers, then added. A comparison is made to see if the index is 3. If not, the process is repeated. Table 10-4 shows the register contents during each step.

Index Values

Perhaps you noticed that only two iterations were completed in Tables 10-3 and 10-4, yet the index incremented to 3. Why did that happen? To answer this

question, we must examine the relationships between loop components and loop count. The order of modification, testing, and processing is not fixed. Figure 10-4 (see page 192) shows some of the possible arrangements.

In Fig. 10-4a, modification and testing of the counter precede the processing. In all these examples, assume that the counter is initialized to 0. How many times is the process repeated if we test for the index being equal to 2? In Fig. 10-4a we see that before the first time the process is executed, the index is set to 1. On the next

Table 10-2 6800 Multiplication by Repetitive Addition

Step	Label	Mnemonic	Operand	Address	Machine Code	Comments
1		LDX	1	0200	CE	1 → index
				0201	00	
				0202	01	
2		LDAA	NUMBER	0203	B6	Number → A
				0204	03	
				0205	00	
3		TAB		0206	16	(A) → B
4	LOOP	ABA		0207	1B	(A) + (B) → A
5		INX		0208	08	Increment index
6		CPX		0209	80	Compare index with test count
				020A	00	
				020B	03	
7		BNE	LOOP	020C	26	If not done, go to next iteration
				020D	F9	

Table 10-3 8085 Loop Analysis

Iteration	Step	Register A	Register B	Register D	Comments*
Before start		?	?	?	
1	1	?	01	?	B is initialized
	2	02	01	?	A receives the number
	3	02	01	?	Number to C also
	4	04	01	?	Add
	5	04	01	04	Partial product to D
	6	04	02	04	Increment index
	7	03	02	04	Test count to A
	8	03	02	04	Compare index with count
	9	03	02	04	Comparison is not satisfied
	10	04	02	04	Restore A
	11	04	02	04	Go to next iteration
2	4	06	02	04	Add
	5	06	02	06	Store answer
	6	06	03	06	Increment index
	7	03	03	06	Test count to A
	8	03	03	06	Compare
	9	03	03	06	Comparison is satisfied, so jump
	12	03	03	06	Halt

* Memory cell 0300_{16} contains 02_{16}.

iteration the count is incremented prior to the test, so the process is only accomplished one time.

Moving to Fig. 10-4b, the first pass through, the count is 0 at the time of the test. After the first iteration, the counter is 1. The second time through, the counter increments to 2. Having reached the decision for the third time, the index now equals 2, and the loop stops. The process was done twice.

Finally, in Fig. 10-4c, the process is done the first time with an index value of 0. The process repeats for an index value of 1, and again for 2, before the test is satisfied. Therefore, the process was iterated three times. Table 10-5 summarizes the manner in which the number of repetitions depends on the arrangements and the index value. See Prob. 10-1 for other loop arrangements that affect the count.

Negative Stepping Index

The figures in the "Counting Loops" section above all used an index that incremented to some terminal value from its initial value. Frequently, a decrementing index

Table 10-4 6800 Loop Analysis

Iteration	Step	Register A	Register B	Register X	Comments
Before start		?	?	?	
1	1	?	?	1	X is initialized
	2	2	?	1	A receives the number
	3	2	2	1	Number to B also
	4	4	2	1	Add
	5	4	2	2	Increment index
	6	4	2	2	Compare index with count
	7	4	2	2	Comparison is not satisfied
2	4	6	2	2	Add
	5	6	2	3	Increment index
	6	6	2	3	Compare index with count
	7	6	2	3	Comparison is satisfied, so branch

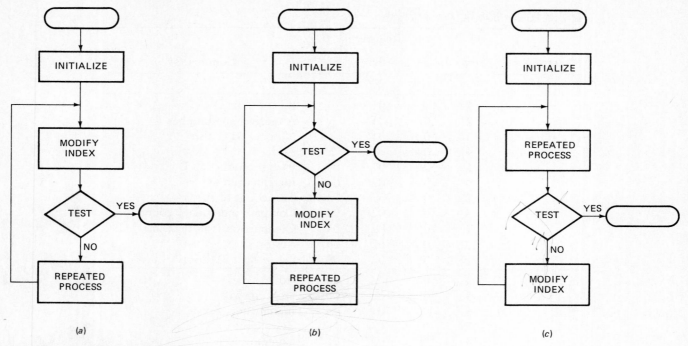

Fig. 10-4 Some loop sequences.

is more useful. The choice of counting up or counting down is made on the basis of the ease of programming and the minimum memory requirements. In the 8085 and 6800, a decrementing loop is usually more efficient. As an example of the memory savings that a decrementing loop can provide, the previous multiplication programs (Tables 10-1 and 10-2) will be recoded with a down-counting index.

As Table 10-6 shows for the 8085, there is a savings of four memory cells with the program rewritten in this way. There would be a further savings if the answer could be left in the accumulator rather than being moved to the D register. In the earlier case the D register was required to hold the answer while the accumulator was used in the comparison. Here, however, no comparison is needed, so the D register storage is redundant.

In the 6800 routine shown in Table 10-7, there are three memory cells saved. The extra comparison instruction required with an incrementing index has been eliminated.

The 6800 routine uses the A register to hold the

count. By double use of the increment instruction, it is possible to add i to n with just a single register.

The number of times a decrementing loop is repeated depends on the component arrangement, in the same way as shown in Table 10-5 for incrementing loops. The only change needed to convert Table 10-5 to decrementing loops is to initialize the counter to the final value shown in that table and then count down to 0. In the present program the order is process–modify–test,

Table 10-5 Loop Repetitions*

Order	Final Index Value	Number of Repetitions
Modify—test—process	N	N − 1
Test—modify—process	N	N
Process—test—modify	N	N + 1

* Assuming that the index is initialized to 0.

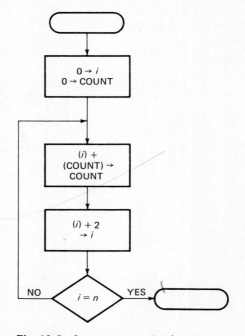

Fig. 10-5 Incorrect counting loop.

Table 10-6   8085 Multiplication by Repetitive Addition (Decrementing Index)

Step	Label	Mnemonic	Operand	Address	Machine Code	Comments
1		MVI B	2	0200	06	$2 \rightarrow$ index
				0201	02	
2		LDA	NUMBR	0202	3A	(Number) $\rightarrow$ A
				0203	00	
				0204	03	
3		MOV	C, A	0205	4F	(A) $\rightarrow$ C
4	LOOP	ADD	C	0206	81	(A) + (C) $\rightarrow$ A
5		MOV	D, A	0207	57	Store result
6		DCR	B	0208	05	(Index) $- 1 \rightarrow$ index
7		JZ	DONE	0209	CA	Decrementing affects status bits; go to
				020A	0F	DONE if index is 0
				020B	02	
8		JMP	LOOP	020C	C3	Go to next iteration
				020D	06	
				020E	02	
9	DONE	HLT		020F	76	Stop

corresponding to the second row in that table. By stepping through the program, we see that the addition is done two times if the starting value of the index is 2.

Variable Stepping Index

Often there will be a need to increment or decrement the index contents by some value other than 1. The index may be incremented or decremented by any number. When this method of indexing is used, care must be exercised in performing the test properly. Figure 10-5 illustrates the problem that can occur if one is not properly concerned with the counting process.

The problem that the flowchart attempts to solve is to produce the sum of all even integers, less than n, where n is a given input to the routine. But there is no requirement that n be even, because the sum is for all positive numbers *less* than n. If n is odd, the test will

never be satisfied and the loop will not terminate. This error would be eliminated if the test were changed to checking for i greater than or equal to n. The test would terminate the loop after the highest valid integer had been added to the previous count regardless of n being even or odd. It is this type of subtle problem that accounts for many computer bugs.

The programmer is anticipating data within certain ranges, but the data does not actually have to satisfy those constraints. There was no stated requirement for n to be even, so an odd number is (or should be) a valid input. The programs that properly calculate the sum are listed in Tables 10-8 and 10-9. (For the 8085, the initial value of n is placed in the A register, and the answer is found in the D register.)

Note that the index is decremented twice to produce a step of 2. This routine uses only single-byte arithmetic. To prevent overflow, the value of n must not exceed

Table 10-7   6800 Multiplication by Repetitive Addition (Decrementing Index)

Step	Label	Mnemonic	Operand	Address	Machine Code	Comments
1		LDX	1	0200	CE	$1 \rightarrow$ index
				0201	00	
				0202	01	
2		LDAA	NUMBER	0203	B6	Number $\rightarrow$ A
				0204	03	
				0205	00	
3		TAB		0206	16	(A) $\rightarrow$ B
4	LOOP	ABA		0207	1B	(A) + (B) $\rightarrow$ A
5		DEX		0208	09	Decrement index
6		BNE	LOOP	0209	26	If not 0, go to next iteration
				020A	FC	

Table 10-8 8085 Variable Stepping Index

Label	Mnemonic	Operand	Address	Machine Code	Comments
	MOV	B, A	0400	47	Store n in register B
	SUI	64	0401	D6	Subtract 1 greater than the maximum legal value
			0402	40	
	JP	ERROR	0403	F2	If A is positive, overflow will occur, so go to error exit
			0404	16	
			0405	04	
	MVI	C, 0	0406	0E	Zero the index
			0407	00	
	MOV C	C	0408	79	Zero the count
LOOP	ADD	C	0409	81	
	INR	C	040A	0C ⎫	
	INR	C	040B	0C ⎭	Increment i by 2
	MOV	D, A	040C	57	Temporarily store the result
	MOV	A, B	040D	78	Obtain n
	SUB	C	040E	91	Subtract i
	JM	END	040F	FA	If result is negative, we have finished
			0410	17	
			0411	04	
	MOV	A, D	0412	7A	Restore count
	JMP	LOOP	0413	C3	Go to next iteration
			0414	09	
			0415	04	
ERROR	CMA		0416	2F	Complement A to set it negative
END	HLT		0417	76	Stop

Notes: n is placed in the A register prior to start. The answer is in A at completion. To prevent overflow, n must be 63 or less; otherwise, the A register is set to a negative value.

Table 10-9 6800 Variable Stepping Index

Label	Mnemonic	Operand	Address	Machine Code	Comments
	LDAA	n	0400	B6	$n \rightarrow$ A
			0401	04	
			0402	0C	
	CMPA	64	0403	81	Check that n is less than 64
			0404	40	
	BGE	ERROR	0405	2C	If A is positive, overflow will occur, so go to error exit
			0406	19	
	LDAA	0	0407	86	Zero the count
			0408	00	
LOOP	INCA		0409	4C	Increment i by 2
			040A	4C	
	CMPA	n	040B	81	
			040C	XX	n is stored here
	BGE	LOOP	040D	2C	If result is positive, repeat
			040E	FA	
			040F		Program continues from here
ERROR			0420		Error exit

Notes: n is placed in cell 040C prior to start. Answer is in A at completion.

63_{10}. A check for the input being within limits is made at the beginning of the routine, and a special output is generated if n is too large. Another error in the input that would not be detected by this test is a negative value for n. By mistake, the person using this routine could insert a negative input. A meaningless answer would be generated in this case.

Counting Loops Review

1. What element is added to the basic loop structure for counting?
2. List three sequences for the parts of a counting loop. How does that order and the terminating value for the index in the test affect the number of repetitions completed for each sequence?
3. What impact does the use of a decrementing index in a counting loop usually have on memory requirements in a microcomputer?
4. What error is frequently made when a variable stepping index is used? How can the mistake be avoided?

NONCOUNTING LOOPS

Every loop need not depend on an index value to stop it. Many computer processes continually repeat until a particular event is detected. For example, consider a microprocessor that is used in a communications system. The system requires that all data being received be tested for errors before any processing is started. The data is 8-bit ASCII characters that are transmitted with odd parity (see Table 10-10). Each character will be placed in the A register by an input instruction. (Here we simply assume that the instruction causes the character to be placed in the accumulator; the input sequence is fully explained in Chap. 12.) The routine will continue to receive characters as long as the parity is odd; if a parity error is ever detected, the processor is to halt. An input instruction does not affect the status register, so the OR operation is needed to set the status

condition bits to reflect the present value in the accumulator. If the parity is odd, the jump causes the processor to repeat the input process.

Noncounting loops are frequently used in I/O processing. The chapter covering that subject provides additional examples. These loops are also used for error decision. For example, the summation program in the previous section could be rewritten to halt on the proper count or when overflow was detected. If the test for overflow were added, the initial verification of the input value would be unnecessary.

Noncounting Loops Review

1. List some conditions that could be used in the test portion of a noncounting loop.
2. Why was an OR instruction required in the parity-checking routine?
3. What instruction(s) could be used to check for overflow in the summation routine, if we wanted to add that test?

TIMING LOOPS

The processor is sometimes too fast in executing its program. When some external system is being controlled, the mechanical devices cannot react as quickly as the MPU. Such devices as valves, synchros, relays, or even the human operator must be given enough time to complete a task before the processor goes on to its next instruction.

Delays are frequently added to programs to allow for this reaction time. Assume that a teletype must be given time for printing between each character that is sent to it. We want to delay the program a minimum of 250 μs between every output. Routines that cause this delay are listed in Tables 10-11 and 10-12.

By referring to the timing data on the instructions, the time elapsed in one iteration of the loop can be calculated. These values are listed in Tables 10-13 and 10-14.

Table 10-10   8085 Parity-Checking Routine

Label	Mnemonic	Operand	Address	Machine Code	Comments
LOOP	IN	0	0600	DB	Receive one character
			0601	00	
	ORI	FF	0602	F6	Cause the parity to be computed
			0603	FF	
	JPO	LOOP	0604	E2	If parity is odd, go to obtain next character
			0605	00	
			0606	06	
	HLT		0607	76	Stop

Table 10-11 8085 Timing Routine

Label	Mnemonic	Operand	Address	Machine Code	Comments
	MVI B	1B	1000	06	$27_{10} \rightarrow i$
			1001	1B	
LOOP	NOP		1002	00	No operation
	DCR	B	1003	05	Decrement counter
	JNZ	LOOP	1004	C2	Repeat if count is not exhausted
			1005	02	
			1006	10	
	HLT		1007	76	Stop

Table 10-12 6800 Timing Routine

Label	Mnemonic	Operand	Address	Machine Code	Comments
	LDAA	3F	1000	B6	$63_{10} \rightarrow A$
			1001	3F	
LOOP	NOP		1002	01	No operation
	DECA		1003	4A	Decrement counter
	BNE	LOOP	1004	26	Repeat if count is not exhausted
			1005	FC	

Table 10-13 8085 Execution Time Delay

Instruction	Delay* (µs)
NOP	2.0
DCR	2.5
JNZ	5.0
Total	9.5

* With 2-MHz clock.

Table 10-14 6800 Execution Time Delay

Instruction	Delay* (µs)
NOP	1.0
DECA	1.0
BNE	2.0
Total	4.0

* With 2-MHz clock.

For the 8085, the total delay each time through the 8085 loop is 9.5 µs. To calculate the number of iterations for a delay of 250 µs, we simply divide: 250 µs total ÷ 9.5 µs per iteration = 26.3 iterations. We actually use 27 iterations because we wanted a minimum of 250 µs.

For the 6800, as shown in Table 10-14, the delay is 4 µs. To calculate the number of iterations, we divide: 250 µs total ÷ 4.0 µs per iteration = 62.5 iterations. In the case of this program, we will round to 63.

The 8085 routine uses two registers—one for the current table address and the other for a loop index. The HL register pair holds the address of the data word being decremented. The B register is used as the index. The index is started with a value of 100_{10} (64_{16}). When the register contains 0, all 100 words have been updated.

Remember that the instruction execution time depends on the clock frequency. Here a standard 2-MHz

clock rate is assumed; suitable adjustments must be made for a slower clock. Furthermore, timing loops of this type are not particularly precise; variations in the clock frequency or contention for the buses, possibly because of an input or output, will affect the accuracy of the delay. Also, we did not include the delay from the MVI or the HLT instructions in the 8085 routine. Generally speaking, delay loops like this one are adequate for I/O timing. If a more precise interval is needed, another method must be used. Chapter 12 discusses other timing techniques.

Timing Loops Review

1. Why are delay loops necessary?
2. If the delay from the first and last instructions of the example were included, what would be the total time interval consumed?

ADDRESS	
m	RECORD 1
m + 1	RECORD 2
m + 2	RECORD 3
m + 3	RECORD 4
⋮	
m + n − 1	RECORD n

Fig. 10-6   A data table.

3. Explain why delay loops should not be used to control the timing of processes that rely on precise time intervals.

ADDRESS MODIFICATION LOOPS

Computers have the powerful ability to manipulate masses of data. When large quantities of data must be processed, a well-organized data structure must be created. One type of data organization that is often used is the *table* or the *array*. Tabular data is placed in consecutive memory cells (see Fig. 10-6). Once the data has been placed in the table, updating is readily accomplished by use of an index. Let a table of 100 records be placed in memory starting at address 0650_{16}. Now we want to change the value of each record in the table. Every data word must be decreased by 1. An *address modification* loop is used for this purpose. (See Table 10-15).

The 6800 routine in Table 10-16 places the starting address of the table in the X register. By just incrementing the X register, we can step through the table. The A register holds the count. The memory content is directly decremented by one instruction.

Address Modification Loops Review

1. Define the term "table."
2. How does the routine determine when all the records in the table have been updated?

NESTED LOOPS

When the process to be repeated is a loop itself, then nesting of iterative procedures is called for. The *nesting* (one loop contained within another loop is "nested" in the outer loop) of two or three loops offers an efficient programming tool. Theoretically, the concept of a loop within a loop can be continued without limit, but as the level of nesting increases, the program becomes difficult to debug and almost impossible to understand. Every level of looping requires its own index if counting loops are used.

A task such as taking a number from a table, rotating the quantity 55_{16} left by that number of bits, and then replacing the original value by the shifted value is a good problem for nested loops. Figure 10-7 gives a flowchart for this routine. The number of left shifts will always be in the range of 1 to 8, and no verification check is required. The table is 10 words long and begins at address 1000_{16}.

In the programs in Tables 10-17 and 10-18 the HL register pair represents the address index i, and the B register the shift count index j. After the HL registers have been set to the starting address of the table, they are used as an index to obtain the shift count. In the inner loop the B register decrements from that value to

Table 10-15   8085 Address Modification

Label	Mnemonic	Operand	Address	Machine Code	Comments
	LHLD	TBADR	0200	2A	Place the starting address of table in HL pair
			0201	0C	
			0202	02	
	MVI B	64	0203	06	Initialize index to 100_{10}
			0204	64	
LOOP	DCR	M	0205	35	Decrement one word in table
	DCX	H	0206	2B	Adjust HL to next table address
	DCR	B	0207	05	Decrement counter
	JNZ	LOOP	0208	C2	Go to next iteration
			0209	05	
			020A	02	
	HLT		020B	76	Stop
TBADR			020C	50	Table's starting address
TBADR + 1			020D	06	

Table 10-16 6800 Address Modification

Label	Mnemonic	Operand	Address	Machine Code	Comments
	LDX	TBADR	0210	FE	Place starting address in X
			0211	02	
			0212	30	
	LDAA	64	0213	86	Initiate A register to 100_{10}
			0214	64	
LOOP	DEC	0	0215	6A	Decrement word in table
			0216	00	
	INX		0217	08	Adjust X to next word
	DECA		0218	4A	Decrement A
	BNE	LOOP	0219	26	Go to next iteration
			021A	FA	
TBADR			0230		Table's starting address

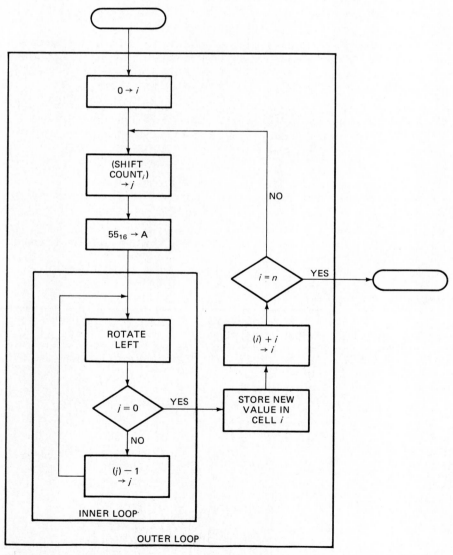

Fig. 10-7 Nested loops.

Table 10-17 8085 Nested Loop Routine

Label	Mnemonic	Operand	Address	Machine Code	Comments
	LHLD	ADDR	2000	2A	Initialize word counter i
			2001	17	
			2002	20	
AGAIN	MOV	B, M	2003	46	Set shift counter j
	MVI A	55	2004	3E	Place shift pattern in A
			2005	55	
NEXT	RLC		2006	07	Rotate left
	DCR	B	2007	05	Decrement j
	JZ	STORE	2008	CA	If $j = 0$, go to store answer
			2009	0E	
			200A	20	
	JMP	NEXT	200B	C3	Go to shift again
			200C	06	
			200D	20	
STORE	MOV	M, A	200E	77	Store answer
	INX	H	200F	23	Increment i
	MVI A	0A	2010	3E	Terminating value for i is 10_{10}
			2011	0A	
	SUB	L	2012	95	Subtract i
	JNZ	AGAIN	2013	C2	If not 0, get next value
			2014	03	
			2015	20	
	HLT		2016	76	Stop
ADDR			2017	00	Table's starting address
			2018	10	

Table 10-18 6800 Nested Loop Routine

Label	Mnemonic	Operand	Address	Machine Code	Comments
	LDX	ADDR	2000	CE	Initialize word counter i
			2001	20	
			2002	20	
AGAIN	LDAB	0	2003	E6	Set shift counter j
			2004	00	
	LDAA	55	2005	86	Place shift pattern in A
			2006	55	
NEXT	ROLA		2007	49	Rotate A left
	DECB		2008	5A	Decrement j
	BEQ	STORE	2009	27	If $j = 0$, store answer
			200A	02	
	BRA	NEXT	200B	20	Go to shift again
			200C	FA	
STORE	STAA	0	200D	A7	Store answer
			200E	00	
	INX		200F	08	Increment j
	CPX	A	2010	8C	Terminating value for i is 10_{10}
			2011	00	
			2012	0A	
	BNE	AGAIN	2013	26	If more to do, form next value
			2014	EE	

0, at which time all rotations have been accomplished. Then the answer is stored and a check is made to see if all 10 (A_{16}) records have been processed. If they have not been, the outer loop is reentered.

For the 6800 routine, the i counter is placed in the X register. The B register serves as the j counter. After the counters are initialized, the pattern is placed in the A register. The inner loop rotates the register the required number of bits. After the result is stored, a check is made to see if all 10 words have been processed. If they have not been, the inner loop is repeated.

Nested Loops Review

1. How many indices would be needed in three nested counting loops?

2. What is the purpose of the outer loop in Tables 10-17 and 10-18? The inner loop?

3. Which index is used for the inner loop? Which register(s) is (are) used to hold that value?

4. How is the termination value for the word count index determined?

CHAPTER SUMMARY

1. A looping, or recursive, process repeats a sequence of instructions until the specified conditions have been met.

2. The variable controlling the number of iterations must be initialized prior to entering the loop.

3. Every loop consists of an initialization section, a process section, and a test section.

4. Counting loops use an index to control the number of cycles. A modification section is added to the basic loop structure to update the index on each pass.

5. The relationship between the initial and final values of the index and the number of repetitions depends on the order of the processing, the modification, and the testing in the loop.

6. The index in a counting loop can decrement as well as increment. In most microprocessors a decrementing loop will usually be more efficient in memory usage than will an incrementing loop.

7. Variable stepping indices are used when the value must be modified in units other than 1. If a variable step is used, the test must be written to properly stop the loop. The simplest way of accomplishing a proper test value is by checking whether it equals or exceeds the final value.

8. Noncounting loops are terminated when a specific event occurs. The status bits are often used as flags to show that the condition was satisfied.

9. Time delays, which slow the processor to allow an external action to be completed, can be implemented by executing a series of instructions in a loop. Timing loops are easily written, but the delay is only an approximation. If precision timing is called for, another method must be used.

10. Address modification loops are well suited for indexing through tables or arrays.

11. Nested loops are used when two or more processes must be repeated. The inner loop runs to completion with each pass through the outer loop. Each nested loop must have a unique index if counting is required.

KEY TERMS AND CONCEPTS

Loops

Recursive processes

Loop components—initialization, processing, and testing

Counting loops

Index

Index modification

Loop count determination

Decrementing index

Variable stepping index

Noncounting loops

Timing loops

Address modification loops

Tables and arrays

Nested loops

10-1 Complete the table (in a manner similar to that used in Table 10-5) for the loop configurations given below. The index is initialized to 0.

Order	Final Index Value	Number of Repetitions
Modify—process—test	N	
Test—process—modify	N	
Process—modify—test	N	

10-2 Write the instructions needed to detect a negative input to the summation program. Begin at address 0406_{16}. The address of the error exit, to be taken if n is less than 0, is $041A_{16}$. Do not rewrite the entire program.

10-3 What should the initial value for the index be in Figs. 10-8a and 10-8b?

10-4 What value should be used in the test portion of the flowcharts for Figs. 10-9a, 10-9b, and 10-9c (see page 202)?

10-5 In Figs. 10-10a and 10-10b (see page 202), how many times is the process done?

10-6 A timing loop is needed to cause a delay of 2 milliseconds (ms). Write a routine, using the same instructions as the loops in Tables 10-11 and 10-12, that will create the appropriate delay. (*Hint:* Consider using the NOP instruction more than once.)

10-7 Draw a table that consists of five records. Each record is 3 bytes long. Then show two ways in which the table could be stored in memory.

10-8 The address modification problem given in this chapter is changed to require that the records only at even addresses be increased by 3. The contents of odd addresses are to remain unchanged. Rewrite the address modification routine for the new requirements.

10-9 A program is needed to do the following:

1. Take the next value from a table.
2. Rotate the quantity 06_{16} right by that number or until the sign bit is set.
3. Replace the original table value by the shifted number.

The table values range from 1 to 8, and no verification of the values is required. The table is 10_{10} words long and begins at address $05AE_{16}$. Prepare a flowchart and then code the routine.

10-10 Write a program to carry out the actions shown in Fig. 10-9c.

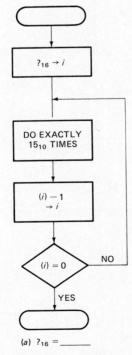

(a) $?_{16} = $ _____

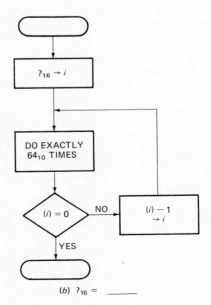

(b) $?_{16} = $ _____

Fig. 10-8 Problem 10-3.

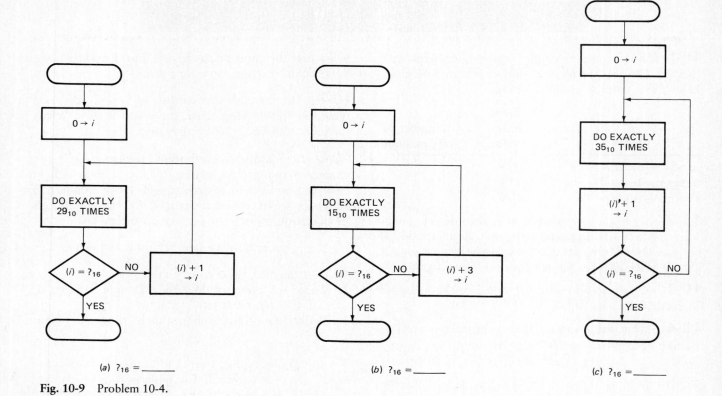

(a) $?_{16} = \underline{\hspace{1cm}}$

(b) $?_{16} = \underline{\hspace{1cm}}$

(c) $?_{16} = \underline{\hspace{1cm}}$

Fig. 10-9 Problem 10-4.

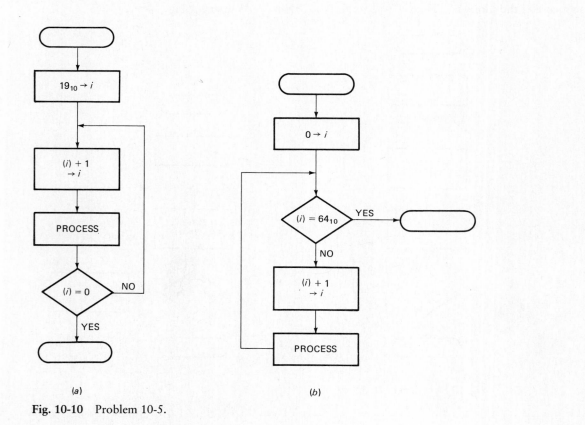

(a)

(b)

Fig. 10-10 Problem 10-5.

SUBROUTINES

Chapters 7, 8, and 9 covered routines for multibyte addition and subtraction, multiplication, and division. The task of rewriting those routines every time we want to perform the arithmetic operations would be quite cumbersome and would also waste a lot of memory space. When a group of instructions is to be used many times in a program, defining these instructions to be a subroutine eliminates the need to rewrite the same code over and over. This chapter investigates the subroutine concept.

CHAPTER OBJECTIVES

Upon completion of this chapter, you should be able to:

1. Describe subroutine construction and referencing.
2. Explain the operation of 8085 and 6800 instructions used to call and return from subroutines.
3. Describe 8085 conditional subroutine calls and returns.
4. Discuss the use of the stack in initiating and terminating subroutines.
5. Show how subroutines can be nested.
6. Describe the process of parameter passing by means of registers or memory.

SUBROUTINES IN GENERAL

A *subroutine* is simply a group of instructions that can be executed many times in one program. The group of instructions is coded like any other set of commands, but it is assigned a unique name, thus allowing the instruction sequence to be referenced as an entity. The name of the subroutine is the label assigned to the first instruction. The label symbolically represents an address, so we reference the routine by that address in the memory.

Figure 11-1 illustrates the subroutine idea. The main routine in a payroll program must perform a multibyte addition three times; after the instruction at addresses 0110_{16}, 0125_{16}, and $01B1_{16}$, the subroutine is referenced, or *called*. At completion of the subroutine, note that the main program sequence must continue from the address immediately following the one calling that subroutine. A distinguishing feature of a subroutine is its ability to *return* to the main program in this manner.

How is this return to an arbitrary address arranged? In the microprocessor the proper exiting from a subroutine relies on the stack. Although there are slight variations, the process is essentially the same for any subroutine call and return. Executing the calling instruction pushes the contents of the program counter on the stack. (Remember that the program counter is set to the address of the *next* instruction.) Then the address of the subroutine is loaded into the program counter register. This action causes the first address of the subroutine to be referenced. The remaining instructions of the subroutine are executed in a normal manner until the return instruction is reached. The return instruction causes the stack to be popped, and the data on top of the stack (the next address in the main program) is placed in the program counter. The main program then continues from the next instruction following the call. A specific, comprehensive example will be given following a more complete description of the unconditional call and return instructions.

🔲 8085 Call Instruction

The call instruction is something like a jump in that the contents of the program counter are changed to transfer control to a new address. In addition, the return address is placed on the stack. The stack is located in RAM, and the stack pointer is set to the address of the item

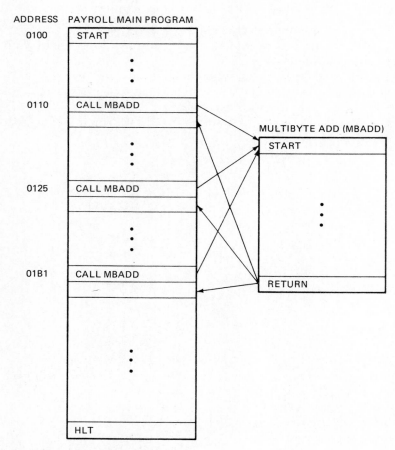

Fig. 11-1 Subroutine example.

currently at the top of the stack. Pushing the new return address on the stack results in three actions:

1. The most significant byte of the program counter value is placed on the stack at the location that is 1 less than the current stack pointer contents.
2. The least significant byte of the program counter is placed on the stack at the location that is 2 less than the current stack pointer contents.
3. The stack pointer is decremented by 2.

Operation code	CD
Mnemonic	CALL
Addressing mode	direct
Status bits affected	none
Clock periods	18
Format	

```
                        Bit number
                    7 6 5 4    3 2 1 0
Memory cell  m    | 1 1 0 0    1 1 0 1 |
            m + 1 |    Low-address byte  |
            m + 2 |    High-address byte |
```

☐ EXAMPLE

Before Execution		After Execution	
Program counter	0400	Program counter	0200
Stack pointer	1025	Stack pointer	1023

Memory

Instruction	0400	CD		0400	CD
	0401	00		0401	00
	0402	02		0402	02
Stack	1022	00		1022	00
	1023	22		1023	03
	1024	FC		1024	04
	1025	EB		1025	EB

The program counter is changed to the starting address of the subroutine (0200_{16}). The address of the next instruction in the main program is 0403_{16} (because the call instruction occupies 3 bytes). That address is pushed on the stack (high byte to location 1024_{16} and low byte to location 1023_{16}). The stack pointer is updated to indicate the new top of stack.

80 8085 Return Instruction

A call instruction must always be paired with a return instruction for the subroutine's referencing to be completed properly; otherwise, a totally confused program would result. The return instruction is always the last one in a subroutine. The return takes the address information previously pushed on the stack and updates the pointer in three steps:

1. The contents of the location equal to the current stack pointer value are placed in the least significant byte of the program counter.
2. The contents of the location equal to the current stack pointer plus 1 are placed in the most significant byte of the program counter.
3. The stack pointer is incremented by 2.

Operation code	C9
Mnemonic	RET
Addressing mode	none
Status bits affected	none
Clock periods	10
Format	

```
                        Bit number
                    7 6 5 4    3 2 1 0
Memory cell  m    | 1 1 0 0    1 0 0 1 |
```

☐ EXAMPLE

Before Execution		After Execution	
Program counter	0240	Program counter	0403
Stack pointer	1023	Stack pointer	1025

Memory

Instruction	0240	C9		0240	C9
	1022	00		1022	00
Stack	1023	03		1023	03
	1024	04		1024	04
	1025	EB		1025	EB

The program counter is set to proceed with execution of the instruction immediately following the last call. The stack pointer indicates the new top of stack.

80 8085 Comprehensive Example

A complete subroutine example will serve to show how the call and the return instructions work together. Figure 11-2a shows the situation prior to calling the subroutine. The subroutine calling instruction is at location 2046_{16} in the main program; the subroutine starting address is 3010_{16}.

After the instruction to reference the subroutine is executed (see Fig. 11-2b), the program counter and the stack pointer have been changed, with the former to the beginning instruction in the routine and the latter to the new top of stack. The return address (2049_{16}) has been pushed on the stack.

When the subroutine is completed (see Fig. 11-2c), the return instruction causes the stack to be popped. The contents of the two top memory cells of the stack are put into the program counter for continuation of the main program. The stack pointer is decremented to reflect the change in stack length.

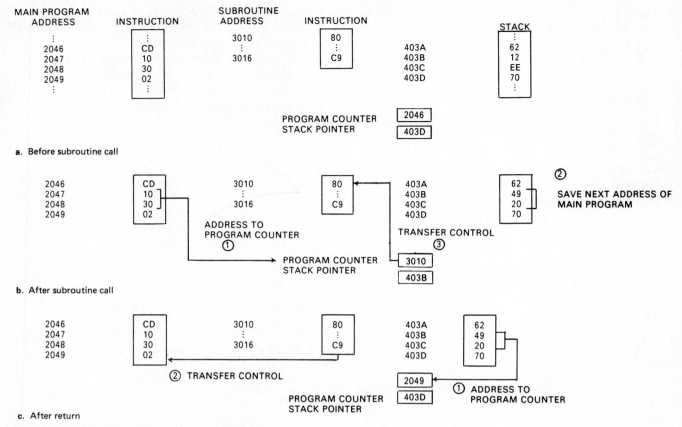

a. Before subroutine call

b. After subroutine call

c. After return

Fig. 11-2 8085 register and memory operations.

68 6800 Jump and Branch to Subroutine

These instructions are a special type of jump or branch. The contents of the program counter are changed to transfer control to the new address. In addition, the return address is placed on the stack. The stack is in RAM, and the stack pointer is set to the current top address on the stack. Pushing the new return address on the stack results in three actions:

1. The most significant byte of the program counter value is placed on the stack at the location that is 1 less than the current stack pointer contents.
2. The least significant byte of the program counter is placed on the stack at the location that is equal to the current stack pointer contents.
3. The stack pointer is decremented by 2.

There are two addressing modes for the jump-to-subroutine instruction and one mode for the branch-to-subroutine instruction. The jump-to-subroutine instruction is described below.

Operation codes   AD, BD
Mnemonic   JSR
Addressing modes   indexed, extended
Status bits affected   none

Clock cycles   4, 3
Format

		Bit number	
		7 6 5 4 3 2 1 0	
Memory cell	m	1 0 1 0 1 1 0 1	
	m + 1	Address modifier byte	

		Bit number	
		7 6 5 4 3 2 1 0	
Memory cell	m	1 0 1 1 1 1 0 1	
	m + 1	High-address byte	
	m + 2	Low-address byte	

☐ EXAMPLE

Before Execution		**After Execution**	
Program counter	0400	Program counter	0200
Stack pointer	1024	Stack pointer	1022
Memory		Memory	

Instruction
0400	BD
0401	02
0402	00

0400	BD
0401	02
0402	00

Stack
1022	00
1023	00
1024	00

1022	00
1023	04
1024	03

The program counter is changed to the starting address of the subroutine (0200_{16}). The address of the next instruction in the main program is 0403_{16} because the extended addressing mode requires 3 bytes. That address is pushed on the stack (low byte to location 1024_{16} and high byte to location 1025_{16}). The stack pointer is updated to the new top of stack.

The branch to subroutine is limited to the same addressing range as a normal branch. It is described below.

Operation code   8D
Mnemonic   BSR
Addressing modes   relative
Status bits affected   none
Clock cycles   8
Format

		Bit number	
		7 6 5 4 3 2 1 0	
Memory cell	m	1 0 0 0 1 1 0 1	
	m + 1	Displacement	

☐ **EXAMPLE**

Before Execution		After Execution	
Program counter	0400	Program counter	044D
Stack pointer	1024	Stack pointer	1022

Memory   Memory

Instruction	0400	8D		0400	8D
	0401	4B		0401	4B
Stack	1022	00		1022	00
	1023	00		1023	04
	1024	00		1024	02

The program counter is changed to the starting address of the subroutine ($044D_{16}$). The address is computed by adding the displacement to the current program counter value plus 2. The address of the next instruction in the main program is 0402_{16} because the relative addressing mode requires 2 bytes. That address is pushed on the stack (low byte to location 1024_{16} and high byte to location 1025_{16}). The stack pointer is updated to the new top of stack.

68 6800 Return Instruction

A jump- or branch-to-subroutine instruction must always be paired with a return instruction for the subroutine's referencing to be completed properly; otherwise, a totally confused program would result. The return instruction is always the last one in a subroutine. The return takes the address information previously pushed on the stack and updates the pointer in three steps:

1. The contents of the location equal to the current stack pointer value plus 1 are placed in the most significant byte of the program counter.

2. The contents of the location equal to the current stack pointer value plus 2 are placed in the least significant byte of the program counter.

3. The stack pointer is incremented by 2.

Operation code   39
Mnemonic   RTS
Addressing modes   inherent
Status bits affected   none
Clock cycles   5
Format

		Bit number	
		7 6 5 4 3 2 1 0	
Memory cell	m	0 0 1 1 1 0 0 1	

☐ **EXAMPLE**

Before Execution		After Execution	
Program counter	0240	Program counter	0402
Stack pointer	1022	Stack pointer	1024

Memory   Memory

Instruction	0240	39		0240	39
Stack	1022	00		1022	00
	1023	04		1023	04
	1024	02		1024	02

The program counter is set to proceed with execution of the instruction immediately following the last subroutine jump. The stack pointer indicates the new top of stack.

68 6800 Comprehensive Example

A complete subroutine example will serve to show how the jump-to-subroutine and return instructions work together. Figure 11-3a shows the situation prior to jumping to the subroutine. The subroutine jump instruction is at location 2046_{16} in the main program; the subroutine starting address is 3010_{16}.

After the instruction to reference the subroutine is executed (see Fig. 11-3b), the program counter is set to the beginning instruction of the routine and the stack pointer is set to the new top of stack. The return address (2049_{16}) has been pushed on the stack.

When the subroutine is completed (Fig. 11-3c), the return instruction causes the stack to be popped. The contents of the two top memory cells of the stack are put into the program counter for continuation of the main program. The stack pointer is decremented to reflect the change in stack length.

Subroutines in General Review

1. Which instruction is used to reference a subroutine? Which is used to exit a subroutine?

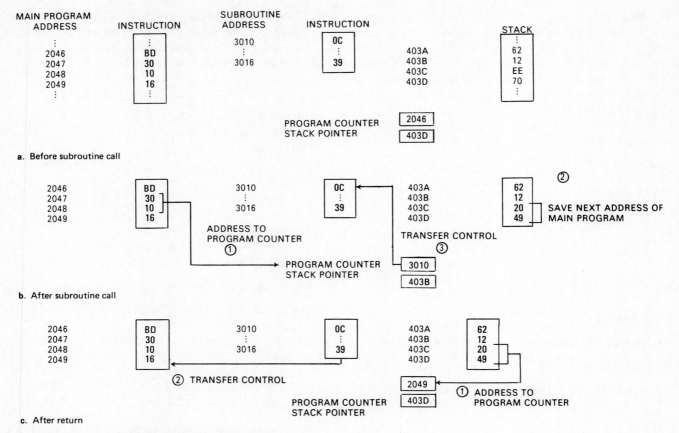

Fig. 11-3 6800 register and memory operations.

2. List the operations performed by each of these two instructions.
3. How is the stack changed after the subroutine call? Why must the stack pointer value be altered in that case?
4. Explain how the next instruction to be executed in the main program is found after a subroutine has finished its processing.
5. Why must the two instructions associated with subroutines always be used as a pair?

80 8085 CONDITIONAL SUBROUTINE CALLS

Just as with jump instructions, the 8085 supports the conditional calling of subroutines. The status register condition is examined in this section to decide whether the subroutine will be called. If the condition is true, the reference is made just as in the unconditional call instruction. None of the calling instructions affects the status register, so it is the responsibility of the program to establish the condition being tested before executing a conditional subroutine instruction. Normally, an arithmetic or a logical instruction will precede the call in order to cause the status bits to be properly set.

80 Call if Carry

If the carry bit is 1, the subroutine is called. Otherwise, the following instruction in the main program is executed immediately.

Operation code	DC
Mnemonic	CC
Addressing mode	direct
Status bits affected	none
Clock periods	18 (9 if the condition is false)
Format	

		Bit number		
		7 6 5 4	3 2 1 0	
Memory cell	m	1 1 0 1	1 1 0 0	
	m + 1	Low-address byte		
	m + 2	High-address byte		

☐ EXAMPLE

Before Execution		After Execution	
Program counter	0B40	Program counter	0A03
Stack pointer	00F0	Stack pointer	00EE
Status register	03	Status register	03

Before Execution			After Execution		
Memory			Memory		
Stack	00EE	00		00EE	43
	00EF	00		00EF	0B
	00F0	00		00F0	00
Instruction	0B40	DC		0B40	DC
	0B41	03		0B41	03
	0B42	0A		0B42	0A

The carry bit was set, thus indicating that there was a carry out of bit 7 from the last operation. The subroutine at $0A03_{16}$ will be referenced by having that address put into the program counter. The next address in the main program ($0B43_{16}$) is stored in the top two cells of the stack and the stack pointer is updated.

80 Call if No Carry

This instruction makes a subroutine reference if the carry bit is cleared. The return address is pushed on the stack in the normal manner if the call is made. A carry bit that is set results in the subroutine not being referenced.

Operation code   D4
Mnemonic   CNC
Addressing mode   direct
Status bits affected   none
Clock periods   18 (9 if the condition is false)
Format

		Bit number		
		7 6 5 4	3 2 1 0	
Memory cell	m	1 1 0 1	0 1 0 0	
	m + 1	Low-address byte		
	m + 2	High-address byte		

☐ EXAMPLE

Before Execution		After Execution	
Program counter	08C2	Program counter	08C5
Stack pointer	01B7	Stack pointer	01B7
Status register	87	Status register	87
Memory	08C2	D4	Memory	08C2	D4
	08C3	20		08C3	20
	08C4	06		08C4	06

The carry bit is set, so that subroutine will not be referenced. Instead, the instruction at $08C5_{16}$ will be executed next.

80 Call if Minus

If the last arithmetic or boolean instruction produced a negative result, thus causing the sign bit to be set, the subroutine is called. No subroutine action follows if the sign bit is 0.

Operation code   FC
Mnemonic   CM
Addressing mode   direct
Status bits affected   none
Clock periods   18 (9 if the condition is false)
Format

		Bit number		
		7 6 5 4	3 2 1 0	
Memory cell	m	1 1 1 1	1 1 0 0	
	m + 1	Low-address byte		
	m + 2	High-address byte		

☐ EXAMPLE

Before Execution		After Execution	
Program counter	2012	Program counter	5905
Stack pointer	0369	Stack pointer	0367
Status register	D2	Status register	D2

Memory			Memory		
Stack	0367	03		0367	15
	0368	00		0368	20
	0369	1D		0369	1D
Instruction	2012	FC		2012	FC
	2013	05		2013	05
	2014	59		2014	59

Because the sign bit is set, a subroutine sequence follows. The return address is saved on the stack, and the program counter is set to the first address in the subprogram.

80 Call if Plus

A subroutine will be called if the last result was positive (sign bit is 0). In case the sign bit is set, the normal program counter incrementing will occur.

Operation code   F4
Mnemonic   CP
Addressing mode   direct
Status bits affected   none
Clock periods   18 (9 if the condition is false)
Format

		Bit number		
		7 6 5 4	3 2 1 0	
Memory cell	m	1 1 1 1	0 1 0 0	
	m + 1	Low-address byte		
	m + 2	High-address byte		

□ EXAMPLE

Before Execution		After Execution	
Program counter	06A8	Program counter	06AB
Stack pointer	8801	Stack pointer	8801
Status register	82	Status register	82
Memory 06A8	F4	Memory 06A8	F4
06A9	20	06A9	20
06AA	0E	06AA	0E

The status bit for the sign is set prior to the conditional call instruction execution; thus no subroutine calling occurs. The following instruction in the main program will immediately be fetched.

80 Call if Zero

An earlier 0 answer, which set the zero condition bit, will cause this conditional command to make a subroutine call. A nonzero value produces the equivalent of a no operation.

Operation code	CC
Mnemonic	CZ
Addressing mode	direct
Status bits affected	none
Clock periods	18 (9 if the condition is false)
Format	Bit number

```
              7 6 5 4   3 2 1 0
Memory cell  m  | 1 1 0 0   1 1 0 0 |
          m + 1 | Low-address byte  |
          m + 2 | High-address byte |
```

□ EXAMPLE

Before Execution		After Execution	
Program counter	34CD	Program counter	1140
Stack pointer	701F	Stack pointer	701D
Status register	56	Status register	56

Memory			Memory		
Instruction	34CD	CC		34CD	CC
	34CE	40		34CE	40
	34CF	11		34CF	11
Stack	701D	00		701D	D0
	701E	00		701E	34
	701F	D2		701F	D2

The call is made because the zero bit was set.

80 Call if Not Zero

A zero condition bit that is clear causes this instruction to make a call. On the other hand, a zero bit that is set disables the calling process.

Operation code	C4
Mnemonic	CNZ
Addressing mode	direct
Status bits affected	none
Clock periods	18 (9 if the condition is false)
Format	Bit number

```
              7 6 5 4   3 2 1 0
Memory cell  m  | 1 1 0 0   0 1 0 0 |
          m + 1 | Low-address byte  |
          m + 2 | High-address byte |
```

□ EXAMPLE

Before Execution		After Execution	
Program counter	0147	Program counter	014A
Stack pointer	08C5	Stack pointer	08C5
Status register	46	Status register	46
Memory 0147	C4	Memory 0147	C4
0148	EC	0148	EC
0149	02	0149	02

No reference is made because the zero status bit is set, thus indicating that the previous result was equal to 0.

80 Call if Parity Even

An even-parity answer to an arithmetic or a logical instruction will set the parity condition bit. A call will be made only if the parity bit is set prior to this conditional command.

Operation code	EC
Mnemonic	CPE
Addressing mode	direct
Status bits affected	none
Clock periods	18 (9 if the condition is false)
Format	Bit number

```
              7 6 5 4   3 2 1 0
Memory cell  m  | 1 1 1 0   1 1 0 0 |
          m + 1 | Low-address byte  |
          m + 2 | High-address byte |
```

□ EXAMPLE

Before Execution		After Execution	
Program counter	0445	Program counter	0EA1
Stack pointer	1182	Stack pointer	1180
Status register	06	Status register	06

Before Execution		After Execution	
Memory		Memory	
	0445 EC		0445 EC
Instruction	0446 A1		0446 A1
	0447 0E		0447 0E
	1180 20		1180 48
Stack	1181 11		1181 04
	1182 4A		1182 4A

The three operations required to make a subroutine call have been completed as a result of the parity bit being set prior to executing the instruction.

80 Call if Parity Odd

An odd-parity indication in the status register triggers this conditional operation. If the bit is set (an indication of even parity), this instruction is essentially ignored.

Operation code	E4
Mnemonic	CPO
Addressing mode	direct
Status bits affected	none
Clock periods	18 (9 if the condition is false)
Format	Bit number

		7 6 5 4	3 2 1 0
Memory cell	m	1 1 1 0	0 1 0 0
	m + 1	Low-address byte	
	m + 2	High-address byte	

□ EXAMPLE

Before Execution		After Execution	
Program counter	09FC	Program counter	09FF
Stack pointer	1187	Stack pointer	1187
Status register	17	Status register	17
Memory	09FC E4	Memory	09FC E4
	09FD 0C		09F0 0C
	09FE 2D		09FE 2D

The parity was even, as shown by a condition bit of 1. No call is made.

80 8085 Conditional Subroutine Calls Review

1. List the conditions that can be tested to decide whether a subroutine should be referenced.
2. Explain the change in the stack and the stack pointer in the example for the CC instruction page 210.
3. For a CM instruction, how is the value that is to be placed in the program counter obtained if the condition is true?

4. What would be the result of a CPE instruction if the preceding instruction had been ADC B? Before the add, the A register was equal to 4_{16} and the status register to 93_{16}.

80 8085 CONDITIONAL RETURN INSTRUCTIONS

The next family of instructions to be discussed provides capabilities for returning from subroutines; these capabilities are parallel to the ones just discussed for calling subroutines. An excellent use for a conditional return is the termination of counting loops. If the subroutine uses an iterative process, like the multiplication routine, for example, the test for final count could be made with a conditional return instruction. One instruction could not only decide if the loop should complete on the current pass but also transfer control back to the main program.

If the condition is satisfied, then popping the stack, incrementing the stack pointer, and loading the program counter proceed in a manner identical to the unconditional return. There is no requirement for matching conditional calls to conditional returns, of course; any combination of conditional and unconditional calling and returning instructions is allowed. The execution time for these instructions is variable. One machine cycle is used to make the decision, and an additional two cycles are needed to fetch the address if the condition is satisfied.

80 Return if Carry

If the carry bit is set, a return will be made to the program that called the subroutine. If the carry bit is not set, operation continues with the instruction following the return-if-carry command.

Operation code	D8
Mnemonic	RC
Addressing mode	none
Status bits affected	none
Clock periods	12 (6 if the condition is false)
Format	Bit number

		7 6 5 4	3 2 1 0
Memory cell	m	1 1 0 1	1 0 0 0

□ EXAMPLE

Before Execution		After Execution	
Program counter	01AD	Program counter	07BB
Stack pointer	2146	Stack pointer	2148
Status register	83	Status register	83

Before Execution		After Execution	
Memory		Memory	
Instruction 01AD	D8	01AD	D8
2146	BB	2146	BB
Stack 2147	07	2147	07
2148	1A	2148	1A

The condition being tested is true. The contents of the cell addressed by the stack pointer go to the lower half of the program counter; the upper half of the counter is loaded from the following location in the stack. Then the stack pointer counts up by 2.

80 Return if No Carry

A 0 value of the condition carry bit causes a return if this instruction is used. No return occurs if that bit is set. The next instruction in the subroutine will be executed instead.

Operation code	D0
Mnemonic	RNC
Addressing mode	none
Status bits affected	none
Clock periods	12 (6 if the condition is false)
Format	Bit number

```
              7 6 5 4   3 2 1 0
Memory cell  m  1 1 0 1   0 0 0 0
```

□ EXAMPLE

Before Execution		After Execution	
Program counter	3111	Program counter	3112
Stack pointer	0A2D	Stack pointer	0A2D
Status register	43	Status register	43
Memory 3111	D0	Memory 3111	D0

The condition is not satisfied, so the program counter merely increments to the next instruction address.

80 Return if Minus

A return is made if the sign bit had been set prior to this instruction. If that bit is clear, no return takes place.

Operation code	F8
Mnemonic	RM
Addressing mode	none
Status bits affected	none
Clock periods	12 (6 if the condition is false)
Format	Bit number

```
              7 6 5 4   3 2 1 0
Memory cell  m  1 1 1 1   1 0 0 0
```

□ EXAMPLE

Before Execution		After Execution	
Program counter	2A36	Program counter	420C
Stack pointer	3014	Stack pointer	3016
Status register	92	Status register	92
Memory		Memory	
Instruction 2A36	F8	2A36	F8
3014	0C	3014	0C
Stack 3015	42	3015	42
3016	90	3016	90

The return to the instruction at $420C_{16}$ in the main program results from the sign status bit being set.

80 Return if Plus

If the sign bit is 0, thus indicating a positive result, the return operation is performed.

Operation code	F0
Mnemonic	RP
Addressing mode	none
Status bits affected	none
Clock periods	12 (6 if the condition is false)
Format	Bit number

```
              7 6 5 4   3 2 1 0
Memory cell  m  1 1 1 1   0 0 0 0
```

□ EXAMPLE

Before Execution		After Execution	
Program counter	0CA2	Program counter	0CA3
Stack pointer	118E	Stack pointer	118E
Status register	86	Status register	86
Memory 0CA2	F0	Memory 0CA2	F0

The sign bit is set, so the return operation is not done. The instruction following the conditional return will be executed next.

80 Return if Zero

The status register is examined, and if the zero condition bit is set, the return is accomplished. If the tested condition is not fulfilled, the next successive instruction follows.

Operation code	C8
Mnemonic	RZ
Addressing mode	none

Status bits affected   none
Clock periods   12 (6 if the condition is not satisfied)
Format   Bit number
                         7 6 5 4   3 2 1 0
          Memory cell m [1 1 0 0   1 0 0 0]

☐ EXAMPLE

	Before Execution			After Execution	
Program counter	4763		Program counter	0E24	
Stack pointer	6211		Stack pointer	6213	
Status register	46		Status register	46	

Memory				Memory		
Instruction	47C3	C8		4763	C8
Stack {	6211	24		6211	24
	6212	0E		6212	0E
	6213	78		6213	78

The previous result was 0 (condition bit is set), so the return goes through. The return address from the stack is moved to the program counter and the pointer value revised.

80 Return if Not Zero

If the zero condition bit shows that the previous answer was other than 0, the return is effective; otherwise, there is no change from normal program counter incrementing.

Operation code   C0
Mnemonic   RNZ
Addressing mode   none
Status bits affected   none
Clock periods   12 (6 if the condition is false)
Format   Bit number
                         7 6 5 4   3 2 1 0
          Memory cell m [1 1 0 0   0 0 0 0]

☐ EXAMPLE

	Before Execution			After Execution	
Program counter	314B		Program counter	314C	
Stack pointer	2182		Stack pointer	2182	
Status register	46		Status register	46	
Memory	314B	C0	Memory	314B	C0

No return is made, because the zero condition bit was set.

80 Return if Parity Even

Even parity in the last arithmetic or logical result (condition bit set) will cause a return. No action is produced if the bit is clear.

Operation code   E8
Mnemonic   RPE
Addressing mode   none
Status bits affected   none
Clock periods   12 (6 if the condition is false)
Format   Bit number
                         7 6 5 4   3 2 1 0
          Memory cell m [1 1 1 0   1 0 0 0]

☐ EXAMPLE

	Before Execution			After Execution	
Program counter	1A84		Program counter	3103	
Stack pointer	53D2		Stack pointer	53D4	
Status register	47		Status register	47	

Memory				Memory		
Instruction	1A84	E8		1A84	E8
Stack {	53D2	03		53D2	03
	53D3	31		53D3	31
	53D4	14		53D4	14

The parity was even, so the stack is popped. The address is loaded into the program counter to transfer back to the calling program.

80 Return if Parity Odd

An odd-parity designation in the status register will allow the return to be made with this instruction.

Operation code   E0
Mnemonic   RPO
Addressing mode   none
Status bits affected   none
Clock periods   12 (6 if the condition is false)
Format   Bit number
                         7 6 5 4   3 2 1 0
          Memory cell m [1 1 1 0   0 0 0 0]

☐ EXAMPLE

	Before Execution			After Execution	
Program counter	4C01		Program counter	4C02	
Stack pointer	0FEE		Stack pointer	0FEE	
Status register	07		Status register	07	
Memory	4C01	E0	Memory	4C01	E0

The parity status bit was set, thus indicating even parity. The return is not taken.

8085 Conditional Return Instructions Review

1. How many machine cycles does the example for the RC instruction require? With a 2-MHz clock, what is the execution time?
2. Why does the return-if-plus example require only six clock periods to execute?
3. Explain the settings of all status register bits in the RM instruction example.
4. What status register setting would have enabled the return in the $E0_{16}$ op code instruction example?

ADVANCED SUBROUTINE CONCEPTS

So far in this chapter we have considered only a main program calling a subroutine. What would we have if one subroutine called another? Can a subroutine call itself? Both situations are handled properly by the microprocessor through the stack. When one subroutine calls another, we refer to the inner one as a *nested subroutine*. If a subroutine can call itself, it is a *recursive subroutine*.

Nested Subroutines

As an example of a nested subroutine, we will use the multiplication programs from Chap. 9 with a slight modification. We only need to add a return instruction at the end of the programs (routines) to convert them

to a subroutine. Remember that the programs work only with positive numbers. We will complete the multiplication capability by writing a routine that checks for a difference in the signs of the multiplier and multiplicand. If they are different, a negative product must be produced. The sign routine will also convert negative multipliers and multiplicands to positive numbers and will then properly adjust the sign of the product. The calling sequence is shown in Fig. 11-4 and in the two programs listed in Tables 11-1 through 11-4. (Only the listing for the multiplication routine are given because these programs were fully discussed in Chap. 9.)

The sequence as shown in Fig. 11-4 begins with calling of the sign program to convert any negative inputs to positive. The sign program calls the multiplication routine, which performs the operation and returns to the sign program. After adjusting the product, the sign subroutine gives control back to the main program. The flowchart for the sign program is given in Fig. 11-5.

8085 Sign Routine

The multiplier must be placed in the C register and the multiplicand in the D register prior to calling. The product will be in the double-length BC register pair on return. Figure 11-6 (see page 218) shows how the stack changes for each call or return. We will assume that an instruction in address 4526_{16} has called the sign program. (Because the call instruction occupies 3 bytes, the next instruction is located at 4529_{16}.) The stack pointer contained 5689_{16} before the process started.

The return address to the main program (4529_{16}) is pushed onto the stack (see Fig. 11-6a). When the SIGN program calls MULT, the return address 1470_{16} is also

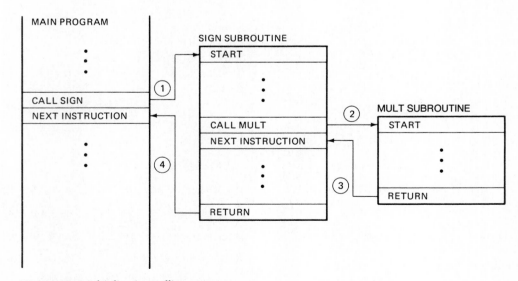

Fig. 11-4 Multiplication calling sequence.

Table 11-1 8085 Sign Routine

Label	Mnemonic	Operand	Address	Machine Code	Comments
SIGN	MOV	A, D	1460	7A	Obtain operand 1
	XRA	B	1461	A8	Exclusive OR with operand 2
	MVI A	0	1462	3E	Clear accumulator
			1463	00	
	JP	STRFLAG	1464	C3	Jump to store sign if positive
			1465	68	
			1466	14	
	CMP	A	1467	BF	Complement A
STRFLAG	STA	FLAG	1468	32	Save results of comparison
			1469	90	
			146A	14	
	CALL	MULT	146B	CD	Call subroutine
			146C	00	
			146D	10	
	LDA	FLAG	1470	3A	If product does not need to be
			1471	90	complemented, return
			1472	14	
	ADI	0	1473	C6	
			1474	00	
	RP		1475	F0	
	MVI A	0	1476	3E	Complement product
			1475	00	
	SUB	C	1476	91	
	MOV	C, A	1477	4F	
	MVI A	0	1478	3E	
			1479	00	
	SBB	B	147A	98	
	MOV	B, A	147B	47	
	RET		147C	C9	
DATA	FLAG		1490		Data storage

Table 11-2 8085 Multiplication Routine

Label	Mnemonic	Operand	Address	Machine Code
MULT	MVI B	0	1000	06
			1001	00
	MVI E	9	1002	1E
			1003	09
MULT1	MOV	A, C	1004	79
	RAR		1005	1F
	MOV	C, M	1006	4E
	DCR	E	1007	1D
	JZ	DONE	1008	CA
			1009	15
			100A	10
	MOV	A, B	100B	78
	JNC	MULT2	100C	D2
			100D	10
			100E	10
	ADD	D	100F	82
MULT2	RAR		1010	1F
	MOV	B, A	1011	47
	JMP	MULT1	1012	C3
			1013	04
			1014	10
DONE	RET		1015	C9

Table 11-3 6800 Sign Routine

Label	Mnemonic	Operand	Address	Machine Code	Comments
	LDAA	MPLR	1460	B6	Obtain operand 1
			1461	11	
			1462	50	
	EORA	MCAND	1463	B8	Exclusive OR with operand 2
			1464	11	
			1465	51	
	BPL	STRFLAG	1466	2A	Branch to store sign if positive
			1467	02	
	LDAA	−1	1468	86	Make A negative
			1469	FF	
STRFLAG	STAA	FLAG	146A	B7	Save results of comparison
			146B	14	
			146C	90	
	JSR	MULT	146D	BD	Call subroutine
			146E	10	
			146F	00	
	TST	FLAG	1470	7D	Check flag
			1471	14	
			1472	90	
	BPL	CONT	1473	2A	If product does not need to be complemented, branch
			1474	02	
	NEGA		1475	40	Complement
	COMB		1476	53	
CONT	RTS		1477	39	Return
FLAG			1490		Data storage

Table 11-4 6800 Multiplication Routine

Label	Mnemonic	Operand	Address	Machine Code
	CLRA		1000	4F
	CLRB		1001	5F
	LDX	8	1002	CE
			1003	00
			1004	08
SHIFT	ASLB		1005	58
	ROLA		1006	49
	ASL	MPLR	1007	78
			1008	11
			1009	50
	BCC	DECR	100A	24
			100B	05
	ADDB	MCAND	100C	FB
			100D	11
			100E	51
	ADCA		100F	89
			1010	00
DECR	DEX		1011	09
	BNE	SHIFT	1012	26
			1013	F1

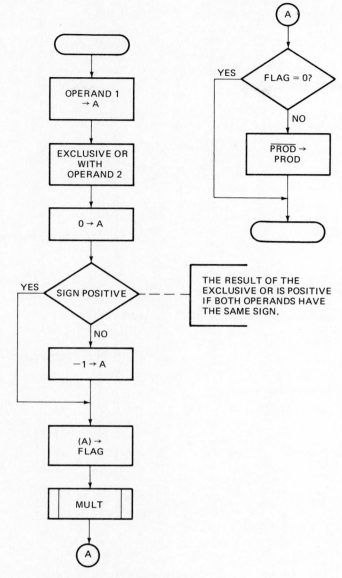

Fig. 11-5 SIGN subroutine flowchart.

placed on the stack and the pointer increased by 2 to show the new top of stack (Fig. 11-6*b*).

Returning is simply a reverse process. To transfer control back to the SIGN program after MULT is through, the stack is popped to load address 1470_{16} into the program counter (see Fig. 11-6*c*). The final return to the main program is made in the same way (see Fig. 11-6*d*).

This process can continue until the stack is completely filled, so that the level of nested subroutines is limited only by the amount of memory available. Of course, the program, the data, and the stack must share the memory. Figure 11-8 shows an efficient way of allocating a 4K RAM to these processes which must compete for memory space. This allocation permits the maxi-

mum program size and maximum stack size simultaneously. Memory is filled when the program and the stack overlap, because the instructions and data fill increasing memory addresses while the stack grows toward decreasing addresses.

68 6800 Sign Routine

The multiplier must be placed in cell 1150_{16} and the multiplicand must be placed in cell 1151_{16} prior to calling this subroutine. The product will be formed in the A and B registers, as explained in Chap. 9. Figure 11-7 shows how the stack changes with each call or

STACK POINTER	STACK ADDRESS	CONTENTS
5687	5685	20
	5686	FF
	5687	29
	5688	45
	5689	A2

a. MAIN PROGRAM CALLS SIGN

STACK POINTER	STACK ADDRESS	CONTENTS
5685	5685	70
	5686	14
	5687	29
	5688	45
	5689	A2

b. SIGN CALLS MULT

STACK POINTER	STACK ADDRESS	CONTENTS	
5687	5685	70	] TO PROGRAM COUNTER
	5686	14	
	5687	29	
	5688	45	
	5689	A2	

c. RETURN FROM MULT

STACK POINTER	STACK ADDRESS	CONTENTS	
5689	5685	70	
	5686	14	
	5687	29	] TO PROGRAM COUNTER
	5688	45	
	5689	A2	

d. RETURN TO MAIN PROGRAM

Fig. 11-6 8085 dynamic stack contents.

STACK POINTER	STACK ADDRESS	CONTENTS
5687	5685	00
	5686	FF
	5687	29
	5688	45
	5689	29

a. MAIN PROGRAM CALLS SIGN

STACK POINTER	STACK ADDRESS	CONTENTS
5685	5685	00
	5686	14
	5687	70
	5688	45
	5689	29

b. SIGN CALLS MULT

STACK POINTER	STACK ADDRESS	CONTENTS	
5687	5685	00	
	5686	14	] TO PROGRAM COUNTER
	5687	70	
	5688	45	
	5689	29	

c. RETURN FROM MULT

STACK POINTER	STACK ADDRESS	CONTENTS	
5689	5685	00	
	5686	14	
	5687	70	
	5688	45	] TO PROGRAM COUNTER
	5689	29	

d. RETURN TO MAIN PROGRAM

Fig. 11-7 6800 dynamic stack contents.

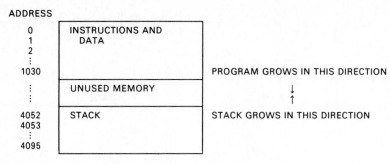

ADDRESS

0	INSTRUCTIONS AND	
1	DATA	
2		
⋮		
1030		PROGRAM GROWS IN THIS DIRECTION
⋮	UNUSED MEMORY	↓
⋮		↑
4052	STACK	STACK GROWS IN THIS DIRECTION
4053		
⋮		
4095		

Fig. 11-8 Memory allocation.

return. We will assume that an instruction at cell 4526_{16} jumped to the subroutine. We will also assume that extended addressing was the mode. (Because the jump to subroutine occupies 3 bytes, the next instruction is located at 4529_{16}.) The stack pointer contained 5689_{16} before the process started.

The return address to the main program (4529_{16}) is pushed on the stack (see Fig. 11-7a). When the SIGN program calls MULT, the return address 1470_{16} is also placed on the stack and the pointer increased by 2 to show the new top of stack (Fig. 11-7b).

Returning is simply a reverse process. To transfer control back to the SIGN program after MULT is through, the stack is popped to load address 1470_{16} into the program counter (see Fig. 11-7c). The final return to the main program is made the same way (Fig. 11-7d).

This process can continue until the stack is completely filled, so that the level of nested subroutines is limited only by the amount of memory available. Of course, the program, the data, and the stack must share the memory. Figure 11-8 shows an efficient way to allocate a 4K RAM to these processes which must compete for memory space. This allocation permits maximum program and stack size simultaneously. Memory is filled when the program and the stack overlap, because the instructions and data fill increasing memory addresses while the stack grows toward decreasing addresses.

Recursive Processes

Some problems are well-suited to a repetitive use of a subroutine. In such cases the nested subroutine calls itself, thus increasing the level of nesting. A simple example of recursion is an algorithm that sums the numbers from 1 to n. We can easily calculate the sum of the jth digit to the previous ones by the formula:

$$\sum_{i=1}^{j} i = j + \sum_{i=1}^{j-1} i \tag{11-1}$$

By continuing this process until j is equal to n, we arrive at the required sum. A recursive subroutine to calculate the sum is listed in Tables 11-5 and 11-6. For the 8085, the value for n must be placed in the B register and the accumulator set to 0 prior to the call. The answer is left in the accumulator. No check for overflow is made, so if

$$\sum_{i=1}^{n} i > 7F_{16} \tag{11-2}$$

the result will be wrong. There is another possible bug in the program if n is not selected properly (see Prob. 11-1). An example of the 8085 stack sequences for $n = 3$ is shown in Fig. 11-9. The pushing and popping sequences guarantee that the instructions will be executed in the proper order and that control will eventu-

Table 11-5 8085 Sum Routine

Instruction	Address	Machine Code	Comments
ADD B	1000	80	Add next number to sum
DCR B	1001	05	Decrement n
CNZ	1002	C4	If nonzero, call again
	1003	00	
	1004	10	
RET	1005	C9	Return

Table 11-6 6800 Sum Routine

Label	Instruction	Address	Machine Code	Comments
SUM	ABA	1000	1B	Add next number to sum
	DECB	1001	5A	Decrement *n*
	BEQ END	1002	27	If nonzero, call again
		1003	02	
	BSR SUM	1004	8D	
		1005	FA	
END	RTS	1006	39	Return

ally return to the main program. We see that the same address (1005_{16}) is placed on the stack twice (see Figs. 11-9b and 11-9c). In fact, that address would be pushed onto the stack every time the sum procedure is called by itself. After the first return (see Fig. 11-9d), the next instruction to be executed is the *same* return. This execution causes the stack to be popped again (see Fig. 11-9e), and for the second time in a row, the instruction at 1005_{16} is performed. Then the address popped from the stack is that of the return to the main program.

This example clearly shows the two characteristics of recursive programs. They are usually quite compact, requiring little memory space; however, they often consume a great deal of running time. The repeated execution of the return instruction at location 1005_{16} is a good illustration of the inefficiency in processor utilization. As *n* gets larger, even more instruction executions are required simply to pop the stack. Because computers are good at repetitive tasks, it may be a good idea to trade off longer running time for memory space. See Prob. 11-2 for another way of dealing with this issue.

For the 6800 version, the value for *n* must be placed in the B accumulator and the A accumulator cleared before the program starts. The answer is left in the A accumulator. No check for overflow is made. Another possible bug in this program is examined in Prob. 11-1. An example of the stack sequences for *n* = 3 is shown in Fig. 11-10. The pushing and popping sequences guarantee that the instructions will be executed in the proper order and that control will eventually return to the main program. We see that the same address (1006_{16}) is placed on the stack twice (see Figs. 11-10b and 11-10c). In fact, that address would be pushed on the stack every time the sum procedure subroutine branched to itself. After the first return (Fig. 11-10d), the next instruction to be executed is the *same* return. This execution causes the stack to be popped again (Fig. 11-10e), and for the second time in a row, the instruction at 1006_{16} is performed. Then the address popped from the stack is that of the return to the main program.

This example clearly shows two characteristics of recursive programs. They are usually quite compact,

requiring little memory space; however, they often consume a great deal of running time. The repeated execution of the return instruction at location 1006_{16} is a good illustration of the inefficiency in processor utilization. As *n* gets larger, even more instruction executions are required simply to pop the stack. Because computers are good at repetitive tasks, it may be a good idea to trade off longer running time for memory space. Problem 11-2 shows another way of dealing with this issue.

Parameter Passing

The input data of all the subroutines used in this chapter were loaded into specific registers before the subroutine was called. The answer was also available in some register on return. Getting the information back and forth between the subroutine and the calling program is more formally designated *parameter passing*. The input and output numbers are the parameters that the subroutine processes.

The number of registers is limited, so if the number of parameters to be passed exceeds the number of registers, another method must be used. A frequently used technique is a *parameter pointer*. In the 8085 the HL register pair can be put to use in that fashion.

Assume that we want to call a subroutine that will arrange 100 numbers in ascending numerical order. The numbers are located in a table that may begin at any memory location. Figure 11-11 shows how the HL registers can be used to point to the starting address. By selecting instructions that use the HL registers to address the operand (such as ADD M; MOV B, M; and SUB M), the routine can efficiently manipulate items in the table. It is obviously the responsibility of the *calling* routine to establish the proper values in the H and the L registers before the subroutine reference.

Sometimes the number of parameters to be passed is variable. Consider a communications system that receives and processes messages of any length. The messages are received in the form of ASCII characters, and

STACK POINTER	STACK ADDRESS	CONTENTS
1027	1020	00
	1021	00
	1022	00
	1023	00
	1024	00
	1025	00
	1026	00
	1027	40
	1028	20

a. Initial call when $n = 3$, return address in main program is 2040_{16}

STACK POINTER	STACK ADDRESS	CONTENTS
1025	1020	00
	1021	00
	1022	00
	1023	00
	1024	00
	1025	05
	1026	10
	1027	40
	1028	20

b. Call when $n = 2$

STACK POINTER	STACK ADDRESS	CONTENTS
1023	1020	00
	1021	00
	1022	00
	1023	05
	1024	10
	1025	05
	1026	10
	1027	40
	1028	20

c. Call when $n = 1$

STACK POINTER	STACK ADDRESS	CONTENTS	
1025	1020	00	
	1021	00	
	1022	00	
	1023	05	⎤ TO PROGRAM COUNTER
	1024	10	⎦
	1025	05	
	1026	10	
	1027	40	
	1028	20	

d. First return

STACK POINTER	STACK ADDRESS	CONTENTS	
1027	1020	00	
	1021	00	
	1022	00	
	1023	05	
	1024	10	
	1025	05	⎤ TO PROGRAM COUNTER
	1026	10	⎦
	1027	40	
	1028	20	

e. Second return

STACK POINTER	STACK ADDRESS	CONTENTS	
1029	1020	00	
	1021	00	
	1022	00	
	1023	05	
	1024	10	
	1025	05	
	1026	10	
	1027	40	⎤ TO PROGRAM COUNTER
	1028	20	⎦

f. Third return to main program

Fig. 11-9   8085 recursive stack processes.

STACK POINTER	STACK ADDRESS	CONTENTS
1026	1020	00
	1021	00
	1022	00
	1023	00
	1024	00
	1025	00
	1026	00
	1027	20
	1028	40

a. Initial call when $n = 3$, return address in main program is 2040_{16}

STACK POINTER	STACK ADDRESS	CONTENTS
1024	1020	00
	1021	00
	1022	00
	1023	00
	1024	00
	1025	10
	1026	06
	1027	20
	1028	40

b. Call when $n = 2$

STACK POINTER	STACK ADDRESS	CONTENTS
1022	1020	00
	1021	00
	1022	00
	1023	10
	1024	06
	1025	10
	1026	06
	1027	20
	1028	40

c. Call when $n = 1$

STACK POINTER	STACK ADDRESS	CONTENTS	
1024	1020	00	
	1021	00	
	1022	00	
	1023	10	⎤
	1024	06	⎦ TO PROGRAM COUNTER
	1025	10	
	1026	06	
	1027	20	
	1028	40	

d. First return

STACK POINTER	STACK ADDRESS	CONTENTS	
1026	1020	00	
	1021	00	
	1022	00	
	1023	10	
	1024	06	
	1025	10	⎤
	1026	06	⎦ TO PROGRAM COUNTER
	1027	20	
	1028	40	

e. Second return

STACK POINTER	STACK ADDRESS	CONTENTS	
1028	1020	00	
	1021	00	
	1022	00	
	1023	10	
	1024	06	
	1025	10	
	1026	06	
	1027	20	⎤
	1028	40	⎦ TO PROGRAM COUNTER

f. Third return to main program

Fig. 11-10　6800 recursive stack processes.

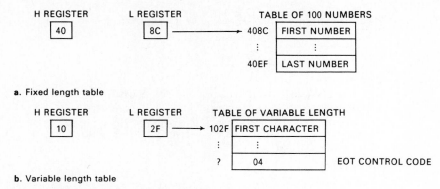

a. Fixed length table

b. Variable length table

Fig. 11-11 Parameter passing with pointers.

every transmission ends with an end-of-text (EOT = 04_{16}) control code. A subroutine is to examine each character for proper parity until the EOT character is encountered. Again, the HL registers can be used to show the starting address of the table, but the end is signaled by the control character.

Exactly the same technique can be used by the subroutine to pass the output parameters. As an example of such a situation, the parity-checking routine above can indicate correct or incorrect parity for each character in an answer table. The answer table is the same length as the character table. The answer table corresponds item for item with the input. Correct parity is shown by a 0 value in that byte of the answer table, and incorrect parity is shown by FF_{16} in the answer table. The HL register pair is set to the starting address of the answer table by the subroutine before the return.

A similar scheme can be used with the 6800. In this case, either the index register or a memory cell would serve as a pointer. In other respects, the action in the 6800 resembles that described for the 8085.

Advanced Subroutine Concepts Review

1. Distinguish between nested and recursive subroutines.
2. How does the SIGN program decide if the product must be complemented?
3. Why was some register, instead of the flag cell, not used to store the decision value temporarily in the SIGN subroutine?
4. Describe the most practical memory allocation scheme when a stack is being used.
5. What limits the number of times a recursive subroutine can call itself?
6. Calculate the number of times the return instruction of the SUM program would be performed if $n = 8$.
7. Discuss the tradeoff of memory space and running time of recursive routines.
8. Explain how a pointer register pair can be used to

pass a fixed or a variable number of parameters to a subroutine.

🔲 OTHER 8085 STACK INSTRUCTIONS

In addition to being useful for calling and returning from subroutines, the stack can also be used for data storage. Normally, such storage would be of a temporary nature when it is unnecessary to declare a memory variable. The stack will hold the information until it is again needed in the calculations.

🔲 Push

Any register pair, or the status register and the accumulator, can be pushed onto the stack by using this instruction. (This is the only command that permits a direct examination of the status bits.) The contents of the first register are saved at the location preceding the stack pointer value and the second register, at the address 2 less than the pointer. The stack pointer is then decremented by 2. Figure 11-12 shows how this operation is performed. As Fig. 11-12 shows, the value in the B, D, H, or program status word (condition bits) is stored at the higher address in the stack. The corresponding register of the pair (C, E, L, or A) is stored in the lower address. The stack pointer is modified to the new top of stack.

Operation Code	Mnemonic
C5	PUSH B
D5	PUSH D
E5	PUSH H
F5	PUSH PSW

Addressing mode register
Status bits affected none
Clock periods 12
Format

	Bit number
	7 6 5 4 3 2 1 0
Memory cell m	1 1 r r 0 1 0 1

	STACK	
STACK POINTER	ADDRESS	CONTENTS
2B3D	2B3B	FF
	2B3C	FF
	2B3D	FF

a. Before execution

	STACK	
STACK POINTER	ADDRESS	CONTENTS
2B3B	2B3B	REGISTER 2 (C, E, L, OR A)
	2B3C	REGISTER 1 (B, D, H, OR PSW)
	2B3D	FF

b. After execution

Fig. 11-12   8085 push instruction.

where rr = 00 for registers B and C
       01 for registers D and E
       10 for registers H and L
       11 for PSW and A registers

□ EXAMPLE

Before Execution		After Execution	
Program counter	2240	Program counter	2241
Stack pointer	3565	Stack pointer	3563
A register	CD	A register	CD
Status register	97	Status register	97

Memory				Memory		
Instruction	2240	F5		2240	F5
Stack	3563	22		3563	CD
	3564	0F		3564	97
	3565	07		3565	07

After the status register is placed in location 3564_{16} and the accumulator in 3563_{16}, the pointer is set to the address for the new top of stack (3563_{16}).

80 Pop

Data can be removed from the stack and placed into a register pair with this command. The byte at the address of the stack pointer is moved to one register of a pair (C, E, L, or A), and the byte from the next higher stack location is placed in the corresponding register for that same pair (B, D, H, or PSW). The stack pointer increments by 2.

Operation Code	Mnemonic
C1	POP B
D1	POP D
E1	POP H
F1	POP PSW

Addressing mode   register
Status bits affected   none (op codes C1, D1, and E1),
                  S, Z, A_C, P, and C (op code F1)

Clock periods   10

Format   Bit number
                   7 6 5 4   3 2 1 0
Memory cell   m | 1 1 r r   0 0 0 1 |

where rr = 00 for registers B and C
       01 for registers D and E
       10 for registers H and L
       11 for PSW and A register

□ EXAMPLE 1   Register pair.

Before Execution		After Execution	
Program counter	10FC	Program counter	10FD
Stack pointer	30FE	Stack pointer	3100
B register	FF	B register	19
C register	00	C register	B0

Memory			Memory		
Instruction	10FC	C1		10FC	C1
Stack	30FE	B0		30FE	B0
	30FF	19		30FF	19
	3100	27		3100	27

□ EXAMPLE 2   Status register and accumulator.

Before Execution		After Execution	
Program counter	027B	Program counter	027C
Stack pointer	058A	Stack pointer	158C
A register	11	A register	00
Status register	02	Status register	86

Memory			Memory		
Instruction	0278	F1		027B	F1
Stack	058A	00		158A	00
	158B	86		158B	86
	158C	FF		158C	FF

There is no requirement for popping the data off the stack and into the same registers that pushed it onto the stack. In fact, a clever means of moving data from one pair of registers to another can be accomplished by using the stack:

PUSH   B
POP   D

This moves the value in the B register to the D register and the contents of the C register to the E register.

80 Load Stack Pointer

The stack pointer was used in all the examples in this chapter, but until now no mention has been made of how the pointer is initiated. If the stack is to be used by a program, either to call subroutines or to push and pop register pairs, the stack pointer must be set to some starting value. Otherwise, it will be equal to some unknown, random address. As Fig. 11-8 showed, this value is frequently the highest memory address, although it does not have to be. Loading the stack pointer is normally one of the first instructions performed in the main program.

One way of loading the stack pointer is with the LXI instruction discussed in Chap. 6. There is also another instruction for the 8085 that places the HL register-pair data in the pointer. Of course, the registers must have been set to the proper values prior to executing this instruction. Once the stack pointer has been initiated, it should not be reloaded because its previous value will be lost.

Operation code   F9
Mnemonic   SPHL
Addressing mode   register
Status bits affected   none
Clock periods   6
Format   Bit number
                                7 6 5 4   3 2 1 0
        Memory cell   m | 1 1 1 1   1 0 0 1 |

☐ EXAMPLE

Before Execution		After Execution	
Program counter	47F1	Program counter	47F2
Stack pointer	021D	Stack pointer	58FF
H register	58	H register	58
L register	FF	L register	FF
Memory 47F1	F9	Memory 47F1	F9

The upper byte of the pointer is set equal to the H register, and the lower byte equal to the L register.

80 Exchange Stack

This command causes the value in the top 2 bytes of the stack and the HL register pair to be interchanged. The L register is swapped with the contents of the location equal to that of the stack pointer and the H register, with the contents of the cell at the pointer address plus 1. The stack pointer value is unchanged.

Operation code   E3
Mnemonic   XTHL
Addressing mode   register
Status bits affected   none
Clock periods   16
Format   Bit number
                                7 6 5 4   3 2 1 0
        Memory cell   m | 1 1 1 0   0 0 1 1 |

☐ EXAMPLE

Before Execution			After Execution		
Program counter		18A9	Program counter		18AA
Stack pointer		2546	Stack pointer		2546
H register		11	H register		01
L register		B0	L register		FF
Memory			Memory		
Instruction	18A9	E3		18A9	E3
Stack	2546	FF		2546	B0
	2547	01		2547	11

The quantities in the stack and the register pair were switched. The stack pointer's final address is equal to the initial one.

80 Other 8085 Stack Instructions Review

1. When the accumulator and the status register are pushed onto the stack, which register goes to the lower address?
2. All the registers and counters in Example 1 of the POP instruction are changed. Explain the reason for their final values.
3. Name two instructions that can be used to load the stack pointer.
4. At what point in the program should the stack pointer be loaded? When should another load stack pointer instruction be executed once the program is running?
5. How is the stack pointer affected by the exchange stack instruction? Explain why this action is logical.

68 OTHER 6800 STACK INSTRUCTIONS

In addition to being useful for jumping to and returning from subroutines, the stack can be used for temporary data storage. The stack can hold the information until it is needed in the calculations.

68 Push Accumulator

Either of the accumulators can be pushed on the stack. The contents of the designated register are pushed on the stack and the stack pointer is decremented by 1.

Operation Code	Mnemonic
36	PSHA
37	PSHB

Addressing mode   inherent
Status bits affected   none
Clock cycles   4
Format   Bit number

		7 6 5 4	3 2 1 0
Memory cell	m	0 0 1 1	0 1 1 r

where r = 0 for A register
r = 1 for B register

☐ EXAMPLE

Before Execution		After Execution	
Program counter	0400	Program counter	0401
Stack pointer	1024	Stack pointer	1023
A register	07	A register	07

Memory			Memory		
Instruction	0400	36		0400	36
	1022	00		1022	00
Stack	1023	00		1023	00
	1024	00		1024	07

The contents of the A register are pushed on the stack and the pointer is updated.

68 Pull Accumulator

Either of the accumulators can be pulled from the stack. For this instruction to work correctly, the register must previously have been pushed on the stack. The contents of the designated register are pulled from the stack and the stack pointer is incremented by 1.

Operation Code	Mnemonic
32	PULA
33	PULB

Operation Code	Mnemonic

Addressing mode   inherent
Status bits affected   none
Clock cycles   4
Format   Bit number

		7 6 5 4	3 2 1 0
Memory cell	m	0 0 1 1	0 0 1 r

where r = 0 for A register
r = 1 for B register

☐ EXAMPLE

Before Execution		After Execution	
Program counter	0400	Program counter	0401
Stack pointer	1023	Stack pointer	1024
A register	AC	A register	07

Memory			Memory		
Instruction	0400	32		0400	32
	1022	00		1022	00
Stack	1023	00		1023	00
	1024	00		1024	07

The pointer is incremented; then the stack is popped and the value placed in the A register.

CHAPTER SUMMARY

1. A subroutine is a group of instructions that is assigned a name. The instructions can be referenced to perform a certain task that is usually repeated many times in a problem.
2. A subroutine is called to reference it. After execution, the subroutine returns control to the address immediately following the call instructions.
3. The stack facilitates calling and returning from subroutines in a microprocessor. The address following the call is pushed on the stack, and then the first address of the subroutine is loaded into the program counter. When the subroutine is completed, the return causes the stack to be popped. The data on top of the stack, the return address, is forced into the program counter. Control is then transferred to the main program.
4. The call and return instructions must always be used as a pair for proper operation.
5. Conditional calling and returning instructions are included in the 8085 repertoire. The subroutine operation will proceed only if the designated condition of the status register is true.
6. The timing for 8085 conditional call and return instructions depends on whether the status being

Table 11-7 8085 Subroutine and Stack Operations

Mnemonic	Machine Code	Number of Bytes	Status Bits Affected				
			C	A$_C$	Z	S	P
CALL	CD	3					
CC	DC	3					
CM	FC	3					
CNC	D4	3					
CNZ	C4	3					
CP	F4	3					
CPE	EC	3					
CPO	E4	3					
CZ	CC	3					
POP, B, D, H, PSW	C1, D1, E1, F1	1		X	X	X	X
PUSH, B, D, H, PSW	C5, D5, E5, F5	1					
RC	D8	1					
RET	C9	1					
RM	F8	1					
RNC	D0	1					
RNZ	C0	1					
RP	F0	1					
RPE	E8	1					
RPO	E0	1					
RZ	C8	1					
SPHL	F9	1					
XTHL	E3	1					

tested for is true. If true, an additional two machine cycles are appended to the instruction to fetch the subroutine address from memory.

7. Subroutines may be nested to any level. Only the RAM space available for the stack limits the number of levels.

8. Allocation of the stack initially to the highest address provides for the maximum utilization of memory space.

9. Recursive subroutines are constructed with the ability of calling themselves. Another return address is added to the stack as a result of each call.

10. Subroutine parameter passing can be implemented by using registers or memory. When memory is used, a parameter pointer shows where the data table starts. The data table need not always have the same length.

11. Registers, including the program status word and the accumulator, can be pushed on the stack. The register values can be restored by popping the stack.

12. The stack pointer must be initiated whenever the program is restarted. Either of two instructions may be used to establish the pointer address.

13. Tables 11-7 and 11-8 list each of the subroutine and stack instructions.

Table 11-8 6800 Subroutine and Stack Operations

Mnemonic	Machine Code	Number of Bytes
BSR	8D	2
JSR	AD, BD	2, 3
PULA	32	1
PULB	33	1
PSHA	36	1
PSHB	37	1
RTS	39	1

Note: None of these instructions affects the status bits.

KEY TERMS AND CONCEPTS

Subroutine

Call

Return

Calling program

Stack usage for subroutines

Unconditional and conditional calls

Unconditional and conditional returns

Nested subroutines

Memory allocation for stack and program

Recursive subroutine

Parameter passing

Parameter pointer

Register pair storage on stack

Loading the stack pointer

Exchange stack and register pair

PROBLEMS

11-1 What would happen if the n input to the SUM subroutine were 0? What if $n = -120$?

11-2 Rewrite the SUM routine by using a loop instead of a recursive subroutine call. Compare the number of memory locations required for each version. Compare the execution times of the two routines for $n = 3$.

11-3 Write a routine equivalent to the SIGN program that properly processes negative dividends and divisors for the division program in Chap. 9, calls the division routine (which has a return instruction appended to it), and corrects the sign of the quotient, if necessary.

11-4 Write an equation expressing the number of times the return instruction of the SUM program is executed for an arbitrary value of n.

11-5 Write the instructions to prevent an error if the condition of Eq. (11-2) is true. These instructions will set the accumulator negative and return if the sum is going to be greater than $7F_{16}$.

11-6 If the n input to the SUM program is 16_{10}, how many recursive calls are made? What value is found in the A register on return?

11-7 The initial call on the SUM program is made from location 3601_{16}. (That is, the op code for the call instruction is at that address.) Show the final configuration of the stack after all calls and returns have been made if $n = 4$. The original stack pointer value is 6400_{16}.

11-8 The end-of-text character in Fig. 11-11b may be received incorrectly. That is, some bits may be erroneously set or cleared because of line noise. Devise a scheme for detecting the end of the parameter table that will be able to accommodate such errors and still find the last character of the text.

AN INTRODUCTION TO INTERFACING AND PERIPHERAL EQUIPMENT

Even the most powerful computers are useless if isolated from their environment. The computer must have a way to accept entry of programs and data so that a new job can be processed. The outcome of this processing must also be communicated to the person who requested the work. There is a further need for data and instruction paths between the processor and memory units within the computer.

Every time signals cross between pieces of equipment or major units, an interface is needed. Much of the day-to-day work on microcomputers involves the fabrication, use, or repair of interface circuitry. When confronted by the myriad of interface circuits that a microcomputer can use, a technician may experience considerable confusion, especially when dealing with combinations of analog, parallel, and serial interfaces.

Despite the seemingly endless variety of interfaces, a few simple concepts are the basis for all of them. A grasp of these concepts will equip you with the understanding needed to troubleshoot even the most complicated microcomputer system.

Once the microcomputer has calculated results, the output must be displayed in some way that a human being can understand. A method for entering data that the machine can read is also needed. Peripheral equipment is used for these functions as well as to transmit data from one place to another and to store it offline. Equipment commonly encountered in microcomputer systems includes printers, CRT terminals and keyboards, modems and floppy- and hard-disk drives, and cartridge or cassette recorders.

CHAPTER OBJECTIVES

Upon completion of this chapter, you should be able to:

1. Explain the role that interfaces play in a microcomputer.
2. Explain why software, as well as hardware, is an important component of the interface.
3. List examples of commonly used interfaces.
4. Discuss the importance of standardization for interfaces.
5. Give several examples of interface designs.
6. Describe the advantages and disadvantages of the various types of printers.
7. Explain the principles of operation of a keyboard.
8. Draw a block diagram for a CRT terminal.
9. Explain why modems are needed in telecommunications.
10. Distinguish between the various kinds of floppy-disk drives available.
11. Explain the operation of magnetic cartridge and cassette recorders.
12. Describe the principles of local area networks.

INTERFACES

Every time a device is connected to a bus or input/output (I/O) port, an interface is created. An *interface* is simply a shared boundary between two systems or units. Obviously, interfaces play an important role in any microcomputer; the method by which memory can be addressed to locate a particular cell is dependent upon its interface to the data, address, and control buses. Similarly, an *I/O port* requires that the same types of signals be applied before data can be sent or received. In the chapters that follow, you will gain an appreciation for the issues that one must deal with in building, troubleshooting, and maintaining microcomputer interfaces.

An important point to keep in mind is that interfacing almost always involves a computer program as well as circuitry. Therefore, we speak of both hardware and software interfacing. The relationship between the two is extremely important because the design of one interacts with the other. A particular hardware interface may make it quite difficult to write a properly running program for the computer. A minor change in the equipment interfacing technique can often dramatically reduce the complexity of the programming task. You may hear people talking of the hardware-software tradeoffs in discussions of these relationships.

Memory interfacing is divided into dealing with read-only and read-write memories. Read-only memories (ROMs) do not allow the stored values to be changed; for that reason, ROM interfacing is simplified because no write circuitry is needed. Read-write memories, also called random-access memories (RAMs), on the other hand, must be able to change the cell contents as well as read out their values. To complicate the problem further, there are dynamic and static RAMs. Static memories will hold the contents in each cell constant as long as power is applied. Dynamic memories, however, must be repeatedly refreshed. Refreshing writes the information back into each location several times per second. A refresh mechanism must be built into the interface of dynamic memories. Bubble and charge-coupled device memories have their own unique interface requirements too.

I/O interfacing is most simply accomplished by an I/O port. Another straightforward I/O interface technique is memory mapping. More sophisticated systems may demand that interrupts be supported. *Interrupts* are signals from an external device that inform the computer of an unscheduled event in a real-time system. Interrupt processing requires that the MPU handle this signal immediately, yet still keep track of what it was doing before the interrupt came along. Because the computer can only perform one operation at a time, the work in progress must be stopped and enough detail about it saved to allow the processor to respond to the interrupt. Then the temporarily stored information is retrieved and the original sequence resumed.

If the speed of transfer between memory and the peripheral equipment is especially critical, direct memory access input/output can be used. With this arrangement, the I/O device can read or write memory contents just like the processor. Implementing any of these methods of data exchange is facilitated by the availability of integrated circuits that supply much of the logic needed to control and respond to signals on the buses.

So far we have only considered *parallel I/O*, but the data can be sent serially, 1 bit at a time, as well. The rules for a *serial I/O* channel are specified in a *protocol*. If the data stream is an unbroken one, *synchronous* protocols are applicable. In contrast, a data stream that starts or stops is suited for *asynchronous* communications. Again, the job of designing, building, and repairing these interfaces is made easier by integrated-circuit receivers and transmitters.

One of the most used peripheral devices for microcomputer I/O is the *teletype*. A special interface for this equipment, called a 20-milliamp (mA) current loop, is frequently encountered in microcomputer systems. By rearranging the elements of the current loop, the communications path between teletype and computer can be made one-way or two-way.

With the wide interest in computer communications, establishing common ways of exchanging data—or *communications standards*—is important for reliability and cost savings. The Electronic Industries Association (EIA) Standard RS-232C provides for a serial interface between the data-handling equipment and the computer. Another widely used standard is the IEEE Standard 488 bus, which is well-suited for instrumentation networks.

The buses within the computer are becoming standardized as well. Possibly one of the best known is the S-100 bus, which has been the basis for many "personal" microcomputers. Manufacturers of microprocessors are also establishing standards within their product lines, and organizations like the Institute for Electrical and Electronics Engineers (IEEE) are furthering standardization efforts.

All of these interfaces are fine if the computer is tied to another digital device, but most equipment is analog. When we want to use a computer to control or sense analog equipment, converters come into play. We can change the digital values to analog voltages or currents with a digital-to-analog (D/A) converter. The continuously varying inputs from sensors can be made understandable to the computer with analog-to-digital (A/D) converters.

This brief overview can only touch on the effects that interfacing has on a microprocessor-based system. The following chapters will help you develop an appreciation of these circuits, which are being used in an ever growing number of applications. The technician who is prepared to work on interfacing circuits will find that the demand for his or her services can only increase as more and more reliance is placed on microcomputer-controlled equipment.

DESIGN EXAMPLES

The frequent need for interfacing can perhaps best be demonstrated by selecting some applications for microprocessors and then sketching out a design approach for each. Many ordinary products using microprocessors will resemble the ones described, but some simplifying assumptions have been made in these designs; therefore, do not expect to find that the "real" equipment works exactly in the manner suggested.

First, let us choose a word processor to make use of our microprocessor. Figure 12-1 shows a system that allows the typist to enter text at a terminal keyboard. While the typist may think that the cathode-ray tube (CRT) is displaying the characters by direct interaction with the keyboard, in fact the microprocessor is responsible. As a key is pressed, the microprocessor receives a notification and must decode its meaning. (The computer does not know that the keys represent letters, numbers, and punctuation marks.) The computer program selects the symbol for CRT display which matches that key and orders the output circuitry to send the symbol to the screen. When received by the terminal electronics, these commands are interpreted as orders to move the electron beam so that the desired character appears on the screen.

Among other actions that the word processor must supply is storing the text as it is typed. Temporary storage is accomplished using the memory, while bulk storage requires the use of floppy disks. (Here we are assuming that two floppy-disk drives are to be used.) Certainly most important to the typist is the ability to

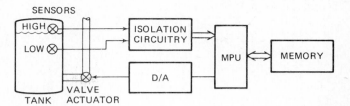

Fig. 12-2 Process controller.

have the text printed on paper. The printer does the hard-copy output.

How many interfaces can you identify in this design? One that is easy to overlook is a ROM interface. Without a program in memory, the processor cannot do anything. At a minimum, a small program that can load other programs must be provided in ROM. Perhaps the entire program for our word processor is in ROM. If so, the typist does not need to reload the program before beginning to type. (Turning the machine off erases RAM contents.) Such a feature (that is, not having to reload) would be a good idea because it would simplify the operation.

Next we will look at a simple process controller. The problem, shown in Fig. 12-2, is to open a valve whenever the liquid level in a tank is above 10,000 gallons (gal) [37,850 liters (L)] and to close the valve whenever the level falls to 8000 gal (30,280 L). Sensors in the tank monitor the two liquid levels. Through the isolation circuitry, the processor is informed when the output of either sensor changes. The processor can then order the valve actuator to open or close. What interfaces are present in the process control application that were not needed in our earlier example (Fig. 12-1)?

A slightly more demanding set of inputs is presented to the data acquisition system of Fig. 12-3. The inputs may be coming from a variety of sensors that are monitoring voltage, pressure, temperature, humidity, and many other parameters. Because the readings are arriving slowly (in comparison to computer speeds), they can all be channeled into a single analog multiplexer. *Multiplexing* is a means of reducing the amount of hardware by using it for several purposes. The program in a multiplexed system is more difficult to write, so we are not getting something for nothing. The program must not only record the reading of the sensor but also figure out which sensor sent the information. The data is recorded on a cartridge magnetic tape unit for offline analysis. The terminal is supplied so the operator can monitor what is happening and make changes in the frequency or types of measurements being recorded.

What if we have a system that is widely dispersed (perhaps there are miles between the individual stations that want to share their data)? A distributed system, like the one in Fig. 12-4, can support communications between processors that are separated by large dis-

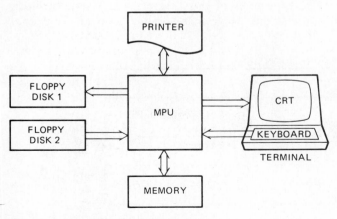

Fig. 12-1 Word processing system.

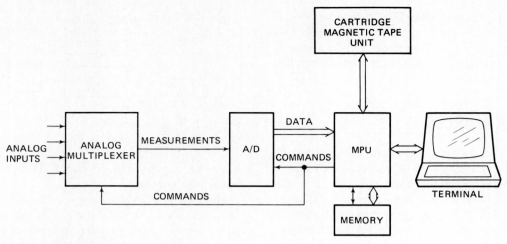

Fig. 12-3 Data acquisition system.

tances. Each processor has access to a serial communications channel; often local area networks or telephone lines are used. Local control is exercised via the operator terminals. The processors can originate or respond to queries by any member of the network. Another advantage of distributed systems is that processors of many different types can be intermixed on the channel. Even large mainframe computers can communicate with microcomputers over the communications channel.

As a final example, let us consider an interactive graphics terminal that is controlled by a bit-sliced processor. Figure 12-5 is a block diagram of the system. Here two separate buses are used: a 32-bit graphics data bus that transfers the high-speed graphics information and a 16-bit bus for peripheral equipment communications.

In addition to the kinds of interfaces we have already seen, we note in Fig. 12-5 that there is an interface module to a host computer. For graphics applications, the host is usually a large computer with considerable capability. The program in the host computer writes instructions, called a display list, into the memory. The microprocessor can then read the memory contents to draw figures and refresh the display. As the drawing takes place, the host computer is free to proceed with

other tasks. The figure stays on the screen until the host modifies some or all of the display list's commands.

Figure 12-6 gives some idea of the many interfaces you may come across in your work on microcomputers. Of course, this is an extreme example. It is unlikely that any one microprocessor would need as many interfaces as shown, but the types of interfaces illustrated are the ones you will often be confronted with. In every case an interaction between the interface and bus occurs that will in some manner affect or be affected by the processor's timing and operations. Because many of the interface operations are software-controlled, you must comprehend how the program can change the signal flow as well as understand what the hardware can do. Throughout the discussions in this and subsequent chapters, an awareness of hardware and software requirements for interfacing is emphasized.

PRINTERS

A printer converts electrical codes into commands for the print head, which impresses the character on paper. Hard-copy units of this type are either serial printers (one character at a time) or line printers. The *serial*

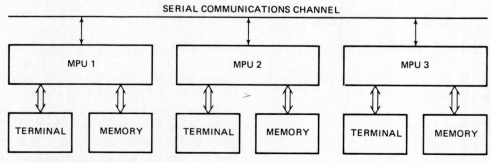

Fig. 12-4 Distributed system.

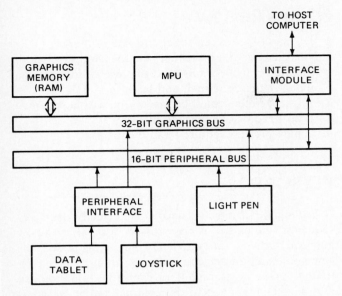

Fig. 12-5 Graphics processing system.

printer has a single print head that moves horizontally across the page. As the head moves to the next position, one character is printed. This type of printer receives the characters one by one from the microcomputer. A *line printer* has a number of print actuators (heads or hammers). Normally there will be one actuator in each print column. When they print, all the actuators hit the paper at once. This printing method means that enough characters must be stored in the print buffer to allow an entire line to be composed; therefore, the computer transmits several characters between each print operation. Figures 12-7 and 12-8 show two printer configurations.

A print line consists of from 48 to 132 characters, depending on the model of printer. Most printers can take paper of varying widths. The print rate can range from a slow 30 characters per second (char/s) to thousands of lines per minute (lines/min). Most printers accept at least a subset of the ASCII code, although other character codes are sometimes encountered.

Printers are further characterized by their printing mechanisms. Either impact or nonimpact heads are used. *Impact printers* employ either (1) front-striking typefaces, which press the ribbon against the paper to print, or (2) rear-striking mechanisms, which have a hammer that forces the paper and ribbon against a type chain. Front-striking impact printers include ball, daisy-wheel, cylinder, and dot-matrix heads. The rear-striking printers require drum, belt, band, or train print mechanisms and can exceed 3000 lines/min. Such high speed is not normally required for microprocessor output.

Nonimpact printers do not have a type face that presses an image onto the paper. Ink-jet printers can produce up to 45,000 lines/min on plain paper; laser printers also use plain paper. Treated papers that change color when subjected to heat or electric fields are necessary for thermal, electrostatic, and electrosensitive printers. A shortcoming of nonimpact printers is their inability to make multiple copies. Table 12-1 summarizes the various types of printers.

Some of the most economical models are the serial impact printers. Because of their cost advantage, these are the types you are most likely to find in a microcomputer installation. The following paragraphs describe their characteristics.

Printers with a cylindrical print head have the character set embossed as a series of rings around the cyl-

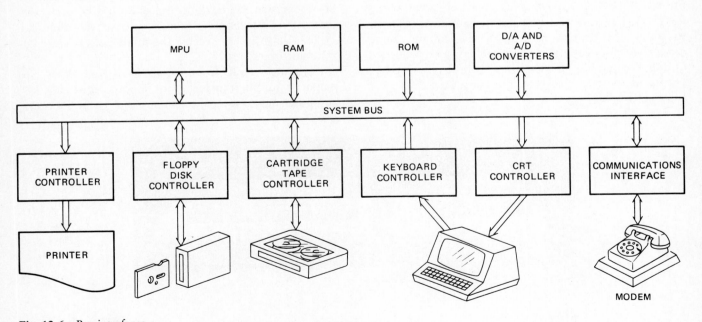

Fig. 12-6 Bus interfaces.

Fig. 12-7 Microline 192 Plus printer manages continuous form and cut sheet paper. *(Courtesy of Okidata)*

inder. The head rotates and shifts up or down to move the selected character into position. Then a hammer strikes the cylinder against the ribbon and paper.

The spherical head, sometimes called the "golfball," has its character set arranged on a ball. The sphere rotates on its axis to position the character. It then strikes the ribbon.

To picture the daisy-wheel head, imagine a wagon wheel with 96 to 128 spokes, each terminated with a print character. The daisy-wheel printer rotates the wheel rapidly to place the character to be printed at the topmost point; then, to print, tip of the arm is struck.

A matrix head uses a column of pins to construct the required character as a series of dots. The character is printed one column at a time as the head moves across the page. The pins are retracted or extended, in order to create the proper pattern for the column being printed. A large variety of fonts can easily be produced by this type of head. Lines can also be compressed or expanded by a control on the printer, as Fig. 12-9 shows.

Printers Review

1. Distinguish between serial and line printers.
2. Characterize the following as either impact or non-impact print mechanisms: daisy wheel, ink jet, cylinder, matrix, thermal, and laser.
3. Which printer would be faster, one with a spherical print head or one with an ink jet?
4. Which printers require treated paper?

KEYBOARDS

A *keyboard* is simply a matrix of normally open key switches. The matrix is crisscrossed by a series of row and column sense lines. When a key is depressed, the row and column intersecting that position become connected (either by grounding or capacitive coupling), so that a voltage applied to the column can be sensed at the appropriate row. The depressed key can be detected by strobing the columns sequentially and scanning the rows. Keyboards are manufactured in a variety of price ranges based on differing technologies.

The simplest keyboards use mechanical contact switches. Low cost and ease of construction characterize these keyboards. Because they are not sealed, they are subject to contact contamination from dust or moisture. Contact bounce takes a considerable amount of time to settle out, so *debouncing* logic or software must be provided to delay until solid closure is established. With gold contacts on the switches, these keys can provide 5 to 10 million operations.

Reed switches use reed relays sealed in glass for contacts. They are opened and closed by the movement of a small magnet toward or away from the contact. Not being exposed to air, the contacts do not become contaminated. The bounce time is also shorter than for mechanical switches because the small reeds have a high resonant frequency.

Keyboards built from saturable-core switches use magnetic toroid transformers similar to those used in computer memories. When no key is pressed, the trans-

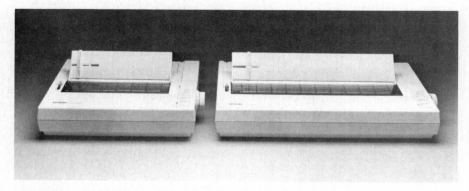

Fig. 12-8 LQ-800 and LQ-1000 dot-matrix printers. *(Courtesy of Epson)*

Table 12-1 Printer Summary

Type	Speed	Print Quality	Cost	Comments
Cylinder	10 char/s	Poor	Low	Noisy
Ball	15 char/s	Excellent	Low	Changeable fonts
Daisy wheel	30–55 char/s	Excellent	Medium	Changeable fonts
Dot matrix	30–330 char/s	Good to poor	Medium	Graphics capability
Thermal	30–120 char/s	Medium	Low	Low noise
Electrosensitive	160–2200 char/s	Poor	Low	Paper wrinkles easily
Electrostatic	300–18,000 lines/min	Excellent	High	Not suited for microcomputers
Laser	4000–14,000 lines/min	Excellent	Medium	Changeable fonts and graphics capability
Ink jet	30 char/s–45,000 lines/min	Good to poor	Low to high	Quiet

formers are saturated, so little of the energy from a high-frequency oscillator is coupled through the transformer. Pressing a key causes a magnet to be displaced, so the toroid is no longer saturated. Then the oscillator energy appears as a voltage at the output. These keyboards are noted for their high reliability.

Another magnetic technology is employed with Hall-effect switches. Here, a magnet is attached to a plunger on each key. Moving the magnet toward or away from a Hall-effect transducer chip produces two output states. These keyboards are high power users because a direct current is needed at all times. Their payoff is that the keyboard is good for more than 100 million operations.

Capacitive-switch keyboards have plates under every key. The plates increase the coupling of other plates connected between an oscillator and amplifier when a key is pressed. As the coupling becomes greater, a much higher output signal is produced. These keyboards are also long-lasting.

Keyboards with membrane switches can be manufactured at the lowest cost. A conductive pattern is laid down on a printed circuit board and overlaid with a Mylar film. The film has holes in it at the key positions. The conductive elastomer sheet on top penetrates these holes when pushed by someone's finger. Contact is made with that portion of the pattern underneath. The keyboards can be formed into thin, sealed assemblies with good reliability.

Keyboards Review

1. Explain how a keyboard is scanned to detect a depressed key.

THIS IS AN EXAMPLE OF COMPRESSED TYPE.

THIS IS AN EXAMPLE OF EXPANDED TYPE

Fig. 12-9 Matrix fonts.

2. What are the major shortcomings of mechanical contact switches?
3. How are reed switches opened and closed?
4. Which keyboard resembles the core memory of a computer?
5. True or false? Hall-effect switches require a magnetic field for operation.
6. Explain how capacitive coupling can be used in a keyboard.

CRT TERMINALS

CRT terminals provide a fast scan display, often accompanied by a keyboard for data input. See Fig. 12-10. Any combination of alphanumeric characters can be displayed on the CRT screen, and some models also provide a graphics capability. The major component of the terminal is, of course, a cathode-ray tube.

The evacuated glass tube has a phosphorescent coat-

Fig. 12-10 WY-60 Terminal. (*Courtesy of Wyse Technology*)

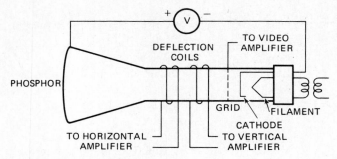

Fig. 12-11 CRT circuits.

ing on the inner surface of the flat screen, as shown in Fig. 12-11. The filament in the neck of the tube heats a cathode, which then produces a flow of electrons by thermionic emission. A high potential between the cathode and screen accelerates the electrons toward the positive screen. When they strike the phosphor, light is emitted.

The beam is positioned under control of electromagnetic coils (as shown in Fig. 12-11) or by deflection plates. If coils are used, the currrent through the coil produces a magnetic field that deflects the beam horizontally or vertically. With electrostatic plates, a voltage is applied across the vertical or horizontal deflection plates. Electrons are attracted toward the more positive plate, causing the beam to move in that direction.

A *monitor* is a CRT together with the necessary electronic circuitry needed to position the beam. As Fig. 12-12 shows, the horizontal oscillator moves the beam across the CRT screen from left to right, then the beam returns rapidly to the left-hand side and repeats the scan. The time that the beam is moving back to the left is called the *horizontal retrace*. The vertical oscillator deflects the beam vertically, resulting in the raster pattern shown in Fig. 12-13. To display a character, the beam intensity must be turned on for the bright areas and off in the dark areas. The video amplifier controls this beam intensity, depending on the input to the amplifier.

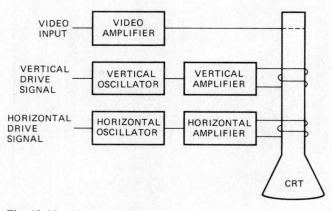

Fig. 12-12 Monitor circuits.

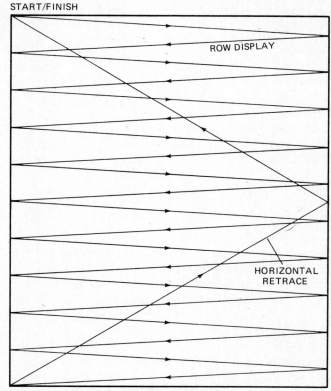

Note: Distance between traces exaggerated for clarity

Fig. 12-13 Raster pattern.

If we combine the monitor with memory to store display information, we have a *terminal*. The terminal will also contain I/O logic so that it can communicate with the computer. Sometimes a keyboard and light pen are also supplied with the terminal.

The terminal display *format* is specified by the maximum number of characters that can be written across the screen and the number of rows of characters on the screen. For example, a terminal may permit 80 characters to be displayed in 64 rows. This arrangement is referred to as the *display page*. Some terminals can store several pages in memory, but only one can be viewed at a time.

To keep the image from blinking, the terminal beam refreshes the display many times a second. A 60-hertz (Hz) *refresh rate* is typical. The total time necessary to draw a full page is then

$$T_{tot} = \frac{1}{60} \text{ Hz} = 16.67 \text{ ms}$$

This time can also be expressed in terms of the number of rows:

$$T_{tot} = T_{row} N + T_{vb} \qquad (12\text{-}1)$$

where T_{row} = time to refresh one row
$\quad\quad\quad N$ = number of rows
$\quad\quad\quad T_{vb}$ = vertical blanking time

If the row refresh time is 246 μs and the vertical blanking time is 900 μs,

$$T_{tot} = (246 \text{ μs})(64) + 900 \text{ μs} = 16.64 \text{ ms}$$

Some terminals will automatically shift the display upward by one row after a page has been filled and another line is transmitted by the computer. This *scrolling* action ensures that the latest information will be viewable for the maximum period of time, although the computer is capable of sending data at a faster rate than we can read even with scrolling.

CRT Terminals Review

1. Describe the operation of the two types of CRT deflection circuitry.
2. True or false? A monitor contains memory and can communicate with the computer.
3. How is the intensity of the electron beam controlled?
4. Define the term "page."

MODEMS

Modems, or *modulators/demodulators,* convert digital data to analog signals for transmission over telephone lines. Medium-speed modems [300 to 1200 bits per second (bps)] use *frequency shift keying (FSK)* for modulation. (Frequency modulation, which has a higher signal-to-noise ratio and requires a wider bandwidth, is used in higher-speed modems.) In FSK, digital values are converted to one of two frequencies by the modulation: a *mark* (1) is represented by a 1200-Hz tone, while a *space* (0) is transmitted as a 2200-Hz tone. These frequencies can readily be transmitted within the 3-kilohertz (kHz) bandwidth of a telephone channel. See Fig. 12-14.

Either dial-up or leased phone lines can be used for the communications channel. Dial-up lines require that either a person or originating computer dial the phone number of the receiving (answering) computer. With leased lines the computers are permanently connected; the computer interfaces with the modem by using one of the digital exchange protocols, such as EIA-RS-232C, IBM, MIL-STD-188C, International Telegraph & Telephone Consultative Committee (CCITT), or Bell Telephone. A *simplex* interface can transmit data in one direction only; one computer acts as the transmitting unit and the other as the receiver. Both can transmit with a *half-duplex* interface, but not simultaneously. A *full-duplex* interface allows for two-way transmission at the same time.

Modems Review

1. Explain how the name "modem" is formed.
2. What is FSK?
3. True or false? A mark representing 0 is transmitted at 1200 Hz.
4. How does a computer interface to the modem?
5. Distinguish between full-duplex and half-duplex communications.

FLOPPY-DISK DRIVES

A *floppy-disk* is a circle of plastic coated with a magnetic surface used for recoding digital data. A drive spins the disk much like a phonorecord. The disk is permanently sealed in its jacket and is highly polished to prevent abrasion from damaging the surface. The standard disk is 8 inches (in) [20.3 centimeters (cm)] in diameter, while the minidisk has a diameter of 5.25 in (13.3 cm). [Other sizes that you may encounter are the 4.12-in (10.5-cm) Eurodisk, 3.25-in (8.3 cm) IBM disk, and 2.55-in (6.5-cm) Olivetti minidisk.] Comparing the two most common disks, the 5.25-in minidisk is smaller and its drive requires less power, but the 8-in disk has 4 times as much data capacity.

There are several types of 5.25-in disks. As listed in Table 12-2, these are the standard, double-density, two-sided, and double-track/double-density disks. The double-density disks can store twice the information of a standard disk. The two-sided disk has twice the number of *tracks,* and the double-track/double-density disk has almost as many.

A *disk drive* provides the mechanical handling for the disk, a drive motor to spin it, and electronics to read

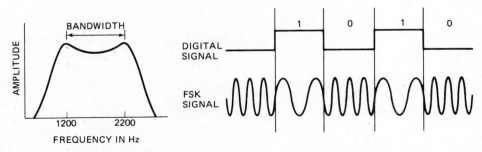

Fig. 12-14 FSK modulation.

Table 12-2 Typical 5.25-in Floppy Disks

	Standard	Double Density	Two-Sided	Double Track/ Double Density
Encoding	FM*	MFM†	FM	MFM
Data rate (kbps)‡	125	250	125	250
Number of tracks	40	40	80	77
Capacity (bytes)	125,000	250,000	250,000	481,250

* Frequency modulation.
† Modified FM.
‡ Kilobits per second (kbps).

or record. Figure 12-15 shows the drive components. The spindle hub engages the center of the disk and imparts the drive motor motion to it. The stepper motor moves the head assembly in or out to position it over the correct track. An index sector light-emitting diode (LED) shines light on the disk, which has an index hole in it to allow the light to pass through to the detector as the hole rotates into position. A write protect switch senses whether the write protect notch on the disk envelope is covered or not. If a disk is write-protected, the computer cannot record on it; write protection prevents any incorrect recording action that could destroy the information previously put on the disk. Electronic circuits provide control of reading and writing as well as of the drive and stepper motors. A controller permits the microprocessor to select any one of several disk drives to use for reading or writing.

A dc drive motor with a servo speed controller and built-in tachometer comprises the drive mechanism. The motor cannot rotate until the interlock in the door latch is closed, to make sure that the disk is properly inserted. The head is made of ceramic material and is mounted on the head assembly. The entire assembly is positioned by a cam, which is driven by the stepping motor in discrete increments. Each step corresponds to the track-to-track spacing on the disk. The control electronics

have many tasks to perform, including detecting the sector index hole, positioning the head over the correct track, loading the head (pressing it against the disk), generating read or write signals, detecting a write-protected disk and informing the computer, and selecting the proper drive for a given operation.

Disk Formats

Disks are formatted to split the surface into blocks of a usable size. All disks are divided into *sectors* like pieces of a pie. Each sector begins at a particular point measured from the index hole. Furthermore, *hard-sectored disks* have an additional index hole to mark the beginning of each sector. *Soft-sectored disks* have only one timing hole. All other sectors begin at a sector mark recorded on the disk by the computer program. Because soft-sectored disks must use part of the surface area for sector marks, they cannot hold as much information as the same-size hard-sectored disks.

Information is stored in concentric, circular *tracks* on the disk surface. For example, there may be 40 tracks in all on one side, with the same number of tracks on the other surface of a double-sided disk. The identically numbered upper and lower tracks of a double-sided floppy disk are sometimes called a "cylinder." The number of sectors that a track is divided into varies; there can be 8, 15, or 26 sectors per track. Depending on the number of sectors, there are then 512, 256, or 128 bytes in a sector. The sector size is also called the "track length."

A sector will always contain a record or part of a record. If the record is too short, the remainder of the bytes in the sector will be filled with 0s. If the record is too long, it will overlap into as many sectors as are needed to hold that number of data bytes. Because of this record-to-track assignment, good practice requires that data be blocked into the correct number of bytes in order to fill a sector completely before writing out. When reading, an entire sector is received at one time.

The IBM soft-sector format is illustrated in Fig. 12-16. With it, track 00 is always used as a system label track identifying the entire floppy disk. Tracks 01

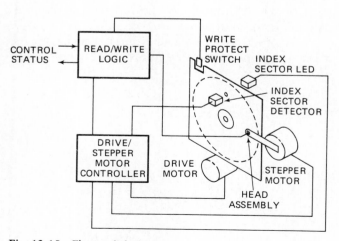

Fig. 12-15 Floppy disk drive.

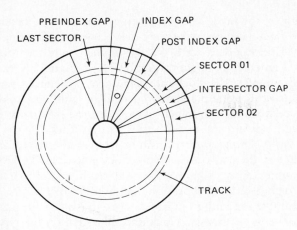

Fig. 12-16 Soft sectored disk format.

PREINDEX GAP
INDEX GAP
LAST SECTOR
POST INDEX GAP
SECTOR 01
INTERSECTOR GAP
SECTOR 02
TRACK

through 74 are used to record data, and tracks 75 and 76 are available as alternates for bad tracks. If track 04, for example, is bad, the data intended for that track is automatically placed on track 75. Whenever a command to read track 04 is issued, track 75 is read instead.

The fields required in an IBM-formatted disk are shown in Fig. 12-17. The identification (ID) field specifies the track number, head number, sector number, and sector length to the disk controller. In addition, a sync field is provided for timing synchronization. The cyclic redundancy check (CRC) allows error checking on the other fields of identification. There are also sync and CRC fields in the data area.

Gaps on the recording surface separate the index hole gap from other sectors and from the ID and data recordings. These gaps provide the electronics with a delay to switch from reading to writing. The gaps also compensate for speed errors between two drives, if the floppy disk was written on a different drive from the one reading it.

Minidisk Formats

A typical format for a mini floppy disk is shown in Fig. 12-18. Here the surface can hold 40 tracks and is divided into 10 soft sectors. Each sector has a length of 256 bytes, so a track holds

$$10 \times 256 = 2560 \text{ bytes} = 20,480 \text{ bits}$$

Because there are 40 tracks, the disk capacity is

$$2560 \text{ bytes per track} \times 40 \text{ tracks} = 102,400 \text{ bytes}$$

The disk spins at 300 revolutions per minute (rpm), so the sector hole passes under the sensor five times per second. At this speed, we can compute the average time to access a random track:

$$T_r = T_{seek} + T_{sector} + T_{data} \qquad (12\text{-}2)$$

where T_r = random-access time
T_{seek} = average seek time to move head over the track
T_{sector} = average time for desired sector to rotate under the head
T_{data} = time to read the data

A particular disk drive, for example, has a T_{seek} of 450 ms, a T_{sector} of 100 ms, and a T_{data} of 20 ms. Therefore, the random-access time is:

$$T_r = 450 + 100 + 20 = 570 \text{ ms}$$

More than half a second is consumed in reading the data in a random way. A more efficient input procedure

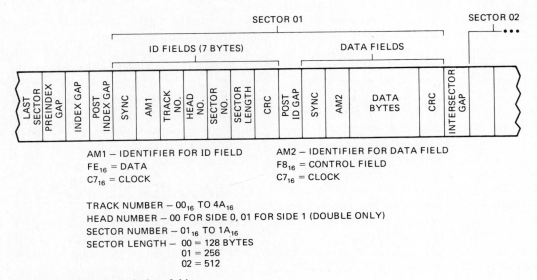

AM1 — IDENTIFIER FOR ID FIELD
FE_{16} = DATA
$C7_{16}$ = CLOCK

AM2 — IDENTIFIER FOR DATA FIELD
$F8_{16}$ = CONTROL FIELD
$C7_{16}$ = CLOCK

TRACK NUMBER — 00_{16} TO $4A_{16}$
HEAD NUMBER — 00 FOR SIDE 0, 01 FOR SIDE 1 (DOUBLE ONLY)
SECTOR NUMBER — 01_{16} TO $1A_{16}$
SECTOR LENGTH — 00 = 128 BYTES
                     01 = 256
                     02 = 512

Fig. 12-17 Floppy disk data fields.

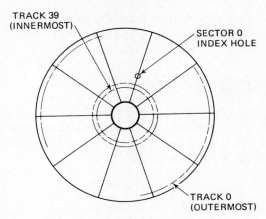

TRACK 39
(INNERMOST)

SECTOR 0
INDEX HOLE

TRACK 0
(OUTERMOST)

Fig. 12-18 Mini floppy disk format.

is to arrange the data to be read sequentially, which eliminates most of the seek and sector time delays.

Floppy-Disk Drives Review

1. Which disk can hold more data, a double-density or a two-sided disk?
2. Explain the head movement mechanism of a floppy-disk drive.
3. How is the index mark detected?
4. What is the purpose of the write protection notch?
5. Explain the difference between hard- and soft-sectored disks.
6. What is another name for the track length?

MAGNETIC TAPE RECORDERS

Cassette and *cartridge recorders* are peripherals often used to record and store microcomputer data offline. The recording medium is a coated tape that is magnetized in one of two states to represent a 1 or 0. Digital recording usually saturates the tape at its positive or negative limits. Saturation results in about 12 decibels (dB) higher output than does audio recording on the same tape. This gain is realized because audio recording uses only 25 percent of the magnetic moment of the tape coating.

In addition to recording 1s and 0s, the digital signals must intermix error detection and correction codes (such as parity or CRC) and timing data. The resulting data stream is shaped and converted to an analog signal in the recording process. The writing actually takes place at the trailing edge of the head gap, where the flux density is highest. The number of bits recorded per inch significantly affects the error rate. Only a single bit error in 10^7 bits would be expected when recording at 800 bits per inch (bpi), but the error rate increases to one in a thousand at 1200 bpi using the identical coding scheme.

As mentioned above, timing is recorded along with data on the tape. There are two methods for recording the clock: using a separate clock track or employing a self-clocking data code. Microcomputer tape recorders are limited to a single track, so only the latter method is of interest. The clock rate is important because a tape recorded on one machine and read by another should be reliable with as much as a 4 percent difference in speed between the two.

Self-clocking codes transition from one level to another at the same time as the clock pulse, so the level changes of the signal allow the reading machine to reconstruct the proper timing. With most codes, a preamble is required in order to establish synchronization between the read clock and the signal on the tape. The preamble is simply a known bit pattern recorded ahead of the data.

One code suitable for this application is the return-to-zero code, or *RZ code*. A positive transition in flux represents a 1 and a negative change a 0. When no bits are being recorded, the head does not put out a signal, leaving the tape in its unmagnetized state. The RZ code is suited for low-density recording. A disadvantage of this type of coding is that unmagnetized tape must be used because no signal is recorded between bits. If a signal were already on a tape (which is quite likely when tapes are used more than once), a confused recording would result. Bulk erasing of the tapes before each use will demagnetize them.

A more practical code is the *biphase code*. There are many variations on this scheme, such as Manchester, phase encoding, and frequency modulation codes. A binary 1 is recorded as two changes in flux direction, while no change in direction represents a 0. A distinct advantage of biphase recording is its sensitivity to drive-motor speed changes.

Magnetic Tape Recorders Review

1. Why is the output from digital recording higher than from analog recording?
2. How does recording density affect error rate?
3. Explain the method used to record the clock.
4. What is the purpose of a preamble?
5. What problem might you encounter in using the RZ code to record a second set of data on a used tape?
6. True or false? Manchester and frequency modulation are RZ codes.

LOCAL-AREA NETWORKS

A *network* is made up of two or more devices that are interconnected to allow them to share information or data processing resources, such as a disk memory. The devices must be *intelligent* in order to operate on a network; that is, they must contain a computer or similar unit to provide control. Applications that use networks include electronic mail, transfer of financial information, process control, and inventory control.

A *local-area network* (LAN) is one of limited geographic range, such as a single building or a building complex. A LAN is unlikely to run more than a few kilometers in extent; in contrast, wide-area networks can be international in range. Although a LAN is limited in area, it may contain thousands of users, also called *nodes*. The physical method of interconnecting nodes is called the *medium*. Commonly used media are coaxial cable and fiber-optic (FO) cable.

One of the factors that has advanced LANs is the standards that are evolving. The description of how a LAN works is sometimes referred to as its *protocol*. One of the most comprehensive is the International Organization for Standardization (ISO) architecture known as the Open Systems Interconnection (OSI). The OSI architecture is shown in Fig. 12-19. As the figure shows, the architecture has seven layers. The standard permits each layer to be implemented in either hardware or software. The implementation must meet the interfacing rules between each layer in order to be valid. This means that as new technology becomes available, a given layer can be implemented in a more efficient manner without disturbing the remainder of the network and without requiring a retrofitting of nodes built from older technology.

The physical and data-link layers of the architecture define the electrical and mechanical features of the connection path. These definitions make possible the transmission and reception of signals through the network. The upper layers are responsible for higher levels of communication, such as establishing links between programs in different nodes, describing how the data will be addressed to the receiving function, sequencing the data sent, and providing network services to the user (either a human or a computer program).

As an example, Ethernet is a LAN that is a collaboration of Digital Equipment Corporation, Xerox Corporation, and Intel Corporation. This LAN specifies how the physical and data-link layers will operate, so any manufacturer can interconnect equipment to the Ethernet. The Ethernet's physical medium is coaxial cable up to 2.8 kilometers (km) long. One reason that Ethernet is a popular LAN is the availability of off-the-shelf ICs that implement the protocol.

LANs can operate in basically two modes. A *baseband* LAN sends all data at the same frequency; for example, a 10-MHz baseband LAN transmits at a frequency equal to the data rate. This transmission technique means that only one signal channel can be sending at one time. It is similar to a serial transmission channel. A *broadband* LAN multiplexes several channels of communications on many separate frequencies; for example, a broadband LAN may have its transmission frequency at video rates (about 100 MHz), while each channel can be limited to 5 to 10 MHz. This means that several channels can share the single LAN cable in a parallel fashion.

LANs are also described by their *topologies,* or the geometric pattern of their nodes. Figure 12-20 shows several common topologies. Each topology has advantages and disadvantages, so the selection must be based on the intended purpose of the LAN. The *star* topology

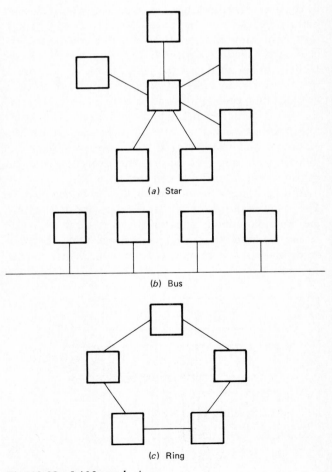

| APPLICATION |
| PRESENTATION |
| SESSION |
| TRANSPORT |
| NETWORK |
| DATA LINK |
| PHYSICAL |

Fig. 12-19   OSI seven layered architecture for LANs.

(a) Star

(b) Bus

(c) Ring

Fig. 12-20   LAN topologies.

(Fig. 12-21a) requires that all data transfers between nodes be routed through a central node. The star is frequently used in fiber-optic networks because star couplers are effective in handling communications based on optical sources. A disadvantage is the single point of failure with the central node. The *bus* topology (Fig. 12-21b) is easily adapted to additional nodes after the network has been fabricated. The control and addressing of transmissions between nodes can become complex in some LANs that use the bus topology. A *ring* topology (Fig. 12-21c) requires that data be passed through all intermediate nodes between the sender and receiver. Data rates can be limited as a result. Another problem of a ring is that a single node failure disables the ring unless some means of failure recovery is built in. On the other hand, rings can be simple to implement.

Regardless of the topology, some means of regulating which node sends information at a given time must be part of the network protocol; otherwise, several nodes may send at once and no communications can take place. Interestingly enough, this is exactly what happens in a *carrier-sense multiple access with collision detect* (CSMA/CD), which is the access method for Ethernet. With CSMA/CD, any node with information to send just puts it on the channel when the node senses that no traffic is being sent; this is the carrier-sense portion of the access method. In other words, the node "listens before it talks." Even so, two or more nodes may transmit at the same time, and this simultaneous use of the channel is called a *collision*. Each node must also "listen while it talks" to detect the collision occurring; this is the collision-detect part of the access method. If a collision occurs, each sending node waits for a brief period (backs off) and then attempts to send the message again. The back-off period is determined by each node generating a random interval to wait, so it is unlikely that the nodes causing the collision will experience another collision when they try again to transmit.

Another access method for LANs is *token passing*. The token is a signal sent over the network that permits the node with the highest priority to be the next user of the medium to transfer a message. Only the node holding the token can use the network. When finished with its data exchange, the node that had control passes the token to the node with the next highest priority.

A protocol that is receiving wide interest has been produced by the IEEE Standard 802 Committee on LAN standards. IEEE Standard 802 covers the network layers shown in Fig. 12-21. The purpose of this standard is to resolve issues not addressed by the OSI layered architecture. Each portion of the standard is designated by a numeral after the decimal point. For example, IEEE Standard 802.1, which establishes common definitions and guidelines, is an overall description of the other standards. IEEE Standard 802.2 describes the logical link control (LLC), which covers the top portion of the data-link layer; it describes how interfacing services are to be provided to the network layer. Within the data-link layer are the medium access control (MAC) sublayer and the LLC sublayer. The remaining standards in this family cover a portion of the data-link layer and various implementations of the physical layer. IEEE Standard 802.3 describes the interface between the data-link and physical layers; it provides the means for data encapsulation (definition of a data frame, address, and error detection) and for MAC. IEEE Standard 802.3 provides for a bus with the CSMA/CD access method. IEEE Standard 802.4 is a definition of a token-passing bus LAN. Its area of coverage is similar to that described for Standard 802.3. IEEE Standard 802.5 defines a token-passing ring, and IEEE Standard 802.6 defines an access method for a metropolitan-area network.

CHAPTER SUMMARY

1. An interface is a shared boundary between two systems or units. The computer program is an important part of the hardware-software tradeoffs in interfacing.
2. Different types of memories vary in their interface requirements. Read-only memories are the least demanding, while dynamic RAMs have a need for read, write, and refresh circuitry. Static RAMs fall between these two in terms of the number of interfaces to be supported.
3. The simplest I/O techniques use ports or memory mapping. If the situation calls for faster responses, interrupts and direct memory access can be used.
4. Input and output can be serial or parallel. Synchronous or asynchronous I/O protocols are useful in serial data communications. The teletype loop is a specialized serial communications channel.
5. Standards for microcomputer data transmission have been established to simplify the job of interconnecting two pieces of equipment. Common interfaces considerably reduce the overall costs of the system.
6. Serial printers type one character at a time, while line printers can type an entire line at once. Print

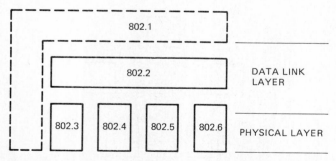

Fig. 12-21 IEEE 802 LAN standards family.

heads in the form of cylinders, balls, daisy wheels, and matrices are used in impact printing mechanisms. Ink-jet, photocopy, electrosensitive, electrostatic, and thermal printers have nonimpact heads.

7. The rows and columns of a keyboard are scanned to detect a depressed key. Switches operating on several different principles are used in the manufacture of keyboards. The technology used in building the keyboard determines its reliability, operating characteristics, and cost.

8. CRT terminals are based on a monitor, together with memory and with I/O electronics to interface with the computer. The rows and columns of characters on the screen make up the display page.

9. Modems convert digital data to analog with a modulation scheme before sending, then demodulate the signals at the receiving end of the channel. A binary 1 is encoded as a mark and a 0 as a space. For medium-speed modems, FSK is usually the means of modulation used.

10. Floppy disks are an economical media for recording data for microcomputers. Sizes most often seen are the 8-in standard disks and 5.25-in minidisks. The disk drive must spin the disk, step the read head to the correct track, record or read data, and control the process. Disks are formatted into tracks and sectors to organize the information written on the magnetic surface.

11. Magnetic cassette and cartridge recorders are also used with microprocessors. As well as preserving the binary values, the coding of data provides timing information. Biphase codes are a widely used scheme for these recorders.

12. Local-area networks permit intelligent nodes within a limited geographic area to interchange information. LANs often use fiber-optic or coaxial cables for interconnection. The rules for using the LAN are described in the protocol. The ISO has defined an OSI protocol with seven layers.

13. LANs can send data in either the baseband or broadband mode. The topology of a network describes its layout. Some topologies are the star, bus, and ring. The access method for a LAN specifies how each node can use the channel. Two common access methods are CSMA/CD and token passing. The IEEE Standard 802 Committee has defined a family of standards for implementing a variety of LANs.

KEY TERMS AND CONCEPTS

Interface

I/O ports

Read-only memory (ROM)

Read-write (or random-access) memory (RAM)

Memory mapping

Interrupts

Direct memory access

Parallel I/O

Serial I/O

Protocol

Teletype loop

Communications standards

Analog interfaces

Serial printers

Line printers

Impact printers

Nonimpact printers

Keyboards

CRT terminals

Monitor

Display page

Refresh rate

Scrolling

Modems

Frequency shift keying (FSK)

Mark

Space

Floppy disk

Disk drive

Sectors

Hard-sectored disks

Soft-sectored disks

Tracks

Cassette and cartridge recorders

Self-clocking codes

RZ code

Biphase code

Network

Local-area network (LAN)

Node

Medium

Protocol

OSI layered architecture

Baseband network

Broadband network

Topology of networks

Star

Bus

Ring

CSMA/CD

Collision

Token passing

IEEE Standard 802 family

12-1 How much time is needed to refresh the CRT display if the row refresh time is 200 μs and there are 40 rows? The vertical blanking time is 800 μs.

12-2 How many rows are there to a page if the vertical blanking time is 900 μs, the row refresh time is 492 μs, and the refresh cycle is 120 Hz?

12-3 A CRT terminal page can display 2048 characters. If there are 32 rows to a page, how many characters are displayed on a line?

12-4 For the display in Prob. 12-3, what is the page refresh time if each character takes 26 μs to be refreshed? The vertical blanking time is 900 μs.

12-5 If a minidisk could hold 512 bytes in each of its 10 sectors, what would the bit capacity of the disk be?

12-6 How long does it take for an entire sector on a standard minidisk to pass under the read head? (Assume that the beginning of the sector is now under the head.)

12-7 On the average, what is the random-access time for track 16 of a minidisk drive with a sector time of 150 ms, data time of 18 ms, and head seek time of 380 ms?

12-8 How much time is saved if data is arranged in two sequential sectors of one track rather than in the random sectors used for the disk drive of Prob. 12-7?

12-9 How long does it take to move the head into position for a 300-rpm minidisk drive if the random-access time is 475 ms? The mean sector time is 85 ms and the data read time is 12 ms.

12-10 What ID fields for track number, head number, sector number, and sector length would be read in the following situation?

Single-sided 15-sector IBM format
Sector 13
Track 34

PARALLEL INPUT/OUTPUT

Even the most powerful computer would be useless if data could not be accepted and answers could not be retrieved. The input/output (I/O) circuitry and software provide these facilities. As you will see, the transfer of data between the microprocessor and the external devices requires a greater awareness of hardware interactions with software than does any other computer operation. The proper timing and sequencing of the signals on the system buses is crucial to the transfer of data. The 8085, 6800, and other processors can perform the data transfer in several different manners. This chapter explores the use of accumulator I/O, of interrupts, and of direct memory access, together with the circuitry required, to move parallel data back and forth.

CHAPTER OBJECTIVES

Upon completion of this chapter, you should be able to:

1. Distinguish between accumulator and memory-mapped I/O.
2. Explain the function of the 8085 input and output instructions.
3. Describe how the 8095 three-state buffer and 8212 I/O port can be used to transfer data.
4. Discuss the use of interrupts in data transfer.
5. Distinguish between single-, multiple-, and vectored-interrupt architectures.
6. Analyze the operation of the 8259 priority interrupt control unit.
7. Define the term "direct memory access."
8. Show how the 8257 direct memory access controller is used in a microcomputer circuit.

I/O CONCEPTS

Before beginning the study of specific I/O methods, let us briefly consider the various methods of exchanging data between the microcomputer and the external devices, often referred to as peripheral equipment.

Data can move either to or from the computer, as shown in Fig. 13-1. The direction is always spoken of relative to that computer. That is, *output* means that the computer is sending and *input* that the computer is receiving. This convention prevents the confusion that sometimes arises when discussing the exchange from the peripheral equipment's point of view. That equipment must receive output data and send input data. Notice in Fig. 13-1 that every device need not handle two-way data exchange. Only device 3 has that ability. Device 1 accepts output data only; a printer is this type of device. Device 2 can only send data; a temperature sensor is this type of device.

The 8085 microprocessor can accept or send data by using either *accumulator I/O* instructions or by *memory-mapped I/O* techniques. (The 6800 can only use memory-mapped I/O.) The input and output instructions and an *I/O port* are used in the former situation, while the peripheral is treated as part of memory in the latter case. An external device, suitably equipped, can notify the processor of any special event by means of *interrupt signals;* the microprocessor must be able to process an interrupt signal at any time. An even more sophisticated I/O device can cause the microcomputer memory to allow that device to read or write data by mimicking the processor on the system buses; the microprocessor and the *direct memory access (DMA)* device share memory accesses in this scheme. The following sections in this chapter more fully explain these techniques.

80 8085 ACCUMULATOR I/O

Accumulator I/O permits transfer of data between the microprocessor and the external device in either direction. Special instructions in the repertoire use the accumulator to send or receive data. Outgoing data must be in the A register before the output instruction is executed, and input data is placed in the accumulator

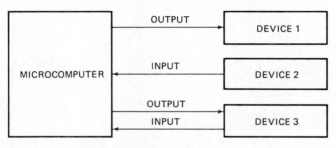

Fig. 13-1 Data transfer directions.

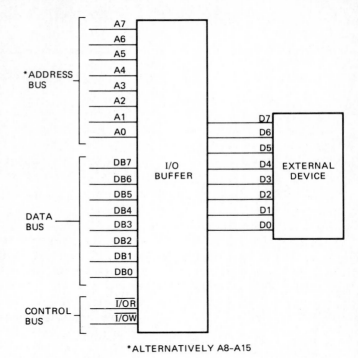

*ALTERNATIVELY A8-A15

Fig. 13-2 I/O port.

upon completion of the input. Accumulator I/O is most similar to the data transfer operations of minicomputers. Many microprocessors do not provide this capability, but the 8085 does support it. As mentioned above, an I/O port is used with accumulator I/O.

The I/O port is a buffer that is connected to the system buses. Figure 13-2 shows a generalized I/O port. Only eight of the address bus lines need be decoded (for reasons that will become apparent when the instructions are discussed). Also, only the appropriate control bus signals need be accepted. In this situation only $\overline{I/OR}$ (input) and $\overline{I/OW}$ (output) are used by the I/O port.

The port must access the system bus at the proper time in the instruction cycle to prevent confusing other users of the buses. By proper sharing of the time available, many I/O ports can be attached to one MPU. The MPU selects the I/O port it wants to access in a manner not very different from reading or writing memory.

80 I/O Instructions

There are two instructions available for accumulator I/O: one for input and the other for output. Each instruction can select up to 256 independent devices; therefore, we can input from a maximum of 256 devices and output to another 256. Some of the devices (device 3 in Fig. 13-1, for example) would need both input and output, while others would require only one or the other. The number associated with each input or output device is called the *device code (DC)*.

The device code is an 8-bit number that uniquely

addresses one peripheral device. Examples might be:

14_{16} (output)	Printer device code
02_{16} (input)	Temperature sensor
02_{16} (output) and $F6_{16}$ (input)	CRT terminal

Note that the input and output device codes need not be the same, as the CRT terminal assignment shows. Furthermore, the same code number may be used for input and output, as above, without any interference between the two.

INPUT The input instruction causes the 8-bit data byte to be read from the I/O port with the device code found in the second word of the instruction. The data is placed in the accumulator. There is no need to clear the A register before this instruction because all bits are changed by reading the input data. No status bits are affected by this instruction.

Operation code	DB
Mnemonic	IN
Addressing mode	immediate
Status bits affected	none
Clock periods	10
Format	

Bit number
7 6 5 4   3 2 1 0

Memory cell m | 1 1 0 1   1 0 1 1 |
m + 1 | Device code |

□ **EXAMPLE**

Before Execution		After Execution	
Program counter	1406	Program counter	1408
A register	03	A register	4A
Memory 1406	DB	Memory 1406	DB
1407	02	1407	02

The device on I/O port number 02_{16} has transmitted $4A_{16}$ to the processor, changing the value of the accumulator.

OUTPUT This instruction sends the current accumulator contents to the equipment connected to the I/O port indicated by the device code.

Operation code	D3
Mnemonic	OUT
Addressing mode	immediate
Status bits affected	none
Clock periods	10
Format	

Bit number
7 6 5 4   3 2 1 0

Memory cell m | 1 1 0 1   0 0 1 1 |
m + 1 | Device code |

□ **EXAMPLE**

Before Execution		After Execution	
Program counter	350A	Program counter	350C
A register	22	A register	22
Memory 350A	D3	Memory 350A	D3
350B	14	350B	14

The A register value (22_{16}) is sent out I/O port number 14_{16}.

80 8085 Accumulator I/O Review

1. List four types of I/O used with microprocessors.
2. Which method of input/output uses an I/O port?
3. Why is it unnecessary for the device to decode more than eight address lines?
4. Where is the device code obtained?

I/O DEVICES

Microprocessors are supported by a family of integrated circuits that helps solve the problems of *interfacing* the microprocessor with the I/O equipment. There are also general-purpose ICs that can be used as well. When connecting any device to the MPU, the output drive capability must be considered.

The fan-out of the MPU is such that the device can drive a maximum current of 1.9 mA. The fan-in of the 7400 series transistor-transistor logic (TTL) is 1.6 mA—very close to the limit. A better choice for interfacing logic would be the 74LS low-power Schottky logic with 0.2- to 0.34-mA fan-in, or the 74L series with 0.1- to 0.16-mA fan-in. Other alternatives are the specially designed devices such as the 8205 decoder and 8212 eight-bit I/O port with a fan-in of 0.15 to 0.25 mA.

If the signals must travel more than 3 in (7.6 cm), the outputs should be buffered. When signal runs are over 12 in (30.5 cm), special bus drivers and termination networks are necessary.

Address Selection

Interpreting every bit of a device code or an address is referred to as *fully decoded address selection*. Otherwise, using *linear selection,* only certain bits can be decoded to generate the device-select pulse. For example, if only the device codes 00_{16} through 07_{16} are used, then only address bits A0 through A2 need be examined. The shortcoming of this latter approach is that someday one may want to expand the system, and increasing the number of bits in the device code might require a major rebuild.

A fully decoded address selection decoder can be constructed using the 74LS30 eight-input NAND gate

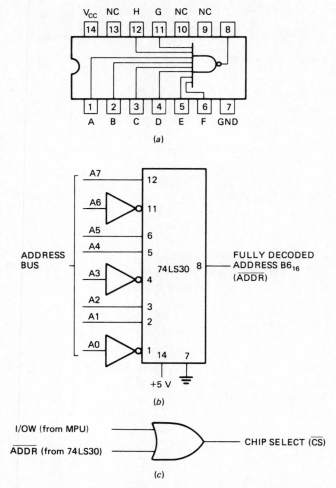

(a)

(b)

I/OW (from MPU)

$\overline{\text{ADDR}}$ (from 74LS30)

CHIP SELECT ($\overline{\text{CS}}$)

(c)

Fig. 13-3 8-bit fully decoded address selection: (*a*) 74LS30, (*b*) decoder, (*c*) generating chip select strobe.

shown in Fig. 13-3*b*. The device code used is $B6_{16}$. The pin assignment for the 74LS30 is shown in Fig. 13-3*a*. The output for this particular NAND may be expressed as

$$\overline{\overline{A7} \cdot \overline{A6} \cdot A5 \cdot A4 \cdot \overline{A3} \cdot A2 \cdot A1 \cdot \overline{A0}} \qquad (13\text{-}1)$$

and only an input of $B6_{16}$ will produce a low output, $\overline{\text{ADDR}}$. Assuming we want to use the decoder with an output device, the chip select signal can be generated by ORing this output ($\overline{\text{ADDR}}$) with the processor's output strobe ($\overline{\text{I/OW}}$), as shown in Fig. 13-3*c*. A low output from the OR gate selects the device.

Buffering

Either input or output signals can be buffered to supply the necessary signal stability. A frequently used IC in microprocessor applications is the three-state *8095 buffer*. Because it is a three-state device, several such buffers can be attached to the data bus, but only one will send an input to the microprocessor at any given

time. Good design practice calls for fully decoding the device code.

The buffer IC is shown in Fig. 13-4*a*. A low input on pins 1 and 15 (DIS1 and DIS2) enables the buffer to transfer data. The chip select ($\overline{\text{CS}}$) signal (from a decoder similar to that of Fig. 13-3) and the processor input ($\overline{\text{I/OR}}$) signal are applied to the enabling inputs. When $\overline{\text{I/OR}}$ and $\overline{\text{CS}}$ go low, *data jamming* occurs: Data is sent, or "jammed," into the MPU.

Two 8095s can be used to provide a full 8-bit data input, as shown in Fig. 13-4*b*. The external device first places the data on the input lines. When the $\overline{\text{CS}}$ and $\overline{\text{I/OR}}$ signals go low, the three-state AND gates are enabled, passing the signals through to the MPU.

I/O Ports

Input/output ports are well-suited for small microprocessor systems or for the special needs of larger systems. The ports usually consist of data latches, buffers, and interrupt logic. The *8212 I/O port* is an 8-bit port with

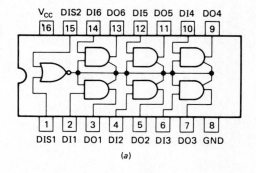

(a)

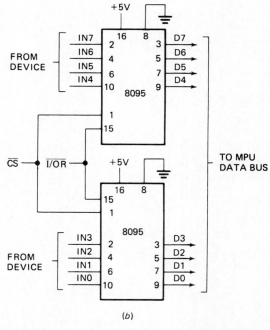

(b)

Fig. 13-4 Input buffer: (*a*) 8095, (*b*) 8-bit data port.

eight D flip-flops for the latches. The Q outputs of the flip-flops are connected to three-state, noninverting output buffers, as shown in Fig. 13-5a. A pin assignment diagram for the port is shown in Fig. 13-5b.

From Fig. 13-5, shown on the next page, and with a little boolean algebra, we can readily determine that:

$$ENB = \overline{DS1} \cdot DS2 + MD$$
$$CK = STB \cdot \overline{MD} + MD \cdot \overline{DS1} \cdot DS2$$
$$SET = \overline{\overline{CLR} + (\overline{DS1} \cdot DS2)}$$
$$\quad = \overline{CLR}(DS1 + \overline{DS2}) \text{ by DeMorgan's theo-}$$
$$\quad\quad \text{rem}$$

A brief description of the 8212 input and output signals is given in Table 13-1.

Next we will analyze the 8212 operation. The 8212 I/O port is selected by setting $\overline{DS1}$ low and DS2 high. Each of the flip-flops will react to the D inputs only when the clock input (CK) is high. When the clock is low, the previous Q output will be held constant.

The mode input (MD) decides whether the IC will be in the output or input mode. If the mode input is high (referred to as the output mode), the output of the buffer enable or gate (gate G) of Fig. 13-5 is high, allowing output data to pass through to the buffers. The D flip-flop input clock is also set high by the output of OR gate D (MD · $\overline{DS1}$ · DS2 is true), so the D flip-flops will react to new inputs. After the propagation delay, the new inputs will appear at the Q output terminal of each flip-flop.

When MD goes low (input mode), the three-state enable line (output of gate G) reacts to the output of gate C. Whenever the device-select inputs are false (that is, $\overline{DS1}$ high or DS2 low), the output of gate G will go low, causing the buffer outputs to float. The clocking of the D flip-flops will then depend on the state of the strobe (STB) input. A high on STB causes clocking of the flip-flops regardless of the state of the device selection inputs. Figure 13-6 summarizes these input mode relationships in a timing diagram.

The D flip-flops can be reset at any time by making the $\overline{CLR}$ input low. For normal operation, $\overline{CLR}$ must be high. The interrupt request signal is used to inform

Table 13-1 8212 Signals

Signal	Description	Type*
DI0–DI7	Data	Input
DO0–DO7	Data	Three-state output
$\overline{DS1}$, DS2	Device select	Input
MD	Mode select	Input
STB	Data strobe	Input
$\overline{CLR}$	Device clear	Input
$\overline{INT}$	Interrupt request	Output

* Input and output are relative to the 8212.

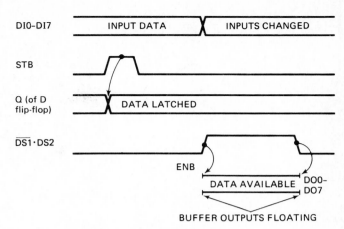

Fig. 13-6 8212 input mode timing diagram.

the processor that the I/O port has new data to send. The processing of interrupts by the processor will be discussed in a later section. For the time being, only the method of setting the signal will be described.

Refer to the simplified diagrams in Fig. 13-7 to follow the sequence of events. In the input mode, STB goes high to clock data from DI0 through DI7 into the flip-flops. When STB falls to the low level, the service request (SR) flip-flop is clocked. With the D input grounded, the Q output must follow. The low Q_{SR} sig-

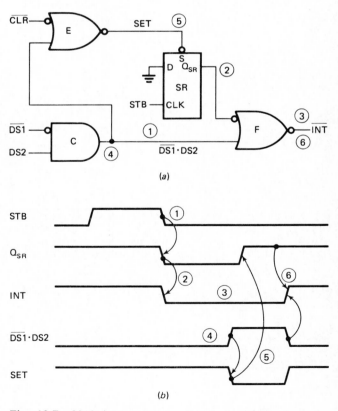

Fig. 13-7 8212 interrupt request: (a) simplified schematic, (b) timing diagram.

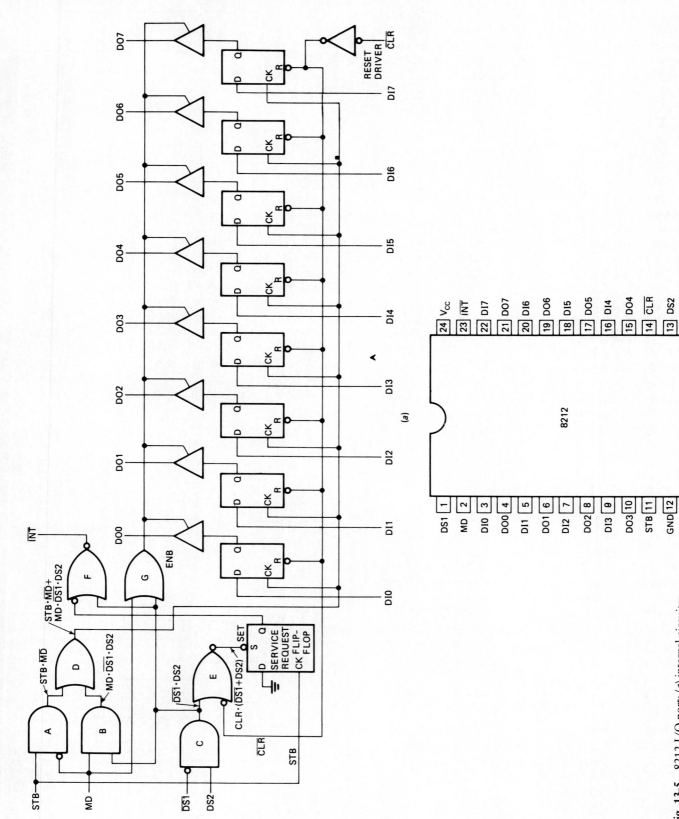

Fig. 13-5 8212 I/O port: (*a*) internal circuitry, (*b*) pin numbering.

nal is inverted in NOR gate F, producing a low $\overline{\text{INT}}$ signal to the MPU. (We are assuming that the device is not selected and thus that $\overline{\text{DS1}} \cdot \text{DS2}$ is low.)

The MPU will respond to the interrupt request by setting $\overline{\text{DS1}} \cdot \text{DS2}$ true to select the device. The high output of gate C produces two actions: The service request flip-flop SET input goes low, forcing Q_{SR} high, and the new high input to NOR gate G will change the state of $\overline{\text{INT}}$ and hold it high.

AN 8212 INPUT PORT The 8212 is a versatile design, so it can be used in various ways. One of the simplest is shown in Fig. 13-8a. While this example shows the use as an input port, appropriate minor modifications would change it to an output port. Because STB is tied high, input data passes through the port continuously. The microprocessor can periodically sample the data lines to read the latest input. The output buffers are enabled by the device selection lines when the processor wants the next input.

AN 8212 OUTPUT PORT WITH HANDSHAKING A slightly more involved 8212 port is shown in Fig. 13-8c. This time the device is used for output, and control signals are exchanged between the processor and device before data transfer begins. Exchange of signals in this way is often called *handshaking*. With MD grounded, the MPU sets STB (after it has stabilized the output data on the bus) to clock the D flip-flops. In response to the high STB, the 8212 accepts the data. When the external device wants to read the data, it sets $\overline{\text{DS1}} \cdot \text{DS2}$ true, enabling the three-state output.

I/O Devices Review

1. Why is the fan-out of the MPU important?
2. List two ways of accommodating the limited drive of the MPU.
3. What should be done with output signal lines that are 16 in (40.6 cm) long?
4. Define "fully decoded address selection."
5. How does the 8095 buffer design provide for placing only one input on the data bus at any time?
6. Describe the operation of the 8212 in the output mode. In the input mode.
7. Why must the MD input be grounded in Fig. 13-7a?
8. What does setting the STB input high in Fig. 13-7c accomplish?

MEMORY-MAPPED I/O

Memory-mapped I/O treats external devices as memory locations, in contrast to accumulator I/O, which assigns them device codes. Because the devices are considered to be memory by the MPU, any of the memory transfer

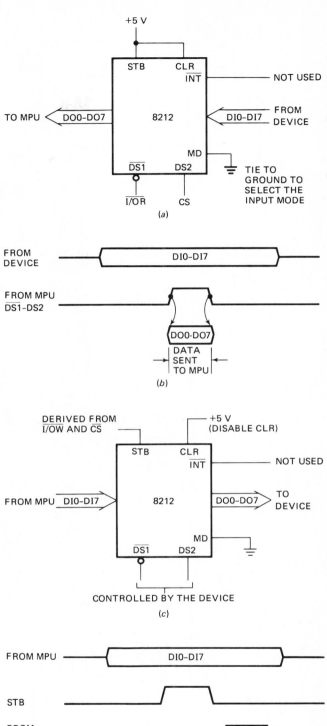

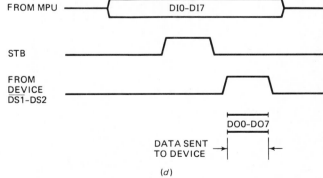

Fig. 13-8 8212 Port with handshaking: (*a*) input port wiring diagram, (*b*) input timing diagram, (*c*) output port wiring diagram, (*d*) output timing diagram.

Table 13-2 Comparison of Accumulator I/O and Memory-Mapped I/O

	Accumulator I/O	Memory-Mapped I/O
Instructions	OUT IN	Any memory-referencing instruction
Control signals	$\overline{I/OW}$ $\overline{I/OR}$	$\overline{MEMW}$ $\overline{MEMR}$
Data transfer	Between accumulator and the device	Between any general register and the device
Device decoding	Device select pulse decoded from 8-bit device code (A0–A7 or A8–A15)	Device select pulse decoded from 16-bit address (A0–A15)
Source of device address	From immediate data byte of the I/O instruction	From the address in an instruction

instructions may be used. Furthermore, any of the general-purpose registers can be used as the source or destination for the data. Table 13-2 compares these two I/O techniques.

There are several advantages to memory-mapped I/O. Being able to use any of the general-purpose registers, instead of just the accumulator, can shorten the program. By storing the 16-bit address for the peripheral device in a register pair and using register-addressed instructions, a memory-mapped I/O transfer can proceed faster than accumulator I/O because the device code need not be fetched from memory. More than 256 device codes are allowed (though more would probably never be required in a microcomputer). Two-byte data transfers are available, and input data can be directly used in arithmetic or logical instructions.

Among the disadvantages of memory-mapped I/O is the need to decode a 16-bit address, even if the device code is only 8 bits long. To clarify this statement, consider how the device with address $F3_{16}$ would distinguish between its address $00F3_{16}$ and $02F3_{16}$, $03F3_{16}$, and so on, unless the upper address byte were also decoded. Some memory addresses are sacrificed for device codes also. The loss may not be a serious problem in a processor that can address a 65K memory.

Figure 13-9 shows the basic difference in control signal usage for memory-mapped and accumulator I/O. The memory and device codes available in each scheme are also indicated, assuming that addresses above 8000_{16} are reserved for devices in the memory-mapped case.

One way to assign the 16-bit address space in a memory-mapped system might be the following:

Bit number

0 = Memory address
1 = I/O device code

The same I/O devices that were used with accumulator I/O can be used with memory mapping. Essentially the only alteration that must be made in the circuits

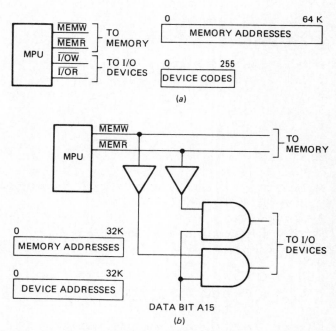

Fig. 13-9 I/O signal comparison: (*a*) accumulator I/O, (*b*) memory-mapped I/O.

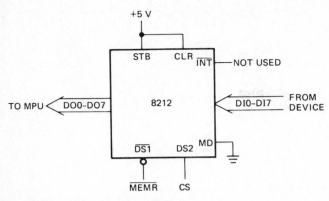

Fig. 13-10 Memory-mapped I/O port.

previously discussed is to change $\overline{I/OR}$ to $\overline{MEMR}$ and $\overline{I/OW}$ to $\overline{MEMW}$. As an illustration of how straightforward the conversion is, Fig. 13-10 shows the 8212 input port of Fig. 13-8a used in this way. Of course, the software must be changed to instructions that use the revised hardware configuration. Instead of the input (IN) instruction, memory data transfer instructions could be used.

Memory-Mapped I/O Review

1. What is the distinguishing characteristic of memory-mapped I/O?
2. True or false? A device with address 0314_{16} must use memory-mapped I/O.
3. List the instructions that can be used with memory-mapped I/O.
4. Discuss the advantages and disadvantages of memory-mapped I/O.
5. What change in the I/O port wiring of Fig. 13-8b must be made to convert it to memory-mapped I/O? What software changes are necessary?

INTERRUPTS

An *interrupt* is a signal that arrives at any time and causes the processor to break out of its normal execution sequence and begin a special interrupt sequence instead. This section describes the types of interrupts that a microprocessor may receive, the instructions available to process and control interrupts, timing and priority of interrupts, and finally a thorough investigation of the 8259 priority interrupt control unit.

MPU Interrupt Configurations

When only a single line is available for input of interrupt signals to the MPU, the configuration is called a *single-interrupt* system. As Fig. 13-11a shows, many devices

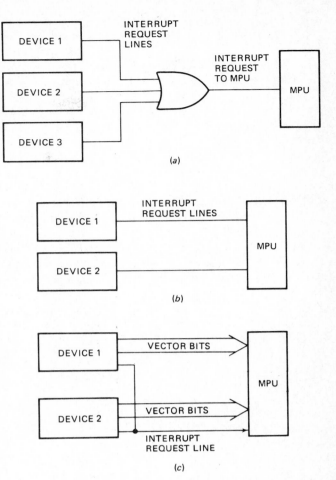

Fig. 13-11 Interrupt request configurations: (a) single, (b) multiple, (c) vectored.

are ORed on one line. The processor must interrogate, or *poll*, the devices to find the particular one that has requested service.

A *multiple-interrupt*–structured microprocessor furnishes several independent interrupt request lines. In this situation, the processor does not need to poll the devices because the one requesting service is uniquely identified. By adding the hardware for multiple interrupts and thus eliminating polling, the programming burden has been reduced. The 6800 is an example of a microprocessor with a multiple-interrupt arrangement. It has two interrupt lines.

Most sophisticated is the *vectored-interrupt* method supported by the 8085 microprocessor. In this architecture, each interrupting device provides a unique address, which specifies the program that services its interrupt. Once again, more complexity of hardware is traded off for simpler software in going to vectored interrupts. Not only must the processor be able to support the vectoring, but the external devices must also be able to supply the vector address in this arrangement.

80 8085 Interrupt-Handling Instructions

The 8085 supplies a substantial capability for accommodating vectored interrupts. When combined with supporting ICs, a powerful I/O handling capability can be constructed. There are two classes of instructions in the 8085 repertoire that relate to interrupts: control and vectoring.

CONTROL INSTRUCTIONS The 8085 contains an interrupt enable flag that dictates whether or not interrupt requests will be honored. If the flag is set, the MPU will recognize and respond to interrupts. When the flag is reset, the processor ignores all interrupt requests. Interrupts are disabled by the RESET signal that starts the processor sequence, so the programmer must enable them. As you might expect, there is one instruction that sets the flag, enable interrupts (EI), and another that clears it, disable interrupts (DI).

Operation code	FB	F3
Mnemonic	EI	DI
Addressing mode	none	
Status bits affected	none	
Clock periods	4	

Format

Bit number
```
 7 6 5 4   3 2 1 0
m 1 1 1 1   1 0 1 1
   Memory cell
```

Bit number
```
 7 6 5 4   3 2 1 0
m 1 1 1 1   0 0 1 1
   Memory cell
```

Examples of the use of these instructions will be presented below under "Comprehensive Interrupt Example."

VECTORED-INTERRUPT INSTRUCTIONS A vectored-interrupt instruction (called the RST instruction) is a special-purpose subroutine call. The instruction is supplied not from computer memory, but by the interrupting device. The device provides a 3-bit number, or *vector*, in the instruction. When one of these instructions is received, the processor enters a special interrupt state. (In all cases we will assume that interrupts are enabled, except when explicitly disabled.) Then the processor causes the program counter to be set to a vector address.

Format

Bit number
```
 7 6 5 4   3 2 1 0
 1 1 v v   v 1 1 1
```

where vvv is the 3-bit vector

vvv	Address
000	0
001	1
010	2
011	3
100	4
101	5
110	6
111	7

In normal use, the vector is used with routines stored in the lower 64 bytes of memory. Each of these routines is 8 bytes long, as indicated by Fig. 13-12. Their length is dictated by the lower 3 bits of the vector address. These routines each service their respective interrupts. Table 13-3 lists the instructions, together with their vector addresses.

Addressing mode	none
Status bits affected	none
Clock periods	11

COMPREHENSIVE INTERRUPT EXAMPLE We will work a comprehensive example showing how the interrupting device causes a particular RST instruction to be executed, in turn forcing control to be transferred to the interrupt-processing routine. We will see that the interrupt-processing routine must execute a return (RET) instruction last to give control back to the main program.

Let the interrupting device be a floppy disk that generates an RST 3 instruction. Decoding the instruction shows that the interrupt vector is 3:

$$RST\ 3 = DF_{16} = 11\underline{01\ 1}111_2$$

$$vvv = 3$$

When the processor recognizes the interrupt request (assuming that the interrupts are enabled), it automat-

ADDRESS$_{16}$	ROUTINE
0000	VECTOR SERVICE ROUTINE 0
0008	VECTOR SERVICE ROUTINE 1
0010	VECTOR SERVICE ROUTINE 2
0018	VECTOR SERVICE ROUTINE 3
0020	VECTOR SERVICE ROUTINE 4
0028	VECTOR SERVICE ROUTINE 5
0030	VECTOR SERVICE ROUTINE 6
0038	VECTOR SERVICE ROUTINE 7

Fig. 13-12 Address of interrupt servicing routines.

Table 13-3 RST Instruction

Operation Code	Mnemonic	Vector	Vector Address$_{16}$
C7	RST 0	0	0000
CF	RST 1	1	0008
D7	RST 2	2	0010
DF	RST 3	3	0018
E7	RST 4	4	0020
EF	RST 5	5	0028
F7	RST 6	6	0030
FF	RST 7	7	0038

ically enters the interrupt state by:

1. Waiting until the current instruction is completed.
2. Clearing the interrupt enable flag. (This action will prevent any other interrupts from disturbing the process.)
3. Taking the RST 3 instruction from the data lines instead of from memory.
4. Pushing the program counter on the stack (just as a normal call instruction would do). The address of the next sequential instruction in the main program is thus saved.
5. Forcing a jump to the 0018_{16} (vector address when vvv = 3).

Figure 13-13 diagrams this series of operations.

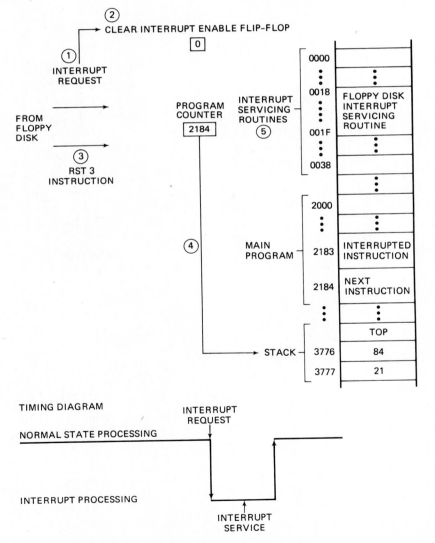

Fig. 13-13 Interrupt processing.

Once we are in this *interrupt-servicing routine*, we must be very careful not to disturb the settings of registers or status bits. If we have to use any register, it must first be pushed on the stack. The stack is popped just prior to returning to the main program, so the register contents before and after the interrupt remain unchanged. Before exiting the interrupt-servicing routine, there are two other tasks that must be completed. First, interrupts must be reenabled if we ever want to receive another (remember that in honoring the interrupt request the processor cleared the flag). Second, as mentioned above, we must execute a return instruction to cause the next address to be popped from the stack and placed in the program counter. Listed in Table 13-4 is a typical interrupt servicing routine. Figure 13-14 is a flowchart for the routine.

As you can see, there is not much memory space for processing. If more is needed, a jump to some other memory location can be made. Then all the memory needed is accessible.

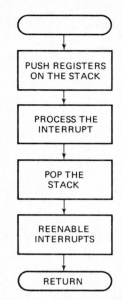

Fig. 13-14 Interrupt servicing routine flowchart.

8085 Interrupt Process Timing

Having discussed the instructions available for interrupt handling and the general sequence of events, we will now look in more detail at the timing and control signals involved. Figure 13-15 shows the relationships between the signals from the microprocessor and the external device.

As explained earlier, the interrupt is initiated by the external device setting the interrupt request signal (INTR) to the processor high. The processor will acknowledge the request, unless interrupts have been disabled by one of these:

1. Disable interrupt instruction
2. Reset condition

3. Previous processor acknowledgment clearing the interrupt enable flag

If interrupts are enabled, the 8085 will acknowledge by terminating the current instruction. Then the interrupt acknowledge machine cycle (as shown in Fig. 13-15) is executed. This six-clock-period cycle is much like an instruction, except that the external device must supply the instruction op code. The $\overline{INTA}$ signal is pulsed low instead of $\overline{RD}$ to obtain the op code. Note that memory is not accessed to obtain the instruction. The program counter is also not changed during the interrupt machine cycle, so the instruction that was being executed continues after the interrupt machine cycle completes.

The $\overline{INTA}$ signal serves both as an acknowledgment to the interrupt request and as a read strobe to fetch the op code. The instruction must be placed on the low-order data lines by the device prior to the middle of T2.

Table 13-4 8085 Interrupt-Servicing Routine

Mnemonic	Address	Operation Code	Comments
PUSH A	0018	F5	Save accumulator and status bits
MVI A, 3	0019	3E⎫	Store indicator of interrupt
	001A	03⎭	vector in D register
MOV D, A	001B	57	
POP A	001C	F1	Restore accumulator and status bits
EI	001D	FB	Reenable interrupts
RET	001E	C9	Return
	001F	—	Not used

8085 Interrupt Request Lines

In addition to the vectored-interrupt line (INTR), the 8085 has four other pins that hardware devices can use to interrupt the microprocessor. These interrupts are similar to the interrupt request, except that the 8085 generates its own interrupt acknowledge instruction when the device sets any of these signals high. Table 13-5 lists the vector addresses for these interrupts.

Most of these interrupts differ from the previously described ones also in that they are individually maskable; that is, the interrupt can only occur if both the interrupt enable flag and the mask bit for that interrupt are both set. You may think of the condition enabling one of these interrupts as

IE AND MASK
where IE = interrupt enable flag
  MASK = individual interrupt enable mask

The TRAP interrupt is an exception and is not maskable. This interrupt is normally used for a major system malfunction, such as low power. The only interrupts are individually maskable.

The RST 5.5 and 6.5 are level-sensitive. This type of sensing means that the interrupt will occur if the input line for the interrupt is set to the high-voltage level. The RST 7.5 interrupt, on the other hand, is edge-sensitive. This interrupt will occur if a signal makes a low-to-high transition on this line. The TRAP input is both level- and edge-sensitive. The masks for these interrupts are set or cleared by means of the RIM and SIM instructions described below under "8085 Interrupt Mask Instructions."

What if several of the interrupts occur simultaneously? The 8085 takes care of that situation with a priority scheme. The priority of the interrupts is listed in Table 13-6. Whichever interrrupt has the highest priority will be serviced first, and the others will have to wait.

Table 13-5 Hardware Interrupt Vectors

Interrupt Line	Vector Address$_{16}$
TRAP	24
RST 5.5	2C
RST 6.5	34
RST 7.5	3C

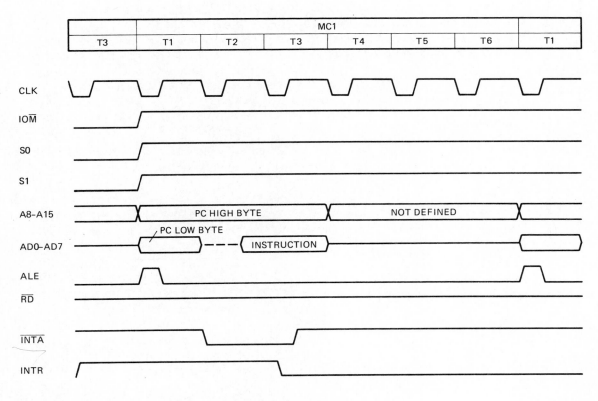

Fig. 13-15 8085 interrupt acknowledgment timing diagram.

Table 13-6 Interrupt Priority

Interrupt	Priority
TRAP	1
RST 7.5	2
RST 6.5	3
RST 5.5	4
INTR	5

80 8085 Interrupt Mask Instructions

The set interrupt mask (SIM) instruction uses the A register. The instruction can program the masks for the RST 5.5, 6.5, and 7.5 interrupts; reset the RST 7.5 input latch; or place serial output data in the serial output data (SOD) latch. The meaning of each bit in the A register for this instruction is shown in Fig. 13-16. Bits 0 through 2 are the masks for the interrupts. Setting any of these bits to 1 enables the respective interrupt. For the masks to be changed, bit 3 must also be set. If this bit is not set, the masks are not updated after the SIM instruction. (Note that the $\overline{RESETIN}$ signal always sets the RST mask bits.) Bit 4 being set causes the RST 7.5 latch to reset. This operation should be performed after any RST 7.5 interrupt occurs in order to allow for the next one.

The SIM instruction also performs serial data output on the SOD line. To output 1 bit, the data is loaded into bit 7 of the A register. Bit 6 of the register must be set as well in order to cause the data to be loaded into the SOD latch.

Operation code   30
Mnemonic   SIM
Addressing mode   immediate
Status bits affected   none
Clock periods   4

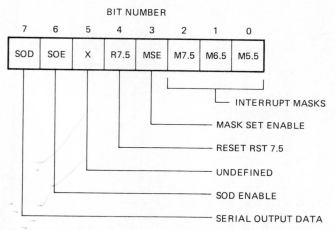

Fig. 13-16 8085 A register before executing SIM instruction.

☐ **EXAMPLE**

Before Execution		After Execution	
Program counter	0350	Program counter	0351
A register	1F	A register	1F
Memory 0350	30	Memory 0350	30

The masks for all interrupts have been set and the latch for the RST 7.5 interrupt has been reset.

The read interrupt mask (RIM) instruction allows us to check the settings of the various mask bits. The A register is used with this instruction. As shown in Fig. 13-17, the lower 3 bits contain the mask bit settings. Bit 3 indicates the state of the interrupt enable flag. Any interrupts that are pending on the RST 5.5, 6.5, or 7.5 lines are shown in bits 4 through 6.

Another use of the RIM instruction is to perform serial data input with the SID line. If data is placed on the SID input pin, it can be read in bit 7 of the A register with this instruction.

Operation code   20
Mnemonic   RIM
Addressing mode   immediate
Status bits affected   none
Clock periods   4
Format

Bit number

7 6 5 4   3 2 1 0

Memory cell   m | 0 0 1 0   0 0 0 0 |

☐ **EXAMPLE**

Before Execution		After Execution	
Program counter	0350	Program counter	0351
A register	00	A register	1F
Memory 0350	20	Memory 0350	20

BIT NUMBER

7	6	5	4	3	2	1	0
SID	I7.5	I6.5	I5.5	IE	M7.5	M6.5	M5.5

                                 └─── INTERRUPT MASKS

                    └─── INTERRUPT ENABLE FLAG

                  └─── PENDING INTERRUPTS

          └─── SERIAL INPUT DATA

Fig. 13-17 8085 A register after executing RIM instruction.

From the contents of the A register after execution of the instruction, we can see that the interrupt enable flag is set and that all RST interrupt masks are enabled.

6800 Interrupt Instructions

The 6800 provides for two types of interrupts: a non-maskable interrupt and a maskable interrupt. The non-maskable interrupt signal ($\overline{\text{NMI}}$) will cause an interrupt any time the external device sets this signal low. This signal is normally used for a major system problem, such as a low power level. The nonmaskable interrupt is edge-sensitive; it will occur when the $\overline{\text{NMI}}$ signal transitions from high-level to low-level. The maskable interrupt line ($\overline{\text{IRQ}}$) will generate an interrupt only if the interrupt enable flag is reset to 0. If the flag is set to 1 and the $\overline{\text{IRQ}}$ signal is low, no interrupt will occur.

The status of the interrupts is checked by the 6800 on each instruction cycle. If an interrupt is pending, the 6800 performs the following operations:

1. Sets the interrupt enable flag, thus preventing any further interrupts.
2. Pushes the contents of the status register, accumulators A and B, index register, and program counter on the stack.
3. Places the address of the instruction appropriate for the type of interrupt in the program counter. Table 13-7 lists the addresses for the interrupts. The programmer sets these addresses to the start of the routines that will serve each type of interrupt.

All these interrupts are controlled by the 6800 instructions. The software interrupt is generated by a special op code described below. The addresses where the various registers are pushed on the stack are relative to the present contents of the stack pointer. Table 13-8 lists the addresses for each register.

The set interrupt mask (SEI) instruction *disables* the $\overline{\text{IRQ}}$ instruction. (Remember that when this bit is set, the interrupts are disabled.)

Operation code	0F
Mnemonic	SEI
Addressing mode	inherent
Status bits affected	interrupt mask
Clock periods	4

Table 13-7 Interrupt Routine Addresses

Type of Interrupt	Addresses$_{16}$
RESET	FFFE, FFFF
NMI	FFFC, FFFD
Software interrupt	FFFA, FFFB
IRQ	FFF8, FFF9

Table 13-8 Stack Addresses for Registers After an Interrupt

Address*	Register
m	PC lower byte
m + 1	PC upper byte
m + 2	X register lower byte
m + 3	X register upper byte
m + 4	A register
m + 5	B register
m + 6	Status register

* Assuming that the SP content is m prior to the interrupt.

Format

Bit number

7 6 5 4   3 2 1 0

Memory cell   m | 0 0 0 0   1 1 1 1 |

□ EXAMPLE

Before Execution		After Execution	
Program counter	0350	Program counter	0351
Status register	C0	Status register	D0
Memory 0350	0F	Memory 0350	0F

The interrupt mask enable bit (bit 4) of the status register is set, and maskable interrupts are disabled.

The clear interrupt mask (CLI) instruction enables the $\overline{\text{IRQ}}$ instruction. (Remember that when this bit is clear, the interrupts are enabled.)

Operation code	0E
Mnemonic	CLI
Addressing mode	inherent
Status bits affected	interrupt mask
Clock periods	4
Format	

Bit number

7 6 5 4   3 2 1 0

Memory cell   m | 0 0 0 0   1 1 1 0 |

□ EXAMPLE

Before Execution		After Execution	
Program counter	0350	Program counter	0351
Status register	D0	Status register	D0
Memory 0350	0E	Memory 0350	0E

The interrupt mask enable bit (bit 4) of the status register is cleared, and maskable interrupts are enabled.

The return-from-interrupt instruction should be the last instruction executed in any interrupt servicing routine. This instruction pops the contents of each of the registers from the stack and restores the state of the microprocessor to what it was before the interrupt happened. This is an instruction that simplifies the work involved in interrupt programming.

		Bit number
Operation code	3B	
Mnemonic	RTI	
Addressing mode	inherent	
Status bits affected	none	
Clock periods	2	
Format		7 6 5 4 3 2 1 0
Memory cell	m	0 0 1 1 1 0 1 1

The programmer can generate an interrupt with an instruction whenever this operation is desired. The instruction pushes all the registers on the stack and executes the instructions at location $FFFA_{16}$ next.

		Bit number
Operation code	3F	
Mnemonic	SWI	
Addressing mode	inherent	
Status bits affected	none	
Clock periods	12	
Format		7 6 5 4 3 2 1 0
Memory cell	m	0 0 1 1 1 1 1 1

Sometimes we want the processor to wait for some external event to take place. Perhaps we are delaying until the operator pushes a button on the console. The wait-for-interrupt instruction causes the processor to pause until the event takes place. This instruction pushes all the registers on the stack and then waits for the next interrupt. The instruction is like a halt instruction, except for the stack operation.

		Bit number
Operation code	3E	
Mnemonic	WAI	
Addressing mode	inherent	
Status bits affected	none	
Clock periods	9	
Format		7 6 5 4 3 2 1 0
Memory cell	m	0 0 1 1 1 1 1 0

68 The Halt State and Interrupts

Recall that the halt instruction causes the processor to stop executing instructions. Once stopped, how is the processor restarted? The halt state can be terminated by an interrupt request (INTR high). In servicing the interrupt, the processor will reference the servicing routine, which will reinitiate operation.

If interrupts are inhibited when the processor halts, the interrupt request will not be acknowledged. What does the operator do then? The only way to leave the halt state, in that case, is to turn the power off and back on again.

Interrupts Review

1. Distinguish between single-, multiple-, and vectored-interrupt configurations. Which configuration requires polling?
2. What instructions control the interrupt enable flip-flop in the 8085 and 6800?
3. How can you determine the entrance address for the servicing routine of an RST instruction?
4. Why must the external device issue an instruction that causes the program counter to be pushed on the stack in response to an interrupt acknowledge?
5. What instructions should be included in every interrupt servicing routine?
6. Describe the timing of interrupt signals in the 8085.
7. How are interrupts handled if the processor is in the halt state?

PRIORITY INTERRUPT CONTROL UNIT

The 8259 *priority interrupt control unit (PICU)* is an NMOS 28-pin DIP designed to work with a microprocessor. All 8259 outputs are TTL-compatible. The 8259 can coordinate a maximum of eight external interrupts, or one device can act as the master for up to eight slave 8259s producing 64 levels of interrupt priority. Such a complex arrangement would not normally be used with a microprocessor, however.

8259 Signals

The pin assignments for the 8259 are shown in Fig. 13-18a, and each of the signals is briefly described in Table 13-9 (see page 262). The 8259 can be used in either a memory-mapped I/O fashion or an I/O port fashion. As Fig. 13-18b shows, bit A15 of the address bus is attached to the A0 input to the chip. You will also see that the 8259 is treated as a device with two addresses—a low address when the A0 input is 0 and a high address when A0 is high.

A system with master-slave 8259s is shown in Fig. 13-19 (see page 262). An important feature to note is that the SP input is high for the master unit and grounded for the slave.

The master services devices 0 through 6, and the slave is connected to IR7 of the master and responds to the interrupts of devices 7 through 14.

8259 Functions

The 8259 not only manages the multiple interrupts but also provides the object code for the call instruction and the 2 address bytes. The address in the last 2 bytes is

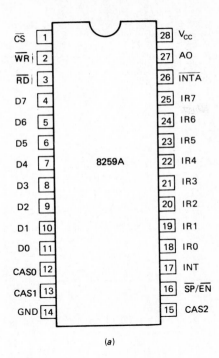

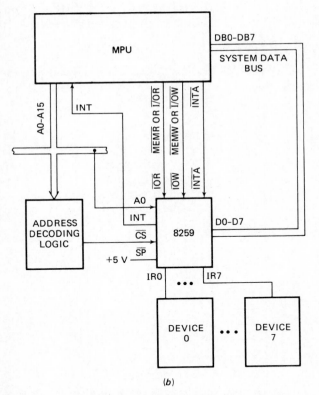

Fig. 13-18 8259 priority interrupt controller: (a) pin assignments, (b) single 8259 system simplified diagram.

the subroutine entrance of the interrupt-handling software.

While the 8259 offers a great deal of flexibility in choosing these addresses, they are not entirely independent. The user has a choice of any starting address for the memory block that contains the interrupt-handling routines. Within that block, the option of allowing either 4 or 8 bytes per routine is offered by the 8259. The memory map for each of these arrangements is shown in Fig. 13-20 (note that the illustration assumes that a starting address of 1000_{16} was selected). Actually, the four-cell option may be most useful, because a jump instruction would normally be placed in that location.

Each entrance cell is uniquely assigned to a given interrupt level. As Fig. 13-20 shows for the first option, cell 1000 is assigned to level 0, cell 1004 to level 2, and so on. The second option is similar, except that the entrances are eight locations apart.

The 8259 also provides for *interrupt priority arbitration;* that is, it arbitrates between simultaneously occurring interrupts to decide which will be serviced first by the processor. This means that if devices 2 and 4 both send interrupts, the 8259 will choose the device with the higher priority and forward its interrupt to the MPU. Such service is typical of any interrupt priority arbitration logic. The 8259, however, carries arbitration a step farther. Not only does it arbitrate at the time the interrupts occur, but it can also prevent a lower-level interrupt from interrupting the servicing routine of a higher level. This means that, once the service routine starts running, it can only be interrupted by a higher-level device. The 8259 offers quite a variety of priority assignment protocols. Each of them is described below. Because the 8259 is a programmable device, each mode must be selected by control signals from the MPU.

FULLY NESTED MODE   The fully nested mode is the default condition: Unless the 8259 is programmed to assume another mode of operation, it will take the fully nested mode. This mode establishes a fixed priority. The priority of a device depends on which IR pin it is connected to. Pin 0 has the highest priority and pin 7 the lowest.

Interrupt priorities never change in the fully nested mode. This means that an interrupt on a lower-priority IR line will never be acknowledged (1) as long as one exists on a higher-priority line or (2) while an interrupt service request for a higher-priority interrupt is being executed.

For example, assume that interrupts are produced by the devices on IR3 and IR6 at the same time. As the timing diagram in Fig. 13-21 on page 263 shows, the priority 6 interrupt does not get to the MPU, although interrupts may be enabled by the MPU until the priority 3 processing is complete. When a priority 2 interrupt occurs, however, the priority 3 processing is suspended and the servicing routine for the device on IR2 is run.

ROTATING PRIORITIES, MODE A   The fixed-priorities scheme of the fully nested mode can result in a poor response to low-level interrupts. In some cases, the

Table 13-9 8259 Signal Description

Name	Purpose	Type
$\overline{CS}$	Device select	Input
A0	I/O port identification	Input
D0–D7	Data bus	Bidirectional, three-state
$\overline{IOR}$	Read control	Input
$\overline{IOW}$	Write control	Input
IR0–IR7	Interrupt requests from external devices	Input
INT	Interrupt request to MPU	Output
$\overline{INTA}$	Interrupt acknowledge	Input
$\overline{SP}$	Master-slave identification (high for master, low for slaves)	Input
C0–C2	Cascade signals to select slaves in multiple 8259 systems	Output (from master)/input (to slaves)

lowest priority may never get access to the processor. With mode A rotating priorities, every level is guaranteed a chance to interrupt the processor. After a given interrupt level has been serviced, it moves to the position of lowest priority. A few examples, shown in Table 13-10, will make it easier to visualize how the priority levels are rearranged. The effect of mode A is to offer equal service to all priority levels. The priorities are rearranged when control codes from the MPU inform the 8259 that processing of the last interrupt has been completed.

ROTATING PRIORITIES, MODE B In this mode, the processor can specify the lowest priority level at any

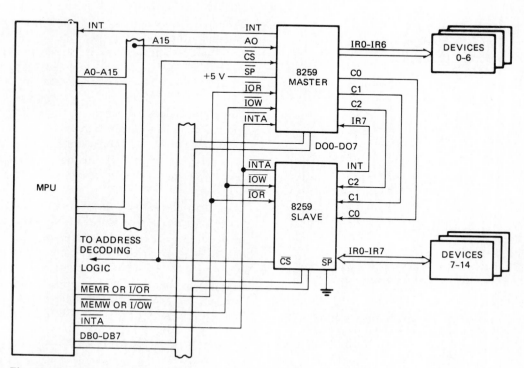

Fig. 13-19 Master-slave 8259 system simplified diagram.

Interrupt Level	Address		
0	1000	C3	← Jump Instruction
	1001	20 ⎤	← Address
	1002	14 ⎦	Not used
	1003		
1	1004	C3	
	1005	60	
	1006	14	
	1007		
2	1008	C3	
	1009	20	
	100A	25	
	100B		
3	100C	C3	
	100D	F0	
	100E	12	
	100F	12	
	⋮	⋮	

(a)

Interrupt Level	Address	
0	1000	C3
	1001	20
	1002	14
	1003	
	1004	
	1005	
	1006	
	1007	
1	1008	C3
	1009	60
	100A	14
	100B	
	100C	
	100D	
	100E	
	100F	
2	1010	C3
	⋮	⋮

(b)

Fig. 13-20 Interrupt address with the 8259: (*a*) option 1-4 cells per entrance, (*b*) option 2-8 cells per entrance.

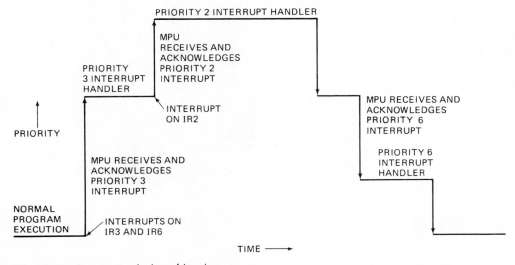

Fig. 13-21 Interrupt priority arbitration.

Table 13-10 Priority Level of Device Interrupt Request Lines

	Lowest							Highest
Initially	IR7	IR6	IR5	IR4	IR3	IR2	IR1	IR0
After an IR3 interrupt is acknowledged	IR3	IR7	IR6	IR5	IR4	IR2	IR1	IR0
After an IR6 interrupt is acknowledged	IR6	IR3	IR7	IR5	IR4	IR2	IR1	IR0

time. The priorities of the other IR lines are then assigned sequentially, but the highest level can be freely chosen. Consider the examples in Table 13-11. As can be seen, the highest-priority IR line is always one greater than the one selected to have lowest priority. Where IR2 is the lowest level, IR3 has the highest; and with IR5 lowest, IR6 is highest.

POLLED MODE The priority arbitration can be bypassed entirely by using the polled mode. Then the 8259 is referenced by the processor to find the status of I/O devices, but no interrupts are generated. When the MPU interrogates the 8259, a status word provides an indication of the highest-level IR line that is requesting an interrupt and an indication that an interrupt request is active. The format for that word is shown here.

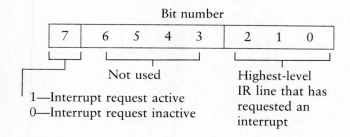

When polling is used in a master-slave configuration, the master is polled first. The slave with an active interrupt is shown in bits 0 to 2. Another polling request from the processor then goes to that slave. For example, the master unit provides a status word of

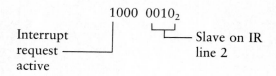

Then slave 2 is polled and responds with

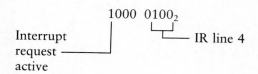

The microprocessor has found that the highest-priority interrupt request is from the device on IR line 4 of slave unit 2.

SIMPLE MASK MODE Masking permits enabling or disabling interrupts on an individual IR line level. There are two *mask modes* available in the 8259, either of which can be superimposed on the fully nested priority or rotating priority modes A or B. In the simple mask mode, the MPU outputs an 8-bit mask—each bit rep-

Table 13-11 Priority Level of Device Interrupt Request Lines

	Lowest							Highest
Initially	IR7	IR6	IR5	IR4	IR3	IR2	IR1	IR0
After the MPU specifies IR2 lowest-level priority	IR2	IR1	IR0	IR7	IR6	IR5	IR4	IR3
After the MPU specifies IR5 lowest-level priority	IR5	IR4	IR3	IR2	IR1	IR0	IR7	IR6

resenting the respective IR line. Any bit that is set disables interrupts on the corresponding IR line:

Bit numbers and IR line numbers

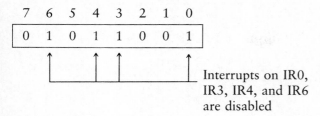

Interrupts on IR0, IR3, IR4, and IR6 are disabled

SPECIAL MASK MODE This mask allows the processor to allow interrupts from a lower-priority-level device to interrupt the service routine of a higher-priority mode. The 8-bit mask is interpreted to mean that 0s will allow that IR level to interrupt a service request for a higher level; 1s in the mask disable this feature.

Bit numbers and IR line numbers

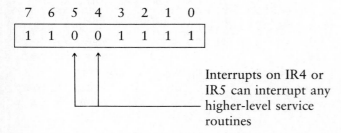

Interrupts on IR4 or IR5 can interrupt any higher-level service routines

8259 Architecture

An understanding of some of the internal registers of the 8259 is necessary before looking into how to program it. As Fig. 13-22 shows, the 8259 has eight functional components. The data bus buffer temporarily holds data transiting between the internal bus and system data bus. The cascade comparator recognizes a slave unit's address. Read-write logic informs the control unit of the direction of data flow.

The interrupt request (IR) and interrupt status (IS) registers maintain the bookkeeping for the priority arbitration logic, as controlled by the processor-supplied mask (if used). The IR register latches all input from the external devices. Any device with a pending interrupt request sets the appropriate bit in the IR register to 1. Only the bit for the highest-level IR line will be set in the IS register. The IS register reflects the result of the arbitration logic. That bit remains set until the interrupt-handling program in the processor clears it by issuing an end-of-interrupt command. Should a higher-level interrupt request come along while that routine is running, its bit is also set in the IS register. If the IS register contains

$$0100 \qquad 1000_2$$

Level 6   Level 3

we know that the interrupt handler for level 6 was interrupted by a request from IR3.

Because the interrupt request from the external device is not latched until the bit is set in the IS register, the device must hold the IR line high until acknowledged. A mask from the processor can prevent bits in the IR and IS registers from being set.

Programming the 8259

The 8259 is programmed by the processor sending a series of initialization and operational control words.

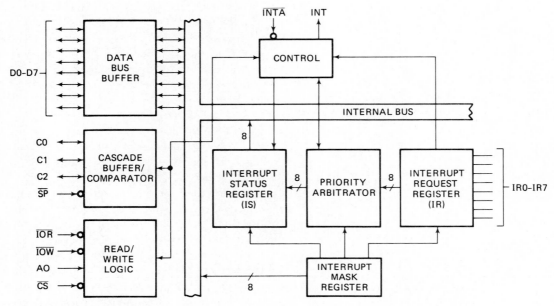

Fig. 13-22 8259 architecture.

The processor addresses the 8259 as two I/O ports or memory locations. All address bits except one are the same for the ports. The final bit is used to set or clear the A0 input.

The initialization sequence of commands that must be sent is diagrammed in Fig. 13-23. Two initialization control words (ICW) are always used. In a master-slave system, a third initialization control word must be sent to the master; then sets of three words are passed to each slave. Finally, options and mask bits can be selected if desired.

Table 13-12 lists the control words for the 8259. After the initialization sequence has been sent, writing data in the high port (A0 = 1) will cause the 8259 to interpret the 8 bits as a mask, unless preceded by ICW1. The operational control words can be sent at any time after the initialization. A typical control word sequence for the configuration shown in Fig. 13-18 is given in Table 13-13 (see page 268).

Priority Interrupt Control Unit Review

1. What are the $\overline{IOR}$ and $\overline{IOW}$ inputs to the 8259 used for?
2. How is the $\overline{SP}$ input used to designate master and slave units?

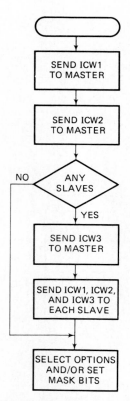

Fig. 13-23 8259 initialization sequence.

3. Describe the two addressing options for the entrances to interrupt-handling routines provided by the 8259.
4. How is the priority of an interrupt level established in the fully nested mode?
5. How does rotating priority mode A differ from mode B?
6. How does the processor locate pending interrupts in the polled mode?
7. How do the two types of masks influence the priority arbitration?
8. List the types of initialization control words that must be issued in a master-slave system with two slaves.

DIRECT MEMORY ACCESS

At times the data transfer to peripheral equipment may be so rapid that interrupts will not provide an adequate data exchange rate. Furthermore, a large number of interrupts will severely reduce the processing speed of the mainline program. In such cases a special controller can be used to perform high-speed transfers between memory and external devices directly. Such a direct memory access (DMA) controller uses the buses in a manner quite similar to that used by the processor.

In a microprocessor system, the hold state is used for direct memory access. DMA may proceed after suspending the processor or by "stretching" clock pulses. We will want to understand how the DMA controller emulates the MPU on the address, data, and control buses. To accomplish the emulation, each DMA channel must have a 16-bit address register and a counter for the number of bytes to transfer. A status register is usually provided as well. Because the processor and external devices cannot simultaneously access memory, one must wait for the other. This *memory cycle stealing* by the external device does slow the processor down, because it cannot execute instructions without accessing memory.

A simplified DMA system is shown in Fig. 13-24 (see page 269). The processor and DMA controller indicate to each other which of them is presently directing the system buses by means of the HOLD and hold acknowledge (HLDA) signals. The devices, in turn, request use of the data bus and are granted it by the control signals between each of the peripherals and the DMA controller. Although the DMA controller is connected to the data bus, data from the external devices does not pass through the controller. Instead, once a device has been granted access to the data bus, data passes directly between the device and memory. The data bus is only used by the DMA controller to accept commands from the processor or to send status information to the processor.

Table 13-12 8259 Control Words

A0 Setting	Control Word	Bit Number	Meaning
0	Initialization control word 1 (ICW1)	0	Not interpreted.
		1	Set, this is only a master 8259 system. Clear, this is a master-slave system.
		2	Set, this is address vector option 1 (four words between entrance cells). Clear, this is address vector option 2 (eight words between entrance cells).
		3	Not interpreted.
		4	Always set.
		5–7	Bits 5–7 of the constant portion of vector address (refer to Fig. 13-20). Bit 5 not interrupted if option 2 was selected.
1	Initialization control word 2 (ICW2)	0–7	Bits 8–15 of the constant portion of the vector address (refer to Fig. 3-20).
1	Initialization control word 3 (ICW3)	0–7	To a master unit: Any bit set means that a slave is attached to that IR line.
		0–2	To a slave unit: Identifies slave's IR line number at the master unit.
		3–7	Not interpreted by slave.
0	Operational control word 2 (OCW2)	0–2	See bits 5–7 for explanation.
		3	Always 0.
		4	Always 0.
		5–7	Operation: 0—No operation. 1—End of interrupt (ignore bits 0–2). 2—No operation. 3—Special end of interrupt; reset the interrupt status (IS) register bit specified in bits 0–2. 4—No operation. 5—End of interrupt; start rotating priority mode A (ignore bits 0–2). 6—Start rotating priority mode B (bits 0–2 specify lowest level). 7—End of interrupt; start rotating priority mode B (bits 0–2 specify lowest level).

Table 13-12 *(cont'd)*   8259 Control Words

A0 Setting	Control Word	Bit Number	Meaning
0	Operational control word 3 (OCW3)	0–1	Set status: 0 — Illegal. 1 — Illegal. 2 — Select reading of the interrupt request (IR) register. 3 — Select reading of the interrupt status (IS) register.
		2	Set, polled mode is selected. Clear, other mode is selected.
		3	Always 1.
		4	Always 0.
		5–6	Mask mode: 0 — Illegal. 1 — Illegal. 2 — Cancel special mask mode. 3 — Select special mask mode.
		7	Not interpreted.

Direct Memory Access Review

1. When is DMA the preferred method of I/O?
2. What state in the MPU is used during direct memory access data transfers?
3. List the registers usually found in a DMA controller.
4. True or false? Data from the peripheral device to be written into memory passes through the DMA controller to the data bus.

THE 8257 DMA CONTROLLER

The 8257 DMA controller, used in MPU systems, supports four DMA channels. Each channel can be assigned to a peripheral device. All signals to or from the NMOS DIP are TTL-compatible. A diagram of pin assignments for the chip is shown in Fig. 13-25. Each of the signals is briefly explained in Table 13-14.

For the 8257 to mimic the processor, it must duplicate

Table 13-13   Control Word Sequence

	A0	Output	Control Word	Meaning
Initialize master in fully nested mode	0	02	ICW1	Master-slave system; eight words between vectors
	1	10	ICW2	Base address for master vector is 1000_{16}
	1	80	ICW3	Slave on IR7
Initialize slave	0	02	ICW1	Master-slave system
	1	18	ICW2	Base address for slave vector is 1800_{16}
	1	07	ICW3	Slave is on IR line 7
	0	A0	OCW2	Rotate priorities mode A with end of interrupt
	0	60	OCW3	Select special mask
	1	02	MASK	Allow level 1 to interrupt level 0 service routine

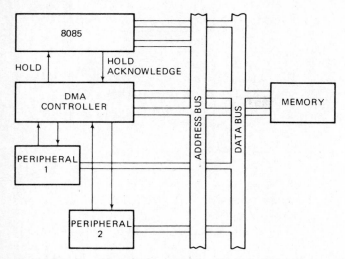

Fig. 13-24 Simplified DMA controller block diagram.

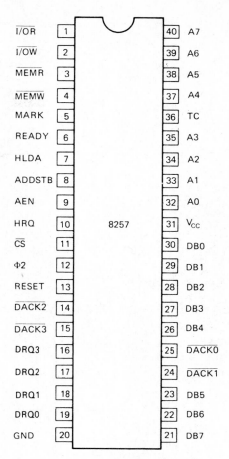

Fig. 13-25 8257 DMA controller.

all signals needed to control memory reading and writing. Table 13-15 compares the 8257 signals with those of the 8085 and 8228. The table indicates that the 8257 multiplexes the upper 8 bits of the address of the data bus. For this reason, an 8212 I/O port (or its equivalent) must be used to demultiplex the data bus output pins from the 8257. A system consisting of the 8085 (with its support chips), 8212, and 8257 is shown in Fig. 13-26. Only signals involved with DMA transfers are included in this illustration. Memory would be connected to the address and system data buses in the normal manner.

Table 13-14 8257 Signal Summary

Signal Name	Meaning	Type
DB0–DB7	Data bus	Three-state bidirectional
A0–A4	Low-order address bus	Three-state, bidirectional
A5–A7	Remaining low-order address bus	Three-state, output
$\overline{\text{I/OR}}$	Processor input strobe	Three-state, bidirectional
$\overline{\text{I/OW}}$	Processor output strobe	Three-state, bidirectional
$\overline{\text{MEMR}}$	Memory read strobe	Three-state, output
$\overline{\text{MEMW}}$	Memory write strobe	Three-state, output
MARK	128-byte count strobe	Output
TC	Terminal count strobe	Output
READY	Memory ready/not ready	Input
HRQ	Hold request to MPU	Output
HLDA	Hold acknowledge from MPU	Input
ADDSTB	Address on data bus strobe	Output
AEN	DMA bus enable/disable	Output
$\overline{\text{CS}}$	Device select	Input
Φ2	Clock	Input
RESET	System reset	Input
DRQ0–DRQ3	Service request from external devices	Input
$\overline{\text{DACK0}}$–$\overline{\text{DACK3}}$	Service acknowledge to external devices	Output

Table 13-15 Comparison of MPU and DMA Signals

8085 Signal	8257 Signal	Purpose
AD0–AD7, A8–A15	A0–A7, DB0–DB7	Address bus
AD0–AD7	DB0–DB7	Data bus
$\overline{\text{I/OR}}$, $\overline{\text{I/OW}}$	$\overline{\text{I/OR}}$, $\overline{\text{I/OW}}$	I/O read and write strobes
$\overline{\text{MEMR}}$, $\overline{\text{MEMW}}$	$\overline{\text{MEMR}}$, $\overline{\text{MEMW}}$	Memory data strobes
READY	READY	Memory ready/not ready
RESET	RESET	System reset

The diagram illustrates how the low-order address bits (A0 through A7) are derived directly from the 8257, but the high-order bits (A8 through A15) are furnished by the 8212 I/O port. It obtains their value by demultiplexing the data bus from the 8257 at the proper time.

8257 Registers

Every DMA channel of the 8257 has two registers. The 16-bit address registers contain the next memory location that will be written or read. The byte count and the direction control satisfy two purposes: The lower 14 bits are the number of bytes that will be transferred,

and bits 14 and 15 indicate the direction of transfer. A ninth register is used by the 8257 for commands, and a tenth for status.

To transfer any block of data by DMA, the starting address, number of words, and direction must be loaded into these registers by the processor. As each word is transferred in the DMA operations, the register contents change:

1. The address register increments to the next memory address.
2. The count register decrements, meaning that 1 byte has been exchanged. (Because the last byte is ex-

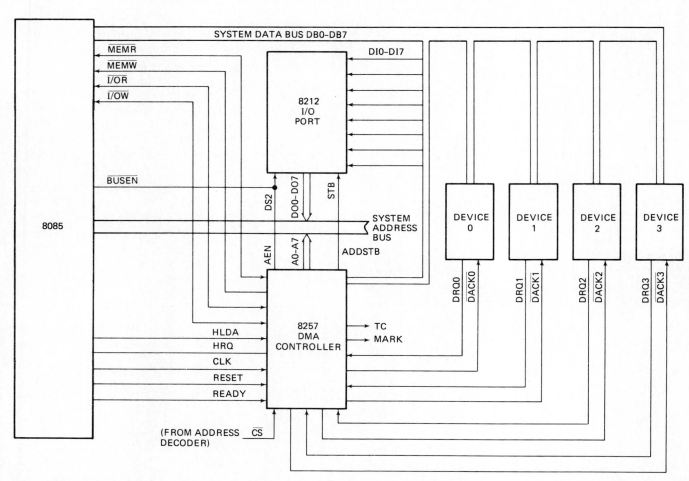

Fig. 13-26 8085 DMA system.

changed on a 0 count, this register should be set to $n - 1$ to transfer n words.)

In order to minimize the pin count on the 8257 package, the address lines are used for a double purpose. In addition to carrying the address information from the 8257, pins A0 through A4 also designate the register to receive data from the processor. Table 13-16 lists the meanings of these bit values. Because the address and byte-count registers are 16 bits long, it takes two output operations to set the values in each. The first output byte goes to the low-order 8 bits and the second output goes to the high-order 8 bits of the designated register. The $\overline{CS}$ signal must be low before the MPU accesses the 8257. (To avoid problems during DMA operations, $\overline{CS}$ must be high. This signal is automatically raised by the 8257 during data transfer.)

Priority Arbitration

What happens if two or more devices attempt to access the 8257 simultaneously? A priority arbitrator, much like the one for interrupts in the above section, "Priority Interrupt Control Unit," decides which device gets acknowledged first. The external devices request service by setting their DRQ signal line high. The acknowledge ($\overline{DACK}$) signal informs the device that its request is being honored.

The priority arbitration scheme to be used is selected by programming the 8257. In the *fixed priority mode,* the device requests are always honored in the same order. The device on DRQ0 has the highest priority, and the one on DRQ3 has the lowest.

The *round-robin mode* guarantees equal service to every device. The low-priority device cannot be locked out by higher-priority ones in this scheme. In the round-robin mode, the last channel that was serviced moves to the bottom of the priority list. Table 13-17 shows the channel priorities for every situation.

Table 13-16 8257 Register Addressing

Bits				
A3	A2	A1	A0	Destination/Source of Data
0	0	0	0	Channel 0 address register
0	0	0	1	Channel 0 byte-count register
0	0	1	0	Channel 1 address register
0	0	1	1	Channel 1 byte-count register
0	1	0	0	Channel 2 address register
0	1	0	1	Channel 2 byte-count register
0	1	1	0	Channel 3 address register
0	1	1	1	Channel 3 byte-count register
1	0	0	0	Command register on output, status register on input
9–15				Not used

Table 13-17 Round-Robin Channel Priority for the 8257

Channel Priority	Initialization	Last Channel Serviced			
		0	1	2	3
Highest	0	1	2	3	0
	1	2	3	0	1
	2	3	0	1	2
Lowest	3	0	1	2	3

DMA Options

The 8257 can transfer data in either a *byte-by-byte transfer* or *burst transfer* mode. The latter method provides the highest data throughput rate. The direction of transfer is specified by the program in the processor. The DMA controller will also allow the device to specify the direction, although this is rarely done.

TRANSFER MODES Under 8257 control, the external device can transfer its data a single byte at a time. In this model the device raises the DRQ signal prior to each transfer. When the DMA controller responds with the $\overline{DACK}$ acknowledgment, the device drops DRQ. To transfer data in a burst mode, the device holds DRQ true until the entire block has been sent or received. Only then is that signal dropped.

TRANSFER DIRECTION The processor specifies the direction of data transfer by the settings of the upper 2 bits in the byte-count register. Table 13-18 is a tabulation of those settings. Note the reversal of meanings of two values when using I/O port addressing instead of memory-mapped addressing. The following subsection, "Programming the 8257," provides more background on these addressing methods.

During a *read* cycle, those contents of a memory location which correspond to the value in the 8257 address register are transferred to the external device. During a *write* cycle, the address register specifies the cell to receive data. The *verify* cycle effectively delays the data transfer, usually giving those external devices which transfer data in blocks more time (possibly to

Table 13-18 Directional Bits

Bit Numbers		8257 Acting as an I/O Port	8257 Acting as a Memory-Mapped Device
15	14		
0	0	Verify cycle	Verify cycle
0	1	Write cycle	Read cycle
1	0	Read cycle	Write cycle
1	1	Not used	Not used

compute a cyclic redundancy check, for example). No data transfer occurs during the verify cycle.

DMA Timing

Figure 13-27 shows the sequence of events that occurs when effecting a DMA data transfer. First, the device raises the DRQ signal to request service. After the priority arbitration logic gives that device highest priority, or if that is the only request, the 8257 sends a true HRQ signal to the MPU. The MPU recognizes the signal as a hold request (HOLD) and responds with hold acknowledge (HLDA); then the 8257 can drop HRQ and set $\overline{DACK}$ true (low), acknowledging the request from the device and giving it access to the data bus.

The address strobe (ADDSTB) output identifies the interval when the high-order address byte is on the data lines in order for the 8212 I/O port to demultiplex it. When the address strobe is high, the high-order byte is routed to bits A8 to A15 of the address bus through the 8212.

The 8257 also provides two other signals that indicate the progress of the data transfer. The terminal count (TC) output becomes high when a byte counter reaches 0. The true TC signal means that the last byte for a given DMA channel is being sent. The MARK output goes true on every 128th byte exchanged. The signal is useful in those floppy disks or tape cassettes which block data in 128- or 256-byte records.

The remainder of the DMA transfer timing diagram is shown in Fig. 13-28. Prior to acknowledging the device, the 8257 has set the proper address on bits A0 to A7 of the address bus and on bits DB0 to DB7 of the data bus. The 8212 latches the latter onto bits A8 to A15 of the address bus. That data remains latched until the next high address strobe. The device receives the $\overline{DACK}$ signal and prepares either to receive or transmit. The data is actually transferred when the appropriate I/O or memory strobe signal goes low.

Programming the 8257

To the programmer, the 8257 appears as either 16 I/O ports or 16 memory locations (listed in Table 13-16).

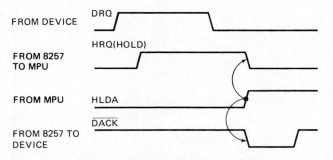

Fig. 13-27 DMA acknowledgment timing diagram.

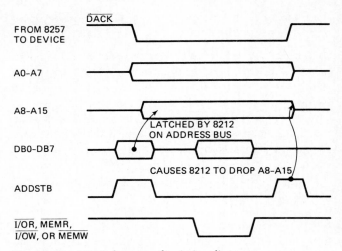

Fig. 13-28 DMA data transfer timing diagram.

Figure 13-29a illustrates the 8257 used as an I/O port. A simple interchange of wires converts the DMA controller to a memory-mapped device, as shown in Fig. 13-29b. The programmer loads the command register with the command for the next DMA operation, after loading the address and byte-count registers. Table 13-19 lists these commands.

☐ **EXAMPLE** An example of programming the 8257 is given here. The 8257 is used as an I/O port in this example. The addresses for the registers are

Address register, channel 0	10_{16}
Byte-count register, channel 0	11_{16}
Command register	18_{16}

MVI	A, 00 ⎫	Send the low byte to the
OUT	10 ⎬	address register, channel 0
MVI	A, 10 ⎫	Send the high byte to the
OUT	10 ⎬	address register, channel 0

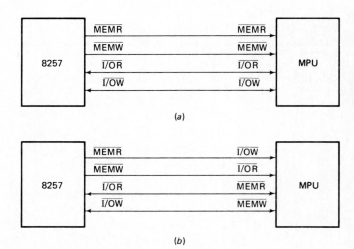

Fig. 13-29 8257 addressing: (a) I/O port, (b) memory mapped.

```
MVI    A, 00 ⎫    Send the low byte to the count
OUT    11    ⎬    register, channel 0
MVI    A, 41 ⎫    Send the high byte to the count
OUT    11    ⎬    register, channel 0
MVI    A, 11 ⎫    Set control register to enable
OUT    18    ⎬    channel 0 round-robin priority
```

The starting address for the transfer will be 1000_{16}. There will be 256_{16} words written. (The byte-count and byte-direction register was set to 4100_{16}, which translates into 100_{16} words to transfer, plus a direction code for the write cycle.) Finally, the bits in the command register are set.

A few features in Table 13-19 require further comment. Bit 5 allows the programmer to choose to extend write pulses. The write pulse can be advanced one clock cycle earlier than normal. This action will give a slow external device more time when sending data to memory.

Setting bit 6 in the command register disables the DMA channel involved when the TC signal goes high. Disabling the channel when the word count is exhausted ensures that the DMA operation stops properly. The channel is reenabled by the processor setting its bit in the command word again. In the autoload option (see the following paragraph), bit 6 does not affect channel 2.

The autoload option is selected with bit 7. The purpose of the autoload is to allow DMA to proceed without reinitiating the address and byte-count registers prior to each record transfer. Autoload works only with DMA channel 2 and requires that channel 3 be reserved as a buffer. The program in the 8085 loads channel 3 with the address, count, and direction for the next channel 2 transfer. When the byte count for channel 2 reaches 0, the register is automatically reloaded with the values from channel 3.

Channel 3		Channel 2
Address register	→	Address register
Byte-count register	→	Byte-count register

The data exchange on channel 2 continues with the new units.

If the address and byte-count registers of channel 2 (instead of channel 3) are loaded in the autoload mode, the information from the channel 2 registers is copied into channel 3. Thereafter, the values of the address and count are refreshed in channel 2 from channel 3.

The condition of the 8257 can be read by executing an input from the same address as the command register (see Table 13-16); the status bits are listed in Table 13-20. If bits 0 through 3 are set, it means that a true terminal-count signal has been issued on that channel. Bit 4 is used with the autoload option. In autoload, the value in the channel 3 registers must not change while the registers are being written into the channel 2 registers. As long as bit 4 is set, the data can be written in channel 3 registers without disturbing the process. Every time the status register is read, all the bits except bit 4 are cleared.

The 8257 DMA Controller Review

1. How many external devices can be connected to the 8257 in normal operations? How many with the autoload option selected?
2. What signals are used by devices to request service? Which signals are used by the 8257 to acknowledge the devices?
3. List the ten 8257 registers. Describe how they are addressed.
4. Distinguish between the fixed and round-robin priority arbitration schemes of the 8257.
5. How does an external device signal that it is using burst mode data transfers?
6. Describe the three transfer direction cycles used by the 8257.
7. Explain the purpose of the HRQ signal in Fig. 13-26.
8. Why is the 8257 permitted to drop the data lines

Table 13-19 Command Register Code Words*

Bit Number	Meaning
0	Set—enable; clear—disable channel 0
1	Set—enable; clear—disable channel 1
2	Set—enable; clear—disable channel 2
3	Set—enable; clear—disable channel 3
4	Clear — fixed priority; set — round-robin priority
5	Clear—normal write pulse; set—extended write pulse
6	Set—for TC disable option
7	Set—autoload option

* Note: The command register is cleared by a system reset.

Table 13-20 8257 Status Registers

Bit Number	Meaning
0	TC status on channel 0
1	TC status on channel 1
2	TC status on channel 2
3	TC status on channel 3
4	Update status
5–7	Not used

representing bits A8 through A15 so early in the timing diagram of Fig. 13-28?

9. How is an 8257 controller addressed as an I/O port distinguished from one addressed by memory-mapped I/O?

10. Why are two outputs necessary to load an address register of the 8257?

11. Explain the result of setting bit 6 in the command register. What happens if bit 7 is also set?

CHAPTER SUMMARY

1. The moving of data between the peripheral devices and the microcomputer is the responsibility of the I/O circuitry and programs. Input and output are always relative to the processor; the computer receives input data and transmits output data.

2. Normally, either accumulator I/O or memory-mapped I/O instructions are used in exchanging information. Accumulator I/O instructions require an I/O port, while memory-mapped commands treat the device as a memory address.

3. Interrupt signals allow the device to request service from the MPU. Direct memory access devices can read or write memory just like the processor can.

4. An I/O port is a buffer between the system buses and the external device. The port is addressed with either the upper or lower eight lines of the address bus. The port address is called its device code.

5. A family of support chips simplifies the task of interfacing the MPU to external equipment. If those devices are not used, low-power Schottky TTL integrated circuits are recommended for use in the interface logic.

6. Fully decoded address selection interprets every bit of the address or device code. Linear selection decodes only a few bits.

7. The 8095 three-state buffer is frequently used on input and output lines. The buffer is enabled by a device selection strobe from the address decoder logic and by an input strobe from the computer.

8. The 8212 I/O port consists of eight D flip-flops used to latch data. Its output is compatible with the three-state system data bus.

9. Devices are addressed as memory locations in a memory-mapped I/O architecture. Memory transfer instructions are used to move data between the processors and the external equipment.

10. The microcomputer can use single, multiple, or vectored interrupts. The 8085 has special instructions in its repertoire to support vectored-interrupt processing, and it has other instructions to control interrupts. A summary of the I/O instructions is provided in Tables 13-21 and 13-22.

Table 13-21   8085 I/O Instructions*

Instruction	Operation Code	Number of Bytes
DI	F3	1
EI	FB	1
IN	DB	2
OUT	D3	2
RST 0	C7	1
RST 1	CF	1
RST 2	D7	1
RST 3	DF	1
RST 4	E7	1
RST 5	EF	1
RST 6	F7	1
RST 7	FF	1

* Status bits are not affected by these instructions.

11. The interrupt device supplies the starting address of the servicing routine in an RST instruction. The processor enters the interrupt state by clearing the interrupt enable flip-flop, taking the next instruction from the data lines, and pushing the program counter on the stack. The servicing routine must reenable interrupts and exit with a return instruction to pop the stack and load the program counter with the address of the instruction following the interrupted one.

12. The external device can respond to an interrupt acknowledgment from the processor by supplying either an RST or CALL instruction.

13. The halt state can be terminated with an interrupt.

14. The 8259 priority interrupt control unit can coordinate up to eight external interrupts. In a master-slave system, even more interrupts can be handled. The 8259 provides arbitration of simultaneous interrupts. The 8259 is initialized and controlled by the microcomputer program.

15. A peripheral can bypass the processor in accessing memory by using direct memory access. The hold state is employed when DMA is used.

16. The 8257 DMA controller can provide four channels for direct memory access. The 8257 modes are selected by the program in the MPU.

Table 13-22   6800 Interrupt Control Instructions

Instruction	Operation Code	Number of Bytes
CLI	0E	1
RTI	3B	1
SEI	0F	1
SWI	3F	1
WAI	3E	1

KEY TERMS AND CONCEPTS

Input/output (I/O)

Peripheral equipment

Accumulator I/O

Memory-mapped I/O

I/O port

Interrupt signals

Direct memory access (DMA)

Device code (DC)

Interfacing

Buffered signals

Fully decoded address selection

Linear selection

8095 buffer

Data jamming

8212 I/O port

Handshaking

Single interrupt

Poll

Multiple interrupt

Vectored interrupt

Interrupt-servicing routine

Halt state

8259 priority interrupt control unit (PICU)

Interrupt priority arbitration

Fully nested mode

Rotating priorities

Polled mode

Mask modes

8257 DMA controller

Fixed priority mode

Round-robin mode

Byte-by-byte transfer

Burst transfer

P R O B L E M S

13-1 A 128-byte block of data is stored in sequential addresses beginning at 1200_{16}. Write a routine to transfer this data to a floppy disk on I/O port 27_{16}. (A loop will be required.)

13-2 How many 74LS00 quad NAND gate ICs can be safely connected to an MPU output?

13-3 If the 74LS30 NAND gate in Fig. 13-3 is to be used to fully decode the device address $D7_{16}$, which inputs require inverters?

13-4 Draw a diagram, similar to Fig. 13-4b, showing how two 8095 buffers can be used for output on the data bus.

13-5 Write a routine to receive a 256-word record from a memory-mapped cassette recorder. The device address is 8237_{16} and data is to be stored beginning at address 0210_{16}.

13-6 The recorder in Prob. 13-5 sends an interrupt whenever a CRC error is detected in the data being sent to the processor. An RST 3 instruction is provided by the device. Write an interrupt-handling routine that will process the interrupt by executing the program of Prob. 13-5 again. Be sure also to reenable interrupts and to take care of other normal interrupt-servicing tasks.

13-7 An 8259 master-slave system consists of two slaves attached to IR6 and IR7 of the master. Devices 0 through 5 are attached to the master, 6 through 13

on the IR6 slave, and 14 through 21 on the IR7 slave. Prepare a table, similar to Table 13-13, with the proper output data to:

1. Initialize the master. Use four words between vector addresses, and use a base address of 4300_{16} for the master.
2. Initialize each slave. The base address for the slave on IR6 is 5100_{16}, and for the slave on IR7 is 5900_{16}.
3. Start rotating priority mode B.
4. Allow interrupts from devices 4 and 5 to interrupt any other service request.
5. Return to the fully nested mode.
6. Cancel the mask of step 4.
7. Start the polling mode.

13-8 There is a simple mask of 51_{16} active in the 8259. Rotating priority mode B is in effect and the current order of priority is

Lowest   Highest

IR5   IR4   IR3   IR2   IR1   IR0   IR7   IR6

The processor issues an OCW2 of $E3_{16}$. When the devices on IR lines 4 and 7 simultaneously request interrupts, which will be serviced first?

13-9 The address for the 8257 channel 2 address register is 50_{16}. Write a program to input 128_{10} words from the floppy disk by DMA transfer. The starting address for storing the data is 0500_{16}. The fixed priority with extended write pulses and the TC disable option are to be selected.

13-10 The CRT terminal is receiving DMA data in the burst mode controlled by channel 1 of the 8257. The floppy disk uses channel 0, also in burst mode. Round-robin priority and the autoload option have been selected. After initialization, the following DMA transfers have occurred:

1. Terminal—read 200_{10} words
2. Floppy disk—verify cycle
3. Floppy disk—read 126_{10} words
4. Terminal—read 350_{10} words

Until this time, no conflicts have occurred, but now the terminal and disk simultaneously request a DMA transfer. The disk wants to write 256_{10} words and the terminal to read 100_{10} words. (a) Which one gets first access to the bus? (b) How many words are transferred? (c) Answer the same questions with the fixed priority mode selected.

CHAPTER 14

SERIAL INPUT/OUTPUT

For some applications, the parallel input/output I/O techniques explained in the previous chapter are not suitable. In those cases, serial data transfer may be more useful. Serial communications are frequently employed when there are long distances between the transmitter and receiver. The most common example of serial data exchange is digital communications by means of telephone lines. Widely separated computers can pass data back and forth in almost no time by using the telephone network. Another example of serial communications is peripheral equipment that can only process data 1 bit at a time. Such devices as printers, CRT terminals, and cassette recorders may be limited to serial data exchange.

CHAPTER OBJECTIVES

Upon completion of this chapter, you should be able to:

1. Draw a simple block diagram of a telecommunications system.
2. Describe the operating principles of serial data receivers-transmitters.
3. Explain how serial bit boundaries are delineated by clock pulses.
4. Distinguish between synchronous and asynchronous serial I/O protocols.
5. List the control signals used with standard modems.
6. Describe the operation of typical synchronous and asynchronous receivers-transmitters.

SERIAL DATA EXCHANGE

The problem confronting us in dealing with serial data transfer from an 8-bit microprocessor is essentially one of *parallel-to-serial conversion:* converting parallel data to serial. As Fig. 14-1 shows, data can be converted by a series of shift register operations. By left-shifting an 8-bit register, a serial bit stream is produced from a parallel word (Fig. 14-1*a*). The most significant bit is made available for transmission first, followed by bit 6, and so on. To assemble a parallel data word from a serial bit stream (*serial-to-parallel conversion*), the process is simple reversed, as Fig. 14-1*b* illustrates.

A serial peripheral is shown in Fig. 14-2. Here, a serial-to-parallel converter is used to change the bit stream from the device into 8-bit words for the computer. For two-way communications, a parallel-to-serial converter is needed for data moving in the other direction.

If the data is to be transmitted by telephone, a device that can convert numerical values to sound must be used, because 1s and 0s cannot be placed directly on the lines. A modem (modulator-demodulator) performs this function. The transmitted bit stream is changed to an audio signal that represents the binary pattern. On the receiving end, the modem changes the audio back to binary digits. Figure 14-3 is a block diagram of a one-way serial communications network. For both units to send or receive data, additional converters must be added. If the system is *half-duplex,* then one station transmits while the other receives. A *full-duplex* system permits simultaneous transmission and reception by both computers.

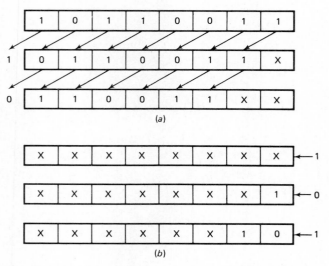

Fig. 14-1 Parallel/serial conversion: (*a*) parallel-to-serial conversion by shifting, (*b*) serial-to-parallel conversion by shifting.

Fig. 14-2 Serial peripheral.

Serial Data Representation

Serial data is transmitted as a series of pulses that are held at either a high or low voltage level for the proper time interval. The pulses must be synchronized with a series of clock pulses to indicate the bit boundaries. Figure 14-4*a* shows how the number 62_{16} would be transmitted in serial format. Here, the data is stable on the trailing edge of the clock. Some communications systems require that the transitions between the 1 and the 0 levels be correct on the leading edge of the clock. Of course, the clock in the transmitter and receiver must use the same frequency (or some multiple of the same frequency).

Many times an additional time period is allowed for the signal settling. This delay is used for the signal to assume its new value before it is sampled. These extra time intervals are called *settling delays,* or *guard times.* Figure 14-4*b* shows how these delays affect transmission and Fig. 14-4*c* shows the impact on reception. Note that attempting to read the data during the settling interval could result in obtaining an erroneous value.

Serial Receiver-Transmitter

There are many integrated circuits available to assist with the exchange of serial information. Later in this chapter, we will look into one such device. At this time, let us consider a somewhat simplified receiver-transmitter to see what functions it must perform. Figure 14-5 shows such a device. Parallel data from the processor is held in a register until it can move into the transmit buffer, which contains the information until it has been shifted onto the serial output line. *Double buffering* with two buffers is used so that the processor can forward word *n* + 1 as word *n* is being transmitted, thus providing a faster data throughput rate.

Serial data being received is shifted into the receive

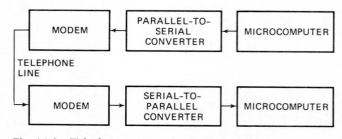

Fig. 14-3 Telephone communications network.

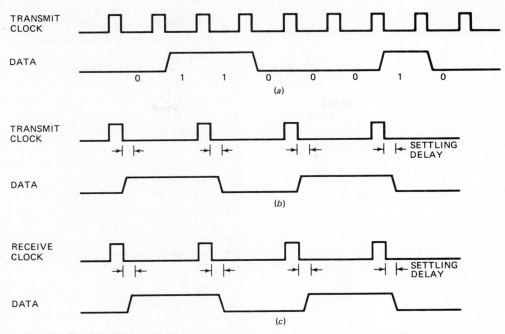

Fig. 14-4 Serial data timing: (*a*) serial data transmission, (*b*) transmission settling delay, (*c*) reception settling delay.

buffer. After this buffer is filled with 8 bits, the parallel word is passed to the receive holding buffer. Double buffering again permits a faster data rate to be maintained. The data then moves to the data register and into the processor.

Control is exercised by means of coded orders sent to the receiver-transmitter. Under program control, the device can be enabled or disabled, change modes, or report status. In the latter case, the status condition codes are forwarded on their unique line to the processor.

Baud Rate

The data rate of a serial channel is equal to the number of characters sent in 1 second (s). For a binary serial channel, the *baud rate* is the same as the number of bits per second (bps) sent. Common baud rates are 300, 1200, 4800, and 9600.

As you may have deduced, the transmit and receive *clock rates* are related to the baud rate. Figure 14-6*a* shows an example of a clock that has the same frequency as the baud rate. Data transitions take place on

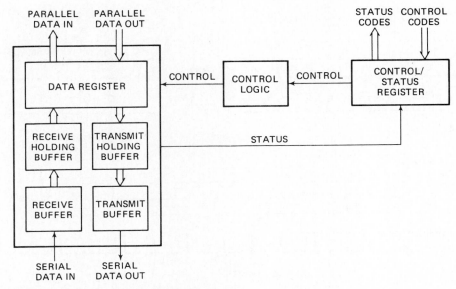

Fig. 14-5 Serial receiver/transmitter.

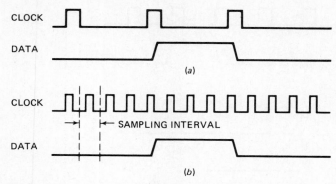

Fig. 14-6 Clock rates: (a) ×1 clock signal, (b) ×4 clock signal.

each clock pulse. This clock is referred to as a ×1 clock signal. A ×4 clock signal is shown in Fig. 14-6b. Now there are four clock pulses for every bit transition. The faster clock rate makes it easier to sample the center portion of the data signal when the voltage level would be most stable. Clock rates of ×16 and ×64 are also frequently encountered.

Synchronization

The clocks in the sending and receiving devices may be running at the same frequency, but out of *synchronization*. Figure 14-7 shows the result of this problem. The receiver only sees the data stream; the transmitter clock is not sent over the channel. If there is a *clock skew* (that is, if the receiver clock is offset, or skewed, in time), it may cause data to be read too early or too late (Fig. 14-7a), as in receive clock pulse 3, which reads too soon. The receiver interprets the data as a 0 when, in fact, a 1 was transmitted during transmit clock pulse 3. This mistake is called a *framing error*.

A special *sync signal* can be sent prior to the start of data, as Fig. 14-7b shows. Until the data was to be sent, the transmitter held the data line high. The high signal is called a *mark*, so the time until data starts is referred to as *marking*. Just before the start of data, the signal goes low for half the width of a normal bit period. If the receiver aligns the trailing edge of its clock with the sync signal, it will be properly phased to read the serial data.

Another synchronization method uses a special *sync character* or pattern. This character would never appear in a normal data stream. The receiver moves a "frame" along the incoming bit sequence until it can recognize the sync character. Figure 14-7c shows the use of a sync pattern. During the "search for sync," the time interval represented by the frame is, in effect, moved earlier or later.

When a ×16 or ×64 clock is used by the receiver, synchronization is not as critical. Even if the receive clock is off a cycle or two from the transmit clock, the skewing is usually not serious enough to miss the center section of the data pulse.

Serial Data Exchange Review

1. Describe the operation of a serial-to-parallel converter.
2. Define the term "modem."
3. Distinguish between half-duplex and full-duplex modes of serial communications.
4. How does a clock transition indicate the bit boundaries of serial data?
5. Why is a settling delay sometimes provided in serial data communications?

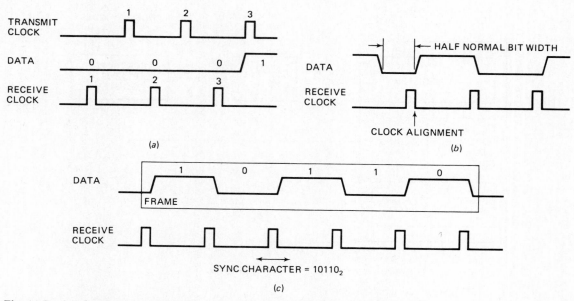

Fig. 14-7 Synchronization: (a) out of sync, (b) sync signal, (c) sync character or pattern.

6. Explain the reason for two transmit and two receive buffers in a receiver-transmitter.
7. What is the baud rate of a serial binary telephone system that sends 1200 bps?
8. What is the advantage of running the receive clock at a higher frequency than the baud rate?
9. Name two methods of synchronization.
10. What does the term "marking" mean?

SYNCHRONOUS SERIAL PROTOCOL

There are several common rules, or *communication protocols,* in use for serial communications. One of these is the *synchronous serial protocol,* which consists of having the transmitter supply data on every clock pulse. Synchronous serial transmission is most often used at data rates above 2000 baud.

Figure 14-8 shows how the receive clock is synchronized with the data. Even when no useful data is being sent over the channel, the transmitter must send data. In such cases the transmitter sends one or more sync characters. The sync character is also used to delineate word boundaries, as shown in the example below (16_{16} is used as the sync character), which uses two sync characters:

|1110 0000||0001 0110||0001 0110||1110 1111|

Word 1   Sync   Sync   Word 2
                character 1   character 2

Synchronous serial receivers normally use a $\times 1$ clock. The clock rate is simply the reciprocal of the baud rate. For example, if the baud rate is 2400, the clock period would be 416.7 µs.

Although the word length shown above (and the word length of most microprocessors) is 8 bits, synchronous serial communications can use any length from 5- to 8-bit words. In addition, a parity bit is frequently appended to the word.

Handshaking

To this point, the discussion has avoided the initialization of communications. Among the unanswered questions are: How does the transmitter tell the receiver to get ready? What if the receiver is turned off? How are errors handled?

In answering these and other questions, we will look at some of the features of a synchronous telephone protocol. Before data is sent, the transmitter and receiver exchange several control characters, an exchange termed *handshaking.* These characters establish the link. Table 14-1 lists a typical message sequence; ASCII control characters are used in this example.

First, the transmitter asks if the receiver is ready (ENQ character). The receiver replies and transmission begins. The *header* consists of the start-of-text character; then the data block is sent. An end-of-block character is followed by two cyclic redundancy check (CRC) codes. The receiver acknowledges receipt of either an even or an odd number of data blocks; for example, the first data block is odd, the second even, and so on. The process repeats until all data is sent. The end-of-transmission character completes the transfer.

Synchronous Serial Protocol Review

1. What is another word with the same meaning as "protocol"?
2. True or false? One would expect a synchronous serial protocol to be used in a 4800-baud communications link.
3. True or false? A $\times 16$ receiver clock is most often used with synchronous serial data transmission.
4. How are words delineated under the synchronous serial protocol?
5. How many bits can be sent in each synchronous serial word (excluding the parity bit)?
6. Define the term "handshaking."

ASYNCHRONOUS SERIAL PROTOCOL

The timing method of *asynchronous serial protocol* allows the transmitter to send only when there is data to transmit; in contrast to synchronous protocols, there is no need to send sync characters to fill periods when no data is ready to send. Asynchronous timing is most often used below 1800 baud. Because every data unit must be indicated by a synchronization indicator, asynchronous data transmission is less efficient than synchronous data transmission.

When the transmitter is not sending data, the data line is set to a mark. When a word is to be transmitted, it is always preceded by a *start bit* (a 0) and terminated by 1, 1½, or 2 *stop bits* (always 1s). The word can range in length from 5 to 8 bits, and a parity bit can be appended.

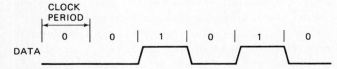

Fig. 14-8 Synchronous serial data.

Table 14-1 Handshaking Protocol With a Telephone

Source	ASCII Control Character	Meaning
Transmitter	ENQ	Are you ready to receive?
Receiver	DC0	Yes (receiver must have been set up in advance).
Transmitter	STX	Start of text.
	Data block	
	ETB	End of block.
	CRC	Cyclic redundancy
	CRC	check sent twice.
Receiver		Receiver has checked data with CRC. No errors have been detected.
		and
	DC1	An even number of data blocks has been received so far.
		or
	DC0	An odd number of data blocks has been received so far.
Transmitter	STX	
	Data block	
	ETB	Repeat until all data has been sent.
	CRC	
	CRC	
Transmitter	EOT	End of transmission.

For example, a standard teletype (TTY) serial character would be transmitted as

0 | X X X X X X X | P | 1 1 |

↑ Start bit   7 Data bits   ↑ Parity bit   Two stop bits

Each TTY character then consists of 11 bits. At the standard rate of 10 char/s, the TTY asynchronous serial data rate is 110 baud.

A reference was made above to 1½ stop bits. How can 1½ bits be represented? Remember that a bit in a serial data stream simply means that the signal is held constant for a certain time interval. To generate 1½ stop bits, the 1 level is just held for 1½ times the normal interval.

Because sync characters are not used in asynchronous timing, there is no framing to be done. Eliminating the framing operation also makes it impossible to encounter a framing error, although other types of errors may occur.

Asynchronous Serial Protocol Review

1. What signal is sent by an asynchronous serial transmitter when it has no data to send?

2. What bits precede a word in this type of timing? What bits follow the word?

3. Why is the standard TTY data rate 110 baud?

4. How can 1½ stop bits be transmitted?

5. True or false? Framing errors never occur when asynchronous data exchange is used.

MODEM CONTROL SIGNALS

A set of signals to initiate data communications between modems has been established. By use of four discrete control lines, a modem can establish that the I/O device, called a *data terminal,* is ready to communicate. Table 14-2 tabulates a typical signal sequence for data terminal transmission. Note that in the standard terminology a modem is called a *data set.*

First, both devices signal that they are ready with low $\overline{DTR}$ and $\overline{DSR}$ lines. When the data terminal has composed the message, it lowers $\overline{RTS}$. After the modem responds with $\overline{CTS}$ true, the exchange begins.

If the modem is the transmitter and the data terminal the receiver, the order of $\overline{DTR}$ and $\overline{DSR}$ is reversed. The modem makes $\overline{RTS}$ true, and the data terminal responds with $\overline{CTS}$.

Table 14-2 Control Signals

Step	Signal	Level	Set By	Meaning
1	$\overline{\text{DTR}}$	Low	Data terminal	Data terminal ready
2	$\overline{\text{DSR}}$	Low	Modem	Data set (modem) ready to receive. Transmission cannot begin until this signal goes low.
3	—	—	—	Text is prepared.
4	$\overline{\text{RTS}}$	Low	Data terminal	Request to send. The data terminal is ready to send to the modem. ($\overline{\text{DSR}}$ and $\overline{\text{DTR}}$ must remain low.)
5	$\overline{\text{CTS}}$	Low	Modem	Clear to send. The modem lowers this signal 2 μs after receipt of $\overline{\text{RST}}$, if ready to receive.
6	—	—	Data terminal	Data is transmitted.

Modem Control Signals Review

1. What is the purpose of the $\overline{\text{DTR}}$ signal?
2. True or false? Upon receipt or an $\overline{\text{RTS}}$ true signal, the receiving unit sets $\overline{\text{CTS}}$ high to indicate that the data can be sent.
3. What is another name for a data set?
4. Name the two other signals that must remain low as long as $\overline{\text{RTS}}$ is low.
5. List the sequence of the standard modem signals for a situation in which the data set transmits.

THE SYNCHRONOUS RECEIVER-TRANSMITTER

There are two basic types of synchronous data transmission. The *character-oriented synchronous data* method is organized to exchange complete character codes. The IBM Bisync protocol is an example of character-oriented synchronous I/O. Table 14-1 gave an example of this communication protocol. Another means of synchronous I/O consists of *bit-oriented synchronous data* protocols, such as SDLC and HDLC (see discussion below). The receiver-transmitters covered in this chapter use bit-oriented synchronous I/O.

SDLC and HDLC Protocols

Before investigating the actual ICs, we will first examine one family of widely used bit synchronous communication protocols. The *synchronous data-link control (SDLC)* protocol is used in networks with a single primary and multiple secondary stations. (The quite similar HDLC protocol is often used in retail store systems.)

Figure 14-9 shows SDLC and HDLC multipoint and point-to-point networks.

The *high-level data-link control (HDLC)* is a standard protocol established by the International Organi-

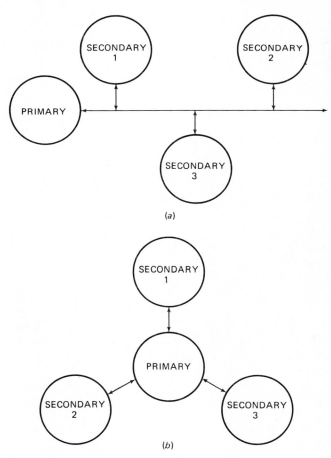

Fig. 14-9 SDLC and HDLC networks: (*a*) multipoint, (*b*) point-to-point.

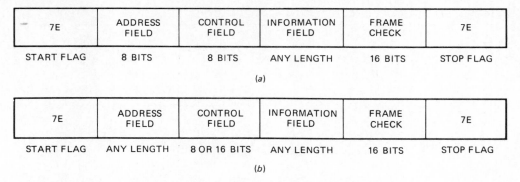

7E	ADDRESS FIELD	CONTROL FIELD	INFORMATION FIELD	FRAME CHECK	7E
START FLAG	8 BITS	8 BITS	ANY LENGTH	16 BITS	STOP FLAG

(a)

7E	ADDRESS FIELD	CONTROL FIELD	INFORMATION FIELD	FRAME CHECK	7E
START FLAG	ANY LENGTH	8 OR 16 BITS	ANY LENGTH	16 BITS	STOP FLAG

(b)

Fig. 14-10 SDLC and HDLC frames: (a) SDLC frame, (b) HDLC frame.

zation for Standardization (ISO). The ISO X.25 packet switching system is implemented by means of the HDLC discipline. SDLC is an IBM protocol used in system network architecture (SNA) communications.

Communication is permitted only between the primary and a secondary station; two secondary stations cannot talk directly to each other. An address field in every message identifies the secondary to receive it or the secondary that sent it. An acknowledgment for messages received correctly is periodically sent by the receiving station.

All messages are formatted into frames, as Fig. 14-10 shows. The first field in any frame is a start flag of $7E_{16}$. The address field identifies the sending or receiving station. The SDLC address field is always 8 bits long, but the HDLC address can be any length. The receiver can determine the length by examining the first bit in each byte of the address. If the first bit is 0, then another address byte follows. If the bit is 1, then the current address byte is the last.

The SDLC control field is always 8 bits. Either 8- or 16-bit control fields are used in HDLC. If the first bit of the field is 0, the field is 16 bits in length. A first-bit value of 1 signals an 8-bit field.

The information field can consist of a bit stream of any length. No breaks in the information field are allowed. If the transmitter does not receive a continual data stream, it will abort the message. (The abort signal is FF_{16} for SDLC and $7F_{16}$ for HDLC.) Control characters can be embedded in the data. For these protocols, control characters are six or more consecutive 1s. To prevent data from looking like control characters, the transmitter automatically inserts a 0 following five consecutive 1s in the data stream (*zero bit insertion*). The receiver automatically strips them off.

The frame-check character is a means of error detection. The character is calculated using the bit pattern of the address, control, and information fields. The frame is terminated by a stop flag of $7E_{16}$. All fields are transmitted least significant bit first, although the user need not be concerned with this requirement. The synchronous I/O device takes care of it in the serial-to-parallel

and parallel-to-serial conversions. Between frames, an idle pattern is transmitted. The idle pattern is a continuous high level on the data line.

The signal conventions to indicate the binary values may use either *nonreturn to zero (NRZ)* or *nonreturn to zero, inverted (NRZI)*. With NRZ, a high level is interpreted as a 1, and a low level as 0. A transition between the high and low levels (in either direction) represents a 0 in NRZI, and no transition a 1. Figure 14-11 illustrates the two conventions.

The Synchronous Receiver-Transmitter Review

1. Name two methods of synchronous data transmission.
2. Distinguish between SDLC and HDLC protocols.
3. True or false? The SDLC protocol permits direct communication between secondary stations.
4. List the fields in an SDLC frame.
5. How would the HDLC receiver be able to tell that the control field is 16 bits long?
6. How does the NRZ convention differ from NRZI?

THE 8251 UNIVERSAL SYNCHRONOUS-ASYNCHRONOUS RECEIVER-TRANSMITTER

The 8251 is a typical synchronous and asynchronous communications interface integrated circuit. The device communicates by using standard synchronous and asyn-

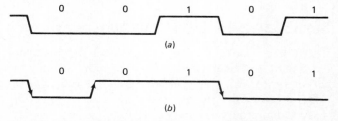

Fig. 14-11 NRZ and NRZI logic: (a) NRZ, (b) NRZI.

chronous protocols. Both half- and full-duplex modes are supported. The device can handle just about every technique used for serial data transmission, including IBM Bisync protocol. The universal synchronous-asynchronous receiver-transmitter (USART) informs the MPU when it is ready to send a character and when a character has been received. The status of the device is always available for the MPU to read.

The characteristics of the 8251 are summarized in Table 14-3. The IC can process data at rates from dc to 64 kHz. Almost any microprocessor can interface to the 8251. As part of its operation, serial data is converted to parallel data and vice versa. Because the 8251 is double-buffered, the load on the processors and the program is reduced.

All the signals for the 8251 are TTL-compatible. The pin configuration for the 28-pin DIP is shown in Fig. 14-12. The use of each of the pins is described in Table 14-4. By means of the data bus buffer, the 8251 interfaces to the 8-bit system data bus. The 8251 is totally under software control. All the options for the communications protocol, as well as the decision to use the synchronous or asynchonous mode, are selected by programming.

Several of the pins serve the purpose of controlling the 8251 communications process. The RESET signal places the 8251 in an idle mode when high. The CLK input generates all timing signals. Usually this signal is supplied by the TTL output of the clock generator. A low on the $\overline{WR}$ line tells the device that the MPU is sending data or control words. Similarly, the $\overline{RD}$ low signal informs the USART that the MPU is reading data or status information. The $\overline{CD}$ input tells the 8251 if the read or write operation involves data (low input) or control and status information (high input). When the 8251 is to perform any operation, it must first be enabled with a low input on the $\overline{CS}$ line.

The USART provides a family of modem control signals. The $\overline{DSR}$ input tests whether the modem is available for data transfer or not. The corresponding $\overline{DTR}$ output lets the modem know when the 8251 is ready to start communicating. The $\overline{RTS}$ output is set low to signal that the 8251 has data to transmit to the

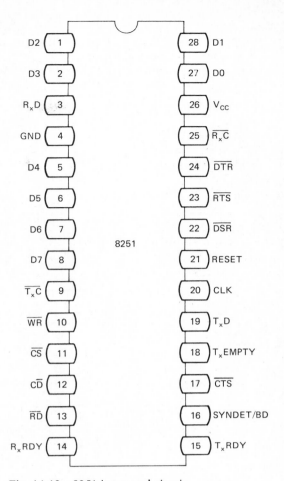

Fig. 14-12 8251 integrated circuit.

Table 14-3 Summary of 8251 Characteristics

Bits per character	5, 6, 7, or 8
Errors detected	Parity, framing, overrun
Synchronous operations:	
Number of sync characters	1 or 2
Baud rate	dc to 64 kHz
Asynchronous operations:	
Clock rate	×1, ×16, or ×64
Stop bits	1, 1½, or 2

Table 14-4 8251 Signals

Signal	Use
DO–D7	Data bus
R_xD	Receive data
$\overline{T_xC}$	Transmitter clock
$\overline{WR}$	Write
$\overline{CS}$	Chip select
$\overline{CD}$	Control/data
$\overline{RD}$	Read
R_xRDY	Receiver ready
$\overline{R_xC}$	Receiver clock
$\overline{DTR}$	Data terminal ready
$\overline{RTS}$	Ready to send
$\overline{DSR}$	Data set ready
RESET	Reset
CLK	Clock
T_xD	Transmit data
T_xEMPTY	Transmitter empty
$\overline{CTS}$	Clear to send
SYNDET/BD	Sync detect/break detect
T_xRDY	Transmitter ready
V_{cc}, GND	Power

modem. The modem provides the $\overline{\text{CTS}}$ input to enable the 8251 transmission of data.

The transmitter section of the 8251 performs the conversion of data received from the processor over the data bus into a serial bit stream. Control of the transmitter section is exercised by another set of signal lines. The T_xRDY output tells the MPU that the USART is ready to accept output data. If the 8251 has completed all transmission, the T_xEMPTY line goes high. In the half-duplex mode, the line can signal the completion of a transmission and alert the processor to prepare to receive. The $\overline{T_x C}$ controls how fast the data is sent; for synchronous transmissions, the baud rate equals this frequency. In the asynchronous mode, the baud rate is a fraction (1, 1/16, or 1/64) of the $\overline{T_x C}$ frequency. Consider the case when the baud rate is 1200 Hz; the value of $\overline{T_x C}$ is:

1200 Hz for ×1
75 Hz for ×16
18.75 Hz for ×64

The receiver section sets the R_xRDY signal high when it has a character to send to the processor. If the processor does not read the data before the next character is sent to the USART, an overrun error will occur and the first character will be lost. The $\overline{R_x C}$ controls the rate of characters being received. In the synchronous mode the baud rate is equal to this frequency. For the asynchronous case, the baud rate is a multiple (×1, ×16, or ×64) of this rate. For a case when the baud

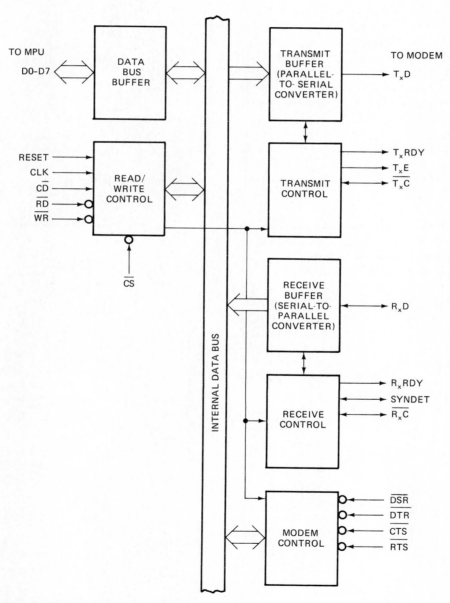

Fig. 14-13 8251 functional diagram.

rate is 75 Hz, the value of $\overline{R_xC}$ is:

75 Hz for $\times 1$
1200 Hz for $\times 16$
4800 Hz for $\times 64$

The SYNDET pin is used only in the synchronous mode. When a sync character is detected, this output will switch to the high level. For the case when the 8251 is programmed for Bisync operations, the signal goes high on the last bit of the second sync character being detected. The line is reset by the RESET signal or upon the status being read. Alternatively, this pin can serve as an input in the external sync detection case. The 8251 begins to build the data word when this signal goes high and the $\overline{R_xC}$ signal transitions to the high level.

The BREAK output is set high when the receiver remains low for two consecutive stop bit sequences (that is, start bits, data, parity, and stop bits). The status can also be detected by reading the device status. A block diagram of the 8251 is shown in Fig. 14-13, which groups all these signals by function.

The key to controlling the 8251 is its programming sequence. Under software control, the synchronous or asynchronous mode and the parity, character-length, and stop bits can all be specified. After the programming

is complete, the 8251 signals the processor that communications can begin by raising the T_xRDY line. Transmission will not start, however, until both the T_x Enable bit command is set by the MPU and the $\overline{CTS}$ input line is set low by the modem. The R_xRDY line also will go high upon receipt of the first character from the modem.

The control instructions to the 8251 establish the mode of operations and the commands to be executed. The mode instruction format is shown in Figs. 14-14 and 14-15. Understanding the 8251 is easiest if we consider it to operate differently (and hence to require different programming) in each mode.

For asynchronous communications, the baud rate, character length, parity, and number of stop bits must be programmed. Referring to Fig. 14-14, we see for example that a mode instruction of $9D_{16}$ will result in:

1½ stop bits (code = 10)
Odd parity (0)
Parity enabled (1)
8-bit character length (11)
$\times 1$ baud-rate factor (01)

The 8251 adds the start bit, parity bit, and proper number of stop bits to the data word sent by the processor. The character is transmitted at the selected baud rate.

The mode instruction for the synchronous mode is shown in Fig. 14-15. With this instruction, the character length, parity, sync detect, and sync character are se-

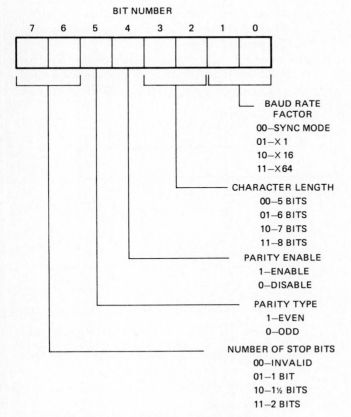

Fig. 14-14 Mode instruction format (asynchronous).

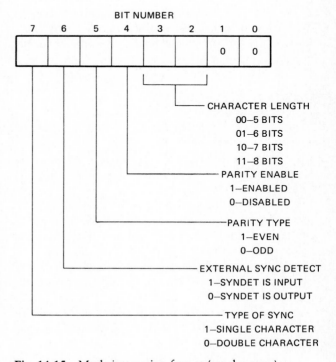

Fig. 14-15 Mode instruction format (synchronous).

lected. For example, a mode instruction of $9C_{16}$ means:

Single sync character (code = 1)
SYNDET is an output (0)
Odd parity (0)
Parity enabled (1)
8-bit character length (11)

After the programming is complete, the T_xD output is set high to request the first character from the MPU. Usually this is the sync character. Once the $\overline{CTS}$ has come from the modem and the transmission has begun, the 8251 must send a continuous data stream. If the MPU does not supply a character, the sync character will be automatically inserted. If sync is ever lost, the processor can command the 8251 to hunt for sync during the time it is receiving.

The command instruction (shown in Fig. 14-16) enables transmission or reception of data, controls modem signals, resets after an error, and orders the 8251 to hunt for sync in the synchronous mode. The status of the 8251 can be determined from the status word, as shown in Fig. 14-17. The status code indicates such errors as parity, overrun, and framing. From the status the processor can also tell when the modem has set the $\overline{DSR}$ signal.

The 8251 USART Review

1. How many power supply voltages does the 8251 require?
2. What is the purpose of the modem control lines?
3. How does the baud rate affect the transmitter clock?
4. What does a high T_xE signal mean?
5. How is the type of parity the 8251 uses controlled?

CHAPTER SUMMARY

1. Data can be converted between serial and parallel forms by means of a shift register.
2. A modem is used to change binary values to an audio signal for transmission. When receiving, the modem reverses the process.
3. Half-duplex communications systems allow one station to transmit and the other to receive at any time. Full duplex provides simultaneous transmission and reception.
4. Serial data is a stream of pulses held at high or low levels for the proper time interval. The pulses are synchronized with a clock.
5. Settling delay periods are allowed in order to ensure that the signal reaches a steady state after transitions.

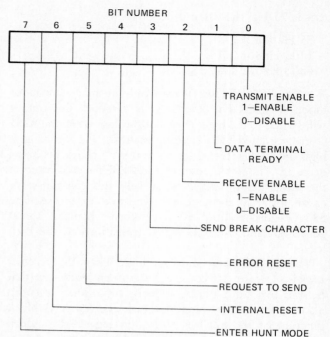

Note: Any bit set to 1 enables the condition

Fig. 14-16 Command instruction format.

6. A serial receiver-transmitter accepts parallel data from the processor and buffers it onto the serial output line. As data comes in on the serial line, it is converted to parallel, then passed to the microprocessor. All modes of the device can be controlled by the program.
7. The baud rate equals the number of bits sent per second in a serial channel. Both the transmitter and receiver clocks must be a multiple of the baud rate.

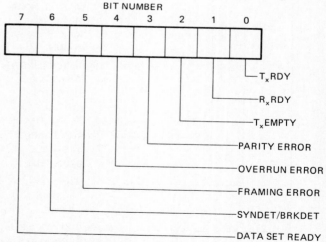

Note: Any bit set to 1 indicates that the status is true

Fig. 14-17 Status word.

8. The receiver must synchronize its clock with the transmitter. If the clocks are badly skewed, a framing error will result. Sync signals are used by the receiver to locate the correct time for clock transitions. Alternatively, sync characters may be used to identify frame boundaries.

9. Synchronous serial transmission is best-suited for faster data rates; asynchronous serial transmission is used in slower communications.

10. In a synchronous system, data is always transmitted. When no useful information is available, the transmitter sends sync characters. Word lengths in these systems can be 5 to 8 bits.

11. Handshaking between stations is required before communications can begin. Control characters exchanged between the transmitter and receiver are employed to initialize the devices.

12. The asynchronous protocol requires the transmitter to send only when there is information furnished by the microcomputer. No sync characters are used. Words are bracketed by start and stop bits.

13. Modem control signals have been established. These signals allow the devices to initiate data exchanges in either direction.

14. Synchronous communications can be either character- or bit-oriented. Among the most popular bit-oriented protocols are SDLC and HDLC.

15. NRZ and NRZI conventions are used in SDLC and HDLC protocols.

16. Integrated-circuit synchronous and asynchronous receiver-transmitters that perform all communications functions are readily available.

KEY TERMS AND CONCEPTS

Parallel-to-serial conversion

Serial-to-parallel conversion

Modem

Half-duplex system

Full-duplex system

Settling delays

Guard times

Double buffering

Baud rate

Clock rates

Synchronization

Clock skew

Framing error

Sync signal

Mark

Sync character

Communication protocols

Synchronous serial protocol

Handshaking

Asynchronous serial protocol

Start bit

Stop bits

Data terminal

Data set

Character-oriented synchronous data

Bit-oriented synchronous data

Synchronous data-link control (SDLC)

High-level data-link control (HDLC)

Zero bit insertion

Nonreturn to zero (NRZ)

Nonreturn to zero, inverted (NRZI)

Universal synchronous-asynchronous receiver-transmitter (USART)

PROBLEMS

14-1 Draw the corresponding NRZ and NRZI waveforms to transmit the number 74_{16}. (Remember that the least significant bit is transmitted first.)

14-2 Show the parallel-to-serial conversion of the first 3 bits of $B7_{16}$. (Refer to Fig. 14-1.)

14-3 In an analogous manner to Prob. 14-2, show the serial-to-parallel conversion of the first 3 bits in the bit stream 0101 1101.

14-4 Draw a serial data waveform representing the data stream $6E_{16}$ sent with a $\times 1$ clock; with a $\times 4$ clock.

14-5 How would the serial data in the following words be transmitted if two sync characters were used to delineate word boundaries? Word 1: 03_{16}; word 2: $C2_{16}$.

14-6 A synchronous serial receiver has a baud rate of 4800. What is its clock frequency?

14-7 An asynchronous serial transmitter sends characters of 8 data bits. Parity and 2 stop bits are used in the system. If 100 characters are sent per second, what is the baud rate?

14-8 Show the format for an SDLC frame if the fields are as listed below:

Frame check	$21E2_{16}$
Information	$46CB09_{16}$
Control field	76_{16}
Address	$F4_{16}$

14-9 How will the control field appear in an HDLC frame if the control information is $6C4E_{16}$?

TELETYPE CURRENT LOOPS

Asynchronous serial data transmission is frequently used between mircoprocessors and teletype (TTY) printers and keyboards. Data from the processor is printed on the paper and can also be punched in paper tape. To send to the MPU, a key is depressed and the coded character is forwarded. Because the teletype may be located a good distance from the microcomputer, a reliable and inexpensive communications channel is desirable. By using serial communications, a simple two-wire cable can be used. This cable is much more economical than an 8-bit parallel line. Low-impedance *current loops* are used as the transmission channel because they are resistant to errors that noise can introduce. Digital signals can be transmitted for distances up to 5000 feet (ft) [1500 meters (m)] over current loops without degrading.

CHAPTER OBJECTIVES

Upon completion of this chapter, you should be able to:

1. Describe the data format used in teletype communications.
2. Explain the mechanical mechanism of the teletype printer and keyboard and relate it to the data input.
3. Decode 7- and 8-bit teletype characters.
4. List the logic levels for 20-mA current loops.
5. Draw a block diagram of a typical teletype current loop.
6. Explain why opto-isolators are required in current loops used with microprocessors.
7. Explain by means of a schematic diagram the input and output circuits used in current loops.
8. Write programs that interface a microprocessor to a teletype printer and keyboard.

TELETYPE CHARACTERISTICS

The serial communication with a teletype is usually run at 110, 150, or 300 baud rates. The transmission from either end of the loop is asynchronous. Figure 15-1 shows a teletype connected to a microprocessor by means of a twisted-pair transmission line. Often the transmission line is shielded to avoid picking up noise. A universal synchronous-asynchronous receiver-transmitter (USART) like the one we studied in Chap. 14 is used as an interface between the parallel I/O of the microprocessor and the serial channel.

The Model 33 Teletype is a good example of the type of peripheral we have been discussing. It can send or receive 10 char/s. Each teletype character sent requires 11 bits. Recall from the last chapter that 1 start bit, 8 data bits, and 2 stop bits comprise each character. Figure 15-2 shows the character format and timing. Because each character consists of 11 bits, and 10 characters are sent per second, the data rate is 110 baud. Later in this chapter we will see how the microprocessor converts the 8 parallel bits in a computer word to the 11 serial bits.

Mechanical Characteristics

Although a teletype appears to be a single piece of equipment, it is actually two separate devices from the microcomputer's point of view. The receiving device is the *printer*, which converts the digital signals to letters. The sending component is the *keyboard*, which generates a bit pattern when a key is pressed. An optional item is the paper-tape reader and punch. If the punch is on when the printer is printing a character, the print bars will also punch through the tape. In an analogous manner, the reader parallels the keyboard operations, allowing data to be transmitted at a faster rate than the operator can type.

PRINTER The printer begins operation after a start bit is detected. The start bit will cause the clutch to engage the mechanical linkages and also enable the selector magnets for decoding. When the 8 data bits arrive (requiring 8 bits $\times$ 9.09 ms per bit = 72.72 ms), they trip the selector magnet, which catches eight spinning, notched wheels. These wheels raise or lower the print bars, selecting the character to be printed. Once the character is in position, the print hammer strikes the

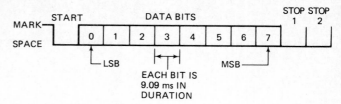

Fig. 15-2 Teletype data format.

head against the ribbon and paper. The stop bits give the printer time to terminate the print operation and prepare for the next start bit.

KEYBOARD The keyboard operations depend on a distributor to produce signals, as shown in Fig. 15-3. Depressing any key causes the keyboard encoder to open or close switches in series with each data bit. The distributor generates the 11 bits by use of a commutator that rotates counterclockwise. The commutator first connects the start contact to the output line. After rotating to the first bit position, the state of the keyboard encoder switch decides whether an open or short circuit is sensed on the output lines. The commutator continues to rotate through each of the other data bit contacts. It finally passes the stop 1 and stop 2 contacts and then waits until the next key is pressed. A synchronous motor turns the commutator and provides the precise 9.09-ms timing. This motor must be well maintained or else sync errors will develop.

CHARACTER SET There are several character sets in use by various pieces of teletype equipment. Most commonly used are 7- or 8-bit ASCII characters. The 7-bit characters will either use bit number 7 as a parity bit or always leave it in the zero state. The *8-bit characters*, as listed in Table 15-1, always set that bit to a 1. The choice of character set does not affect the hardware interface because 8 data bits must be sent regardless of coding. The software that processes the characters must, however, be programmed to use the appropriate character set.

Teletype Characteristics Review

1. Why are teletype current loops used?
2. How many bits are needed for each teletype character? How are they used?
3. What delimits the start and stop of each bit in a character?

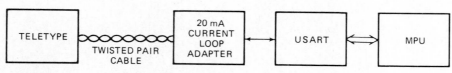

Fig. 15-1 Teletype communications channel.

4. Explain how the keyboard distributor encodes each character.

CURRENT LOOPS

Data signals from the processor move through the USART, which converts them to serial, and through the current loop converter, which changes them from TTL levels to currents. Instead of using high and low voltage levels, current loops represent the two data states by the presence or absence of current flow. A logic 1 is indicated by a 20-mA current, logic 0 by no current.

The current loop in Fig. 15-4 shows the important features for the circuit.

The current flows from the converter to the negative terminal of the printer. The printer's positive terminal is connected to the negative terminal of the keyboard. From the keyboard, the circuit leads to the ground terminal of the current regulator, which produces the current flowing in the loop with the aid of a +15-V power supply. Finally, the circuit is completed at the negative terminal of the converter.

20-mA Converter

The *20-mA converter* used in this circuit provides the necessary voltage isolation between the microprocessor and current loop. By employing an *opto-isolator* (also called an "optical isolator"), voltage isolation of several thousand volts can be achieved, although such high voltages would never appear in the circuit. The opto-isolator works much like a relay. The infrared light-emitting diode (LED) converts the incoming signal to

Table 15-1 8-Bit Teletype Characters

Character	Code	Character	Code
0	B0	O	CF
1	B1	P	D0
2	B2	Q	D1
3	B3	R	D2
4	B4	S	D3
5	B5	T	D4
6	B6	U	D5
7	B7	V	D6
8	B8	W	D7
9	B9	X	D8
		Y	D9
A	C1	Z	DA
B	C2		
C	C3	.	AE
D	C4	,	AC
E	C5	?	BF
F	C6	=	BD
G	C7	*	AA
H	C8	$	A4
I	C9	%	A5
J	CA	!	A1
K	CB	'	A7
L	CC	SP	A0
M	CD	LF	8A
N	CE	CR	8D

light. The light is sensed by a light-sensitive semiconductor, such as a photoresistive detector or phototransistor. That component, in turn, acts as a switch and produces the correct output conditions.

The converter is a discrete component circuit that has seven inputs or outputs, as shown in Fig. 15-5*a*. Two leads are for the TTL input and output. The 20-mA input and output connections are made at the appropriate positive and negative terminal pairs. Another input is the common 20-mA current sink termination. A +5-V power supply is required, and the remaining pin is usually attached to ground.

Three separate circuits are actually used in the converter. The current-to-TTL conversion is performed by the circuit shown in Fig. 15-5*b*. Diode D1 is just used to prevent damage in case the loop is connected with reverse polarity. An opto-isolator, such as the 4N35, provides the isolation, as was explained above. When current flows in the loop, the LED in the 4N35 is forward-biased, causing it to emit light. Light striking the phototransistor causes it to saturate with a collector-emitter voltage V_{CE} of about 0.3 V. This low voltage applied to the Schmitt trigger inverter (one of the six inverters in a 7414) produces a high at the TTL output.

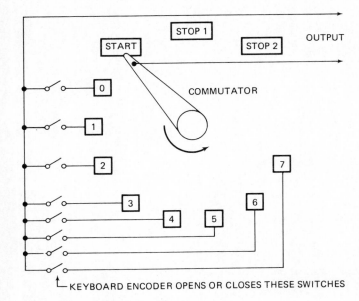

Fig. 15-3 Keyboard distributor.

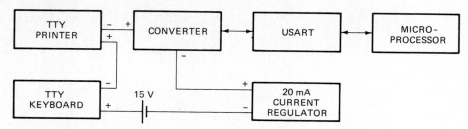

Fig. 15-4 Current loop.

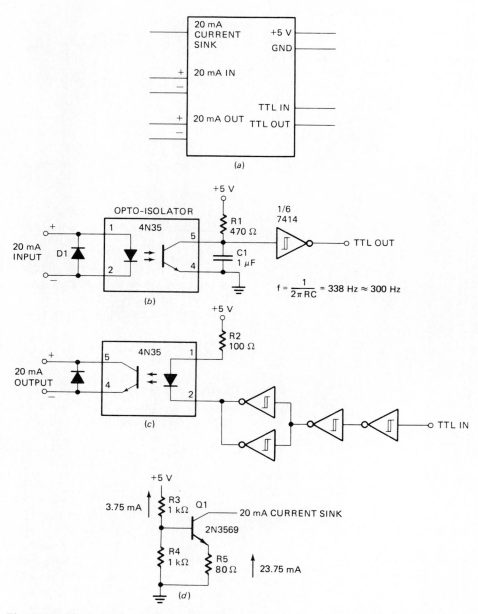

Fig. 15-5 20mA current loop converter: (*a*) pin configuration, (*b*) current-to-TTL converter, (*c*) TTL-to-current converter, (*d*) current sink.

If no current flows in the loop, the LED does not emit and the phototransistor is off. Then $+5$ V appears at the inverter input and the TTL output is low. The data rate is controlled by the value of C1. With the 1-microfarad (μF) value shown, a data rate in the range of direct current to 300 bps can be maintained. Selecting a smaller capacitor will increase the data rate; a value of 0.01 μF will allow the converter to run at up to 40K bps. As the data rate increases, however, so does the noise.

TTL-to-current conversion is the purpose of the circuit in Fig. 15-5c. The TTL input is applied to the opto-isolator through a network of Schmitt trigger inverters. The output transistor of the optical isolator acts as a switch in the current loop. A low TTL input passing through the three inverter stages appears as a $+5$-V level on pin 2 of the opto-isolator. This voltage reverse-biases the LED, causing the phototransistor to remain off. With the transistor off, no current can flow in the loop. On the other hand, a high at the TTL input produces a low voltage at the cathode of the LED. The LED is forward-biased, so it emits, saturating the transistor. Now current can flow in the loop. (See Prob. 15-8.) D2 protects this circuit in the same way as D1 in Fig. 15-5b.

The current sink (Fig. 15-5d) is a simple one-transistor circuit. Q1 is normally held on by the power supply. The transistor provides a low-impedance path to ground.

The converter can drive up to 10 TTL gates (fan-out = 10) but can only accept a single input. A current less than 3 mA in the loop will be recognized as a logic 0; current more than 15 mA is a logic 1.

Current Loops Review

1. How is a logic 1 represented in a current loop? A logic 0?
2. Why is an opto-isolator used in the 20-mA converter? Explain briefly how the opto-isolator works.
3. What effect does current flowing into the circuit shown in Fig. 15-5b have? What current is produced when the TTL input shown in Fig. 15-5c is low?
4. How does changing the value of C1 in Fig. 15-5b from 1 to 0.01 μF affect the baud rate?

SYSTEM OPERATION

The teletype circuit can be used in either half- or full-duplex modes. Figure 15-6 shows the half-duplex configuration. In a half-duplex system, either the teletype or processor can transmit, but not at the same time. Basically, the loop is a series circuit. The 20-mA input runs to the printer and through the keyboard and the power supply to ground. The circuit is completed through the sink and the 20-mA output. In this case, we are using the USART that was studied in Chap. 14.

Full-duplex operation (Fig. 15-7) calls for two current loops and two power supplies. Now the microcomputer and teletype can both transmit simultaneously. The keyboard loop terminates at the 20-mA input and the printer loop at the 20-mA output. Serial data passes in both directions between the USART and TTL input and output terminals.

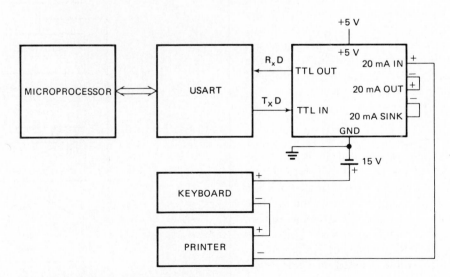

Fig. 15-6 Half-duplex teletype system.

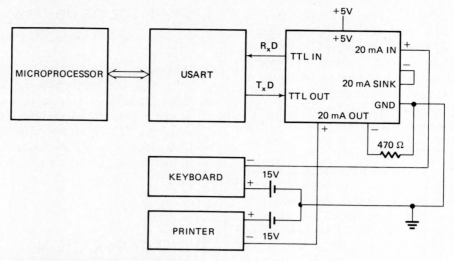

Fig. 15-7 Full-duplex teletype system.

System Operation Review

1. How are the connections of the teletype and 20-mA converter changed in going from half-duplex to full-duplex operation?
2. Why are two power supplies needed in the full-duplex mode?
3. Describe the purpose of each loop in the full-duplex configuration.

SOFTWARE INTERFACING TO TELETYPES

Many of the tasks required to interface a processor can be done by either hardware or software. For example, the appending and checking of the parity bit can be a function of either the USART or the microprocessor program. Another one of these tasks is controlling the timing to send the serial bits of a character at 9.09 ms.

In this section we will see how the program can provide the timing accuracy required and also how the 8-bit character stored in memory can be used to generate the 11 bits needed for the teletype character.

Output

A flowchart for the teletype output routine is shown in Fig. 15-8. In the first step a counter is set to 11 to maintain a count of the number of bits sent. Each bit is transmitted with a 9.09-ms delay between them. After each bit has been sent, the counter is decremented. If the counter is not 0, the loop is reentered to send the next character. When the counter reaches 0, the routine terminates. The 8085 program is listed in Table 15-2. There is a main program and a delay subroutine in the table. Considering first the main program, the character

to be sent must be in the E register before entering the routine. A series of rotate accumulator instructions will be used to shift the bits out one by one. Only the least significant bit of I/O port $0F_{16}$ is used, so the USART need only deal with a single bit, as Fig. 15-9 shows. Because of the simple interface, an AND gate can be used instead of a USART. (Although not in the program listing, the stack pointer must be properly initialized so that the subroutine call works correctly.)

After the counter has been initialized and the char-

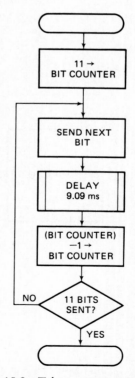

Fig. 15-8 Teletype output routine.

Table 15-2 8085 Teletype Output Routine

Label	Mnemonic	Address	Operation Code	Comment
	MVI D, 11	1000	16	Set bit counter to 11
		1001	0B	
	MOV A, E	1002	7B	Place data in accumulator
	ORA A	1003	B7	Clear carry bit
	RAL	1004	17	Carry A bit 0 of accumulator to act as start bit
LOOP	OUT 0F	1005	D3	Send data on port $0F_{16}$
		1006	0F	
	CALL DELAY	1007	CD	9.1-ms delay subroutine
		1008	50	
		1009	10	
	RAR	100A	1F	
	STC	100B	37	Set carry for stop bits
	DCR D	100C	15	Decrement bit counter
	JNZ LOOP	100D	C2	Is counter 0? If not, go to send next character
		100E	05	
		100F	10	
	HLT	1010	76	Stop
DELAY	MVI B, 6	1050	06	Load outer loop counter to perform outer loop six
		1051	06	times
OUTLOOP	MVI C, 202	1052	0E	Load inner loop counter
		1053	CA	to perform inner loop 202 times
INLOOP	DCR C	1054	0D	Decrement inner counter
	JNZ INLOOP	1055	C2	If not 0, go to decrement again
		1056	54	
		1057	10	
	DCR B	1058	05	Decrement outer counter
	JNZ OUTLOOP	1059	C2	If not 0, go to decrement again
		105A	52	
		105B	10	
	RET	105C	C9	Return

acter placed in the accumulator (address 1002_{16}), the A register is ORed with itself. This operation does not change the accumulator, but it does clear the carry bit. The RAL instruction on the next line moves the carry bit (which was 0) to the LSB of the accumulator and shifts the MSB of the accumulator to the carry bit position. See Fig. 15-10a.

The output instruction places the accumulator contents on the data lines. Only data bit 0 is passed to the teletype, and that is a 0 for the start bit. The delay subroutine, which we will examine later, introduces the

proper delay and the accumulator is rotated right, returning the MSB to bit 7 of the accumulator, as Fig. 15-10b shows.

Next, the carry bit is set, so the next right shift will bring a 1 into the MSB of the A register to act as one of the stop bits (Fig. 15-10c). Because 11 bits have not been transmitted, the loop is repeated. When the RAR instruction is reached again, the set carry bit moves into the accumulator (Fig. 15-10d). The same process repeats until all data bits and 2 stop bits have been sent. By use of the carry status, we were able to insert the

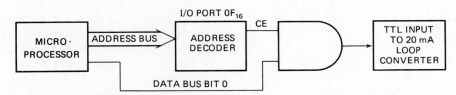

Fig. 15-9 Simplified teletype output circuit.

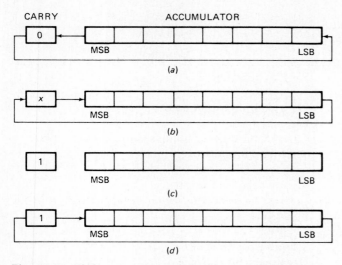

Fig. 15-10 Shift patterns: (*a*) bringing zero into the LSB position, (*b*) restoring MSB, (*c*) setting carry to act as stop bits, (*d*) moving stop bits into accumulator.

stop and start bits to convert the 8 data bits into a complete teletype character.

Now we will see how the delay was created. If our 8085 has a 2-MHz clock, then we can use the execution rate of two instructions to cause the delay. We will use the DCR and JNZ instructions, which have execution times of

DCR	2.5 μs
JNZ	5.0 μs
Total	7.5 μs

To create a delay of approximately 9.1 ms, we have to divide by the instruction delay:

$$\frac{9.1 \text{ ms}}{7.5 \text{ μs}} = 1213 \tag{15-1}$$

Because the largest number we can use in a DCR instruction is FF_{16} (255_{10}), we must perform the decrementing loop several times. As the program shows, we can use an outer loop that repeats an inner loop six times. By setting the inner counter to 202_{10}, we have

$$6 \times 202 = 1212$$

which is close enough to the value in Eq. (15-1). It is worthwhile emphasizing that this technique is an approximation and assumes that no wait states or interrupts occur. In reality it may be necessary to adjust the count in cell 1053 up or down slightly to create the desired delay.

Input

When the processor is receiving, the teletype provides the data with correct timing. The processor just waits for the bits to arrive. One method that could be used

would be to attach the data received (DR) pin from the USART to bit 7 of the data bus. (Bit 0 will be used to receive the serial input.) The processor would stay in a loop of the three following instructions:

REPEAT	IN	0F	Input from port 0F
	ORA		Set status bits
	JP	REPEAT	Input again if not negative

When the DR line goes high, it will set the sign bit. Sensing a negative value means that a new bit has been sent by the teletype.

After recognizing the start bit, the processor receives the serial data bits and packs them into a byte. After all eight data bits arrive, the two stop bits are accepted, and the procedure is complete.

Software Interfacing to Teletypes Review

1. Name two tasks required in a teletype interface that either hardware or software can perform.
2. How does the output software produce the 11 teletype character bits from a data byte?
3. What technique was used by the output program to convert parallel data to serial?
4. Which data bit is sent to the teletype first in the output routine?
5. Why is a simple AND gate adequate for the output circuit shown in Fig. 15-9?
6. How does the software produce a 9.1-ms delay between bits?
7. True or false? The teletype input routine must contain a 9.09-ms delay loop.

CHAPTER SUMMARY

1. Current loops are used in teletype communications channels. Baud rates of 110, 150, or 300 are commonly used by these asynchronous serial channels. A USART interfaces between the processor and the current loop.
2. Each character is sent by 11 bits: 1 start bit, 8 data bits, and 2 stop bits. Each bit level is held for 9.09 ms.
3. The selector magnet of the printer is controlled by the data bits, which cause the magnet to engage notches on eight notched wheels that raise or lower the print bars, thus selecting the character to be printed. Once the character is set on the print bars, a hammer strikes the head against the paper.
4. The keyboard distributor converts the key depressed to outgoing signals. The encoder opens or closes switches that control current flow as the commutator rotates.

5. Several character sets are used by various teletypes. The 7- and 8-bit ASCII codes are frequently encountered.
6. A 20-mA converter changes transmitted TTL levels to currents and changes received currents back to TTL levels. A logic 1 in a current loop is shown by current flow of 20 mA. No current means that a logic 0 is being sent.
7. Voltage isolation in the converter is the reason for including an opto-isolator in the circuit.
8. Current loops permit teletypes to operate in either half- or full-duplex modes.
9. Software can take over many of the jobs necessary in interfacing. By adding more software to the program, the hardware can be simplified a great deal, but the processor and memory are then dedicated to the interfacing task part of the time.

KEY TERMS AND CONCEPTS

Current loops	Stop bits	Keyboard	20-mA converter
Start bit	Printer	8-bit characters	Opto-isolator

PROBLEMS

15-1 The 8-bit ASCII character for the letter I is to be transmitted. Show the carry status bit and the accumulator values for the first 3 bits sent using the output routine.

15-2 What character does CC_{16} represent in 8-bit ASCII code? What is the purpose of the MSB if this were a 7-bit ASCII code that used parity?

15-3 How should the output routine be changed if we want to have 12-ms delays between character bits for an experimental teletype?

15-4 Write the code needed by the input routine to store the 8 data bits in memory cell 0200_{16}. (Remember that the LSB is received first and that bit 7 is used by the DR line to signal when the bit has been received.)

15-5 Draw a block diagram of a teletype output circuit that replaces the AND gate shown in Fig. 15-9 with the USART.

15-6 Repeat Prob. 15-5 for the input circuit.

15-7 If the teletype is sending the 7-bit ASCII character M (without parity), what would be the state of the encoder switches shown in Fig. 15-3?

15-8 Assume that the LED shown in Fig. 15-5c drops 1.8 V and that the resistance of the output stages of the inverters is zero. The maximum current that each inverter can sink in the low-output state is 16 mA. Explain why two inverters must be paralleled in this circuit.

15-9 The V_{CE} of the phototransistor shown in Fig. 15-5b is 0.3 V. Assume that the only resistance in the circuit is R1 of 470 Ω. How long after the phototransistor is cut off does the input to the inverter reach 5 V?

15-10 What is the voltage on the base of Q1 in Fig. 15-5d? When current flows into the circuit, what is the emitter voltage if V_{CE} is 0.2 V and the transistor has negligible internal resistance in comparison to R5?

EIA STANDARD
RS-232C INTERFACE

The most widely used serial communications interface is the *RS-232C interface*. This interface is defined in an Electronic Industries Association (EIA) standard that specifies the interconnection of the *data terminal equipment (DTE)* and *data communications equipment (DCE)*. When the interface is used between a microcomputer and peripheral, the computer is usually the DCE and the peripheral the DTE. This chapter describes the RS-232C circuits and then shows how they can be used in various configurations. Circuits that can convert between TTL or 20-mA current loops and the RS-232C are also discussed.

CHAPTER OBJECTIVES

Upon completion of this chapter, you should be able to:

1. List the basic capabilities of the RS-232C interface.
2. Describe the four types of lines specified in the standard.
3. List the voltage levels used for logic and control signals.
4. Distinguish between primary and secondary channels.
5. Define the purpose of each signal in the RS-232C specification.
6. Group the signals by category.
7. Draw a timing diagram for a typical RS-232C handshaking situation.
8. Explain the electrical and mechanical characteristics of the standard.
9. Use a circuit diagram to explain how RS-232C signals can be converted to either TTL or 20-mA current loop levels.

RS-232C CAPABILITIES

This interface specification is quite general in its application. While it assigns the serial signals to specific pins on the connector, it does not restrict the type of data that can be sent. Any character length, bit code, and bit sequence can be used. Either synchronous or asynchronous communications may be employed. The interface is intended for fairly short cables [about 50 ft (15 m)] between the computer and peripheral.

Data rates of up to 20K baud can be supported. The most frequently encountered rates are listed in Table 16-1. The reference for the interface is EIA Standard RS-232C, "Interface between Data Terminal Equipment and Data Communications Equipment Employing Serial Binary Data Interchange."

Four types of lines are presented in the specification:

Data signals
Control signals
Timing signals
Signal grounds (returns)

The data signals represent a logic 1 with a voltage between -3 and -25 V. A logic 0 is a voltage greater than $+3$ V and less than $+25$ V. Any voltage in the range of -3 to $+3$ V is an undefined level. Control signals are on if the voltage is $+3$ to $+25$ V and are off between -3 and -25 V.

There are two kinds of channels that may possibly be included in an RS-232C interface. *Primary channels* run at the higher signal rate and are intended to transfer data. *Secondary channels* run at a slower rate and provide control information. Secondary channels are further subdivided into (1) *auxiliary channels,* whose data direction is independent of the primary and who are controlled by a set of secondary control circuits, and (2) *backward channels,* which always transmit in a direction opposite to the primary channel.

Table 16-1 RS-232C Baud Rates

Rate (baud)	Common Use
50	
75	
110	
150	Teletype
300	
600	
1,200	
2,400	
4,800	CRT terminal
9,600	
19,200	

RS-232C Capabilities Review

1. True or false? RS-232C channels are ideally suited for communicating between a microcomputer and a CRT display that is 300 ft away.
2. What is the highest data rate recommended for RS-232C signals?
3. List the types of lines specified by the EIA standard.
4. Describe the RS-232C logic and control voltage levels.
5. Distinguish between a primary and a secondary channel.

SIGNAL DESCRIPTION

There is a maximum of 25 signal lines, or circuits, in the RS-232C connector. Of these, two are grounds, four are data signals, twelve are control signals, and three are timing signals. The remaining lines are either reserved or unassigned. Table 16-2 lists all the signals by pin number and gives the circuit nomenclature and common abbreviation. Table 16-3 groups the signals by category.

Data Signals

The TRANSMITTED DATA signal (BA circuit) is generated by the DTE. The data terminal must hold this signal in the 1 state during the interval between characters or words and when no data is being transmitted. The data terminal cannot send this signal until all the following control signals (if implemented) are: REQUEST TO SEND (CA circuit), CLEAR TO SEND (CB circuit), DATA SET READY (CC circuit), and DATA TERMINAL READY (CD circuit). As already noted and as shown in Table 16-2, the common designator for the TRANSMITTED DATA signal is TXD.

The RECEIVED DATA signal (BB circuit) is sent by the DCE. The signal must be held at the logic 1 level whenever the RECEIVED LINE SIGNAL DETECTOR signal (CF circuit) is off. In a half-duplex system, this signal is held at logic 1 when REQUEST TO SEND (CA circuit) is on and for a brief interval following the on-to-off transition of CA in order to allow for completion of transmission and for the delay due to line reflections. As noted in Table 16-2, the RECEIVED DATA signal is commonly abbreviated RXD.

The secondary channel has data signals equivalent to the two above. The SECONDARY TRANSMITTED DATA signal (SBA circuit) is equivalent to the TRANSMITTED DATA signal, and the SECONDARY RECEIVED DATA signal (SBB circuit) is an analog of the RECEIVED DATA signal.

Control Signals

The first control signal is REQUEST TO SEND (CA circuit), which is originated by the DTE. For one-way or duplex

Table 16-2 RS-232C Signals

Pin Number	Circuit	Common Abbreviation	Description
1	AA	—	Protective ground
2	BA	TXD	Transmitted data
3	BB	RXD	Received data
4	CA	RTS	Request to send
5	CB	CTS	Clear to send
6	CC	DSR	Data set ready
7	AB	—	Signal ground (common return)
8	CF	DCD	Received line signal detector
9	—	—	Reserved for data set testing
10	—	—	Reserved for data set testing
11	—	—	Unassigned
12	SCF	—	Secondary received line signal detector
13	SCB	—	Secondary clear to send
14	SBA	—	Secondry transmitted data
15	DB	—	Transmission signal element timing (DCE source)
16	SBB	—	Secondary received data
17	DD	—	Receiver signal element timing (DCE source)
18	—	—	Unassigned
19	SCA	—	Secondary request to send
20	CD	DTR	Data terminal ready
21	CG	—	Signal quality detector
22	CE	—	Ring indicator
23*	CH/CI	—	Data signal rate selector (DTE/DCE source)
24	DA	—	Transmit signal element timing (DTE source)
25	—	—	Unassigned

* Only one of these two signals is tied to pin 23.

channels, an on condition holds the DCE in the transmit mode. In half-duplex channels, the on condition maintains the equipment in the transmit mode and inhibits the receive mode; when off, the signal enables the receive mode. Once REQUEST TO SEND has been turned off, it cannot be turned on again until CLEAR TO SEND (CB circuit) has been turned off by the DCE. The common abbreviation for REQUEST TO SEND is RTS.

The DCE transmits CLEAR TO SEND (CB circuit) in response to an on condition on the DATA SET READY (CC circuit) and REQUEST TO SEND (CA circuit) control lines. No data should be sent when this control is off. The abbreviation for this signal is CTS.

The status of the DCE is presented by DATA SET READY (CC circuit). The signal is on when the equipment (1) is connected to the channel, (2) is not in test, talk, or the dial mode, and (3) has completed the timing functions and answer tones (if applicable). The on condition does not mean that the communications circuit has been established, but only that the local equipment is ready. The abbreviation is DSR.

When the data terminal set is ready, it connects the DCE to the channel with the DATA TERMINAL READY (CD circuit) control. When the signal goes off, the DCE is removed from the channel after completing any in-progress transmission. This control is abbreviated DTR.

The on state of the RING INDICATOR signal (CE circuit) from the DCE means that a ringing signal is being received. When the DCE is receiving a signal that meets its suitability criteria, the RECEIVED LINE SIGNAL DETECTOR (CF circuit) is transmitted in the on state. This signal goes off when no signal or an unsuitable signal is received. This signal is also called data carrier detected (which is why it is abbreviated DCD).

Table 16-3 RS-232C Signals by Category

Circuit	CCITT Equivalent	Ground	Data From DCE	Data To DCE	Control From DCE	Control To DCE	Timing From DCE	Timing To DCE
AA	101	X						
AB	102	X						
BA	103			X				
BB	104		X					
CA	105					X		
CB	106				X			
CC	107				X			
CD	108.2					X		
CE	125				X			
CF	109				X			
CG	110				X			
CH	111					X		
CI	112				X			
DA	113							X
DB	114						X	
DD	115						X	
SBA	118			X				
SBB	119		X					
SCA	120					X		
SCB	121				X			
SCF	122				X			

The SIGNAL QUALITY DETECTOR signal (CG circuit) from the DCE is on when there is no reason to believe that a data error has occurred, and off when there is a high probability of an error. The DCE uses the DATA SIGNAL RATE SELECTOR (CH or CI circuits) to designate which of two data signaling rates (in the case of dual-rate data sets) will be used. An on condition selects the faster rate. The source of this signal can be either DTE or DCE, but not both.

The SECONDARY REQUEST TO SEND control (SCA circuit) is equivalent to REQUEST TO SEND as described above, except that this control applies to the secondary channel. In a similar manner, the SECONDARY CLEAR TO SEND (SCB circuit) corresponds to CLEAR TO SEND. Finally, the SECONDARY RECEIVED LINE SIGNAL DETECTOR (SCF circuit) provides the same operations on the secondary channel as the RECEIVED LINE SIGNAL DETECTOR.

Timing Signals

The TRANSMITTER SIGNAL ELEMENT TIMING (DTE SOURCE) signal (DA circuit) is sent by the data terminal to indicate the center of each bit on the transmitted data line. A corresponding signal from the DCE, TRANSMITTER SIGNAL ELEMENT TIMING (DCE SOURCE) (DB circuit), is used by the data terminal to change the data on the transmitted data line when the DB signal makes a transition from off to on. The RECEIVER SIGNAL ELEMENT TIMING (DD circuit) is sent by the DCE to indicate the center of each bit on the received data line. A transition of on to off marks the center.

Grounds

The PROTECTIVE GROUND (AA circuit) connects to the equipment frame and may be connected to external grounds. The SIGNAL GROUND (or COMMON RETURN) (AB circuit) establishes a common ground reference potential for all RS-232C signals (except the protective ground). This circuit must be brought to one point and may be connected to the AA ground by an internal wire strap.

Selection

Not all the signals provided need be implemented by a piece of equipment. In fact, most communications systems do not implement them all. A very minimal system with only three signals is shown in Fig. 16-1a. Figure

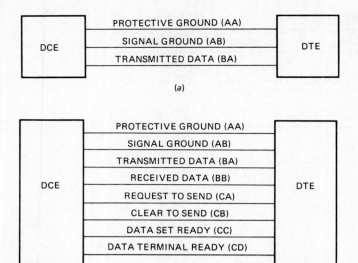

Fig. 16-1 RS-232C communications channels: (a) minimal system, (b) typical system.

16-1b is a more typical eight-signal channel system. Tables 16-4 and 16-5 list other options.

Handshaking

The initialization of communications on an RS-232C channel requires the exchange of a series of control signals. Figure 16-2 is an example of how the DTE and DCE can start the interchange. The REQUEST TO SEND is raised by the terminal. When the DCE responds with CLEAR TO SEND, the terminal responds with DATA TERMINAL READY, which stays high as long as data is transmitted. (The REQUEST TO SEND line can be reset after CLEAR TO SEND drops.)

Signal Description Review

1. Which two signals are used to transmit or receive data on the primary channel?
2. Can data transmission begin with the control signal states: RTS on, CTS on, DCD off? (These are the only control signals implemented.)
3. What is another name frequently used for the RE-CEIVED LINE SIGNAL DETECTOR?
4. Which timing signal may be used to indicate the center of each bit transmitted by the data terminal?
5. Distinguish between the purpose of the PROTECTIVE GROUND (AA circuit) and the SIGNAL GROUND (AB circuit).
6. True or false? Every RS-232C interface must provide 25 lines in the cable.

Table 16-4 RS-232C Interfaces

Configuration	Interface*
Transmit only	A
Transmit only†	B
Receive only	C
Half duplex	D
Full duplex†	D
Full duplex	E
Primary channel transmit only†; secondary channel receive only	F
Primary channel transmit only; secondary channel receive only	H
Primary channel receive only; secondary channel transmit only†	G
Primary channel receive only; secondary channel transmit only	I
Primary channel transmit only†; half-duplex secondary channel	J
Primary channel receive only; half-duplex secondary channel	K
Half-duplex primary channel; half-duplex secondary channel	L
Full-duplex secondary channel†; full-duplex secondary channel	L
Full-duplex primary channel; full-duplex secondary channel	M
Special	Z

* See Table 16-5.
† The CA signal (request to send) is included in the selection.

ELECTRICAL CHARACTERISTICS

In regard to *electrical characteristics*, the equivalent circuit for all RS-232C line drivers and receivers is shown in Fig. 16-3. The same circuit is used for all signal lines regardless of their being used for data, control, or timing.

Each line driver must be able to withstand an open circuit or a short circuit between that signal line and any other conductor in that cable without sustaining damage to itself or damaging any associated equipment.

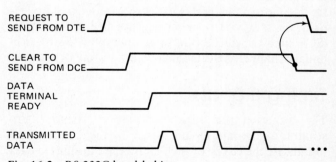

Fig. 16-2 RS-232C handshaking.

Table 16-5 RS-232C Data Communications Channels

Circuit	A	B	C	D	E	F	G	H	I	J	K	L	M	Z
AA	*	*	*	*	*	*	*	*	*	*	*	*	*	*
AB	X	X	X	X	X	X	X	X	X	X	X	X	X	X
BA	X	X		X	X	X		X		X		X	X	S
BB			X	X	X		X		X		X	X	X	S
CA		X		X		X				X		X		S
CB	X	X		X	X	X		X		X		X	X	S
CC	X	X	X	X	X	X	X	X	X	X	X	X	X	S
CD	Y	Y	Y	Y	Y	Y	Y	Y	Y	Y	Y	Y	Y	S
CE	Y	Y	Y	Y	Y	Y	Y	Y	Y	Y	Y	Y	Y	S
CF			X	X	X		X		X		X	X	X	S
CG														S
CH/CI														S
DA/DB	Z	Z		Z	Z	Z		Z		Z	Z	Z	Z	S
DD			Z	Z	Z		Z		Z		Z	Z	Z	S
SBA							X		X	X	X	X	X	S
SBB						X		X		X	X	X	X	S
SCA							X			X	X	X		S
SCB							X		X	X	X	X	X	S
SCF						X		X		X	X	X	X	S

* optional.
X—must be included.
Y—switched service circuits only.
Z—synchronous channel circuits only.
S—as specified by supplier.

Furthermore, any passive, noninductive load between the signal line and any other line (including the signal ground) must not damage the driver. All line receivers must be able to withstand a ±25-V input.

The load resistance of the receiver (R_R) must be between 3000 and 7000 Ω when measured with a voltage of less than 25 V. The total effective capacitance of the receiver (C_R) must be equal to or less than 2.5 nanofarads (nF). The reactive component of the load must not be inductive. This restriction means that relays cannot be used.

When implemented, the REQUEST TO SEND, DATA SET READY, DATA TERMINAL READY, and SECONDARY RE-QUEST TO SEND shall be used to detect either a power-off condition or a disconnect in the channel cable.

The power-off source impedance of the driver must be greater than 300 Ω. The driver voltage must, of course, be within the range of −25 to +25 V. The driver's internal resistance (R_D) and effective capacitance (C_D) are not specified, but a short between any two conductors in the interconnecting cable must not produce a current in excess of 0.5 A.

When the receiver is as specified, the voltage at the interface point V_I shall be within ±5 to ±15 V. All signals must pass through the region without reversal in direction. No signal can exceed a rate of change of more than 30 V/µs.

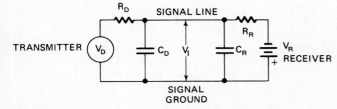

Fig. 16-3 Line driver and receiver equivalent circuit.

Electrical Characteristics Review

1. Explain the meaning of each component of the equivalent circuit shown in Fig. 16-3.
2. What are the limits of the receiver's dc load resistance?
3. True or false? A receiver effective capacitance of

1000 picofarads (pF) is acceptable in an RS-232C interface.

4. What maximum current is allowed if the transmitted data line is accidentally allowed to contact the signal ground?

MECHANICAL CHARACTERISTICS

There is a great deal of flexibility in the mechanical characteristics and structure of the connector. The connector must be in the form of a plug, and the female end is associated with the DCE. Extension cables are permitted if the load capacitance C_L at the interface point is less than 2.5 nF.

Any 25-pin connector may be used, but most manufacturers select one in the DB-25 series that is a subminiature, rectangular connector. Some part numbers are DB-25P or DB-25S of the TRW Cinch and ITT Cannon line of connectors and the AMP 17-81250-0 or 17-91250-0 connectors.

CONVERTING RS-232C LEVELS

We will be using the RS-232C interface with a microcomputer, so there is a requirement to convert between TTL and RS-232C voltages. There is also a requirement to invert the logic levels because a 1 is positive in TTL and negative in the RS-232C channel. There are many ways available to perform the level changing, including integrated circuits.

Several circuits for converting TTL to RS-232C levels are shown in Fig. 16-4. Figure 16-4a uses an operational amplifier, such as a 741. The biasing of the noninverting input is selected halfway between the minimum value for a high TTL input and the maximum value of a low TTL output:

TTL high-output min	2.4 V
TTL low-output max	− 0.4 V
Difference	2.0 V

Half of difference = 1.0 V

TTL low-output max + half difference
$$= 0.4 + 1.0 = 1.4 \text{ V}$$

The TTL input is applied at the inverting input of the operational amplifier (op amp). A high signal input will produce an output of about − 8 V, and a low input an output of + 8 V.

The transistor circuit in Fig. 16-4b uses an inverter to reverse the logic-level states. A TTL high is applied to the base of Q_1, turning both it and Q_2 off. Because no current flows, the output is − 12 V. A low input to the inverter turns both transistors on. The output will be about + 4 V.

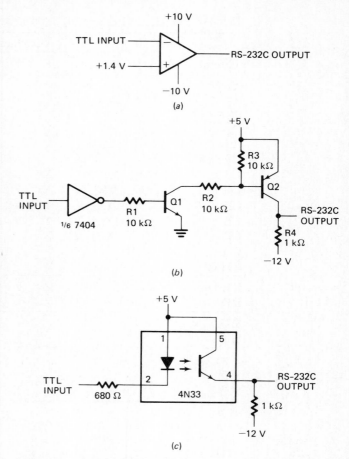

Fig. 16-4 TTL-to-RS-232C converters: (a) op-amp, (b) transistor, (c) opto-isolator.

An opto-isolator can be used to perform the conversion, as shown in Fig. 16-4c. A low TTL input will forward-bias the LED. The light striking the phototransistor will cause it to conduct, pulling the output up to almost + 5 V. When the TTL input is high, the LED is reverse-biased and the transistor off. A voltage of − 12 V appears at the output.

Conversion from RS-232C to TTL is readily accomplished by the circuit shown in Fig. 16-5. When a negative input (logic on) is applied to the base of Q_1, turning it off, the power supply voltage of + 5 V is seen at the TTL output. A positive RS-232C signal will, on

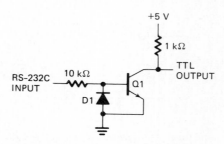

Fig. 16-5 RS-232C-to-TTL converter.

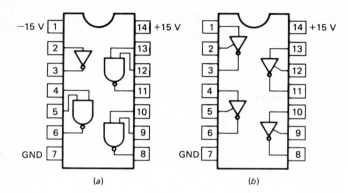

Fig. 16-6   Integrated circuit converters.

the other hand, saturate the transistor, pulling the output to almost ground potential.

The integrated circuits shown in Fig. 16-6 also perform these level changes. The IC in Fig. 16-6a converts TTL levels to RS-232C levels. This dual in-line package (DIP) also acts as an RS-232C driver. There are three NAND gates and one inverter on the chip. The IC in Fig. 16-6b reverses the process of changing RS-232C levels back to TTL levels. This integrated circuit can be used as an RS-232C receiver. The additional inputs to the inverters (pins 2, 5, 9, and 12) are controlling signals enabling each of them independently.

It is also possible to convert between RS-232C voltages and teletype loop currents. Figure 16-7a illustrates a current-loop–to–RS-232C conversion circuit. When current is flowing, the LED lights and turns on the transistor. This action produces a negative voltage on the output. No current flow causes the transistor to switch off, thus connecting the +12 V to the output. The voltages applied to the opto-isolator need not be +12 and −12 V. Any convenient values in the 3- to 15-V range will do.

The RS-232C–to–current-loop converter shown in Fig. 16-7b uses two 7404 inverters to drive the LED. The diodes limit the input voltage of the first inverter to a range of 0 to +5 V. As the input goes positive, the LED is reversed-biased and the transistor opens the loop. A negative input puts a low on the cathode of

the LED, causing it to emit light. This action makes the transistor conduct and close the loop.

Converting RS-232C Levels Review

1. Why must RS-232C voltages be inverted to interface with TTL circuits?
2. Why is the diode D_1 required on the input shown in Fig. 16-5?
3. What is the reason for the control inputs to the inverters of the IC of Fig. 16-6b?
4. Why are two series inverters used on the RS-232C input shown in Fig. 16-7b?

CHAPTER SUMMARY

1. The RS-232C standard specifies the purpose for each of 25 lines in a cable, but it does not place limits on the type of data, character length, bit code, or bit sequence. Serial synchronous or asynchronous communication with data rates up to 20K baud can be supported by the signal lines.
2. The specification provides for grounds, data signals, control signals, and timing signals. Data levels use −3 to −25 V for a 1 and +3 to +25 V for a 0. Voltages from −3 to +3 V are undefined; control signals are on if the voltage is +3 to +25 V and off if the voltage is −3 to −25 V.
3. Primary channels are higher-speed than secondary channels and are used to transfer data. Secondary channels, intended for control, may be either auxiliary or backward channels.
4. There are four data signals, 12 control signals, three timing signals, and two grounds provided by RS-232C channels.
5. Electrical specifications for the RS-232C interface include transmitter and receiver voltages, resistance, and capacitance. All loads must be noninductive. Provision to prevent damage in case of shorts must be built into the driver and receiver.

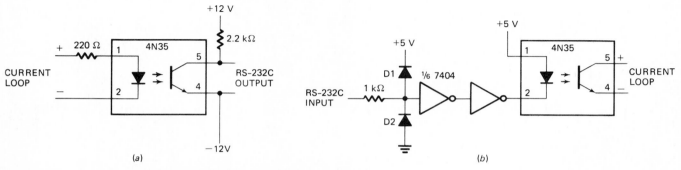

Fig. 16-7   RS-232C and current loop converters: (a) current loop to RS-232C converter, (b) RS-232C to current loop converter.

6. Mechanically, the builder of an RS-232C interface is given plenty of latitude. The type of connector is not specified, and an extension cable is permitted.

7. Discrete component and integrated circuits can be used to shift levels between RS-232C and TTL voltages. The RS-232C signals can also be converted to 20-mA loop currents.

KEY TERMS AND CONCEPTS

RS-232C interface

Data terminal equipment (DTE)

Data communications equipment (DCE)

Primary channels

Secondary channels

Auxiliary channels

Backward channels

Data signals

Transmitted data (TXD)

Received data (RXD)

Request to send (RTS)

Control signals

Clear to send (CTS)

Data set ready (DSR)

Data terminal ready (DTR)

Received line signal detector (DCD)

Timing signals

Protective ground

Signal ground, or common return

Electrical characteristics

Mechanical characteristics

P R O B L E M S

16-1 Draw a handshaking timing diagram for the initialization of an RS-232C communications sequence for the system shown in Fig. 16-1b.

16-2 The RS-232C interface is being repaired by a technician. At the time when RTS is on ($+15$ V) and DSR is off (-15 V), the technician accidentally shorts the two pins with a screwdriver. What current flows between the lines?

16-3 The DCE detected a parity error in the last 8 bits of data transmitted. Draw a timing diagram of the situation if the following lines are implemented:

AA	CB
AB	CC
BA	CD
BB	CG
CA	

16-4 If the dc load resistance of an RS-232C interface is 5 kΩ and the receiver capacitance is the maximum allowable value, what is the RC time constant of the load?

16-5 An RS-232C system uses $+25$ V for a logic 0 and -25 V for a logic 1. Assuming that the time constant of the load is the only factor determining the rise time from the 1 to 0 state, would the following receiver values provide acceptable operation?

$R_R = 3$ kΩ
$C_R = 50$ pF
$V_R = 0$ V

16-6 What biasing voltage would you select for the op-amp TTL–to–RS-232C converter if the TTL integrated circuit you were using had a minimum high output of 2.8 V and a maximum low of 0.3 V?

16-7 Assume that $V_{CE,SAT}$ of Q_1 and Q_2 shown in Fig. 16-4b is 0.3 V. The voltage levels from the 7404 inverter are

High: 3.0 V
Low: 0 V

Find the current in each resistor when the TTL input is low. (The voltage drop between the base and emitter of Q_1 and the emitter to base of Q_2 in saturation is 0.7 V.)

16-8 If the Q_1 in Fig. 16-5 has the same parameters as those in Prob. 16-7 and the forward-bias voltage drop of D_1 is 0.7 V, find the currents in the circuit when the input equals -4 V. When the input equals $+5$ V.

16-9 The diodes of the RS-232C–to–current-loop converter drop 0.6 V when forward-biased. What is the voltage at the cathode of D_2 when the input is -10 V? When it is $+10$ V?

16-10 What is the current through the 1-kΩ resistor for each input in Prob. 16-9?

IEEE-488 GENERAL-PURPOSE INTERFACE BUS

The general-purpose interface bus (GPIB) supports a wide latitude of functions. Originally conceived for programmable instrumentation, the bus is also suited for data transfer between the microcomputer and its peripheral equipment. The bus is defined in IEEE Standard 488 (1978). This standard specifies the functional requirements for the bus as well as its electrical and mechanical characteristics. The bus's operational use, however, is device-dependent and is left up to the equipment designer.

CHAPTER OBJECTIVES

Upon completion of this chapter, you should be able to:

1. List the capabilities of the IEEE-488 bus.
2. Describe the signal lines used by the bus.
3. Explain the functional partitioning of the bus interface.
4. Discuss the commands in the bus repertoire.
5. Show how messages are coded.
6. Distinguish between local and remote messages.
7. Describe the electrical and mechanical characteristics of the IEEE-488 bus.
8. Explain some typical operational bus transactions and give examples of both hardware and software interface processing.

IEEE-488 BUS OVERVIEW

The GPIB uses parallel data transfer, in contrast to the serial transmission used by the RS-232C interface. The basic data unit is 1 byte, which is sent from one system component to another. Members of the bus can be programmable or not.

In many ways the bus can be thought of as a party line. It uses a handshaking sequence to carry on communications. Three signals are used to perform the handshaking. Hewlett Packard has patented this process, but it licenses it to other developers of GPIB hardware.

As the IEEE-488 bus has evolved, it has been known by a variety of names (such as the HPIB, the IEC BUS, the plus bus, and the ANSI MC 1.1 bus). A maximum of 15 devices can be attached to the bus at any one time. The total transmission length must be less than 60 ft (20 m), with no more than 6 ft (2 m) between any two units.

The original IEEE Standard 488 of 1975 was updated in 1978. The update was largely editorial, with few technical changes. One of the modifications allowed the standard low voltage for drivers to increase from 0.4 to 0.5 V to accommodate Schottky devices introduced since the original standard was issued. Another change recommended coded markings on the instruments; these identifiers would define the I/O capability, so the operator would not have to refer to the user's manual to find this information.

BUS STRUCTURE

The GPIB is a transparent communications channel, allowing equipment of various manufacturers to be interconnected in a single network. Regardless of their simplicity or complexity, all the devices talk or listen in the same way.

The data is transferred point to point and does not require relay through a controller. Devices can be *listeners* (receivers), *talkers* (senders), *controllers,* or any combination. Each device has a unique address. There are 31 primary addresses to select from and 961 secondary (2-byte) addresses possible.

Bus Signals

Three sets of bus signals comprise the 16 lines in the cable: The bidirectional data bus contains the eight lines used to transfer each data byte, as shown in Fig. 17-1. Control of the data is exercised by the three-wire *handshaking bus*. Other control signals are transmitted on the *general interface management bus*, which consists of five lines.

As you can see, there can be a diverse mix of communications abilities among the bus units. The most complex, such as a microprocessor, can talk, listen, and control the bus. Simpler devices, like a digital multimeter, can talk and listen. Simplest of all is one-way equipment, such as a listen-only signal generator or a talk-only counter.

The individual lines are listed in Table 17-1. The data input/output lines are numbered DIO1 through DIO8. These lines, of course, carry the message bits.

The next set of signals (used in the handshaking cycle) executes an *interlocked sequence* of control-and-status information exchanges, which means that one event in the sequence must occur before the next one can begin. The first of these signals is DAV, which indicates that information is available and valid on the DIO lines. A device signals its readiness to accept data by the state of the NRFD signal. The third line, NDAC, shows when data has been accepted by the device.

The ATN general-management signal tells how to interpret the DIO lines and which device should respond. A quiescent state, usually necessary at start-up, can be established with the IFC signal. When a device needs service on the bus, it can signal with SRQ and request a break in the current sequence of events. The REN signal can lock out control of a device from its front-panel switches. The EOF signal is used for two purposes: It can either indicate the end of a multibyte data transfer or, used with ATN, it means that a polling

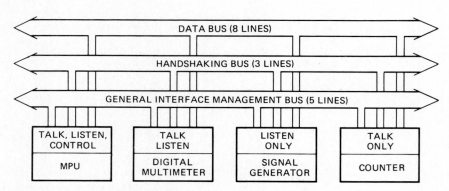

Fig. 17-1 IEEE-488 bus signals.

Table 17-1 GPIB Data and Control Buses

Bus	Line	Signal
Data bus	DIO1	Data input/output 1
	DIO2	Data input/output 2
	DIO3	Data input/output 3
	DIO4	Data input/output 4
	DIO5	Data input/output 5
	DIO6	Data input/output 6
	DIO7	Data input/output 7
	DIO8	Data input/output 8
Data-byte transfer	DAV	Data valid
control	NRFD	Not ready for data
(handshaking)	NDAC	No data accepted
General interface	ATN	Attention
management	IFC	Interface clear
	SRQ	Service request
	REN	Remote enable
	EOI	End or identify

sequence is to be executed (the polling will be explained under "Parallel Polling" on page 314).

Functional Partitioning

The IEEE-488 specification divides an equipment item into several component areas (*functional partitioning*). The immediate connection to the bus is made through drivers and receivers, as Fig. 17-2 shows. The drivers and receivers exchange data by means of the message-coding section, which transfers its signals to the device through a collection of interface functions (which are fully described in the following section, "Functional Repertoire").

Briefly, the interface functions regulate the state of the bus control circuitry. The functions are mutually independent, so only one state is active at a time. A repertoire of the functions is specified by means of state diagrams. Even so, the functions do not necessarily have to be implemented by flip-flops.

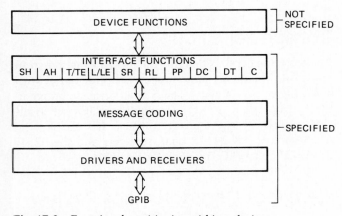

Fig. 17-2 Functional partitioning within a device.

On the other side of the interface functions are the device functions. Here, the type of measurement the instrument can make, its modes of operation, its capabilities, and its precision are controlled. Note that the specification for the GPIB covers all portions of the device except for this last one.

Bus Structure Review

1. List the three sets of signal buses that comprise the 16 lines.
2. Define the term "interlocked sequence."
3. How does IEEE Standard 488 partition a device that is capable of communication on the bus?
4. What signal can be used to establish a quiescent state at initiation?
5. What is the purpose of the DAV signal?

FUNCTIONAL REPERTOIRE

The entire functional repertoire that the interface can perform is listed in Table 17-2. Keep in mind that these are only possibilities. Any particular device may be capable of only a few of them, or it may implement the entire repertoire. A description of each function is provided in the following discussion. Each function uses one or more of the bus lines to carry out the action.

The source handshake controls the talking device and allows it to transfer a data message. All transfer between source and acceptor handshaking devices originate with this function. The acceptor handshake is returned by the listening device(s). If more than one listener is involved, the slowest one determines the return rate.

Device-dependent data is sent by means of the talker or the extended talker. The talker is only active when addressed by a single byte. The extended talker requires a 2-byte address. The corresponding listener function receives device-dependent data with a single-byte address (listener) or 2-byte address (extended listener).

Table 17-2 Functional Repertoire

Interface Function	Symbol
Source handshake	SH
Acceptor handshake	AH
Talker or extended talker	T/TE
Listener or extended listener	L/LE
Service request	SR
Remote local	RL
Parallel poll	PP
Device clear	DC
Device trigger	DT
Controller	C

A device can obtain the notice of the controller with a service request. The SR signal is sent as a single-bit reply in the status byte during a serial poll.

The remaining functions all have to do with controller operations. The remote local allows the front-panel (manual) controls on the instrument to be enabled or disabled. The parallel polling mode allows each of eight devices to send a status bit on the DIO lines. The device, or a group of devices, can be cleared and initialized by the device clear sequence; then operation can be started remotely with the device trigger. The controller function can initiate device addresses, send universal commands, and transmit addressed commands. There can be more than one controller on the bus, but only one can be actively issuing commands. All others must be in the controller idle state.

Messages

Messages can be categorized as either local or remote. *Local messages* are those sent between the device and the interface functional logic. *Remote messages* are those sent between the device and the bus.

Remote messages will cause a state transition in some interface functions. Alternatively, remote messages can be device-dependent for internal control, and any type of remote message can be used. (Specific examples of remote messages are provided in Table 17-5.)

Messages must be encoded and decoded. The coding section shown in Fig. 17-2 translates the remote messages to or from interface signal line voltages. Because this translation is part of the specification, only a certain set of remote messages is allowed.

In normal operations, two devices may transmit remote messages simultaneously. A result may be that the two messages come into conflict and the conflict must be resolved. The resolution is based on the fact that there are two types of transfers: active and passive. The active value always overrides the passive in the event of conflict.

Functional Repertoire Review

1. What function is used to originate all data transfers between a talker and listener?
2. What is the purpose of the SR function? When is this signal sent?
3. Explain the difference between local and remote messages.
4. Which section of the device in Fig. 17-2 translates remote messages to or from signal line voltages?

ELECTRICAL CHARACTERISTICS

In regard to electrical characteristics, the IEEE-488 bus uses TTL levels for all signals. The specifications cover drivers and receivers, load termination and capacitance,

Table 17-3 Driver Output Stages

Output	Signals
Open-collector only	SRQ, NRFD, and NDAC
Open-collector or three-state	DAV, IFC, ATN, REN, EOI, and DIO (except when parallel polling is used)

grounding, and cables. A logic 0 is defined as a high state and a logic 1 as a low state.

Open-collector drivers can be used for all signals, as indicated by Table 17-3. For higher speed, three-state devices are allowed, with the exception of SRQ, NRFD, and NDAC signals. When parallel polling is used, the DIO lines must also be open-collector.

The driver low-voltage level must be 0.5 V or less, with a minimum of 0 V. In the low state, the driver must be able to sink +48 mA without damage. A high output is defined as equal to or greater than 2.4 V at −5.2 mA. Maximum voltage is limited to 5.0 V. All electrical measurements are to be made at the device connector between the signal and logic ground.

Receiver input voltage in the low state will be between −0.6 and 0.8 V. A high input will range from 2.0 to 5.5 V. All receivers must limit negative excursions. Most often a diode clamp is used.

Every signal line is to be terminated in a resistive load. These loads serve to establish a steady-state voltage when all three-state drivers on a particular line are in the high-impedance state. The capacitive load limit is 100 pF within each device.

The 24-conductor bus should be constructed to minimize cross talk between the signal lines and to minimize susceptibility to external noise. The resistance of each line must be no more than 0.14 Ω/m, but the common logic ground cannot exceed 0.085 Ω/m. The overall shield resistance is limited to 0.0085 Ω. The shield on the cable is grounded.

Transceiver Circuit

The recommended I/O circuit for the GPIB is shown in Fig. 17-3. The driver uses an open-collector buffer with a 48-mA drive capacity. The Schmitt trigger buffer in the receiver offers good noise immunity. ICs are available to provide the interface; typical ICs include the MC3440P or MC3441P quad receivers and the 8291, described under "IC Interfaces" on p. 316.

Electrical Characteristics Review

1. List the voltage levels for high and low voltages on the IEEE-488 bus.

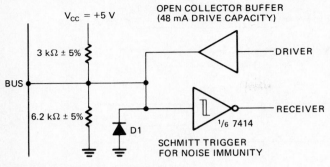

Fig. 17-3 Recommended I/O circuit.

2. True or false? Use of three-state drivers for higher speed is permitted on all signal lines.
3. What is the ground reference for all electrical measurements?
4. Why are signal lines terminated in a resistive load?
5. Explain the purpose of the Schmitt trigger in the recommended transceiver circuit.

MECHANICAL CHARACTERISTICS

The connecter specified for the bus is a rack-and-panel type. Each cable is terminated with both a plug and receptacle, as shown in Fig. 17-4. This configuration makes it easy to daisy-chain from one instrument to another.

The connector voltage rating is 200 V dc, and the current rating is 5 amps (A) per contact. Contact resistance must be less than 10 milliohms (mΩ). The contact material is to be gold over copper. Insulation resistance must exceed 10 gigohms (GΩ).

There are 24 contacts arranged in two rows of 12 connectors. The surfaces must be self-wiping. The pin assignments are listed in Table 17-4. In addition to signal lines, there is an earth ground for the shield and grounds or returns for the control signals. The grounds form a twisted pair with their respective signal lines.

BUS OPERATIONS

Flowcharts of *bus operations*, that show corresponding actions for the talker and the listeners on the bus, are illustrated in Fig. 17-5. The talker sets DAV high to respond to the collective NDAC low signal from all

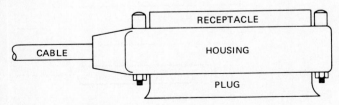

Fig. 17-4 Connector housing.

Table 17-4 Connector Pin Assignments

Pin	Signal
1	DIO1
2	DIO2
3	DIO3
4	DIO4
5	EOI
6	DAV
7	NRFD
8	NDAC
9	IFC
10	SRQ
11	ATN
12	SHIELD (earth ground)
13	DIO5
14	DIO6
15	DIO7
16	DIO8
17	REN
18	DAV ground
19	NRFD ground
20	NDAC ground
21	IFC ground
22	SRQ ground
23	ATN ground
24	LOGIC ground

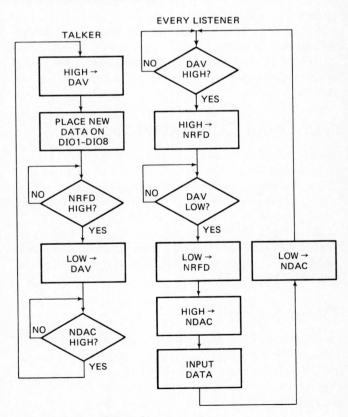

Fig. 17-5 Flowcharts of bus operations.

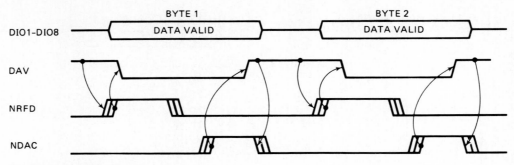

Fig. 17-6 Timing diagram.

listeners and to indicate that data is being changed. Upon sensing the high DAV signal, each listener will raise NRFD. Until all listeners respond, the talker waits.

After this condition is satisfied, the talker drops DAV to signify that the data is valid. As each listener inputs the data, it pulls NDAC low and allows NRFD to go high. Sensing that NDAC is low from all listeners, the talker repeats the cycle for the next data word.

Figure 17-6 shows a timing diagram for the communications exchange. Notice that only the last listener raising or lowering NRFD or NDAC actually produces a change in the signal level.

Now the reason for the three handshaking signals mentioned at the first of this chapter (under "IEEE-488 Bus Overview") becomes more obvious. They permit more than one listener on the bus. The open-collector buffer outputs let all listeners signal one talker or controller. The collective change in signal levels lets them independently sample data, yet provides a way of denoting the completion of all inputs. For example, as each listener accepts data it stops pulling NDAC low, which allows the resistive load to pull NDAC up to 3.3 V (Fig. 17-3).

Controller Communications

Communication between a controller and the listeners is quite similar to that used by the talker. In this case, ATN is used to distinguish between commands (ATN true) and data (ATN false). The instruments listening must respond to ATN signals within 200 ns.

Thus, in a minimal interface, only the data lines (DIO1 through DIO8), DAV, NRFD, and NDAC are needed. If a controller is used, then IFC and ATN are added.

Other Signals

A talker labels the last byte in a data transfer with a monitor bit. When EOI is set to 1, the listeners know that the transfer has been completed.

A controller can disable the front-panel controls of an instrument with the REN signal. As long as this line is held true (low), remote control is in effect. Only when REN is allowed to rise does the instrument revert to manual control. The switching between remote and local control is quite rapid—within 100 μs. Upon initiation, both ATN and REN are set true.

Service can be requested by an instrument sending a true SRQ signal to the controller. This input acts as an interrupt. Control then proceeds by a preselected rule, parallel polling, or serial polling. These control words are recommended in the appendix of IEEE Standard 488 but are not considered to be a formal part of it.

Parallel Polling

A controller can poll (ask the instruments for data) in a parallel fashion. A maximum of eight instruments can be polled, because each is assigned a unique bit on the data bus. To enter this state, the controller simultaneously drops EOI and ATN. Each instrument responds by transmitting 1 bit of status information. The meaning of each 1 or 0 status signal depends on the type of instrument involved. For example, a low could be an OK status reply. Figure 17-7 depicts the parallel polling timing.

A Typical Message Sequence

A list of remote messages is provided in Table 17-5. Each message is a unique combination of data and control signals. In the case of the first message, ACG, bits 5 through 7 of the data bus must be 0 and all others are "don't care" settings. To understand the application of some of these signals, consider a multimember bus.

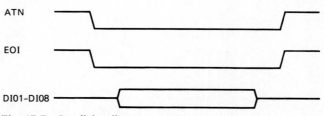

Fig. 17-7 Parallel polling sequence.

Table 17-5 Remote-Message List

Mne-monic	Name	Type	Class	DIO 8	7	6	5	4	3	2	1	DAV	NRFD	NDAC	ATN	EOI	SRQ	IFC	REN
ACG	Address command group	M	C	X	0	0	0	X	X	X	X	X	X	X	X	X	X	X	X
ATN	Attention	U	U	X	X	X	X	X	X	X	X	X	X	X	1	X	X	X	X
DAB	Data byte	M	D	D	D	D	D	D	D	D	D	X	X	X	X	X	X	X	X
DAC	Data accepted	U	H	X	X	X	X	X	X	X	X	X	X	0	X	X	X	X	X
DAV	Data valid	U	H	X	X	X	X	X	X	X	X	1	X	X	X	X	X	X	X
DCL	Device clear	M	U	X	0	0	1	0	1	0	0	X	X	X	X	X	X	X	X
END	End	U	S	X	X	X	X	X	X	X	X	X	X	X	X	1	X	X	X
EOS	End of string	M	D	E	E	E	E	E	E	E	E	X	X	X	X	X	X	X	X
GET	Group execute trigger	M	C	X	0	0	0	1	0	0	0	X	X	X	X	X	X	X	X
GTL	Go to local	M	C	X	0	0	0	0	0	0	1	X	X	X	X	X	X	X	X
IDY	Identify	U	U	X	X	X	X	X	X	X	X	X	X	X	X	1	X	X	X
IFC	Interface clear	U	U	X	X	X	X	X	X	X	X	X	X	X	X	X	X	1	X
LAG	Listen address group	M	A	X	0	1	X	X	X	X	X	X	X	X	X	X	X	X	X
LLO	Local lockout	M	U	X	0	0	1	0	0	0	1	X	X	X	X	X	X	X	X
MLA	My listen address	M	A	X	0	1	L	L	L	L	L	X	X	X	X	X	X	X	X
MTA	My talk address	M	A	X	1	0	T	T	T	T	T	X	X	X	X	X	X	X	X
MSA	My secondary address	M	2	X	1	1	S	S	S	S	S	X	X	X	X	X	X	X	X
NUL	Null byte	M	D	0	0	0	0	0	0	0	0	X	X	X	X	X	X	X	X
OSA	Other secondary address	M	2	(OSA = SCG and $\overline{\text{MSA}}$)															
OTA	Other talk address	M	A	(OTA = TAG and $\overline{\text{MTA}}$)															
PCG	Primary command group	M	—	(PCC = ACG or UCG and LAG and TAG)															
PPC	Parallel poll configure	M	C	X	0	0	0	0	1	0	1	X	X	X	X	X	X	X	X
PPE	Parallel poll enable	M	2	X	1	1	0	Y	P	P	P	X	X	X	X	X	X	X	X
PPD	Parallel poll disable	M	2	X	1	1	1	D	D	D	D	X	X	X	X	X	X	X	X
PPR 1	Parallel poll response 1	U	S	X	X	X	X	X	X	X	1	X	X	X	X	X	X	X	X
PPR 2	Parallel poll response 2	U	S	X	X	X	X	X	X	1	X	X	X	X	X	X	X	X	X
PPR 3	Parallel poll response 3	U	S	X	X	X	X	X	1	X	X	X	X	X	X	X	X	X	X
PPR 4	Parallel poll response 4	U	S	X	X	X	X	1	X	X	X	X	X	X	X	X	X	X	X
PPR 5	Parallel poll response 5	U	S	X	X	X	1	X	X	X	X	X	X	X	X	X	X	X	X
PPR 6	Parallel poll response 6	U	S	X	X	1	X	X	X	X	X	X	X	X	X	X	X	X	X
PPR 7	Parallel poll response 7	U	S	X	1	X	X	X	X	X	X	X	X	X	X	X	X	X	X
PPR 8	Parallel poll response 8	U	S	1	X	X	X	X	X	X	X	X	X	X	X	X	X	X	X
PPU	Parallel poll unconfigure	M	U	X	0	0	1	0	1	0	1	X	X	X	X	X	X	X	X
REN	Remote enable	U	U	X	X	X	X	X	X	X	X	X	X	X	X	X	X	X	1
RFD	Ready for data	U	H	X	X	X	X	X	X	X	X	X	0	X	X	X	X	X	X
RQS	Request for service	U	S	X	1	X	X	X	X	X	X	X	X	X	X	X	X	X	X
SCG	Secondary command group	M	2	X	1	1	X	X	X	X	X	X	X	X	X	X	X	X	X
SDC	Selected device clear	M	C	X	0	0	0	0	1	0	0	X	X	X	X	X	X	X	X
SPD	Serial poll disable	M	U	X	0	0	1	1	0	0	1	X	X	X	X	X	X	X	X
SPE	Serial poll enable	M	U	X	0	0	1	1	0	0	0	X	X	X	X	X	X	X	X
SRQ	Service request	U	S	X	X	X	X	X	X	X	X	X	X	X	X	X	1	X	X
STB	Status byte	M	S	R	X	R	R	R	R	R	R	X	X	X	X	X	X	X	X
TCT	Take control	M	C	X	0	0	0	1	0	0	1	X	X	X	X	X	X	X	X

Table 17-5 (cont'd)

Mne-monic	Name	Type	Class	DIO 8	7	6	5	4	3	2	1	DAV	NRFD	NDAC	ATN	EOI	SRQ	IFC	REN
TAG	Talk address group	M	A	X	1	0	X	X	X	X	X	X	X	X	X	X	X	X	X
UCG	Universal command group	M	U	X	0	0	1	X	X	X	X	X	X	X	X	X	X	X	X
UNL	Unlisten	M	A	X	0	1	1	1	1	1	1	X	X	X	X	X	X	X	X
UNT	Untalk	M	A	X	1	0	1	1	1	1	1	X	X	X	X	X	X	X	X

Notes:
Type:
 M—multiline
 U—single (uniline) message
Class:
 C—addressed command
 A—address (talk or listen)
 D—device-dependent
 H—handshake
 U—universal command
 2—secondary
 S—status

Signals:
 0—high-level state
 1—low-level state
 D—device-dependent bits
 E—device-dependent code in EOS message
 L—device-dependent listen address
 T—device-dependent talk address
 S—device-dependent secondary address
 X—don't care
 P—specify the PPR message to be sent when parallel poll is executed
 Y—sense of PPR (either 0 or 1)
 R—device-dependent status

A microprocessor acts as a controller and talker on a bus with listeners and other talkers.

Figure 17-8 is a flowchart of the initial series of events. First, the processor sends the IFC message (sets bit true) to clear all interface logic. Next, the DCL message causes each device to enter a start state. Assume that next the processor wants to signal the first instrument. The MPU sends the listen address of that instrument followed by the programmable commands to the device.

The processor then sends a stop listening message (UNL) followed by the address and data for the next instrument. This procedure is repeated until all devices have been addressed.

Then the MPU sends the talk address for the first talker. The other talker, in turn, sends data to the addressed listener. The data codes sent to the device by either the controller or talker can use ASCII or the 7-bit ISO codes listed in Table 17-6.

In most cases, Table 17-6 is just a repeat of the messages in Table 17-5 in a somewhat different form. Consider GTL, for example; in both tables, the code for "go to local" is 01_{16}. In other cases, a range of addresses is provided; the listen (MLA) address is shown to range from 02_{16} to $3E_{16}$ in Table 17-6. This range corresponds to the LLLLL field of Table 17-5.

IC Interfaces

A number of integrated-circuit interfacing chips are now available. The Intel 8291 talker-listener chip shown in Fig. 17-9 is typical. It is controlled by a microprocessor

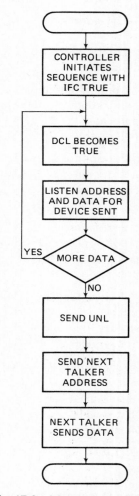

Fig. 17-8 Message sequence.

Table 17-6 ISO 7-Bit Code

DIO1–DIO4 (hexadecimal)	DIO5–DIO8 (hexadecimal)							
	0	1	2	3	4	5	6	7
0								
1	GTL	LLO						
2								
3								
4	SPC	DCL						
5	PPC	PPU	MLA assigned to device	MLA assigned to device	MTA assigned to device	MTA assigned to device	Defined by PCG code	Defined by PCG code
6								
7								
8	GET	SPE						
9	TCT	SPD						
A								
B								
C								
D								
E								
F				UNL		UNT		
	Address command group	Universal command group	Listen address group		Talk address group		Secondary command group	
	Primary command group							

to perform all the functions of a talker or listener. The 8291 can provide the complete handshaking sequence for either a source or accepting instrument and also handles all addressing modes.

Two of the registers in the IC are for data transfer to the microprocessor, while the 14 others support the control, status, and addressing required by the bus interface standard.

The 8291 can also request service, parallel-poll, and send device clear, trigger, and local and remote commands. The IC recognizes primary or secondary addresses. The 8291 can read or write memory data with-

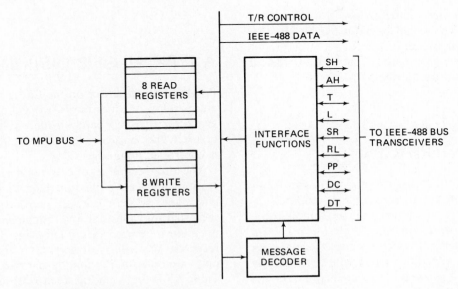

Fig. 17-9 8291 Talker/Listener.

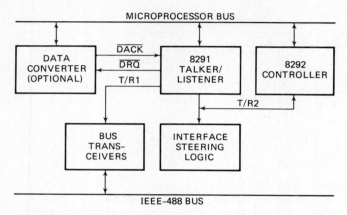

Fig. 17-10 IEEE-488 interface.

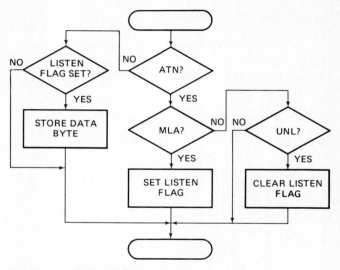

Fig. 17-11 IEEE-488 listener program.

out direct MPU action if an optional DMA controller chip is supplied.

Figure 17-10 shows a bus interface system that uses DMA. The 8292 in the diagram supplements the 8291 by doing the controller actions. The 8292 initializes the bus with the IFC signal. It can then follow with the commands shown in Fig. 17-8, for example.

Bus Operations Review

1. How is the talker able to determine that all listeners have received the last data word and that the data lines can be changed?
2. Explain how it is possible to have multiple listeners on the bus. (Use the timing diagram given in Fig. 17-6.)
3. How can a listener tell the difference between commands and data from a controller?
4. What label is placed on the last byte in a sequence from a talker?
5. Describe the parallel polling process.
6. What are the levels of all lines on the bus for the unlisten remote message?
7. How are the remote messages (Table 17-5) related to the ISO 7-bit codes (Table 17-6)?

SOFTWARE INTERFACES

Instead of using ICs to recognize and process the bus signals, a program in the microprocessor could be substituted. A flowchart for a program to complete the listener functions is shown in Fig. 17-11. This program is initiated by an interrupt which signifies that data has been received. The program first checks to see if the input is an attention message. If so, it then checks for its address in the data bits. If the address matches its

own, it sets an indicator for the listening. If the data is not a match for its own address, the program asks if this could be a UNL message. If so, it clears the listen indicator that had been set by a previous message. If the ATN signal is not true, the program verifies that it is in the listen state and accepts the data byte as a unique command. Note that if none of these conditions is satisfied, the program exits without doing any processing.

Softwear Interfaces Review

1. What event initiates the software listening program?
2. What remote messages must be received before any data will be accepted?
3. What is the result of receiving a UNL message?

A TYPICAL GPIB INSTRUMENT

Programming a device on the bus is straightforward to an operator. As an example, we will consider a function generator that can be controlled by the bus. The generator works basically the same on the bus as when it is controlled manually.

The programming process requires first that all operations to be performed be defined. Then the program is designed. Afterward the description is converted to the program codes that the instrument uses. Finally the program is written in the language that the controller requires. We will assume that our function generator only responds to the unique data commands listed in Table 17-7 and that the controller uses ASCII coded commands. The listen addresses for the device is 34_{16}.

Table 17-7 Instrument Unique Data Commands

Command	ASCII Code
Function	FU
Sine wave	1
Square wave	2
Triangle wave	3
Frequency	FR
Hz	HZ
kHz	KHZ
MHz	MHZ
Amplitude	AM
Volts peak to peak	VP
Volts rms	VR

A command to address the function generator to listen and provide a 10-kHz sine wave with an amplitude in root-mean-square (rms) value of 5 V rms could be written as:

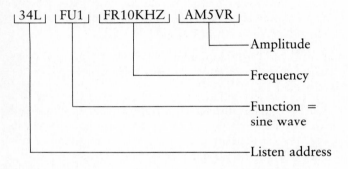

A 60-Hz square wave with 2.5-V peak-to-peak excursion could be provided by the command

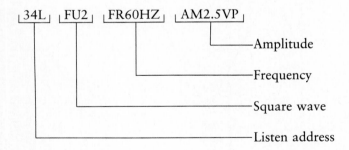

Most instruments would have a much larger repertoire of commands. Especially lacking in this case is the ability to report status. To perform that function, the generator would require a talk address.

The controller gains control of the instrument by forcing it to the remote mode. This state change is effected by setting ATN and REN true and sending the listen address of 34 for that device. Then any string of data messages can be addressed to the generator.

As each command is received, the generator processes it and responds. The listener function must also respond to the general commands listed in Table 17-5. In this manner, the generator can be programmed to initialize (DCL), respond to a serial poll (SPE), unlisten (UNL), untalk (UNT), and so on.

A PRACTICAL NOTE

Although the IEEE-488 bus specification standardizes a great number of the mechanical, electrical, and logical interfaces, others are optional or not defined. The result may be that two instruments may not be able to communicate directly over the bus. Unfortunately, this problem has even been observed in two instruments from the same manufacturer.

The reason for this incompatibility stems from device-dependent program codes, output data formats, and data coding. For example, one instrument may use binary while another uses BCD.

To prevent such problems, be sure to note these conflicts in the equipment manuals. Do not assume that a claim of IEEE-488 compatibility necessarily implies that two devices can communicate on the bus.

CHAPTER SUMMARY

1. The IEEE-488 bus transfers data bytes in parallel. Three signals accomplish the handshaking necessary to communicate.
2. Devices performing any combination of talkers, listeners, or controllers can communicate on the bus. Each will have a unique address.
3. Three sets of signals comprise the GPIB: data, handshaking, and general interface management.
4. An interlocked sequence of control and status exchanges runs the bus.
5. Any IEEE-488-compatible equipment item is subdivided into these partitions: driver and receiver, message coding, interface functions, and device functions. All partitions except the device-dependent functions are specified.
6. Ten functions that the GPIB can support are listed in the repertoire. These functions include those required for handshaking, talking, listening, requesting service, remote controlling, polling, clearing, and triggering.
7. The electrical and mechanical characteristics constrain the designer to certain types of drivers, terminations, receivers, and connectors.
8. In operation, a specific series of signals exchanged between a talker and listener synchronizes the time when data is valid and when data can change. Parallel polling is used to obtain status from up to eight instruments at one time.
9. The bus logic can be implemented in either hardware or software.

General-purpose interface bus (GPIB)

Listeners

Talkers

Controllers

Data bus

Handshaking bus

General interface management bus

Interlocked sequence

Functional partitioning

Functional repertoire

Electrical characteristics

Mechanical characteristics

Bus operations

Parallel polling

IC interfaces

Software interface

PROBLEMS

17-1 Assume that the voltage on the bus line is -0.4 V. What current is flowing through the two resistors shown in Figure 17-3?

17-2 A high voltage is placed on the bus line in Fig. 17-3. If the voltage is 5.2 V, what is the input voltage to the receiver amplifier? What current flows in the 3-kΩ resistor?

17-3 Because of a malfunction, -2.0 V appears on the bus line of Fig. 17-3. What are the voltages across the resistors if D_1 requires a forward bias of 0.7 V to conduct? Assuming that all current flows into the driver, how much current will it sink?

17-4 Draw a timing diagram similar to that shown in Fig. 17-6 for a bus system consisting of two listeners and one talker. Assume that DAV is low for 0.5 μs and high for 1 μs. Listener 1 always responds 0.1 μs before listener 2.

Note: Use the remote-message list in Table 17-5 to answer Probs. 17-8 through 17-9.

17-5 What would be the state of the data bus and other signals for a DCL command?

17-6 How would device 13_{10} send its listen address in the MLA message?

17-7 Assume that to disable a parallel polling sequence, a device requires a data code of 11_{10}. Show the data content of the PPD message required.

17-8 A controller commands talker 26_{10} to take control with the appropriate remote message. What are the settings of the data bus and REN line?

17-9 A programmable calculator receives a command of BF_{16}. How would this remote message be interpreted?

17-10 What instruction would be used to command the function generator to produce the signal shown in Fig. 17-12? (The function generator was discussed under "A Typical GPIB Instrument" on p. 318.)

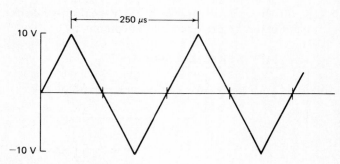

Fig. 17-12 Problem 17-10.

MICROCOMPUTER BUSES

This chapter investigates bus standards that make it possible to construct a customized microcomputer simply by plugging in the proper selection of printed circuit cards. These buses are used within the computer to interconnect modules such as the processor, ROM, and RAM. In contrast to an external bus between equipment, such as the IEEE-488 bus, the microcomputer bus is within the computer cabinet. Although more components are used in a microcomputer built with one of these buses, overall costs can be reduced by their application. Cost reduction results from the existing support documentation, maintenance aids, standard enclosures, power supplies, and printed circuit cards. A large family of plug-compatible modules can be developed if the bus is mass-produced. Microcomputers that use a bus are very adaptable to change. An obsolete board can be removed and a new design substituted. Maintenance is also simplified by the module-swapping approach.

CHAPTER OBJECTIVES

Upon completion of this chapter, you should be able to:

1. Distinguish between unidirectional and bidirectional computer buses.
2. Explain the purpose of bus drivers and receivers.
3. Describe the general capabilities of two widely used buses.
4. Explain the use of the various signal lines of the bus.
5. Show how a collection of modules can be integrated into a complete microcomputer.

MULTIPLEXED BUSES

A microcomputer bus is a collection of conductors that serve as a standard communication path between the modules comprising the computer. The bus is multiplexed so that any member on it can originate or receive messages. The communication paths provided by the bus include the address, data, control, and power lines.

Bus connections are made to the long edge of a rectangular printed circuit board (PCB), or card. The PC card serves to interconnect and support the electronic components. The card height is measured from the bus connector to the opposite side. The width is the distance between the sides perpendicular to the connector.

The cards slide into a cage which supports them and which also provides the *motherboard,* or backplane that holds the receptacles for the card plugs. The guides on the holder must support the cards with precise spacing. This precision means that the width dimension of the PCB is critical in avoiding a loose fit.

The tops of the cards stick up above the cage. Frequently test points, displays, and switches are mounted on the top for maintenance operations. These features allow the technician to check the card without removing it from the cage. Extender boards are available to assist the technician. The extender connects to the PCB, increasing its height, so the card is outside the cage frame. The extended card remains connected to the bus at the same time the circuit is accessible for signal tracing.

Figure 18-1a shows a *daisy-chain multiplexed bus.* A loop is formed, interconnecting every module in the system. Each module acts as a source and acceptor for signals not addressed to it. The addressed acceptor recognizes that the data is intended for it and does not pass the data on. A daisy chain forms a unidirectional bus. This limitation prevents the daisy chain from being used for data transfer, but daisy chains are used in addressing on some buses.

The *party-line bus* offers direct access between any modules on the bus. There is only one source and one acceptor for each message. The party line is bidirectional, so it is often used for data exchange.

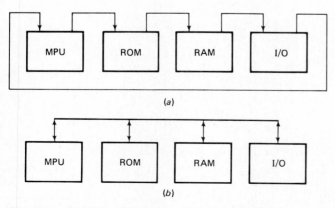

(a)

(b)

Fig. 18-1 Multiplexed buses: (a) daisy chaining, (b) party line.

Bus Signals

The type of information being sent and the receiving module must be specified for every message transmitted. Control signals supply this necessary coordination. Another important control function is *bus arbitration.* Arbitration avoids the problem of having two transmitters using the bus at once. A priority auction is used by the arbitration circuitry to decide which of two transmitters simultaneously requesting the bus will be granted access.

With *synchronous bus control,* only one member (usually the microprocessor) originates all control and timing signals. Other bus members synchronize their operations to those signals when transmitting or receiving. If control and timing are generated jointly by the source and acceptor, *asynchronous bus control* is being used. Handshaking is frequently associated with asynchronous bus control. An example of a handshaking signal sequence is listed in Table 18-1.

Drivers

Special circuits called *drivers* are employed to connect or disconnect sources placing signals on the bus. The drivers ensure electrical compatibility among all bus members. The drivers also offer a higher current drive for the signals than the output circuits of the processor are capable of, so the signals are more likely to reach their destination without error.

A driver is designed to drive one standard TTL load. A key attribute of the bus is its capacitive loading. The stray bus capacitance limits its bandwidth and therefore its maximum operating speed. A microcomputer with a 2-μs cycle time requires a bus with a capacitive load of less than 100 pF in each line.

Several types of drivers are shown in Fig. 18-2. The logical OR driver includes a digital multiplexer that selects the source for the signal to be put on the bus. (These examples show single-bit operation only. Parallel circuits can be added to make the bus as wide as necessary.) The logical OR driver can only be used on a unidirectional bus because one of the sources is always connected to the bus. It is not a good choice for modules that are widely separated. Also, once this type of driver is constructed, adding more sources is difficult.

A wired-OR driver uses open-collector gates directly wired to the bus. Recall that the transistor in the output

Table 18-1 Handshaking Signals

Source	Acceptor
Prepare to receive (Places data on bus)	Ready to receive
Data ready (Data lines dropped)	Data accepted

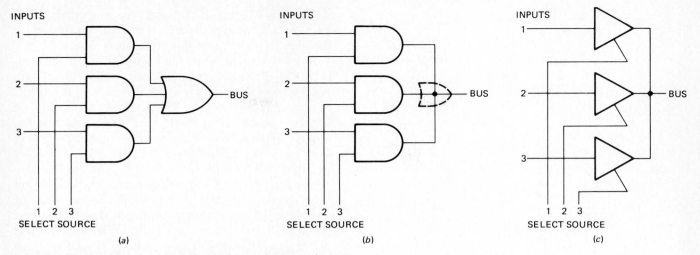

Fig. 18-2 Driver circuits: (*a*) logical OR, (*b*) wired OR, (*c*) three-state.

stage of an open-collector gate will determine the logic level on the bus. The output transistor of all the gates that are not selected will be off, so only the selected gate controls the level. If the output transistor in that gate is on, the bus is pulled low; otherwise, the bus is high. Because the wired-OR driver permits the condition in which no source is being selected, this driver can be used on a bidirectional bus.

The three-state driver offers three output conditions: high, low, and high-impedance output. When any gate is enabled, its input appears at the output terminal. If the gate is disabled, the output is in the high-impedance state, and we say that the output lines are floating. The three-state driver can be either a source or a sink on a bidirectional bus.

Receivers

The proper type of receiver can be quite effective in reducing the capacitive loading and can thus offer higher-speed operation. The loading on the bus increases with the number of receivers that are simultaneously enabled. If an enable line is provided for the receiver, it can be set to a high-impedance state when there is no incoming message.

A simple receiver is illustrated in Fig. 18-3. The bus signal is passed only through the gate selected. By placing the address on the selection line, the one receiver to accept the message is designated.

Bus Circuits

A practical bus transceiver is shown in Fig. 18-4a. A *transceiver* is a combined driver and receiver. These circuits find frequent use when I/O devices are to be connected to the bus. A bidirectional data path is offered, and a number of transceivers can be placed on the bus because they are three-state devices.

The circuit shown in Fig. 18-4b is a *bidirectional driver*. Four of these drivers are usually packaged in a single IC. The quad driver can source or sink 4 bits on the bus. The amplifier acts as a buffer that boosts the driver capacity. This latter attribute is particularly effective on heavily loaded buses. Table 18-2 summarizes two widely used microcomputer buses.

Multiplexed Buses Review

1. Define the term "bus."
2. If the PC card for a bus module is 5 in × 10 in (12.7 cm × 25.4 cm), what is its width?
3. Distinguish between daisy-chain and party-line buses.
4. True or false? Most bidirectional buses use daisy-chain loops.
5. Explain the purpose of bus arbitration.
6. Why are drivers used for bus communication?
7. Explain why wired OR drivers can be used on a bidirectional bus and logical OR drivers cannot.

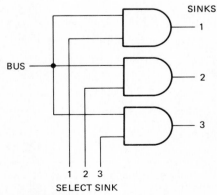

Fig. 18-3 Receiver circuits.

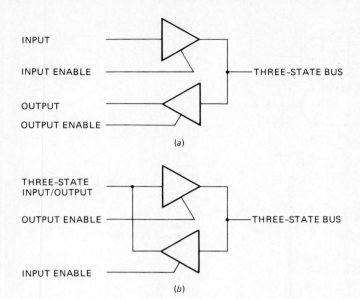

Fig. 18-4 (a) Bus transceiver, (b) bidirectional driver.

THE S-100 BUS

The *S-100 bus,* also known as the IEEE-696 bus, is a parallel bus widely used in personal computers. Sometimes called the "hobby bus," the S-100 was invented by MITS for the 8080-based Altair 8800 microcomputer. The name originated from the 100 lines that make up the bus. After its introduction, the bus was used by IMSAI, Polymorphic, Processor Technology, and others in their equipment. Today there are more than 700 boards or modules for the bus that are produced by over 100 manufacturers. So you can see that there are a lot of S-100 buses in operation. Some of the lines are logically identical to those of the 8080A, while others are related to 8080A signals or uniquely defined by MITS.

Table 18-2 Typical Buses

Characteristics	S-100	Multibus*
Originator	MITS	Intel
Lines	100	86
Address	16	16
Data	16†	16
Control	38	15
Interrupts	8	8
Grounds	2	8
Power	4	16
Spare	16	7
Number of supply voltages	3	5

* Multibus is a trademark of Intel Corporation.
† Eight in each direction.

An overall listing of the signals is provided in Table 18-3. Pins 1 through 50 are on the component side of the board and 51 through 100 on the foil side.

The power distributed on the bus is unregulated, so each board must regulate it locally. There are advantages to distributing power in this manner. The distribution circuitry is simplified and the noise coupling between boards is reduced. The boards cost more, though, because individual regulators must be supplied. The $+8$ V is regulated to $+5$ V, the $+16$ to $+12$ V, and the -16 to -12 V.

The data bus is divided into separate input and output lines. Data input is used to transfer data to the processor (the master) from another module (the slave). Data output reverses the process. For both sets of lines, bit 0 is the least significant bit. The availability of unidirectional data buses offers no advantage, and eight additional pins on the connector are required to provide the separate buses. The separate buses are frequently wired together on many peripheral modules. Figure 18-5 shows how the output bus is enabled by $\overline{\text{DODSB}}$. Until that signal is pulled low, the three-state drivers have floating outputs.

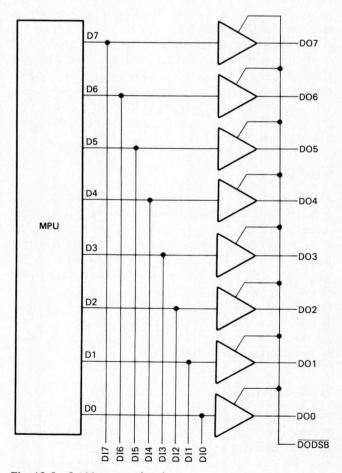

Fig. 18-5 S-100 output data bus.

Table 18-3 S-100 Bus Signals

Pin	Purpose	Comments	Pin	Purpose	Comments
1	+8 V	Unregulated power	43	DI7	Data in 7
2	+16 V	Unregulated power	44	SM1	Machine cycle 1 (instruction fetch)
3	XRDY	External ready input to MPU			
4	VI0	Vectored-interrupt 0	45	SOUT	Output; status signal indicating that the address bus holds the output device code
5	VI1	Vectored-interrupt 1			
6	VI2	Vectored-interrupt 2			
7	VI3	Vectored-interrupt 3	46	SINP	Input; status signal indicating that the address bus holds the input device code
8	VI4	Vectored-interrupt 4			
9	VI5	Vectored-interrupt 5			
10	VI6	Vectored-interrupt 6	47	SMEMR	Memory read; status signal indicating that a memory read will occur
11	VI7	Vectored-interrupt 7			
12	—	Undefined			
13	—	Undefined	48	SHLTA	Halt; status signal in response to an HLT instruction
14	—	Undefined			
15	—	Undefined	49	$\overline{\text{CLOCK}}$	Inverted Φ2 clock
16	—	Undefined	50	GND	Ground
17	—	Undefined	51	+8 V	Unregulated +5-V power (same as pin 1)
18	$\overline{\text{STATDSB}}$	Status disable; strobe for three-state buffers on status lines			
19	$\overline{\text{C/CDSB}}$	Command/control disable; strobe for the three-state command/control buffers	52	−16 V	Unregulated power
			53	$\overline{\text{SSWI}}$	Sense switch input from panel
			54	$\overline{\text{EXTCLR}}$	External clear to I/O devices
20	UNPROT	Unprotect; input to memory protect flip-flop	55	—	Undefined
			56	—	Undefined
21	SS	MPU is executing in single step (one instruction at a time)	57	—	Undefined
			58	—	Undefined
			59	—	Undefined
22	$\overline{\text{ADDRDSB}}$	Address disable; strobe for three-state buffers on address lines	60	—	Undefined
			61	—	Undefined
23	$\overline{\text{DODSB}}$	Data output disable; strobe for three-state output on data lines	62	—	Undefined
			63	—	Undefined
24	Φ2	Phase 2 clock	64	—	Undefined
25	Φ1	Phase 1 clock	65	—	Undefined
26	PHLDA	Hold acknowledge Processor command/control signal	66	—	Undefined
			67	—	Undefined
27	PWAIT	Wait; processor command/control signal	68	MWRITE	Memory write; data is to be placed in memory
			69	$\overline{\text{PS}}$	Memory protect flip-flop status
28	PINTE	Interrupt enable; processor command/control signal	70	PROT	Input to memory protect flip-flop
			71	RUN	Indicates that MPU is in the run mode
29	A5	Address line 5			
30	A4	Address line 4	72	PRDY	Processor ready input
31	A3	Address line 3	73	$\overline{\text{PINT}}$	Interrupt request
32	A15	Address line 15	74	$\overline{\text{PHOLD}}$	Processor command/control input to enter hold state
33	A12	Address line 12			
34	A9	Address line 9	75	$\overline{\text{PRESET}}$	Reset processor command/control input
35	DO1	Data out 1			
36	DO0	Data out 0	76	PSYNC	Sync processor command control output
37	A10	Address line 10			
38	DO4	Data out 4	77	$\overline{\text{PWR}}$	Write processor command/control output
39	DO5	Data out 5			
40	DO6	Data out 6	78	PDBIN	Data bus input processor command/control signal
41	DI2	Data in 2			
42	DI3	Data in 3	79	A0	Address line 0

Table 18-3 *(cont'd)*

Pin	Purpose	Comments	Pin	Purpose	Comments
80	A1	Address line 1	91	DI4	Data in 4
81	A2	Address line 2	92	DI5	Data in 5
82	A6	Address line 6	93	DI6	Data in 6
83	A7	Address line 7	94	DI1	Data in 1
84	A8	Address line 8	95	DI0	Data in 0
85	A13	Address line 13	96	SINTA	Interrupt acknowledge output
86	A14	Address line 14	97	$\overline{\text{SWO}}$	Write out status signal
87	A11	Address line 11	98	SSTACK	Stack status signal
88	DO2	Data out 2	99	$\overline{\text{POC}}$	Power on clear
89	DO3	Data out 3	100	GND	Ground
90	DO7	Data out 7			

The address bus is a standard 16-bit buffered bus. As Fig. 18-6 shows, bits A0 through A15 correspond to the 8080A address pins. A three-state buffer is used on the lines. The $\overline{\text{ADDRDSB}}$ signal enables the buffers when true.

The command/control bus, shown in Fig. 18-7, buffers six signals used to control the other bus information. Any member of the bus, and the front-panel switches of the microcomputers, can originate these signals. The PINTE signal represents the status of the interrupt enable flag of the processor. Hold acknowledge (PHLDA) is generated by the processor when it enters the hold state. A low $\overline{\text{PWR}}$ signal means that a write operation to memory or to an I/O device will occur. Data on the address and output buses must not change while this signal is low. When the processor is in the wait state, PWAIT is high. PDBIN is used to indicate that the addressed device should place its data on the data input bus. PSYNC corresponds to the 8080A SYNC signal, which indicates the beginning of a machine cycle. Figure 18-7 also shows how the command/control outputs are derived from the 8080A. $\overline{\text{C/CDSB}}$ must be true before any of these signals will appear on the bus.

The status bus signals in Fig. 18-8 are typically latched by an 8212 I/O port. All the status signals are derived from the status byte sent by the 8080A. The SMEMR signal is used to designate that a memory read will occur next. The memory write (MWRITE) signal is derived from SMEMR. A true SINP signal means that the address bus is set to the input device address. Similarly, the SOUT signal indicates that the output device code is on the address bus. An instruction-fetching cycle (M1) is indicated by SM1 going high. When the processor halts, it sets SHLTA high. The stack pointer address is on the address bus when SSTACK is true. A write operation is indicated by $\overline{\text{SWO}}$, and an interrupt request is acknowledged by use of SINTA.

The control signals are buffered and latched also. PRDY/XRDY corresponds to the READY output of 8080A, PHOLD to HOLD, PINT to INT (interrupt request), and PRESET to RESET. All these S-100 signals are identical to the 8080A signals.

Some other signals are the two clock phases, $\Phi 1$ and $\Phi 2$, and $\overline{\text{CLOCK}}$ ($\Phi 2$ inverted). The $\overline{\text{POC}}$ signal indicates that power is being applied to the processor when true. The vectored interrupts, VI0 through VI7, are intended to reference the eight vector addresses in the 8080A using the RST instruction.

The original computer for which the bus was designed had a series of switches on the front panel that controlled some of the bus signals. Data in memory could be altered if UNPROT were true and was protected against change when PROT was true. Momentary contact switches to originate the $\overline{\text{PRESET}}$ or $\overline{\text{EXTCLR}}$ were also provided. The mode of operation depended on the state of the RUN and SS switch. A final signal, $\overline{\text{SSWI}}$, is used to coordinate data transfer to the front-panel sense switches.

Electrical Specifications

The voltages and currents for high and low levels on the bus are listed in Table 18-4 (see page 328). Because the levels are not specified, the values listed should be considered typical of what one would expect for TTL compatibility. Capacitive loading on any signal line should not exceed 25 pF. Positive current means that the module is acting as a sink. Bus drivers and receivers on each PCB should be placed close to their S-100 bus connectors.

Mechanical Specifications

The S-100 is implemented by use of a motherboard consisting of 100 parallel foil strips that interconnect several 100-pin receptacles. The individual printed circuit cards plug into the motherboard by use of an edge connector.

Figure 18-9 (see page 328) shows the S-100 mechanical configuration. The S-100 bus connector consists of a 100-pin plug with conductors at $1/8$-in (0.3-cm) spacing.

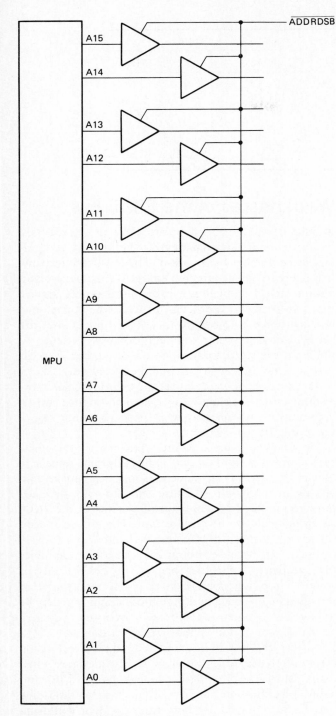

Fig. 18-6 S-100 address bus.

There are 50 pins on each side of the board. Boards are separated by ³/₄ in (1.9 cm) along the motherboard, with component height restricted to 0.55 in (1.4 cm). The board thickness is 0.062 in (0.16 cm).

S-100 Timing

The S-100 bus timing is quite similar to that of the 8080A. Timing diagrams for memory read and write

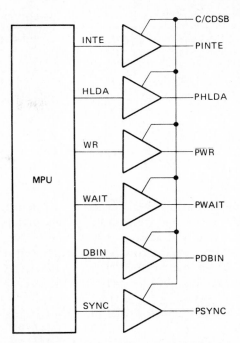

Fig. 18-7 S-100 command/control bus.

are shown in Fig. 18-10 (see page 329). The read operation is signaled by the true state of SMEMR and the false state of $\overline{PWR}$. The data is accepted by the memory cell addressed by A0 through A15 when DBIN goes high.

A write operation requires that SMEMR be low. The addressed memory will respond with the data when PWR becomes true. (Write operations may also be controlled by MWRITE.) The status codes appear on the data lines during T1 of the instruction cycle, as with normal 8080A operations.

Other operations that use the bus are those for exchanging bus control and interrupting the processor. To request bus control, the device forces $\overline{PHOLD}$ true. When the processor has entered the hold state, it relinquishes the bus with the acknowledgment, PHLDA. Then the requesting device disables the processor bus drivers (Figs. 18-5 through 18-8) with $\overline{DODSB}$, $\overline{ADDRDSB}$, C/CDSB, and $\overline{STATDSB}$ signals. The device

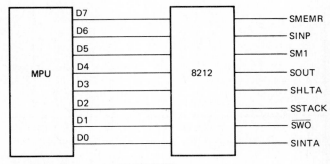

All signals are enabled by $\overline{STATUSDSB}$

Fig. 18-8 S-100 status bus.

Table 18-4 S-100 Electrical Characteristics

	Voltage (V)		Current	
	Max	Min	Max	Min
Driver				
High	+5.5	+2.4		−12 mA
Low	+0.5	0		+24 mA
Receiver				
High	+5.5	+2.0	+40 μA	
Low	+0.8	−0.6	−0.8 mA	

then has complete control of the bus. The bus is surrendered by raising the disable signals and PHOLD. The processor will regain control of the bus at that time. Unfortunately, two devices can request and gain control of the bus at once in this manner. To correct this shortcoming, the user must provide bus arbitration logic.

Interrupts are signaled with a low $\overline{\text{PINT}}$ signal. When the current instruction is completed, the MPU sets the interrupt acknowledge status, SINTA. The interrupted device then supplies the next instruction (usually RST or CALL) on the data input bus.

Example of an S-100 System

A microcomputer that uses the S-100 bus is shown in Fig. 18-11. Three modules plus the power supply form the computer. The processor is provided with the control and status buses and the normal address and data buses.

The memory is controlled by the status of MWRITE and SMEMR, while the I/O controller module requires $\overline{\text{PWR}}$, SOUT, PDBIN, and SINP for its operations. As you will notice, two modules may use quite different status and control signals to communicate with the processor. In addition to the control, status, address, and data lines, power will be distributed to each module by means of the bus.

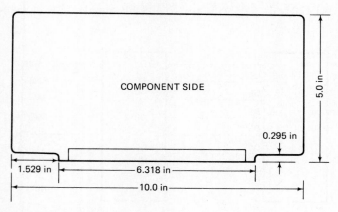

COMPONENT SIDE

5.0 in

0.295 in

1.529 in — 6.318 in — 10.0 in

Fig. 18-9 S-100 board.

Weaknesses of the S-100 Bus

In spite of the S-100's popularity, the technician must be aware of its shortcomings to be able to properly service equipment built with it. The most serious problem likely to be encountered concerns the power distribution pins. Unplugging a board with power applied (not a recommended practice) provides the opportunity to touch −18 V (pin 1) to the +8-V (pin 2) line with subsequent spectacular, although expensive, results. At the least, the regulators will be damaged, but every IC with a +5-V power input could be wiped out.

Variations in power level for the boards located more distantly from the supply can sometimes induce current variations. A module may work properly in one slot of the motherboard but not in another.

Manufacturers have picked up some of the unassigned pins on the bus and applied special signals to them. The use of the undefined pins can make two boards incompatible. Because the bus was designed prior to the 8228 system controller, many of the S-100 control signals are now redundant. There is no specification for the use of the vectored interrupts (pins 4 through 11). Because the rapidly changing clock lines run parallel to control signals, a great deal of noise is coupled into the control lines, often requiring that shielding be provided and that good design practices be followed. No signals should use a frequency equal to the clock rate or double that rate, for example.

Because the bus is not buffered, capacitive loading can severely degrade the signals. The designer must derive such simple 8080A signals as $\overline{\text{MEMR}}$ and $\overline{\text{MEMW}}$ because they are not on the bus. Making some signals true high and others true low is a confusing convention and makes it difficult to OR two or more signals of opposite polarity together. The lack of arbitration when two devices request bus control is a serious obstacle in direct memory access designs.

The S-100 Bus Review

1. True or false? The S-100 bus provides separate unidirectional input and output data lines.
2. Explain how the output data bus is enabled.

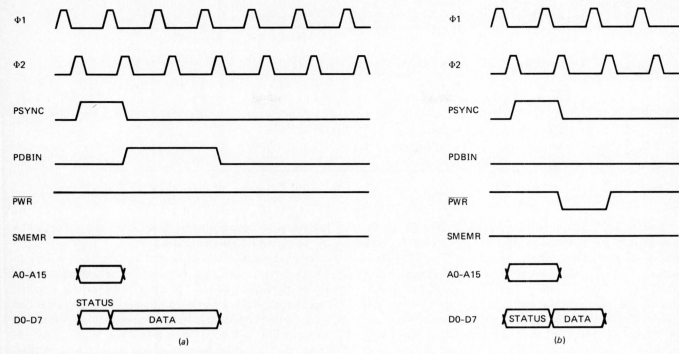

Fig. 18-10 S-100 timing: (*a*) read, (*b*) write.

3. What is the purpose of the PINTE control signal?
4. Which signal on the bus corresponds to the 8080A SYNC pulse?
5. How is the memory write signal, MWRITE, derived?
6. Distinguish between SINP and SOUT.
7. List the maximum and minimum driver voltage levels.
8. Explain the method used to transfer bus control.

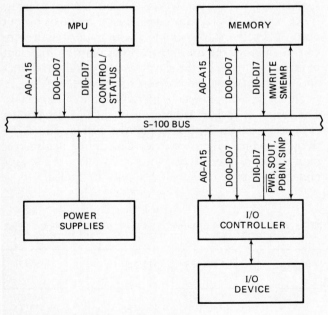

Fig. 18-11 S-100 microcomputer.

THE MULTIBUS

The *Multibus*, also called the IEEE-796 bus, provides a mechanism for quickly connecting single-board computers; memory, digital or analog I/O boards; and peripheral controllers. This bus is specified and supported by the Intel Corporation. Table 18-5 lists some of the modules available for operation on the Multibus. In building a microcomputer, one simply selects the mix of components that will satisfy the requirements of the application. Card cages, power supplies, and cabinets are produced by the manufacturer as well.

The Multibus carries five types of signals: There is a 20-line address bus, a 16-line bidirectional data bus, eight multilevel interrupt lines, control and timing lines, and power distribution lines. The address and data bus are three-state, while the interrupt lines are open-collector.

Modules on the bus operate as either masters or slaves. A master module transmits commands and designates addresses. Another way of defining this relationship is to say that a master module can control the bus; a slave cannot. Arbitration logic is built in to handle requests from multiple masters. The speed of data transfer is not synchronous with the bus clock, so a faster rate is possible. The data rates of the master and slave are the controlling factors. For that reason, a slow master unit can have the same opportunity to gain bus access as a fast master module can. Once a master has bus control, either single- or multiple-word transfers are allowed.

Table 18-5 Typical Multibus Modules

Designation	Description	Power Requirements (Max)			
		+5 V	+12 V	−5 V	−12 V
80/24	Microcomputer	4.7 mA	300 mA	180 mA	120 mA
80/30	Microcomputer	4.6	350	95	150
032	32K RAM	3.2	600	40	
464	64K EPROM	1600			
88/45	Communications processor	5100	20	20	
215	Winchester disk controller	3350	150	30	

Table 18-6 lists the signals carried by the Multibus. The signals are assigned to pins in the P1 primary connector or the P2 secondary connector. The P1 signals include address, data, control, interrupt, and power lines. The P2 signals in the auxiliary connector are optional and are used for battery (backup) power and memory protection. Most of the signals on the bus use negative logic; that is, they are true when low. With negative logic, the possibility of issuing an incorrect command is lessened because TTL devices produce high outputs when not driven. Therefore, invalid true outputs will not be issued when one bus master takes control from another.

Primary Signal Lines

The initialization signal is the system reset command. Most often used in start-up operations, the $\overline{\text{INIT}}$ signal would probably be a result of the operator pressing a front-panel switch.

The address bus, $\overline{\text{ADR0}}$–$\overline{\text{ADR13}}$, is numbered in the hexadecimal (0_{16} through 13_{16}), so there are 20 lines in all. An 8-bit microprocessor would normally only use 16 address lines ($\overline{\text{ADR0}}$–$\overline{\text{ADRF}}$) for memory operations and 8 address lines ($\overline{\text{ADR0}}$–$\overline{\text{ADR7}}$) for I/O port addressing. The Multibus can also support 16-bit microprocessors. Then all 20 address lines are needed for referencing memory, and 12 lines are used for I/O port designation ($\overline{\text{ADR0}}$–$\overline{\text{ADRB}}$).

Inhibit lines are provided so that both RAM and ROM can be assigned identical memory addresses. The $\overline{\text{INH1}}$ signal inhibits the read-write memory from responding to the memory address. The $\overline{\text{INH2}}$ signal performs an identical function for ROM. Some uses for the inhibit signals are to allow either ROM or RAM to share the same memory addresses, to allow for an auxiliary ROM with the same addresses as the primary ROM, or to allow memory-mapped I/O ports to override ROM.

The bidirectional data lines are the paths for data moving between the processor and memory or an I/O port. A 16-bit-wide bus is available, but 8-bit microprocessors use only the least significant 8 bits. The byte

high enable signal must be true when the upper 8 bits of the data bus are being used.

Seven bus lines are dedicated to priority resolution. The negative edge of the bus clock synchronizes the bus arbitration (also called "priority resolution") circuits. The constant clock has a 100-ns period and is intended for general-purpose use by any module. The priority in and out lines are used for priority resolution; they are connected in daisy-chain fashion, as shown in Fig. 18-12. With this arrangement, the physical card position establishes the priority for a given master. When a master gains control, it uses $\overline{\text{BUSY}}$ as an indication to other masters, preventing them from requesting the bus. When the bus is not busy, the module wanting to use it makes its requirement known with the $\overline{\text{BREQ}}$ signal. The master currently in control is made aware of another master needing the bus with the $\overline{\text{CREQ}}$ line.

Another group of bus lines is assigned to coordinate the transfer of information. Two sets of read and write signals are available: one set for memory operations and the other for I/O devices. The $\overline{\text{MRDC}}$ and $\overline{\text{MWTC}}$ signals are associated with strobing memory, while $\overline{\text{IORC}}$ and $\overline{\text{IOWC}}$ do the same for an input or output port. When the slave completes the read or write operation, it sends the transfer acknowledgment. Interrupt requests are made by the slave using the multilevel lines and are granted by the processor sending $\overline{\text{INTA}}$.

The power supply bus carries voltage to all modules. The design of each board must provide bulk decoupling capacitors on the board to prevent current surges on the power bus. High-frequency decoupling is also recommended. Values of 22 μF for +5- and +12-V pins and 10 μF for −5- and −12-V pins are typical.

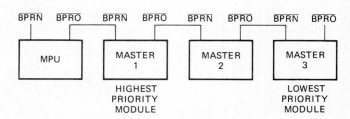

Fig. 18-12 Multibus priority signals.

Table 18-6 Multibus Signals

Name	Symbol	Source	Purpose
P1 signals:			
Initialization	$\overline{\text{INIT}}$	Master/external switch	Resets system
Address line	$\overline{\text{ADR0}}$–$\overline{\text{ADR13}}$ (numbered 0–13_{16})	Master	Memory and I/O address
Inhibit RAM signal	$\overline{\text{INH1}}$	Master	Prevents RAM response
Inhibit ROM signal	$\overline{\text{INH2}}$	Master	Prevents ROM response
Data lines	$\overline{\text{DAT0}}$–$\overline{\text{DATF}}$	Master/slave	Bidirectional data to or from memory or I/O port
Byte high enable	$\overline{\text{BHEN}}$	Master	Used with 16-bit memory and I/O transfers
Bus clock	$\overline{\text{BCLK}}$	Bus control	Negative edge is used to sync bus priority resolution circuits
Constant clock	$\overline{\text{CCLK}}$	Bus control	General-purpose clock
Bus priority in	$\overline{\text{BPRN}}$	Bus control	Indicates to a particular master that it has highest priority
Bus priority out	$\overline{\text{BPRO}}$	Master	Used in daisy-chain priority resolution schemes
Bus busy	$\overline{\text{BUSY}}$	Master	Indicates bus is in use
Bus request	$\overline{\text{BREQ}}$	Master	Indicates that a master requires use of the bus
Common request	$\overline{\text{CREQ}}$	Master	Informs current bus master that another master wants to use the bus
Memory read	$\overline{\text{MRDC}}$	Master	Address of a memory location to be read is on the address bus
Memory write	$\overline{\text{MWTC}}$	Master	Address of a memory location to be written is on the address bus
I/O read command	$\overline{\text{IORC}}$	Master	Address of an input port to be read has been placed on the address bus
I/O write command	$\overline{\text{IOWC}}$	Master	Address of an output port to be written has been placed on the address bus
Transfer acknowledge	$\overline{\text{XACK}}$	Slave	Response when specified read-write operation has been completed
Interrupt request	$\overline{\text{INT0}}$–$\overline{\text{INT7}}$	Slave	Multilevel parallel interrupt request lines
Interrupt acknowledge	$\overline{\text{INTA}}$	Master	Requests transfer of interrupt information
P2 signals:			
AC low	$\overline{\text{ACLO}}$	Power supply	AC input voltage too low
Power fail interrupt	$\overline{\text{PFIN}}$	External power fail circuit	Power failure
Power fail sense	$\overline{\text{PFSN}}$	External power fail circuit	Output of a latch indicating that a power failure has occurred
Power fail reset	$\overline{\text{PFSR}}$	External power fail circuit	Resets the power failure sense latch
Address latch enable	ALE	Master	From 8085 or 8086 as an auxiliary address latch
Halt	$\overline{\text{HALT}}$	Master	MPU has halted
Wait state	$\overline{\text{WAIT}}$	Master	Master processor is in the wait state
Auxiliary reset	$\overline{\text{AUXRESET}}$	External	Initiates power-up sequence
Memory protect	$\overline{\text{MPRO}}$	External	Prevents memory operations when power is uncertain

Optional Signal Lines

The optional P2 signals are not bused to the backplane, so a separate connector is required for each board that uses these signals. A power failure warning is provided by the ACLO signal. Normally this signal becomes true 3 ms before the dc power falls below acceptable levels. Restoring the power to within 95 percent of rated voltage disables this signal. An external power source (battery) provides the voltage to interrupt the processor with $\overline{\text{PFIN}}$ and to indicate that power has failed with $\overline{\text{PFSN}}$. The latter signal remains true until reset by $\overline{\text{PFSR}}$.

Memory contents cannot be altered if $\overline{\text{MPRO}}$ is low. This signal is used when the dc voltage level is unreliable. An auxiliary address latch (ALE) is available if the microprocessor is an 8085 or 8086. When the MPU halts, it produces a low on the halt line. The $\overline{\text{WAIT}}$ signal indicates that the processor is in the wait state. Finally, an auxiliary reset signal is available to initiate the power-up sequence.

Data Transfer

Reading and writing of data on the Multibus is limited to a maximum rate of 5 MHz. A more typical rate is 2 MHz to allow for bus arbitration and memory access time. The timing diagram for reading data is shown in Fig. 18-13. Depending on whether memory or an input device is to supply the data, the $\overline{\text{IORC}}$ or $\overline{\text{MRDC}}$ line is selected. The address must be stable 50 ns before either of these commands goes low. The slave replies by placing the data on the bus and pulling the acknowledge signal low.

Write timing resembles the read in many ways. Figure 18-14 shows that $\overline{\text{IOWC}}$ or $\overline{\text{MWTC}}$ signals the addressed memory or output port that the data is ready to be sampled. Data is applied to the bus at the same time as the address. When the data has been sampled, the slave signals with $\overline{\text{XACK}}$.

The interrupt lines $\overline{\text{INT0}}$–$\overline{\text{INT7}}$ allow a slave to interrupt the processor. These are two schemes for interrupting possible. Bus vectored interrupts transfer the vector address over the Multibus address lines from the

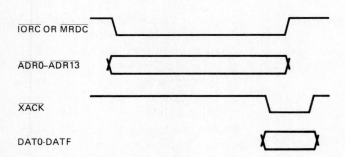

Fig. 18-13 Multibus read timing.

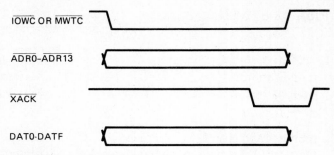

Fig. 18-14 Multibus write timing.

slave to the master using the $\overline{\text{INTA}}$ command for synchronization. The other type of vectored interrupt requires that the interrupt controller of the master generate the vector address and transfer it to the processor over the local bus. No address appears on the Multibus.

Electrical Specifications

The output voltage levels for all drivers on the bus must be in the range of 2.0 to 5.25 V for a high, and 0 to 0.45 V for a low. The receivers must accept a range of 2.0 to 5.5 V as a high, and −0.5 to 0.8 V as a low. The drive current, output stage, and termination for all signals are specified and listed in Table 18-7. Almost all bused signals are three-state. The tolerance of all power supply voltages is ±1 percent, with the ripple not to exceed 25 mV peak-to-peak (P-P). Drivers and receivers should be located as close as possible to their Multibus pin connections.

Mechanical Specifications

The motherboard supports the 86-pin receptacles that mate with the plug on each board. The auxiliary connector is not connected into the system bus. Board thickness is 0.062 in (0.16 cm), and spacing between the boards is 0.6 in (1.5 cm). Component height is limited to 0.4 in (1.02 cm). Figure 18-15 is a diagram

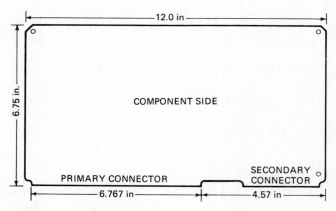

Fig. 18-15 Multibus board.

Table 18-7 Multibus Electrical Specifications

Signals	Output Stage	Minimum Driver Current (mA)	Maximum Receiver Current (mA)	Termination (Ω)
DAT0–DATF	Three-state	16	−0.8	2200
ADR0–ADR13	Three-state	16	−0.8	2200
MRDC MWTC	Three-state	32	−2	1000
IORC, IOWC	Three-state	32	−2	1000
XACK	Three-state	32	−2	510
INH1, INH2	Open-collector	16	−2	1000
BCLK, CCLK	Three-state	48	−2	220 and 330
BREQ	Three-state	5	2	100
BPRO	Three-state	5	−1.6	—
BPRN	Three-state	5	−2	—
BUSY, CBRQ	Open-collector	32	−2	1000
INIT	Open-collector	32	−2	2200
INTA	Three-state	32	−2	1000
INT0–INT7	Open-collector	16	−1.6	1000
PFSR, PFSN	Three-state	16	−1.6	1000
ACLO	Open-collector	16	−1.6	1000
PFIN	Open-collector	16	−1.6	1000
MPRO	Three-state	16	−1.6	1000
AUXRESET	—	—	−2	—

of the most important dimensions. The Multibus connector is an 86-pin plug, and the secondary bus connector has 60 pins.

The Multibus Review

1. Distinguish between P1 and P2 Multibus signals.
2. Which signal indicates that a system reset has occurred?
3. Explain how both 8- and 16-bit microprocessors can effectively communicate over the Multibus.
4. Why is it possible to assign identical addresses to ROM and RAM?
5. Describe the bus arbitration scheme. What establishes the priority of a master module?

CHAPTER SUMMARY

1. A microcomputer bus is a collection of conductors used to communicate between modules of the computer. Any member can be the transmitter or receiver of data or control signals. Power is also distributed by the bus.

2. The bus is implemented on a motherboard (or backplane), which accepts the plugs of PC cards.
3. A daisy-chain bus is unidirectional, so it cannot be used to carry data. The bidirectional party-line bus can be used for data exchange.
4. Arbitration or priority resolution logic selects one of the modules competing for bus access.
5. The processor controls the timing on a synchronous bus, while handshaking is necessary on an asynchronous bus.
6. Several types of drivers—including logical OR, wired-OR, and three-state—are found on multiplexed buses.
7. The proper receiver can substantially enhance bus performance by reducing capacitive loading.
8. The S-100 bus is the basis for many personal computers. This bus features unidirectional data paths. Many of the S-100 signals correspond to those of the 8080A. The remaining signals can be grouped into an address bus, command/control bus, status bus, and power bus.
9. The Multibus is a standardized computer bus used with 8- and 16-bit processors. Five groups of signals are carried on the bus. These groups include address, data, interrupt, control, and power distribution buses.

KEY TERMS AND CONCEPTS

Multiplexed bus	Bus arbitration	Transceiver
Motherboard	Synchronous bus control	Bidirectional driver
Backplane	Asynchronous bus control	S-100 bus
Daisy-chain multiplexed bus	Drivers	Multibus
Party-line bus		

PROBLEMS

18-1 Assume that you are checking the operation of a Multibus slave module and find that its interrupt output is attached to $\overline{INT2}$. What address is an 8085 will be referenced when the interrupt occurs?

18-2 If the processor shown in Fig. 18-1a is sending an output to the I/O controller, what delays will be encountered if the propagation times are as listed below?

	Receive (μs)	Transmit (μs)
MPU	0.5	0.7
ROM	0.2	0.2
RAM	0.3	0.35
I/O port	1.5	1.0

18-3 Compute the delay time between the processor and I/O port of Prob. 18-2 if the party-line bus shown in Fig. 18-1b is substituted for the daisy chain.

18-4 What is the bus level in Fig. 18-2a if the inputs are as listed below?

Inputs		Selection	
1	H	1	L
2	H	2	H
3	L	3	L

18-5 If the inputs to all gates shown in Fig. 18-2b are high, but no gate is selected, what is the level of the bus?

18-6 If the bus shown in Fig. 18-2c is in the low state, what can you say about the state of the selection lines?

18-7 Let the input to the bidirectional driver shown in Fig. 18-4b be high. What effect does a low input on the bus have if the enable input line is true?

18-8 What can be said about the levels of the command/control signals on the S-100 bus if the following 8080A signal levels exist?

INTE	L
$\overline{WR}$	H
WAIT	L
SYNC	H
$\overline{C/CDSB}$	H

18-9 All three masters shown in Fig. 18-12 issue a low signal on $\overline{BREQ}$. Assume that the $\overline{BPRN}$ input to master 3 is grounded by a malfunction. Which master(s) is (are) granted bus control?

18-10 The memory addresses for a ROM and RAM on the Multibus are identical. What value appears in the 8085 accumulator in the situation described below?

Program Counter	RAM		ROM	
1051	1051	3A	1051	3A
	1052	54	1052	54
	1053	10	1053	10
	1054	00	1054	FF

$\overline{BHEN}$	H
$\overline{INH1}$	L
$\overline{INH2}$	H
$\overline{BCLK}$	L

ANALOG INTERFACES

A major class of microcomputer applications requires that the computer control, interpret, monitor, or generate signals for analog devices. The objective of analog interfacing is to bridge the gap between the digital signals of the processor system and the varying voltages or currents of the analog equipment. These systems call for solutions that are compatible with the timing, voltage, current, and loading requirements on both sides of the interface.

At times we may be fortunate enough to find that the analog component can accept the same levels used by the microprocessor although this method can generally only be used with simple devices. More complex analog equipment calls for a conversion process before signals can be exchanged with the computer. In this chapter we will investigate various means of using interfaces to satisfactorily couple the computer to analog equipment.

CHAPTER OBJECTIVES

Upon completion of this chapter, you should be able to:

1. Show how to connect a microcomputer directly to simple analog components.
2. Draw a block diagram of a digital-to-analog converter.
3. List the basic types of digital-to-analog converters.
4. Explain the operation of a multiplying digital-to-analog converter.
5. Calculate the output voltage of a digital-to-analog converter.
6. Program a microcomputer to generate a variety of analog waveforms.
7. Explain the purpose for double-buffering a digital-to-analog converter.
8. List typical types of analog-to-digital converters.
9. Compare the output waveform of the counter analog-to-digital converter to that of the successive approximation analog-to-digital converter.
10. Program a microcomputer to perform data sampling.
11. Describe the characteristics of analog interface devices.
12. Explain the purpose of sample-and-hold integrated circuits.
13. Explain the principles of operation for voltage-to-frequency converters.

THE SIMPLE ANALOG INTERFACE

Sometimes we find that the job of interfacing to an analog device is straightforward because the digital voltages can be used without change. Such a case is shown in Fig. 19-1. Here, the speaker is our analog device. We simply want the computer to produce a series of signals that generates a tone from the speaker.

There is not even a data output in this circuit. The device code on the address bus acts as a trigger for each tone sample. When the correct device code is recognized, the low output of the decoder is NORed with the $\overline{OUT}$ signal clocking the D flip-flop. On each clock pulse, the previous output is fed back and complemented. The TTL flip-flop acts as a driver for the speaker. By complementing the output in this way, we avoid the necessity of a data output. The speaker input is therefore a series of square waves. By adjusting the time between output instructions, we can change the tone of the sound generated.

A program for this interface is listed in Table 19-1. By changing the delay interval, the speaker output frequency can be varied. Decreasing the value in locations 1003_{16} and 1004_{16} increases the frequency, and increasing this value lowers the frequency.

We can calculate the approximate frequency (F) by the formula

$$F = \frac{1}{\text{delay interval}}$$

$$= \frac{1}{(n)\,(7.5\ \mu s)} \tag{19-1}$$

where n = the value in cells 1003_{16} and 1004_{16} (in decimal).

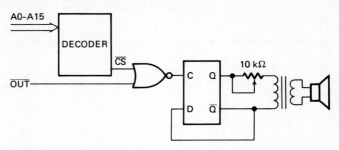

Fig. 19-1 Audio generator.

The Simple Analog Interface Review

1. How is the drive current for the speaker produced in this circuit?
2. Why is there no need for a data output?
3. Describe the relationship between the computer program and the audio frequency from the speaker.
4. What causes the signal to alternate between the high and low voltage?

DIGITAL-TO-ANALOG CONVERTERS

A key element in a *digital-to-analog (D/A) converter*, as well as in many of the other devices we will study in this chapter, is an operational amplifier. The op amp serves the dual purpose of buffering the output and of decoupling from the load. As a buffer, the amplifier acts to collect and store the output signal. The loading effects of the downstream circuitry are eliminated by the decoupling of the op amp.

Table 19-1 8085 Audio Generator Program

Label	Mnemonic	Operand	Address	Code	Comment
NEXT	OUT	10	1000	D3	Device code is 10
			1001	10	
	LXI H	FFFF	1002	21	
			1003	FF	Delay
			1004	FF	
LOOP	DCX H		1005	2B	
	MVI A	00	1006	3E	
			1007	00	Test for zero bit
	ADD L		1008	85	
	ADD H		1009	84	
	JNZ	LOOP	100A	C2	
			100B	05	
			100C	10	
	JMP	NEXT	100D	C3	Repeat
			100E	00	
			100F	10	

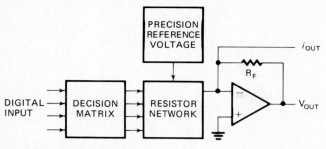

Fig. 19-2 D/A converter.

Figure 19-2 shows a generalized D/A converter. A digital input consisting of several bits is applied to the decision matrix. The matrix is, in fact, a collection of logic gates. Voltage is connected to the resistor stage for one state of the input and is not connected for the other state. The matrix can be thought of as switches that open or close as directed by the digital input. If there are n bits of the input, then there are n switches in the matrix. The number of switches determines the *resolution* of the converter. The more bits in the input, the smaller the increments that the output voltage can be divided into.

The resistor network (Fig. 19-2) is arranged to weight the incoming current that is passed through the closed switches in the decision matrix. Common weighting schemes accommodate either binary or binary-coded decimal (BCD) inputs. The reference voltage is the source of the drive for the resistor network. This reference must be accurately maintained at its assigned voltage if an accurate conversion is to be accomplished. A Zener diode is often used to provide a constant voltage level.

D/A converters with an input level compatible with TTL or CMOS integrated circuits are readily available. With these characteristics, interfacing with 7400 TTL integrated circuits or microcomputers is easy. The converter itself is an integrated circuit that can be ordered in flatpack, TO "can," or dual-in-line package configurations.

Converters that accept supply voltages of 5 to 35 V, or more, are available. Almost all of them operate reliably over a wide range of temperatures.

D/A Converter Output

The output range of a D/A converter can be found if the number of input bits and the reference voltage are known. Assuming a binary input is used,

$$V_{out} = \frac{\text{binary input}}{2^n} \cdot V_{ref} \qquad (19\text{-}2)$$

where n = number of input bits.

For example, consider a 3-bit converter that uses a reference voltage of 4 V. Table 19-2 lists the output

Table 19-2 D/A Outputs

Binary Input	Output Voltage (V)
000	0
001	0.5
010	1.0
011	1.5
100	2.0
101	2.5
110	3.0
111	3.5

values resulting from any input. As the table shows, the least significant bit (001_2) represents 0.5 V. This voltage is the resolution of the converter. No smaller voltage steps can be produced. Each output level is exactly that voltage increment above the preceding one. Also note that the full-scale output (when the input is all 1s) is not 4 V. The D/A full-scale output is always one LSB less than the reference voltage.

Input Coding

The number of steps in the output is related to the digital input code. In the case of our 3-bit converter (Table 19-2), *binary coding* was used. As mentioned at the start of this section, BCD is frequently encountered as well. In BCD, each decimal digit is represented by 4 bits. These bits must always fall within the limits of 0000 to 1001 for each decimal digit. If a converter had a two-digit BCD input, the lowest input value expressed in bits would be 0000 0000, and the full scale input would be 1001 1001, representing 99.

Other converters use *complement* number systems. Both 1's and 2's complement binary converters can be obtained. Depending on the converter, the output may or may not be negative voltage. Two examples of 1's complement converters are provided in Table 19-3. Both use references of 8 V.

Yet another popular coding scheme is *offset binary*. In it, some midpoint value is selected as the zero voltage output. In this way both positive and negative (bipolar) outputs can be produced. Table 19-4 gives an example.

Table 19-3 Input Coding

Converter	1's Complement Binary Input		Output Voltage (V)
A	0 0 0 0	0 0 0 0	0
	1 1 1 1	1 1 1 1	−7.5
B	0 0 0 0	0 0 0 0	0
	1 1 1 1	1 1 1 1	+7.5

Table 19-4 Offset Binary Converter

Binary Input	Output Voltage (V)
000	−1.0
001	−0.75
010	−0.50
011	−0.25
100	0
101	0.25
110	0.5
111	0.75

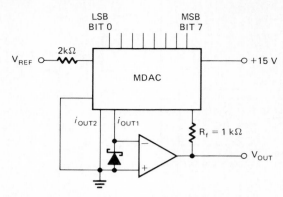

Fig. 19-3 Digital two-quadrant MDAC circuit.

Types of D/A Converters

The most frequently encountered converters use either *weighted resistor* or *resistor ladder networks*. The weighted resistor converters use a series of resistors to develop current from each input bit. The resistors' values are obtained by doubling their value in going from one bit to the next. If the resistor for the MSB is 10 kΩ, then the resistor for the next lower bit would be 20 kΩ, and so on. The LSB resistor is then $(10K)(2^{n-1})$. The resistor ladder uses only two values for its resistors. If R represents one value, then the other is $2R$.

MULTIPLYING D/A CONVERTERS *Multiplying D/A converters (MDACs)* are equivalent to digitally controlled potentiometers. The MDAC has both an analog and a digital input. The analog input is multiplied by a fraction represented by the digital input to yield the output voltage:

$$V_{out} = \frac{\text{digital input}}{2^n} \cdot V_{analog} \qquad (19\text{-}3)$$

The digital input is assumed to have a radix point to the left of the MSB. Let an 8-bit MDAC have an analog input of 12 V and a digital input of 1100 0000. Placing the radix point to the left of the MSB,

$$0.1100\ 0000_2 = 0.75_{10}$$

Therefore, $V_{out} = (12\text{ V})(0.75) = 9\text{ V}$

Multiplying D/A converters are classed as either *two-* or *four-quadrant devices*, with a further subdivision made in two-quadrant devices. *Digital two-quadrant MDACs* are most common, but they are not as versatile as the other types. The output voltage always either increases or decreases from zero. The digital input ranges over positive and negative values (bipolar).

Analog two-quadrant MDACs are analogous to a three-terminal pot. The digital codes are limited to either an increasing or a decreasing range, but the amplitude of the output signal includes positive and negative values.

Four-quadrant MDACs allow both the digital controlling input signal and the output signal to take on positive and negative values. In addition to varying the amplitude, the four-quadrant MDAC can change the signal phase by 180° as well.

A circuit for a digital two-quadrant MDAC is shown in Fig. 19-3. At the maximum limit, the signal is at its negative extreme. When the digital count reaches zero, the output also goes to zero.

COMPANDING D/A CONVERTERS A variation of the MDAC is the *companding (compression/expansion function) D/A converter*. The companding converter permits the 8-bit input from a microcomputer to achieve a low signal-to-quantizing error over a 40-dB range, which would be impossible by just using linear coding. This type of converter is an implementation of the Bell System μ-255 logarithm companding law. The output can be expressed as

$$y = 0.18 \ln (1 + \mu x) \qquad (19\text{-}4)$$

where y = output
  x = normalized input
  μ = 255

Obviously, the law is named for the constant, μ.

The operation of the converter is best shown by an example. Let the 8-bit input be defined as

Bit number	7	6 5 4	3 2 1 0
	Sign	Chord number	Step size

The sign bit denotes positive or negative values (1 = negative). The chord is one of the eight line segments that symmetrically form a linear approximation of the transfer function; see Fig. 19-4. The 3 bits allow us to specify which of the eight chords is currently being designated. The last 4 bits indicate one of 16 step sizes for the designated chord. The cumulative transfer function is usually tabulated in a form similar to that given in Table 19-5. Assume that we input a positive chord designator of 3 and a step size of 1. Reading from the chart, we see that the length of that chord in the transfer function will be 247 units. (This length means that the

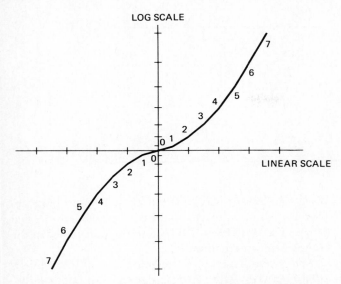

Fig. 19-4 Companding D/A converter transfer function.

LOG SCALE

LINEAR SCALE

Chord 0: $\dfrac{1}{2^{12}} = 0.025\%$

Chord 7: $\dfrac{1}{2^5} = 3.2\%$

Thus an input of a step size 1 and chord of 0 (represented as 1,0) will give us a resolution of 0.025 percent, which is the same as would be produced by a 12-bit D/A converter. The increment using chord 7 is 3.2 percent—the same as that of a 5-bit D/A converter.

Let us continue this example, using the notation V_{out} (step, chord) to indicate the output. The output voltage can be calculated as

$$V_{out} \text{ (step, chord)} = \frac{\text{chart (step, chord)}}{8031} \cdot V_{ref} \quad (19\text{-}5)$$

Let the output voltage range be -12 to $+12$ V. (This means that V_{ref} is either -12 or $+12$ V, depending on sign.)

$$V_{out} (1,0) = \left(\frac{2}{8031}\right)(12 \text{ V}) = 0.003 \text{ V}$$

equivalent to

$$V_{out} = 0.00025 \,(12 \text{ V}) = 0.003 \text{ V}$$
$$= 0.025\% \text{ full-scale voltage}$$

Another case showing the step-size increment is

$$V_{out} (0,7) = \frac{(4191)}{(8031)}(12 \text{ V}) = 6.26 \text{ V}$$

$$V_{out} (1,7) = \frac{(4447)}{(8031)}(12 \text{ V}) = 6.64 \text{ V}$$

$$V_{out} (1,7) - V_{out} (0,7) = \text{voltage increment}$$
$$= 0.38 \text{V}$$
$$= 3.2\% \text{ of full scale}$$
$$= (2^{1/5})(12 \text{ V})$$

output will be 247/8031 times the positive full-scale value.) By changing the chord designator and step size, the shape of the transfer function can be modified.

To show the equivalence of the units used on the chart, we note that the maximum length is 8031; therefore, one unit represents

$$\frac{1}{8031} = 0.0125\%$$

of full scale, so incrementing by two units in the 0 chord column is the same as 0.025 percent of full scale (2 × 0.0125 percent), and the 256 units in the 7 chord column represent 3.2 percent of full scale (256 × 0.0125 percent). These same units result for the resolution indicated.

Table 19-5 Cumulative Transfer Function

Step Size	Chord							
	0	1	2	3	4	5	6	7
0	0	33	99	231	495	1023	2079	4191
1	2	37	107	247	527	1087	2207	4447
2	4	41	115	263	559	1151	2335	4703
·	·	·	·	·	·	·	·	·
·	·	·	·	·	·	·	·	·
·	·	·	·	·	·	·	·	·
·								
15	30	93	219	471	975	1983	3999	8031
Increment	2	4	8	16	32	64	128	256
Resolution (bits)	12	11	10	9	8	7	6	5
Increment as a percentage of full scale	0.025	0.05	0.1	0.2	0.4	0.8	1.6	3.2

⟨‾‾‾⟩: maximum

Table 19-6 Typical D/A Converters

Manufacturer	Model	Bits	Conversion Time (ns)	Range
PMI	DAC-01	6	3000	± 5 V
PMI	DOC-03	10	1500	0.10 V
Analog devices	AD 7522 (multiplying)	10	500	± 5 mA
Motorola	1406L	6	150	± 1 mA
Motorola	MC1408L8	8	300	± 1 mA
National	DA1200	12	1500	10 V

A summary of the variety of D/A converters on the market appears in Table 19-6. The resolution range of from 6 to 12 bits covers most ordinary requirements.

Programming for D/A Converters

Once the D/A interface has been constructed for the microcomputer, a variety of waveforms and functions can be generated simply by changing the program in the computer. Figure 19-5 shows an interface to an 8-bit D/A converter that uses a 74100 eight-bit latch. The 74100 is composed of eight identical D flip-flops. Data placed on the input of any latch is transferred to the output terminal and the level is maintained until the next input is received.

The inputs to the latch are the data bus bits. When the latch is enabled by the device select and $\overline{\text{OUT}}$ signals, the information on the data bus is fed to the D/A converter. The converter transforms the digital input into an analog voltage. The analog output will track the values sent by the microcomputer.

The waveform generated depends on two aspects of the program. The period of the signal results from the time it takes to execute one complete pass through the program, as shown in Fig. 19-6. The amplitude is determined by the maximum value of the output.

SQUARE-WAVE GENERATION   The program to produce a square wave from the circuit shown in Fig. 19-5 is listed in Table 19-7. The program relies on the complement instruction.

The accumulator is zeroed initially, and this value is sent to the converter. After a delay (instructions in addresses 1004_{16} to $100E_{16}$), the accumulator is changed to its 1's complement (FF_{16}). This value is equivalent to the maximum full-scale output of the D/A converter. Thus the square wave alternates between zero and full-scale output with a period of twice the delay loop. We can calculate this delay by knowing the time it takes to execute the instructions in the loop. (We will assume that the microprocessor is running with a 2-MHz clock.)

DCX	2.5 μs
MVI	3.5
ADD L	2.0
ADD M	2.0
JNZ	5.0
	15.0 μs

and $FFFF_{16} = 65535_{10}$

so $65535 \times 15 \ \mu s = 0.98$ s

The period of the square wave will be approximately 2 s.

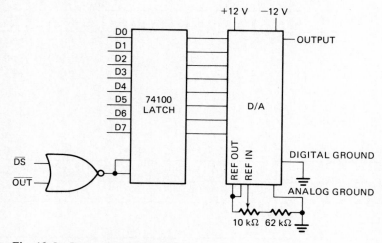

Fig. 19-5   D/A converter interface.

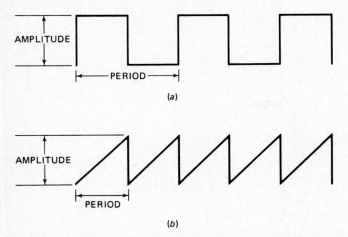

Fig. 19-6 Waveforms: (a) symmetrical square wave, (b) sawtooth wave.

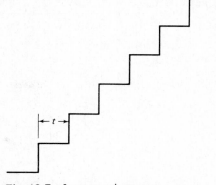

Fig. 19-7 Incrementing ramp.

SAWTOOTH-WAVE GENERATION
A sawtooth, or ramp, function can be generated almost as easily. In this program, we simply increment the accumulator, letting it overflow (see Table 19-8 on page 342). Every time it goes from FF_{16} to 0, the output changes from its maximum to its minimum value. In this case, the delay is placed between each step to control the slope of the ramp; see Fig. 19-7.

In actuality the wave is a stairstep function, but the resolution of the D/A converter is sufficiently small to approximate a linearly increasing slope.

In this situation the period can be found by multiplying the delay in each step by the number of steps, which is FF_{16} (255_{10}). The delay at each step is 127_{10} ($7F_{16}$) $\times$ 7.5 μs.

We have:

$$255 \text{ steps} \times (127 \times 7.5 \ \mu\text{s per step}) = 0.24 \text{ s}$$

This time means that the period is about a quarter of a second. The amplitude increases to full scale, then drops to zero and begins to count up again at the completion of each period.

We can easily make this program generate a decreasing sawtooth instead. Just changing the instruction at cell 1008 to DCR A accomplishes this modification. Now the accumulator decrements to zero and underflows to all 1s.

Table 19-7 Square-Wave Program

Label	Mnemonic	Operand	Address	Code	Comments
	MVI A	0	1000	3E	Zero the accumulator
			1001	00	
NEXT	OUT	12	1002	D3	Output the next value
			1003	12	
	LXI H	FFFF	1004	21	Loop count A HL
			1005	FF	
			1006	FF	
LOOP	DCX H		1007	2B	Decrement
	MVI A	00	1008	3E	
			1009	00	
	ADD L		100A	85	
	ADD H		100B	84	Test for zero bit
	JNZ	LOOP	100C	C2	
			100D	07	
			100E	10	
	CMA		100F	2F	Complement accumulator
	JMP	NEXT	1020	C3	
			1021	02	
			1022	10	

Table 19-8 8085 Sawtooth-Wave Program

Label	Mnemonic	Operand	Address	Code	Comments
NEXT	OUT	12	1000	D3	Output the next value
			1001	12	
	MVI B	7F	1002	06	Loop count → B
			1003	7F	
LOOP	DCR B		1004	05	Decrement
	JNZ	LOOP	1005	C2	Delay loop
			1006	04	
			1007	10	
	INR A		1008	3C	Increment accumulator
	JMP	NEXT	1009	C3	Repeat
			100A	00	
			100B	10	

DOUBLE BUFFERING The scheme we described above works fine with D/A converters that have inputs not exceeding the data bus width, that is, 8 bits or less. What if we have a 10- or 12-bit A/D converter, though? A thought that comes immediately to mind is to address the low 8 bits and upper bits of input separately and output the two sets of bits to separate devices.

Consider how this approach would work with a 12-bit D/A converter producing a sawtooth output. Assuming that the accumulator starts at 0, we have Table 19-9. This method seems to work fine. But consider what happens in going from $0000\ 1111\ 1111_2$ to $0001\ 0000\ 0000_2$. The lower half is changed to 0 before the upper becomes 0001; therefore, the output will drop to zero, causing a *glitch* every time the lower 8 bits increment to 0. A related difficulty is observed when the counter

is going from all 1s back to 0. We could observe that the data lines change as follows:

$1111\ 1111\ 1111_2$	Initial
$1111\ 0000\ 0000_2$	Lower half increments
$0000\ 0000\ 0000_2$	Upper half becomes 0

We can prevent both of these problems by use of a *double buffer*, as shown in Fig. 19-8.

Latches 1 and 2 hold the new value for the D/A converter, but they are not applied to the input terminals until latches 3 and 4 are strobed. By ensuring that both the upper and the lower sets of bits have been assigned their correct values prior to applying either to the D/A converter, we eliminate the glitches that were previously a problem. A program fragment to output the value

Table 19-9 Double Buffering a 12-Bit D/A Converter

Action	Accumulator	B Register (Temporary Storage)	11	10	9	8	7	6	5	4	3	2	1	0
Output lower 8 bits	00	?	?	?	?	?	0	0	0	0	0	0	0	0
Save value	00	00												
Output upper 4 bits	00	00	0	0	0	0	0	0	0	0	0	0	0	0
Switch A and B	00	00												
Increment A	01	00												
Output lower	01	00	0	0	0	0	0	0	0	0	0	0	0	1
Switch A and B	00	01												
Output upper	00	01	0	0	0	0	0	0	0	0	0	0	0	1
Switch A and B	01	00												
Increment A	10	00												
Output lower	10	00	0	0	0	0	0	0	0	0	0	0	1	0
Switch A and B	00	10												
Output upper	00	10	0	0	0	0	0	0	0	0	0	0	1	0
.	.	.												
.	.	.												
.	.	.												

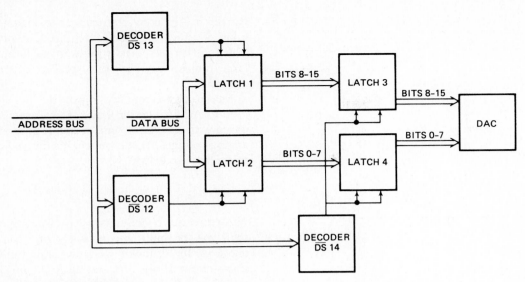

Fig. 19-8 Double buffer.

$17F7_{16}$ to the 12-bit D/A converter is as follows:

MVI A, F7   Lower bits
OUT 12   Output to latch 2
MVI A, 17   Upper bits
OUT 13   Output to latch 1
OUT 14   Enable latches 3 and 4

Only on the last output do the data bits change the D/A converter input. Double buffering is so frequently necessary that many D/A converters have the twin sets of latches built into the package.

Digital-to-Analog Converters Review

1. Explain the purpose for each component of a D/A converter.
2. Distinguish between binary and offset binary input coding.
3. Describe the operation of a multiplying D/A converter.
4. Why is the companding D/A converter considered to be an implementation of the μ-255 law?
5. What determines the period of a waveform generated by a computer program? How is the amplitude defined?

ANALOG-TO-DIGITAL CONVERTERS

Now let us discuss devices that can provide inputs to the computer that are samples of analog voltages. With an *analog-to-digital (A/D) converter*, physical processes can be monitored by the computer program. The pro-

gram simply inputs data from the converter at some interval to obtain its readings. These readings could represent a temperature, voltage, current, pressure, or some other important parameter of the system being controlled.

Several types of integrated-circuit A/D converters are manufactured. Some of them use a feedback loop that has a D/A converter in the loop. Figure 19-9 illustrates their principle of operation. The *counter* A/D converter feeds the output of a comparator to the control circuitry that senses when the digital estimate equals or exceeds the analog input. A counter is used to produce the digital estimate, giving the converter its name. The output is produced slowly in a stairstep manner, as Fig. 19-10a shows. The counter A/D converter is popular despite its slowness because of its simplicity and low cost.

Another widely used converter is the *successive approximation* converter. Here the comparator inputs are also the unknown analog voltage and the output of a D/A converter. A bit-by-bit comparison is made, starting with the MSB set high. If the resulting digital value exceeds the analog 1, that bit is turned off. Then the process continues with the next lower bit, and so on, until all bits have been used. Figure 19-10b shows how

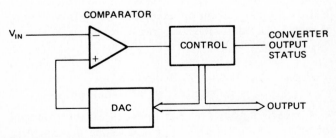

Fig. 19-9 A/D converter concept.

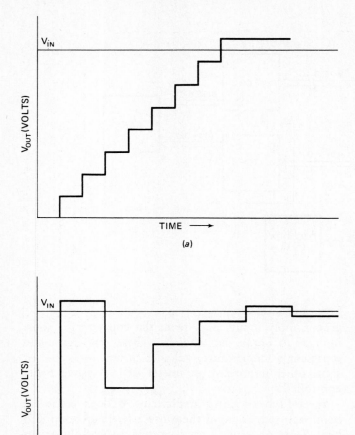

Fig. 19-10 A/D converter outputs: (a) counter, (b) successive approximation.

the output develops. A good voltage reference and D/A converter are required in the successive approximation converter, but the cost is justified by the speed of conversion, which is in the range of 10 to 20 μs.

The *parallel* A/D converter performs the process simultaneously. The digital result is a summation from many separate comparators, so operation can be continuous, with new samples of the analog signal being constantly fed into the converter. This type of converter is used for sampling rates in excess of 10 MHz, although it is costly. The resolution of the parallel A/D converter is related to the number of comparators:

$$C = 2^{n/2+1} - 2 \qquad (19\text{-}6)$$

where C = number of comparators
        n = number of bits of resolution

A *tracking* A/D converter operates on the principle of a servo loop. In fact, it is also called a servo A/D

converter. The converter tracks the analog input, but it takes considerable time to acquire and lock the signal. This time lag is especially pronounced if the input makes large jumps. Even so, this style of converter is very accurate.

An op-amp integrator forms the basis of the *integrating* A/D converter. Here, a reference time is compared with a variable time, which is proportional to the analog voltage. The output can be derived from a count of the time intervals:

$$V_{in} = \frac{T_{in}}{T_{ref}} \cdot V_{ref} \qquad (19\text{-}7)$$

This converter is quite insensitive to component values, so it can be built inexpensively and has good noise rejection. Its disadvantage is the slow time for conversion—about 10 ms. Integrating A/D converters are frequently used as panel voltmeters.

Data Sampling

A straightforward A/D converter that can be used in a computer sampling system is shown in Fig. 19-11. The two 8212 I/O ports interface the data bus to the converter.

The program used to drive this circuit is given in Table 19-10. The output to device 23 starts the converter and causes it to convert one sample. As long as the $\overline{BUSY}$ is low, the device is performing the conversion, so the program loops until that signal (received as data bit 0) goes high. Finally, a sample is accepted by the input from device 22.

A list of typical A/D converters is provided in Table 19-11. This collection suggests some of the ranges in resolution, conversion time, and voltage range that can be found today.

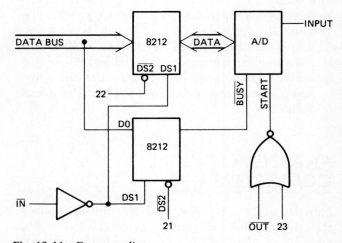

Fig. 19-11 Data sampling.

Table 19-10 8085 A/D Conversion Program

Label	Mnemonic	Operand	Address	Code	Comments
	OUT	23	1000	D3	Start conversion
			1001	23	
LOOP	IN	21	1002	DB	Input $\overline{BUSY}$
			1003	21	
	ANI	01	1004	E6	Get bit 0
			1005	01	
	JZ	LOOP	1006	CA	If still busy, check
			1007	02	again
			1008	10	
	IN	22	1009	DB	Sample A/D converter
			100A	22	output

Analog-to-Digital Converters Review

1. Distinguish between counter, successive approximation, parallel, tracking, and integrating A/D converters.
2. Give another name for a servo A/D converter.
3. Explain the purpose of the $\overline{BUSY}$ input of the A/D converter shown in Fig. 19-11.
4. How is the program in a microprocessor able to determine that the conversion process has been completed in a data-sampling system?

CHARACTERISTICS OF CONVERTERS

Specifications for converters are usually expressed in terms that have a specialized meaning. Knowing this terminology makes it possible for you to read and understand data books for the converters. An appreciation of the limits and capabilities of a particular converter model will allow you to judge whether a specific use is within its design limits and whether a different model could be used as a substitute.

Most of the specifications are expressed as errors in the output. These errors are generally determined by measuring the deviation of the actual output from the idealized value expected. Some of these errors, such as gain and zero scale, can be removed or reduced by adjustment. The others are inherent limits of the device. Probably the most important of the latter is linearity, followed closely by drift.

The *gain,* or full-scale, error is the difference in the actual full-scale range from the ideal full-scale range. This range is the span of voltage or current values over which the converter can be used, such as 1 to 10 V. *Zero-scale* (sometimes called *offset*) *error* is the shift in the transfer function by some dc bias (see Fig. 19-12a). As stated above, the offset error can be removed by adjustment so that the output is zero when the input is grounded.

Linearity, more than any other parameter, is the measure of converter quality. It is the limit of performance. Linearity is measured by finding the deviation of the transfer function from a straight line extending from zero to full scale. The maximum deviation is expressed as a percentage of full-scale range or in terms of the LSB value. Almost any converter should limit its linearity error to less than 1 percent. See Fig. 19-12b.

Drift results from the variation in output as a result of temperature. Changes in temperature can affect linearity, offset, and gain. The total drift can be calculated from the temperature coefficients provided in manufacturers' data sheets.

Table 19-11 A/D Converters

Manufacturer	Model	Bits	Conversion Time (ms)	Voltage Range (V)
Analog Devices	ADC 1100	10 (BCD)	42	± 0.1999
Analog Devices	ADC 141	14	40	± 10
Analogic	AN 2313	10	6.7	± 2
Datel	ADC E10B	10	1.25	± 10

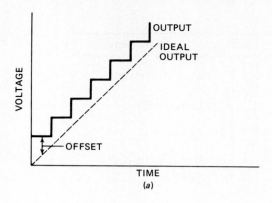

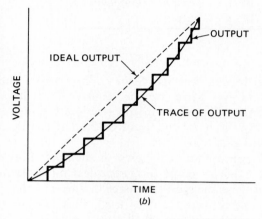

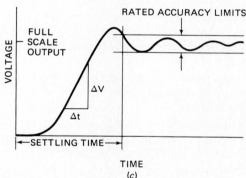

Fig. 19-12 Converter characteristics: (*a*) offset error, (*b*) linearity error, (*c*) slew rate.

$$D = (TC_L + TC_O + TC_G) \times \Delta T \qquad (19\text{-}8)$$

where D = drift in parts per million (ppm)
TC_L = linearity temperature coefficient
TC_O = offset temperature coefficient
TC_G = gain temperature coefficient
ΔT = change in temperature, °C

Low values for the coefficients are required for accurate conversion over any spread of temperatures.

A *monotonic* converter is one for which the output always increases or remains at the last value for an increase in the input. The monotonic parameter is especially important for successive approximation and counter A/D converters.

Resolution should be a familiar concept to you by now. It can be expressed as the number of states into which the digital input or output can be divided. It can be expressed as

$$\text{Resolution} = \frac{\text{full-scale range}}{2^n} \qquad (19\text{-}9)$$

$$= \text{value of the LSB} \qquad (19\text{-}10)$$

where n = number of digital bits. The full-scale analog input range is used to calculate the resolution of A/D converters and output units for D/A converters. A useful formula for the value of the most significant bit is

$$\text{MSB} = \frac{(2^{n-1})(\text{full-scale range})}{2^n - 1} \qquad (19\text{-}11)$$

Absolute accuracy expresses the difference between an ideal full-scale output and that measured. (Do not confuse this value with the relative accuracy, which is another term for linearity.)

How fast does a converter respond to a change of input? This question is answered by the slew rate, settling time, and aperture error specifications. The *slew rate* of a D/A converter is expressed as the rate of change in output for large input-signal changes, as shown in Fig. 19-12*c*. This change of output per unit time is often rated in volts per microsecond:

$$\text{Slew rate} = \frac{\Delta v}{\Delta t} \qquad (19\text{-}12)$$

The time elapsed before the output of a D/A converter stabilizes into its rated accuracy limits is the *settling time.* You can think of the settling time as the period needed for overshoots to damp out. This parameter is one of the best indications of the converter speed.

Aperture errors of an A/D converter result from variations in the input during the sampling time. Because every converter has a nonzero slew rate, the input signal may change its value before the conversion has been completed. (The aperture error of an A/D converter is a counterpart of the slew rate in the D/A converter.) The sample-and-hold circuit described in the following section is frequently used to overcome the aperture error.

Characteristics of Converters Review

1. List the errors that can usually be adjusted out of a converter.
2. Which is the most important characteristic in rating a D/A converter?
3. True or false? Large temperature coefficients are required for accurate conversion.
4. Define the term "monotonic."

5. Distinguish between absolute and relative accuracy in a converter.
6. How does the slew rate affect the speed of conversion? In what way does the settling time enter into the question?
7. Would a small aperture time be desirable in an A/D converter? Explain.

SAMPLE-AND-HOLD CIRCUITS

As noted in the discussion on A/D converter aperture time, a rapidly varying input signal cannot be accurately converted. In that case, we need a voltage memory device that can "freeze" the input level for some specified period. The *sample-and-hold (S/H) circuit* performs this function when it is used as a *front end* for a converter. As Fig. 19-13 shows, there are two intervals of interest. During the sample period, the S/H obtains an estimate of the incoming signal. This value is then held at a constant level until the clock indicates that the next sample is to be taken.

As you can see, there are two techniques used in constructing a sample-and-hold circuit. The *sampling* type of S/H abruptly changes to the new output value, while the *tracking* type of S/H follows the signal to its new value.

There are many other uses for the S/H besides holding the signal steady for the A/D converter. The S/H circuit

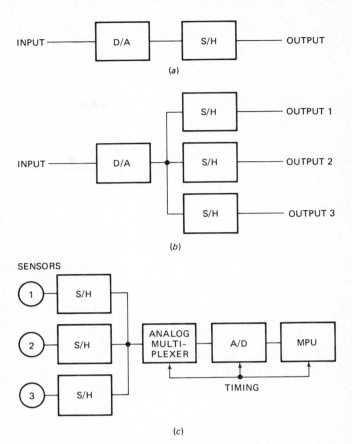

Fig. 19-14   S/H applications: (*a*) eliminate D/A transients, (*b*) fanout D/A converter, (*c*) multiplexing.

can also be used to eliminate transients on the output of a D/A converter (Fig. 19-14*a*). Yet another use is to increase the fan-out of the voltages generated by a D/A converter (Fig. 19-14*b*).

A common problem that occurs in process control is monitoring many sensors by a microcomputer. Figure 19-14*c* shows how many sensors can be sampled with a single A/D converter and one computer I/O port. With this configuration, a minimal amount of hardware is used to do the job. The computer program signals the analog multiplexer, which allows only one of the sensor inputs to pass through to the converter at any time. The processor accepts the digital input, knowing that this value is to be associated with the sensor requested from the multiplexer.

Sample-and-Hold Characteristics

Just as with converters, the performance of an S/H can be assessed by investigating its characteristics. Linearity is the most important measure for the S/H and, as with the converter, the linearity of an S/H is the variation of its output from an ideal straight line. The *dc offset* is the difference in input and output voltages with the

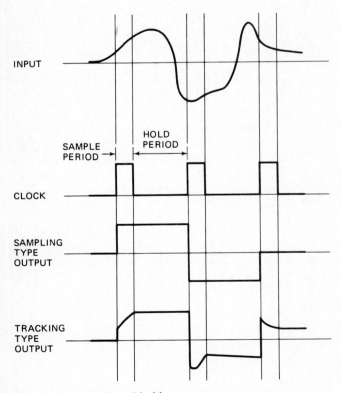

Fig. 19-13   Sample-and-hold.

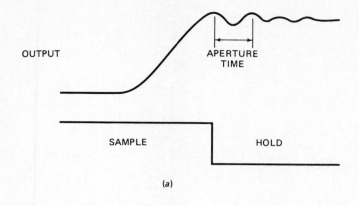

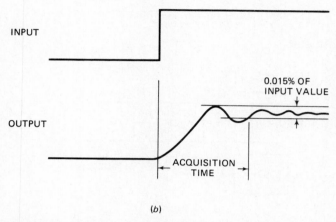

Fig. 19-15 Aperture and acquisition time: (*a*) aperture time, (*b*) acquisition time.

input terminal grounded. Just as with converters, the offset error can be removed by adjustment.

The slew rate for an S/H is measured similarly to that for a converter. The rate of change in voltage with time is a key element in the speed of sampling. Aperture time, however, is measured a little differently. As Fig. 19-15*a* shows, the aperture time is the duration required for switching from the sample mode to the hold mode. Another timing measure is the *acquisition time*, shown in Fig. 19-15*b*. This measure specifies the time required to obtain a sample from the hold mode until the new output is within 0.01 percent of the input voltage.

Sample-and-Hold Circuits Review

1. Explain the purpose of the S/H circuit.
2. Distinguish between sampling and tracking S/H devices.
3. How can the S/H be used to remove transient voltages from a D/A converter output?
4. Describe how an analog multiplexer can be used with several S/H circuits to monitor many sensors.
5. How does the aperture time definition for an S/H differ from that of an A/D converter?
6. True or false? Short acquisition times are not demanded of most sample-and-hold circuits.

VOLTAGE-TO-FREQUENCY CONVERTERS

Converters that work on an entirely different principle can also be used for analog-to-digital conversion. The *voltage-to-frequency (V/F) converter* changes an input voltage to a frequency that is proportional to the input. This output frequency is TTL-compatible. A microprocessor program estimates the analog voltage by counting the pulses per unit time.

Because some time must elapse while a count is made, V/F conversion is a relatively slow process. The converter is, however, useful for many purposes in spite of this limitation. Integration of the input signal is readily achieved, as is summing out random noise (which is integrated to zero). With the V/F converter, the TTL output simplifies interfacing to the processor. Another characteristic that makes V/F converters highly effective is their accuracy. Table 19-12 lists some VF converters available at low cost.

The components of a charge-balancing V/F converter are shown in Fig. 19-16. The input signal combined with the common input causes the integrator to generate a ramp waveform. When the negative-going ramp drops below the threshold voltage, the trigger fires. The trigger, in turn, causes the one-shot to produce a pulse that saturates the output transistor and also forces the integrator to output a positive-going ramp. When the ramp again reaches the input level, the cycle repeats.

Table 19-12 V/F Converters

Manufacturer	Mode	Full-scale Accuracy (%)	Frequency Range (KHz)	Output Drive (mA)
Intech	A-8400	±15	100	2
Analog Device	AD537J	±7	150	20
Teledyne	9400	±10	100	10
Raytheon	RC4151	±10	100	3
Burr Brown	VFC32	±5	500	8

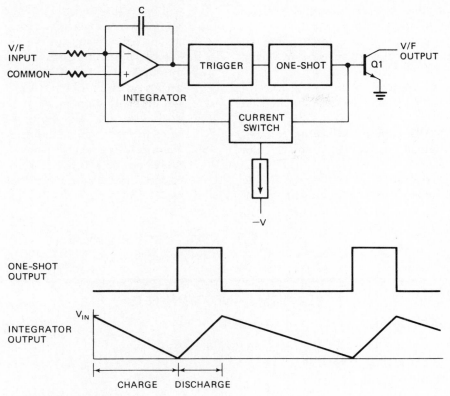

Fig. 19-16   V/F converter.

The time necessary for the ramp voltage to complete one cycle depends on how much difference exists between the input signal voltage and the trigger voltage. If these voltages are close in value, little time is required for the ramp to transit between them, and the output frequency is high. If these voltages are far apart, the duration is longer, making the output frequency lower.

A microcomputer circuit using a V/F converter is shown in Fig. 19-17. A pull-up resistor is used to interface the V/F converter to the 7400 gate. The reset line (a 1-bit output line) from the processor synchronizes the V/F output with the counting program.

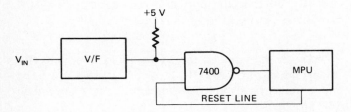

Note: The reset line is a control output from the microprocessor (not to be confused with the RESET signal used to initialize the 8085 or 6800).

Fig. 19-17   Microcomputer with V/F converter.

Voltage-to-Frequency Converters Review

1. List some advantages of V/F converters.
2. True or false? The V/F converter is well-suited to circumstances calling for rapid conversion.
3. Explain the operation of the charge-balancing V/F converter.

CHAPTER SUMMARY

1. If the analog system is a simple one, the processor may be directly connected to it. Only in cases where the voltages and currents are compatible can this method be applied.
2. A D/A converter can be thought of as being constructed from a decision matrix, voltage reference, resistor network, and op amp. The outputs of the converter are TTL or CMOS levels that readily accommodate microprocessor interfacing.
3. D/A converter outputs are coded as binary, BCD, 1's or 2's complement, and offset binary.
4. Multiplying D/A converters combine the analog input with a digital fraction to extend their range. Digital and analog two- and four-quadrant

MDACs are available. Companding converters are a special class of multiplying converters.

5. By changing the program in the microcomputer, the same circuit can be used to generate many different waveforms.

6. Double buffering is needed to prevent glitches in D/A converters that have inputs wider than the data bus.

7. The families of A/D converters include counter, successive approximation, parallel, tracking, and integrating converters.

8. Errors in converters can be classed as adjustable and inherent. Errors such as offset and gain can be eliminated by adjustment. Inherent errors limit the accuracy of conversion. Most important of the inherent errors is linearity.

9. Sample-and-hold circuits are employed to eliminate aperture errors of A/D converters. These circuits are also useful for eliminating transients, providing fan-out, and sampling many sensors. Errors of S/H devices include dc offset, acquisition time, slew rate, aperture time, and linearity.

10. Voltage-to-frequency converters offer accurate, noise-free A/D conversion. These converters are easy to interface to a processor.

KEY TERMS AND CONCEPTS

Digital-to-analog (D/A) converter

Resolution

Input coding

Offset binary

Multiplying D/A converters (MDACs)

Two- or four-quadrant devices

Companding (compression/ expansion function) D/A converter

Waveform generation

Double buffer

Analog-to-digital (A/D) converter

Gain

Offset

Linearity

Drift

Monotonic

Absolute accuracy

Slew rate

Settling time

Aperture error

Sample-and-hold (S/H) circuit

Sampling S/H

Tracking S/H

DC offset

Acquisition time

Voltage-to-frequency (V/F) converters

PROBLEMS

19-1 What is the resolution of a 10-bit D/A converter with an output range of 0 to 5 V?

19-2 If the binary input to the converter in Prob. 19-1 is $1001\ 0111_2$ and the reference voltage is 5 V, what is the output?

19-3 The output voltage of the MDAC in Fig. 19-3 is equal to the product of I_{out1} with R_f. What is the current into the inverting terminal of the op amp if the reference voltage is 10 V and the digital input is 11 1010_2?

19-4 What is the output of the companding D/A converter discussed in this chapter if its range is -12 to $+12$ V and the input is $1010\ 0000_2$?

19-5 If the input to the companding D/A converter is increased from $0001\ 0110_2$ to $0010\ 0110_2$, how large an increment is produced in the output as a percentage of full scale?

19-6 Change the square-wave program to generate a wave with a period of ½ s and an amplitude of one-quarter the full-scale output of the converter.

19-7 How many comparators are required in a 10-bit parallel A/D converter?

19-8 What is the input voltage to an integrating A/D converter with a reference time of 1 μs and a reference voltage of 12 V if the measured time interval is 397 ns?

19-9 Find the D/A converter drift resulting from the temperature decreasing from 75 to 68°F. The manufacturer lists the following characteristics for the converter:

Temperature Coefficient
Linearity   2.94
Offset   1.72
Gain   1.03

19-10 Find the slew rate for the converter with a switching characteristic, as shown in Fig. 19-18.

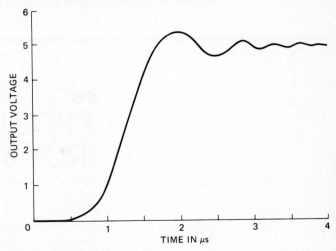

Fig. 19-18 Problem 19-10.

SUPPORT DEVICES
AND TROUBLESHOOTING

The range of tasks that a microcomputer can perform need not be limited to those supported by custom-built interface circuits. There are hundreds of supporting chips available to supplement the more basic types of I/O devices. These supporting chips provide special functions, such as encrypting and decrypting the digital information. Peripheral controllers are another large class of supporting ICs. The peripheral controllers simplify the job of interfacing the processor to a floppy-disk drive, CRT terminal and keyboard, printers, and cassette recorders. There are even interfacing circuits for games that are driven by microprocessors.

Skills in troubleshooting microcomputer interfaces will become one of your most important assets as you continue to work in the electronics field. A variety of new test equipment has been developed to assist you in isolating circuit failures, but the standard voltmeter and oscilloscope that you have been using for years will continue to be important aids in servicing microcomputers. Diagnostic programs are another significant type of problem-identification support. More than any of these tools, however, your judgment and experience will become the prime means you should rely on in repairing these circuits. Often a few minutes spent thinking logically about the symptoms can find the problem hours earlier than would be possible if you immediately start connecting test equipment and pulling ICs from their sockets.

CHAPTER OBJECTIVES

Upon completion of this chapter, you should be able to:

1. Explain the principles of data encryption.
2. Describe the operation of an encryption/decryption support chip.
3. Explain the operation of a floppy-disk controller.
4. List the requirements for interfacing to the CRT of a display terminal.
5. List the steps in logically troubleshooting a microcomputer.
6. Explain how a pulser can be used to inject signals into microprocessor circuits.
7. Describe the use of a logic probe in analyzing digital circuitry.
8. Discuss the modes of operation for logic analyzers and specify when each mode should be used.
9. Explain how in-circuit emulators can be used for fault isolation.
10. Give examples of software diagnostic programs and describe their advantages and disadvantages.

DATA ENCRYPTION UNIT

In many cases, the information being processed by the computer is quite sensitive. For example, banks may wish to prevent unauthorized people from gaining knowledge of electronic funds transfers, or businesses may want to protect their trade secrets from competitors. Encryption of the data can mask the information content from those not authorized to have access to it, yet allow those with the key to readily read the data.

Data encryption is based on a reversible algorithm that can use one of a large number of possible mathematical transforms that scramble, or encrypt, the original bit sequence. By converting the data to an apparently random pattern, the algorithm makes reading it impossible without reversing the process. *Decryption,* the process of converting the data back to the original message, requires knowledge of that specific transform which encrypted the bit stream. The *key* identifies the specific transform to be used.

The *data encryption unit (DEU)* incorporates a product cipher developed by IBM. The cipher is based on the work of Horst Feister. The cryptographic procedure requires 16 alternate rounds of key-controller substitutions and permutations of the original bits. The crypto process was accepted by the National Bureau of Standards (NBS) in July 1977. A complete description of the *NBS algorithm* is given in the NBS algorithm publication, *Federal Information Processing Data Encryption Standard.*

Even if a person has complete knowledge of the algorithm, the cipher cannot be broken without the key because there are such a large number of possible sequences. In some ways the cipher can be compared to a combination lock. Knowing how the lock works internally makes it no easier to open without the combination.

Encryption or decryption groups 8 bytes into 64-bit data blocks, then operates on the block as a unit. The key consists of 56 bits. The resulting transformed data is also a 64-bit block. Figure 20-1 illustrates the rounds of encryption. There are 16 rounds required in all. In the first, the right-most 32 bits of data are transformed by the kernel function as specified by a value derived from the key. The results are summed with the left-most 32 bits and a swap of the right and left half of the bits is made. In round 2 a similar process occurs, and so on until round 16. After the last round, one more data switch is needed before the final output is developed. Decrypting uses exactly the same key and algorithm.

Although a microprocessor could implement the algorithm, the time required to do all the arithmetic would be excessive, resulting in quite slow encryption. A more efficient means of accomplishing the encryption is to use an integrated circuit developed to implement the NBS standard.

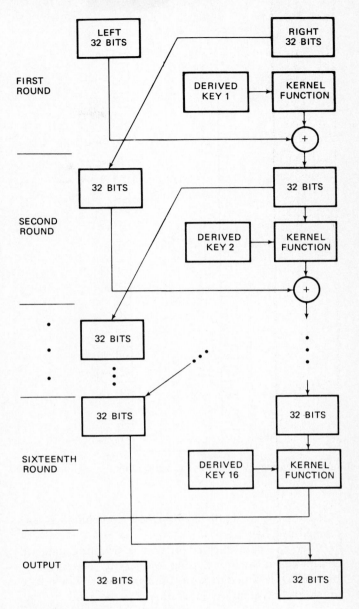

Fig. 20-1   Encryption algorithm.

One such device is the 8294 data encryption unit. Its pin diagram is shown in Fig. 20-2. The 40-pin DIP requires only a single +5-V power supply. A brief description of each signal is listed in Table 20-1.

Timing for the transforms is supplied by an external crystal or an LC oscillator through the X1 and X2 inputs. The chip is enabled for reading or writing with the $\overline{CS}$ input. The unit is forced to an idle condition whenever $\overline{RESET}$ becomes low. A high-frequency SYNC signal, with a frequency equal to the clock divided by 15, is supplied for use by external circuits, if desired.

The most efficient way of moving data through the device is by direct memory access, by means of the DMA request (DRQ) and acknowledge ($\overline{DACK}$) signals pro-

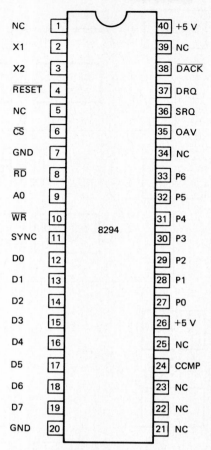

Fig. 20-2 Data encryption unit.

vided for use with the 8257 DMA controller, as explained in Chap. 13.

When the data encryption unit is awaiting data or commands at the input buffer, the service request interrupt (SRQ) is issued to inform the processor. When data or status information is available to be read by the microprocessor from the 8294 output buffer, an OAV interrupt occurs. After the encrypting or decrypting conversation on a 64-bit block has been completed, the encryption unit sends a CCMP interrupt. A 7-bit output port, which is completely independent from the crypto process, is provided in the 8294. The output pins P0 through P6 can be used in this fashion.

To program the 8294, one must follow the steps outlined in Fig. 20-3. First, the mode of operation command must be issued and the interrupts enabled. Then the key is entered. Although the key is only 56 bits long, each 7-bit segment is sent with a parity bit, so sending 64 bits is required to change the key. Next the unit is told to run the data through the transforms. Upon completion, the data encryption unit interrupts the processor, which then reads the results and can transform another block. The process continues until the processor runs out of data.

A more detailed breakdown of the data encryption unit will better describe the steps in the program. There are several registers in the 8294 that can be read or written. The command input buffer receives all the instructions. Each command is tabulated in Table 20-2. The command for setting the mode and enabling the interrupts permits the user to individually control the output available, the service request, and the conversion completion interrupts. At any point these interrupts can be allowed or locked out. DMA transfers can be enabled or disabled in a like manner.

When a key is to be entered, it must be preceded by the appropriate command. The key is entered most significant byte first, with odd parity on each byte. Either the encrypt or decrypt mode is selected prior to beginning operation. With DMA transfers, the unit can then automatically obtain its data from memory once the processor initializes the DMA read and write channels.

The reading of the registers to obtain data or status and the writing of data or commands are controlled by

Table 20-1 Data Encryption Unit Signals

Signal Name	Purpose	Input or Output
D0–D7	Data bus	Bidirectional
$\overline{\text{RD}}$	Read strobe	Input
$\overline{\text{WR}}$	Write strobe	Input
A0	Control/data select	Input
$\overline{\text{RESET}}$	Initialization	Input
X1, X2	Frequency reference	Input
SYNC	High frequency	Output
DRQ	DMA request	Input
$\overline{\text{DACK}}$	DMA acknowledge	Output
SRQ, OAV, CCMP	Interrupt requests	Output
P0–P6	Output port	Output
$\overline{\text{CS}}$	Chip select	Input

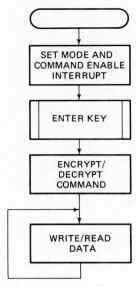

SET MODE AND COMMAND ENABLE INTERRUPT

ENTER KEY

ENCRYPT/ DECRYPT COMMAND

WRITE/READ DATA

Fig. 20-3 8294 programming.

four pins, as Table 20-3 shows. The use of these registers will be demonstrated by entering a key and encrypting or decrypting. The data input buffer is used for inserting a key, data for encryption or decryption, and the DMA block count. The output buffer is the register for results.

The status buffer consists of five flags that indicate the states within the chip. The output buffer full flag (OBF) is set when there is data to be read and is reset when the buffer is empty. The input buffer full flag (IBF) is a 1 when writing is in progress and a 0 afterward.

The mode is indicated by the DEC flag, which is 0 for decryption and 1 for encryption. The completion flag (CF) is used to signal the end of an 8-byte-block data transfer, can replace the CCMP interrupt, and in conjunction with the key parity error (KPE) flag indicates the parity correctness of key entries.

Figure 20-4 shows the use of the various registers in entering a key. First, the program waits until the input buffer is full. Next, an enter key command is sent. Again, a delay is allowed while the command is read, then 1 byte of the key is entered. After all key bits are sent, the CF and KPE flags are checked to ensure that the new key was received correctly.

The encryption and decryption flowchart is shown in Fig. 20-5. Here, the sequence of sending the data bytes out is much the same as for sending key bytes. After all bytes have been sent, a wait for either the completion flag or an interrupt is incurred. Then the processed data is retrieved 1 byte at a time.

Data Encryption Unit Review

1. Define the term "data encryption."
2. What are desirable characteristics of an encryption algorithm?
3. Explain how the data is transposed in 32-bit units on each round of the NBS encryption process.
4. What is the purpose of the SRQ interrupt?
5. Describe the steps that a program for the data encryption unit must execute.
6. How do the read, write, chip select, and A0 pins control the reading or writing of register data?

Table 20-2 Data Encryption Unit Commands

Command	Function
40	Enter new key; followed by 8-byte key (each key byte must have odd parity using LSB)
30	Encrypt data
20	Decrypt data
0X	Set mode, enable interrupts, or allow DMA transfers for value of X

X			
0	none	8	OAV
1	CCMP	9	OAV, CCMP
2	DMA	A	OAV, DMA
3	DMA, CCMP	B	OAV, DMA, CCMP
4	SRQ	C	OAV, SRQ
5	SRQ, CCMP	D	OAV, SRQ, CCMP
6	SRQ, DMA	E	OAV, SRQ, DMA
7	SRQ, DMA, CCMP	F	all

Various*	Write to output port.

* MSB of command must be a 1; remaining bits are output on P6–P0, respectively.

Table 20-3 Accessing Registers

Register	Signal			
	$\overline{\text{RD}}$	$\overline{\text{WR}}$	$\overline{\text{CS}}$	A0
Data input buffer	1	0	0	0
Data output buffer	0	1	0	0
Command input buffer	1	0	0	1
Status output buffer	0	1	0	1

FLOPPY-DISK CONTROLLER

Floppy disks are one of the most common peripherals used to load and store microcomputer programs, as was explained in Chap. 12. *Floppy-disk controller* devices can interface from one to four drives to the microprocessors. The chips can also unload many error detection and correction tasks from the processor. We will use the Intel 8271 to illustrate the important concepts of floppy-disk control.

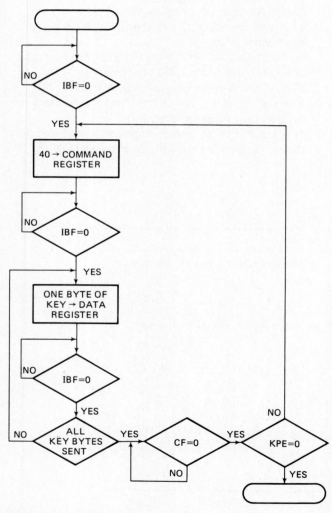

Fig. 20-4 Entering a key.

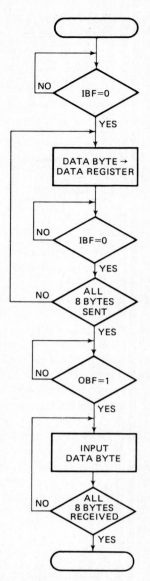

Fig. 20-5 Encryption and decryption flowchart.

The Intel 8271 can read, write, or scan the disk for a specified bit pattern. The controller is packaged as a 40-pin DIP and requires a +5-V supply. A 2- or 4-MHz square-wave clock input is necessary for timing.

A block diagram of the controller is shown in Fig. 20-6. The data buffer supports the 8-bit data bus input and output. A DMA controller is supplied in order to fetch or store data from memory. The disk interface is composed of a serial controller and a drive controller. A description of all signals is provided in Table 20-4.

Many of the signals are the same as we have seen on other microprocessor support ICs. In particular, the data bus, reset, chip select, interrupt request, read, write, and DMA lines perform the usual functions. The microprocessor interface has five registers used with A0, A1, $\overline{\text{RD}}$, and $\overline{\text{WR}}$.

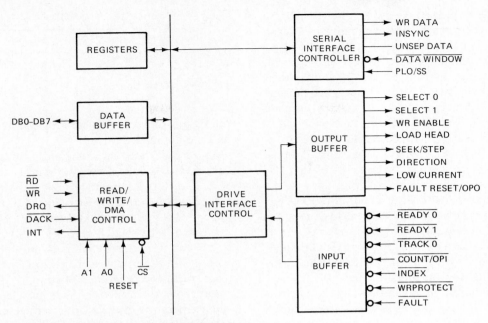

Fig. 20-6 Floppy disk controller block diagram.

Table 20-4 Floppy-Disk Controller Signals

Name	Function	Direction
DB0–DB7	Three-state data bus	Bidirectional
RESET	Select idle state	Input
$\overline{CS}$	Chip select	Input
A0–A1	Interface register select	Input
INT	Service request interrupt	Output
DRQ	DMA request	Output
$\overline{DACK}$	DMA acknowledge	Input
$\overline{WR}$	Write command	Input
$\overline{RD}$	Read command	Input
WR DATA	Write disk data	Output
INSYNC	Input data sync has been achieved	Output
UNSEP DATA	Unseparated data (the combined clock and data input)	Input
$\overline{DATA\ WINDOW}$	Data window established	Input
PLO/SS	Data separator specifier	Input
SELECT 0, SELECT 1	Drive select	Output
WR ENABLE	Write enable	Output
LOAD HEAD	Signal drive to press the head against the disk	Output
SEEK/STEP	Seek control	Output
DIRECTION	Seek direction (high means inward, low means outward)	Output
LOW CURRENT	Track 43 or higher selected	Output
FAULT RESET/OPO	Error condition reset	Output
$\overline{READY\ 0}$, $\overline{READY\ 1}$	Specified drive ready	Input
$\overline{TRACK\ 0}$	Head is positioned over track 00	Input
$\overline{COUNT/OPI}$	Stepping pulse	Input
$\overline{INDEX}$	Disk index position	Input
$\overline{WR\ PROTECT}$	Disk is write-protected	Input
$\overline{FAULT}$	Unsafe condition	Input

The registers are selected by the settings of A0 and A1. The operation code for the command to be performed and the number of the drive to be used are placed in the command register. Up to five amplifying parameters for a command can be used by sending them to the parameter register. The results register the outcome of the last command, such as successful or unsuccessful completion. The status of the controller can be read from the status register. Such conditions as register full or empty, requests for DMA or interrupts, and busy state can be determined from the contents of that register.

Transfer of data to the disk is usually by DMA (although not required by the 8271) because of the data rate. One byte can be sent or received in 32 μs, so an entire block of 128, 256, or 512 bytes can be exchanged rapidly. The use of DMA request and acknowledge signals is the same as was explained in Chap. 13.

Drive commands rely on clock pulses to reconstruct input data. All data is written between clock pulses. Figure 20-7a is a timing diagram of the combined signal. If the data bit is a 0, there will be a full-bit time between high pulses. However, if the data bit is a 1, there is only a half-bit time from one high pulse to the next. This sequence makes it possible to detect missing clock pulses, as the figure shows.

The DATA WINDOW signal is separated from the data stream by using a circuit such as that shown in Fig. 20-7b. The window is sampled on the leading edge of unseparated data to detect whether the delay since the previous pulse was a half- or full-bit time. As the block is read, the controller automatically establishes sync using the sync field in the identification (ID) or data portion of the block. It also computes and verifies

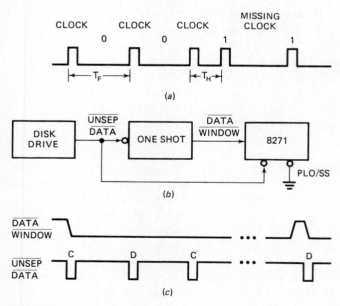

Fig. 20-7 Data timing.

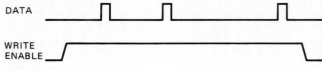

Fig. 20-8 Write timing.

the ID information and CRC for both the identification and the data fields.

In writing data, the controller builds the composite (unseparated) data block by interleaving clock pulses with data bits. Computation of the identification and CRC fields are done for each block, and these codes are appended to the data field. Figure 20-8 shows a timing diagram for writing. When WR ENABLE is high, the electronics in the drive will pass the data stream to the write head. When that signal is low, the head reads the magnetically recorded information.

Other control functions that must be performed include generation of the head step rate, load time, setting time delay, unload delay, and monitoring of the drive. To initialize the drive, the controller pulses the seek/step high and the direction line for the desired movement (high is inward). The head then steps in or out one track for each seek/step pulse. Alternatively, the count line can supply the pulses and the seek/step line be held high until the head is in position. When the head reaches its maximum outward limit (track 00), the track 0 line becomes true.

The head seek settling time, that is, the time from the last step until reading or writing is possible, can be programmed to be from 0 to 225 ms for 8-in drives and to 510 ms for minidrives. The head load settling time, when the head is placed in contact with the disk, can also be programmed for 0 to 60 ms for large disks, and for 0 to 120 ms for minis.

The drive being selected is specified by the select 0 and select 1 lines. When recording on the inner tracks (track numbers higher than 43), the low-current pin output is active to compensate for the lower velocity of disk surface (as compared with the outer tracks).

Every disk has a write protect notch. When the floppy disk is write-protected, the $\overline{\text{WR PROTECT}}$ signal becomes true, preventing the controller from writing. An interrupt is also sent to the processor to inform it of the incorrect situation. Another signal that detects problems in writing is the write fault, which indicates that data integrity is questionable. The processor is also interrupted for this condition, which is reset with the write fault reset signal.

Each drive signals its readiness for operation with the $\overline{\text{READY 0}}$ and $\overline{\text{READY 1}}$ lines. The drive selected must be ready before data is read or written. If not, a processor interrupt results and the operation terminates. One other quite useful service provided by the controller is alternate-track recording. If one of the tracks is found to be bad, the controller will automatically record on tracks 75 or 76. Whenever the processor requests to input that data, the correct alternate track will be read.

Operating the disk drives requires that a command be issued; then the operation is carried out. Last, the results must be checked for proper conditions. To send a command, the status register is checked to ensure that the command busy bit is not set. The DMA channel is initiated and a write op code transmitted to the command register, followed by the necessary parameter. (Between each parameter write, the status register is examined and a wait incurred as long as the parameter full bit is set.)

The operation is carried out under DMA, so the processor need not involve itself with the data transfer. After the operation, the command byte is examined for a successful result. If the result is not successful, the status and result registers allow the program to interpret

the type of error that occurred. A failure could be caused by a clock error, DMA late timing, drive not ready, or attempting to write on a protected disk.

Floppy-Disk Controller Review

1. Describe how the number of a floppy-disk drive to be read is specified.
2. Explain the format for unseparated data.
3. How does the controller detect a missing clock pulse?
4. How is the head moved to the correct track?
5. What is an alternate track?

CRT CONTROLLER

A general-purpose interface to a CRT terminal can greatly simplify the output of character information from the microprocessor. Such a *CRT controller* is used with raster scan displays, which were described in Chap. 12. The controller refreshes the display by buffering information from the computer memory. As the character is buffered out, the controller keeps track of where it is writing on the screen.

The Intel 8275 is composed of a DMA controller and data buffer for the computer interface, together with timing and control logic for the video terminal. The processor interface is a conventional DMA input/output controller. Figure 20-9 is a block diagram of the 8275. The signals are listed in Table 20-5.

Table 20-5 8275 CRT Controller Signals

Signal	Purpose
DB0–DB7	Three-state data bus
DRQ, $\overline{\text{DACK}}$	DMA control signals
IRQ	Interrupt request
$\overline{\text{RD}}$, $\overline{\text{WR}}$	Read/write strobes
A0	Select command registers or parameter registers
$\overline{\text{CS}}$	Chip select
CCLK	Character clock from the dot timing
CC0–CC6	Character codes
LC0–LC3	Line count
LA0–LA1	Line attribute codes
HRTC	Horizontal retrace interval
VRTC	Vertical retrace interval
HLGT	Highlight (to intensify the display at the current position)
RVV	Reverse video (black characters on a white background)
LTEN	Light enable (to underline)
VSP	Video suppression (blank video signal)
GPA0–GPA1	General-purpose attribute codes
LPEN	Light-pen input

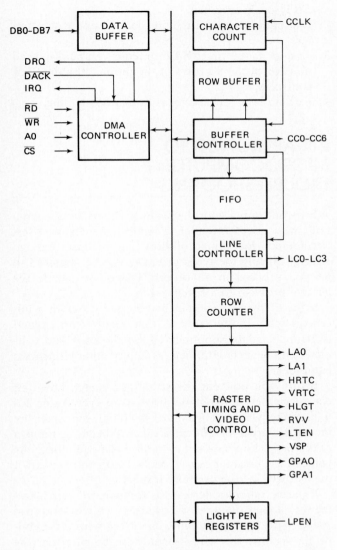

Fig. 20-9 CRT controller block diagram.

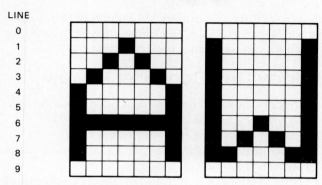

Fig. 20-10   10-line character.

Each display character is retrieved from memory on a row-by-row basis. The character counter determines the number of characters to be written on a row, while the line counter maintains the number of horizontal lines (sweeps) in a row. See Fig. 20-10 for an example. The number of rows that make up the entire screen is programmed using the row counter.

The display format, as shown in Fig. 20-11, is variable and under program control. The number of characters can range from 1 to 80 in a row, and up to 64 rows can be displayed on the screen. As Fig. 20-10 indicated, the line counter increments as each line of the character is sent to the screen. The 8275 controller can use from 1 to 16 lines to draw a character, and underlining is provided. The line counter simply cycles through its count repeatedly for each character. The line counter increments during the horizontal retrace after the character counter has reached the maximum value for the number of characters in a row. A timing diagram is shown in Fig. 20-12. When the retrace signal goes high, the line counter takes on its next value.

The CRT controller requires a character generator and dot timing and interface to produce the video, sync, and intensity voltages for the CRT. Figure 20-13 shows

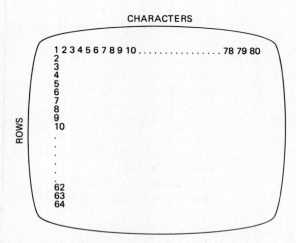

Fig. 20-11   CRT format.

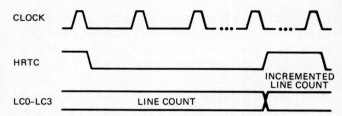

Fig. 20-12   Line counter timing.

a typical system. The line counter and character codes select the position on the screen and the type of character that the character generator supplies. The dot-timing logic supplies a clock so that all of the devices can stay synchronized with the scan position on the terminal screen.

CRT Controller Review

1. How is the number of characters per row on the CRT screen specified?
2. Distinguish between the line counter and row counter.
3. True or false? Up to 64 characters can be displayed on each of the 80 rows of the terminal by the CRT controller.
4. Explain how a character is drawn line by line.

AN APPROACH TO MICROCOMPUTER TROUBLESHOOTING

When confronted with the problem of tracking down a fault in a microcomputer, a technician may well feel bewildered. Just think of how many things can go wrong! Luckily the types of errors can be classified to let you proceed in an orderly fashion to isolate the general problem to a specific chip.

Some of the test equipment you will use with a microcomputer is the same as that required in general electronics troubleshooting. The oscilloscope and voltmeter can be as helpful here as in any other electronics equipment.

Before you pull out the scope and meter, however, consider an even better tool first—your eyes. Table 20-6 lists the problems you are likely to encounter by increasing order of difficulty. *Always* begin at the top of the table. You may not even need test equipment. As you can see, no equipment is needed until halfway down the list, if you look carefully instead.

If the circuit board looks OK, compare the chip placement to a logic diagram. Should this be a wire-wrapped breadboard for a prototype, check the wiring for continuity against the wire list and also be sure that the power and ground buses are properly isolated. Either a

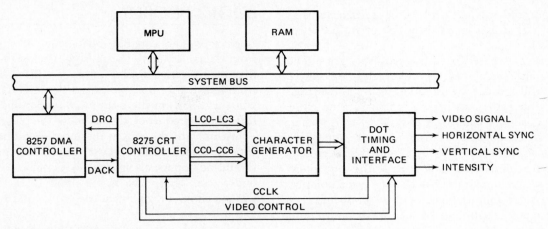

Fig. 20-13 CRT system.

voltmeter or a buzzer (in series with a battery) can be used for these tests. Also verify that the power supply outputs are correct.

Logic probes and pulsers will readily detect stuck or floating lines. These small testers are also a good way to find shorts. If you have gotten this far and still have not found the problem, heavy artillery is called for. An oscilloscope may be of help in tracking down noisy lines, an incorrect clock period, or glitches. More than likely a logic analyzer or in-circuit emulator may be needed, especially if the computer being tested is a prototype.

Do not forget that the computer can be programmed to isolate faults also, that is, provided it is operating at least in partial fashion. If the front panel of the computer allows you to inspect register and memory contents, use it also as a diagnostic aid.

An Approach to Microcomputer Troubleshooting Review

1. What is the first step in troubleshooting any microprocessor-based equipment?
2. List the most common, and easiest to find, microcomputer faults.
3. How would you test the continuity of a prototype breadboard?
4. Explain a method for identifying lines that are stuck in a high state.
5. What faults are best found with an oscilloscope?

PULSERS

A *pulser* is a hand-held signal generator with a metal tip that is to be touched to the pin of an IC. Usually about 5 in (12.5 cm) long and weighing a few ounces, the pulser can generate a signal of either positive or negative polarity. The pulser comes with alligator clips to connect to the power supply. Any voltage in the region of $+4$ to $+18$ V is suitable, provided only that it match V_{CC} of the chip.

To operate the pulser, simply touch the tip to the pin, then press the button (for less than 1 s). A pulse will be produced at the tip. If the button is held down continuously, a series of pulses at about 100 Hz is produced. The LED on the case flashes each time a pulse is generated. For TTL circuits, the pulse width is in the 1- to 2-μs range, and it is lengthened to 10 μs in the CMOS mode.

As small as it is, the pulser has considerable drive. It can fan out to at least 50 TTL loads. Furthermore, a pulser can withstand overvoltages, pulse into short circuits, and even let you reverse the polarity on the power-

Table 20-6 Troubleshooting Guide

Level	What to Look For
Easy	Not plugged in
	IC in socket backwards
	Wrong type of IC in socket
	Lead on IC bent underneath or broken off
Moderate	Solder bridge
	Cold solder joint
	Broken trace
	Power supply voltage out of tolerance
	Stuck line (high or low)
	Floating line
Difficult	Noisy switch
	Bad connector
	Bad socket
	Timing glitch
	Bus conflict (especially data bus)
	Loading
	Noise

supply inputs by mistake—all without damage. The three-state output is isolated from the circuit by better than 250 kΩ.

Its operation is based on a comparator circuit. The polarity-sensing circuit selects either sink or source pulses that will activate the test point (cause it to change state). A comparator matches the voltage at the point to the power supply voltage. If the test point is higher, the output of the pulser goes low; otherwise, a positive going pulse is produced. After each pulse has been sent out, another comparison is made. If the test point changed state, the next pulse will have reversed polarity. In this way a continuous trigger can be produced.

In use, the power supply cable acts as the return path for the output pulse as well as providing operating voltage. Always clip the power leads close to the test point to prevent ground loops. (Ground loops can cause false triggering of the circuit being tested.) Some pulsers come with an auxiliary ground clip to be used next to the tip to prevent such problems. If the auxiliary clip is used, the pulser is not to be grounded at the power supply.

Figure 20-14 shows an example of the pulser in use. It triggers the HOLD input of the 8085. The test for a response (HLDA) uses a logic probe (described in the following section). Because the pulser has such a high fan-out, it will override any inputs to the HOLD input—regardless of the states of downstream logic. This handy feature of the pulser makes it unnecessary to disconnect other signals being fed to the pin being pulsed.

The pulser can also be used to replace the system clock in single-phase circuits. By clocking the circuit, you can step the logic through an entire cycle of its states. Logic probes can then sample the outputs at several key test points.

Pulsers Review

1. What voltage range can the pulser be used with?
2. What would happen if you reversed the polarity of the power supply leads to a pulser?
3. Distinguish between the effects of pressing the pulser button for less than a second and holding it down continuously.
4. How can the pulser trigger a circuit even though downstream gates are holding the input in the low state?

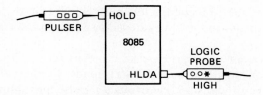

Fig. 20-14 Testing the HOLD input of the 8085.

LOGIC PROBES

Logic probes are capable of detecting and storing pulses from digital circuits. The pulse is latched by a flip-flop that controls the display of three LEDs. A transition from negative to positive causes the high LED to light, while a change in the opposite direction lights the low LED. High-frequency signals blink the pulse LED.

Just as with the pulser, the logic probe has alligator clips to attach to the power supply. The power leads should be connected as close as possible to the circuit under test. The probe is set either to the TTL level, which defines a high signal level as greater than 2.25 V and a low as less than 0.8 V, or to the MOS level, for which a high is a level greater than 70 percent of the power supply voltage and a low is less than 30 percent of that voltage. Levels in the region in between are not defined.

To use the probe, choose the level appropriate for the IC being tested, then touch the output pin. In the pulse mode, the LEDs will light on each pulse. For short pulses, switch to the memory mode, in which the latch can catch pulses as narrow as 100 ns. When using the memory mode, first contact the pin, then switch the memory on. If the probe is not in contact when the memory is switched on, the floating tip will trigger an erroneous indication when brought into contact.

The LEDs can give more information than just the level of the signal, as shown in Table 20-7. Of course, a steady light on the high or low LED means that the signal is not changing. If all LEDs are off, the tip is in contact with an open circuit. Pulse trains cause the high and low LEDs to light with the pulse LED blinking if the frequency is less than 100 Hz. The duty cycle of the pulse train can be estimated by the ratio of the time the pulse LED is on and off. For pulses from 100 Hz to 10 MHz, only the pulse LED is blinking.

The logic probe is quite simple to work with, so figuring out why it does not give the proper indications is straightforward. If none of the LEDs gives an indication, first check that power is applied to the equipment. Next, verify that the power supply cable of the probe is properly connected. (If leads are crossed, the

Table 20-7 Logic Probe Indications

LED Indicator			
High	**Low**	**Pulse**	**Meaning**
On	Off	Off	Steady high signal
Off	On	Off	Steady low signal
Off	Off	Off	Open circuit
On	On	Blink	Pulse train (frequency less than 100 kHz)
Off	Off	Blink	High-frequency pulse train

probe will not be damaged by the reverse polarity, but it will not indicate either.) A final possibility to consider is that the signal exceeds the measuring ability of the probe. In that case, select a different piece of test equipment, such as an oscilloscope.

Logic Probes Review

1. Why can logic probes be used with either TTL or MOS circuits?
2. Explain the meaning of each of the LED indicators on the probe.
3. Why must the probe tip be in contact with the pin before switching on the memory mode?
4. Using a logic probe, how can you distinguish a 90-kHz pulse train from a 900-kHz pulse train?

LOGIC ANALYZERS

A *logic analyzer* is a recording device that accepts a multiple number of input channels of data. Each channel represents the signals from any digital device. The devices can be either TTL, ECL, or CMOS technologies, and the analyzer will correctly interpret the logic levels. Typical analyzers can accept 8 to 16 channels of data up to 50 MHz or more. Once recorded in the random-access memory of the analyzer, the data can be displayed in many different ways. No data is lost when it is viewed on the built-in CRT or on an external scope.

The display is able to present the stored information in several formats. Each display is useful for detecting a particular type of fault. The format choices include pulse-train, binary, and map formats and various computer output.

Pulse-train format displays are well-suited for finding timing faults. Because many channels are recorded simultaneously, the timing relationship between the pulses is available as well as the time of transition. Many times, faults in microcomputers are caused by a particular signal changing levels just a little too early or late. Such a problem can easily be spotted on the display. The horizontal dimension of the display represents the duration (time) of the recording, as Fig. 20-15a shows. The vertical dimension represents each of the 16 channels. By designating a point on the horizontal scale with the cursor, the user can expand the display by a factor of 10 or 20 times to examine fine details or time relationships (Fig. 20-15b).

The *binary data format* display is simply a listing of the logic analyzer's memory contents, as Fig. 20-16 shows. The left-hand area of the display is the memory address. Any consecutive 16 memory locations can be viewed at once. The middle of each row lists the 2-byte memory contents in binary. The same value is converted

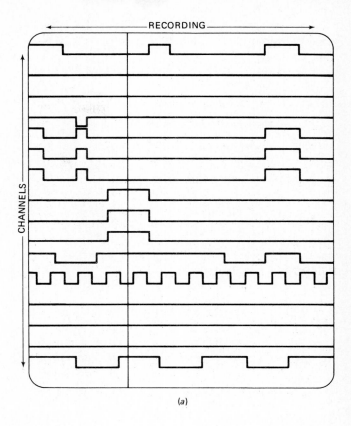

(a)

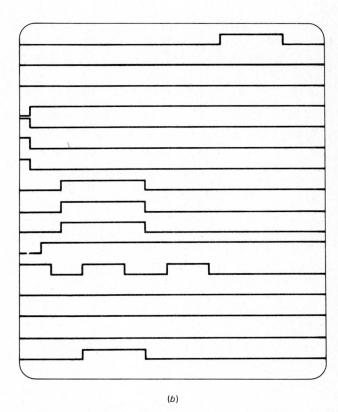

(b)

Fig. 20-15 Pulse train display: (a) normal scale, (b) ×20 magnification.

001	1111	1111	1111	1100	FFFC
002	1111	1111	1111	1101	FFFD
003	0111	0101	0000	0000	7500
004	1000	0000	0000	0100	8004
005	1000	0000	0000	0011	8003
006	1000	0000	0000	0010	8002
007	1000	0000	0000	0001	8001
008	1000	0000	0000	0000	8000
009	0111	0000	1100	0000	70C0
010	0111	0000	1101	0000	70D0
011	0111	1111	0000	0000	7F00
012	0111	0000	0000	0110	7006
013	1111	1111	1111	1111	FFFF
014	0101	0101	0101	0101	5555
015	0000	0000	0000	0000	0000
016	0111	0000	0100	0000	7040

Fig. 20-16 Binary display.

to hexadecimal or octal and displayed to the right. This display format is best-suited for software checkout.

The *map format* display gives an *x-y* presentation of the memory contents. Each word is divided into two equal groups of bits. For example, if the memory word length is 16 bits, the upper byte is displayed on the *y* axis and the lower byte on the *x* axis (see Fig. 20-17). The image that results is a *signature* for the circuit in its present state. If any output changes value, there will be a difference in the map. Normally the map format is used at the beginning of a troubleshooting session to find out where the error might be, and then the pulse train or binary mode is used for a detailed analysis of the problem.

Many analyzers also provide a serial output channel. The memory contents of the analyzer can be read directly by a computer using this channel. Testing of complicated circuitry can be computer-driven, with the

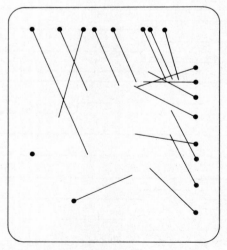

Fig. 20-17 Map display.

responses to the test inputs being monitored on this channel.

Some analyzers provide a comparison mode to enhance the diagnostic power of the equipment. In the *comparison mode*, the data recorded in memory is matched against each new recording of the same data. Any difference between the stored value and the latest reading is highlighted on the display. In this manner, a cyclic check for a fault can be run until its next occurrence is detected.

The analyzer readily allows the technician control of the sampling process. Sampling can begin at a selected time to cover the period that precedes and follows a specific event if *pretrigger recording* is chosen. With *delayed recording*, information is gathered after the event, similar to delay sweep triggering of an oscilloscope (except the timing of the analyzer can be controlled more precisely).

The input probes for the analyzer must present a low capacitive load, as well as a high impedance, to the circuit under test. Values in the neighborhood of 1 MΩ and 10 pF can be considered typical. The probes for each channel often have spring-loaded hooks to clip on the output lead. Cables about 10 ft (3 m) long connect the probes to the analyzer chassis.

Data is recorded as a binary value. The threshold voltage is established by a comparator that converts any input voltage above the threshold to a 1. All other inputs become 0s. The threshold can be set to the correct value for TTL, ECL, or MOS circuits.

In the *sampling mode*, 1 bit of data is recorded for each channel on each clock pulse. This method of sampling is best for synchronous circuits. Any signal change between clock pulses is ignored (as it should be in a synchronous circuit). For testing asynchronous circuits, the *latch mode* is provided. By latching, the data noise spikes or glitches can be detected. The analyzer records a bit and flags the event whenever there is a change in any channel that exceeds the threshold in between clock pulses. Although a bit is recorded when the noise spike occurs, the duration of the spike is not detectable using the logic analyzer. Only that a transition has taken place on one of the input channels can be read.

Another flexible feature of analyzers lies in the methods available for *clocking*. With *manual* clocking, a sample is made every time the operator pushes a button. *External* clocking permits a single event to dictate the time to sample. Most variation is provided by the *internal* clock, which responds to a particular bit pattern combination of the input data. Each bit can be set for on, off, or don't care. For example, we may be monitoring the address bus and want to sample when the address reaches $3B_{16}$. Simply by dialing in the number, the technician causes the analyzer to sample when the address is $3B_{16}$. Another variation of the same idea is to cause the data to be sampled as long as it does *not* equal the preset value.

Logic Analyzers Review

1. List the display formats of the logic analyzer.
2. Which format is best for debugging software?
3. Explain the structure of the map display.
4. What is a circuit signature?
5. When should the sampling mode be used? The latch mode?
6. How is the analyzer clock derived?

IN-CIRCUIT EMULATORS

An *in-circuit emulator (ICE)* is a module that plugs into the socket of the microcomputer as a replacement for the processor. By removing the microprocessor and inserting the emulator in its place, a powerful diagnostic capability is provided. A cable runs from the ICE to a microprocessor development system. This system also simulates ROM, RAM, and I/O operations to check out the hardware and software of a prototype system.

With the emulator in place, the MPU's registers and the RAM contents can be examined or modified. The program can be run in single step (one instruction at a time) or at full speed. *Breakpoints* can be inserted to cause the program to stop whenever a predefined event occurs. Such events may include reading or writing in a specified memory address or executing a particular instruction. After the breakpoint, the operator gains control from the program and may inspect or change register and memory values. Input or output of data can also be carefully monitored.

When the ICE is to be used, only a few actions are needed to change over from the normal microcomputer configuration to one with the emulator installed. First, the computer is unplugged. Next, the computer system clock or the ICE clock is selected. The microprocessor is removed and the in-circuit emulator put in; then the ground connection from the ICE to computer ground is made. In the power-up sequence, the microcomputer is turned on first, followed by applying power to the ICE development system. After forcing a reset signal, the computer is ready to begin running the program. Results will be shown on the development system display.

In-Circuit Emulators Review

1. List the test capabilities that an in-circuit emulator provides.
2. What steps are required before an emulator can be used?

3. If you wanted to step through a program one instruction at a time, would a logic analyzer or an ICE be more appropriate?
4. Define the term "breakpoint."

SOFTWARE DIAGNOSTICS

With the versatility of the microcomputer, faults can often be detected with computer programs (*software diagnostics*). Unfortunately, software checkout utility programs cannot be run unless at least a portion of RAM is operating reliably and much of the control and arithmetic logic is also usable. Some microcomputers are equipped with a microprogram ROM program to verify that enough of the circuits are operable to begin running the diagnostic programs.

These programs can thoroughly exercise the processor by executing every instruction, then examining memory functions, and finally verifying peripheral equipment operation. Some RAMs have been known to experience a sensitivity to certain bit patterns. When one of these patterns is stored, incorrect values are obtained when the data is read later. Sometimes writing into one address will change the value of another location.

Because the number of bit patterns that can be stored in microcomputer memory is large, for practical purposes an exhaustive test of every pattern cannot be made. The number of possible patterns is

$$\text{Number of memory patterns} = 2^W \times M \qquad (12\text{-}1)$$

where
W = word size
M = memory size

For example, a 32K memory on an 8-bit computer can store a possible

$$(2^8)\,(32,768) = 8,388,608$$

different patterns. If we could verify one pattern in 30 ms, it would take almost 70 hours just to test one memory. Obviously, a shortcut is needed.

Most often, patterns that represent worst-case conditions are used for memory testing. Patterns of all 0s, all 1s, and alternating 1s and 0s are frequently used. Some diagnostic programs divide the memory into zones and apply the patterns in a checkerboard fashion.

A Microprocessor Diagnostic Program

As an example of the type of program used for diagnostic work, Table 20-8 lists a test program for the 8085 shift logic. The four rotate instructions (RAL, RAR, RLC, and RRC) are each used one time to verify

Table 20-8 8085 Shift Diagnostic Program

Label	Mnemonic	Operand	Address	Machine Code	Comments
	LDA	PATTERN	1000	3A	Shift pattern → A
			1001	33	
			1002	10	
	RLC		1003	07	Rotate left
	CPI	55	1004	FE	Compare with correct value
			1005	55	
	JZ	TEST 2	1006	CA	Go to TEST 2 if OK
			1007	0C	
			1008	10	
	MVI A	01	1009	3E	Error code → A
			100A	01	
	HLT		100B	76	Stop
TEST 2	LDA	PATTERN	100C	3A	Shift pattern → A
			100D	33	
			100E	10	
	RRC		100F	0F	Rotate right (clear carry)
	CPI	55	1010	FE	Compare with correct value
			1011	55	
	JZ	TEST 3	1012	CA	Go to TEST 3 if OK
			1013	18	
			1014	10	
	MVI A	02	1015	3E	Error Code → A
			1016	02	
	HLT		1017	76	Stop
TEST 3	LDA A	PATTERN	1018	3A	Shift pattern → A
			1019	33	
			101A	10	
	RAL		101B	17	Rotate left through carry (set carry)
	CPI	54	101C	FE	Compare with correct value
			101D	54	
	JZ	TEST 4	101E	CA	Go to TEST 4 if OK
			101F	24	
			1020	10	
	MVI A	03	1021	3E	Error code → A
			1022	03	
	HLT		1023	76	Stop
TEST 4	LDA	PATTERN	1024	3A	Shift pattern → A
			1025	33	
			1026	10	
	RAR		1027	1F	Rotate right through carry
	CPI	55	1028	FE	Compare with correct value
			1029	55	
	JZ	END	102A	CA	End test if OK
			102B	30	
			102C	10	
	MVI A	04	102D	3E	Error code → A
			102E	04	
	HLT		102F	76	Stop
END	MVI A	00	1030	3E	Clear A
			1031	00	
	HLT		1032	76	Stop
PATTERN		AA	1033	AA	

that the proper result is produced. If it is, the program then tests the next instruction in sequence; otherwise, the program stops with a code number in the accumulator indicating which instruction failed. If all instructions execute correctly, the program stops with the accumulator cleared. The error indications are as follows:

A Register	Instruction That Failed
1	RLC
2	RRC
3	RAL
4	RAR

A Memory Diagnostic Program

An example of a memory diagnostic program is given in Table 20-9. The program starts the test at the location stored in the LOWER LIMIT variable location and ends the test at that cell which is one less than the UPPER LIMIT variable location. (For example, if the LOWER LIMIT is 1005 and the UPPER LIMIT 1015, the cells tested will be those in the range 1005 to 1014.) All 0s are written and read from each cell. If the test fails, the HL register pair contains the address, and the accumulator value is the number that is supposed to be in the memory cell. If the test is successful, the program halts with a value of 01 in the accumulator. Obviously, this

Table 20-9 Memory Diagnostic Program

Label	Mnemonic	Operand	Address	Machine Code	Comments
	LHLD	LOWER LIMIT	0000	2A	Lower limit → HL
			0001	1D	
			0002	00	
LOOP	MVI A	00	0003	3E	0 → A
			0004	00	
	MOV M, A		0005	77	Store value in memory
	CMP M		0006	BE	Compare memory value to A
	INX H		0007	23	
	JZ	NEXT	0008	CA	Increment count Go to next cell if OK
			0009	0C	
			000A	00	
	HLT		000B	76	Otherwise, stop (error)
NEXT	LDA	UPPER LIMIT	000C	3A	Check L value. Is this the last cell?
			000D	1F	
			000E	00	
	CMP L		000F	BD	
	JNZ	LOOP	0010	C2	If not, repeat test
			0011	03	
			0012	00	
	LDA	UPPER LIMIT + 1	0013		
			0014	3A	
			0015	20	Check H value
			0016	00	
	CMP H			BC	
	JNZ	LOOP	0017	C2	Is this the last cell? If not, repeat the test
			0018	03	
			0019	00	
	MVI A	01	001A	3E	1 → A
			001B	01	
	HLT		001C	76	Stop
LOWER LIMIT			001D		
			001E		
UPPER LIMIT			0001F		
			0020		

program cannot test the memory area where the diagnostic routine itself resides.

Software Diagnostics Review

1. Describe the type of testing that software diagnostic programs can support.
2. Why is exhaustive pattern testing of memories not practical?
3. What patterns are frequently used for memory tests?
4. What would happen if the memory diagnostic program given in this chapter were used between the limits of 0000_{16} and $1A2F_{16}$?
5. Why does the shift diagnostic program not need to check the contents of the carry register?

CHAPTER SUMMARY

1. Data encryption is useful in preventing the disclosure of sensitive material. Encryption is based on a reversible transform of the bit sequence. To perform the proper transform, one must know the key; otherwise, the cipher cannot be decrypted.
2. The data encryption unit is an implementation of the NBS encryption algorithm. The mathematical processes of encryption and decryption are automatically performed by this circuit.
3. The floppy-disk controller can direct one of several drives to read or write on the rotating magnetic surface. Important disk operations include separating data from clocking signals, stepping the head to the correct track, loading the head against the surface, calculating identification and CRC data, and maintaining correct time relationships.

4. A CRT terminal interface can be constructed easily by use of an interface chip. The CRT controller has logic to clock out the proper dot pattern for each line of characters. The controller will maintain a count of the proper number of characters in one row and the total number of rows on the screen. The signals required to time the trace on the screen are also provided by the controller.
5. Logical troubleshooting can save you time. Look first for the obvious failures before using test equipment. Proceed in a step-by-step manner.
6. A pulser can generate a signal to trigger a logic circuit at any point. Its high fan-out overwhelms the effects of downstream gates. Either single pulses or a series can be produced.
7. Logic probes can indicate the presence of a large number of different signals in digital circuits. Based on the indicator LEDs, the technician can readily identify signal levels.
8. Logic analyzers record signals obtained from many channels at once. This feature makes analyzers invaluable in diagnosing problems on the data, address, or control buses of a microcomputer. Display formats for pulse trains, binary data, and maps are provided.
9. An in-circuit emulator replaces the processor to permit inspection and changing of register or memory contents, controlling I/O, or inserting breakpoints in the program. Any RAM, ROM, or I/O operation can be simulated with this test equipment. The program can be run in single-step or full-speed modes when the emulator is in place.
10. Software diagnostics can provide almost limitless troubleshooting assistance, provided that enough memory and processor circuits are operable to execute the instructions. Even using the speed of the computer, however, exhaustive tests are not practical.

KEY TERMS AND CONCEPTS

Data encryption unit (DEU)	Pulse-train format	Sampling mode
NBS algorithm	Binary data format	Latch mode
Floppy-disk controller	Map format	Clocking
CRT controller	Signature	In-circuit emulator (ICE)
Pulser	Comparison mode	Breakpoints
Logic probes	Pretrigger recording	Software diagnostics
Logic analyzer	Delayed recording	

20-1 Given the key below, calculate the proper parity for each byte for entry into the data encryption unit.

Byte	Value$_{16}$
1	E8
2	12
3	76
4	FC
5	CC
6	BA
7	04
8	56

20-2 In checking the unseparated data for the first 4 bits of input, the floppy disk controller notes the following sequence of bit times following the true $\overline{\text{DATA}}$ $\overline{\text{WINDOW}}$ signal:

Full-bit time
Full-bit time
Half-bit time
Full-bit time
Full-bit time
Half-bit time

What are the values for the first 4 bits? Were any clock pulses missing? If so, which one(s)?

20-3 If the option of pulsing the seek/step signal is used to move the head from track 07 to track 39, how many pulses of the signal are required?

20-4 How many different memory patterns could be stored in a 16-bit memory with a capacity of 64 K? If each pattern of the memory could be tested in 25 ms, how long would it take to completely test the memory?

20-5 If the pattern for the shift diagnostic program were to be changed to 55_{16}, what modification would be necessary in the listing?

20-6 Change the memory diagnostic program so

that it tests the ability of the RAM to store all 1s in each cell.

20-7 Assume that the shift diagnostic program is being run and that a logic analyzer is attached to the address bus. Show the contents of the binary display after the first three instructions have been executed (that is, the instructions in cells 1000_{16} through 1005_{16}).

20-8 If a pulser and logic probe are applied to the circuit shown in Fig. 20-18, what indications would the probe give?

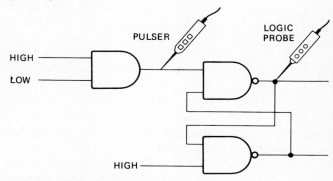

Fig. 20-18 Problem 20-8.

20-9 Assume that a logic probe is to be used to test a CMOS circuit that has a V_{CC} of $+12$ V. What minimum voltage must a pulse have to register as a high level on the probe? As a low level?

20-10 A logic probe is connected to a TTL circuit and gives the following indications:

1. All LEDs off, except that high is steady.

Followed by:

2. The high and low LEDs are steady while the pulse indicator is blinking.

Draw the pulse train that produced these indications. (Show voltage levels and time intervals.)

AN INTRODUCTION TO 16- AND 32-BIT MICROPROCESSORS

Increasing scales of integration of circuits have brought about more capable microprocessors having all the features of a powerful mainframe computer on a chip. These processors work according to the principles of the 8-bit machines that you already know about. The larger word size makes it possible to perform more sophisticated calculations in a shorter time; consequently, these devices are rapidly replacing medium to large computers that are built from component circuits. A computer that easily fits on a desk top can duplicate the functions of a machine that would have occupied much more space 10 years ago, and the desktop version costs only a fraction of the large computer's price.

This chapter provides an overview of the new concepts involved in the 16- and 32-bit microprocessors. Some of the typical chips will be examined to see how processing is controlled and how memory access is managed. Because these processors are upwardly compatible with the 8-bit MPU, you will see a direct correlation to their operations in the smaller-word-size chips.

CHAPTER OBJECTIVES

Upon completion of this chapter, you should be able to:

1. List the major new capabilities of 16- and 32-bit microprocessors.
2. Describe the means of addressing memory used by these processors.
3. Compare the types of operations in 8- and 16-bit microprocessors.
4. Explain how the 16- and 32-bit processors are upward-compatible with the 8-bit processors.
5. Describe how a numerical coprocessor functions.

THE 80186 MICROPROCESSOR

The 80186 microprocessor is a 16-bit computer on a chip. This MPU can directly address 1 megabyte (Mbyte) of memory by means of 24 operand addressing modes. The operations can be performed on data comprised of a bit, a byte, a word, or a block of many words. The operands can be either 8 or 16 bits, with or without a sign. The 80186 can carry out binary or decimal arithmetic operations, including multiplication and division. (Remember that we had to write a subroutine to multiply or divide with the 8-bit microprocessors.) The 80186 is provided with the capability of working in conjunction with a *numerical coprocessor*, such as the 8087; the numerical coprocessor directly executes more involved mathematical functions, thus increasing the program execution rate. Each of these features will be considered in this section.

The 80186 integrates onto a single chip six functions that were separate ICs in the 8-bit processor. These functions include clock generation, interrupt control, timers, DMA, bus interfacing, and chip select/ready generation for external devices; of course, the 80186 also supplies the MPU operations. Figure 21-1 shows the architecture of the 80186. The result of integrating all these functions on the chip is a simpler computer system to interface with the remainder of the computer system.

Referring to Fig. 21-1, we can see the reason why the 80186 is a 16-bit machine. The data bus is 16 bits wide. The data and address buses are multiplexed for the lower 16 bits of the address. The upper 4 bits of the address bus are also used to carry status information. The internal bus of the 80186 must also provide a 16-bit-wide path for data.

Another MPU quite similar to the 80186 is the 80188. Although the 80188 has an 8-bit external data bus, in most other respects it is the same as the 80186. The following discussion thus applies in most respects to the 80188 as well as to the 80186.

Microprocessing Unit

The 80186 MPU shares common architectural features with the earlier 8086 and 8088 as well as with the more powerful 80286. The entire object code written for the 8086 will run on the 80186 without modification, although the timing may differ. Being able to run the software from the 8086 makes the 80186 upward-compatible with that machine; in fact, the 80186 can run much of the 8085 software too. Because of its increased functionality, the 80186 is replacing the 8086 in new designs, and by being able to run the same software, it can make for significant costs savings in these new designs.

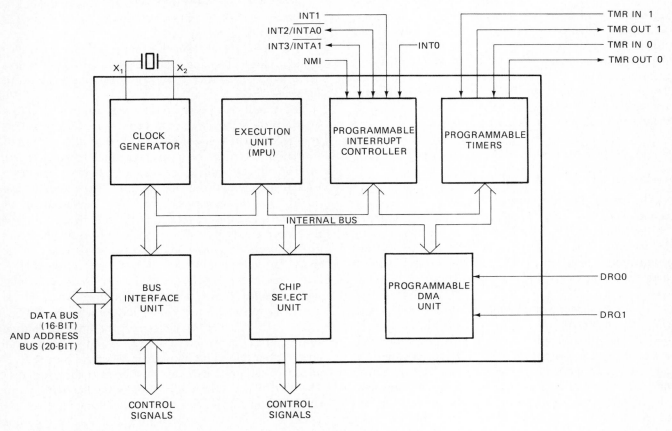

Fig. 21-1 80186 block diagram.

The 80186 MPU has a set of general-purpose 16-bit registers (AX, BX, CX, and DX) that can also be used in an 8-bit mode. There is also a set of 16-bit pointer registers (SI, DI, BP, and SP), which are used for arithmetic and for accessing memory.

ADDRESSING MEMORY Now let's consider how the 80186 can directly address memory as large as 1 Mbyte. The address range must be 00000_{16} to $FFFFF_{16}$, but the word size is only 16 bits. How, then, can a 20-bit address be handled? The answer is to use a *segment value* that establishes a base for an area of memory. This addressing approach is often referred to as *paging* memory. The segment value is a 20-bit number that says where we begin addressing from. Addresses above the segment value are an *offset*; for example, if the offset is 3, we are located at a *physical address* that is three locations above the segment value.

More specifically, Fig. 21-2 shows how the segment value and the offset combine to form the physical address. The segment value always ends in the hexadecimal digit 0. For this reason, we can indicate the segment value with just four hexadecimal digits. Before adding the offset, we shift the segment value 4 bits to the left (in effect creating a least significant hexadecimal digit of 0). Then we add the offset. The offset is provided by some combination of the instruction pointer register, other pointer registers, and immediate values. (Do you see how this addressing resembles the addressing mode used by the 6800 in branching?) The 20-bit sum of the segment value and the offset forms the physical address that is actually placed on the address bus to access memory. If the addition produces a carry, it is ignored. To illustrate the concept better, let us assume that the segment value is $7CB5_{16}$ and that the offset is $2E39_{16}$. Computing the physical address, we have:

Segment value	$7CB50_{16}$
Offset	$+ \ 2E39_{16}$
Physical address	$7F989_{16}$

The arithmetic-logic unit (ALU) executes its instructions in 16-bit units to compute results or perform boolean functions. The ALU also moves data among the various registers, memory, or I/O. New instructions support high-speed memory movements of blocks of data by means of *string-move* instructions or by *block I/O*.

Working in conjunction with the *bus interface unit* (Fig. 21-1), the ALU can achieve faster throughput by *overlapping* the instruction fetching; that is, as the ALU is executing one instruction, the bus interface unit obtains the next sequential instruction and places it in a quence. Since the MPU does not have to wait for memory access to fetch the next instruction, there is a gain in speed. Can you think of a case where this means of overlapping will not increase the throughput? Consider

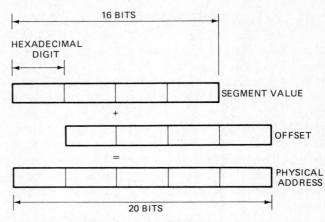

Fig. 21-2 Physical address in the 80186.

a jump instruction. In this case the next sequential instruction is not the appropriate one to execute, so the MPU will have to wait for the memory access from the address in the jump instruction. Because jumps are relatively infrequent in a program, there is a significant speed increase from this technique in spite of the occasional inefficiency in the case of a jump.

The *direct memory access (DMA)* unit supplies byte or word transfers on two independent high-speed channels. There are separate 20-bit pointers for the source and destination of data for each channel. The capability to increment, decrement, or count with any of the pointers is supplied. The transfer count for each channel is also maintained by the DMA unit.

Timers on the 80186 chip can be programmed to control external or internal events. Two of the timers serve as *event timers*, while the third functions as an *interrupt timer*.

The principle means of interrupt control with the 80186 is the separate *interrupt controller* function. This controller arbitrates among all the external and internal sources of interrupts to determine which has the highest priority. It can also be cascaded as a master to two 8259A interrupt controller chips. Alternatively, the 80186 interrupt controller can also be slaved to an external interrupt controller. With this flexibility, any type of interrupt priority scheme can be implemented.

The *clock generator* supplies a crystal oscillator at twice the desired MPU rate. For example, if the 80186 is to run at the 8-MHz rate, the oscillator frequency will be 16 MHz. Signals are also supplied by the clock generator to synchronize other devices with the MPU.

The *chip select/ready generator* provides six output control lines for memory addressing and seven control lines for peripheral unit addressing. For the purposes of memory selection, memory is split into three groups. The size of each group is programmable within the entire 20-bit addressing range. Upper memory is assigned to ROM code, which is executed after a system reset to start the microcomputer. Lower memory is as-

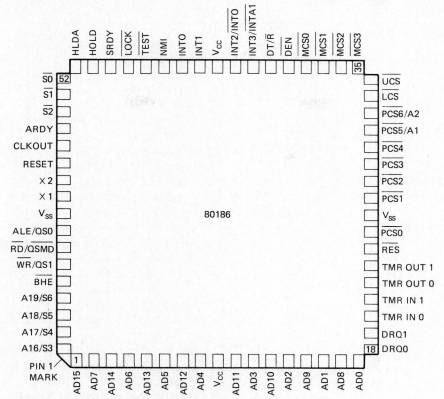

Fig. 21-3   80186 pin layout (bottom view).

signed to interrupt vector addresses. Finally, middle memory, which is usually the largest-size group, is the main program memory. The size of any of these groups is a multiple of 128-byte blocks above a programmable *base address*. Thus one could start at an address of 00000_{16} and specify three blocks; inclusive addresses would then be 00000_{16} through $0007F_{16}$.

The 80186 processor is packaged in a 68-lead chip-carrier configuration, as shown in Fig. 21-3. Each of the signals is listed in Table 21-1 (see page 374). At this point, it is not necessary to understand all the signals in detail. Looking through the table, you will see a number of controls that resemble those of the 8-bit machines.

REGISTER SET
The register set for the 80186 is shown in Fig. 21-4. There are sets of general registers, of segment registers, and of status and control registers. The 8 general registers are used for arithmetic and as pointers. The first four can be split into 8-bit registers as well. The AX and DX registers have special meanings for multiplication, division, and I/O instructions. The CX register is involved in looping, shifting, repeating, and counting instructions. The BX and BP registers indicate the base address for a memory block, while the SI and DI registers serve as indexes. Finally, the SP register is the stack pointer.

The starting address for instructions is contained in the code segment selector register. This and all other segments are 64 Kbytes long. (Recall the discussion

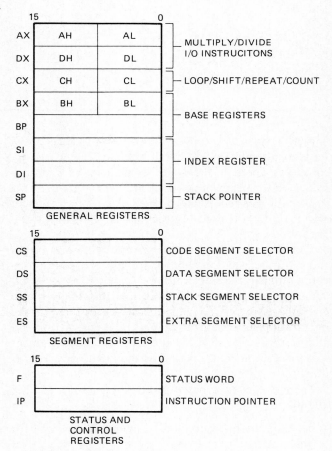

Fig. 21-4   80186 registers.

Table 21-1 80186 Signal Descriptions

Symbol	Pin(s)	Function
V_{CC}	9, 43	+5-V power
V_{SS}	26, 60	Ground
X1, X2	59, 58	Crystal inputs
$\overline{RES}$	24	System reset
$\overline{TEST}$	47	Control execution during WAIT instruction
TMR IN 0, TMR IN 1	20, 21	Timer inputs
DRQ0, DRQ1	18, 19	DMA request
NMI	46	Nonmaskable interrupt
INT0, INT1, INT2$\overline{INTA0}$, INT3$\overline{INTA1}$	45, 44, 42, 41	Maskable interrupts
A19–S6, A18–S5, A17–S4, A16–S3	65, 66, 67, 68	Upper 4 bits of address bus and status lines
AD15–AD0	10–17, 1–8	Multiplexed address and data bus
$\overline{BHE}$/S7	64	Controls word or byte transfer on data bus
ALE/QS0	61	Address latch enable and queue status 0
$\overline{WR}$/QS1	63	Write strobe and queue status 1
$\overline{RD}$/QSMD	62	Read strobe and queue status
ARDY	55	Asynchronous ready
SRDY	49	Synchronous ready
$\overline{LOCK}$	48	Prevents other system bus masters from gaining control of the system bus
$\overline{S0}$, $\overline{S1}$, $\overline{S2}$	52, 53, 54	Bus cycle status indicators
HOLD	50	Request another bus master for use of local bus
HLDA	51	Hold acknowledge
$\overline{UCS}$	34	Upper-range memory chip select
$\overline{MCS0-3}$	38, 37, 36, 35	Midrange memory chip select
$\overline{LCS}$	33	Low-range memory chip select
$\overline{PCS0}$, $\overline{PCS1-4}$	25, 27, 28, 29, 30	Peripheral chip select 0–4
$\overline{PCS5}$/A1	31	Peripheral chip select 5 and latched A1 signal
$\overline{PCS6}$/A2		Peripheral chip select 6 and latched A2 signal
$\overline{DTR}$	40	Data transfer and receive
$\overline{DEN}$	39	Data enable

earlier in this section about using segment values as the basis for the physical address.) The data segment selector shows where the local data segment starts. The stack is located by means of the stack segment selector. String instruction references are based on the extra segment selector, which is used together with the DI index register.

The status word register serves the same purpose as the status register on 8-bit processors. In addition to containing such status indicators as carry, parity, zero, auxiliary carry, sign, and overflow, this register also controls interrupts. The instruction pointer contains the offset address for the next sequential instruction. By adding this value to the contents of the code segment selector, the physical address of the next instruction is found.

There are eight types of addressing modes for the 80186:

1. The *register* operand mode provides the operand for the instruction in one of the 8- or 16-bit general registers.

2. For the *immediate* operand mode, the operand is included in the instruction. Several modes specify the operand location by means of a base address combined with a displacement and an index. The base address will be found in the BX or BP registers. The displacement is an 8- or 16-bit value in the instruction, similar to the 6800's branch instructions. The index will be the contents of the SI or DI registers.

3. *Direct* addressing supplies a displacement as part of the instruction.

4. For the *register indirect* mode, the offset is contained in either the BX, BP, DI, or SI register.

5. In the *based* mode the operand offset is the sum of a displacement and the contents of the BP or BX registers.

6. The *indexed* mode adds the displacement in the instruction to the SI or DI register contents.

7. More involved is the *based indexed* mode, which forms the sum of the contents of a base register and the index register.

8. The most flexible case is the *based indexed mode*

with displacement, which sums the base register's contents with the index register and adds the displacement.

With all these addressing options, you can appreciate how difficult programming a 16-bit microprocessor would be using assembly or machine code.

Operations in the 80186 can be performed on eight types of data.

1. The simplest is a signed *integer* of 8 or 16 bits. Two's complement arithmetic is used. (With a numerical coprocessor, 32- and 64-bit integers can be supported.)
2. An *ordinal* is an unsigned 8- or 16-bit value.
3. *Pointers* are 16 or 32 bits in length; a pointer is formed from a 16-bit segment base added to a 16-bit offset.
4. A *string* is a sequence of bytes from 1 to 65536 bytes long.
5. Character values can be represented by *ASCII* and are 1 byte in length.

6. Another numerical representation is *BCD*, with 1 byte representing the digits 0 through 9.
7. *Packed BCD* squeezes two digits into 1 byte.
8. *Floating-point numbers* are signed 32-, 64-, or 80-bit real numbers.

Numerical Coprocessors

High-speed arithmetic operations can be added to the basic 80186 MPU to achieve improved performance in applications with extensive calculations. By means of *benchmark* programs, the execution times of a variety of hardware configurations can be compared. Speed increases of 40 to 1 have been realized using the 80186 and the 8087 in double-precision matrix-multiplication benchmark routines.

We will consider the 8087 coprocessor as a typical example of this type of device. Figure 21-5 shows how the 8087 interfaces to the 80186. The 82188 is an integrated bus controller that allows multiple master devices to share the system buses.

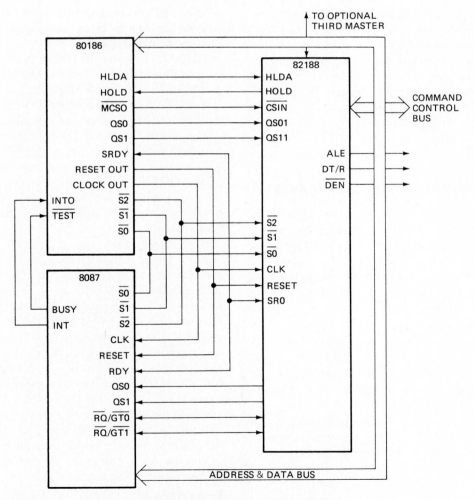

Fig. 21-5 Mathematical coprocessor interface with the 80186.

The 8087 provides arithmetic, trigonometric, exponential, and logarithmic instructions that augment the repertoire of the microprocessor. The 8087 operates on integers and real numbers up to 64 bits in length. Table 21-2 lists the instructions supported.

The 8087 supports all 24 addressing modes of the 80186 processor, so the data can be forwarded to the coprocessor without modification. The coprocessor also conforms to the proposed IEEE standard for floating-point numerical processing. Data can be in the form of 8-, 16-, 32-, or 64-bit integers; 32-, 64-, or 80-bit floating-point real numbers; or 18-bit BCD numbers.

The 8087 is paralleled with the 80186. The status lines (S0 through S2) and queue status lines (QS0 and QS1) supply the communications between the devices. The 8087 monitors and decodes instructions in synchronization with the processor, without the MPU being burdened. Local data transfers are done by the 8087 using one of the request lines to handshake on. When one of the 68 instructions that the 8087 is to execute occurs in the program, the 80186 treats that operation as an escape instruction and lets the 8087 carry it out.

The computations in the 8087 take place in a register stack. This stack has eight 80-bit registers, numbered R1 to R8. With registers of this size, the 8087 can deal with the 80-bit data. In addition, there are control and status registers, an instruction pointer, a data pointer, and a tag-word register. The tag word indicates the meaning for the contents of the R1 through R8 registers. When the registers are used in an instruction, usually only the top one or two registers on the stack are involved. The top of the stack is shown by the contents of a stack pointer.

The 80186 Microprocessor Review

1. What types of data can the 80186 manipulate?
2. Describe some differences between an 8-bit microprocessor you are familiar with and the 80186.
3. What is the purpose of the 8087?
4. What are the six additional functions integrated into the 80186?

Table 21-2 8087 Instructions

Instruction	Operand
Add/subtract	Integer or floating point
Multiply (single and extended precision)	Integer or floating point
Divide	Integer or floating point
Compare	Integer or floating point
Load/store	Integer or floating point
Square root	Integer
Tangent	Floating point
Exponentiation/logarithm	Floating point

5. How does the 80188 differ from the 80186?
6. List the general-purpose registers for the processor.
7. Explain how 80186 addressing is performed.

THE 80286 MICROPROCESSOR

The 80286 is a more advanced product than the 80186 in that the 80286 offers management of large memories. The address space for the 80286 is 16 Mbytes of physical memory. Even that size is not a limit because the 80286 provides each program up to 1 gigabyte (Gbyte) of virtual memory, which is a technique that allows multiple programs and data to be stored in the same physical memory in a timesharing fashion. In this way each program can operate as though it had a huge memory area and the processor can take care of all the effort involved in doing the sharing.

The 80286 offers two operating modes as well. In the *real-address* mode the 80286 is fully compatible with all software for the 8086 and 80186; in this mode, memory size is limited to 1 Mbyte for compatibility. The *protected virtual address* mode permits the 80286 to take full advantage of the larger memory area, at a cost of no longer being compatible with the earlier microprocessor software.

Figure 21-6 shows the 80286 pin locations. Each pin is briefly described in Table 21-3. Clock rates for the 80286 can be 4, 6, or 8 MHz. A numerical coprocessor is available to work with the MPU in a manner similar to that of the 8087 previously discussed in this chapter.

The 80286 has much the same instruction repertoire and data-handling capacity as the 80186, so the details will not be repeated here. The most interesting feature of the 80286 is its memory management functions in the protected virtual mode. The 80286 is placed in this mode by setting the protection enable (PE) bit of the status word by means of the load machine status word (LMSW) instruction.

The 1-Gbyte memory is mapped in to 16-Mbyte physical memory segments, which can be addressed by the A23–A0 bus. The protected mode uses 32-bit *pointers* to the memory segment. Each pointer consists of a 16-bit selector and a 16-bit offset portion. The *selector* is an index to a table in memory, not to the upper 16-bits of a memory address (as in the case of the 80186). The memory table contains the 24-bit base address. The offset is added to the base to form the physical address. Figure 21-7 shows how the address is formed. For example, if the word in the memory table indicated by the selector contains $187DF3_{16}$ and the offset is $3EA6_{16}$, the physical memory address would be $18BC99_{16}$.

The use for a particular area of memory is defined by *descriptors*. The segment descriptors establish code, stack, data, special system data, and control transfer operations memory areas. The access to each area is

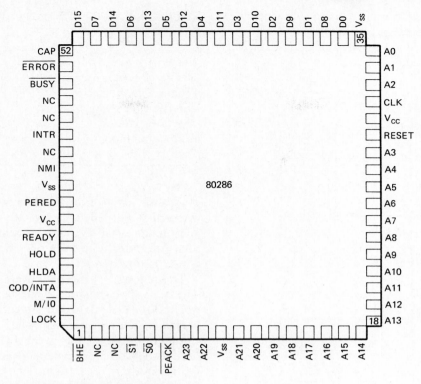

Fig. 21-6 80286 pin configuration.

Table 21-3 80286 Pin Description

Symbol	Function
CLK	System clock
D15–D0	Data bus
A23–A0	Address bus
$\overline{\text{BHE}}$	Bus high enable
$\overline{\text{S1}}$, $\overline{\text{S0}}$	Bus cycle status
$\text{M}\overline{\text{IO}}$	Memory or I/O select
COD/$\overline{\text{INTA}}$	Code or interrupt acknowledge
$\overline{\text{LOCK}}$	Bus lock
$\overline{\text{READY}}$	Bus ready
HOLD, HLDA	Hold request and acknowledge
INTR	Interrupt request
NMI	Nonmaskable interrupt request
PEREQ, $\overline{\text{PEACK}}$	Processor extension operand request and acknowledge
$\overline{\text{BUSY}}$, $\overline{\text{ERROR}}$	Processor extension busy and error indicator
RESET	System reset
V_{SS}	System ground
V_{CC}	System power
CAP	Substrate filter capacitor (a 0.047-μF $\pm$20% capacitor must be connected to this pin)

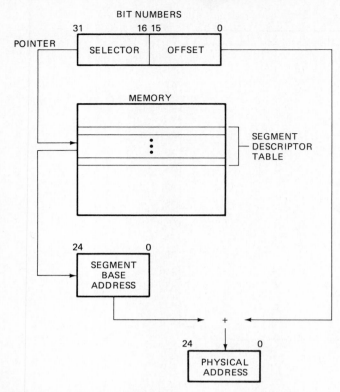

Fig. 21-7 80286 protected mode memory address formation.

limited to only that software with an established reason for referencing it. In this way many programs can share memory in a multiprocessor system.

The 80286 Microprocessor Review

1. Distinguish between physical memory and virtual memory.
2. Which addressing mode would be used to execute a program written for the 80286?
3. How much memory can the 80287 address? Explain how this is done.

THE 68020 MICROPROCESSOR

Next we will discuss an example of a 32-bit microprocessor. The 68020 is implemented with 32-bit data paths, registers, and address bus. The 68020 is upward-compatible with earlier models in the 68000 family. It is supported by the 68881 coprocessor with full IEEE floating-point capabilities.

The address and data buses in the 68020 are not multiplexed, so data and addresses can be sent simultaneously on their respective buses. This organization results in higher rates of data transfer.

The characteristics of the 68020 are listed in Table 21-4. The block diagram of the microprocessor in Fig. 21-8 shows its major components. The bus controller

Table 21-4 68020 Characteristics

Item	Specification
Memory support	Virtual
Data and address registers	16
Program counter	32-bit
Direct-address range	4-Gbyte
Processor clock	12- or 16-MHz
Addressing modes	18
Data types	7

loads instructions from the data bus into the instruction prefetch and decode unit and into the instruction cache. The timing of all events is governed by the sequencer and the control unit. The operations are performed in the execution unit.

The registers of the 68020 are shown in Fig. 21-9. There are two classes of registers: *user registers* for application programs and *supervisor registers* for operating-system programs. The data registers (D0 through D7) are 32 bits in length, but they can also be used as 16- or 8-bit general registers. There is also a 64-bit mode of operation. The address registers (A0 through A6) can be either stack pointers or base address registers. Either the data or the address registers can serve as index registers. The stack pointer register, program counter register, and condition code (status) register perform in the manner you already know.

The supervisor program registers are convenient for performing system programming functions, such as I/O and interrupt handling. The two stack pointers are re-

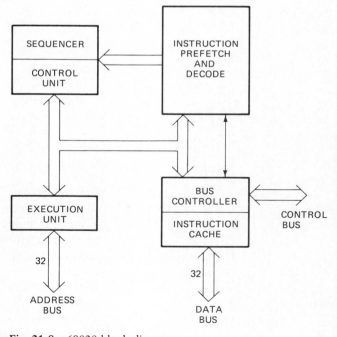

Fig. 21-8 68020 block diagram.

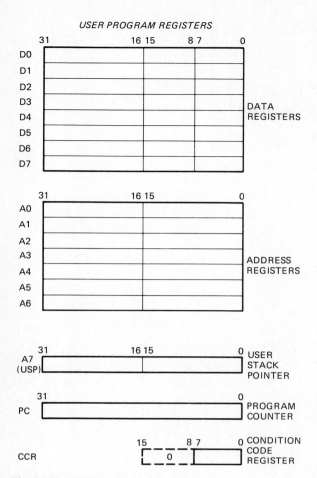

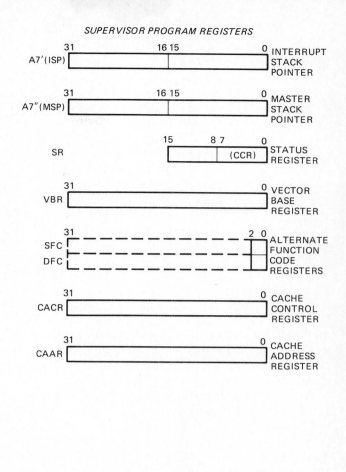

Fig. 21-9 68020 registers.

served for interrupt and operating-system operations. The vector base register shows the address of the exception vector table in memory in order to support multiple vector tables. The two function code registers permit supervisor programs to reach any address in memory. The cache registers permit the program to manipulate the cache section of the processor. The use of cache can speed up program execution. In addition to the normal status codes, the status register indicates when the processor is in the trace mode, supervisor state, and master interrupt state.

The data types that the 68020 can process include bit, bit field (maximum of 32 bits long), BCD digit, byte, word (16 bits), double word (32 bits), and quad word (64 bits). When equipped with the coprocessor, the 68020 also supports floating-point numbers.

Addressing flexibility is offered by the 18 modes the 68020 has. These modes are variations of nine types: register direct, register indirect, register indirect with indexing, memory indirect, program counter indirect with displacement, program counter indirect with indexing, program counter memory indirect, absolute, and immediate. Various means of incrementing an index are supplied. In addition, certain instructions imply addressing in terms of using a stack pointer, program counter, or status register.

The instruction set of the 68020 is quite rich to allow programmers to take full advantage of the power in the processor. Multiplication, division, and BCD arithmetic are just a few of the advanced features of the MPU.

By means of virtual memory techniques, the 68020 can address 4,294,967,296 memory locations. Of course, not every microcomputer need have that much memory. Even when there is less memory available, the microprocessor can take complete advantage of it. For a processor to use virtual memory, operating-system software must support this resource. Only the program running in the supervisory state can assign memory to an application program. The concept is similar to that of the 80286 microprocessor. The instructions that affect memory usage are referred to as *privileged* instructions; therefore, only the operating-system software running in the supervisory mode can execute a privileged instruction.

One of the reasons that the 68020 is so fast is its *pipelined architecture*. Figure 21-10 shows how instructions are decoded in stages. The instructions are fetched from memory and placed in the instruction cache on

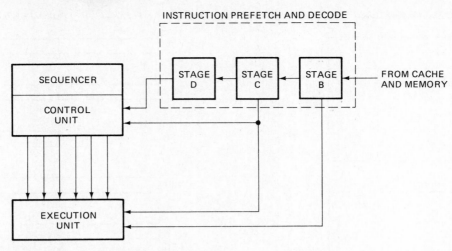

Fig. 21-10 68020 pipelined architecture.

the 68020 chip. From there the instruction is prefetched into stage B. The instruction decoding proceeds in steps as the instruction is sent down the *instruction pipe*. In stage D the instruction is fully decoded, but if the instruction involves immediate data only, the instruction can be executed directly from stage C. This will save time in decoding the instruction. Also, three instructions are in the pipeline being interpreted at all times. This means that the processor does not have to wait all the time necessary for fetching and decoding the instruction. In this way, concurrent operations can occur on up to three words of a single instruction or on three separate instructions.

The 68020 Microprocessor Review

1. What type of memory support is provided by the 68020?

2. How much memory can the 68020 address?

3. Why does the 68020 have two classes of registers?

4. Describe the pipelined architecture of the 68020.

CHAPTER SUMMARY

1. The 80186 is an example of a 16-bit microprocessor. It can directly address 1 Mbyte of memory in 24 modes. Data operations can be performed on a bit, byte, word, or block.

2. Arithmetic operations in the 80186 repertoire include multiplication and division.

3. The 8087 coprocessor works in conjunction with the 80186 for more involved mathematical functions.

4. The 80186 chip provides clock generation, interrupt control, timers, DMA, bus interfacing, and chip select/ready generation.

5. The 80186 is upward-compatible with the 8086.

6. Memory in the 80186 is paged.

7. The 80186 MPU, together with the bus interface unit, increases throughout by overlapping instruction fetching.

8. Memory assignments for the 80186 divide into areas for interrupt vectors, ROM code, and main program memory.

9. The 80286 handles physical memories as large as 16 Mbytes and provides up to 1 Gbyte of virtual memory.

10. The 80286 operating in the real-address mode can execute programs written for the 80186 and 8086.

11. The 68020 is a 32-bit microprocessor. It works with the 68881 coprocessor. The direct-addressing range is 4 Gbytes.

12. The 68020 has two classes of registers for the application programs and the operating system to use.

13. The pipelined architecture of the 68020 results in high-speed operations.

KEY TERMS AND CONCEPTS

Numerical coprocessor

Upward compatibility

Segment value

Paging

Offset

Physical address

String

String move

Block I/O

Bus interface unit

Overlapping instruction fetch

Direct memory access unit

Event timers

Interrupt timer

Interrupt controller

Clock generator

Chip select/ready generator

Base address

Ordinal

Virtual memory

Real-address mode

Protected virtual address mode

Memory descriptors

User registers

Supervisor registers

Privileged instruction

Pipeline architecture

Instruction pipe

P R O B L E M S

21-1 The problems below refer to the address generation in the 80186 MPU. Supply the missing values. (All numbers are hexadecimal.)

Segment Value	Offset	Physical Address
1. 61E9	A3C4	?
2.	B1E3	F170
3. D79	612F	?
4. B53E	?	C98A
5. 27A8	491	?
6. 69D2	?	F237
7.	19BE	5544
8. E624	AD6	?
9.	3416	512D
10. 9420	A875	?

APPENDIX

While many of the examples given in the text are based on the 8085 micro-processor, with little or no change most apply to the 8080 and Z80 processors as well. The following sections will comment on the differences between the 8085 and the other processors to indicate how the examples might be modified for those machines.

THE 8080A MICROPROCESSOR

Figure A-1 is the pin assignment for the 8080A. As you can see, the 8080A is a 40-pin dual in-line package (DIP). The purpose of each pin is described in Table A-1. The address lines (A0 through A15) comprise the three-state address bus. Addresses set on these lines indicate the binary location in memory of data to be read or written. The address lines can also designate a particular I/O device to be used in data transfers external to the microcomputer. Consisting of three-state lines, the address lines can *float* (switch to the high-impedance state) to allow other users on the bus to exchange data without interfering with the MPU.

The bidirectional data lines form the data bus for the 8 bits of information being sent or received by the microprocessor. Input/output data to or from the processor is transferred by means of this bus also. Two *clock phases*, Φ1 and Φ2, are used by the microprocessor to delineate the clock periods, T, of Fig. A-2. These periods are derived from the two phases, as shown in Fig. A-3. The beginning of each period is indicated by the leading edge of Φ1.

A separate SYNC pulse is produced to identify T1 during every machine cycle. The SYNC signal rises on the leading edge of the first Φ2 pulse during each machine cycle and falls on the leading edge of the second Φ2 pulse. Arrows on the timing diagram (Fig. A-3) show this cause and effect. As Φ2 goes high the first time, it causes SYNC to switch to the high state. On the second Φ2 transition, SYNC returns to the original low level. While synchronizing clocking signals can be quite involved, they are easily generated using the 8224 clock-signal-generator integrated circuit.

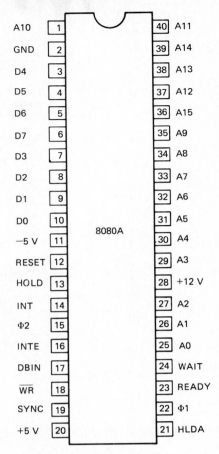

Fig. A-1 8080A integrated circuit.

Table A-1 8080A Signals

Signal Name	Purpose	Type of Data	Other Characteristics
A0–A15	Address lines	Output	Three-state system bus
D0–D7	Data lines	Bidirectional	Three-state bus
DBIN	Data input strobe	Output	System bus
HOLD	Hold state request	Input	System bus
HLDA	Hold acknowledge	Output	System bus
INT	Interrupt request	Input	System bus
INTE	Interrupt acknowledge	Output	System bus
READY	Data input stable	Input	System bus
RESET	Reset MPU	Input	System bus
SYNC	Machine cycle Synchronizer	Output	
WAIT	MPU in wait state	Output	System bus
$\overline{\text{WR}}$	Data output strobe	Output	System bus
Φ1, Φ2	Clock signals	Input	

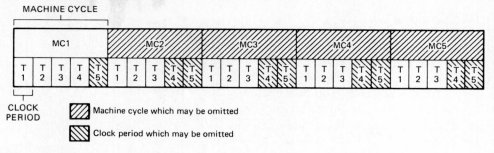

Fig. A-2 Machine cycles.

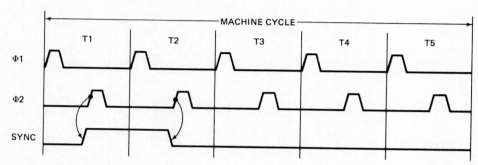

Fig. A-3 Clock periods.

During any machine cycle, clock periods T1 through T3 are reserved from memory references. The use of these clock periods is illustrated in Fig. A-4a. The remaining time periods in the machine cycle, T4 and T5, are available for MPU functions not involving memory or for use by external logic.

In addition, there is a special meaning of MC1 for any instruction: It is during this machine cycle that the instruction is fetched. As Fig. A-4b shows, T1, T2, and T3 are used to obtain the instruction. This timing is a special case of memory referencing during the first three clock periods. It is in the T4 interval that the program counter will increment and the instruction be decoded. The remaining period T5 is optional; that is, for some instructions the MPU can use this time for other operations; otherwise, T5 is canceled.

Identifying Operations

With all the different tasks accomplished by the 8080A, how can external devices keep track of what is happening? Actually this seemingly complex problem is solved quite simply. During T2 of every machine cycle, the processor signals the operation to be performed on the data bus. A code on the 8-bit data bus informs all devices of what is to take place.

A timing diagram of these signals is shown in Fig. A-5a. The status signals are stable when both Φ1 and SYNC are high. From this fact the simple circuit shown in Fig. A-5b can be constructed to trigger an external device to sample the data lines at the proper time. The read status strobe goes high only during the proper interval of T2.

The meaning of each bit in the status message is listed in Table A-2. As you can see, each data bit (D0 through D7) is assigned a unique meaning in the status code. For example, if D1 is high, the instruction will use the data bus to transmit information to memory or an external device.

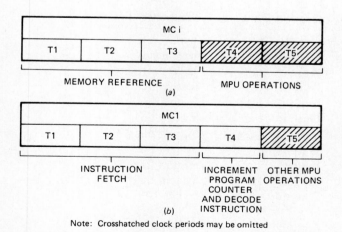

Note: Crosshatched clock periods may be omitted

Fig. A-4 Instruction execution timing: (a) other than MC1, (b) MC1.

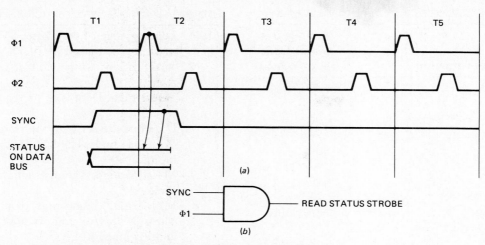

Fig. A-5 Status signal timing: (*a*) timing diagram, (*b*) circuit.

Each microinstruction sequence usually requires more than one operation. Several status bits are set to provide a complete indication of the operations to be performed. As Table A-3 shows (page 386), the code on the data lines uniquely identifies every microinstruction sequence. Consider the instruction fetch with its code of $A2_{16}$. Status bits 7, 5, and 1 are set. Referring back to Table A-2, we see that these bits indicate memory reading, fetching the first byte of an instruction, and *not* writing. (Remember that $\overline{WO}$ must be low to be true.) These three operations are those required for fetching an instruction.

To aid the hardware designer in the use of the status bits during T2, the 8228 system controller was developed. This IC automatically handles these status signals and converts them to command lines on the control bus.

Instruction Fetching

Let us analyze the instruction-fetching microprogram in more detail to gain a further understanding of the timing

Table A-2 Status Bits Set During T2

Data Bus Bit	Status Indication	Meaning
D0	INTA	Acknowledge signal for interrupt request.
D1	$\overline{WR}$	The data bus will be used for a write operation either to memory or to an external device.
D2	STACK	The address bus now holds the stack pointer address.
D3	HLTA	Acknowledge signal for the HALT instruction.
D4	OUT	The address bus now indicates the output device that should accept data when $\overline{WO}$ is low.
D5	M1	MPU is in the fetch cycle of the first byte of an instruction.
D6	INP	The address bus now indicates the input device that should place data on the bus when DBIN goes high.
D7	MEMR	The data bus will be used for reading from memory.

Table A-3 Status Codes for the Microinstructions

Type of Microinstruction	Address Bus Status Code (hexadecimal)
Instruction fetch	A2
Memory read	82
Memory write	00
Stack read	86
Stack write	04
Input read	42
Output write	10
Interrupt acknowledge	23
Halt acknowledge	8A or 0A
Interrupt acknowledge while halted	2B or 23

relationships in the MPU. The sequence of events is specified in Table A-4. A timing diagram showing each period of MC1 is shown in Fig. A-6. During T1, the clock phases and SYNC pulse indicate the start of a machine cycle. The WAIT line is low, allowing the processor to proceed without delay. Because this is a read operation, $\overline{\text{WR}}$ is held high.

At about the same time the processor sets the status code on the data lines for instruction fetching ($A2_{16}$ from Table A-3). The memory address of the instruction is placed on the address lines. (The instruction address

Table A-4 Single-Byte Instruction Fetching

T1: 1. Leading edge of Φ2 causes SYNC to rise, marking the period of T1.
    2. WAIT is low, so the MPU is not in the wait state.
    3. $\overline{\text{WR}}$ is high. Data is to be read (not written) from memory.
    4. Data bits are set with the status code.
      $\overline{\text{WO}}$ (D1) high. The MPU is expecting an input.
      M1 (D5) high. The instruction is in the fetch cycle.
      MEMR (D7) high. Input from memory.
    5. The appropriate memory address is set on the address lines, A0–A15.

T2: 1. Memory uses Φ1 ANDed with SYNC to read status from the data bus.
    2. DBIN high causes the data bus to be ready to receive input. (The signal stays high until the rising edge of Φ2 during T3.)

T3: 1. MPU stores the instruction in the instruction register, where the control section will interpret it.
    2. The data lines are floated during T3, making it available to external logic.

T4: 1. The data bus is floated during T4.
    2. The program counter is incremented.

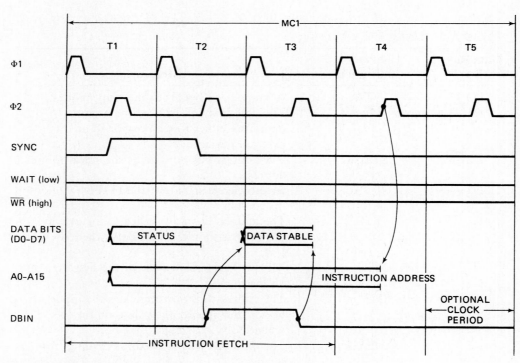

Fig. A-6 Instruction fetch timing.

was obtained from the program counter.) In the next clock period the memory can anticipate an input operation by ANDing Φ1 with SYNC to generate a status read strobe. DBIN goes high, indicating that the data bus is ready to receive data; the processor floats the bus in preparation for the data transfer. At the beginning of T3, memory data must be stable on the lines so that the processor can move the instruction into the instruction register. The data bus is floated by the memory after Φ2 of the third period to make it available to other users. It is in T4 that the processor counts up the program counter and also floats the address bus. T5 is an optional period in the machine cycle that may or may not be used, depending on the instruction.

Reading Memory Data

The microprogram for reading memory uses practically the same procedures as the instruction-fetching sequence. There are only two changes. First, some machine cycle other than M1 would be used. Second, the status code set on the data lines during T1 would be 82_{16} because the M1 status bit (D5) is 0. Of course, every memory read operation adds one machine cycle to the instruction execution time.

Writing Memory Data

The operations for sending a byte of data from the processor to memory have many similarities to those required for reading. The sequence is listed in Table A-5 and a timing diagram provided in Fig. A-7. The first difference occurs during step 4 of T1. The status code on the data lines is all 0s. With $\overline{\text{WO}}$ low, we know

Table A-5 Writing Data in Memory

T1:	1. Leading edge of Φ2 causes SYNC to rise, marking the period as T1.
	2. WAIT is low, so the MPU is not in the wait state.
	3. $\overline{\text{WR}}$ is high until the time to write.
	4. All data bits are 0.
	5. The appropriate memory address is set on the address lines, A0–A15.
T2:	1. Memory uses Φ2 ANDed with SYNC to read status from the data bus.
	2. DBIN remains low.
T3:	1. $\overline{\text{WR}}$ goes low.
	2. The data is transferred from memory to the data bus and then to the processor.
T4:	1. The data and address buses are floated during T4.
	2. The program counter is incremented.

that this will be a write operation. During T2 the processor sets the data to be placed in memory on the data lines. (The memory already has the address available on the address bus.) When $\overline{\text{WR}}$ goes low during T3, the memory accepts the data.

THE 8224 CLOCK GENERATOR

The 8224 provides the 8080A with its Φ1 and Φ2 clock phases. This IC also creates READY and RESET inputs

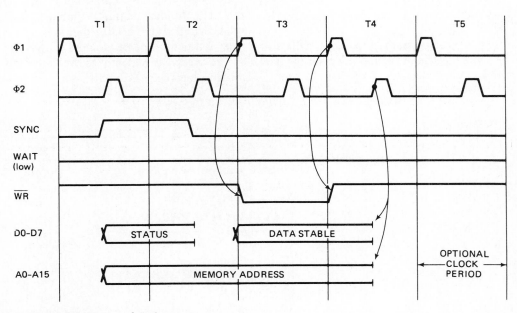

Fig. A-7 Memory read timing.

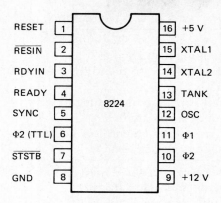

RESET	1	16	+5 V
RESIN	2	15	XTAL1
RDYIN	3	14	XTAL2
READY	4	13	TANK
SYNC	5	12	OSC
Φ2 (TTL)	6	11	Φ1
STSTB	7	10	Φ2
GND	8	9	+12 V

8224

Fig. A-8 8224 IC.

properly synchronized with Φ2, as required by the MPU. The pin arrangement of the 8224 is shown in Fig. A-8 and the signals described in Table A-6.

The XTAL and TANK inputs are associated with the crystal that must be used to generate the clock phases. The 8224 produces the nonoverlapping Φ1 and Φ2 pulses, which swing between +11 and +0.3 V. Because these voltages are not TTL-compatible, separate TTL-level outputs of Φ2 (TTL) and OSC are provided.

The clock frequency of the 8224, and therefore of the 8080A, depends on a crystal oscillator. The crystal frequency must be exactly 9 times the required clock period. The standard clock period for the 8080A is 500 ns, which means that the crystal frequency should be 18 MHz. Each clock period is divided into nine segments. Each segment is then equal to one crystal oscillation period. If a supporting LC network is used with an overtone mode crystal, the TANK input to the 8224 is used.

Control Signals

There are two sets of corresponding control signals handled by the 8224. The external-logic-supplied RESIN is converted to a synchronized RESET to be sent to the 8080A. Similarly, RDYIN from another device is translated to READY by the 8224. In addition, the 8224 sends a signal to the 8228.

RESET It would be difficult for external logic to synchronize the RESET signal input with Φ2, so the 8224 provides that service for the system. Furthermore, it converts a slowly varying input of RESIN to a sharply rising RESET output by use of an internal Schmitt trigger. The output goes to the high level in synchronism with Φ2 when RESIN falls below a threshold value.

READY The 8224 will accept an asynchronous RDYIN signal also. RDYIN can arrive at any time in the interval between successive Φ2 pulses. The 8224 will generate a READY signal to coincide with the leading edge of the next Φ2 pulse.

STSTB A status probe signal is sent from the 8224 to the 8228 system controller. This signal is produced as a result of the SYNC input from the 8080A. As long as the three ICs are being used to form the microcomputer, this signal is of little interest to the user.

THE 8228 SYSTEM CONTROLLER AND BUS DRIVER

The 8228 provides most of the bus signals in an 8080A-based microcomputer. The 8228 is a bidirectional bus driver combined with signal generation logic. The pin configuration of this IC is shown in Fig. A-9. Many of the signals are those provided by the 8080A or the 8224, already described. The signals are summarized in Table A-7. As we will see, the 8228 was developed to overcome the pin count limitation on the 8080A. To minimize the number of pins, control and data signals are multiplexed on the 8080A data bus. The 8228 basically acts as a demultiplexer for the signals.

The 8228 provides a bidirectional buffer for data moving between the 8080A and the system data bus.

Table A-6 8224 Signals

Name	Purpose	Type
OSC	Crystal oscillator waveform	Output
RDYIN	Ready signal	Input
READY	Control signal to 8080A	Output
RESET	Control signal to 8080A	Output
RESIN	Reset signal	Input
STSTB	Sync signal	Output
SYNC	Control signal	Input
XTAL1, XTAL2, TANK	External crystal connections	Input
Φ1, Φ2	Clock signals	Output
Φ2 (TTL)	TTL-compatible clock	Output

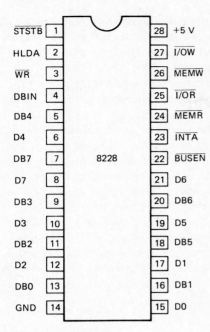

```
STSTB    1          28  +5 V
HLDA     2          27  I/OW
WR       3          26  MEMW
DBIN     4          25  I/OR
DB4      5          24  MEMR
D4       6          23  INTA
DB7      7   8228   22  BUSEN
D7       8          21  D6
DB3      9          20  DB6
D3      10          19  D5
DB2     11          18  DB5
D2      12          17  D1
DB0     13          16  DB1
GND     14          15  D0
```

Fig. A-9 8228 IC.

The 8080A internal microprocessor bus signals are designated D0 through D7. These bidirectional signals are passed through the bus driver to become the data on the system bus used by external logic. The corresponding system data bus lines are labeled DB0 through DB7.

The 8228 combines three 8080A control signals ($\overline{WR}$, DBIN, and HLDA) with status codes on the microprocessor data lines during T2 to generate the system control bus signals.

These signals are generated by combinatorial logic, as shown in Table A-8. Note that all system bus signals use negative logic; that is, $\overline{MEMR}$, $\overline{MEMW}$, $\overline{I/OR}$, $\overline{I/OW}$, and $\overline{INTA}$ are all true when low. The 8228 produces $\overline{MEMR}$ by ANDing MEMR (which is bit D7 on

Table A-7 8228 Signals

Name	Purpose	Type
$\overline{BUSEN}$	Data bus float/enable control	Input
DBIN	Data input strobe	Input
D0–D7	Microprocessor data bus	Bidirectional
DB0–DB7	System data bus	Bidirectional
HLDA	Hold acknowledge	Input
$\overline{I/OR}$	I/O read control	Output
$\overline{I/OW}$	I/O write control	Output
$\overline{INTA}$	Interrupt acknowledge	Output
$\overline{MEMR}$	Memory read control	Output
$\overline{MEMW}$	Memory write control	Output
$\overline{STSTB}$	Status strobe	Input
$\overline{WR}$	Data output strobe	Input

the data bus during T2) with DBIN from the 8080A. Other system bus signals are also derived from 8080A signals.

An example of the 8228 signals used for fetching an instruction from memory followed by writing into memory is shown in the timing diagram of Fig. A-10. The signal to read, $\overline{MEMR}$, results from the MEMR bit being set in the status code during T1 and MC1 and from DBIN going high during T2. (The 8228 must latch the status codes so that they will be available during T2.) The $\overline{MEMR}$ signal is synchronized with the input $\overline{STSTB}$ (from the 8224). The true state of $\overline{MEMR}$ is a read strobe for memory that places the data on the system data bus lines; the 8228 then relays the data to the processor on the internal data bus during T2 and T3 until $\overline{MEMR}$ goes high again. The writing of memory takes place in MC2. Then $\overline{WR}$ causes $\overline{MEMW}$ to become true (low) and memory accepts the data at the location specified by the address bus.

A system diagram for a complete microprocessor comprised of three ICs is shown in Fig. A-11. The address bus, internal and system data buses, and system control bus are shown in the diagram. Three power supply voltages are used by the 8080A, while the 8228 shares two of them, and the 8228 requires only +5 V. A common ground is also necessary for the three ICs.

THE Z80 MICROPROCESSOR

All of the 8085 instructions are a subset of the Z80 repertoire. This provision means that the 8085 programs will also run on the Z80. (The Z80 has 158 instructions, while the 8085 has 78.) Although the operation codes are identical, you will note that different mnemonics are used in Z80 manuals. The Z80 requires only a +5-V power supply and uses a single-phase clock. Clock logic is on the chip.

As shown in Fig. A-12 (page 392) and listed in Table A-9 (page 390), the Z80 does not separate read and write into memory or I/O operations. An I/O or memory selection pulse is provided to distinguish between them, as with the

Table A-8 System Control Bus Signals

Inputs	System Control Bus Output
MEMR (D7) and DBIN	$\overline{MEMR}$
OUT (D4) and WR	$\overline{MEMW}$
INP (D6) and DBIN	$\overline{I/OR}$
OUT (D4) AND $\overline{WR}$	$\overline{I/OW}$
INTA (D0)	$\overline{INTA}$

Table A-9 Z80 Signals

Signal	Description
D0–D7	Three-state data bus
A0–A15	Three-state address bus
$\overline{RD}$, $\overline{WR}$	Read/write strobes
$\overline{M1}$	Instruction-fetching cycle
$\overline{MREQ}$	Memory access indicator
$\overline{IORQ}$	I/O operation indicator
$\overline{RFSH}$	Dynamic memory refresh indicator
$\overline{HALT}$	MPU in halt state
$\overline{WAIT}$	Wait state request
$\overline{INT}$	Interrupt request
$\overline{NMI}$	Nonmaskable interrupt request
$\overline{RESET}$	Reset MPU input
$\overline{BUSRQ}$	Request for control of the data, address, and control buses
$\overline{BUSAK}$	Bus acknowledge
Φ	Clock input

8085. A nonmaskable interrupt, which is usually used to detect power failure, is supported. The Z80 also supplies a dynamic memory refresh signal, simplifying the interface to dynamic RAM.

This processor has more registers than the 8085 and has expanded the addressing modes. The additional registers are indicated in Fig. A-13. The alternate set of registers (indicated by prime marks, such as A′ and E′) can be used in exactly the same way as the main set, doubling the number of programmable registers. The alternate set is also convenient to reserve for interrupt-servicing routines. Then no registers need be saved before processing the interrupt.

The interrupt vector register extends the interrupt-processing capacity of the MPU. The refresh counter indexes the address when rewriting the values into dynamic memories, which is necessary to prevent data loss. Thus separate memory refresh circuitry is eliminated from the microcomputer.

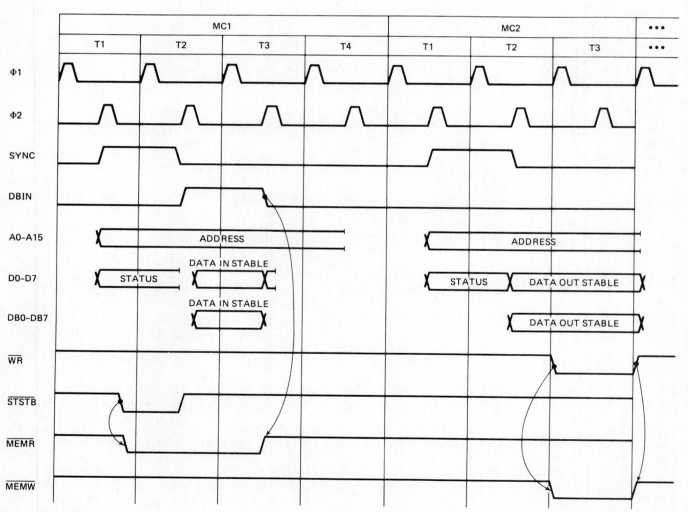

Fig. A-10 8228 timing.

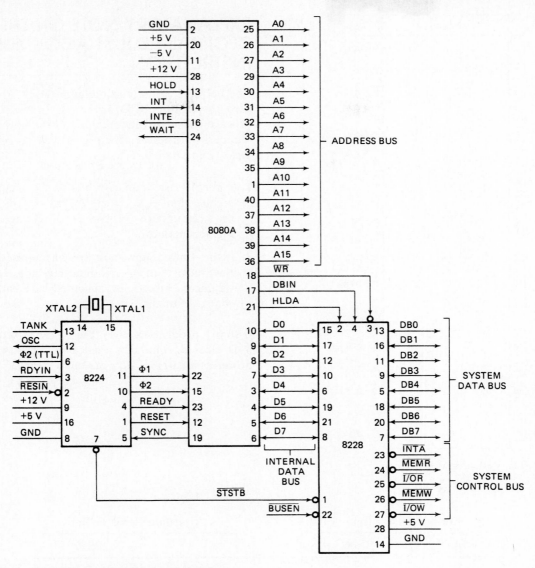

Fig. A-11 808A microcomputer system.

The index registers allow the address of the operand to be offset by a displacement value. This programming feature is frequently applied to table or list processing and also frees the register pairs for other purposes. The operand address in an indexed instruction is calculated as

$$\text{Address} = (IX) + D$$

or

(A-1)

$$\text{Address} = (IY) + D$$

where (IX) = contents of the X index register
(IY) = contents of the Y index register
D = displacement, a signed 8-bit value to be added to the index; the data can be located within ± 128 bytes of the index register contents

The relative jump instruction also uses a displacement. This instruction allows the programmer to branch to an address equal to

$$\text{Address} = (PC) + 2 + D$$

(A-2)

where (PC) = contents of the program counter
D = displacement

Individual bits can be manipulated by a group of instructions that can set or reset any single bit in a word. Block move instructions can transfer any number of contiguous memory cells to another memory area or to an output port. The block compare can scan a memory area for a specific data value. The Z80 status register provides a subtraction indicator, so the DAA instruction used in BCD arithmetic programs is simplified.

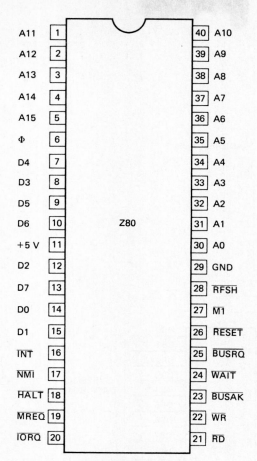

Fig. A-12 Z80 integrated circuit.

EXPLANATORY NOTE ON THE DECIMAL ADJUST ACCUMULATOR INSTRUCTION

The decimal adjust accumulator (DAA) instruction is used to perform BCD arithmetic in the 8085. When necessary, this instruction modifies the sum of two BCD numbers to produce a correct answer. To do so requires a two-step procedure:

1. If the 4 least significant bits of the accumulator are greater than 9, or if the A_C bit is 1, 6 is added to the accumulator; otherwise, no change is made to the accumulator.

2. If the 4 most significant bits of the accumulator are now more than 9, or if the carry bit is 1, the 4 most significant bits are incremented by 6; otherwise, no change is made.

If step 1 produces a carry, the A_C bit is set; otherwise, it is cleared. Similarly, the carry bit is set if step 2 produces a carry; if not, the bit is cleared.

Main Register Set

A	PSW
B	C
D	E
H	L

Alternate Register Set

A′	PSW′
B′	E′
D′	E′
H′	L′

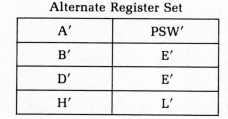

SP	
PC	
IX	X index register
IY	Y index register
IV	R

Interrupt vector address   Dynamic memory refresh counter

Fig. A-13 Z80 registers.

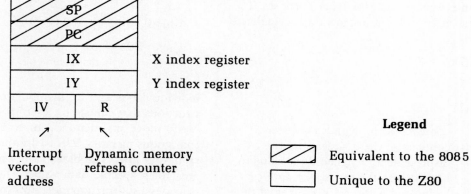

Legend

░ Equivalent to the 8085

☐ Unique to the Z80

□ **EXAMPLE** Initially the accumulator is $7A_{16}$, and both A_C and the carry bits are cleared. When DAA is executed, the following occurs:

STEP 1.
$$A = 7A$$
Four least significant bits are greater than 9

add 6
$$\frac{+\ 6}{80}$$

STEP 2.
$$A = 80$$
Four most significant bits are not greater than 9, so no further operations are performed

INDEX

A register (*see* Accumulator)
Accumulator, 4, 56–57, 76, 92
  6800, 104
Accumulator input/output, 246–247
Add instruction, 70, 87, 132–136
Addend, 30
Addition, 30–31
  multibyte, 164–166, 169–172
Address bus, 3
  6800, 75
  8085, 55
Address modification loop, 197–198
Address selection, 247–248
Addressing, memory, 10–13, 105–106
  8085, 93–95
Addressing modes:
  6800, 106–107
  8085, 94–95
ALU (*see* Arithmetic-logic unit)
American Standard Code for Information Interchange (ASCII), 37–39
Analog interfacing, 336
Analog-to-digital (A/D) converter, 343–346
AND, 140
Arithmetic, 30–33
Arithmetic-logic unit (ALU), 4, 6
  register (RALU), 14–15
Array, 197
ASCII (American Standard Code for Information Interchange), 37–39
Asynchronous protocol, 230
Asynchronous serial protocol, 281–282
Augend, 30
Auxiliary carry bit, 121

Base, 25
Baseband local-area network, 241
Baud rate, 279, 301
BCD (binary-coded decimal), 37
Bidirectional bus, 2

Bidirectional bus driver, 68–69, 85
Binary, 25–36
Binary-coded decimal (BCD), 37
Binary-coded decimal (BCD) arithmetic, 146–148, 169–173
Biphase code, 240
Bisync protocol, 283
Bit numbering, 4
Bit-sliced microprocessor, 13–15, 22
Boolean instructions, 140–145
Borrow, 30
Branch instruction, 156–164
Broadband local-area network, 241
Bubble memory, 68, 85
Buffer, 62–64, 248
Bug, 44
Bus, 2–3, 322–333
  address, 3
    6800, 75
    8085, 55
  bidirectional, 2
  control, 3
  data, 2
    6800, 75
    8085, 55
  demultiplexing system: 6800, 79–81
    8085, 62–64
  IEEE-488, 310–319
  Multibus, 329–333
  multiplexed, 2, 322–324
  S-100, 324–329
Bus contention, 66, 83–85
Bus drivers, 85, 322–323
  bidirectional, 68–69, 85
Bus interfaces, 232, 233
Bus network, 242
Byte, 2

Call instruction, 8085, 204–206
Call subroutine, 204, 206–207
Carry, 30

Carry bit, 121, 123–124
Carry flag, 5
Cartridge tape recorder, 240
Cassette tape recorder, 240
Cathode-ray tube (CRT), 235–236
Cathode-ray tube (CRT) controller, 359–360
Cathode-ray tube (CRT) terminal, 235–237
CCD (charge-coupled device), 85
Charge-coupled device (CCD), 85
Charge-coupled device (CCD) memory, 66–67
Check sum, 40
Chip-select (CS) input, 10
Clear instruction, 131–132
Clock periods and phases, 6
Clock signal:
    6800, 77–79
    8085, 57–61
Codes, 36–40
Coding, 46
    program, 95–104
Column address strobe, 12–13
Communication standard, 230
Compare instruction, 148–151
Complement accumulator instruction, 127
Complement instruction, 130–131
Complement systems, 33–35
Conditional call and return instruction, 208–214
Control:
    6800, 75–76
    timing and, 56, 79
Control bus, 3
Control read-only memory (CROM), 7
Control section, 6–7
Control-signal generator, 15
Conversion, number system, 26–30
Counting loops, 189–195
CRC (cyclic redundancy check), 40, 239, 240
CRT (cathode-ray tube), 235–236
Current loop, 293–295
Cyclic redundancy check (CRC), 40, 239, 240
Cylinder print head, 233–234

Daisy-wheel print head, 234
Data acquisition system, 231–232
Data bus, 2
    6800, 75
    8085, 55
Data encryption unit, 353–355
Data set, 282
Data terminal, 282
Debouncing logic keyboard, 234
Debugging, 46, 148–150
Decimal adjust accumulator instruction, 392–393
Decoding addresses, 12–13
Decrement instruction, 126–127, 129–130
Deflection plate, 236
Demultiplexing system buses:
    6800, 79–81
    8085, 62–64

Device code, 246–247
Diagnostic software, 365–368
Difference, 30
Digit-by-digit algorithm, 29–30
Digital computer, 2
Digital-to-analog (D/A) converter, 336–343
Direct memory access (DMA), 15, 17, 230, 246, 266–273
Disk drive, 237–240
Display page, 236
Distributed system, 232
Dividend, 32
Division, 32–33
Division algorithm, 183–185
Divisor, 32
DMA (see Direct memory access)
Documentation, program, 46
Dot-matrix print head, 234
Double-precision arithmetic, 35–36
Drivers, bus, 85, 322–323
    bidirectional, 68–69, 85
Dynamic memory, 10
Dynamic random-access memory, 12–13

8048, 19–20
8080A, 18, 383–389
8085, 55–61
8086, 20
80186, 371–376
80286, 376–378
Electromagnetic deflection, 236
Error detection and correction (EDAC) codes, 39–40
Ethernet, 241
Exchange instruction, 100
Exchange stack instruction, 225
Exclusive OR, 142
Explosion algorithm, 27–28

First-in last-out (FILO), 4
Flag, 5
Floppy-disk controller, 356–359
Floppy-disk drive, 237–240
Flowcharts, 45–48
Frequency shift keying (FSK), 237
FSK (frequency shift keying), 237
Full-duplex interface, 237
Full-duplex system, 278
Fully decoded addressing, 11–13

General Purpose Interface Bus (GPIB) (see IEEE-488 bus)
Graphics processor system, 232–233
Grouping, number system conversion by, 26–27

Half-duplex interface, 237

Half-duplex system, 278
Halt, 69
Halt instruction, 102
Halt state, 61, 78, 260
Handshaking, 281
    signals exchanged as, 251
Handshaking protocol, 282
Hexadecimal, 25–36
High-level data-link control (HDLC) protocol, 283
Hold state, 60–61, 78

ICE (in-circuit emulator), 365
IEEE-488 bus, 310–319
Impact printer, 233
In-circuit emulator (ICE), 365
Increment instruction, 123–127
Index, loop, 189
Index register, 4, 76
Initialization for loops, 189
Input/output (I/O), 15–17
    memory-mapped, 246, 251–253
Input/output (I/O) concepts, 246
Input/output (I/O) device designation, 94
Input/output (I/O) devices, 247–251
Input/output (I/O) instructions, 246–247
Input/output (I/O) port, 230, 246, 248–251
Instruction cycle, 6
Instruction execution, 6800, 77
Instruction fetching, 6, 57–59
Instruction formats, 69, 86
Instruction notation:
    6800, 104–106
    8085, 92
Instruction register, 4
Interface, 230–232
Interrupts, 15–17, 230, 246, 253–266
I/O (see Input/output entries)

Jump instruction, 101–102, 113, 156–164

Keyboards, 234–235

Label, 95, 107
LAN (local-area network), 240–242
Least significant bit (LSB), 4
Line printer, 233
Linear selection addressing, 10–11
Load accumulator instruction, 108–110
Load instruction, 87, 96–98, 110–111
Load stack pointer instruction, 225
Local-area network (LAN), 240–242
Logic analyzer, 363–365
Logic probe, 362–363

Loop functions, 188–189
Loops:
    address modification, 197
    counting, 189–195
    nested, 197–200
    noncounting, 195
    timing, 195–197
LSB (least significant bit), 4

Machine code, 69
Machine cycle, 57–58
Magnetic tape recoder, 240
Manchester code, 240
Mark, 237
Masking, 144–145
Memory, 2, 7, 10–13
    bubble, 68, 85
    charge-coupled device (CCD), 66–67
    virtual, 21
Memory addressing, 93–95, 105–106
Memory cycle stealing, 17
Memory designation, 92–93, 104–105
Memory map, 10–11, 64–66
    6800, 81–83
Memory-mapped input/output, 246, 251–253
Memory reading, 59
Memory writing, 59
Microcomputer, definition of, 2
Microinstruction, 7
Microprocessor:
    bit-sliced, 13–15, 22
    eight-bit, 18–21
    four-bit, 18
    sixteen-bit, 20–21
Microprocessor unit (MPU), 2
Microprogram, 7
Minuend, 30
Mnemonic code, 69, 95
Modem, 237, 282–283
Monitor, 236
Most significant bit (MSB), 4
Move instruction, 70, 98–100
MPU (microprocessor unit), 2
MSB (most significant bit), 4
Multibus, 329–333
Multibyte addition, 164–166, 169–172
Multibyte subtraction, 166–173
Multiplexed bus, 2, 322–324
Multiplexing, 231
Multiplicand, 32
Multiplication, 32
Multiplication algorithm, 181–183
Multiplier, 32

Nested loops, 197–200
Nested subroutines, 214–219

Network, 240
  ring, 242
  star, 241–242
Newton algorithm, 49–50
No operation instruction, 96, 108
Noncounting loops, 195
Nonimpact printer, 233
Notation, instruction:
  6800, 104–105
  8085, 92
Number systems, 25–36
Numerical coprocessors, 375–376

Octal, 25–36
1's complement, 33–34
Open Systems Interconnection (OSI), 241
Operand, 6, 10, 107
Operation code, 69, 95, 107
Opto-isolator, 293
OR, 140
  exclusive, 142
OSI (Open Systems Interconnection), 241
Overflow, 176
Overflow bit, 122, 124–125

Parallel input/output, 230
Parallel-to-serial converter, 278
Parameter passing, 220–223
Parity, 39
Parity bit, 122
Parity flag, 5
PICU (priority interrupt control unit), 260–266
Polynomial expansion, 26
Pop instruction, 224–225
Popping the stack, 4
Positional number system, 25
Printers, 232–234
Priority interrupt control unit (PICU), 260–266
Process control, 231
Product, 32
Program, 2
Program counter, 4, 57, 76–77
Program status word, 57
Programmed input/output, 15–16
Programming, 43–51
  introduction to, 69–71, 85–88, 95–104, 108–116
Protocol, 230, 241, 281–284
Pull accumulator instruction, 226
Pulser, 361–362
Push accumulator instruction, 226
Push instruction, 223–224
Pushing the stack, 4

Quotient, 32

Radix, 25
Radix point, 25
RALU (register arithmetic-logic unit), 14–15
RAM (see Random-access memory)
Random-access memory (RAM), 2
  dynamic, 12–13
RAS (row-address strobe), 12–13
Raster pattern, 236
Read-only memory (ROM), 2, 10
  control (CROM), 7
Receivers, 323
Recursion, 188
Recursive subroutine, 219–222
Refresh rate, 236
Refreshing memory, 13
Register, 4–5, 92, 104
  status, 5, 76–77, 121–123
Register arithmetic-logic unit (RALU), 14–15
Reset signal, 61, 79
Return from subroutine, 204, 205, 207
Ring network, 242
ROM (see Read-only memory)
Rotate accumulator instruction, 175, 177–181
Rounding, 28
Row-address strobe (RAS), 12–13
RS-232C standard, 300–308

S-100 bus, 324–329
Sample-and-hold (S/H) circuit, 347–348
Scaling, 176
Scrolling, 237
Self-clocking code, 240
Sequencer, 14
Serial data exchange, 278–280
Serial input/output, 230
Serial printer, 232–233
Serial-to-parallel converter, 278
Shifting concepts, 176–177
Sign bit, 121–122
Simplex, 237
6500, 20
6800, 19, 75–79
68000, 21
68020, 378–380
Space, 237
Spherical print head, 234
Split addressing cycle, 12
Stack, 204
Stack errors, 5
Stack instruction, 223–226
Stack overflow, 5
Stack pointer, 4, 57, 76
Stack underflow, 5
Star network, 241–242
Static memory, 10
Status register, 5, 76–77, 121–123
Store instruction, 70, 87, 100–101, 112–113
Subroutines, 44, 204
  call, 204, 206–207

Subroutines *(continued)*
 conditional call, 208–214
 nested, 214–219
 recursive, 219–220
 return from, 204, 205, 207
Subtraction, 30–31, 35
 multibyte, 166–173
Subtraction instruction, 136–140
Subtrahend, 30
Sum, 30
Synchronization, 280
Synchronous data-link control (SDLC) protocol, 283
Synchronous protocol, 230
Synchronous receiver-transmitter, 283–288
Synchronous serial protocol, 281

Table, 197
Teletype characteristics, 292–293
Terminal, CRT, 235–237
Three-state bus, 2
Timing and control, 56, 79
Timing loops, 195–197
Top-down programming, 44
Transceiver, 323
Transfer accumulator instruction, 110

Transfer instruction, 111–112
Troubleshooting, 360–361
2900, 22
2's complement, 34–35

Universal synchronous-asynchronous receiver-transmitter (USART), 284–285

Virtual memory, 21
Voltage-to-frequency (V/F) converter, 348–349

Wait-for-interrupt instruction, 87
Wait state, 60, 77
Word processing system, 231
Word size, 2

Z80, 20, 389–392
Z8000, 20–21
Zero bit, 122